L,65a
023.2
BRUM

W9-BZP-864

NEAL-SCHUMAN DIRECTORY of
PUBLIC LIBRARY
JOB DESCRIPTIONS

Removed from
Division of Libraries

REBECCA BRUMLEY

PROPERTY OF
DELAWARE DIVISION OF LIBRARIES

58789672

Neal-Schuman Publishers, Inc.
New York   London

Published by Neal-Schuman Publishers, Inc.
100 William St., Suite 2004
New York, NY 10038

Copyright © 2005 Neal-Schuman Publishers, Inc.

All rights reserved. Reproduction of this book, in whole or in part, without written permission of the publisher, is prohibited.

Printed and bound in the United States of America.

The paper used in this publication meets the minimum requirements of American National Standard for Information Sciences—Permanence of Paper for Printed Library Materials, ANSI Z39.48-1992.

PROPERTY OF
DELAWARE DIVISION OF LIBRARIES

Library of Congress Cataloging-in-Publication Data

Brumley, Rebecca, 1959-
  The Neal-Schuman directory of public library job descriptions / Rebecca Brumley.
    p. cm.
  Includes bibliographical references and index.
  ISBN 1–55570–523–5 (alk. paper)
  1. Librarians—Job descriptions—United States. 2. Library employees—Job descriptions—United States. I. Title.
Z682.25.B76 2005
023'.2—dc22

For Jack and Charlie Brumley, whose mere presence is a cause for celebration, and for my brothers, who weathered many storms and whose love got me safely to shore.

A painter must paint, a musician must make music, a writer must write in order to be fulfilled. A person must be what a person was meant to be in order to be happy.

—Abraham Maslow

CONTENTS

PREFACE

Managers in all professions, including libraries, often possess an avoid-at-all costs attitude towards the prospect of inventing or revising job descriptions. This administrative nightmare requires careful—sometimes agonizing—hours of discussion detailing duties, responsibilities, knowledge, skills, abilities, and physical requirements as well as knowledge of and proper attention to Equal Employment Opportunity Commission requirements. With few guidelines to follow, this demanding task can often become even more laborious. Once completed, or the position filled, the descriptions are often filed away and rarely, if ever, referred to again. A lucky handful of libraries hire outside human resource specialists who perform countless interviews and job analyses. But in the end, the institution receives a hefty bill and only an outsider's idea of a description that may or may not meet their real needs.

I compiled *The Neal-Schuman Directory of Public Library Job Descriptions* to provide the help, guidance, and examples that can turn the process into a rewarding experience for both the library and the staff. In the pages that follow, you will find 273 effective job descriptions from 92 public libraries across the United States.

The *Directory* is divided into 20 major job categories representing the diversity of positions and functions employed by today's public libraries. Several categories include unpaid positions (volunteers, foundation and board members) because, to serve effectively, even those who work outside of the payroll system need to know what their roles entail, the time commitment involved, and their responsibilities and duties. These are the 20 categories of job descriptions:

- Administration
- Adult and Reference Services
- Archives and Special Collections
- Automation, Information Technology, and Web Services
- Children's and Youth Services
- Circulation Services
- Community Relations and Marketing
- Design and Graphic Services
- Facilities and Maintenance Services
- Library Board Members
- Library Foundation Members
- Mail and Delivery Services
- Office Staff
- Outreach and Extension Services
- Security Services
- Technical Services

- Training Specialties
- Volunteers—Public Services
- Volunteers—Support Services
- Volunteers—Miscellaneous Positions

Within each broad category are the individual job titles and between one and six different job descriptions for each. Entries begin with statistics about the library, including the name; city; population size; and number of volumes, titles, and periodical subscriptions culled from *The American Library Directory 2003–2004*. Next, each entry is divided into the following standardized areas:

- Reports To
- General Summary
- Essential Functions and Responsibilities
- Additional Job Duties
- Knowledge, Skills, and Abilities
- Physical and Mental Requirements
- Tools and Equipment Used
- Work Environment
- Supervisory Responsibilities
- Education, Experience, and Training
- Additional Qualifications
- License and Certification Requirements
- Position Hours
- Disclaimers

The Directory retains the job description's original wording except for revised headings to improve clarity.

The Neal-Schuman Directory of Public Library Job Descriptions includes a "Job Description Writer's Toolbox" to help with the ins-and-outs of writing job descriptions. The following tools are included:

- Tool 1, "Understanding the Equal Employment Opportunity Commission, Job Descriptions, and Essential Functions," explains the importance of the EEOC and the necessity of clearly, carefully defined essential functions in job descriptions.
- Tool 2, "Tips for Creating Well-Written Job Descriptions," outlines the features of effective job descriptions, explains their importance to libraries, and provides tips for thinking and drafting accurate statements.
- Tool 3, "Sample Job Description Questionnaire," provides a resource against which job drafts can be checked and improved.
- Tool 4, "Active Verbs to Employ in a Successful Job Description," lists over 250 verbs that most precisely convey the duties of a library professional.

The companion CD-ROM reproduces all of the entries in Microsoft Word. Because jobs are sometimes combined at libraries or their descriptions don't exactly fit the desired duties, they can be cut, rearranged, or even combined.

Throughout my inquiries I crossed paths with various Internet sites promising to craft a "one-size-fits-all" description for only $99. Generic job descriptions have no place in today's public library. Every library has unique needs—be it a small one that consolidates many tasks into one job, or a large research counterpart with very specialized positions. One size cannot fit all.

The Neal-Schuman Directory of Public Library Job Descriptions is a collaborative resource. Librarians have always had a collective knowledge—shared ideas, best practices, and anecdotes of what failed and what worked. I am reminded of a note for my last book, *The Public Library Manager's Forms, Policies, and Procedure Manual with CD-ROM,* sent from Shirley Vonderhaar from James Kennedy Public Library in Dyersville, Iowa. She said it best on her returned "Permission to Reprint" form: "Like many policies in many libraries, it is the distillation of the wisdom of our peers, if you see your hand in our policy, thank you for your help." If you encounter a familiar description, know that every librarian who uses it shares in the gratitude to its creator. I hope the profession continues to share and circulate knowledge.

During my research for *The Directory*, I was impressed by the great number of institutions revising their job descriptions. Using inaccurate, out-of-date descriptions is not only ineffective; in today's litigious society, it is dangerous. It only takes one disgruntled employee or overlooked candidate to initiate a potentially costly and lengthy law suit. Keeping up-to-date, accurate, and clearly worded descriptions on file may be the best prevention to becoming entangled in such a suit.

ACKNOWLEDGMENTS

I would like to especially thank my wonderful editor, Michael Kelley, and Director of Publishing at Neal-Schuman, Charles Harmon, for their creative talents and constant encouragement. A special thanks goes to Lisa Lipton and the staff at Dallas Public Library for their faithful support and friendship.

I'd like to express my gratitude to the many libraries across the country that generously permitted reproduction of job descriptions. (For a complete list, please see page 343.). A big thanks to all of them!

THE QUICK GUIDE

1

ARRANGEMENT OF THE MATERIAL

The most challenging part of compiling the information in the *Neal-Schuman Directory of Public Library Job Descriptions* was how to organize the material so the reader could most easily find the needed descriptions. Unlike most directories, this subject matter does not lend itself to a simple alphabetical listing.

There are thousands of public libraries across America. While each of them features the same *types* of jobs, depending on the size and mission of the individual institution, there may be many different job titles for a person performing roughly the same duties. A library assistant in one place might be called a library associate in another, or, a librarian technician in a third.

Some readers will want to search through a variety of job descriptions to determine the correct mix of elements that suit their individual needs. I arrange the material schematically. An index is provided for a quick look up of specific jobs.

The job descriptions in the directory are arranged from the most general to the most specific. All of the more than 275 different descriptions are grouped into 20 major job categories that one might find in an American library. Within each of the 20 categories, the positions are divided by title. Under title, they are listed by individual job description.

For more information turn to "Two Methods to Find the Right Job Description" on page 4.

The downloadable, customizable Word document version of the directory on the CD-ROM mirrors this arrangement.

The "Job Description Writer's Tool Box" (pages 321–344) features a useful compendium of support materials. Tools include "Tips for Creating a Well-Written Job Description," a sample "Job Description Questionnaire" for a current employee to use to describe his or her job, and a list of active verbs to use in job descriptions.

Two Methods for Finding the Right Job Description

There are two basic methods for searching in *The Neal-Schuman Directory of Public Library Job Descriptions.*

METHOD 1:

STEP 1: Select one of the twenty major job descriptions (see contents, page v, or list on page 13).
STEP 2: Narrow the search to the closest job title within the category (pp.5–11).
STEP 3: Find the best job description under the title.
        For example, let's search for a job description for a public library Webmaster.
STEP 1: Select the category "Part IV: Automation, Information Technology, and Web Services."
STEP 2: Narrow the search to job title "4.0 Internet—Webmaster."
STEP 3: Find the best job description under that job title: "4.1 Webmaster."

METHOD 2:

STEP 1: Decide what title you think most people might use for this job.
STEP 2: Turn to the Index of Job Titles on page 345.
STEP 3: Look for the job title that most closely matches and turn to that page.
        For example, let's search for a job description for a public library Webmaster.
STEP 1: Decide that the best title is "Webmaster."
STEP 2: Turn to the Index of Job Titles.
        Under "Webmaster" it says:
        "Webmaster: see also Automation, Information Technology, and Web Services"
        Turn to "Automation, Information Technology, and Web Services" and find "Webmaster."
STEP 3: Find the indexed page number corresponding to "Webmaster."

Complete List of Major Job Categories, Titles, and Descriptions

I. Administration

directors, assistant directors, and various central administrators

1.0 Assistant County Librarian
  1.1 Assistant County Librarian
    1.1.1 Job Description (JD)
2.0 Assistant Director
  2.1 Assistant Director
    2.1.1
    2.1.2
3.0 Director
  3.1 Library Director
    3.1.1
    3.1.2
    3.1.3
    3.1.4
  3.2 Deputy Library Director
    3.2.1
  3.3 Director Reporting to Library Board
    3.3.1
  3.4 Director Reporting to City Manager
    3.4.1
4.0 Administrative Services Director
  4.1 Administrative Services Director
    4.1.1
5.0 Division Administrator
  5.1 Audiovisual and Maintenance Administrator
    5.1.1
  5.2 Central Library and Division Administrator
    5.2.1
    5.2.2 Central Library Administrator
  5.3 Library Services Administrator
    5.3.1 JD

  5.4 Publications Administrator
    5.4.1
6.0 System Coordinator
  6.1 System Coordinator
    6.1.1

II. Adult and Reference Services

administrators, librarians, library associates, specialists, technicians, and assistants; subject specialists, such as music, art, and humanities; service specialists, such as adult literacy, foreign language; and audiovisual specialists

1.0 Adult Services Director
  1.1 Adult Services Director
    1.1.1
2.0 Branch, Neighborhood, and Extension Services Director
  2.1 Neighborhood Libraries Director
    2.1.1
    2.1.2
3.0 Library Assistant
  3.1 Branch Library Assistant
    3.1.1
  3.2 Literacy Project Library Assistant
    3.2.1
  3.3 Reference Library Assistant
    3.3.1
    3.3.2
    3.3.3
4.0 Library Associate
  4.1 Branch Library Associate
    4.1.1

5

4.2 Reference Associate
  4.2.1
  4.2.2
5.0 Librarian
5.1 Reference Librarian
  5.1.1
  5.1.2
  5.1.3
  5.1.4
  5.1.5
  5.1.6
  5.1.7
5.2 Manager/Department Head
  5.2.1
  5.2.2
  5.2.3
  5.2.4
  5.2.5 Librarian, Reference Department Head
5.3 Senior Librarian
  5.3.1
5.4 Audiovisual Librarian
  5.4.1
5.5 Branch Librarian, MLS Desirable Not Required
  5.5.1
5.6 Branch Librarian
  5.6.1
5.7 Branch Manager
  5.7.1
5.8 Branch Librarian with Supervisory Responsibilities
  5.8.1
  5.8.1
5.9 Extra Help Librarian
  5.9.1
5.10 Humanities Reference Librarian
  5.10.1
5.11 Language Specialist Librarian
  5.11.1
5.12, Literacy Coordinator Librarian
  5.12.1
5.13 Literacy Specialist Librarian
  5.13.1
5.14 Music and Art Librarian
  5.14.1
5.15 Science and Social Sciences Librarian
  5.15.1
5.16 Substitute Librarian
  4.16.1
5.17 Genealogy Librarian
  5.17.1
6.0 Specialist
6.1 Library Specialist
  6.1.1
  6.1.2

7.0 Technician
7.1 Library Technician
  7.1.1
  7.1.2

III. Archives and Special Collections
archivists; genealogy and local history librarians; and map, museum, and manuscript curators

1.0 Archivist
1.1 Archivist
  1.1.1
1.2 Genealogy/Local History Archivist
  1.2.1
1.3 Archivist/Librarian
  1.3.1
2.0 Curator
2.1 Manuscript Curator
  2.1.1
2.2 Map Curator
  2.2.1
2.3. Museum Curator
  2.3.1
  2.3.2

IV. Automation, Information Technology, and Web Services
technology and automation administrators, information system managers, assistants, technicians, help desk workers, systems coordinators, and Web-masters

1.0 Administrator
1.1 Automation and Technology Administrator
  1.1.1
1.2 Technology Administrator
  1.2.1
1.3 Head of Technology Services/Assistant County Librarian
  1.3.1
1.4 Technology and Automated Circulation Systems Administrator
  1.4.1
2.0 Assistant
2.1 Automation Assistant
  2.1.1
3.0 Manager
3.1 Information Systems Manager
  3.1.1
4.0 Internet and Intranet Administrator
4.1 Webmaster
  4.1.1
4.2 Internet and Intranet Administrator
  4.1.2
5.0 Librarian
5.1 Technology Librarian
  5.1.1

6.0 Systems
  6.1 Systems Coordinator
    6.1.1
    6.1.2
7.0 Technicians
  7.1 Automation and Technology Technician
    7.1.1
  7.2 Computer Technician
    7.2.1
    7.2.2
  7.3 Help Desk Technician
    8.3.1

V. Children's and Youth Services

administrators, supervisors, and managers; program coordinators; summer reading assistants; young adult and children's librarians; and early childhood and children's specialists

1.0 Administrator
  1.1 Youth and Community Administrator
    1.1.1
  1.2 Children's Collections and Community Programs Administrator
    1.2.1
2.0 Library Assistant
  2.1 Children's Library Assistant
    2.1.1
    2.1.2
  2.2 Children's Summer Reading Assistant
    2.2.1
  2.3 Youth Library Assistant
    2.3.1
  2.4 Young Adult Library Assistant
    2.4.1
3.0 Associate
  3.1 Children's Associate
    3.1.1
4.0 Clerk
  4.1 Youth Clerk
    4.1.1
5.0 Coordinator
  5.1 Program Coordinator
    5.1.1
6.0 Librarian
  6.1 Children's Librarian
    6.1.1
    6.1.2
  6.2 Children's Librarian, Branch Supervisor
    6.2.1
  6.3 Children's Services Manager
    6.3.1
    6.3.2
  6.4 Youth Librarian
    6.4.1

    6.4.2
  6.5 Youth Librarian Manager/Department Head
    6.5.1
    6.5.2
  6.6 Youth Librarian with Supervisory Responsibilities
    6.6.1
7.0 Specialist
  7.1 Youth Specialist
    7.1.1
  7.2 Early Childhood Specialist
    7.2.1

VI. Circulation Services

circulation administrators, managers, coordinators, clerks, pages, and midrange positions at the library associate, assistant, and specialist level

1.0 Administrator
  1.1 Circulation Administrator
    1.1.1 JD
2.0 Library Assistant
  2.1 Reception and Information Assistant
    2.1.1 JD
  2.2 Circulation Assistant
    2.2.1 JD
    2.2.2 JD
3.0 Associate
  3.1 Circulation Associate
    3.1.1 JD
4.0 Clerk
  4.1 Circulation Clerk
    4.1.1 JD
  4.2 Public Services Clerk
    4.2.1 JD
  4.3 Clerk with Supervisory Responsibilities
    4.3.1 JD
5.0 Coordinator
  5.1 Circulation Coordinator
    5.1.1 JD
  5.2 Staffing Coordinator
    5.2.1 JD
6.0 Manager
  6.1 Circulation Manager,
    6.1.1 JD
7.0 Page, Shelver, and Aide
  7.1. Aide
    7.1.1 JD
    7.1.2 JD
    7.1.3 JD

7.2 Circulation Page/Shelver
   7.2.1
   7.2.2 Circulation Page
   7.2.3 Page
   7.2.4 Shelver
   7.2.5 Shelver
7.3 Lead Page
   7.3.1 JD
7.4 Film Page,and Sound Shelver
   7.4.1 JD
8.0 Specialist
8.1 Circulation Specialist
   8.1.1 JD

VII. Community Relations and Marketing

community development, marketing, and public relations coordinators; librarians, assistants, managers, and communication specialists

1.0 Community Relations and Development Coordinator
1.1 Community Relations Coordinator
   1.1.1
   1.1.2
2.0 Librarian
2.1 Community Development Librarian
   2.1.1
3.0 Marketing Research Assistant
3.1 Assistant
   3.1.1
4.0 Marketing
4.1 Marketing Manager
   4.1.1
4.2 Marketing and Communications Manager
   4.2.1
5.0 Public Relations
5.1 Public Relations Supervisor
   5.1.1
5.2 Public Relations Officer
   5.2.1
5.3 Public Relations Assistant
   5.3.1
6.0 Senior Specialist
6.1 Communications and Marketing Senior Specialist
   6.1.1

VIII. Design and Graphic Services

desktop publishing specialists and graphic designers
1.0 Desktop Publishing
1.1 Desktop Publishing Specialist
   1.1.1
2.0 Graphic Design
2.1 Graphics Designer
   2.1.1
   2.1.2
3.0 Graphic Designer II
3.1 Graphic Designer II

   3.1.1
4.0 Specialist
4.1 Graphic Design Specialist
   4.1.1

IX. Facilities and Maintenance Services

facilities managers, custodial and building assistants, and maintenance specialists

1.0 Building Maintenance
1.1 Building Maintenance and Custodial Specialist
   1.1.1
1.2 Custodial and Maintenance Assistant
   1.2.1
2.0 Managers
2.1 Facilities Manager
   2.1.1
   2.1.2
2.2 Maintenance and Custodial Manager
   2.2.1

X. Library Board Members

board and trustees, members and officers

1.0 Library Board Member and Trustee
1.1 Public Library Trustee
   1.1.1
   1.1.2
   1.1.3
2.0 Officer
2.1 Board of Library Commissioners Officer
   2.1.1

XI. Library Foundation Members

board members and directors

1.0 Foundation Director
1.1 Foundation Director
   1.1.1
2.0 Foundation Board Member
2.1 Board Member
   2.1.1

XII. Mail and Delivery Services

delivery drivers and shipping and receiving personnel
1.0 Delivery Driver
1.1 Delivery Driver
   1.1.1
   1.1.2
   1.1.3
2.0 Shipping and Receiving
2.1 Shipping and Receiving Manager
   2.1.1

2.2 Shipping and Receiving Clerk
2.2.1

XIII. Office Staff
secretaries, assistants, officer managers, administrative assistants, typists

1.0 Assistant
1.1 Assistant to Director
1.1.1
1.2 Administrative Assistant
1.2.1
1.3 Office Assistant
1.3.1
1.3.2
1.3.3
2.0 Office Manager
2.1 Office Manager
2.1.1
3.0 Secretary
3.1 Secretary
3.1.1
3.1.2
3.2 Branch Secretary
3.2.1
3.3 Executive Secretary
3.3.1
4.0 Typist
4.1 Typist
4.1.1

XIV. Outreach and Extension Services
bookmobile personnel, outreach librarians, and programming coordinators

1.0 Bookmobile
1.1 Bookmobile Assistant
1.1.1
1.1.2 Bookmobile Associate
1.2 Bookmobile Librarian
1.2.1
1.3 Bookmobile Specialist
4.3.1
2.0 Outreach Coordinator
2.1 Outreach Coordinator
2.1.1
2.2 Programming Coordinator
2.2.1
2.3 Regional Programming Coordinator
2.3.1
3.0 Outreach Librarian
3.1.1 Outreach Librarian
3.1.2 Extension Services Librarian
3.1.1
3.1.2

XV. Security Services
security clerks, guards, and afternoon guards

1.0 Security Guard
1.1 Afternoon Security Guard
1.1.1
1.2 Security Monitor Clerk
1.2.1
1.3 Security Officer
1.3.1
1.3.2
1.3.3

XVI. Technical Services
technical services administrators, cataloging librarians, acquisitions, interlibary loan clerks, processing clerks, assistants, book repairers, and collection development librarians, managers, and technicians

1.0 Administrator
1.1 Technical Services Administrator
1.1.1
2.0 Library Assistant
2.1 Cataloging Assistant
2.1.1
2.2 General Library Assistant
2.2.1
2.2.2
3.0 Library Associate
3.1 Senior Library Associate
3.1.1
4.0 Preservation—Book Repairer
4.1 Book Repairer
4.1.1
5.0 Purchasing
5.1 Buyer
5.1.1
5.1.2
6.0 Clerk
6.1 Acquisitions Clerk
6.1.1
6.2 General Clerk
6.2.1
6.3 Interlibrary Loan Clerk
6.3.1
6.4 Processing Clerk
6.4.1
6.4.2
6.5 Audiovisual Processing Clerk
6.5.1
7.0 Acquisitions Librarian
7.1 Acquisitions Librarian
7.1.1
8.0 Cataloging Librarian
8.1 Cataloging Librarian—General
8.1.1
8.1.2
8.1.3
8.2 Cataloging Librarian—Rare Books

The Job Descriptions

I. ADMINISTRATION

Included in this section are directors, assistant directors, and various central library administrators. Other administrators can be found under the various departments below.

1.0 ASSISTANT COUNTY LIBRARIAN

1.1 ASSISTANT COUNTY LIBRARIAN

1.1.1 Assistant County Librarian

Library Name: Tippecanoe County Public Library
Library Location: La Fayette, Indiana
Population Served: 104,310
Number of Volumes: 297,091
Number of Titles: N/A
Number of Periodical Subscriptions: 1,947

Reports to

SUPERVISOR: Library Director

General Summary

JOB OBJECTIVE:

Assist the director in furthering the library's mission and accomplishing the goals established in the long range plan. Provide leadership to the library staff and represent the library in the community in a professional manner. Aid in the daily operation and management of the library, its materials, facilities, and staff, efficiently and effectively.

Essential Functions and Responsibilities

Assist the Director with planning, goal setting, preparation of administrative and budget reports, research and implementation of the directives of the Board of Trustees

Assist in the coordination of the goals, staff, services, and budgets of the library's Departments

Assist in the management of the day to day operations of the library in consultation with the director

Coordinate the public relations efforts of the departments and assist tin the overall Marketing of the library

Conduct various personnel management activities, including interviewing and hiring professional staff, advise managers regarding personnel actions or problems, make recommendations regarding personnel such as appointments, transfers, promotions, pay increase, and disciplinary actions

Consult with department managers and Administrative Team regarding planning and developing projects or services; communicates with managers any plans, Policies, and procedures as adopted through regular meetings, memos, or Individual consultation

Research and implement special projects on an ad hoc basis in concert with other Relevant personnel

Coordinate staff development opportunities and advise department heads on Planning and training programs for staff

Oversee ADA compliance as it relates to library services

Participate in managing the library's collections of materials

Know, apply and assist in the development of, library policies

Deal with disturbances and problem users

Understand the necessity of, and maintain, the confidentiality of library use

Promote a service-oriented outlook among all staff

Participate effectively and contribute to the discussions and decisions of the Administrative Team

Act as liaison with the Friends of the Library; assist the group with its planning, goal setting, budgeting, and programming

Act as liaison to the regional library networks

Represent the library to community and civic organizations

Participate in state and national library associations

Administer all library operations and activities in the absence of the director

Attend board meetings

Other duties as assigned and/or required

Knowledge, Skills, and Abilities

Must have a broad knowledge of the principles and details of librarianship, personnel practice, administration, public relations, and financial management

Must be able to keep track of the latest trends and technology in library services

Must be able to analyze and compare the products of vendors and their credibility

Must have problem solving skills, particularly the ability to zero in on problems in areas not dealt with before, and accelerate into the learning curve in order to solve them

Must be able to effectively ascertain and handle problematic situations

Must have the ability to plan, orchestrate, and implement services and projects

Must be able to establish and maintain effective working and advisory relationships

Must be able to speak and write effectively

Physical and Mental Requirements

Must be able to work at a computer terminal for 55 minutes at a time

Tools and Equipment Used

Personal Computer

Education, Experience, and Training

QUALIFICATIONS:

Education:

MLS from an ALA accredited school

Previous experience:

Three years of supervisory or management experience as assistant director or Department Head of a public library

License and Certification Requirements

License/Certification:
Indiana Certificate of Librarianship II

2.0 ASSISTANT DIRECTOR

2.1 ASSISTANT DIRECTOR

2.1.1 Assistant Director

Library Name: Williamsburg Regional Library System
Library Location: Williamsburg, Virginia
Population Served: 60,100
Number of Volumes: 261,243
Number of Titles: N/A
Number of Periodical Subscriptions: 562

General Summary

JOB OBJECTIVE:
Under the supervision of the Library Director, the Assistant Library Director serves as second-in-command of the Williamsburg Regional Library. The Assistant Library Director participates in preparing the annual Williamsburg Regional Library budget, is a member of the library's management team; and supervises a major library department.

Essential Functions and Responsibilities

Performs duties of director in director's absence at director's discretion, including public relations, personnel, and budget duties.

Supervises and evaluates the staff of a major library department.

Supervises and evaluates other library department heads as required by library organization chart.

Assists director and finance director in preparing the annual library budget.

Keeps abreast of advances in technology, and plans for applications to improve and enhance library services.

Prepares monthly, statistical, and special reports; collects and analyzes pertinent data.

Improves the quality of library services through individual and general staff development by attending relevant meetings, workshops, training sessions, and visiting other sites.

Participates in library-wide planning and decision making as a member of the library management team.

Performs other duties as required.

Knowledge, Skills, and Abilities

Ability to plan, organize and administer a department.

Comprehensive knowledge of the principles, practices, and techniques of library services and personnel management.

Desire and ability to serve the public with friendliness, tact, and diplomacy.

Excellent written and oral communication skills.

Ability to work well under pressure. Ability to delegate work effectively.

Ability to set own priorities for work to be done, and meet deadlines.

Ability to establish and maintain effective working relationships with staff members, vendors, technicians, government officials and staff, and the general public.

Physical and Mental Requirements

Administers work typically sitting in an office and standing at a public service desk, with occasional walking, light lifting and other limited physical activities. Frequent sustained operation of office equipment is required.

Regular contact is made with staff members, vendors, technicians, government officials and staff, and the general public. The job occurs in the library buildings.

Tools and Equipment Used

Computer and other office equipment as required.

Education, Experience, and Training

MINIMUM QUALIFICATIONS:
Master of Library Science degree from ALA-accredited library school. Minimum of three years of library experience. Supervisory experience at a departmental level required.

Additional Qualifications

NECESSARY SPECIAL QUALIFICATIONS:
Requires the ability to travel among various library sites.

Position Hours

WORK SCHEDULE:
Full-time, exempt position; 40 hours per week; includes some evenings and weekends.

2.1.2 Assistant Library Director

Library Name: Goffstown Public Library
Library Location: Goffstown, New Hampshire
Population Served: 16,929
Number of Volumes: 36,000
Number of Titles: N/A
Number of Periodical Subscriptions: 125

Reports to

Accountability: Reports to the Library Director.

General Summary

JOB OBJECTIVE: The Assistant Library Director supervises the daily operations of reference and adult services and technical services staff. Directs the library in the absence of the Library Director. Participates in the formulation of library policies and procedures and in the selection and evaluation of library staff. Significant interaction with the public.

Essential Functions and Responsibilities

Duties and Responsibilities: The following functions are considered essential for this position:

Plan and implement Outreach Service connecting Goffstown Public Library with the community.

Supervise and participate in all aspects of Adult Services, including Reference, Circulation, and Technical Services.

Assist in planning and implementation of adult programming.

Participate in collection development and materials selection, including periodicals and serials.

Help to develop policies and procedures for improved library services.

Help to select and evaluate staff members, develop staff schedules.

Coordinate and help develop library's presence on the Internet.

Use current technologies in support of information services, including but not limited to database searching, Internet and CD-ROM. Instructs other staff members in the proper use of such resources.

Attends professional meetings at the discretion of the Library Director.

Performs other related duties as assigned.

Physical and Mental Requirements

Job requires some lifting, frequent walking and stair climbing, along with the ability to climb on stools and ladders to retrieve materials on high shelves. Ability to listen, understand, and interpret patron and staff requests and questions critical. Self motivation, a professional attitude, and a sense of commitment are necessary. Ability to work with the public.

Tools and Equipment Used

Equipment Used: Computer terminals/keyboards, microcomputers and peripherals, typewriters, laser scanners, photocopiers, calculators, facsimile machine, and small hand tools.

Work Environment

Environment: Inside 99% (indoors) Outside: 1% (outdoors)

Normal hours of duty: As scheduled, regularly including one or two evenings per week and Saturdays in a rotation.

Education, Experience, and Training

VOCATIONAL PREPARATION REQUIREMENTS

M.L.S. or equivalent graduate degree from an institution accredited by the American Library Association. Minimum of three years progressive professional experience required including at least 1-2

years in a supervisory capacity. Good communication skills, computer literacy and knowledge of reference tools and searching techniques are necessary.

3.0 DIRECTOR

3.1 LIBRARY DIRECTOR

3.1.1 Library Director

Library Name: Murray Public Library
Library Location: Murray, Utah
Population Served: 34,024
Number of Volumes: N/A
Number of Titles: 74,554
Number of Periodical Subscriptions: 281

General Summary

JOB OBJECTIVE:

Under broad policy guidance and direction from the Library Board, performs professional and administrative duties in planning, developing, implementing, and directing public library services for the Murray City Public Library. These duties include budget preparation, evaluation, personnel, collection development, community relations, and facility maintenance.

Essential Functions and Responsibilities

*— Administers board policies; make policy recommendations to board; provides staff support and information to board.

*— Prepares department budget for Library Board approval; monitors and approves expenditures as directed by the Library Board; administers gifts, state and federal monies.

*— Supervises department personnel directly or through subordinates; hires and trains employees; assigns and monitors work; evaluates personnel; disciplines employees as necessary.

*— Evaluates library services and makes recommendations for improvements; works with elected officials, school officials, and civic organizations to develop programs and resolve problems.

*— Administers maintenance of library facilities and equipment; works with architects and planners on facility development.

— Reviews and approves selection of all materials for purchase.

*— Participates in professional meetings, classes, conferences, and workshops, locally and nationally.

*— Participates in organizational management through the committee process.

— Reads professional materials to update and maintain knowledge and skills.

— Performs other related duties as assigned.

Additional Job Duties

This is a management position. Accountable for all activities, programs, and services of the department.

Knowledge, Skills, and Abilities

— Thorough knowledge of the theories, principles, and objectives of library science.

— Thorough knowledge of library organization theories.

— Thorough knowledge of current trends and developments in the library field.

— Knowledge of and experience with effective participative management techniques.

— Considerable knowledge of management principles and practices.

— Knowledge of supervision, training, and staff utilization principles.

— Thorough knowledge of library reference sources, print and online.

— Considerable knowledge of children's, young adult, and adult literature.

— Considerable knowledge of online automation.

— Considerable knowledge of cataloging and classification.

— Working knowledge of public relations procedures.

— Working knowledge of budgetary and accounting processes of the department.

— Ability to plan, organize, supervise, and evaluate the work of employees in diversified library activities.

— Broad experience in collection development and programming.

— Substantial skills related to the organization of people, processes, and tools in a public library setting.

— Superior human relations and communication skills.

— Ability to establish and maintain effective and harmonious working relationships with employees, other agencies, and the general public.

— Ability to communicate effectively, verbally and in writing.

— Ability to follow written and verbal communications.

— Ability to develop and carry out program services.

— Ability to digest and condense information and ideas.

Physical and Mental Requirements

The physical demands described here are representative of those that must be met by an employee to successfully perform the essential functions of this job. Reasonable accommodations may be made to enable individuals with disabilities to perform the essential functions.

— While performing the duties of this job, the employee is frequently required to walk, sit and talk or hear. The employee is occasionally required to use hands to finger, handle, feel or operate objects, tools, or controls; and reach with hands and arms. The employee is occasionally required to climb or balance; stoop, kneel, crouch, or crawl.

— The employee must occasionally lift and/or move up to 25 pounds. Specific vision abilities required by this job include close vision, distance vision, color vision, peripheral vision, depth perception, and the ability to adjust focus to both print and electronic text.

Tools and Equipment Used

— Library computer system; personal computer, including world wide web search engines and the library's web site, word processing and database management software; calculator; copy and fax machine; phone; automobile.

Work Environment

The work environment characteristics described here are representative of those an employee encounters while performing the essential functions of this job. Reasonable accommodations may be made to enable individuals with disabilities to perform the essential functions.

— Work is performed primarily in an office setting. The noise level in the work environment is generally quiet.

Education, Experience, and Training

Education and Experience

— Completion of a Master's Degree in Library science, and a minimum of five years of experience as a librarian in an increasingly responsible supervisory and/or administrative position; substantial experience in public services and dealing with the public; or an equivalent combination of education and experience which provides the required knowledge and abilities.

Special Requirements

— None

3.1.2 Library Director

Library Name: Amherst County Public Library
Library Location: Amherst, Virginia
Population Served: 28,578
Number of Volumes: 39,000
Number of Titles: N/A
Number of Periodical Subscriptions: 105

General Summary

JOB OBJECTIVE

Performs professional library duties in planning and directing all the activities of the county library system.

Work is performed under the adopted policies of the Library Board of Trustees; the employee reports to and is responsible to the Library Board of Trustees.

Supervision extends to all library personnel, whether direct or indirect.

Distinguishing Features of the Class

An employee in this position is responsible for maintaining a professional work relationship with the Library Board and the community; for developing and coordinating programs; for employing, training, and supervising library staff; for preparing and administering the library budget; for overseeing operations of the main and the branch libraries; and for representing the library at meetings and conferences.

Essential Functions and Responsibilities

Plans, organizes, and directs the policies and operations of county library services.

Prepares and administers the library budget in consultation with the Library Board of Trustees.

Determines new library acquisitions.

Selects, trains, directs, and evaluates staff; initiates personnel actions for staff.

Prepares and processes administrative and financial reports and actions.

Supervises maintenance of files and records.

Arranges for facility and equipment acquisition and maintenance.

Implements library security policies and procedures.

Maintains relations with the Friends of the Library at each library.

Reports to the Library Board of Trustees on the activities of the library and the library staff.

Represents the Library in meetings and events.

Resolves patron or community user issues and problems.

Additional Job Duties

Performs related work as required.

Knowledge, Skills, and Abilities

Knowledge of principles, concepts, and practices of library science and of library operation as applied to the operation of a county library system.

Ability to plan, organize, and direct a county library system; to plan, train, and supervise the work of staff;

To speak and to write effectively;

To establish and to maintain effective working relationships with Trustees, County employees, staff, patrons, and others encountered in the work.

Physical and Mental Requirements

Requires sitting, standing, walking, climbing, stooping, bending/twisting, and reaching; talking and hearing clearly, including use of the telephone; lifting and carrying 50 pounds or less; pushing and pulling objects weighing 50 to 80 pounds on wheels; fingering for typing, writing, filing, sorting, shelving, and processing; vision to see all levels of shelving and vision to see while typing or using a computer; mobility to travel to meetings outside the library.

Education, Experience, and Training

Master's Degree in Library Science. Progressively responsible professional library experience, preferably with public libraries; supervisory duties required.

License and Certification Requirements

Possession of a Librarian's Certificate issued by the Virginia Board for the Certification of Librarians and a Master's Degree

in Library Science from an American Library Association accredited institution.

Position Hours

Unusual Demands
Position may require working evenings and weekends.

3.1.3 Library Director

Library Name: Weld Library District
Library Location: Greeley, Colorado
Population Served: 137,888
Number of Volumes: 360,019
Number of Titles: N/A
Number of Periodical Subscriptions: 711

General Summary

JOB OBJECTIVE

Performs executive and administrative work directing all operations and activities of the Weld Library District, a multi-site, comprehensive service system serving Weld County communities. The Director plans, organizes, directs, evaluates, and reviews the Library's resources, services, and programs to respond to the needs of the community. Work includes planning and implementing the District's short and long-range goals, developing and monitoring budget resources, and oversight of staff and services. Work includes frequent contact with the Board and local and state leaders regarding library services, funding and collaborative efforts, as well as contact with member library directors to plan and discuss services. Work is performed under executive direction of the Library Board, in accordance with board policies and objectives and is reviewed for results obtained. Supervision extends to the entire staff of the library system.

Essential Functions and Responsibilities

Any one position may not include all of the duties listed nor do the listed examples include all duties, which may be found in positions of this class. Allocation of positions to this class will be determined on the amount of time spent in performing the primary duties.

Confers with the Library Board on policies and long-range library programs; recommends new policies to the Library Board and advises Board of new concepts in organization, procedures, equipment, and technology through periodic reports; prepares reports for and advises the Board on progress toward goals, budget issues and planning.

Leads the management team in goal setting, personnel administration, program initiation, training, problem solving and achievement of objectives; initiates change within the District by developing and implementing new systems, programs and technologies.

Plans, develops, directs and implements library services for the District. Develops long range plans and specific annual goals and objectives; coordinates cooperative services for member libraries; develops organizational policies for the District; evaluates library services and determines future action; oversees collection development.

Directs budget preparation and administration; negotiates and oversees contracts for services provided to the library; develops plans for capital expenditures; researches or supervises the preparation of statistical reports regarding library operation, finances and programs.

Oversees the employment, retention, promotion, transfer, and termination of library personnel consistent with approved personnel policies, rules and regulations, and serves as final authority on all personnel matters; provides leadership and training for Library staff.

Represents the library system at various professional conferences and public meetings; makes presentations, gives speeches, attends and chairs meetings; works with State Library and State Legislature to achieve progressive library legislation and funding for public libraries and on collaborative efforts.

Knowledge, Skills, and Abilities

Comprehensive knowledge of the principles, methods, and practices of professional library science and administration.

Comprehensive knowledge of public management principles as they relate to library operations and administration budgeting, planning, personnel administration, and fund raising.

Thorough knowledge of reader interest levels and group and community interests, and a wide knowledge of professional library literature, multi-media, and library technology.

Thorough knowledge of the principles, practices, theory and applications of public personnel management.

Ability to organize, direct, and evaluate the work of a large staff of professional, paraprofessional, and other library personnel which compose the library system.

Ability to analyze library system services in relation to needs of the community and to redirect library services consistent with changing public needs and established library policy.

Ability to establish and maintain effective working relationships with community leaders, public officials, professional groups, and the general public.

Ability to communicate effectively, both orally and in writing.

Ability to analyze issues and make informed recommendations to the board of directors and/or decisions in the daily operations of the district.

Thorough knowledge of the principles, practices, theory and applications of public personnel management.

Physical and Mental Requirements

Work is primarily performed in an office environment. Work is essentially sedentary with occasional walking, standing, bending, safely carrying items under 25 pounds. Work requires commuting between various District sites.

Education, Experience, and Training

MINIMUM QUALIFICATIONS

Work requires possession of a master's degree in library science including, or supplemented by, coursework in management or public administration, and extensive progressively more responsible experience in professional library management, some of which shall have been as a manager or director, or an equivalent combination of education and/or experience. thats.

> 3.1.4 Library Director
>
> **Library Name:** Woodland Public Library
> **Library Location:** Woodland, California
> **Population Served:** 46,300
> **Number of Volumes:** 95,372
> **Number of Titles:** N/A
> **Number of Periodical Subscriptions:** 237

Reports to

SUPERVISION RECEIVED AND EXERCISED

Policy direction is provided by the Library Board of Trustees. Receives administrative direction from the City Manager. Exercises direct and indirect supervision over assigned staff.

General Summary

JOB OBJECTIVE

To plan, organize, and direct the operations and activities of the City's library system.

Essential Functions and Responsibilities

EXAMPLES OF DUTIES

The following are typical illustrations of duties encompassed by the job class, not an all-inclusive or limiting list:

ESSENTIAL JOB FUNCTIONS:

Plan, organize, and direct the operations and activities of the City's library system.

Develop and coordinate programs of service to meet community needs including plans for efficient and economical use of labor, buildings, equipment and materials.

Attend meetings of and prepare reports for the Library Board of Trustees and provide technical and professional advice and recommendations related to levels of service and other library-related matters.

Prepare and direct the preparation of various statistical reports to the City Council and state and federal reports; coordinates special studies on a variety of complex problems which require a high degree of technical competence and political awareness.

Prepare and present reports to Council; provide technical and professional advice and recommendations related to levels of service and other library related matters; direct preparation of relevant reports and research.

Assure that positive public relations and effective working relationships are maintained by the Department with the general public, other governmental agencies, the City Council, City departments, and the media.

In consultation with the City Manager and City Council, assure that the department has adequate resources to fulfill its mission through proper budget planning and execution, personnel selection, and training and development.

Review work methods and interdepartmental procedures to ensure effective work flow and compliance with established policies and procedures.

Promote and maintain safety in the work place.

Represent the Library before the City Council, the community and at professional meetings as requested.

Serve as Acting City Manager as assigned.

Perform related duties as assigned.

Knowledge, Skills, and Abilities

Knowledge of:

Principles and practices of organization, administration, budgeting and personnel management, including principles and practices of library science, automation and collection.

Organizational and management practices as applied to the analysis and evaluation of programs, policies, and operational needs.

Library classification, circulation, distributing, cataloging and reference techniques and practices; automated library systems and data bases.

Operation and programs of a personal computer.

Skill to:

Analyze feasibility of projects and proposed programs; prepare complete and accurate reports.

Persuade and motivate individuals and groups toward the successful accomplishment of shared goals and objectives.

Delegate responsibility; schedule and program work on a long-term basis.

Communicate clearly and concisely, both orally and in writing.

Efficiently operate a personal computer.

Establish and maintain effective work relationships with those contacted in the performance of required duties.

Ability to:

Develop and implement library services which will meet the changing needs of the community; use financial, technological and staff resources effectively for the planning, programming and promoting of services; set priorities, work well under pressure and meet deadlines.

Deal patiently and tactfully with other department directors, elected officials, outside agencies, citizens, and the press.

Analyze a variety of administrative and organizational problems and make sound policy and procedure interpretations and recommendations.

Meet the physical requirements necessary to safely and effectively perform the assigned duties.

Supervisory Responsibilities

SUPERVISION RECEIVED AND EXERCISED

Policy direction is provided by the Library Board of Trustees. Receives administrative direction from the City Manager. Exercises direct and indirect supervision over assigned staff.

Education, Experience, and Training

Any combination of education and experience that would likely provide the required knowledge and abilities is qualifying. A typical way to obtain the knowledge and abilities would be:

Education

Possession of a Master's of Library Science Degree from an accredited college or university is required in addition to a Bachelor's Degree with major course work in library services or related field;

Experience:

Five years of increasingly responsible experience in professional public library administration, including at least three years of responsible administrative/management experience.

3.2 DEPUTY LIBRARY DIRECTOR

3.2.1 Deputy Library Director

Library Name: Des Moines Public Library
Library Location: Des Moines, Iowa
Population Served: 198,682
Number of Volumes: 427,008
Number of Titles: N/A
Periodical Subscriptions: 1,051

General Summary

JOB OBJECTIVE:

Manages library public services; performs directly related work as required.

Distinguishing Features of the Class

The principal function of an employee in this class is to manage public services including all library locations, outreach, collection management, and is responsible for the development of library services to serve library district patrons. The work is performed under the direct supervision of the Library Director but extensive leeway is granted for the exercise of independent judgment and initiative. Supervision is exercised over the work of employees in the class of Supervising Librarian. The nature of the work performed requires that an employee in this class establishes and maintains effective working relationships with department heads, other library employees, and the general public. The principal duties of this class are performed in a general office environment.

Essential Functions and Responsibilities

Examples of Essential Work (Illustrative Only):

Plans, directs and supervises library public services operations and activities;

Provides advice, direction, and interpretation of library policies, mission, values, and strategic direction;

Coordinates public service activities and programs to produce efficient, effective library public services;

Ensures maintenance of a viable collection of library materials that meets the needs of patrons in the library service area;

Participates in system-wide management decisions, including labor relations and contract negotiations for the collective bargaining unit;

Analyzes library public services needs and recommends new and improved policies, procedures, practices, equipment, facilities and staffing;

Provides estimates and forecasts of library operations to assist in long-range planning and analyzes library statistics, historical records and other applicable information;

Develops goals, plans and measurements for public services operations;

Maintains effective relations with library friends groups and governmental jurisdictions in the service area;

Participates in professional library organizations concerned with trends and innovations related to public library patron needs and services;

Trains and coaches staff in public service issues;

Compiles, tracks, and analyses the library materials budget;

Prepares and submits regular and special required reports on public library operations;

Serves on city-wide committees and task forces as assigned;

Acts for the Library Director, as assigned;

Provides needed information and demonstrations concerning how to perform certain work tasks to new employees in the same or similar class of positions;

Keeps immediate supervisor and designated others fully and accurately informed concerning work progress, including present and potential work problems and suggestions for new or improved ways of addressing such problems;

Attends meetings, conferences, workshops and training sessions and reviews publications and audio-visual materials to become and remain current on the principles, practices and new developments in assigned work areas;

Responds to citizens' questions and comments in a courteous and timely manner;

Communicates and coordinates regularly with appropriate others to maximize the effectiveness and efficiency of interdepartmental operations and activities;

Performs other directly related duties consistent with the role and function of the classification.

Knowledge, Skills, and Abilities

Required Knowledge, Skills and Abilities:

Comprehensive knowledge of library public service functions, procedures, policies and organization;

Thorough knowledge of community and political wants, needs, processes and procedures that affect the public services offered by the library;

Thorough knowledge of the materials collections in the library district;

Thorough knowledge of automated on-line library systems utilized by the library district;

Skill in public speaking and presentations;

Skill in leadership, motivation, and coordination of the work of others;

Ability to communicate effectively with others, both orally and in writing, using both technical and non-technical language;

Ability to understand and follow oral and/or written policies, procedures and instructions;

Ability to prepare and present accurate and reliable reports containing findings and recommendations;

Ability to operate a personal computer using standard or customized software applications appropriate to assigned tasks;

Ability to use logical and creative thought processes to develop solutions according to written specifications and/or oral instructions;

Ability to perform a wide variety of duties and responsibilities with accuracy and speed under the pressure of time-sensitive deadlines;

Ability and willingness to quickly learn and put to use new skills and knowledge brought about by rapidly changing information and/or technology;

Integrity, ingenuity and inventiveness in the performance of assigned tasks.

Physical and Mental Requirements

Essential Physical Abilities:

Sufficient clarity of speech and hearing or other communication capabilities, with or without reasonable accommodation, which permits the employee to communicate effectively;

Sufficient vision or other powers of observation, with or without reasonable accommodation, which permits the employee to produce and review a wide variety of technical and training materials, written correspondence, reports and related materials in both electronic and hard copy form;

Sufficient manual dexterity with or without reasonable accommodation, which permits the employee to operate a keyboard;

Sufficient personal mobility and physical reflexes, with or without reasonable accommodation, which permits the employee to monitor and supervise library operations at various locations on a regular basis, and to attend library system, City, community, and public meetings at various locations.

Education, Experience, and Training

Acceptable Experience and Training:

Graduation from an accredited college or university with a Master of Library Science Degree; and

Extensive management experience in a public library environment; or any equivalent combination of experience and training which provides the knowledge, skills and abilities necessary to perform the work.

License and Certification Requirements

Candidates for positions in this class must pass a post-employment offer physical examination and drug screen;

Possession of a valid Iowa driver's license or evidence of equivalent mobility.

3.3 DIRECTOR REPORTING TO LIBRARY BOARD

3.3.1 Director Reporting to Library Board

Library Name: Bay County Library System
Library Location: Bay City, Michigan
Population Served: 111,489
Number of Volumes: 290,577
Number of Titles: N/A
Number of Periodical Subscriptions: 781

Reports to

Bay County Library System Board of Trustees

General Summary

Under the direction of the Library Board, is directly responsible for the administration and management of the Bay County Library System.

Essential Functions and Responsibilities

Oversees and evaluates the operation of the multi-branch library system

Develops library policies, procedures, and practices, and implements and administers them upon approval of the Library Board.

Formulates library goals and objectives in conjunction with the Library Board and plans library services designed to meet them.

Prepares an annual budget for approval by the Library Board and County Commission, and administers and monitors the expenditure of funds.

Leads, directs, and supervises the staff of the Bay County Library System, directly and through other supervisory personnel.

Develops and implements effective administrative programs and procedures in collaboration with the management team.

Promotes staff development at all levels.

Implements Board personnel policies, including recruiting, interviewing, hiring, orienting, and overseeing training of new employees, reviewing, evaluating performance, and termination decisions.

Facilitates labor management relations, represents the library in union contract negotiations, handles grievances, administers collective bargaining agreements.

Maintains confidentiality of all patron records and transactions.

Solicits bids for services and purchases, presenting all contracts and recommendations to the Library Board.

Oversees the preparation of timely reports on usage, financials, circulation, services and programs for the Library Board, state library, and other governmental units.

Responsible for collection development and maintenance.

Develops and oversees library technology and automation while balancing new and traditional formats and services.

Serves as a spokesperson and advocate for the library throughout the community.

Oversees fundraising activities for the library.

Enforces library "Rules of Conduct" and takes appropriate action in case of infringement.

Represents and maintains active involvement by the Library within the Mideastern Library Cooperative and Valley Library Consortium.

Coordinates system services with those of the regional cooperative, state library, school districts, and other nearby systems.

Represents the Library at meetings and conferences of state, regional, and national professional library associations.

Oversees maintenance and improvement of library facilities, property, and equipment to assure compliance with federal, state, and local code and safety regulations.

Approves all purchases for payment.

Implements regular library staff meetings.

Attends all Board of Trustees meetings.

Knowledge, Skills, and Abilities

Extensive knowledge of current principles, methods, and practices of a public library.

Knowledge of community needs and interest levels.

Knowledge of print, electronic, audiovisual and information formats, technologies, and resources.

Ability to plan, analyze, evaluate, supervise, and direct library needs and services.

Interpersonal and oral and written communication skills necessary to establish and maintain effective working relationships with community leaders, public officials, professional groups, library employees, and the general public.

Knowledge of hardware and software systems necessary for the operation of the library and management of its resources.

Ability to use electronic means of communication and information transfer.

Ability to make decisions and take appropriate action to assure implementation.

Physical and Mental Requirements

Ability to meet certain physical requirements successfully to perform the essential functions of the job. Functions include (but are not necessarily limited to):

Occasional lifting or carrying objects weighing up to 25 pounds for short distances.

Reaching, including overhead reaching.

Mobility.

Ability to use a computer keyboard and mouse.

Ability to exchange information in person or on the telephone.

Supervisory Responsibilities

Supervises: All Library Staff

Education, Experience, and Training

Qualifications:

Masters Degree in Library Science and Information Science from an American Library Association-accredited program. A second degree in public or business administration is preferred.

At least 8 years experience in a public library in an administrative or supervisory capacity.

Additional Qualifications

Additional duties/responsibilities as required or assigned by the Library Board.

3.4 DIRECTOR REPORTING TO CITY MANAGER

3.4.1 Director Reporting to City Manager

Library Name: Palo Alto City Library
Library Location: Palo Alto, California
Population Served: 60,800
Number of Volumes: 238,636
Number of Titles: 166,858
Number of Periodical Subscriptions: 952

Reports to

City Manager

General Summary

JOB OBJECTIVE: Under the general direction of the City Manager, manages, operates, directs, and controls a continuing municipal library system providing reading, reference, and related informational services for the residents of Palo Alto.

DISTINGUISHING FEATURES: The Director of Libraries is a one-position managerial classification charged with the overall responsibility for planning, organizing, implementing, and evaluating city-wide library and related information service programs within a branch library system. The requirement to perform budgetary analysis and preparation, as well as policy and procedure analysis and implementation, are key elements of this position. Emphasis is also placed upon the incumbent's ability to develop and maintain efficient and effective operating techniques within a highly visible, service-oriented municipal organization.

Essential Functions and Responsibilities

Essential and other important responsibilities and duties may include, but are not limited to, the following:

Directly, and through subordinate supervisors, plans, organizes, directs, monitors, and evaluates the overall library operation, including establishing selection processes and procedures for new employees, in-service training programs, departmental orientation; develops, reviews, and conducts personnel performance appraisals.

Reviews and approves adult and children's service programs and activities, library publications and publication schedules, material selection policies, and all material purchase requests.

Reviews and approves technical services activities, including material selection, purchase and maintenance standards and procedures, insuring that materials meet the criteria of the ALA Bill of Rights and are available in sufficient quantity.

Analyzes needs, develops and implements plans for growth, use, and development of library facilities in accordance with the needs of the residents of the community.

Prepares and monitors Annual Operating and Capital Improvements budgets, reviewing and exercising final approval authority over all library expenditures; establishes and monitors inventory control systems for all library furnishings and material; reviews and analyzes fee structure and fee collection process for adequacy and control.

Acts as Library department liaison with community groups to ensure that appropriate and sufficient contact is maintained to adequately assess the community's library service needs.

Works with other City departments to insure that the Libraries are organized and operated efficiently and effectively and in a manner consistent with the goals of continuing employee development, optimum service delivery, and professional standards; insures that employee selection standards and procedures are consistent with the City's Affirmative Action goals and policies.

Perform related duties and responsibilities as required.

Knowledge, Skills, and Abilities

Ability to plan, organize, direct and implement programs and activities in the library field and related community services field;

Stimulate creativity and executive change as needed;

Analyze, formulate and implement departmental budget;

Work effectively and cooperatively with a variety of city/community programs;

Successfully supervise the work of others;

Effectively evaluate book collection needs for the city's library system;

Write clearly.

Knowledge of principles of management and organization;

Principles and practices of librarianship, including problems and procedures in operating a branch library system, and professional services such as cataloging, reference, and bibliographic work; Modern library plant and equipment requirements;

Library programs and their relationship to community needs; Adult and juvenile books, periodicals, reference, and bibliographic works;

Principles of training and supervision.

Ability to communicate with others and to assimilate and understand information, in a manner consistent with the essential job functions.

Ability to operate assigned equipment.

Ability to make sound decisions in a manner consistent with the essential job functions.

Ability to communicate effectively, orally and in writing, in English language with wide variety of people.

Ability to work varied schedule as required.

Work Environment

WORKING CONDITIONS: Work in office environment; sustained posture in seated position for prolonged periods of time; travel to other locations frequently.

Supervisory Responsibilities

SUPERVISES: Supervising Librarian Staff Secretary Manager, Main Library Services

Education, Experience, and Training

MINIMUM QUALIFICATIONS: Sufficient education, training and/or work experience to demonstrate possession of the following knowledge, skills, and abilities which would typically be acquired through:

Possession of a Master's degree in Library Science and ten years of increasingly responsible public library experience, five of which must have been in a managerial capacity.

4.0 ADMINISTRATIVE SERVICES DIRECTOR

4.1 ADMINISTRATIVE SERVICES DIRECTOR

4.1.1 Administrative Services Director

Library Name: Williamsburg Regional Library System
Library Location: Williamsburg, Virginia
Population Served: 60,100
Number of Volumes: 261,243
Number of Titles: N/A
Number of Periodical Subscriptions: 562

General Summary

JOB OBJECTIVE:

Under the supervision of the Library Director, the Director of Administrative Services is responsible for overseeing the operations of the Library Administrative Office. This includes the supervision of library administrative assistants, working with the Board of Trustees, Foundation Board and Friends of the Library and assisting the Library Director and department heads with projects and operations.

Essential Functions and Responsibilities

Administers all functions of the administrative office, including hiring, training, scheduling, supervising, and evaluating library administrative assistants.

Complies and maintains computerized monthly statistical report; helps compile information for the annual State Library report.

Works closely with the Board of Trustees, Foundation Board, and Friends of the Library in the preparation of meeting agendas, informational packets, minutes of meetings, and correspondence.

Is responsible for working with library staff, the Library Director, and the Board of Trustees on the development and promulgation of Library policy. Keeps library policy manual current.

Performs and supervises library administrative assistants on a variety of special projects, as required, such as coordinating employee recognition events, conducting employee and public surveys, researching information regarding policies and procedures, and developing new programs and services.

Is responsible for new employee orientation to the library's mission, goals, organizational structure, etc.

Assists library departments in employee selection. May serve on interview committees.

Performs other duties as needed.

Knowledge, Skills, and Abilities

Ability to plan, organize, and administer a department.

Comprehensive knowledge of the principles, practices, and techniques of library management.

Ability to compile and analyze information, including statistical data, and make recommendations.

Excellent written and oral communication skills.

Ability to be an active and sensitive listener.

Ability to work under pressure.

Ability to delegate work effectively.

Ability to set own priorities for work to be done and meet deadlines.

Ability to establish and maintain effective working relationships with employees, department heads, supervisors, board members, government employees and officials, and representatives from the private sector or other municipalities, and the general public.

Work Environment

The job occurs in the library buildings. Administers work typically sitting in an office, with occasional walking, light lifting, and other limited physical activities; some operation of computer and other office equipment is required. Regular contact is made with employees, various boards, government officials and personnel, and the general public.

Education, Experience, and Training

MINIMUM QUALIFICATIONS:

Bachelor's degree in business management or closely related field and five years increasingly responsible experience in library management; supervisory experiences; or any equivalent combination of acceptable education and experience providing the required knowledge, skills, and abilities.

Additional Qualifications

NECESSARY SPECIAL QUALIFICATIONS:

Requires the ability to travel among various library sites.

5.0 DIVISION ADMINISTRATOR

5.1 AUDIOVISUAL AND MAINTENANCE ADMINISTRATOR

> ### 5.1.1 Audiovisual and Maintenance Administrator
>
> **Library Name:** Williamsburg Regional Library System
> **Library Location:** Williamsburg, Virginia
> **Population Served:** 60,100
> **Number of Volumes:** 261,243
> **Number of Titles:** N/A
> **Number of Periodical Subscriptions:** 562

General Summary

JOB OBJECTIVE:

Under the supervision of the Library Director, the Maintenance and Audiovisual Director is responsible for overseeing the custodial and maintenance services for the two facilities and the bookmobile, supervising the HVAC and building maintenance staff and for coordinating and assisting in the provision of audiovisual services to the Library's program services department.

Essential Functions and Responsibilities

Administers all functions of the custodial and maintenance services for two library facilities, including hiring, training, scheduling, supervising, and evaluating the HVAC and building maintenance staff.

Oversees building maintenance budget requests and spending. Develops capital improvements budgets in consultation with Collection Services Director for major building maintenance and repair projects.

Assesses, oversees, and provides staff with audiovisual and theatrical equipment training needs.

Oversees maintenance, repair, rental, and replacement of audiovisual and theatrical equipment; ensures that required piano tunings are scheduled and completed; initiates purchase orders for these purposes. Trains staff in the maintenance and repair of selected equipment.

In consultation with the Program Services Director and other appropriate staff, establishes procedures for the repair of audiovisual materials; oversees and trains staff and volunteers to perform timely repairs.

May participate in library-wide committees or projects.

Performs other duties as needed.

Knowledge, Skills, and Abilities

Ability to plan, organize, and administer a department.

Comprehensive knowledge of the principles, practices, and techniques of library and building maintenance management.

Expertise in theatrical lighting, sound, and other audiovisual equipment.

Excellent written and oral communication skills.

Ability to work under pressure.

Ability to delegate work effectively.

Ability to set own priorities for work to be done and meet deadlines.

Ability to establish and maintain effective working relationships with library staff.

Work Environment

JOB LOCATION AND EQUIPMENT NEEDED

The job occurs in and around the library buildings. Considerable contact is made with employees and the public. Administers work typically moving, using, lifting, and adjusting a variety of light to heavy equipment and materials associated with the requirements of the job, including frequent sustained operation of custodial equipment.

Education, Experience, and Training

MINIMUM QUALIFICATIONS:

Associates degree with experience in building maintenance and theatrical lighting, sounds, and audiovisual; or any equivalent combination of acceptable education and experience providing required knowledge, skills, and abilities.

Additional Qualifications

NECESSARY SPECIAL QUALIFICATIONS:

Requires the ability to travel among various library sites and to lift 50 pounds.

5.2 CENTRAL LIBRARY AND DIVISION ADMINISTRATOR

5.2.1 Central Library and Division Administrator

Library Location: Boston Public Library
Population Served: 574,283
Number of Volumes: 7,954,358
Number of Titles: N/A
Number of Periodical Subscriptions: 29,026

Reports to

Chief of Public Services

General Summary

JOB OBJECTIVE:

Under the general direction of the Chief of Public Services, provides leadership to and administers Central Library public service operations within the framework of goals, policies and procedures established by the Board of Library Trustees and the Strategic Process Team. Works closely with all parts of the organization to ensure excellent public service delivery. Member of the Senior Management Team.

Essential Functions and Responsibilities

Coordinates and provides general direction and administration of public services in Boston Public Library's Central Library, to meet the diverse user needs of scholars, children, adults and families seeking a range of materials and services including research, popular and life long learning.

Provides leadership that inspires and promotes Central Library staff involvement in organizational change through collaborative problem solving processes.

Sets goals and standards for Central Library public service operations including all subject departments, format departments, collection access services; evaluates the work of Central Library department heads; ensures operational effectiveness through continuous quality improvement where appropriate; oversees and ensures adherence to all applicable Library policies and guidelines.

Helps formulate and interpret management decisions, directions, policies and procedures to staff and the public; relays public and staff needs and suggestions to Chief of Public Services.

Makes continuous and periodic studies of the Central Library's community, evaluates the library's effectiveness in meeting community needs, and assumes responsibility for establishing unique community partnerships.

Serves as liaison to the City-Wide Friends. Attends their meetings, provides information about Central Library needs and goals, facilitates communication between the Friends and the Library.

Works with the Program Services Office to deliver programs, exhibits and events, and shares in the library's public relations and publicity efforts to encourage Central Library usage.

Works with the Human Resources Division to recruit, hire, and evaluate central library staff, and to take disciplinary action where warranted.

Works with the Financial Services Division by assisting in the formulation, management and deployment of Central Library budget.

Works with Facilities to identify and resolve building access and related service issues.

Works with the Technology Division by assisting in the planning, management and deployment of technological and electronic resources in the Central Library.

Coordinates with Technical Services and the Collection Development Manager to efficiently select, acquire, and deliver to the public a collection responsive to the full range of user needs.

Assists in long-range and short-term strategic planning for the library including capital projects, community outreach activities, and implementing and managing organizational change. Uses management information to improve service delivery and decision-making.

Serves as backup to the Chief of Public Services.

Serves and represents the Library on appropriate community, state, regional and national committees or related activities.

Performs related functions as assigned.

Knowledge, Skills, and Abilities

Extensive knowledge of the principles and practices of public library work.

Knowledge of library trends and best practices for superior service delivery.

Demonstrated ability and willingness to lead teams and work in teams, to analyze professional and managerial problems and recommend workable solutions, and to organize work effectively and direct personnel.

Considerable knowledge of user interests and needs, and a broad knowledge of books, authors and non-book materials and online resources.

Superior oral and written communication skills.

Experience in hiring and evaluating staff.

Exceptional interpersonal skills and creative problem solving ability.

A sense of humor and a positive and enthusiastic approach to public services and library leadership.

Ability to balance the diverse user needs of a Central Library that serves scholars, children, adults and families in a multicultural, urban environment.

Education, Experience, and Training

Education – Bachelor Degree from an accredited college or university and a Masters Degree in Library Science from an ALA accredited library school.

Experience – 10 years of related library experience, including 5 years at a supervisory and/or management level, which reflects initiative and responsiveness to the dynamic nature of public library services.

Additional Qualifications

Desired attributes—Adaptability; self-directed; ability to organize and delegate competing priorities; an open-honest communicator who inspires trust and one who seeks and sparks creative contributions from others.

Requirements: Must be a Resident of the City of Boston upon first day of hire.

5.2.2 Central Library Administrator

Library Name: Phoenix Public Library
Library Location: Phoenix, Arizona
Population Served: 1,350,435
Number of Volumes: 2,015,587
Number of Titles: 734,921
Number of Periodical Subscriptions: 4,500

General Summary

JOB OBJECTIVE:

The fundamental reason this classification exists is to administer the activities of the Central Library and its grounds, the branch libraries, or the Technical Services Division. The administrator plans, directs, and evaluates public service systems and facilities to meet present and future library service needs. Supervision is exercised over professional and supervisory personnel. Work is performed under the general direction of the City Librarian in accordance with professional standards and established division policies and procedures.

Essential Functions and Responsibilities

Supervises professional, paraprofessional, clerical, and protective service employees engaged in providing library services;

Plans and directs the operation of the Central Library, the branch libraries, or Technical Services;

Formulates goals, policies, objectives, plans, and procedures for public library services;

Monitors and evaluates the effectiveness of service programs;

Prepares divisional budget requests and participates in development of the annual library budget;

Monitors and controls expenditures through the budget year;

Directs or prepares studies and reports to support recommendations for policy changes or procedural improvements;

Investigates new library systems techniques to determine their applicability to the Phoenix Public Library System;

Maintains administrative controls to ensure adequate physical security of library property;

Coordinates custodial and maintenance requirements of the Central Library or the branch libraries with the Public Works Department;

Conducts automation and other supplier vendor contract negotiations, coordinates contracts with the City Attorney's Office, and monitors contracts;

Supervises professional and supervisory personnel who operate technical services sections and provide support to the public services units of the Library;

Keeps aware of current developments in library operational techniques and procedures and revises division methods as appropriate;

Confers with other library administrators on issues of common interest;

Analyzes, plans, and participates in the development of capital improvement projects;

Demonstrates continuous effort to improve operations, decrease turnaround times, streamline work processes, and work cooperatively and jointly to provide quality seamless customer service.

Knowledge, Skills, and Abilities

Knowledge of:

Principles and theories of library science.

Principles and practices of library administration, municipal budgeting, supervision, and personnel administration.

Means of determining community needs and interests, and methods for providing requested resources.

Principles and applications of computers, automation and data communications as they relate to library systems.

Leadership styles and skills.

Ability to:

Perform a broad range of supervisory responsibilities over others.

Communicate orally, in the English language, with customers, clients, City official and the public by phone or in person in a one-to-one or group setting.

Comprehend and make inferences from written material.

Produce written documents with clearly organized thoughts using proper sentence construction, punctuation, and grammar.

Analyze professional and administrative problems, make recommendations, and take appropriate action.

Conduct and direct research and evaluate the results.

Interpret library policies, objectives, and facilities to community groups, public officials, professional groups, and the general public.

Work cooperatively with others.

Work safely without presenting a direct threat to self or others.

Additional Requirements:

Some positions require the use of personal or City vehicles on City business. Individuals must be physically capable of operating the vehicles safely, possess a valid driver's license and have an acceptable driving record. Use of a personal vehicle for City business will be prohibited if the employee is not authorized to drive a City vehicle or if the employee does not have personal insurance coverage.

Some positions will require the performance of other essential and marginal functions depending upon work location, assignment, or shift.

Education, Experience, and Training

Four years experience directing professional library work and a master's degree in library science from an American Library Association (ALA) accredited institution. Other combinations of experience and education that meet the minimum requirements may be substituted.

5.3 LIBRARY SERVICES ADMINISTRATOR

5.3.1 Library Services Administrator

Library Name: Phoenix Public Library
Library Location: Phoenix, Arizona
Population Served: 1,350,435
Number of Volumes: 2,015,587
Number of Titles: 734,921
Number of Periodical Subscriptions: 4,500

General Summary

JOB OBJECTIVE:

The fundamental reason this classification exists is to administer the activities of the Central Library and its grounds, the branch libraries, or the Technical Services Division. The administrator plans, directs, and evaluates public service systems and facilities to meet present and future library service needs. Supervision is exercised over professional and supervisory personnel. Work is performed under the general direction of the City Librarian in accordance with professional standards and established division policies and procedures.

Essential Functions and Responsibilities

Supervises professional, paraprofessional, clerical, and protective service employees engaged in providing library services;

Plans and directs the operation of the Central Library, the branch libraries, or Technical Services;

Formulates goals, policies, objectives, plans, and procedures for public library services;

Monitors and evaluates the effectiveness of service programs;

Prepares divisional budget requests and participates in development of the annual library budget;

Monitors and controls expenditures through the budget year;

Directs or prepares studies and reports to support recommendations for policy changes or procedural improvements;

Investigates new library systems techniques to determine their applicability to the Phoenix Public Library System;

Maintains administrative controls to ensure adequate physical security of library property;

Coordinates custodial and maintenance requirements of the Central Library or the branch libraries with the Public Works Department;

Conducts automation and other supplier vendor contract negotiations, coordinates contracts with the City Attorney's Office, and monitors contracts;

Supervises professional and supervisory personnel who operate technical services sections and provide support to the public services units of the Library;

Keeps aware of current developments in library operational techniques and procedures and revises division methods as appropriate;

Confers with other library administrators on issues of common interest;

Analyzes, plans, and participates in the development of capital improvement projects;

Demonstrates continuous effort to improve operations, decrease turnaround times, streamline work processes, and work cooperatively and jointly to provide quality seamless customer service.

Knowledge, Skills, and Abilities

Knowledge of:

Principles and theories of library science.

Principles and practices of library administration, municipal budgeting, supervision, and personnel administration.

Means of determining community needs and interests, and methods for providing requested resources.

Principles and applications of computers, automation and datacommunications as they relate to library systems.

Leadership styles and skills.

Ability to:

Perform a broad range of supervisory responsibilities over others.

Communicate orally, in the English language, with customers, clients, City official and the public by phone or in person in a one-to-one or group setting.

Comprehend and make inferences from written material.

Produce written documents with clearly organized thoughts using proper sentence construction, punctuation, and grammar.

Analyze professional and administrative problems, make recommendations, and take appropriate action.

Conduct and direct research and evaluate the results.

Interpret library policies, objectives, and facilities to community groups, public officials, professional groups, and the general public.

Work cooperatively with others.

Work safely without presenting a direct threat to self or others.

Education, Experience, and Training

ACCEPTABLE EXPERIENCE AND TRAINING:

Four years experience directing professional library work and a master's degree in library science from an American Library Association (ALA) accredited institution. Other combinations of experience and education that meet the minimum requirements may be substituted.

Additional Qualifications

Some positions require the use of personal or City vehicles on City business. Individuals must be physically capable of operating the vehicles safely, possess a valid driver's license and have an acceptable driving record. Use of a personal vehicle for City business will be prohibited if the employee is not authorized to drive a City vehicle or if the employee does not have personal insurance coverage.

Some positions will require the performance of other essential and marginal functions depending upon work location, assignment, or shift.

5.4 PUBLICATIONS ADMINISTRATOR

5.4.1 Publications Administrator

Library Name: Williamsburg Regional Library System
Library Location: Williamsburg, Virginia
Population Served: 60,100
Number of Volumes: 261,243
Number of Titles: N/A
Number of Periodical Subscriptions: 562

General Summary

JOB OBJECTIVE:

Under the supervision of the Program Services Director the Publications and Graphics Administrator helps prepare and disseminate a variety of graphic and informational materials supporting the programs and services of the library system. Also maintains scrapbooks and files of library history, news articles and feature stories.

Essential Functions and Responsibilities

Assists in preparation of graphic materials which include newsletters, flyers, posters, ads, reports, booklists, and other promotional and informational materials; assists in dissemination of same.

Helps oversee printing of promotional and informational materials; assists in obtaining bids for printing services.

Assists with preparation of timely news releases and distribution of same to various media.

Creates and maintains library signs and bulletin boards at both libraries.

Develops computer web pages and uses other media to help promote library services and programs.

Organizes, maintains, and keeps current scrapbooks and files of all media items of historical interest, including news articles and feature stories about the libraries.

May participate in library-wide committees or projects.

Performs other related duties as required.

Knowledge, Skills, and Abilities

Demonstrated expertise in graphic design and advertising, including camera-ready art.

Thorough knowledge of printing process, including print specification.

Expertise in IBM word processing (WordPerfect preferred) and related graphics software.

Excellent written and verbal communication skills, including accurate proofreading.

Ability to organize work, set priorities, use time effectively, work independently, and meet deadlines.

Ability to establish and maintain effective working relationships with employees, vendors, printers, media personnel, and the general public.

Ability to analyze and to creatively solve problems related to the position.

Ability to work with enthusiasm and initiative.

Tools and Equipment Used

Frequent sustained operation of graphic tools, computer and other office equipment.

Work Environment

The job is located in two libraries. Administers work typically sitting in an office, with occasional walking, light lifting, and other limited physical activities. Regular contact is made with employees, vendors, printers, media personnel, and the general public.

Education, Experience, and Training

MINIMUM QUALIFICATIONS:

Undergraduate degree or combination of higher education and experience in pertinent fields to provide necessary expertise.

Additional Qualifications

Requires the ability to travel among various library sites.

6.0 SYSTEM COORDINATOR

6.1 SYSTEM COORDINATOR

6.1.1 System Coordinator

Library Name: Manitowoc-Calumet Library System
Library Location: Manitowoc, Wisconsin
Population Served: 58,213
Number of Volumes: 195,166
Number of Titles: N/A
Number of Periodical Subscriptions: 395

Reports to

REPORTS TO System Director
UNION STATUS: Non-Represented
FLSA STATUS: Exempt

General Summary

JOB OBJECTIVE: Under general direction from the System Director, plans, develops, manages, and evaluates the overall activities of the Manitowoc-Calumet Library System and oversees or performs the day to day operations of the System. Administers and manages the System's service programs; develops and manages the System budget; supervises System staff. Develops and prepares System plans, reports, compliance documentation, and library agreements. Monitors and maintains compliance with all statutory requirements for Wisconsin public library systems. Writes and implements grants. Participates on the MPL/MCLS management team and coordinates activities of the System with those of other units of the Resource Library and other libraries within the System area.

Essential Functions and Responsibilities

PRINCIPAL DUTIES AND RESPONSIBILITIES: The following list identifies principal duties and responsibilities of the job. It is not a definitive list and other similar duties may be assigned. An asterisk (*) before any of the following items indicates duties and responsibilities which are not "essential functions" of the job as defined by the Americans with Disabilities Act.

Plans, develops, manages and evaluates the overall activities of the Manitowoc-Calumet Library System, and works to assure that MCLS complies with all statutory requirements for Wisconsin public library systems.

Coordinates and maintains service programs for backup reference and interlibrary loan, referral of reference and interlibrary loan requests, "same services" from member libraries, in-service training, delivery and communications, agreements with adjacent systems, professional consultation, users with special needs,

cooperation with other types of libraries, library technology and resource sharing, collection development, services to youth, and any other service programs included in the System plan.

Provides and performs administrative support services to facilitate the functioning of the System board, System Director, System office routines, and the System in general. Makes recommendations to the System Director for the improvement of the operations of the Manitowoc-Calumet Library System. Coordinates activities of the System with those of other units of the System Resource Library (MPL) and other libraries within the System area. Assists the System Director and functions in the Director's absence, if assigned.

Develops and writes the System's annual plan, annual report, and other required plans and reports, with input and review by the System Director and MCLS member librarians as appropriate. Plans, writes, administers, and implements grants and other proposals for the System. Compiles, maintains, reports, and interprets statistics relevant to the System's service programs.

Prepares and administers the budget for each System service program and the System as a whole, subject to the review of the System Director. Performs managerial and technical duties related to budgetary control such as authorizing invoices for payment, receiving and allocating revenues, scheduling and preparing for an annual audit, etc.

Negotiates, writes, implements, and monitors agreements with the System's member counties and libraries; the System Resource Library; and other libraries, library systems, and library organizations. Develops and administers any budget processes necessary to maintain specific agreements.

Supervises and schedules MCLS staff. Evaluates MCLS staff in conjunction with the System Director. Team interviews and makes hiring recommendations to the System Director. Develops and implements plans for training of MCLS staff, and involves staff from member libraries, as appropriate. Interprets management decisions, directives, policies and regulations to staff; communicates staff needs and suggestions to the Director. When necessary, handles progressive discipline of staff through the level of written warnings and makes recommendations for further discipline up to and including firing to the System Director.

Keeps informed on current trends and developments affecting libraries, and disseminates such information to System staff, member libraries, and the System Board. Serves as a general consultant for member libraries.

Monitors legislative developments affecting libraries, maintains contacts with legislators and officials, and advocates for libraries and library systems.

Organizes and conducts meetings. Represents MCLS at regional and state meetings relevant to system services and attends other library-related meetings, workshops, in-service programs, etc., as necessary.

Serves as continuing education validator for recertification of public librarians in the System.

Provides public relations for the System. Confers with the MPL Public Relations Supervisor regarding publicity and public relations. Encourages the use of system services and resources by other area libraries and the public.

Provides professional back-up to System interlibrary loan staff. Assists with difficult reference questions, verification, etc. Drives system van, as needed. Assists with the other work of MCLS and performs work of other MCLS staff, as needed. May perform work of another member of the MCLS/MPL management team, as assigned.

Serves on the Participants Council of the Manitowoc-Calumet Library Automated Resource Sharing Consortium (LARS). May provide supportive services in assistance to the operation of LARS.

Selects materials purchased by the System. May assist in the selection of materials for Manitowoc Public Library.

Acts as a cooperative member of the MCLS/MPL management team. Cooperates with MPL Public Services Coordinator in coordinating the public services and collection management efforts of the library and with MPL Automation & Technology Coordinator in collection maintenance, automation efforts, and LARS. Confers with the MPL Circulation Services Supervisor and MPL Technical Services Department Head about automation and support services; with MPL Information & Adult Services Department Head, and MPL Youth Services Department Head about public service needs and collection management issues; and with MPL Business Office Supervisor about personnel and financial issues.

Deals with problem patrons in the System Resource Library (MPL), particularly those who disrupt normal use or operation of the Library, or attempt to unlawfully remove library materials from premises. Assists with maintenance of building security. For example: enforces library policies for patron behavior; responds to alarms; completes Incident Reports and calls police or other official assistance, when necessary.

Additional Job Duties

Initiative and resourcefulness to take acceptable risks, make appropriate decisions, and exercise proper authority. Ability to present clear explanations of established policies and procedures. Ability to think and act appropriately under pressure. Willingness and ability to grant logical exceptions to policies and procedures when warranted. Willingness to maintain confidentiality when appropriate and to be held accountable.

Ability to develop work-related goals and objectives. Willingness to develop job-related abilities, skills and knowledge. Willingness and ability to keep abreast of changing technologies and procedures, and to assume responsibilities required by introduction of different services and equipment.

Willingness and ability to understand and support the fundamental principles of library services, such as offering open access to library materials in any format for people of all ages; providing materials representing as many points of view as possible; and protecting a patron's right to privacy in dealings with MCLS and with respect to records maintained by the System.

Knowledge, Skills, and Abilities

Thorough knowledge of the principles and practices of modern library administration and management as well as current library system/consortium practices, and ability to apply these to library system setting. Willingness and ability to contribute to and lead on-going development of System-wide philosophy, mission and services, and ability to provide consultation on the development of library philosophy, goals and services.

Thorough knowledge of public library planning practices and their application to system services. Ability to analyze and evaluate current conditions and make logical evaluations of future needs. Ability to develop and execute short-range plans. Ability to synthesize and creatively adapt trends in technology, publishing, information retrieval and library science to planning for the System.

Ability and willingness to assume a leadership role in a group setting. Ability to establish and maintain effective working relationships with the System Director and Trustees, directors and trustees of other member libraries, MPL Management Team members, other member library staff members, sales representatives, community and state officials, agency representatives, and the public. Ability to work in the MCLS/MPL/LARS team setting. Willingness to assist and support coworkers, contribute ideas, and maintain flexibility. Ability to adapt to a rapidly changing environment.

Ability to make realistic budget proposals, to operate within established budgetary guidelines, and to identify and analyze budgetary impact of services.

Commitment to and skill in supervising people. Thorough knowledge of supervisory and training techniques. Willingness and ability to provide a positive managerial example. Willingness and ability to foster an environment in which employees are self-motivated and can exhibit high morale. Capacity to recognize and utilize talents of others. Fairness when distributing workload, responsibility, and authority. Ability to identify proper work assignments for subordinates and willingness to follow-up to ensure proper completion.

Ability to set realistic standards for employees and to encourage productive and efficient performance. Conscientiousness when appraising performance, counseling employees, writing and administering performance appraisals, and making personnel recommendations.

Skill in managing departmental workflow, including ability to identify, negotiate, establish, communicate, and apply priorities. Skill in performing and supervising routine and non-routine procedures involving many steps. Ability to give and follow complex written and/or verbal instructions and to pay close attention to detail. Willingness to provide professional and managerial support to the System Director. Ability to accept delegation and to work under general supervisory direction.

Ability to communicate effectively. Skill in interpersonal communication and public speaking. Capacity to be easily understood on voice telephone. Ability to do technical writing for procedures, proposals, reports, etc.

Ability to interact effectively with the MCLS/MPL/LARS automated systems. Skill in using microcomputers and related software. Knowledge of database, spreadsheet and word processing software programs. Knowledge of or ability to quickly learn current software programs as these apply to job responsibilities.

Knowledge of and ability to use modern library technology. Interest in emerging technologies.

Knowledge of reference practices and collection development tools and theory. Ability to apply this knowledge as a consultant, as requested by member libraries.

Physical and Mental Requirements

Sometimes (up to 25% of work time) lifts and/or transports objects weighing 5 to 35 pounds; pushes or pulls carts loaded with materials weighing more than 150 pounds.

Sometimes (up to 25% of work time) works with equipment and performs procedures where carelessness may result in minor cuts, bruises, or muscle strains.

Occasionally (up to 10% of work time) works in bookstack areas where there is exposure to dust, newsprint, etc.

Occasionally (up to 10% of work time) retrieves and/or shelves objects weighing 5 to 20 pounds from all shelving levels.

Occasionally (up to 10% of work time) works with vehicles and equipment, and performs procedures where carelessness may result in traffic accident and/or cuts, bruises, muscle strains, or other injuries.

Occasionally (up to 10% of work time) drives full-size cargo-type van, truck, and/or other System vehicle up to 120 miles per trip in all types of weather, getting in and out of van at least 20 times per trip.

Work Environment

WORKING CONDITIONS:
Usually (up to 100% of work time) works in shared office environment with considerable staff contact, both in person and via phone, fax and email. Occasionally (up to 10% of work time) has direct contact with the public.

Usually (up to 100% of work time) works in close proximity with terminals and other similar electronic equipment.

Usually (up to 100% of work time) maintains work environment. For example: vacuuming computer areas, dusting, recycling paper; cleaning up after programs. Infrequently (as situation requires) assists with building emergencies which may involve cleaning up snow, bodily fluids, etc.

Education, Experience, and Training

MINIMUM QUALIFICATIONS:
Master's degree in library science from an A.L.A.-accredited school.

Eligibility for Grade 1 Wisconsin Library Certificate.

3 years post-M.L.S. managerial experience in a library system, consortium, or public library setting, 1 year in a supervisory role, and one year in administration; or, equivalent education/experience mix as determined by the System Director. Demonstrated ability to supervise staff, preferably in a union environment.

Additional Qualifications

Demonstrable possession of knowledge, skills, abilities, and capacities identified in "Job Specifications" section, above.

Capacity to work under conditions described in "Working Conditions" section, above.

License and Certification Requirements

Possession of or ability to attain a valid Wisconsin driver's license and good driving record with no accidents or citations for major violations within the last three years, and ability to obtain other appropriate licenses if required. Ability to maintain a valid Wisconsin driver's license and a good driving record with no accidents or citations for major violations either on or off the job.

Willingness, physical capacity and mechanical aptitude to drive a large cargo-type van, truck and/or other System vehicles or personal vehicle in normal Wisconsin weather conditions.

Must comply at all times with the System's "Drug-Free Workplace" policy and be willing to submit to drug and alcohol testing if involved in any traffic accident while operating any System vehicle.

Position Hours

Salaried full-time, typically working at least 80 hours per two-week pay period on a flexible schedule which may vary from day to day. May be scheduled to work days, evenings, Saturdays, and Sundays.

II. ADULT AND REFERENCE SERVICES

Included in this section are administrators, reference librarians, library associates, specialists, technicians and assistants, subject specialists, literacy librarians, foreign language specialist and audiovisual librarian.

1.0 ADULT SERVICES DIRECTOR

1.1 ADULT SERVICES DIRECTOR

1.1.1 Adult Services Director

Library Name: Anacortes Public Library
Library Location: Anacortes, Washington
Population Served: 14,500
Number of Volumes: N/A
Number of Titles: 55,565
Number of Periodical Subscriptions: 126

Reports to

Library Director

General Summary

JOB OBJECTIVE: This is a full-time, exempt professional position responsible for the development of the library's adult and young adult collections. This position also coordinates staff training and development and is responsible for the public service-functions of the library.

LEVEL OF AUTHORITY: Performs duties with only general direction and defined latitude for independent action and decisions commensurate with demonstrated ability. Errors in judgment could have substantial impact on library's fiscal condition and the public's acceptance of programs, personnel and facilities.

Essential Functions and Responsibilities

Research and recommend adult Library programs to the Director. Contact various agencies, as necessary and as directed, for assistance in such programs. Assist in the preparation of appropriate supporting materials for financial assistance.

Prepare and monitor budget for areas of responsibility, generating budget reports and analyses as required.

Hire and, in turn, plan, schedule, supervise and evaluate the work of the inter-library loan staff and the public services supervisor.

As directed, review and select books and other informational materials for purchase and distribution in the Library's adult collection. Catalog and classify incoming materials.

Provide reference service as scheduled or as time permits.

Respond to public inquiries in a courteous manner. Provide information within scope of knowledge or refer to other staff as appropriate.

Coordinate staff training programs, to include technology updates, safety and career development.

Write news releases and prepare articles relative to areas of responsibility.

Maintain records and statistics related to the Library's adult collection and patronage.

Act as Director in his/her absence.

Additional Job Duties

Attend staff and community meetings as required, often outside regular working hours.

Work with public-service supervisor in reviewing public-service clerks, pages, and performance.

May perform portions of the work of higher classified positions, as assigned.

May perform portions of the work of lower classified positions, as needed.

Work closely with Friends of the Library in purchases using their funds.

Must be able to drive an automobile in the course of Library business.

Knowledge, Skills, and Abilities

Attention to detail and accuracy.

Ability to communicate effectively, patiently and courteously with City employees, patrons and other community members.

Ability to handle multiple activities or interruptions at once and to work positively and effectively within a team model.

Ability to work a schedule including weekday, evening, weekends and morning hours.

Ability to supervise staff.

Ability to enforce Library rules.

Physical and Mental Requirements

Physical

Strength, for example, to push loaded book cart weighing approximately 300 pounds on level floor and up ramp, to lift or maneuver onto cart loads up to 50 pounds and to carry cartons of books up and down stairs.

Ability to bend, stoop and lift for prolonged periods in cramped spaces.

Stamina, for example, to stand for prolonged periods up to six hours in a shift. High energy to deal with the public for sustained periods while maintaining positive and enthusiastic communication.

Ability to sit and use computer workstation, including keyboard and visual display terminal, for extended periods of time.

Tools and Equipment Used

Audio-visual equipment, such as; cassette recorder, VCR and film and slide projectors; Office equipment, such as; personal computer and associated software, modem, typewriter, adding machine, microfiche reader, paper cutter, fax, copier, telephone and postage meter.

Work Environment

Work is performed primarily in indoor office setting, in community meeting rooms and at the library, in frequently dusty atmosphere with potential exposure to airborne pathogens.

Education, Experience, and Training

QUALIFICATIONS:

Technical

Must have a master's degree in Library or Information Science from an American Library Association accredited college or university.

Must have previous related experience sufficient to demonstrate thorough competency and extensive knowledge of the principles and practices of Library management.

Must have ability to plan, schedule, supervise and evaluate the work of assigned staff for proficient performance and high morale.

Must be bondable.

Must possess a valid Washington State driver's license.

Must have computer ability to adequately utilize automated library cataloging, circulation and other systems.

Must maintain professional and technical expertise through participation in continuing education.

Additional Qualifications

OTHER:

As an absolute condition of employment, employees are required upon hire to sign a drug-free workplace agreement and an agreement not to use tobacco products of any kind while on the job.

The statements contained in this job description reflect general details as necessary to describe the principal functions of this job, the level of knowledge and skill typically required and the scope of responsibility. It should not be considered an all-inclusive listing of work requirements. Individuals may perform other duties as assigned, including work in other functional areas to cover absences or provide relief, to equalize peak work periods or otherwise to balance the workload.

2.0 BRANCH, NEIGHBORHOOD, AND EXTENSION SERVICES DIRECTOR

2.1 NEIGHBORHOOD LIBRARIES DIRECTOR

2.1.1 Neighborhood Libraries Director

Library Name: Seattle Public Library
Library Location: Seattle, Washington
Population Served: 608,150
Number of Volumes: 2,553,934
Number of Titles: N/A
Number of Periodical Subscriptions: 9,719

General Summary

JOB OBJECTIVE:

The Director of Neighborhood Libraries reports to the City Librarian and is a member of the Library Leadership Team. The Director of Neighborhood Libraries provides leadership to the system's current 22 (soon to be 27) neighborhood libraries, to ensure that the best possible library resources and services are being provided in the city's neighborhood libraries. The Director also plays a key role in system-wide strategic planning and directs the activities of 19 Branch Managers, 3 Managing Librarians and a half-time Administrative Assistant.

Essential Functions and Responsibilities

Plan, organize, direct and evaluate the effectiveness of Neighborhood Library programs and operations; oversee the use and allocation of the budget and other resources; and direct the training, development, evaluation and use of staff resources to ensure that patrons receive high-quality, responsive customer service.

Provide leadership that inspires and promotes neighborhood library staff involvement in organizational change through collaborative problem solving processes like the Joint Labor Management Partnership Agreement.

Working with the City Librarian and members of the Library Leadership Team, assume responsibility for how staff and the public perceive the Library.

Support intellectual freedom.

Set goals and standards for branch operations; evaluate the work of the Branch Managers; ensure operational effectiveness through continuous quality improvement where appropriate; and oversee and ensure adherence to all applicable Library policies, procedures and guidelines.

Ensure effective communication and collaboration between Neighborhood Library Services and all other Library divisions, and with patrons, other governmental organizations, community agencies and special interest groups throughout the Seattle community.

Assist the City Librarian in long-range and short-term strategic planning for the Library, including capital projects, community outreach activities, and implementing and managing organizational change.

Knowledge, Skills, and Abilities

Knowledge of and proven experience applying effective management practices and principles in a public library setting, including personnel administration, budget development, strategic planning, and project management.

Current knowledge of relevant and emerging issues, including involvement with local, state, and national library groups.

The ability to lead effectively by example, inspire staff, and promote enthusiastic teamwork.

Exceptional interpersonal skills and creative problem-solving ability.

Exceptional written and oral communication skills, including experience in public speaking.

Positive and enthusiastic approach to public service and library leadership.

Education, Experience, and Training

QUALIFICATIONS

An MLS from an ALA-accredited library school, or Washington State certification as a librarian, and directly related, increasingly responsible public library management experience at a managerial or director level.

> ### 2.1.2 Neighborhood Libraries Director
>
> **Library Name:** Milwaukee Public Library
> **Library Location:** Milwaukee, Wisconsin
> **Population Served:** 608,150
> **Number of Volumes:** 2,553,934
> **Number of Titles:** N/A
> **Number of Periodical Subscriptions:** 9,719

Reports to

SUPERVISION RECEIVED: (Indicate the extent to which work assignments and methods are outlined, reviewed, and approved by others.)

Receives broad administrative direction from the City Librarian, with wide latitude for exercise of discretion and initiative. Subject to prior approval of new plans and policies and general review of results. Name and title of Immediate Supervisor: City Librarian

General Summary

JOB FUNCTION:

The incumbent serves as third in command of the Milwaukee Public Library System, and as administrator of the Neighborhood Libraries and Extension Services Bureau. The Manager of Neighborhood and Extension Services assumes full responsibility for all units of the library in the absence of the City Librarian and Manager of Central Library Services.

Responsible for the daily direction of the twelve neighborhood libraries, the Mobile Library and Outreach Services unit, the Automotive Services unit, and the Wisconsin Regional Library for the Blind and Physically Handicapped.

The Milwaukee Public Library is committed to providing the highest quality of service to internal and external customers. In meeting this commitment, employees are expected to be knowledgeable, competent, dependable and courteous in the performance of their job responsibilities, and to work cooperatively as part of a team.

Essential Functions and Responsibilities

DESCRIPTION OF JOB: (Describe the specific duties and responsibilities of the job as accurately and completely as possible. Use additional sheet if necessary.)

DUTIES AND RESPONSIBILITIES: (Break job into component parts as you would describe it to the incumbent. Indicate the approximate percentage of time devoted to each major task or group of related tasks. List the most important duties and responsibilities first. Include responsibilities related to employee safety and affirmative action goals for management positions.)

65% 1. Administration

Works with the City Librarian and Manager of Central Library Services in carrying out the policies, programs, and long range plans of the Library's Board of Trustees. Works with the City Librarian, Manager of Central Library Services, Library Business Operations Manager, and Extension Services Coordinator in developing the annual budget for the maintenance of existing programs and services. Works with Administration and staff in the development and maintenance of library services in Extension Services.

Consults with and advises the Business Operations Manager and the building maintenance supervisors regarding Neighborhood Libraries and Extension Services improvements, maintenance and repairs, and the replacement and repair of shelving, furnishing and equipment. Develops specifications for new technical equipment. Works with the City Librarian and Manager of Central Library Services in the development of the capitol improvements budget on matters affecting the Neighborhood Libraries and Extension Services Bureau.

Works with and advises the Communications and Marketing Coordinator regarding Neighborhood Libraries and Extension Services program and events, exhibits, signage, public program announcements and related items.

Works with and advises the Library Foundation Director regarding Neighborhood Libraries and Extension Services funding needs to provide funds for collections and services.

Works with and advises the Library Foundation Director regarding Neighborhood Libraries and Extension Services' funding needs to provide funds for collections and services.

Works with the Literacy Coordinator and extension managers in the development and implementation of the Library's literacy program.

Works with and advises young adult librarians with collection development, programs, and services for YA patrons.

Receives, investigates, evaluates and acts upon difficult complaints and suggestions from citizens and organizations pertaining to Neighborhood Libraries and Extension Services. Applies and interprets Library Board and city policies in complex situations

Investigates security incidents and advises City Librarian and Neighborhood Library and Extension Services agencies on action when code of conduct policy is violated.

Judiciously draws upon the Library's special trust funds and endowments for further improvement of the collections and working with the Foundation, seeks special grants and donations from private and public sources for this purpose.

Works with the Coordinator of Extension Services, managers and staff in providing quality library service to the public and in building teams and improving communication at each library.

20% 2. Staff Development

Selects, trains and evaluates administrative and reference personnel involved in the Neighborhood Libraries and Extension Services Bureau. Answers bargaining unit grievances. Coaches extension managers and supervisors on customer service and communication skills.

10% 3. Collection Development and Maintenance

Possesses overall responsibility for the maintenance and development of the collections in each extension services agency. Evaluates bibliographic services and operation to ensure effective public access. Serves as liaison to research level users, university faculty, business and industry, and government. Has responsibility for collection organization at each extension agency. Maintains overall responsibility for book selection criteria, as well as non-book materials for community based organizations.

5% 4 Miscellaneous

Represents the library in community and professional meetings. Maintains active membership in professional organizations, may hold office. Keeps current with and contributes to technical and professional literature. Maintains liaison with other major urban libraries throughout the nation. Serves as liaison with other special libraries and information agencies, community groups and local officials. Performs other related duties as assigned.

Knowledge, Skills, and Abilities

1. Strong customer service orientation
2. Thorough knowledge of modern public library goals, organization, practices, policies, goals, services, administration and reference services.
3. Demonstrated ability in innovative programming, public service development and complex budget development and management.
4. Knowledge and skill in using large diversified reference collections and in exploiting the reference value of books and non-book materials.
5. Ability to function as team leader to plan, organize, direct, coordinate, coach and supervise the work of others.
6. Ability to speak before audiences and to write for publications.
7. Understanding of the social responsibilities of an urban public library in an era of information explosion and technological change.

8. Familiarity with research methods and extensive knowledge of the development, preservation and organization of research and reference collections.
9. Flexibility and skill in encouraging staff to solve problems that stand in the way of providing quality public service.
10. Successful experience in obtaining outside funding highly desirable.

Physical and Mental Requirements

PHYSICAL DEMANDS OF POSITION: List the physical demands which are representative of those that must be met to successfully perform the essential function of the job. Reasonable accommodations may be made to enable individuals with disabilities to perform the essential functions.

1. Frequently standing, walking, sitting, reaching in front of body, and using hand, wrist and fingers simultaneously (i.e.: computer entry);
2. Sometimes stooping, twisting, reaching overhead, and climbing on to motor vehicles;
3. On occasion kneeling and climbing stairs
4. Usually lifting objects weighing up to 10 pounds and on occasion up to 20 pounds. Maximum weight lifted to hip height, shoulder height or above shoulders:20 pounds. Maximum weight lifted and carried without assistance: 10 pounds.
5. Sometimes pushing/pulling objects or loads weighing up to 20 pounds and on occasion up to 50 pounds. Maximum weight pushed/pulled without wheels or assistance: 10 pounds
6. Usually talking and hearing ordinary conversation in both quiet and noisy environments
7. Usual need for near vision at 20" or less (i.e. computer entry, reading); Frequent need for far vision at 20" or more (i.e. driving);
8. Frequent travel to outside meetings and engagements

MENTAL REQUIREMENTS: List the mental requirements, which are, representative of those that must be met to successfully perform the essential function of the job. Reasonable accommodations may be made to enable individuals with disabilities to perform the essential functions.

1. Communication Skills: effectively communicate ideas and information both in written and oral form.
2. Time Management: set priorities in order to meet assignment deadlines.
3. Problem Solving: develop feasible, realistic solutions to problems, recommend actions designed to prevent problems from occurring.
4. Planning and Organizing: develop long-range plans to solve complex problems or take advantage of opportunities; establish systematic methods of accomplishing goals.
5. Analytical Ability: identify problems and opportunities; review possible alternative courses of action before selection; utilize available information resources in decision making.
6. Creative Decision Making: effectively evaluates or makes independent decisions based upon experience, knowledge or training,

Tools and Equipment Used

EQUIPMENT USED: List equipment, which is representative of that which would be used to successfully perform the essential function of the job. Reasonable accommodations may be made to enable individuals with disabilities to perform the essential functions.

Computer terminal or networked personal computer and peripheral equipment including printers, typewriter, telephone, photocopier, fax machine, calculator, book truck.

SUPPLEMENTARY INFORMATION: (Indicate any other information which further explains the importance, difficulty, or responsibility of the position.)

Work Environment

I. ENVIRONMENTAL/WORKING CONDITIONS: List the conditions, which are, representative of those that must be met to successfully perform the essential function of the job. Reasonable accommodations may be made to enable individuals with disabilities to perform the essential functions.

1. Inside work environment
2. Flexible work hours; rotating work shift; some evening and weekend hours, work in excess of 40 hours per week as necessary
3. Sometimes dusty work conditions

Supervisory Responsibilities

SUPERVISION EXERCISED:

167 Total number of employees for whom responsible, either directly or indirectly.

Direct Supervision. List the number and titles of personnel directly supervised. Specify the kind and extent of supervision exercised by indicating one or more of the following: (a) assign duties; (b) outline methods; (c) direct work in process; (d) check or inspect completed work; (e) sign or approve work; (f) make hiring recommendations; (g) prepare performance appraisals; (h) take disciplinary action or effectively recommend such.

Provides direction to the Coordinator of Extension Services and the managers/supervisors of the twelve neighborhood libraries, Regional Library for the Blind and Physically Handicapped, Mobile Library and Outreach Services, and the Automotive Services unit by assigning duties, outlining methods, overseeing work flow in general, taking disciplinary action at the administrative level for these units, issuing commendations, and being available for consultation on problems that arise. Through these managers/supervisors indirectly supervises the staff of these units.

Education, Experience, and Training

1. MLS from a library school accredited by the American Library Association or approved by the Department of Employee Relations. 2. Five years of progressively responsible professional experience, including at least three as an administrator of a large branch or independent community library, or as an administrator of a major library division or as coordinator in a major subject area.

3.0 LIBRARY ASSISTANT

3.1 BRANCH LIBRARY ASSISTANT

3.1.1 Branch Library Assistant

Library Name: St. Clair County Library System
Library Location: Port Huron, Michigan
Population Served: 160,708
Number of Volumes: 432,880
Number of Titles: 206,173
Periodical Subscriptions: 560

Reports to

SUPERVISION RECEIVED:

Work is performed under the general supervision of the Branch Librarian or Department Head.

General Summary

JOB OBJECTIVE:

Assists Branch Librarian or Department Head with the day-to-day operation of the branch including circulation, reference, material selection and processing, special programming, public computer assistance and outreach. Position may constitute work at the Main Library in various departments and/or at a branch library.

Essential Functions and Responsibilities

Typical Work: (An employee in this classification may be called upon to perform the following tasks which are illustrative and not exhaustive in nature.)

Gives friendly and helpful service to library users.

Conducts circulation activity, entering data into computer, searching and checking customer files, including registering new patrons.

Checks library materials in and out using the library's automated library system.

Fills requests for reserved materials.

Performs miscellaneous material collection related duties within context of department/branch needs.

Provides research assistance to patrons, helping them to gain access to both manual and computer generated information.

Provides input into and may be asked to facilitate new and innovative programs to create interest in and enjoyment of the library.

Performs a wide variety of routine clerical tasks including maintaining records and collecting and recording fines.

Attends training courses and undertakes special training activities as directed.

May represent the library at various promotional events and activities.

Performs other duties as assigned by supervisor.

Knowledge, Skills, and Abilities

Desired Qualifications: A proactive public service initiative with strong communication and interaction skills and the ability to relate to people of all ages. Knowledge, interest and appreciation of literature and other sources of information available at the library. Ability to provide research assistance. Ability to assist in organizing activities and to perform routine tasks. Ability to use computers and perform data entry. Exhibits flexibility and possesses a high degree of patience and tolerance. Willingness to further credentials by additional education and workshops. The qualified candidate must possess a valid state of Michigan operator license and maintain this license during employment in the position.

Supervisory Responsibilities

SUPERVISION EXERCISED
Supervision is exercised over Library Pages when appropriate.

Education, Experience, and Training

Experience Needed: High School diploma or equivalent required, with college level studies, computer training and library experience highly desired.

3.2 LITERACY PROJECT LIBRARY ASSISTANT

3.2.1 Literacy Project Library Assistant

Library Name: Escondido Public Library
Library Location: Escondido, California
Population Served: 136,956
Number of Volumes: N/A
Number of Titles: 281,548
Number of Periodical Subscriptions: 320

Reports to

Supervision
Supervision is received from the Literacy Project Assistant II. Supervises groups of children during ELLI class activities.

General Summary

JOB OBJECTIVE:
Under administrative direction, assists in the planning, preparation, and implementation of the English Language and Literacy Intensive (ELLI) Project.

Essential Functions and Responsibilities

Conducts school and community outreach activities for the ELLI Project;
Works with individual students or small groups;

Distributes ELLI public relations materials and classroom curricula;
Coordinates an oral reading recording project with students;
Assists with processing of ELLI materials;
Assists with planning for children's learning activities in the library setting;
Records statistics and assists in preparing quarterly project reports.

Knowledge, Skills, and Abilities

Knowledge of:
Early childhood development and children's literature;
Basic computer office programs;
Spanish language and customs;
Community needs and their relationship to literacy materials and services;
Principal and practices of customer service and public relations.
Ability to:
Conduct community outreach and collaborate with school administration and teachers;
Relate effectively to individuals from diverse backgrounds;
Coordinate assigned programs and services with those of other Library and City programs and departments;
Display excellent written and oral communications skills;
Communicate clearly and effectively in English and Spanish, both orally and in writing;
Make public presentations;
Work both independently and in a team, exercise good judgment, and take initiative;
Establish and maintain effective working relationships with local school districts, Library staff, and a wide variety of community organizations and individuals.

Physical and Mental Requirements

COMMUNICATION:
VISION (may be correctable) to see computer screens, books, observe customers and situations.
HEARING of telephone and personal conversations with customers, fire and security alarms, sound equipment.
SPEAKING clearly to converse with customers.
WRITING to complete forms and notes to assist customers.
PHYSICAL: CONTINUOUS walking; lifting objects weighing up to 10 lbs.; fine finger dexterity and light pressure to operate keyboards, calculators, telephones; pinch grasp to hold books, writing materials.
FREQUENT standing, sitting, bending and stooping, squatting, reaching above and at shoulder level, pushing/pulling, twisting at waist, upward and downward flexion of neck, side-to-side turning of neck; lifting objects weighing 11-15 lbs. from below waist to above shoulders and transporting distances up to 500 yards; moderate wrist torque to operate and adjust equipment such as printers, computers.
OCCASIONAL climbing, kneeling; lifting objects weighing 26-50 lbs. from below waist to waist level, with or without assistance, and transporting distances up to 10 feet.

INFREQUENT crawling, balancing above ground, lifting objects weighing 26-50 lbs. From chest level to above shoulder level, with or without assistance, and transporting distances up to 10 feet; lifting objects weighing 51-75 lbs. from below waist to shoulder level, with assistance, and transporting distances up to 5 feet; strong grasp to lift equipment or boxes of books.

Work Environment

ENVIRONMENTAL: Exposure to heat and humidity working outdoors at special events; noise of crowds and groups of people; temperature variations, within the building and from indoors to outdoors; possible mechanical hazards of equipment and large quantities of books and papers.

Occasional overtime may be required for adequate staffing of library facilities, and incumbents may be required to work weekends, nights and holidays. Work is performed primarily indoors at school sites as well as library facilities. Work setting is formal, team-oriented, having both routine and variable tasks. Work pace and pressure in variable, but frequently fast-paced and high pressure.

Education, Experience, and Training

Education and Experience – Equivalent to two years of full-time college coursework in child development, early childhood education, or similar field and one year of paid or volunteer experience working with children in an educational capacity.

Additional Qualifications

License and Certification Requirements – Must possess a valid Class C California Driver's license or be able to arrange transportation as required. Fluent verbal and written English/Spanish bilingual ability is required. Must be willing to work occasional evenings and weekends.

3.3 REFERENCE LIBRARY ASSISTANT

3.3.1 Reference Library Assistant

Library name: West Chicago Public Library District
Library Location: West Chicago, Illinois
Population Served: 22,337
Number of Volumes: 81,851
Number of Titles: N/A
Number of Periodical Subscriptions: 238

General Summary

JOB OBJECTIVE:

This is a paraprofessional Library position. The Adult Services Assistant performs a wide variety of clerical and paraprofessional tasks necessary in planning and implementing the Library's Adult Services programs and activities.

Essential Functions and Responsibilities

General Duties:

Provides reference desk assistance, answering reference questions and providing reader's advisory service.

Assists Library patrons with the use of on-line catalogs, databases, and computers.

Assists in promoting the Adult Services collection through designing and constructing displays, signage, and bookmarks.

Performs general administrative duties for the Adult Services department, i.e., answering phones, filing, photocopying, stocking patron supplies, and general straightening of furniture and equipment, as well as plant watering.

Performs other duties as required or assigned.

Specific Duties (may be responsible for one or more):

Assists in collection development by reading reviews and making recommendations for purchases.

Assists patrons in obtaining materials not found in the Library's collection by searching computerized databases and initiating direct loan or inter-Library loan requests.

Maintains and updates the pamphlet file, especially in areas of local history or interest.

Maintains public viewing areas.

Registers patrons for Internet and computer use. Verifies valid Library card and signed Internet agreement.

Maintains the memorial book program by coordinating book selections and keeping records and files.

Prepares the Library newsletter and submits press releases to the local newspaper.

Maintains the college financial loan forms and college catalogs.

Maintains the magazine collection and arranges for replacements as necessary.

Additional Job Duties

Prints, cuts, and stocks bookmarks for the Circulation desk.

Logs patrons onto to the Internet.

Allows patrons access to other Library services, i.e., study rooms, PCs, etc.

Physical and Mental Requirements

Requires sitting, standing, stooping, bending, and lifting/moving books and carts up to 40 pounds.

Must be able to communicate effectively in English, both orally and in writing.

Must be able to hear, comprehend and respond to Library patrons both in person and in telephone conversations.

Must have visual ability to see computer screens.

Requires good hand dexterity for computer.

Requires mental alertness, focus, and attention to details.

Knowledge, Skills, and Abilities

Skills:

Demonstrated ability in interpersonal and communication skills to satisfy positive interaction with patrons, staff, and others.

Ability to type and operate equipment, i.e., computer, calculator, printers, copiers, microfilm/fiche readers, microphone, and multi-media projectors.

Knowledge of word processing, spreadsheet, and database software.

Ability to prioritize work, remain focused, and pay close attention to detail.

Ability to communicate in Spanish, both verbally and in writing, is a plus.

Work Environment

Indoor conditions

Must maintain professional manner when dealing with patrons, staff, and others.

Must be able to work independently as well as with a team.

Must be flexible, creative, patient, and have a sense of humor.

May be required to work evenings and weekends.

Education, Experience, and Training

MINIMUM QUALIFICATIONS REQUIRED:

Education: Library Technical Certificate (LTA) and/or Bachelor's degree.

Experience: Two years Library experience, or one year reference experience.

Disclaimers

NOTE: This job description describes the nature and level of assignments given in this position. This is not an exhaustive list of duties; additional related duties may be assigned.

3.3.2 Reference Library Assistant

Library Name: Phoenix Public Library
Library Location: Phoenix, Arizona
Population Served: 1,350,435
Number of Volumes: 2,015,587
Number of Titles: 734,921
Number of Periodical Subscriptions: 4,500

General Summary

JOB OBJECTIVE:

The fundamental reason this classification exists is to provide highly skilled reference service either directly for library users or in service support areas in the Central Library or a branch. Work requires the application of basic professional knowledge and techniques of library science to a variety of assignments, including descriptive cataloging, acquisition of library materials, and response to information requests from library users. Employees work independently under the general supervision of a Librarian.

Essential Functions and Responsibilities

Retrieves information from an on-line computer catalog by operating a keyboard or obtains information from written documents in order to help library users find books or information;

Assists and trains library users in the use of the on-line computer catalog system;

Answers questions and provides service for routine reference requests;

Finds and provides answers for library users' reference questions at the information service desks at the Central Library;

Refers complex reference questions to the appropriate specialized Librarian;

Assists library users who have disabilities in the use of specialized equipment, such as magnifiers, computerized personal readers with synthesized speech, and Braille embossers, when assigned to the Central Library's Special Needs Center;

Reads computer cataloging information from a screen or printout, reconciles information with material being cataloged or acquired in the library, and makes necessary changes to the information when assigned to a cataloging/acquiring activity of the Central Library;

Demonstrates continuous effort to improve operations, decrease turnaround times, streamline work processes, and work cooperatively and jointly to provide quality seamless customer service.

Additional Job Duties

Some positions require the use of personal or City vehicles on City business. Individuals must be physically capable of operating the vehicles safely, possess a valid driver's license and have an acceptable driving record. Use of a personal vehicle for City business will be prohibited if the employee is not authorized to drive a City vehicle or if the employee does not have personal insurance coverage.

Some positions will require the performance of other essential and marginal functions depending upon work location, assignment, or shift.

Knowledge, Skills, and Abilities

KNOWLEDGE OF:

Principles, practices, methods, and materials of public libraries.

Principles and practices of customer service.

Basic library reference resources.
ABILITY TO:
Conduct effective reference interviews with library users.
Operate microcomputers and library automated systems.
Work cooperatively with other City employees and the general public.
Communicate in the English language by phone or in person in a one-to-one or group setting.
Comprehend and make inferences from written material.
Learn job-related material primarily through oral instruction and observation which takes place mainly in an on-the-job training setting.
Work safely without presenting a direct threat to self or others.

Education, Experience, and Training

ACCEPTABLE EXPERIENCE AND TRAINING:
Bachelor's degree in a program that imparts a broad liberal education. Other combinations of experience and education that meet the minimum requirements may be substituted.

3.3.3 Reference Library Assistant

Library name: Ellensburg Public Library
Library Location: Ellensburg, Washington
Population Served: 15,400
Number of Volumes: 59,000
Number of Titles: 53,000
Number of Periodical Subscriptions: 188

Reports to

LIBRARY ASSOCIATE
TYPE OF SUPERVISION RECEIVED:
Quantity and quality of employee's work is subject to a close check by the circulation supervisor.

General Summary

JOB OBJECTIVE:
Assist patrons to locate and check out library materials, maintain accurate patron records, check in returned items and maintain shelf order.

Register patrons for library cards, provide information about library circulation policies; assist patrons with the computer catalog and locating items, check library materials out, check in returned items, collect payment of fines and fees; sort and shelve returned items, keep items in order on the shelves, search for missing items, answer basic reference questions by using standard reference sources; provide information on library programs and services. Perform duties in outreach circulation, interlibrary loans, reserves, Local History collection, typing and filing; process magazines, paperbacks and other uncataloged items; new book processing, mending, book jackets, etc.

Essential Functions and Responsibilities

All of the following are to be performed while adhering to City of Ellensburg operational policies, safety rules, and procedures.
Patron Service:
Register patrons and issue library cards; refer problems to supervisor
Inform patrons on library circulation policies, fines, fees, etc.
Demonstrate use of computer catalog and assist patrons in use
Locate items in catalog and on shelves for patrons
Assist patrons in placing holds or interlibrary loan requests
Notify patrons when reserved items, interlibrary loans are received
Collect and record payment of fines and fees; refer damaged items to supervisor
Check items out to patrons
Locate information for patrons using standard reference sources in books and CD ROM databases to answer questions; refer to reference staff as needed
Provide access to items in closed stacks of Local History collection when appropriate
Provide information about library programs and services, orally and with flyers
Answer telephone inquiries
Operate library equipment as appropriate
Assist patrons with summer reading program information and materials
Report behavior problems to supervisor or person in charge, or take appropriate action
Collection duties:
Check items in accurately to clear patron records; empty book drop and check items in
Review physical condition of items for completeness, damages, soil, mending, etc.
Sort materials into collection divisions
Place sorted items onto carts and return items to library shelves in correct order
Read shelves to maintain correct shelf order of all items; search for missing items
Process new paperbacks, magazines, and other uncataloged materials
Mend, recover and relabel older items as needed
Keep Local History collection in order
Remove items from tables, check in and reshelve as appropriate
Office Duties:
Maintain supply of forms, paper, pens, tape, labels, etc., or request from supervisor
Keep desks, cabinets, and work areas, supplies and equipment orderly for shared use
Perform opening and closing procedures as instructed by supervisor
Report problems with equipment or building systems to supervisor and director
Miscellaneous; or special assignments:
Attend staff training workshops and regular monthly meetings

Assist in sending fax requests and processing interlibrary loans
Provide circulation service for rotating and outreach collections
Take requests for photo prints, tapes, etc.
Perform missing item searches
Create booklists and/or book mark flyers
Clean equipment and maintain library appearance
Other duties may be assigned.

This is a representative sample—not to imply a complete listing of responsibilities and tasks.

Additional Job Duties

KEY RELATIONSHIPS:

The key relationships described here are representative of those an employee encounters while performing the essential functions of this job.

While performing the duties of this job, the employee will provide information to and collect information from the public, educators and researchers. Children are a significant proportion of the public. Contact will be made by telephone and in person.

The employee will solve problems and negotiate solutions within policy guidelines with the public, educators and researchers. Contact will be made by telephone or in person.

Knowledge, Skills, and Abilities

LANGUAGE SKILLS:

Ability to read and interpret documents such as safety rules, operating and maintenance instructions, and procedure manuals. Ability to write routine reports and correspondence. Ability to speak effectively before groups of customers or employees of organization.

MATHEMATICAL SKILLS:

Ability to add, subtract, multiply, and divide in all units of measure, using whole numbers, common fractions, and decimals.

NECESSARY KNOWLEDGE, SKILLS AND ABILITIES:

A) Some knowledge of general office practice and procedures; some knowledge of library organization and purpose; knowledge of alphabetical and whole/decimal number filing;

B) Skill in keyboard and computer data entry; operation of listed tools and equipment; ability to maintain confidentiality of patron records.

C) Ability to be courteous and tactful with the general public; Ability to communicate effectively, verbally and in writing; to implement policy and procedure; to exercise initiative and judgment in completing tasks; to organize various activities; ability to establish and maintain effective working relationships with employees, supervisors, and the general public.

Physical and Mental Requirements

PHYSICAL DEMANDS:

The physical demands described here are representative of those that must be met by an employee to successfully perform the essential functions of this job. Reasonable accommodations may be made to enable individuals with disabilities to perform the essential functions.

While performing the duties of this job, the employee is regularly required to stand; walk; sit; use hands to finger, handle, or feel objects, tools, or controls; reach with hands and arms; climb or balance; stoop, kneel, crouch, or crawl; and talk or hear. The employee is occasionally required to taste or smell.

The employee must regularly lift and/or move up to 50 pounds and occasionally lift and/or move more than 50 pounds. Specific vision abilities required by this job include close vision, distance vision, color vision, peripheral vision, depth perception, and the ability to adjust focus. Tasks affected include shelving books, computer work, watching patrons while working, shelving by using colored dots, and processing books.

Tools and Equipment Used

Personal computer, printer, cash register, book carts, calculator, typewriter, copy and fax machine; phone, audio-visual equipment, microfilm reader/printer

Work Environment

The work environment characteristics described here are representative of those an employee encounters while performing the essential functions of this job. Reasonable accommodations may be made to enable individuals with disabilities to perform the essential functions.

While performing the duties of this job, the employee is regularly exposed to airborne particles. The employee occasionally works in outside weather conditions for brief periods and is exposed to wet and/or humid conditions or extreme heat, and risk of electrical shock. Sharp utensils are used in some tasks.

The noise level in the work environment is usually moderate.

Supervisory Responsibilities

None.

Education, Experience, and Training

To perform this job successfully, an individual must be able to perform each essential duty satisfactorily. The requirements listed below are representative of the knowledge, skill, and/or ability required. Reasonable accommodations may be made to enable individuals with disabilities to perform the essential functions.

High school diploma or general education degree (GED); one year related experience and/or training; or equivalent combination of education and experience.

Disclaimers

Job profiles are not intended, nor should they be construed to be, an exhaustive list of all responsibilities, tasks, skills, efforts, working conditions or similar behaviors, attributes or requirements associated with a job. A job profile is not a comprehensive job description. It is intended for the sole purpose of acquainting a person who is unfamiliar with such position with a brief overview of the position's general direction and scope. This position profile is confidential, is intended for internal use only and may not be copied or reproduced by anyone for any purpose without written permission from the Director of Personnel or the City Manager.

NOTICE: The above job profile does not include all essential and nonessential duties of this job. All employees with disabilities are encouraged to contact the Personnel Department to review and discuss the essential and nonessential functions of the job. An employee with a disability can evaluate the job in greater detail to determine if she/he can safely perform the essential function of this job with or without reasonable accommodation.

4.0 LIBRARY ASSOCIATE

4.1 BRANCH LIBRARY ASSOCIATE

4.1.1 Branch Library Associate

Library Name: Cecil County Public Library
Library Location: Elkton, Maryland
Population Served: 80,600
Number of Volumes: 224,182
Number of Titles: 94,293
Number of Periodical Subscriptions: 201

General Summary

JOB OBJECTIVE:

Provides information services and programming in a library branch. Manages one or more projects. May manage day-to-day operations in a library branch. Makes decisions based on published policies, but refers unusual situations to supervisor. Receives supervision from local branch manager and Branch Services Librarian.

Essential Functions and Responsibilities

Provides reader guidance and reference service to patrons.
Circulates materials and registers borrowers.
Responsible for daily cash handling procedures.
Monitors and maintains collection. Shelves books.
Manages one or more projects.
May manage day to day operations in a branch library.
May provide outreach services.
May plan and conduct programs, book talks, or school visits.
Markets library materials and services. Merchandises collections.
Works well with supervisors to develop and implement department or branch goals within overall system goals.
Monitors and maintains branch PCs and software.
Helps public sign up for and use of public computers, Office software and the Internet.

Gives basic instructions to public in use of library hardware, software, catalog and services.
Maintains facility and reports problems to appropriate staff.
Maintain accurate service statistics.
Performs ongoing assignments of moderate to high difficulty.
Other duties as assigned.

Additional Job Duties

Promotes and maintains high standard of customer service.
Performs job in keeping with the policies and procedures of the Cecil County Public Library.
Maintains courteous, friendly, and constructive relationships with patrons and staff.

Knowledge, Skills, and Abilities

CRITICAL SKILLS/EXPERIENCE:

Excellent written and verbal communications skills.
Excellent customer service skills.
Ability to work with patrons from all walks of life in a courteous and diplomatic manner.
Ability to analyze and perform and/or manage a wide variety of library projects.
Good knowledge of personal computer operations, windows operating system, Office software and the use of the Internet.
Willingness and ability to acquire knowledge of advanced library computer systems and applications.
Knowledge of books, authors, current events.
Ability to reach, bend and lift up to 20 lbs.
Ability to push/pull a rolling book carts.

Tools and Equipment Used

EQUIPMENT:

Personal computers, scanners, printers, photocopier, date stamps, book trucks, fax machine, telephone, security system.

Work Environment

Works in normal heat and light conditions with some exposure to seasonal draft conditions. Some eye fatigue from working at computer terminals; physical fatigue from working at counter height (39") work surface and from repetitive lifting of books, moving wand and pushing carts. Some stress from constant public contact.

Education, Experience, and Training

CRITICAL SKILLS/EXPERIENCE:

Baccalaureate Degree from an accredited college.
Introductory knowledge of library systems, of alpha numeric filing, of the Dewey Decimal System, of reference materials and methods available to assist patrons.
Within two years of appointment, each Library Associate II shall have successfully completed Library Associates' in-service

training or six credit hours of formal academic course work in library science. Such training may have been received prior to the date of appointment. Training provided by CCPL off-site in Maryland.

Additional Qualifications

DESIRABLE ADDITIONAL QUALIFICATIONS
Experience working in a public library.
Experience developing programs and managing projects.

4.2 REFERENCE ASSOCIATE

4.2.1 Reference Associate

Library Name: Ellensburg Public Library
Library Location: Ellensburg, Washington
Population Served: 15,400
Number of Volumes: 59,000
Number of Titles: 53,00
Number of Periodical Subscriptions: 188

Reports to

Library Director
TYPE OF SUPERVISION RECEIVED:
Employee is under the general supervision of the Library Director.

General Summary

JOB OBJECTIVE:

Provide reference services and coordinate reference activities with heads of other principal library divisions; assist Director in achieving goals and objectives of quality library service.

Responsible for planning and coordination of activities of a principal division or function within the library. Direct patron service for reference activities and researching the library collection and resources. Responsible for installation, use, and staff training in computerized resources such as Internet, CD ROM databases, PC software for patron use. Provide staff training in reference and research. Responsible for creation of internal resources, such as local information, fugitive facts file; Organize uncataloged government documents and ephemeral reference materials. Provide reader advisory service and bibliographical lists for patron use. Train and supervise volunteers assigned to reference.

Essential Functions and Responsibilities

All of the following are to be performed while adhering to City of Ellensburg operational policies, safety rules, and procedures.
Reference Coordination:
Implement policies for reference service; assist in Policy development
Develop procedures to accomplish division work
Provide reasonably close supervision on quality and quantity of reference work
Implement use of automation system as it applies to reference service
Provide staff training and coordination in research
Prepare statistical reports on reference service; prepare reports for Director as needed
Provide reference and consulting help to other public libraries in the County
Maintain reference forms, supplies, and other materials as needed
Maintain orderliness of desks, cabinets, supplies and equipment for shared staff use
Patron Service:
Interview patrons to determine information needs
Analyze needs and identify appropriate sources to fulfill those needs
Assist patrons in use of library resources; explain print and computer sources
Assist patrons in use of library computers, readers, copier, and other equipment
Serve patrons from special collections, such as Local History
Demonstrate use of library catalog, CD ROMS, Internet and other resources; assist Director with outreach efforts on library services
Locate items in catalog and on shelves as needed; Assist patrons with holds
Locate information using standard reference sources in books and CD-ROM and electronic databases; consult with Director and Librarian as needed
Assist school librarians in use of the library DialPac and related activities
Provide information about library programs and services, orally and with flyers
Answer telephone inquiries
Enforce library rules of behavior; take appropriate action in case of misbehavior; keep Director informed
Collection/Computer Support Duties:
Provide input on purchase of CD ROM and reference materials; and software and hardware as appropriate
Implement use of PC software to produce reader advisory and publicity materials

Install CD-ROMs in reference computers; complete data as needed to install

Apply knowledge of computer technology to reference services

Maintain supply inventory for public computers; diagnose problems and maintain hardware and software

Assist in use of office software programs such as spreadsheets, word processing, etc.

Read professional journals, computer publications to maintain knowledge

Miscellaneous:

In charge of the library in absence of Director, Head of Circulation/ Collection Support, Children's Librarian; or as assigned evening and weekend hours

Assist Head of Circulation at check out desk as scheduled or when requested

Conduct tours and orientation sessions for patron groups/classes as needed

Assist with special projects, such as Web Page development, grants, etc.

Attend workshops, conferences, training; weekly and monthly library staff meetings

Provide reference reviews/information at monthly staff meetings

Prepare informational flyers on reference and Internet services

Other duties may be assigned.

This is a representative sample—not to imply a complete listing of responsibilities and tasks.

Additional Job Duties

KEY RELATIONSHIPS:

The key relationships described here are representative of those an employee encounters while performing the essential functions of this job.

While performing the duties of this job, the employee will provide information to and collect information from library patrons, other libraries, and other agencies for information purposes. Children are a significant proportion of the public. Contact will be made by telephone and in person and in writing.

The employee will coordinate projects and activities with other libraries and agencies by telephone, in person, or in writing.

The employee will solve problems and negotiate solutions within policy guidelines with the public, other libraries and agencies by telephone, in person, or in writing.

Knowledge, Skills, and Abilities

A) Knowledge of general office practice and procedures; considerable knowledge of basic principles of library practices and procedures, considerable knowledge of library reference practices, principles, and classification systems; considerable knowledge of reference resources and the library collection; knowledge of personal computer software and equipment; working knowledge of principles of supervision and personnel practices;

B) Interviewing skills to determine patron needs; Skill in using automated library systems; skill in keyboard and computer data entry; skill in library data base searching; operation and maintenance of listed tools and equipment; skill in public relations; constantly accesses sensitive information required to perform job tasks, requiring the ability to maintain confidentiality.

C) Ability to be courteous and tactful with the general public; Ability to communicate effectively, verbally and in writing; to implement policy and procedure; to exercise initiative and judgment in completing tasks; to organize various activities; Ability to work independently, exercising initiative and judgment in directing the work of others; ability to establish and maintain effective working relationships with patrons, employees, supervisors, and the general public.

Physical and Mental Requirements

PHYSICAL DEMANDS:

The physical demands described here are representative of those that must be met by an employee to successfully perform the essential functions of this job. Reasonable accommodations may be made to enable individuals with disabilities to perform the essential functions.

While performing the duties of this job, the employee is regularly required to stand; walk; sit; use hands to finger, handle, or feel objects, tools, or controls; The employee is frequently required to reach with hands and arms; climb or balance; stoop, kneel, crouch, or crawl; and talk or hear. The employee is occasionally required to taste or smell.

The employee must regularly lift and/or move up to 25 pounds and occasionally lift and/or move more than 50 pounds. Specific vision abilities required by this job include close vision, distance vision, color vision, peripheral vision, depth perception, and the ability to adjust focus. Tasks affected include, computer work, researching print and non-print sources; watching patrons while working; creating lists, flyers, forms, and posters.

Tools and Equipment Used

Automated library system, personal computer, printer, software programs, phone and fax; audio-visual equipment, microfilm reader/printer, Kurzweil reading machine, cash register, calculator, copier

Work Environment

The work environment characteristics described here are representative of those an employee encounters while performing the essential functions of this job. Reasonable accommodations may be made to enable individuals with disabilities to perform the essential functions.

While performing the duties of this job, the employee is regularly exposed to airborne particles. The employee is occasionally exposed to risk of electrical shock by working a considerable amount of time at computer terminal and associated equipment.

The noise level in the work environment is usually moderate.

Supervisory Responsibilities

Assist Library Assistants (5-6) and part time Reference Specialist, when engaged in reference activities. Plan the scope of the unit's work with the Director, determine appropriate assignment of work to volunteers; provide training opportunities and materials for staff; monitor quality and quantity of reference work accomplished; refer complaints and problems to Director. Coordinate activities of reference unit with heads of circulation, children's services, and collection support services.

Education, Experience, and Training

QUALIFICATION REQUIREMENTS:

To perform this job successfully, an individual must be able to perform each essential duty satisfactorily. The requirements listed below are representative of the knowledge, skill, and/or ability required. Reasonable accommodations may be made to enable individuals with disabilities to perform the essential functions.

EDUCATION and/or EXPERIENCE:

Bachelor's degree (B.A.) from four year college or university; and two to four years of related experience and/or training working in reference services including supervision; or equivalent combination of education and experience.

LANGUAGE SKILLS:

Ability to read, analyze and interpret general business periodicals, professional journals, technical procedures, or governmental regulations. Ability to write reports, business correspondence, and procedure manuals. Ability to effectively present information and respond to questions from clients, customers, and the general public.

MATHEMATICAL SKILLS:

Ability to calculate figures and amounts such as interest, percentages, area, circumference, and volume. Ability to apply concepts of basic algebra and geometry.

License and Certification Requirements

SPECIAL REQUIREMENTS:

Certification in First Aid and CPR; Valid State driver's license or ability to obtain one.

Disclaimers

Job profiles are not intended, nor should they be construed to be, an exhaustive list of all responsibilities, tasks, skills, efforts, working conditions or similar behaviors, attributes or requirements associated with a job. A job profile is not a comprehensive job description. It is intended for the sole purpose of acquainting a person who is unfamiliar with such position with a brief overview of the position's general direction and scope. This position profile is confidential, is intended for internal use only and may not be copied or reproduced by anyone for any purpose without written permission from the Director of Personnel or the City Manager.

4.2.2 Reference Associate

Library Name: Palo Alto City Library
Library Location: Palo Alto, California
Population Served: 60,800
Number of Volumes: 238,636
Number of Titles: 166,858
Number of Periodical Subscriptions: 952

Reports to

Various Library Managers or Supervisors

General Summary

JOB OBJECTIVE:

Under general direction performs responsible library activities on a paraprofessional level in a library or technical area.

DISTINGUISHING FEATURES: Library Associates are found in the Library Division within the Department of Community Services and are distinguished by the paraprofessional nature of the position combining broad knowledge of library organization, public service, purchasing procedures, computerized systems and library clerical support activities. Incumbents work with minimal supervision and are assigned to a particular unit or library with defined tasks. The position requires frequent use of independent judgment, and is the highest paraprofessional position found within the Library Division.

Essential Functions and Responsibilities

Essential and other important responsibilities and duties may include, but are not limited to, the following:

Essential Functions:

When working in Public Service:

Performs circulation tasks required to serve the public, including the following: checks materials out and in; registers and updates files of borrowers; checks status of patron accounts using the Library's automated system; accepts payments for fines, bills and fees; tabulates and records daily cash register receipts; works to resolve patron complaints

Provides reader's advisory service to assist users in identifying library materials of interest; assists the public in use of a variety of library equipment

Provides basic reference service using the resources available in the Neighborhood Library and providing referral of patrons to the Resource Libraries as appropriate

Recommends additions to the collection of books and media in the Neighborhood Libraries; may select and deselect materials in an assigned area

Prepares, displays and marketing presentations of library materials

Shelves library materials and maintains the general order and attractiveness of the library facilities

Provides direct daily guidance to other staff in the Neighborhood Library by allocating assignments and scheduling staff

Troubleshoots minor equipment problems; reports major equipment problems and follows through to ensure equipment functionality

Monitors condition of and reports problems with the physical facility

Uses library technology to provide patron services, to monitor use statistics and to develop information for supervisors and managers

When working in Technical Services:

Maintains computer files for all types of library materials in the library computer systems: adds, deletes, or corrects bibliographic and inventory information and trouble shoots as required

Enters bibliographic data into online systems using library standards for identification and description of items

Initiates orders and payments. Communicates both orally and in writing with vendors to execute work, solve problems and/or questions. Refers further communication to supervisor as appropriate

Receives requests for book or other media from library staff, searches available bibliographic sources to verify publication data; searches library files to prevent duplication of acquisitions.

Creates and produces various reports, documents and correspondence

Establishes and maintains complex record keeping system for control of all library materials contracts and purchases, identifying accounts, subprograms, fund encumbrances; establishes and monitors payment schedules, applies direct charges, discounts, and indirect cost factors; verifies and approves classification of charges and credits

Maintains up-to-date acquisition files for staff use including creation of new records in the library computer system on orders, cancellations, back orders, and tracking for high demand titles

Assists in the preparation and issuance of comprehensive bid proposal documents

Related Functions in both areas:

Collects information for and prepares detailed statistical and status reports of various kinds as needed

Receives, sorts, distributes library mail

Participates on Library, City or cooperative library system committees

Performs related duties and responsibilities as required

Interviews, trains, schedules, and coordinates the work of hourly and volunteer staff. May train, schedule, and assign work to other staff as needed.

Knowledge, Skills, and Abilities

Knowledge of public library operations and processes

Knowledge of the basic principles and practices of public libraries

Ability to train and direct work of clerical, temporary and/or volunteer employees

Ability to develop work schedules and to respond to changes in the schedule effectively

Ability to communicate effectively orally with a wide variety of people

Ability to use assigned equipment, including computers and communication equipment, and the Library's automated equipment

Ability to make sound decisions in a manner consistent with the essential job functions

Ability to interpret and apply procedures and policies of the library, organize work assignments, recognize priorities, understand and follow written and oral directions

Ability to use independent and sound judgment to resolve problems

Ability to effectively communicate complex data both orally and in writing to public, staff and vendors

Ability to type and/or use computer terminal or word processing system effectively and to learn operation of computerized system

Ability to work accurately with numbers; identify and correct computational errors

Ability to utilize computers and software systems

When working in Public Service:

Ability to work a varied schedule as required

Work Environment

WORKING CONDITIONS: Work in a library environment; sustained posture in a standing or seated position for prolonged periods of time; bending, lifting and pushing may be required; some positions may include prolonged usage of computer equipment.

Supervisory Responsibilities

SUPERVISES: Non-supervisory position, may assign work to clerical, temporary and/or volunteer staff

Education, Experience, and Training

MINIMUM QUALIFICATIONS: Sufficient education, training and/or work experience to demonstrate possession of the following knowledge, skills, and abilities which would typically be acquired through:

High school graduate and two years of college or equivalent work experience preferred and six semester hours of library science courses relevant to particular position available

Or two years relevant experience in a library.

5.0 LIBRARIAN

5.1 REFERENCE LIBRARIAN

5.1.1 Reference Librarian

Library Name: Phoenix Public Library
Library Location: Phoenix, Arizona
Population Served: 1,350,435
Number of Volumes: 2,015,587
Number of Titles: 734,921
Number of Periodical Subscriptions: 4,500

General Summary

JOB OBJECTIVE:

The fundamental reason this classification exists is to perform entry level professional library work by applying the full scope of basic library knowledge and techniques in the performance of duties. Work involves analyzing the public's library needs, selecting library material, applying bibliographic control techniques to library materials, advising the public in their use of library materials, and handling reference and information search requests. Work is performed in accordance with established policies and accepted library practices and procedures. Some positions supervise a shift of Library Assistants, Library Circulation Attendants, and Library Clerks working at a branch library or a section of the Central Library when the regular supervisor is absent. Work is performed independently and guidance is received from a Librarian III or other section head through review and coordination of plans and programs and frequent conferences.

Essential Functions and Responsibilities

Answers reference questions and performs readers' advisory services;

Reviews assigned media and selects books and other library materials for purchase on the basis of established selection criteria and the needs of library users;

Verifies book orders for exact bibliographic data and related information to ensure proper ordering;

Participates in library committee work and contributes to cooperative efforts in producing recommended reading lists and selection lists;

When assigned, assumes shift responsibility for a branch library or a Central Library section when the supervisor is absent and the performance of his or her function is required;

Technical Services Checks the work products of Library Assistants, Library Technical Assistants, and Remote Computer Terminal Operators for quality control purposes;

Trains clerical staff in acquisition policies and procedures, and the operation of various automated systems;

Supervises and participates in the acquisition of books, reference materials, video and audio media, and other materials including selecting, ordering, receiving, paying and vendor monitoring;

Supervises the Acquisitions Center in the absence of the Acquisitions Center Supervisor;

Performs original cataloging of library materials;

Demonstrates continuous effort to improve operations, decrease turnaround times, streamline work processes, and work cooperatively and jointly to provide quality seamless customer service.

Knowledge, Skills, and Abilities

Knowledge of:

Principles and practices of public libraries.

Principles and techniques of library materials selection and cataloging.

Books, publishing, the book trade, and book review media.

Basic reference tools and services.

Automated library information retrieval systems.

Ability to:

Analyze, evaluate, and appropriately select popular level library materials.

Find answers to general reference questions that are answerable from materials in the library's collections.

Work cooperatively with other City employees and the general public.

Communicate in the English language by phone or in person in a one-to-one or group setting.

Comprehend and make inferences from written material.

Enter or retrieve information from a computer by operating a keyboard.

Work safely without presenting a direct threat to self or others.

Education, Experience, and Training

ACCEPTABLE EXPERIENCE AND TRAINING:

A master's degree in library science from an American Library Association (ALA) accredited institution. Other combinations of experience and education that meet the minimum requirements may be substituted.

Additional Qualifications

Some positions require the use of personal or City vehicles on City business. Individuals must be physically capable of operating the vehicles safely, possess a valid driver's license and have an acceptable driving record. Use of a personal vehicle for

City business will be prohibited if the employee is not authorized to drive a City vehicle or if the employee does not have personal insurance coverage.

Some positions will require the performance of other essential and marginal functions depending upon work location, assignment, or shift. Some positions require use of personal or City vehicle.

5.1.2 Reference Librarian

Library Name: Phoenix Public Library
Library Location: Phoenix, Arizona
Population Served: 1,350,435
Number of Volumes: 2,015,587
Number of Titles: 734,921
Number of Periodical Subscriptions: 4,500

General Summary

JOB OBJECTIVE:

The fundamental reason this classification exists is to perform a full range of professional library work at the Central Library or at a branch library. Work is performed independently in accordance with general policies and accepted professional practices. The advanced difficulty of work assignments and the greater independence with which work is performed differentiates this class from the Librarian I class. Supervision, advice and support are received from a Librarian IV or Librarian III through discussion of plans, problems, and available resources, and performance is evaluated on results obtained.

Essential Functions and Responsibilities

Seeks information from users and potential users of information and library materials about their library needs and interests;

Reviews media and selects books and other library materials for purchase on the basis of established selection criteria and the needs of library users;

Answers reference questions and performs readers' advisory services;

Participates in library committee work and contributes to cooperative efforts in producing recommended reading lists and selection lists;

Assumes the responsibilities of the branch or section head in his or her absence;

Demonstrates continuous effort to improve operations, decrease turnaround times, streamline work processes, and work cooperatively and jointly to provide quality seamless customer service.

Knowledge, Skills, and Abilities

Knowledge of:

Professional library theories, issues and trends.

Principles and practices of public library operation and library materials selection.

Specific subject field or type of library material.

Sources of information on advanced and specialized library materials as well as the general book trade and review media.

Specialized bibliographic and reference tools as well as general reference tools and services.

Library professional publications and the literature of librarianship.

Research techniques and practices.

Ability to:

Analyze professional problems and take appropriate action.

Analyze, evaluate and appropriately select specialized and advanced level library materials as well as popular level materials.

Find answers to specialized and advanced level reference questions in area of specialization as well as to general reference questions.

Keep up-to-date with current professional issues and developments.

Work cooperatively with other City employees and the general public.

Communicate in the English language by phone or in person in a one-to-one or group setting.

Comprehends and makes inferences from written material.

Produce written documents with clearly organized thoughts using proper sentence construction, punctuation and grammar.

Work safely without presenting a direct threat to self or others.

Education, Experience, and Training

ACCEPTABLE EXPERIENCE AND TRAINING:

A master's degree in library science with two years of experience in professional library work or a second master's degree in the area of specialization for subject specialist positions. Degrees must be from an American Library Association (ALA) accredited institution. Other combinations of experience and education that meet the minimum requirements may be substituted.

Additional Qualifications

Some positions require the use of personal or City vehicles on City business. Individuals must be physically capable of operating the vehicles safely, possess a valid driver's license and have an acceptable driving record. Use of a personal vehicle for City business will be prohibited if the employee is not authorized to drive a City vehicle or if the employee does not have personal insurance coverage.

Some positions will require the performance of other essential and marginal functions depending upon work location, assignment, or shift. Some positions require use of personal or City vehicle.

5.1.3 Reference Librarian

Library Name: Mission Viejo
Library Location: Mission Viejo, California
Population Served: 98,000
Number of Volumes: 133,664
Number of Titles: N/A
Number of Periodical Subscriptions: 271

General Summary

DEPARTMENT/DIVISION: LIBRARY SERVICES/VARIES
JOB OBJECTIVE:

Under direction, performs a variety of professional duties involved in planning, coordinating and implementing library services and programs; provide complex professional and technical library services to the community; and perform other related work as necessary.

DISTINGUISHING CHARACTERISTICS:
None.

Essential Functions and Responsibilities

Management reserves the right to add, modify, change or rescind the work assignments of different positions and to make reasonable accommodations so that qualified employees can perform the essential functions of the job.

Coordinate and implement library services programs and regular and special event programs and services and prepare and distribute publicity items.

Interpret and apply library policies and procedures for customers and staff; access and retrieve information for library customers and staff as requested and research and respond to difficult or technical reference questions, referring questions as appropriate; advise and assist library customers in the use of library services and tools.

May participate in the evaluation, selection, acquisition, retention, discarding, or special handling of library materials; use the automated cataloging system to catalog and classify a variety of library materials.

Direct and participate in the compiling of library activity reports and statistics.

Maintain a liaison with other librarians in the community and perform special reading and research to stay abreast of current library practices.

Provide staff support to the Senior Librarian-Public Services.

In addition, when assigned to Children's Services:

Advise children in locating and choosing appropriate materials and advise children, parents and teachers in selecting materials for youth.

Instruct children in the use of electronic reference sources.

Implement a variety of library-related literature-based and educational programs and activities for children including, story-times, library tours, and instructional classes in library use and prepare reading lists and bibliographies.

Develop promotional materials and displays for the children's department; give facility tours to promote the library.

Read reviews of new books, periodicals and other media and participate in the selection of library materials and perform special reading and research to keep abreast of current practices in the field.

In addition, when assigned to Reference:

Participate in all aspects of reference services including online and other electronic searching; telephone reference, municipal reference, and reader's advisory.

Read reviews of new books, periodicals and other media and participate in the selection of library materials and perform special reading and research to keep abreast of current practices in the field.

Prepare instructional brochures, reading lists, bibliographies, and special indexes.

Instruct adults and young adults in the use of electronic reference sources.

In addition, when assigned to Technical Services:

Participate in the acquisition and processing operations for receiving and incorporating materials into the library's collection.

Catalog and classify a variety of library materials using OCLC or other related on-line cataloging systems and ensure staff training in its use and perform bibliographic searches for cataloging data.

Recommend and implement revisions to existing catalog.

Additional Job Duties

May supervise library operations during evening and weekend hours in the absence of Senior Librarian or full-time Librarian.

Perform related duties and responsibilities as assigned.

Knowledge, Skills, and Abilities

Knowledge of:

Library services programs and available resources.

Modern office practices, methods, and computer equipment.

Recent developments, current literature, and sources of information related to library services program planning and administration.

Principles and practices of professional library work, including methods, practices, and techniques of library reference, technical services and/or children's library services.

Principles, techniques, and procedures in cataloging, indexing, classifying, and organizing library materials and those used in bibliographic research.

Applications of automated library circulation system and general library materials selection standards.

Principles and procedures of record keeping.

Pertinent federal, state, and local laws, codes, and regulations including administrative and departmental policies and procedures.

Principles and practices used in dealing with the public and techniques used in public relations.

General principles of risk management related to the functions of the assigned area.

Safe driving principles and practices.

Safe work practices.

Skill to:

Operate modern office equipment including computer equipment and software programs.

Operate a motor vehicle safely.

Ability to:

Coordinate, direct, and implement library services programs suited to the needs of the community.

Recommend and implement goals, objectives, and practices for providing effective and efficient library services programs.

Prepare and maintain accurate and complete records.

Respond to requests and inquiries from the general public.

Prepare clear and concise reports.

Meet and deal tactfully and effectively with the public.

Interpret and apply federal, state, and local, administrative, and departmental laws, codes, regulations, policies, and procedures.

Independently compose correspondence and memoranda and access, retrieve, enter, and update information using a computer terminal.

Work evenings and weekends.

Communicate clearly and concisely, both orally and in writing.

Understand and carry out oral and written instructions.

Establish, maintain and foster positive and harmonious working relationships with those contacted in the course of work.

Physical and Mental Requirements

The sensory demands of the job typically require speaking, hearing, touching and seeing. This is primarily a sedentary office classification although standing in work areas and walking between work areas may be required. Finger dexterity is needed to access, enter and retrieve data using a computer keyboard, typewriter keyboard or calculator and to operate standard office equipment. Positions in this classification occasionally bend, stoop, kneel, reach, push and pull drawers open and closed to retrieve and file information. Positions in this classification occasionally lift and carry reports and records that typically weigh less than 20 pounds.

Work Environment

Environmental Elements:

Employees work in an office environment with moderate noise levels, controlled temperature conditions and no direct exposure to hazardous physical substances. Employees may interact with upset staff and/or public and private representatives in interpreting and enforcing departmental policies and procedures.

Supervisory Responsibilities

May exercise technical and functional supervision over technical, clerical and volunteer staff.

Education, Experience, and Training

Any combination equivalent to experience and training that would provide the required knowledge, skills, and abilities would be qualifying. A typical way to obtain the knowledge, skill, and abilities would be:

Experience:

Two (2) years of related experience.

Training:

Requires a Master's degree from an accredited college or university with major course work in library science or a related field. Candidates close to completing the education requirement may also apply, however, copies of transcripts must be submitted at time of filing, and proof of MLS is required prior to appointment.

License and Certificate Requirements

Possession of, or ability to obtain, and maintain, a valid California Driver's License may be required.

5.1.4 Reference Librarian

Library Name: Weld Library District
Library Location: Greeley, Colorado
Population Served: 137,888
Number of Volumes: 360,019
Number of Titles: N/A
Number of Periodical Subscriptions: 711

General Summary

JOB OBJECTIVE:

This is a professional library work assisting library patron with reference questions, developing and maintaining collections. The Librarian is responsible for providing quality public service by directing library patrons to their information needs, planning, developing and implementing library programs and collections responsive to the library clientele. Work includes identifying services and implementing them in a fiscally sound manner. Supervision may be exercised over library assistants or volunteers. Work is performed under the general supervision of a Library Branch Manager with considerable freedom to assist patrons in the assigned area. Work requires extensive contact with library staff, library users, vendors, professional organizations and associates, and community groups. Branch librarians are required to work a flexible schedule, which includes evenings and weekends in support of public service hours.

Essential Functions and Responsibilities

Guides and assists patrons in locating answers to their questions using a variety of available resources; performs reference interviews and readers advisory services.

Instructs and advises patrons in using the on-line catalog system, understanding the classification system and reference material procedures, finding materials, and evaluating Internet and other resources available.

Develops assigned areas of collection; develops, justifies, and evaluates budget for assigned area of collection; orders all related materials, verifies order information, coordinates orders.

Assess patron needs; plans, develops, implements and evaluates programming and activities and promotes the use of materials through displays, bibliographies, book talks and related activities; publicizes services through links on the web.

Explains various program requirements to volunteers or District staff; trains volunteers and staff in techniques and procedures.

Establishes and maintains contact with patrons and modifies library services consistent with community and public needs as well as established library policy.

Monitors use and request for equipment and supplies; arranges for their proper custody and use; troubleshoots technical problems.

Assists in budget development and evaluation of reference function.

Attends and participates in staff meetings.

Prepares periodic statistical reports.

Maintains an awareness of developments in the profession.

May provide assistance to Spanish-speaking patrons in Spanish.

Physical and Mental Requirements

Work requires bending, standing, stooping and lifting, and reaching high bookshelves for long periods. Work may require pushing or pulling filled library carts and lifting up to 50 lbs. of materials.

Education, Experience, and Training

MINIMUM QUALIFICATIONS

Possession of a master's degree in library science (MLS) is required. Some experience in professional library work; or any equivalent combination of experience, which provides the required knowledge, skills and abilities.

Thorough knowledge of professional library principles, methods, materials and practices, especially as they relate to the field of specialization in which work is performed.

Thorough knowledge of sources and procedures used in reference and bibliographic research.

Thorough knowledge of rules and regulations, professional library procedures, practices and standards, applicable legislation applying to library operations and material access and site directives at specific libraries.

Thorough professional knowledge of reader interest levels, books and authors, periodicals and pamphlet materials, and library guides and publications.

Considerable knowledge of interviewing and problem solving techniques.

Ability to train and lead staff as required by the assignment.

Ability to communicate effectively orally and in writing.

Ability to effectively promote community interest in the field or department of specialization, or in the services provided by a library unit.

Ability to establish and maintain effective working relationships with staff, library customers, and various external clients.

Ability to work with the public for extended periods of time, maintaining a positive, pleasant demeanor and providing friendly, courteous services to library patrons.

Ability to analyze, evaluate and recommend collection development acquisitions.

Ability to operate a computer efficiently.

Ability to communicate effectively orally and in writing in Spanish desired.

License and Certification Requirements

English/Spanish fluency is desirable. Some positions may require a driver's license.

5.1.5 Reference Librarian

Library Name: Manchester Public Library Mary Cheney Library
Library Location: Manchester, Connecticut
Population Served: 54,740
Number of Volumes: 208,997
Number of Titles: N/A
Number of Periodical Subscriptions: 350

Reports to

Librarian II

General Summary

JOB OBJECTIVE:

This professional position is responsible for assisting in the administration and operation of a major section of the library such as reference, circulation and children's and performing specialized professional work. A person in this position also administers the entire library in the absence of a librarian in a more responsible position. Responsibilities include helping develop, coordinate and implement programs to improve service availability and quality consistent with library policies and management guidelines. Other routine work involves keeping current of new technologies and methods, directing, reviewing and evaluating the work of less senior staff, providing for the overall care and maintenance of the collections, attending meetings and workshops and communicating with customers, co-workers and other agencies. Regularly scheduled night and weekend work is expected. The work is subject to review according to the Town's personnel plan through observation, reports and the results achieved.

Essential Functions and Responsibilities

Assists with the development and implementation of programs, strategies and methodologies to increase customer awareness of library resources and appropriate self-sufficiency and monitors the results achieved.

Regularly reads book reviews, publishers catalogues and researches other information sources to identify materials to meet customer needs, enrich the library's collections, and correct deficiencies.

Continuously develops a strong knowledge of the library collection and materials, its strengths and weaknesses and how to find items using the best access methods assigned areas.

Manages, organizes and maintains materials and equipment under his/her care.

He/she assesses department needs and initiates preparation of requisitions for equipment, materials and supplies.

Is responsible for administering all library facilities in the absence of Librarians II or other administrative personnel.

Prepares statistical and other reports regarding library operations and use.

Assists customers with developing needed information by answering questions, identifying potential information sources, recommending specific items, materials or sources and referring them to other appropriate assistance resources such as reference specialists, interlibrary loan materials, manual and automated information or resource databases and staff.

Oversees customers and their use of the library and its resources maintaining the appropriate atmosphere and discipline depending upon the area and the customers being served.

Additional Job Duties

Attends staff and other inter and intra agency meetings to coordinate programs and activities and to increase professional knowledge and skills.

Performs related work as required as well as other duties as may be assigned from time to time and which are consistent with this classification.

Knowledge, Skills, and Abilities

A well developed knowledge of the principles and practices of library work particularly related to assigned areas of expertise such as reference, circulation or children's services and a strong working knowledge of the library's computerized systems.

Able to identify customer needs and requirements, initiate the development of policies, procedures, programs and activities to meet those needs and monitor ongoing performance in the attainment of objectives.

Works in a pleasant and effective manner with customers, coworkers, other departments and agencies.

Communicates effectively orally, in writing and by listening in the modes of conversation, speaking to small groups, preparing formal and informal written reports and hearing and reading instructions, concerns or customer complaints.

Has a strong professional interest in reading, literature and library science.

Physical and Mental Requirements

Assists library customers in their use of the library performing work which is moderately physically demanding and administers the library collection wherever materials may be located including obtaining and replacing books from shelving in the stacks and on all levels, walking and standing for extended time periods (two to four hours) and carrying a reasonable selection of materials between places where they are stored and places where they are used within library facilities and property.

Able to communicate effectively orally, in writing and by listening in the modes of public speaking, speaking with small groups, providing instruction, counseling and direction, and in preparing notes, memorandum, correspondence and reports. This includes the direct and personal use of office computers.

Able to receive, understand, interpret and carry out library policies and procedures.

He/she must be able to hear normal sounds, distinguish sound as voice patterns and communicate through human speech.

Ongoing intellectual effort is required to maintain a current knowledge of library resources, learning, literature and information resources.

Education, Experience, and Training

Minimum Training And Experience

To be considered for this position an applicant must have a master's degree in library science, not less than three (3) years of library experience and a strong knowledge of automated library systems.

Disclaimers

(The above description is illustrative. It is intended as a guide for personnel actions and must not be taken as a complete itemizing of all facets of any job.)

5.1.6 Reference Librarian

Library Name: Milford Public Library
Library Location: Milford, Connecticut
Population Served: 52,000
Number of Volumes: 106,242
Number of Titles: N/A
Number of Periodical Subscriptions: 250

General Summary

JOB OBJECTIVE:

This is professional library work related to the developing, organizing, maintenance, and use of the Library's collection. Under the direction of the Head Librarian and/or Assistant Head Librarian may function as the supervisor of one of the Library's Departments: Reference, Children's, Technical Services, or

Media. Supervises employees within his/her Department through training, scheduling, assigning work, etc.

Essential Functions and Responsibilities

Illustrative Duties

Applies the basic principles of Library Science which are taught as part of the Master's Degree program.

Performs a variety of professional library duties in carrying out major assignments within the operations of the library system.

Accepts assignments and is qualified to work in any department within the Library organization.

Responsible for overseeing applicable clerical procedures and for the training, supervision, and scheduling of assigned library staff. Utilizes current library advances such as computer technology, shared databases, and circulation systems to organize and locate library materials.

Prepares statistical and informational reports.

Attends professional meetings and may represent the Library at professional organizations.

Assumes authority in the absence of the Head Librarian and/or Assistant Head Librarian in accordance with established Library policy.

Performs related work as required.

If assigned to Reference Department:

Provides professional reference services by assisting patrons in the location and use of various library materials and equipment.

Uses interlibrary loan or other appropriate referrals to aid and direct patrons.

Selects materials for inclusion in the collection with emphasis on the reference collection; removes outdated material.

Oversees the history and genealogy collection: assists patrons in its use and performs limited genealogical searches.

Promotes library services through tours and programs.

Performs other duties as assigned.

If assigned to Children's Department:

Provides professional children's services by assisting patrons in the location and use of various juvenile library materials and equipment within the Children's Room.

Plans and presents programs for children, parents, and schools.

Selects materials for inclusion in the collection with emphasis on the children's collection; maintains the collection through weeding, binding, etc.

Performs other duties as assigned.

If assigned to Technical Services Department

Provides professional services in the cataloging and classification of library materials.

Utilizes a computerized, shared database and circulation system such as the software developed by the General Accounting and Computing Corporation (GEAC) in order to enter library materials into the database in accordance with established procedures and standards such as the Machine Readable Catalog (MARC) format.

Selects materials for inclusion in the Library's collection with emphasis on the non-fiction area; maintains the collection through weeding, binding, etc.

Establishes procedures for dealing with book suppliers: monitors library book account.

Oversees the procedures for the processing of new materials.

Performs other duties as assigned.

If assigned to Media Department provides professional media services by assisting patrons in the location and use of various library media materials and equipment.

Plans and presents programs for adults.

Selects materials for inclusion in the collection with emphasis on the media collection; maintains the collection through weeding, repairs, etc.

Provides professional cataloging and classification of media materials in accordance with appropriate media materials systems such as the Alpha numeric system for classifying recordings (ANSCR system).

Oversees the processing of media materials.

Resolves media item circulation problems.

Performs other duties as assigned.

Knowledge, Skills, and Abilities

Professional knowledge of library practices and procedures.

Knowledge of any specialized field of library science.

Knowledge of and ability to be trained in the various technological advances in the library profession such as the utilization of computerized equipment and computer applications.

Ability to meet the public tactfully.

Ability to work with fellow employees.

Ability to supervise assigned personnel.

Education, Experience, and Training

Qualifications

Master's Degree in Library Science from a college or university accredited by the American Library Association is required.

One year of professional library experience is required; additional professional experience desired.

5.1.7 Reference Librarian

Library Name: Woodland Public Library
Library Location: Woodland, California
Population Served: 46,300
Number of Volumes: 95,372
Number of Titles: N/A
Number of Periodical Subscriptions: 237

Reports to

SUPERVISION RECEIVED AND EXERCISED

Direction is provided by the Library Services Director. Responsibilities may require functional supervision of lower level library personnel.

General Summary

JOB OBJECTIVE:

To perform a variety of professional librarian duties in the activities of the library including reference, cataloging, and inter-library loans related to adult, young adult, and children's services.

DISTINGUISHING CHARACTERISTICS

Librarian I: This is the entry level class in the professional library series. Work may involve responsibility for assignments in any library program area which requires the application of fundamental library science principles and practices. Assignments are generally limited in scope and within the design and procedural framework established by higher level employees. However, as experience is acquired, the employee performs with increasing independence. Librarian II: This is the journey level class in the professional library series. Positions in this class are flexibly staffed and are normally filled by advancement from the lower class of Librarian I, or, when filled from the outside, require prior professional library work experience. Appointment to the higher class requires that the employee be performing substantially the full range of duties for the class and meet the qualification standards for the class. Work in this class is distinguished from that of a Librarian I by the greater complexity of the assignments received and by the greater independence with which an incumbent is expected to operate.

Essential Functions and Responsibilities

EXAMPLES OF DUTIES

The following are typical illustrations of duties encompassed by the job class, not an all-inclusive or limiting list:

ESSENTIAL JOB FUNCTIONS:

Assist in the development, implementation, and evaluation of young adult's, children's, adult and other library programs and services.

Assess patron needs and advise them in making effective use of library resources and services; assist patrons of all ages by answering reference questions and selecting print and non-print materials.

Organize, maintain and index a variety of reference materials including government documents, maps and pamphlets.

As a Children's Librarian: Plan, organize and present children's programs including storytelling, book readings, video showings, crafts, and puppet shows, family programs and classes on children's literature and parenting; provide outreach programs to city schools.

Review new publications and collection materials and select materials for acquisition and/or disposition as appropriate.

Regular and consistent attendance.

Work cooperatively with others.

Prepare publicity, coordinate the publication of brochures and coordinate the dissemination of library program publicity.

Attend and represent the library at professional meetings as required.

Compile library activity reports and statistics; assist in preparing the library budget.

Plan, direct and supervise the work of staff involved in assigned library section.

Perform related duties as assigned.

Knowledge, Skills, and Abilities

QUALIFICATIONS

Librarian I

Knowledge of:

General principles and practices of professional library work including methods, practices and techniques of library classification and cataloging.

Patron advisory methods and practices.

Children's and young adult services as a specialized part of the library field; children's and young adult literature.

Modern office procedures and methods including automated library systems.

Operation and programs of a personal computer

Skill to:

Provide information to the general public regarding library department services.

Efficiently operate a personal computer; prepare effective displays and other visual material.

Develop programs that are responsible to community needs.

Perform technical library tasks.

Communicate clearly and concisely, both orally and in writing.

Establish and maintain effective work relationships with those contacted in the performance of required duties.

Ability to:

Develop cooperative public relations with co-workers and the general public.

Select books and materials to meet patrons needs.

Work weekend and evening shifts as assigned.

Meet the physical requirements necessary to safely and effectively perform the assigned duties.

Education, Experience, and Training

Any combination of education and experience that would likely provide the required knowledge and abilities is qualifying. A typical way to obtain the knowledge and abilities would be:

Education:

Possession of a Master of Library Sciences Degree from an accredited college or university.

Experience:

None Required

Knowledge, Skills, and Abilities

Librarian II

In addition to the qualifications for Librarian I:

Knowledge of:

Policies, procedures and functions of the library system.

Print and non-print materials, reference materials, journals, documents, and electronic resources and their appropriateness in recreational reading/research needs.

Computerized cataloging, bibliographic and circulation system data bases and rules for entry of material.

Principles and practices of supervision and training.

Skill to:

Plan, direct and review the work of assigned staff.

Ability to:

Relate well to children, young adult's, and adult alike; exercise creativity in program development.

Assess library patron needs and provide accurate and appropriate information.

Plan and implement specialized programs, including the performance of outreach work.

Supervisory Responsibilities

SUPERVISION RECEIVED AND EXERCISED

Direction is provided by the Library Services Director. Responsibilities may require functional

supervision of lower level library personnel.

Education, Experience, and Training

Experience:

Two years performing duties comparable to those of a Librarian I in the City of Woodland.

5.2 MANAGER/DEPARTMENT HEAD

5.2.1 Manager

Library Name: Manchester Public Library Mary Cheney Library

Library Location: Manchester, Connecticut

Population Served: 54,740

Number of Volumes: 208,997

Number of Titles: N/A

Number of Periodical Subscriptions: 350

Reports to

Library Director

General Summary

JOB OBJECTIVE:

This professional position is responsible for administering and operating a major section of the library such as reference, circulation or children's and performing specialized professional and supervisory work. Responsibilities include initiating, developing, coordinating and implementing programs to improve service availability and quality consistent with library policies and management guidelines. Other routine work involves drafting operating policies and procedures for approval, assisting in the preparation and administration of the division's operating and capital budgets, keeping current of new technologies and methods, directing, reviewing and evaluating the work of subordinates, providing for the overall care and maintenance of the collections under his/her care, assisting in hiring staff, attending meetings and communicating with customers, co-workers and other agencies. Regularly scheduled night and weekend work is expected. The work is subject to review according to the Town's personnel plan through observation, reports and the results achieved.

Essential Functions and Responsibilities

Initiates the development and implementation of programs to increase customer awareness of library resources and appropriate self-sufficiency.

Develops and recommends policies and procedures to improve operations.

Monitors and reports the results achieved.

Manages the assigned staff consistent with delegated responsibilities performing tasks such as scheduling assignments, training and directing staff in the implementation of library policies, procedures, standards and services.

Provides for their professional development.

Evaluates performance and applies positive and negative discipline as appropriate to achieve desired results.

Regularly reads book reviews, publishers catalogues and researches other information sources to identify materials to meet customer needs, enrich the library's collections and correct deficiencies.

Continuously develops a strong knowledge of the library collection and materials, its strengths and weaknesses and how to find items using the best access methods, particularly in areas of expertise.

Manages, organizes and maintains or provides for the care of materials and equipment under his/her stewardship by or providing for the organization of inventories, the maintenance and repair of items, the acquisition of needed and the removal of obsolete items.

Assesses department needs and prepares requisitions for equipment, materials and supplies.

Assists customers with developing needed information by answering questions, identifying potential information sources, recommending specific items, materials or sources and referring them to other appropriate assistance such as reference specialists, interlibrary loan, manual and automated information databases and staff.

Oversees customers and their use of the library maintaining the appropriate atmosphere and discipline depending upon the area and the customers being served.

Attends staff and other inter and intra agency meetings to coordinate programs and activities and to increase professional knowledge and skills.

Prepares or provides for the preparation of statistical and other reports regarding library operations and use.

Additional Job Duties

Performs related work as required, as well as other duties as may be assigned from time to time and which are consistent with this classification.

Knowledge, Skills, and Abilities

A strong knowledge of the principles and practices of library work and of the library's computerized systems, particularly related to an assigned area of expertise such as reference, circulation or children's services.

The ability to identify customer needs and requirements, initiate and develop policies, procedures, programs and activities to meet those needs and monitors ongoing performance in the attainment of objectives.

Works in a pleasant and effective manner with customers, co-workers, other departments and agencies.

Ability to supervise while establishing and maintaining effective working relationships with superiors, subordinates, other employees and customers.

A strong professional interest in reading, literature and library science.

Physical and Mental Requirements

Assists library customers in their use of the library performing work which is moderately physically demanding and administers the library collection wherever materials may be located including obtaining and replacing books from shelving in the stacks and on all levels, walking and standing for extended time periods (two to four hours) and carrying a reasonable selection of materials between places where they are stored and places where they are used within library facilities and property.

Able to communicate effectively orally, in writing and by listening in the modes of public speaking, speaking with small groups, providing instruction, counseling and direction, and in preparing notes, memorandum, correspondence and reports. This includes the direct and personal use of office computers.

Able to receive, understand, interpret and carry out library policies and procedures.

He/she must be able to hear normal sounds, distinguish sound as voice patterns and communicate through human speech.

Ongoing intellectual effort is required to maintain a current knowledge of library resources, learning, literature and information resources.

Education, Experience, and Training

Minimum Training and Experience

To be considered for this position an applicant must have a master's degree in library science, not less than three (3) years of library professional level experience, a strong knowledge of automated library systems and supervisory experience.

(The above description is illustrative. It is intended as a guide for personnel actions and must not be taken as a complete itemizing of all facets of any job.)

5.2.2 Manager/Department Head

Library Name: Portage County Public Library
Library Location: Stevens Point, Wisconsin
Population Served: 67,378
Number of Volumes: 157,918
Number of Titles: N/A
Number of Periodical Subscriptions: N/A

Reports to

Reports to Library Director Summary: Manages the Adult Services Department

Essential Functions and Responsibilities

Selects and orders Adult Services materials.

Maintains statistics and records of the Adult Services Department.

Replaces lost or damaged Adult Services materials.

Weeds and replaces Adult Services collection.

Conducts reference interviews and offers readers' advisory help for library patrons.

Assists patrons in locating and using print and non-print resources.

Assists with programs, displays and exhibits for adult patrons.

Maintains reference materials, such as library forms, brochures, tax forms, and handouts.

Serves at the Circulation Desk by checking materials in and out, entering patron card registrations, handling inquiries regarding overdues, and other tasks as assigned.

Performs general operational procedures, such as opening and closing the library.

Other tasks and duties as assigned by Library Director.

Knowledge, Skills, and Abilities

Computer Skills:

Knowledge of and familiarity with various computer programs including word processing and desktop publishing programs.

Knowledge of and familiarity with microcomputer hardware and microcomputer installation and basic troubleshooting.

Communication Skills:

Ability to communicate effectively with staff and the public and maintain effective public relations.

Ability to comprehend and follow instructions from supervisor, verbally and in written form.

Mental Skills:

Analytical skills – identify problems and potential areas for improvement; utilize available information sources in decision-making.

Problem solving skills – develop feasible, realistic solutions to problems.

Planning and organizational skills – develop long-range plans and establish methods for accomplishing goals.

Communication skills – effectively communicate ideas and information both in written and oral forms and in Standard English.

Reading ability – effectively read and understand memoranda, reports, and bulletins.

Mathematical ability – calculate basic arithmetic problems.

Time management – set priorities and follow through to meet assignment deadlines.

Physical and Mental Requirements

The physical demands described here are representative of those that must be met by an employee to successfully perform the essential functions of this job. Reasonable accommodations may be made to enable individuals with disabilities to perform the essential functions. The physical demands of the job may require the employee to:

Bend, twist, stretch and reach.

Talk and hear, use the telephone.

Have far vision at 20 feet or farther, near vision at 20 inches or less.

Lift and carry 50 pounds or less.

Handle processing, pick up and shelve books.

Push and pull objects weighing 50-80 pounds on wheels.

Type, write, file, sort and process materials.

Move around the library.

Work Environment

The work environment characteristics described here are representative of a typical public library. Efforts are made to ensure that patrons and staff will be in a comfortable room temperature. The library takes up two floors, but does not have an elevator, so stairs must be used. Overhead storage is sometimes used, and there is a low to moderate noise level. Reasonable accommodations may be made to enable individuals with disabilities to perform the essential functions.

Supervisory Responsibilities

Assumes daily supervision of the Adult Services Department staff.

Trains Adult Services personnel.

Supervises long term staff planning.

Assigns tasks to Adult Services Staff.

Appraises Adult Services staff performance.

Writes instructions and trains Adult Services staff on changes in procedures.

Addresses complaints and resolves problems arising in the Adult Services Department.

Reviews PLDL policies and employee law as they pertain to the Adult Services Department.

Other tasks and duties as assigned by Library Director.

Education, Experience, and Training

This position requires a Bachelors Degree from an accredited college or university. Hiring is contingent on proof of such.

Should have considerable knowledge of library operations, services, and materials, including a depth of knowledge on issues, topics, and writers of special interest to adults.

Ability to understand library policies and procedures and apply them to library operations.

Additional Qualifications

To perform this job successfully, an individual must be able to perform each essential and supervisory responsibility satisfactorily. The requirements listed below are representative of the knowledge, skill, and/or ability required. Reasonable accommodations may be made to enable individuals with disabilities to perform the essential functions.

License and Certification Requirements

Certificates, Licenses, Registrations:

Upon hiring, the employee must be able to obtain a Limited Professional Certification, Class A or B, (Level IV or V), from the Library of Michigan within the 90-day probationary period.

5.2.3 Manager/Department Head

Library Name: Woodland Public Library
Library Location: Woodland, California
Population Served: 46,300
Number of Volumes: 95,372
Number of Titles: N/A
Number of Periodical Subscriptions: 237

General Summary

JOB OBJECTIVE:

To plan, organize and supervise personnel in the day-to-day activities of the library;

oversee the maintenance of Library building, grounds and equipment.

Essential Functions and Responsibilities

The following are typical illustrations of duties encompassed by the job class, not an all inclusive or limiting list:

To plan, organize and supervise library personnel in the day-to-day activities of the library:

Review work methods and interdepartmental procedures to ensure effective work flow and compliance with established policies and procedures; select, train and evaluate assigned personnel; work with employees to correct deficiencies.

Oversee the maintenance of the Library building, grounds and computer equipment, including the coordination and monitoring of outside maintenance contracts and work performed.

Perform the most complex professional librarian duties including reference, cataloging and inter-library loans.

Assess patron needs and advise them in making effective use of library resources and services; assist patrons of all ages by answering reference questions and selecting print and non-print materials.

Prepare comprehensive and complex departmental reports by researching, summarizing, and analyzing information from a variety of sources; conduct periodic surveys on library usage.

Regular and consistent attendance.

Work cooperatively with others.

Participate in the development and implementation of goals, objectives, policies and priorities including current and advanced library activities; assist in the preparation, analysis, and administration of program budgets.

Develop and maintain appropriate procedure manuals.

Represent the Library in organizations, community, and professional meetings as required.

Promote and maintain safety in the work place.

Serve as Acting Library Director as assigned.

Perform related duties as assigned.

Knowledge, Skills, and Abilities

QUALIFICATIONS

Knowledge of:

Principles, laws, policies, methods, and practices of public library administration.

Principles and practices of contract administration, management and supervision.

Library classification, circulation, distributing, cataloging and reference techniques and practices.

Patron advisory methods and practices.

Statistical research and reporting methods, techniques and procedures.

Safety principles, practices and procedures.

Operation and programs of a personal computer.

Skill to:

Plan, coordinate, and prioritize a variety of projects.

Persuade and motivate individuals and groups toward the successful accomplishment of shared goals and objectives.

Provide information to the general public regarding library department services.

Perform complex professional library work in the absence of supervision.

Communicate clearly and concisely, both orally and in writing.

Collect and analyze data and develop complex reports.

Supervise and evaluate assigned staff.

Effectively operate a personal computer.

Establish and maintain effective work relationships with those contacted in the performance of required duties.

Ability to:

Manage, direct, coordinate and evaluate the work of professional and technical personnel.

Develop cooperative public relations with contractors, other City departments, business owners, and the general public.

Analyze and compile technical and statistical information; prepare clear and concise technical reports.

Analyze problems, identify alternative solutions, project consequences of proposed actions and implement recommendations in support of goals.

Ensure compliance with Federal, state and local rules, laws and regulations.

Understand and implement effective facility maintenance practices.

Meet the physical requirements necessary to safely and effectively perform the assigned duties.

Supervisory Responsibilities

SUPERVISION RECEIVED AND EXERCISED

Direction is provided by the Library Services Director. Responsibilities include direct and indirect supervision of professional, technical and clerical staff.

Education, Experience, and Training

Education and Experience:

Any combination of experience and training that would likely provide the required knowledge and abilities is qualifying. A typical way to obtain the knowledge and abilities would be:

Education:

Possession of a Master of Library Sciences Degree from an accredited college or university.

Experience:

Three years of increasingly responsible experience in professional public library administration.

5.2.4 Manager/Department Head

Library Name: Helen M. Plum Memorial Library

Library Location: Lombard, Illinois

Population Served: 42,322

Number of Volumes: 210,815

Number of Titles: N/A

Number of Periodical Subscriptions: 358

Reports to

RELATIONSHIPS: Reports to the Library Director

General Summary

This job description is meant to be a general guide to the responsibilities and duties of the job and is not intended to list every possible task an employee may be called upon to perform.

Essential Functions and Responsibilities

Planning, implementing and supervising the Adult Services Department in accordance with the mission statement, policies, goals and objectives of the Helen M. Plum Memorial Library.

Coordinating a library program designed to interest people over the age of 14 in the use of the Library.

Supervising and training all departmental staff.

Screening and hiring job applicants in consultation with the Director.

Explaining Library personnel policies and procedures.

Alerting Adult Services staff to staff development opportunities and scheduling same.

Processing personnel records such as time sheets, sick leave, vacation, etc.

Keeping track of the gain and use of compensatory and holiday time.

Performing Adult Services employee evaluations and recommending position and salary placement.

Preparing work schedules and revising as needed.

Scheduling and conducting department meetings.

Orienting and training Adult Services staff in all aspects of their work.

Training Adult Services staff in the use of reference materials, electronic and print.

Planning and managing the daily operations of the department.

Preparing and implementing departmental goals and objectives.

Supervising reference and reader's advisory service given in the department.

Ensuring that requests for material available outside the Library (ILL, SLS requests, etc.) are handled properly.

Developing Adult Services policies in conjunction with the Director.

Acting as consultant on reference and reader's advisory questions.

Overseeing the departmental collection management program.

Having overall responsibility for the acquisition of all materials for the department.

Evaluating the collection on a regular basis and coordinating the weeding process.

Participating in collection management.

Selecting, weeding and maintaining assigned areas of the Adult Services collection.

Data entry of orders into the online catalog.

Working with the Acquisition Clerk and Head of Technical Processing on departmental orders.

Working with the Adult Cataloger and Head of Technical Processing on cataloging of departmental materials.

Working with the Processing Clerk and Head of Technical Processing on the processing of departmental materials.

Approving invoices for adult materials as needed.

Participating in budget related activities on behalf of the department.

Preparing the annual departmental budget recommendations.

In conjunction with the other department heads and the Director, developing a library-wide budget.

Implementing the working budget pertaining to the Department. Researching and recommending new equipment and furniture for purchase.

Keeping a running account of the monies encumbered and spent on programs, publicity and departmental training and travel.

Coordinating library and departmental surveys.

Planning for and creating new services, and revising or canceling existing ones to meet current needs.

Regularly reviewing the need for physical improvements in the Department relating to the use of space, appearance, and maintenance, and calling these to the attention of the proper person.

In this department these areas include:

Adult stacks and study areas

Quiet study area in the addition

Skylight area

Adult Services offices

Bulletin Boards—Friends and Library

Typing rooms

Browsing area

Periodical storage

Developing and evaluating procedures for Department using input from staff members

Maintaining appropriate records and preparing regular and special reports to the Director and the Library Board of Trustees.

Advising and working with the Adult Services staff in the preparation of booklists and bibliographies.

Working with those outside the Adult Services Department.

Acting as intermediary in communications between the Adult Services staff and the Director.

Communicating with other department heads on interdepartmental concerns and/or problems.

Advising the Director in the management of the Library as a member of the Advisory Committee.

Attending monthly meetings of the Library Board of Trustees.

Attending and participating in professional organizations and meetings and reading professional literature.

Writing reports of meetings attended.

Advising the interlibrary loan clerk on problems with the service.

Serving as an Adult Services librarian.

Providing reference and reader's advisory service to all Library patrons to satisfy their informational and recreational needs.

Conducting a reference interview.

Answering reference inquiries in person, via e-mail, and over the phone.

Recording inquiries about reference problems that cannot be answered at the time and following through on answering the request within a reasonable amount of time.

Assisting patrons with questions and requests that cannot be answered in house by using ILL, metropolitan area sources, long distance telephone reference, etc.

Assisting and instructing patrons in using the automated catalog including, but not limited to, bibliographic searching, the use of the suggestion box, viewing a patron record, requesting an item, the establishment of a PIN number, and searching other libraries.

Assisting patrons in using various CD-ROM and online databases, indexes, reference and circulating collections.

Showing patrons the location of materials on shelf when necessary.

Taking reserves for materials already checked out.

Reading or examining new library materials to stay current in the literature and trends.

Communicating availability of DLS special services to patron.

Doing online searching as needed including Internet, bibliographic databases such as DLS/MAGIC, COD, IO, Firstsearch, and other online databases.

Answering direct loan requests made by DLS libraries.

Advising Blind and Physically Handicapped patrons.

Accepting suggestions for purchase from patrons and routing them to the correct selector/department.

Scheduling, planning and presenting class and group visits.

Promoting literature through reader's advisory, using knowledge of adult and teen literature and reference materials.

Acting as Person in Charge when designated by the Director.

Having a working knowledge of library policies and procedures.

Handling emergencies that cannot wait until later.

Making written reports of situations in which s/he has acted as PIC.

Performing closing procedures when Monitors are not present.

Advising and instructing the Monitors.

Planning and assisting in the development and execution of adult and teen programs in cooperation with the other staff members.

Additional Job Duties

Other important responsibilities and duties:

Helping patrons with computer workstation hardware and software problems, with the assistance of the Automation Manager.

Having a working knowledge of the tasks done by those in the department and filling in for absent staff members as needed.

Covering public service desks for other departments during their staff meetings.

Preparing subject and specialized user bibliographies.

Helping with publicity.

Checking out A-V equipment to patrons.

Servicing the typing/quiet study rooms.

Assisting patrons with A-V and other equipment in the department.

Assisting patrons with the Internet.

As part of a team, creating displays to highlight collections and promote programs.

Knowledge, Skills, and Abilities

Committed to excellence in library service to adults and teenagers.

A knowledge of professional practices, procedures and techniques of library service, particularly as they apply to adults and teenagers.

Service oriented and able to work cooperatively with other staff and patrons in a pleasant, mature and courteous manner at all times.

Able to exercise initiative, tact, leadership and independent judgment.

Skill in both written and oral communication.

Well-organized, innovative and creative.

Able to foster and maintain the high standards of public service.

Skill in the interviewing process and in training, supervising and evaluating the work of others.

Knowledge of adult books and materials and their organization.

Skill in the use of reference tools in Adult Services and the ability to interpret questions.

Knowledge and skill in the use of the Library computer system and personal computer operations.

Skill in the use of the Internet.

Adaptable, flexible, able to deal with change.

Professional in appearance and demeanor.

Education, Experience, and Training

Required: ALA accredited MLS degree.

A minimum of 3 years experience in public library reference work with adults and teenagers.

A minimum of 2 years administrative experience, supervising others.

Desirable: Computer literate. Courses or experience in the use of various computer software applications and hardware uses.

5.2.5 Librarian, Reference Department Head

Library Name: Manitowoc Public Library
Library Location: Manitowoc, Wisconsin
Population Served: 58,213
Number of Volumes: 195,166
Number of Titles: N/A
Number of Periodical Subscriptions: 395

General Summary

JOB OBJECTIVE:

Under general direction from Public Services Coordinator, plans, develops, implements and evaluates the Library's program of information and adult services for the community. Administers and manages department; supervises departmental staff; develops and manages departmental budget; provides direct service to the public. Participates on the Library's management team and assists in administration of the Library. Participates in Library's collection development and marketing efforts. Handles large-scale, on-going projects for the Library, as assigned, and serves as Emergency/Disaster Plan Coordinator. Acts as liaison between the Library and community groups. Performs work of other departmental staff, as needed. May perform work of another member of the Library's management team, as assigned.

Essential Functions and Responsibilities

The following list identifies principal duties and responsibilities of the job. It is not a definitive list and other similar duties may be assigned. An asterisk (*) before any of the following items indicates duties and responsibilities which are not "essential functions" of the job as defined by the Americans with Disabilities Act.

1. Plans, develops, implements and evaluates the Library's program of information and adult services for the community by: budgeting and expending resources (personnel, space, money, etc.); developing a range of public services and programs; directing marketing strategies. Establishes departmental priorities. Administers and manages departmental budget and plan of departmental services. Writes project proposals and grants, and implements programs. Analyzes technological advances and recommends appropriate applications. Works with Coordinators and Director on short- and long-range planning and coordinates departmental plans within Library's goals, objectives and policies.

2. Participates on the Library's management team and assists in administration of the Library. Attends meetings and communicates decisions with staff, as appropriate. Provides professional and managerial support to supervisor and other members of the management team. Assists in establishing and meeting goals and objectives for the Library. Recommends policies and administrative actions to Coordinators and Library Director. Communicates with other members of the management team about departmental issues and priorities. Acts as consultant for MCLS and other libraries, as delegated or assigned.

3. Guides overall functions and direction of the department. Administers and manages departmental budget and plan of departmental services. Directs development and implementation of departmental procedures and routines. Writes (or supervises writing by other staff) project proposals and grants, and implements programs.

4. Supervises and schedules departmental staff. Manages Reference Desk schedule. Evaluates departmental staff in conjunction with Coordinator. Team interviews and makes hiring recommendations to Library Director. Develops and implements plans for training departmental staff, and involves staff from other departments, as appropriate. When necessary, handles progressive discipline of staff through the level of written warnings and makes recommendations for further discipline up to and including firing to the Library Director.

5. Under direction of the Public Services Coordinator, participates in the Library's collection development efforts, including selection, deselection, marketing, evaluation and reconsideration. Attends committee meetings and may chair meetings, as delegated or assigned. Assists in on-going development and statement of collection philosophy. Assumes responsibility for specific areas of the collection, as delegated or assigned.

6. Directs development of programs and tours, including training programs for patrons in the use of the Library. Participates in the Library's coordinated marketing efforts. Plans and implements marketing strategies for departmental services and collections.

7. Handles large-scale, on-going projects for the Library, as assigned. Serves as Emergency/Disaster Plan Coordinator for the Library.

8. Provides direct service to the public. Assists patrons at the Reference Desk and over telephone by providing reference, readers' and AV advisory, local information, referral, and electronic information services. Assists with maintenance of building and building security. Acts as liaison between the Library and community groups, as assigned.

*9. Performs work of other departmental staff, as needed. May perform work of another member of the Library's management team, as assigned.

Knowledge, Skills, and Abilities

JOB SPECIFICATIONS:

1. Knowledge of public library administrative and managerial practices, and ability to apply these to an information and adult services department. Willingness to contribute to on-going development of Library-wide philosophy, mission and services, and ability to lead development of departmental philosophy, goals and services.

2. Knowledge of public library planning and role-setting practices and their application to information and adult services. Ability to analyze and evaluate current conditions and make logical evaluations of future needs. Ability to plan and execute short-range plans. Ability to synthesize and creatively adapt trends in technology, publishing, information retrieval and library science to planning for the department and the organization. Skill in negotiating for resources to meet departmental needs.

3. Ability to assume a leadership role in a group setting. Ability to establish and maintain effective working relationships with the Library Director, Public Services Coordinator, Management Team members, other library staff members, sales representatives, community officials, agency representatives, and the public. Ability to work in the Library's team setting. Willingness to assist and support coworkers, contribute ideas, and maintain flexibility. Ability to adapt to a rapidly changing environment.

4. Commitment to and skill in supervising people. Knowledge of supervisory and training techniques. Willingness and ability to provide positive managerial example. Willingness and ability to foster environment in which employees are self-motivated and can exhibit high morale. Capacity to recognize and utilize talents of others. Fairness when distributing workload, responsibility, and authority. Ability to identify proper work assignments for subordinates and willingness to follow-up to ensure proper completion.

5. Ability to set realistic standards for employees and to encourage productive and efficient performance.

Conscientiousness when appraising performance, counseling employees, writing and administering performance appraisals, and making personnel recommendations.

6. Skill in managing departmental workflow, including ability to identify, negotiate, establish, communicate, and apply priorities. Skill in performing and supervising routine and non-routine procedures involving many steps. Ability to give and follow complex written and/or verbal instructions and to pay close attention to detail. Willingness to provide professional and managerial support to supervisor. Ability to accept delegation and to work under general supervisory direction.

7. Ability to make realistic budget proposals, to operate within established budgetary guidelines, and to identify and analyze budgetary impact of services.

8. Ability to communicate effectively. Skill in interpersonal communication. Ability to do technical writing for procedures, proposals, reports, etc.

9. Initiative and resourcefulness to take acceptable risks, make appropriate decisions, and exercise proper authority. Ability to present clear explanations of established policies and procedures. Ability to think and act appropriately under pressure. Willingness and ability to grant logical exceptions to policies and procedures when warranted. Willingness to maintain confidentiality when appropriate and to be held accountable.

10. Ability to provide courteous and timely public service to patrons of various ages, interests, backgrounds, and levels of library expertise. Ability to conduct a reference interview to determine patron needs. Capacity to be easily understood on voice telephone. Knowledge of popular authors, artists, and subject areas to facilitate patron question negotiation. Knowledge of reference tools, methodologies, and philosophy. Ability to provide instruction and encouragement in use of library resources to patrons individually and in groups.

11. Understanding of collection development tools and theory. Knowledge of publishers, popular authors, artists, and subject areas to facilitate collection development. Willingness and ability to understand and contribute to on-going development of local collection philosophy.

12. Ability to interact effectively with the Library's automated systems. Skill in using microcomputers and related software. Basic knowledge of database, spreadsheet and word processing software programs. Knowledge of or ability to quickly learn Library's current software programs as these apply to job responsibilities.

13. Ability to develop work-related goals and objectives. Willingness to develop job-related abilities, skills and knowledge. Willingness and ability to keep abreast of changing technologies and procedures, and to assume responsibilities required by introduction of different services and equipment.

14. Willingness and ability to understand and support the fundamental principles of library services, such as offering open access to library materials for people of all ages; providing materials representing as many points of view as possible; and protecting a patron's right to privacy in dealings with the library and with respect to records maintained by library.

Work Environment

1. Usually (up to 100% of work time) works in environment with considerable public and staff contact and rapid turn-over at service desk or, when not at service desk, in shared office environment.

2. Usually (up to 100% of work time) works in close proximity with terminals and other similar electronic equipment.

3. Usually (up to 100% of work time) maintains work environment. For example: vacuuming computer areas, dusting, recycling paper; cleaning up after programs. Infrequently (as situation requires) assists with building emergencies which may involve cleaning up snow, bodily fluids, etc.

4. Sometimes (up to 25% of work time) lifts and/or transports objects weighing 5 to 20 pounds; pushes or pulls carts loaded with materials weighing more than 150 pounds. Retrieves and/or shelves objects weighing 5 to 20 pounds from all shelving levels.

5. Sometimes (up to 25% of work time) works with equipment and performs procedures where carelessness may result in minor cuts, bruises, or muscle strains.

6. Sometimes (up to 25% of work time) works in bookstack areas where there is exposure to dust, newsprint, etc.

Education, Experience, and Training

MINIMUM QUALIFICATIONS:

1. Master's degree in library science from an A.L.A.-accredited school.

2. 3 years post-M.L.S. managerial experience in a public library setting; or, equivalent education / experience mix as determined by the Library Director. Demonstrated ability to supervise staff, preferably in a union environment.

3. Demonstrable possession of knowledge, skills, abilities, and capacities identified in "Job Specifications" section, above.

4. Capacity to work under conditions described in "Working Conditions" section, above.

Position Hours

POSITION HOURS: Salaried full-time, typically working at least 80 hours per two-week pay period on a flexible schedule which varies from week to week. May be scheduled to work days, evenings, Saturdays, and Sundays.

5.3 SENIOR LIBRARIAN

5.3.1 Senior Librarian

Library Name: Mission Viejo Library
Library Location: Mission Viejo, California
Population Served: 98,000
Number of Volumes: 133,664
Number of Titles: N/A
Number of Periodical Subscriptions: 271

General Summary

DEPARTMENT/DIVISION: LIBRARY SERVICES/VARIES
JOB OBJECTIVE:

Under administrative direction, manage, supervise, and coordinate the programs, activities, and services of the City Library; coordinate assigned activities with other City departments and outside agencies; provide complex administrative support to the Director of Library Services; and perform other related work as necessary.

DISTINGUISHING CHARACTERISTICS:
None.

Essential Functions and Responsibilities

Management reserves the right to add, modify, change or rescind the work assignments of different positions and to make reasonable accommodations so that qualified employees can perform the essential functions of the job.

Assume management responsibility for all services and activities of the City Library and assigned Division.

Manage and participate in the development and implementation of goals, objectives, policies, and priorities for assigned programs.

Recommend, within Departmental policy, appropriate service and staffing levels; recommend and administer policies and procedures.

Monitor and evaluate the efficiency and effectiveness of service delivery methods and procedures.

Assess and monitor workload, administrative support systems, and internal reporting relationships; identify opportunities for improvement; direct the implementation of improvements.

Select, train, motivate, and evaluate assigned personnel; provide or coordinate staff training; work with employees to correct deficiencies; implement discipline and termination procedures.

Plan, direct, coordinate, and review the work of the City Library and assigned division.

Meet with staff to identify and resolve problems, assign work activities, projects and programs; monitor workflow; review and evaluate work products, methods and procedures.

Manage and participate in the development and administration of the City Library and assigned division annual budget and grants; direct the forecast of additional funds needed for staffing, equipment, materials, and supplies.

Direct the monitoring of and approve expenditures; direct and implement adjustments as necessary.

Serve as liaison for the City Library and Library Services Division with other City departments, divisions, and outside agencies; negotiate and resolve significant and controversial issues.

Provide staff assistance to Director of Library Service; prepare and present staff reports and other necessary correspondence.

Assess community needs; determine scope and nature of required library programs, collections, and services; develop and coordinate long-term plan of services.

Plan, organize, and oversee the implementation and maintenance of automated library functions; plan and direct the utilization of data processing techniques to library personnel.

Coordinate library services activities with other libraries on a system wide basis.

Develop, administer, and evaluate service contracts.

Administer and evaluate activities and services provided by contractors; evaluate the adequacy of rates for library service programs.

Coordinate and direct the maintenance of Library facilities and equipment; administer and evaluate adequacy of building criteria to meet the requirements of future library development.

Conduct a variety of organizational studies, investigations, and operational studies; recommend modifications to library services programs, policies, and procedures as appropriate.

Participate in a variety of boards and commissions; attend and participate in professional group meetings; stay abreast of new trends and innovations in the field of library services.

Prepare press releases; make presentations; promote use of library services.

Respond to and resolve difficult and sensitive inquiries and complaints.

In addition, when assigned to Public Services:

Assume management responsibility for all services and activities of the City Library and Library Services Division, including administration, reference, children's services, and circulation services programs.

In addition, when assigned to Support Services:

Assume management responsibility for all services and activities of the City Library's Support Services, including acquisitions, serials, OPACs, cataloging, processing, reference, automated systems, and circulation services.

Continuously monitor and evaluate the efficiency and effectiveness of service delivery methods and procedures including circulation services.

Serve as Library's liaison between City's Information Technology Division in coordinating the implementation, administration and application of the library's automated system (DYNIX) and its associated services and modules; troubleshoot circulation equipment.

Participate in the planning and development of the future growth of the library's technology, including the facilitation of remote patron access, linked systems and shared databases.

Additional Job Duties

Participate in the selection of library materials.

Provide library users with advisory services and answer reference questions.

Perform related duties and responsibilities as assigned.

Knowledge, Skills, and Abilities

Knowledge of:

Operational characteristics, services, and activities of a library services program.

Organizational and management practices as applied to the analysis and evaluation of programs, policies and operational needs.

Modern and complex principles and practices of library program development and administration.

Recent developments, current literature, and sources of information related to library services and program planning and administration.

Organization, objectives, programs services and technology of a modem public library system.

Current practices and procedures of the library profession, including availability of printed media and non-print informational services.

Principles, laws, policies, methods and practices of public library administration.

Principles of personnel selection, supervision, training, and performance evaluation.

Principles and practices of budget preparation and administration.

Pertinent Federal, State, and local laws, codes, and regulations.

Library automation and information retrieval systems.

Library programs and services and their relationship to community needs.

Nationally held standards for quality library services.

In addition, when assigned to Support Services:

Principles, practices, techniques and characteristics, services and activities of a library's technical services including, but not limited to, OCLC, DYNIX or other automated systems, Internet, Z39.50, PAC for Windows, AACR2R, LCSH, MARC, IP/FTP, WebPac, technology planning, vendor relations, RFP's, database licensing, automated integrated/linked library systems, Y2K issues, and other applications of technology in the public library setting.

General principles of risk management related to the functions of the assigned area.

Safe driving principles and practices.

Safe work practices.

Skill to:

Operate modern office equipment including computer equipment and software programs.

Operate a motor vehicle safely.

Ability to:

Select, supervise, train, evaluate, manage and coordinate the work of professional, paraprofessional, clerical, part-time/seasonal/temporary and volunteer staff.

Recommend and implement goals, objectives and practices for providing effective and efficient library services and programs.

Interpret, explain and ensure compliance with City Library services, policies and procedures.

Provide administrative and professional leadership and direction for the City Library and Support Services.

Analyze problems, identify alternative solutions, project consequences of proposed actions, and implement recommendations in support of goals.

Research, analyze, and evaluate new service delivery methods, procedures, and techniques.

Assess needs, prepare long-term plans and provide alternate methods for implementation.

Administer the activities, services, and operations of a city library.

Coordinate, direct, and implement library services and programs suited to the needs of the community.

Elicit community and organizational support of library programs; present material to the general public.

Prepare and administer large and complex budgets.

Prepare clear and concise administrative and financial reports.

Interpret and apply Federal, State, and local policies, procedures, laws, and regulations.

Prepare, analyze, and recommend appropriate alternatives related to City administrative affairs.

Communicate clearly and concisely, both orally and in writing.

Understand and carry out oral and written instructions.

Establish, maintain and foster positive and harmonious working relationships with those contacted in the course of work.

In addition, when assigned to Support Services:

Evaluate technological choices and recommend action.

Resolve staff/patron problems and issues related to automated resources and services.

Physical and Mental Requirements

Physical and Sensory Elements:

The sensory demands of the job typically require speaking, hearing, touching and seeing. This is primarily a sedentary office classification although standing in work areas and walking between work areas may be required. Finger dexterity is needed to access, enter and retrieve data using a computer keyboard, typewriter keyboard or calculator and to operate standard office equipment. Positions in this classification occasionally bend, stoop, kneel, reach, push and pull drawers open and closed to retrieve and file information. Positions in this classification occasionally lift and carry reports and records that typically weigh less than 20 pounds.

Work Environment

Employees work in an office environment with moderate noise levels, controlled temperature conditions and no direct exposure to hazardous physical substances. Employees may interact with upset staff and/or public and private representatives in interpreting and enforcing departmental policies and procedures.

Supervisory Responsibilities

SUPERVISION EXERCISED:

Exercises direct supervision over professional, technical and clerical staff.

Education, Experience, and Training

Any combination equivalent to experience and training that would provide the required knowledge, skills, and abilities would be qualifying. A typical way to obtain the knowledge, skill, and abilities would be:

Experience:

Five (5) years of increasingly responsible professional preferably in a library setting, including at least two (2) years of supervisory experience.

Training:

Equivalent to a Master's degree from an accredited college or university with major course work in library science or a related field.

License and Certification Requirements

Possession of, or ability to obtain, and maintain, a valid California Driver's License may be required.

5.4 AUDIOVISUAL LIBRARIAN

5.4.1 Audiovisual Librarian

Library Name: St. Clair County Library System
Library Location: Port Hudson, Michigan
Population Served: 160,708
Number of Volumes: 432,880
Number of Titles: 206,173
Periodical Subscriptions: 560

Reports to

SUPERVISION RECEIVED Work is performed under the general supervision of the Adult Services Coordinator or the director or other designated person.

General Summary

JOB OBJECTIVE:

This position works with limited supervision performing Reference Department duties. This position is also responsible for coordinating and implementing assignments with regard to audiovisual material.

Essential Functions and Responsibilities

Typical Work:

Responsible for Reference Desk duties providing Library customers with requested information.

Performs readers advisory and is instrumental in the selection, organization and access of library materials.

Assists and instructs Library customers in using the public access catalog, Internet, LAN and additional technological databases.

Provides bibliographic assistance and education to Library customers.

Participates in information literacy and library instruction programs.

Develops and maintains the reference collection for assigned classification areas.

Contributes to the development of the general collection and works on collection management projects as necessary.

Participates in continuing education, conference, workshops, seminars, or other activities that enhance professional knowledge.

Other duties may be assigned.

Additional Job Duties

Oversees the operation of Audiovisual Department routines and reports on departmental activities.

Demonstrates awareness of current developments and trends in audiovisual services, systems and equipment.

Contributes to the development of the audiovisual collection and works on collection management projects as necessary.

Evaluates audiovisual collection expansion and shelving requirements as needed

Supervisory Responsibilities

SUPERVISION EXERCISED Library Staff during scheduled evening and weekends when Librarian 1A is highest authority.

Education, Experience, and Training

Graduate degree in Information (Library) Science from an ALA accredited school.

The qualified candidate must possess a valid State of Michigan operator license and maintain this license during employment in the position.

Additional Qualifications

Desired Qualifications:

Knowledge of the principles and practices of professional library responsibilities.

Strong interpersonal skills with the ability to relate to all diversities of employees and customers.

High level of energy and enthusiasm for the work assigned.

5.5 BRANCH LIBRARIAN, MLS DESIRABLE NOT REQUIRED

5.5.1 Branch Librarian, MLS Desirable Not Required

Library Name: St. Clair County Library System
Library Location: Port Huron, Michigan
Population Served: 160,708
Number of Volumes: 432,880
Number of Titles: 206,173
Periodical Subscriptions: 560

Reports to

SUPERVISION RECEIVED; Work is performed under the general supervision of the branch coordinator, assistant director, or the Director.

General Summary

Manages the operation of a branch Library of the St. Clair County Library System; this includes supervision of all branch staff programs, collections, services, outreach and facilities.

Essential Functions and Responsibilities

Typical Work: Supervises and trains assistant staff in all library operations, assigning work as needed.

Provides reference and readers advisory service to the public utilizing on-line reference databases, the Internet, and print reference resources.

Selects, maintains, and evaluates the library collection to meet the needs of the local and county community according to the county library's materials selection guidelines and policies

Oversees the circulation of materials according to policies established, assuring this function is handled with consistency and accuracy by all staff.

Develops and implements or works with assistants in developing new and innovative programs at the branch designed to create interest and enjoyment of the Library.

Is responsible for maintaining patron records according to county library practices, policies, and procedures and adheres to the privacy guidelines established.

Teaches the public how to use the on-line catalog to find materials and to place holds. Teaches the public other tools such as computer databases, microfilm readers, the Internet, use of copy

machines, self-checkout machines, etc. to enable them to become independent library users.

Follows county library procedures for the collection of and the accounting for funds received from the public and remits these to the business office of either the county or the local municipality as appropriate.

Prepares and posts work schedules for all branch staff according to county library procedures and reviews and authorizes time cards accurately and on time.

Oversees the library facility informing the local municipality/township of needed repairs, safety concerns, or required improvements of the physical plant.

Acts as liaison to the local advisory board, municipal council, Library Friends and other local groups to promote the interests of the library branch and the entire library system.

Oversees material processing: cataloging, bar coding, labeling, shelving and assigns work appropriately among staff.

Generates and maintains branch records, statistics, and reports as required.

Works with Community Relations Department to promote services by providing information on library services, facilities, rules, and activities.

Acquires a thorough knowledge of the community and its demographics so that library service can meet the specific needs of the community.

Enforces policies and procedures of the St. Clair County Library System and any other local or county governance related to the operation of the branch library.

Communicates the branch library concerns, activities and needs to the branch coordinator and the library director.

Furthers credentials and skills by regular attendance of work related training.

Attends meetings as required.

Performs other duties as assigned by branch coordinator or the director.

Physical and Mental Requirements

The physical demands described are representative of those that must be met by an employee to successfully perform the essential functions of this position. Reasonable accommodations may be made to enable individuals with disabilities to perform the essential functions.

While performing the duties of this job, the employee is regularly required to sit, talk and hear. The employee is required to stand, walk and operate a computer. The employee is occasionally required to push carts with materials and stoop in an ergonomically correct manner. The employee must occasionally lift and/or move materials up to 35 pounds. Specific vision requirement required by this job includes close vision and depth perception.

Work Environment

The work environment characteristics described are representative of those that an employee encounters while performing the essential functions of this position. Reasonable accommodations may be made to enable individuals with disabilities to perform the essential functions.

The noise level in the work environment is moderate, with many interruptions. The position requires working with a very diverse cross-section of the public.

Supervisory Responsibilities

SUPERVISION EXERCISED

Supervision is exercised over Assistant Branch Librarians and Library Pages. (Branch staff)

Education, Experience, and Training

Knowledge, interest, and appreciation of Literature and other sources of information available at the library; a proactive public service initiative with strong communication and interaction skills and the ability to relate to people of all ages; a demonstrated aptitude for library procedures and practices; solid experience with PC computer, Microsoft Office products, email, on-line public access catalogs, and internet searching; skill in organization, management and planning; ability and experience in scheduling and supervision, at least one year of supervisory experience is preferred; flexibility and possessing a high degree of patience and tolerance; ability to keep accurate records and reports.

Experience Needed: A four-year Bachelor's Degree is required. Possessing a current Library of Michigan Level V Limited Professional Certificate is highly preferable. Having or working towards a Master's Degree in Library and Information Science is highly desirable. Successful experience in a public library in a position of equivalent responsibility and demonstrating mastery of library skills, as listed under "Representative Job Duties" may substitute for up to two years of educational requirements. The qualified candidate must possess a valid State of Michigan operator license and maintain this license during employment in the position.

Disclaimers

The information contained in this job description is for compliance with the American with Disabilities Act (A.D.A.) and is not an exhaustive list of duties performed for this position. Additional duties may be assigned.

5.6 BRANCH LIBRARIAN

5.6.1 Branch Librarian

Library Name: Richland County Public Library
Library Location: Columbia, South Carolina
Population Served: 320,700
Number of Volumes: 1,059,806
Number of Titles: N/A
Periodical Subscriptions: 2,840

Essential Functions and Responsibilities

Assists Branch Manager with professional and managerial duties in the operation of the branch, in cooperation with other professional staff; may serve as person in charge of branch in absence of Branch Manager, as well as any other times as needed;

Assists with overseeing maintenance of building and grounds;

Assists with responsibilities related to operation of automated functions and equipment, notifying Chief and/or Technology Department Staff when problems occur;

Resolves circulation problems, including dealing with complex circulation situations (out of county registrations, non-resident property owners, fines and lost book problems);

Interprets and communicates library policies and procedures to patrons;

Plans and conducts programs for children and adults such as story times, film showings, etc.;

Answers reference questions, and provides professional reference services to patrons;

Provides referral services as appropriate; coordinates, trains, and supervises staff conducting programs for children and adults;

Selects material for a specific collection area and assists with deacquisitions; Assists with supervision and training of all professional and paraprofessional staff;

Assists branch manager with interviewing and hiring of new staff;

May interview, hire, and train volunteers;

Assists library patrons by checking in and out library materials, renewing materials, issuing library cards, etc., using automated library system;

Assists patrons in finding and using library materials;

Maintains statistical records and reports;

Provides advisory services and bibliographic instruction.

Education, Experience, and Training

Minimum qualifications:

ALA-accredited MLS degree; eligible for or holds SC Librarian certification; specialized subject knowledge or skills developed through work experience where appropriate for this position; SC driver's license with safe driving record; ability to perform job functions.

5.7 BRANCH MANAGER

5.7.1 Branch Manager

Library Name: Pasco County Library System
Library Location: Hudson, Florida
Population Served: 344,765
Number of Volumes: 528,463
Number of Titles: 406,236
Number of Periodical Subscriptions: 2,117

General Summary

JOB OBJECTIVE:

Managerial and technical work in planning, organizing, and directing of a single location or a specific service of the County library system. Responsible for planning operations in regards to a specific location or service, determining, assessing, and addressing the library and community needs. This position is distinguished from a Librarian I position by a broader range of responsibilities, ability to make independent judgments, and the supervisory responsibility for Librarian I personnel as well as other levels of staff.

Essential Functions and Responsibilities

(Essential functions are fundamental job duties. They do not include marginal tasks, which are also performed but are incidental to the primary functions.)

Plans, analyzes, and evaluates library services and operations; recommends and takes appropriate action. Actively participates in fulfilling system-wide goals and implementing policies. Participates in the selection and training of subordinate staff and professionals and evaluates their performance. Coordinates staff schedule and payroll records for the assigned service unit. Works effectively with Library administration and other supervisors or coordinators. Supplies budgetary information and monitors expenditures regarding service unit. Interprets goals and policies to subordinate staff and to patrons and individuals outside of the library. Resolves conflicts with patrons and the general public. Represents the Library at meetings, conferences, presentations and workshops. If assigned to a branch library, monitors physical maintenance and determines need for repairs and improve-

ments. Develops community partnerships for the assigned service unit. Prepares reports and publications. Performs related work as required.

Knowledge, Skills, and Abilities

Knowledge of the principles and methods of professional public library service and operations.

Knowledge of principles and practices for providing customer services. Knowledge of reference and information procedures and practices.

Knowledge of library technology.

Knowledge of supervisory techniques and practices.

Ability to establish and maintain positive, effective working relationships.

Ability to apply logic and reasoning to problem resolution.

Ability to effectively manage time.

Ability to motivate, develop, train, and direct personnel.

Ability to deal with details.

Ability to work without close supervision.

Ability to deal with diverse elements simultaneously.

Ability to understand and apply highly complex policies and procedures.

Ability to plan and assign work. Ability to operate equipment and technology.

Physical and Mental Requirements

Job requires walking, standing, sitting, bending, stooping, and reaching. Requires use of a video display monitor, keyboard, and mouse. Job requires lifting of up to 20 pounds and pushing of loaded book truck with up to 35 pounds of pressure. Ability to communicate effectively using speaking, hearing, writing, and vision skills.

Education, Experience, and Training

Must possess a Masters in Library Science from a college or university accredited by the American Library Association. Experience with library automation systems and/or personal computers and software including database and/or Internet experience. Three years of professional library experience in a public library system including two years supervisory experience. A comparable amount of directly related experience may be substituted for the minimum educational requirements.

License and Certification Requirements

Must possess a valid driver's license. ALL APPLICANTS MUST BE ABLE TO ACCEPT CHANGES IN WORK SCHEDULE AND LOCATIONS TO MEET THE CHANGING NEEDS OF THE COUNTY. INDIVIDUALS HIRED MAY BE REQUIRED TO COMPLY WITH THE U.S. IMMIGRATION REFORM AND CONTROL ACT OF 1986.

Position Hours

MUST BE ABLE TO WORK EVENINGS AND SATURDAYS.

5.8 BRANCH LIBRARIAN WITH SUPERVISORY RESPONSIBILITIES

5.8.1 Branch Librarian with Supervisory Responsibilities

Library Name: Genesee District Library
Library Location: Genesee, Michigan
Population Served: 318,250
Number of Volumes: 686,139
Number of Titles: N/A
Number of Periodical Subscriptions: 425

General Summary

JOB OBJECTIVE:

Performs professional librarian duties, which include public service, collection development, program development, training and direction to patrons, staff and volunteers; performs related duties as required. On occasion may be required to work at other locations of the Genesee District Library System.

Essential Functions and Responsibilities

Manages the operations of the branch including responsibilities for implementation and monitoring of all library procedures to meet the needs and interests of patrons. Tasks include, but are not limited to circulation, interloan, technological, reference and all related library procedures.

• Provides direction and supervision to the staff and volunteers assigned to the branch and updates them on new procedures.

• Operates the computerized library system, including all C.D., Internet and other on-line reference services.

• Provides instruction and assistance to patrons on the use of all library services, independently and in a classroom setting.

• Responds to reference questions, or refers the questions to Headquarters when appropriate.

• Handles patron complaints and requests with discretion and good judgement.

• Maintains a well-balanced collection by participating in the book selection process, as needed, and by weeding the collection.

• Develops a thorough working knowledge of all GDL equipment used in the library.

• Communicates and builds strong community bonds by working with local community leaders.

• Tactfully communicates concern about the building and site to the local contact person and the administrative staff to assure proper building maintenance and operation.

• Markets the library by developing and/or assisting with public service oriented programming and press interviews.

• Maintains orderliness in the overall appearance of the branch.

• Prepares and maintains required reports and records using approved formats in a timely fashion.

• Must demonstrate an interest in life-long learning by maintaining an interest in new library services and trends via reading, seminars, workshops, etcetera.

Knowledge, Skills, and Abilities

• Master's Degree in Library or Information Science from an American Library Association accredited library school.

• Possession of Level II Professional Librarian Certificate for the State of Michigan within ninety (90) days of hire; must meet requirements for continued renewal of Certificate.

AND

• Superior interpersonal and communication skills, both written and verbal.

• Ability to get along with diverse personalities, tactful, good reasoning abilities and sound judgement.

• General computer proficiency, including knowledge of library software and Microsoft products.

Physical and Mental Requirements

The physical demands described here are representative of those that must be met by an employee to successfully perform the essential duties of this job. Reasonable accommodations may be made to enable individuals with disabilities to perform the essential functions.

While performing the duties of this job, the employee will frequently, sit, stand and walk. The employee is occasionally required to stoop, kneel, and reach forward and above the head. The employee will occasionally lift and/or move up to fifty (50) pounds such as boxes of books and equipment. Specific vision abilities required by this job include close vision.

Work Environment

The noise level in the work environment is usually quiet and work is performed indoors.

License and Certification Requirements

SPECIAL REQUIREMENTS

Possession of a valid driver's license and must have insured vehicle for use on Library business.

Disclaimers

*The above statements are intended to describe the general nature and level of work being performed by personnel assigned to this classification. They are not to be construed as an exhaustive list of all duties performed by personnel so classified.

5.9 EXTRA HELP LIBRARIAN

5.9.1 Extra Help Librarian

Library Name: Solano County Library
Library Location: Fairfield, California
Population Served: 373,100
Number of Volumes: 569,516
Number of Titles: 526,809
Number of Periodical Subscriptions: 1,006

General Summary

JOB OBJECTIVE:

This is an Extra Help position. An employee appointed to an extra help must meet all the requirements of the corresponding regular position. An extra help employee is a person who is employed for the purpose of relieving or augmenting regular staff in the accomplishment of work. Extra Help employees cannot work more than 999 hours in a fiscal year. Extra help employees are excluded from civil service and shall not have the rights to regular or continued employment.

Essential Functions and Responsibilities

TYPICAL DUTIES MAY INCLUDE BUT ARE NOT LIMITED TO THE FOLLOWING:

1. Maintains library collection of books, documents, audiovisual, and other materials; participates in material selection and places orders; weeds materials collection by evaluating current and potential user service needs; catalogs and classifies materials as necessary.

2. Researches and answers general and/or complex reference questions for customers; provides suggestions for titles and/or authors of interest in a variety of subject areas; instructs and assists in the use of reference and general library resources; compiles bibliographies and webliographies as requested.

3. Plans and conducts programs for specific customer groups such as children, young adults, or adults; conducts class visits and maintains relationships with local schools and other community groups; coordinates and conducts special projects involving library promotion and outreach activity; promotes and participates in national programming efforts.

4. Participates in various public relations activities; develops, coordinates, prepares and creates a variety of displays; assembles and maintains displays, bulletin boards, and other visual aids in assigned areas; writes newspaper articles and press releases to promote library services.

5. Performs cataloging tasks in accordance with generally accepted library principles; monitors and adjusts workflow of the cataloging and processing units; assists in forming policy for technical services and cataloging and processing units; creates original descriptive cataloging in machine readable format; analyses subject content and assigns nationally accepted headings; assigns classification numbers; reviews and updates cataloged materials; trains and oversees assigned staff.

6. Performs acquisitions tasks to acquire new materials for the collection; manages funds associated with materials acquisition; monitors and adjusts workflow of the acquisition unit; assists in forming policy for technical services and acquisitions; merges, organizes and edits data on online ordering systems; trains and oversees assigned staff.

7. May write proposals and grant requests for special library needs; attends various meetings; assists in ensuring facilities are properly maintained.

8. Interviews, trains, supervise, and evaluates support personnel including adult and student volunteers and/or student assistants. May assist in training professional staff.

9. Manages, reviews and prepares for processing publicly donated books and other materials.

10. Acts as supervisor or manager in their absence; monitors and assumes responsibility for the safety of the public and security of the building; prepares incident reports as necessary.

11. Maintains professional knowledge in applicable areas and keeps abreast of changes in job-related trends; makes recommendations for the implementation of changes; reads and interprets professional literature; attends training programs. Workshops and seminars as appropriate.

Education, Experience, and Training

1. Possession of a Master's Degree in Library Science from an accredited college or university is required.

2. AND one (1) year of professional library experience.

PLEASE NOTE THE FOLLOWING:

Any applicant, who indicates that they have a college degree or have taken any college units, must provide proof, even though the position does not require a degree or college units.

A copy of your college transcripts or diploma must be submitted with your application. Candidates who attended a college or university that is accredited by a foreign or non-U.S. accrediting agency must have their educational units evaluated by an educational evaluation service. The results must be submitted to the Human Resources Department no later than the close of the recruitment. Please contact your local college or university to learn where you can obtain this service.

Knowledge, Skills, and Abilities

Knowledge of the professional practices, procedures and techniques of library science including general reference, classification, cataloging, acquisition, circulation, collection development, adult and children's library work; reader interest levels and popular books and authors; the major fields of learning; publisher and dealer practices and methods; on-line automated library search and reference systems. Ability to select books and fill the current and potential needs of the community served and individual patrons; performs reference readers' advisory and/or catalog work; use and explain the use of catalogs, guides and other library resources; establish and maintain cooperative working relationships with associated and library patrons; direct a children's or adult program; communicate effectively both verbally and in writing; develop and promote special library services to meet current and prospective community needs; train and supervise support staff; maintain complex records and prepare reports; make routine arithmetical calculations.

5.10 HUMANITIES REFERENCE LIBRARIAN

5.10.1 Humanities Reference Librarian

Library Name: Seattle Public Library
Library Location: Seattle, Washington
Population Served: 608,150
Number of Volumes: 2,553,934
Number of Titles: N/A
Number of Periodical Subscriptions: 9,719

General Summary

JOB OBJECTIVE:
The Humanities Department is the largest subject department in the Central Library. Located on the first floor, the collection includes the following topics:

Literature and Classic Fiction	Library Science
Genealogy	Philosophy and Religion
History and Biography	Travel and Maps
Law	

The Humanities Department houses an extensive foreign language collection, including books, periodicals, and audiotapes in many of the world's major languages. The successful candidate will be involved in Reader's Advisory, Fiction and Literature and will market fiction and promote books and reading. This person will also serve on the Fiction and 800s selection team.

Essential Functions and Responsibilities

Conduct effective reference interview to determine needs, consistently using Model Reference Behaviors.

Learn new information technology and explore how it can be applied to enhance public service.

Tell the library's story to the community in every way possible so that users and potential users know about the Library's resources.

Responsible for the maintenance of portions of the Humanities web page which will include recommending appropriate sites and reporting changes to the web liaison.

Knowledge, Skills, and Abilities

Candidates must be able to demonstrate that they possess the following:

Knowledge of Reader's Advisory services.

Ability to independently manage departmental or library-wide projects.

Broad, general knowledge of information resources and services available throughout the Library, including those available on the Internet.

Working knowledge of networked PCs in the Windows environment and of new and emerging information resource and delivery technologies.

The ability to be flexible, handle multiple competing priorities and assignments, adapt to change, and work effectively in an environment of constant change and transition.

Ability to work harmoniously with a diverse work team and public.

Education, Experience, and Training

Masters of Library Science (undergraduate degree in English, Literature or related field desirable).

Fluency in a foreign language or American Sign Language desirable.

Equivalent education/experience may substitute for the stated requirements.

Experience in public speaking and formal writing skills.

Additional Qualifications

Commitment to library instruction as integral to the delivery of information services in the public library.

A commitment to public service, exceptional interpersonal communication, problem-solving, customer relations and teamwork skills.

Commitment to intellectual freedom.

5.11 LANGUAGE SPECIALIST LIBRARIAN

5.11.1 Language Specialist Librarian

Library Name: Seattle Public Library
Library Location: Seattle, Washington
Population Served: 570,800
Number of Volumes: 999,555
Number of Titles: 899,185
Periodical Subscriptions: N/A

General Summary

JOB OBJECTIVE:
Assigned to the Literacy, ESL, and World Languages Department in the Central Library, the Senior Librarian has primary responsibility for providing information and reference, readers' advisory, and outreach services to meet the educational, recreational and cultural information needs of the community, while acting as a resource within the Library system. The Senior Librarian will have a lead role in the development, maintenance, and marketing of the Library's Vietnamese language collections.

Working in cooperation with staff of other departments, the Senior Librarian will also help develop bilingual programs that are of interest to Seattle's Vietnamese-speaking communities, and will assist in the selection of Vietnamese language materials in alternative formats such as compact discs, audio cassettes, video cassettes and CD-ROM products.

Essential Functions and Responsibilities

Public Service

Provide a full range of services to patrons and internal customers, in person at public service desks and by phone, while ensuring that each individual library user receives the highest possible standard of customer service.

Responsible for developing and implementing innovative services and programs for Vietnamese-speaking user groups.

Educate patrons about library programs, services and resources, and teaching them how to effectively use the full range of library technology and resources available to them.

Outreach

Develop and maintain creative, productive and effective relationships with schools, community, business and other target groups, government and civic agencies, current and potential library users.

Represent the Library to a wide range of individuals and organizations, including those who are Vietnamese speaking, to introduce and promote Library services, identify emerging community issues and needs, develop recommendations, and assist in implementing innovative services and programs to meet those needs.

Resource Development and Instruction

Assist with developing and maintaining Vietnamese language and other materials, collections and related information resources, including print publications, electronic resources, and a wide variety of other information media.

Researching new information needs and developing creative responses using innovative resources and delivery service methods (e.g., electronic resources such as on-line database searching, CD-ROM products, the Internet, etc.).

Language Expertise:

Serve as a Vietnamese language specialist for the Library and will provide assistance to patrons and internal customers on a range of activities, from providing reference or translation services to participating in the development and implementation of bilingual and community outreach programs.

Knowledge, Skills, and Abilities

Knowledge of Informational Resources

Current working knowledge of technological innovations and library applications, especially the ability to use on-line, CD-ROM, Internet and World Wide Web searching methods and information re-sources.

Knowledge of, and experience with, DYNIX library automation or a similar system.

Education, Experience, and Training

Required Qualifications:

Masters Degree in Library Science

MLS from an ALA-accredited library school, or Washington State Certification as a Librarian.

Language Expertise:

Must be able to read, write and speak both Vietnamese and English fluently. Additional language expertise is favorable.

Training and/or Experience/Knowledge and Ability Required:

Education, training or experience in providing public service.

Additional Qualifications

Excellent Customer Service and Communication Skills:

The successful candidate will possess exceptional interpersonal communication, problem-solving, customer relations and teamwork skills.

Ability to communicate clearly, diplomatically, and in a friendly and positive manner, orally and in writing, with library users from diverse ethnic, socio-economic and cultural backgrounds, as well as with neighborhood-based or special interest groups.

Experience in public speaking and formal writing skills are highly desired.

Possess a sense of humor and the ability to demonstrate a positive and enthusiastic commitment to public service.

5.12 LITERACY COORDINATOR LIBRARIAN

5.12.1 Literacy Coordinator Librarian

Library Name: Escondido Public Library
Library Location: Escondido, California
Population Served: 136,956
Number of Volumes: N/A
Number of Titles: 281,548
Number of Periodical Subscriptions: 320

General Summary

JOB OBJECTIVE:

Under general supervision, plans, coordinates, supervises, organizes and directs the literacy services division of the library; performs related work as assigned.

Essential Functions and Responsibilities

REPRESENTATIVE DUTIES

The following duties are typical for this classification. Incumbents may not perform all of the listed duties and/or may be required to perform additional or different duties from those set forth below to address business needs and changing business practices.

Assists in developing and implementing goals, objectives, policies, programs, procedures, and work standards for library literacy services.

Directs and may participate in tutor and learner recruitment and oversees evaluation of learner assessment tests.

Oversees and supervises selection and review of library literacy materials and resources.

Arranges, coordinates and/or conducts training sessions for volunteer tutors and learners

Assesses effectiveness of services and programs by developing surveys and conducting periodic progress visits with program participants and implements changes in response to results.

Continues and sustains an active public awareness campaign by speaking to community groups, writing public press releases, conducting television and/or radio interviews, and developing and disseminating public relations and recruitment materials such as brochures, flyers, videos and newsletters.

Plans, coordinates, supervises and conducts literacy special events and participates in library special events as appropriate.

Develops and maintains collaborative relationships with area businesses and organizations, in order to promote and expand library literacy services and programs.

Assists in the development and preparation of grant applications and coordinates submission of required reports and documents.

Proposes programs and projects to meet identified needs, implements, oversees and evaluates grant projects.

Develops annual budget requirements for literacy services and grant projects and monitors expenditures.

Plans, organizes, directs, supervises and reviews work of literacy support staff, volunteers, tutors, contract and grant-funded positions.

Serves as liaison, and may serve as a committee member, to community agencies and other literacy groups such as the San Diego Council on Literacy, California Literacy, Inc. and other State Library committees.

Monitors new developments in the literacy field; incorporates new developments, as appropriate, into programs and services.

Participates with senior level library staff in developing and implementing general goals for the library.

Depending on area of assignment, duties may also include:

Performs related work as required.

Participates in activities of professional associations as time and budget permits.

Knowledge, Skills, and Abilities

The following generally describes the knowledge and ability required to enter the job and/or be learned within a short period of time in order to successfully perform the assigned duties.

Knowledge of:

Principles and practices of adult and family literacy services including learning disabilities in the adult population.

Principles and practices of project management and administration.

Supervisory principles and practices including training and evaluation.

Library objectives and procedures.

Principles and practices of budget development and implementation.

Grant-writing techniques.

Principles and techniques of positive customer service and public relations.

Ability to:

Demonstrate an awareness and appreciation of a diverse community, interacting and communicating successfully with people from a variety of backgrounds both individually and in groups.

Establish and maintain effective working relations with adult learners and their families, volunteers, tutors, library staff and a wide variety of community professionals and organizations.

Elicit community and organizational support for programs.

Effectively select, train, and evaluate paraprofessional support staff, contract and grant-funded staff, and volunteers.

Effectively plan, organize, and direct the work of paraprofessional staff, contract and grant-funded staff, and volunteers.

Plan, organize, implement and evaluate service programs and activities.

Prepare and administer program budgets.

Interpret and explain City policies and procedures.

Recognize successful methods and programs for teaching literacy skills and adapt them to the needs of adults and families in the literacy program.

Prepare clear and concise reports, correspondence and other written materials; maintain accurate records.

Communicate clearly and effectively both orally and in writing.

Contribute to a successful team effort.

Develop appropriate and effective collections/resources within literacy services.

Conduct research using print media and electronic resources.

Ability to use computer equipment and applications such as Microsoft Office, Internet, and e-mail.

Physical and Mental Requirements

CONTINUOUS walking; lifting objects weighing up to 10 lbs. from below the waist to above shoulder level and transporting distances up to 500 yards; fine finger dexterity and light pressure to operate keyboards, calculators, telephones; pinch grasp to hold books, writing materials.

FREQUENT standing, sitting, bending and stooping, squatting, reaching above and at shoulder level, pushing/pulling, twisting at waist, upward and downward flexion of neck, side-to-side turning of neck; lifting objects weighing 11-15 lbs. from below waist to waist level, with or without assistance, and transporting distances up to 10 feet.

INFREQUENT crawling, balancing above ground, lifting objects weighing 26-50 lbs. from chest level to above shoulder level, with or without assistance, and transporting distances up to 10 feet; lifting objects weighing 51-75 lbs. from below waist to shoulder level, with assistance, and transporting distances up to 5 feet; strong grasp to lift equipment or boxes of books.

Communication:

VISION (may be correctable) to see computer screens, books, observe customers and situations.

HEARING of telephone and personal conversations with customers, fire and security alarms, sound equipment.

SPEAKING clearly to converse with customers.

WRITING to complete forms and notes to assist customers. Incumbents must occasionally deal with difficult customers in library facilities, including impaired persons or people attempting to steal items.

Work Environment

The conditions herein are representative of those that must be met by an employee to successfully perform the essential functions of this job. Reasonable accommodations may be made to enable individuals with disabilities to perform the essential job functions.

Environment: Exposure to heat and humidity working outdoors at special events; noise of crowds and groups of people; temperature variations within the building and from indoors to outdoors; possible mechanical hazards of equipment and large quantities of books and papers. Work is performed in 80-hour work periods, with unscheduled breaks. Occasional overtime my be required for adequate staffing of library facilities, and incumbents may be required to work weekends, nights and holidays. Work is performed primarily indoors at library facilities. Work setting is formal, team oriented, having both routine and variable tasks. Work pace and pressure is variable, but frequently fast-paced and high pressure.

Education, Experience, and Training

Any combination of education and experience that would likely provide the required knowledge and abilities is qualifying. A typical way to obtain the knowledge and abilities would be:

Education/Training:

Graduation from an accredited four-year college or university with a degree in Education, Public Administration or related field.

Experience:

Five years of progressively responsible experience in the field of literacy, education, public administration, or related field. Direct experience in the management of an adult or family literacy program in a library setting is desirable. A Master's Degree in Library Science,

Reading Education or a related field may be substituted for two years experience.

License and Certification Requirements

May be required to possess a valid Class C California driver's license. English/Spanish bilingual ability is desirable.

Position Hours

Must be willing to work evenings and weekends.

Disclaimers

Class specifications are intended to present a descriptive list of the range of duties performed by employees in the class. Specifications are not intended to reflect all duties performed within the job.

5.13 LITERACY SPECIALIST LIBRARIAN

5.13.1 Literacy Specialist Librarian

Library Name: Boston Public Library
Library Location: Boston, Massachusetts
Population Served: 574,283
Number of Volumes: 7,954,358
Number of Titles: N/A
Number of Periodical Subscriptions: 29,026

Reports to

Reports to Ranking staff member

Essential Functions and Responsibilities

Under supervision and within the framework of the library's policies and practices, to assume responsibility for the effective execution of programs and services in support of ESOL/ABE and Family Literacy within the Library's broader program of services to a diverse population characteristic to an urban setting, performing work which requires substantial application of professional knowledge and experience.

Additional Job Duties

Initiates, develops, plans and implements the Library's programs and services which support ESOL/ABE and Family Literacy.

Provides extensive readers' advisory and reference services for individuals and families in need of literacy services or those engaged in progressive reading and basic skills development.

Develops interactive relationships, and coordinates library programs and services with community based organizations, especially those which offer instructional programs and support services for individuals engaged in basic skills and literacy development.

Assumes responsibility for collection development at the Dudley Literacy Center, manages the appropriate materials budget; provides recommendations for the selection and acquisition of books and non-print materials for the Library's Literacy Resource Collections.

Initiates, develops and implements an on-going program of outreach activities to stimulate use of the Library's literacy resources at the Dudley Literacy Center.

Provides instruction to increase patron skills in the use of book resources and electronic databases available in the Dudley Literacy Center.

Trains, supervises and evaluates volunteers engaged in library-based literacy instruction, tutoring, translation and other support services at the Dudley Literacy Center.

Compiles annotated lists and bibliographies involving book and non-print materials.

Assumes responsibility for oral presentations and written reports on literacy services activities within the branch library.

Actively participates in appropriate system-wide committees, training and other professional activities.

May be called upon to represent the library on citywide and statewide committees.

Assists in training and supervising professional and non-professional staff.

Performs other related and comparable duties, as assigned.

Supervisory Responsibilities

Supervises: As assigned, professional and non-professional staff and community volunteers.

Education, Experience, and Training

Minimum Qualifications

A bachelor's degree from a recognized college or university and a master's degree in library science from an accredited library school. In exceptional instances specialized education, training and/or experience may be substituted for part or all of the educational requirements.

Two years of professional library experience including substantial experience in working with individuals or groups engaged in literacy education and in working collaboratively with community based organizations, or any equivalent combination of education, experience and training sufficient to indicate ability to do the work.

Broad knowledge of library policies, practices and procedures; extensive knowledge of book and non-print materials and specialized resources related to the literacy field; extensive knowledge of general bibliographic tools and of specialized resources related to literacy; demonstrated knowledge of outreach techniques and demonstrated interest in library work related to literacy; demonstrated interest in community library work and willingness to develop strong, interactive community relationships; demonstrated ability to assume responsibility and to carry out assignments independently. Proven oral and written communication skills. Demonstrated ability to work well with staff and public in a multicultural environment; initiative; good judgment; dependability; tact; courtesy.

Additional Qualifications

Requirements: Must be a Resident of the City of Boston upon first day of hire

5.14 MUSIC AND ART LIBRARIAN

5.14.1 Music and Art Librarian

Library Name: Brand Library and Art Center, Glendale Public Library
Library Location: Glendale, California
Population Served: 199,022
Number of Volumes: 709,044
Number of Titles: N/A
Number of Periodical Subscriptions: 737

General Summary

Education, Experience, and Training

Minimum Qualifications

A bachelor's degree from a recognized college or university and a master's degree in library science from an accredited library school. In exceptional instances specialized education, training and/or experience may be substituted for part or all of the educational requirements.

Two years of professional library experience including substantial experience in working with individuals or groups engaged in literacy education and in working collaboratively with community based organizations, or any equivalent combination of education, experience and training sufficient to indicate ability to do the work.

Broad knowledge of library policies, practices and procedures; extensive knowledge of book and non-print materials and specialized resources related to the literacy field; extensive knowledge of general bibliographic tools and of specialized resources related to literacy; demonstrated knowledge of outreach techniques and demonstrated interest in library work related to literacy; demonstrated interest in community library work and willingness to develop strong, interactive community relationships; demonstrated ability to assume responsibility and to carry out assignments independently. Proven oral and written communication skills. Demonstrated ability to work well with staff and public in a multicultural environment; initiative; good judgment; dependability; tact; courtesy.

Under the supervision of a Library Administrator, this mid-management position is responsible for managing the operations of the Brand Art and Music Library. As part of the Library's management team, this position actively participates in projects, committees and decision-making related to the entire library system.

Essential Functions and Responsibilities

Essential functions include, but are not limited to:

Oversees public operations and ensures outstanding customer service.

Advises staff on collection management for art and music materials.

Oversees art and music programming, including a professional community gallery and recital hall.

Serves as liaison to the Library's support group and to the City of Glendale's Arts and Culture Commission.

Coordinates Library activities with other City divisions, other libraries and other agencies.

Acts as a public representative and advocate for the section.

Develops policies and procedures for the section.

Creates long-range plans for all functions of the library including the building plan for the facility.

Develops and monitors section budgets and reports.

Seeks and writes grants.

Trains, supervises, and evaluates professional and support staff.

Recommends, initiates and implements personnel actions.

Performs advanced professional library work that requires the use of independent judgment in the application of professional library practices.

Works on art or music reference desks as needed.

Assumes responsibility for ensuring the duties of the position are performed in a safe, efficient manner.

Performs other related duties as assigned or as the situation requires.

Knowledge, Skills, and Abilities

Knowledge of principles, trends, terminology and practices of modern library work.

Knowledge of reference materials in the fields of art and music.

Knowledge of the principles and methods of cataloging and classification.

Skill in effective oral and written communication.

Skill in problem solving and ability to think analytically.

Ability to apply professional knowledge to the practical problems faced on the job.

Ability to effectively supervise, review and evaluate employees' job performance, and to organize and direct workflow.

Ability to establish smooth working relationships with a wide variety of people, including staff, coworkers, general public, community groups and the support group of Brand Library.

Ability to exercise sound judgment in difficult or stressful situations.

Ability to foster a teamwork environment and resolve interpersonal conflicts. Ability to interact effectively with a variety of temperaments.

Ability to learn new library technology and train staff and public in its use.

Ability to organize and direct the work of subordinates.

Ability to prepare and monitor budget information.

Ability to read, write, comprehend and communicate directions in English.

Education, Experience, and Training

Qualifications: Required: Bachelor's Degree in any field and a Master's Degree in Library Science from an accredited college or university.

Four years of professional library work, including two years supervisory experience and two years of professional experience within an art or music library.

An equivalent combination of experience, education and/or training may substitute for the listed minimum requirements.

Preferred: Degree in the fine arts and/or music desirable.

Bilingual ability in Spanish and/or Armenian is desirable.

Additional Qualifications

Possesses a wide range of knowledge and library experience.

Possesses interest in art and music.

Possesses strong leadership ability.

Supportive of change.

Willing to work overtime as needed.

Willingness to assume responsibility for maintaining a safe working environment. Willingness to attract new audiences to Brand Arts Center.

Willingness to initiate, recommend and carry out personnel actions.

License and Certification Requirements

Valid California Class C Driver's License is required.

5.15 SCIENCE AND SOCIAL SCIENCES LIBRARIAN

5.15.1 Science and Social Sciences Librarian

Library Name: Seattle Public Library
Library Location: Seattle, Washington
Population Served: 608,150
Number of Volumes: 2,553,934
Number of Titles: N/A
Number of Periodical Subscriptions: 9,719

Essential Functions and Responsibilities

Public Service

Provide general reference, information, referral, program and readers' advisory services to the general public, in person and by the telephone.

Provide assistance in the physical sciences, life and health sciences, in sports and recreation, and in the fields of sociology, education, psychology, parapsychology, and family life.

Provide assistance to the job hunter.

Knowledge of appropriate employment resources in a variety of formats, including electronic resources, is required.

Outreach

Perform a variety of outreach activities in collaboration and/or support of local social service, employment and youth agencies assisting individuals in securing employment.

Resource Development

Active participation in developing and maintaining the Career/Education Center collections and information resources.

Contribute to the development of new and innovative ways to assist job seekers through electronic resources including the remote user.

Knowledge, Skills, and Abilities

Ability to contribute creative and innovative program content and/or outreach approaches to providing employment assistance.

Knowledge of and the ability to identify current trends in employment practices, educational requirements and programs to meet basic, local market, job requirements, and other governmental or private agencies which can provide additional employment assistance.

Working knowledge of PCs in a Windows environment, and of technological innovations and library applications, especially the ability to use on-line, CD-ROM, Internet and World Wide Web searching methods and information resources.

Ability to be flexible, handle multiple competing priorities and tasks, adapt to change, and work effectively in a fast-paced, high-volume environment.

Education, Experience, and Training

Qualifications

MLS from an ALA-accredited library school, or Washington State certification as a librarian.

Experience in public speaking and formal writing skills are required.

Additional Qualifications

Commitment to intellectual freedom.

A commitment to public service, exceptional interpersonal communication, problem-solving, customer relations and teamwork skills.

5.16 SUBSTITUTE LIBRARIAN

5.16.1 Substitute Librarian

Library Name: Mission Viejo
Library Location: Mission Viejo, California
Population Served: 98,000
Number of Volumes: 133,664
Number of Titles: N/A
Number of Periodical Subscriptions: 271

General Summary

DEPARTMENT/DIVISION: LIBRARY SERVICES/VARIES

Education, Experience, and Training

Minimum Qualifications

A bachelor's degree from a recognized college or university and a master's degree in library science from an accredited library school. In exceptional instances specialized education, training and/or experience may be substituted for part or all of the educational requirements.

Two years of professional library experience including substantial experience in working with individuals or groups engaged in literacy education and in working collaboratively with community based organizations, or any equivalent combination of education, experience and training sufficient to indicate ability to do the work.

Broad knowledge of library policies, practices and procedures; extensive knowledge of book and non-print materials and specialized resources related to the literacy field; extensive knowledge of general bibliographic tools and of specialized resources related to literacy; demonstrated knowledge of outreach techniques and demonstrated interest in library work related to literacy; demonstrated interest in community library work and willingness to develop strong, interactive community relationships; demonstrated ability to assume responsibility and to carry out assignments independently. Proven oral and written communication skills. Demonstrated ability to work well with staff and public in a multicultural environment; initiative; good judgment; dependability; tact; courtesy.

Under direction, performs a variety of professional duties involved in planning, coordinating and implementing library services and programs; provide complex professional and technical library services to the community; and perform other related work as necessary.

DISTINGUISHING CHARACTERISTICS:
None.

Essential Functions and Responsibilities

Management reserves the right to add, modify, change or rescind the work assignments of different positions and to make reasonable accommodations so that qualified employees can perform the essential functions of the job.

Coordinate and implement library services programs and regular and special event programs and services and prepare and distribute publicity items.

Interpret and apply library policies and procedures for customers and staff; access and retrieve information for library customers and staff as requested and research and respond to difficult or technical reference questions, referring questions as appropriate; advise and assist library customers in the use of library services and tools.

May participate in the evaluation, selection, acquisition, retention, discarding, or special handling of library materials; use the automated cataloging system to catalog and classify a variety of library materials.

Direct and participate in the compiling of library activity reports and statistics.

Maintain a liaison with other librarians in the community and perform special reading and research to stay abreast of current library practices.

Provide staff support to the Senior Librarian-Public Services.

In addition, when assigned to Children's Services:

Advise children in locating and choosing appropriate materials and advise children, parents and teachers in selecting materials for youth.

Instruct children in the use of electronic reference sources.

Implement a variety of library-related literature-based and educational programs and activities for children including, story-times, library tours, and instructional classes in library use and prepare reading lists and bibliographies.

Develop promotional materials and displays for the children's department; give facility tours to promote the library.

Read reviews of new books, periodicals and other media and participate in the selection of library materials and perform special reading and research to keep abreast of current practices in the field.

In addition, when assigned to Reference:

Participate in all aspects of reference services including online and other electronic searching; telephone reference, municipal reference, and reader's advisory.

Read reviews of new books, periodicals and other media and participate in the selection of library materials and perform special reading and research to keep abreast of current practices in the field.

Prepare instructional brochures, reading lists, bibliographies, and special indexes.

Instruct adults and young adults in the use of electronic reference sources.

In addition, when assigned to Technical Services:

Participate in the acquisition and processing operations for receiving and incorporating materials into the library's collection.

Catalog and classify a variety of library materials using OCLC or other related on-line cataloging systems and ensure staff training in its use and perform bibliographic searches for cataloging data.

Recommend and implement revisions to existing catalog.

Additional Job Duties

OTHER JOB RELATED DUTIES:

May supervise library operations during evening and weekend hours in the absence of Senior Librarian or full-time Librarian.

Perform related duties and responsibilities as assigned.

Knowledge, Skills, and Abilities

Knowledge of:

Library services programs and available resources.

Modern office practices, methods, and computer equipment.

Recent developments, current literature, and sources of information related to library services program planning and administration.

Principles and practices of professional library work, including methods, practices, and techniques of library reference, technical services and/or children's library services.

Principles, techniques, and procedures in cataloging, indexing, classifying, and organizing library materials and those used in bibliographic research.

Applications of automated library circulation system and general library materials selection standards.

Principles and procedures of record keeping.

Pertinent federal, state, and local laws, codes, and regulations including administrative and departmental policies and procedures.

Principles and practices used in dealing with the public and techniques used in public relations.

General principles of risk management related to the functions of the assigned area.

Safe driving principles and practices.

Safe work practices.

Skill to:

Operate modern office equipment including computer equipment and software programs.

Operate a motor vehicle safely.

Ability to:

Coordinate, direct, and implement library services programs suited to the needs of the community.

Recommend and implement goals, objectives, and practices for providing effective and efficient library services programs.

Prepare and maintain accurate and complete records.

Respond to requests and inquiries from the general public.

Prepare clear and concise reports.

Meet and deal tactfully and effectively with the public.

Interpret and apply federal, state, and local, administrative, and departmental laws, codes, regulations, policies, and procedures.

Independently compose correspondence and memoranda and access, retrieve, enter, and update information using a computer terminal.

Work evenings and weekends.

Communicate clearly and concisely, both orally and in writing.

Understand and carry out oral and written instructions.

Establish, maintain and foster positive and harmonious working relationships with those contacted in the course of work.

Physical and Mental Requirements

Physical and Sensory Elements:

The sensory demands of the job typically require speaking, hearing, touching and seeing. This is primarily a sedentary office classification although standing in work areas and walking between work areas may be required. Finger dexterity is needed to access, enter and retrieve data using a computer keyboard, typewriter keyboard or calculator and to operate standard office equipment. Positions in this classification occasionally bend, stoop, kneel, reach, push and pull drawers open and closed to retrieve and file information. Positions in this classification occasionally lift and carry reports and records that typically weigh less than 20 pounds.

Work Environment

Employees work in an office environment with moderate noise levels, controlled temperature conditions and no direct exposure to hazardous physical substances. Employees may interact with upset staff and/or public and private representatives in interpreting and enforcing departmental policies and procedures.

Supervisory Responsibilities

SUPERVISION EXERCISED:

May exercise technical and functional supervision over technical, clerical and volunteer staff.

Education, Experience, and Training

Any combination equivalent to experience and training that would provide the required knowledge, skills, and abilities would be qualifying. A typical way to obtain the knowledge, skill, and abilities would be:

Experience:

Two (2) years of related experience.

Training:

Requires a Master's degree from an accredited college or university with major course work in library science or a related field. Candidates close to completing the education requirement may also apply, however, copies of transcripts must be submitted at time of filing, and proof of MLS is required prior to appointment.

License and Certification Requirements

Possession of, or ability to obtain, and maintain, a valid California Driver's License may be required.

5.17 GENEALOGY LIBRARIAN

5.17.1 Genealogy Librarian

Library Name: Seattle Public Library
Library Location: Seattle, Washington
Population Served: 608,150
Number of Volumes: 2,553,934
Number of Titles: N/A
Number of Periodical Subscriptions: 9,719

General Summary

SPL is recognized as having the largest and most comprehensive genealogy collection in the State of Washington. The Librarian will function as an integral part of a small team of specialists in the busy Genealogy Section of the Humanities Department, assisting patrons with genealogical and directory research. The individual selected for this position will be expected to continually develop and expand his or her knowledge in this subject area in order to respond to extensive user demand for these services. SPL's organizational priorities include a major emphasis on excellence in customer service, and on building and maintaining strong and effective community relations. That means the successful candidate for our position must bring superior interpersonal and communication skills for developing positive working relationships with all patrons and groups served, as well as other SPL staff. The ideal candidate will be computer literate and willing to learn and grow with constantly changing technology in order to effectively serve our patrons. Other key characteristics we seek are exceptional problem-solving skills, flexibility, and an obvious enthusiasm for public service.

Essential Functions and Responsibilities

The Librarian assigned to the Genealogy Unit will:

Provide information and reference services in the genealogy/directories area to public library users by telephone, letter, E-mail and in person;

Assist patrons in locating and using a wide variety of library resources, including those in electronic formats;

Perform bibliographic searches and other reference work in the subject areas of genealogy and directories;

Provide related Internet instruction and tours of the genealogy area;

Assist with the maintenance and development of the genealogy/directories collection;

Process inter-library loan requests relating to genealogy and directory materials;

Assist, as needed, with special projects or assignments and in providing a range of other related library services to patrons who use the Humanities Department and its resources.

Knowledge, Skills, and Abilities

Candidates must have:

Working knowledge of a range of basic and ready reference library information resources used in performing genealogical searches;

Current working knowledge of PC's in a Windows environment, and of technological innovations and library applications, especially the ability to use CD-ROM products AND a variety of printed and computerized circulation and on-line information retrieval technologies, including Internet resources, WWW searching methods and information resources, email, etc.

Knowledge of, and experience with, DYNIX library automation or a similar system is highly desirable.

Excellent Customer Service and Communication Skills

The successful candidate will

Demonstrate a real commitment to public service;

Possess exceptional interpersonal, communication, problem solving, customer relations and teamwork skills;

Be able to communicate clearly, diplomatically, and in a friendly and positive manner, under time and service pressures, with library users from diverse ethnic, socioeconomic and cultural backgrounds. Customer service experience involving multilingual and diverse populations is highly desirable.

Other Required Skills and Abilities

Candidates should also possess:

Effective listening skills and a sincere interest in helping people research and explore their family histories;

Flexibility and the ability to handle multiple competing priorities and tasks;

The ability to exercise initiative and work effectively, both independently and in a team environment, under extremely busy conditions.

Fluency in Asian, Eastern European or Spanish languages, or American Sign Language is highly desirable. Finally, the successful candidate MUST possess a sense of humor and a positive and enthusiastic approach to public service.

Education, Experience, and Training

In their application materials, candidates must demonstrate that they possess the following:

MLS: To be considered, candidates must have an MLS from an ALA-accredited library school, or Washington State Certification as a Librarian.

Commitment to Intellectual Freedom

Candidates must have either education, training or experience in providing public service, plus:

Training and study in the subject area of genealogy AND/OR in-depth and documentable experience in performing genealogical research; Experience in making oral presentations and/or teaching is highly desirable. Experience in performing genealogical research;

6.0 SPECIALIST

6.1 LIBRARY SPECIALIST

6.1.1 Library Specialist

Library Name: Neill Public Library
Library Location: Pullman, Washington
Population Served: 24,675
Number of Volumes: 60,247
Number of Titles: N/A
Number of Periodical Subscriptions: 145

General Summary

JOB OBJECTIVE:

Performs professional and technical library work in the coordination and performance of one or more specific library programs, such as reference, collection development, adult or youth services, technical services or library systems administration.

CLASSIFICATION SUMMARY:

The principal function of an employee in this class is dependent upon the division to which the employee is assigned. In Community and Youth Services, the Library Specialist is responsible for program development, reference and collection development. In Technical Services, the Library Specialist is responsible for cataloging, bibliographic entry and maintenance of collections and serves as the main back up for systems administration. In all cases, the Library Specialist serves as a back up to the Library Division Manager. As such, the Library Specialist may supervise the work of staff and volunteers on a regular or sporadic basis. The work in this class differs from that of Library Assistants and Library Technicians by the direct responsibility for professional services of a major programmatic area of library operations, such as reference/patron services or technical/systems services. The work is performed under the general direction of a Library Division Manager with much independence granted to perform the assigned function. The principal duties of the class are performed in a general office or library environment.

Essential Functions and Responsibilities

Reference and Collection Development

Provides information desk services to answer reference questions; explains library services including internet, CD-ROM and print materials, and refers patrons to other community resources, as needed; suggests reading materials, provides patrons with bibliographic information; develops, clarifies and implements reference policies and procedures; assists in the development of the collection plan for adult or youth collections; reads review media, recommends new material for purchase; reviews and assesses collections using various tools such as Dynix-generated circulation lists, bibliographic tools and general knowledge; develops, coordinates and implements weeding projects; reviews materials processing for accuracy of subject headings and series entries; prepares orders for new materials; prepares various reports for collection development and library planning; processes and performs original cataloging; maintains cataloging authority files to insure clean, correct cataloging lists.

Programming and Public Services

Develops and presents youth programming at the library or off site; plans, coordinates and presents special programs, such as summer reading programs, book talks, book clubs, display themes, calendar of events, etc.; assists teachers, parents and school groups with special library presentations, youth council meetings, library tours or programs; plans and writes brochures, flyers, signs, and articles on new books for the newspaper or other distribution; coordinates volunteer help to assist with special programs or projects; researches, generates and updates online Best Seller Lists for public access catalog; provides patron assistance in searching library database or accessing the Internet.

Technical Services

Reviews and verifies the accuracy of bibliographic and authority records and all materials added to the collection; generates collection development and circulation reports; processes and performs original cataloging; supervises temporary and volunteer technical services staff; coordinates technical service activities with other library divisions; assists public with circulation services; trains and directs the daily activities of staff performing binding, mending and finishing work.

Systems Administration

Serves as main back-up for systems administration; implements system software upgrades; maintains web server PC/Software and Internet access; troubleshoots system difficulties; installs hardware and software equipment; performs monthly operating systems and Webserver backup; maintains disk usage report; monitors backup system; changes transaction assurance process as needed for continuous backup system; runs system software utilities; updates and maintains library defined system parameters as needed; works with the Systems Administrator to update and change subsystems and agency records, codes, types and stats to maintain statistical accuracy for collection development; maintains system documentation; provides staff and patron assistance for use of software and equipment.

Attends work on a regular and dependable basis.

Interacts in a professional and respectful manner with city staff and the public.

Additional Job Duties

As a back-up to the Library Division Manager: Trains other library staff; participates in hiring and selection process of library staff; supervises staff on a regular or sporadic basis; participates in staff meetings or other planning sessions; assists with the preparation and maintenance of library policies, procedures and operating manuals.

Knowledge, Skills, and Abilities

Current development, trends and practices in reference services and materials including technological developments;

Library collection classification and selection techniques;

Equipment and facilities required in a comprehensive library system, including online cataloging, bibliographic procedures and circulation systems;

Community library needs and resources;

Adult and/or children's literature, specific genres, reading preferences and publishing trends;

LANS and PC security, operating systems, website management and PC application software (for technical services position);

Library cataloging techniques, including classifying, processing, authority control and MARC records (for technical services positions).

Ability to:

Coordinate and direct special library programs in assigned area;

Develop creative displays and visuals, flyers, brochures or other media;

Relate well to a variety of people of diverse ages, backgrounds and interests;

Work on multiple projects at a time;

Effectively identify problems and modify procedures to improve service to the public;

Learn, and develop proficiency in, the operation and maintenance of the library's cataloging, web and Internet servers, PC's and related hardware and software;

Provide quality library services and to meet and deal with library patrons in a calm, pleasant, and courteous manner;

Work independently;

Communicate effectively;

Establish and maintain effective working relationships with supervisor, co-workers, and the general public;

Work a flexible schedule that includes evenings and weekends;

Interact in a professional and respectful manner with city staff and the public;

Physically perform the essential functions of the job.

Tools and Equipment Used

Personal computer, Computerized library information systems, Internet and multiple online databases, copy machine, typewriter, telephone, modem, fax machine.

Work Environment

(The work environment characteristics described here are representative of those an employee encounters while performing the essential functions of this job. Reasonable accommodations may be made to enable individuals with disabilities to perform the essential functions.)

Work is performed primarily in an office environment while sitting at a desk or computer terminal or while standing at a counter for extended periods of time. Physical exertion may be required to replace or retrieve materials from shelves, high and low, and to service computer equipment. Sufficient vision or other powers of observation are essential to permit the employee to read and sort library materials and provide public services.

Education, Experience, and Training

MINIMUM QUALIFICATIONS:

Bachelor's Degree with a minimum of three years of library experience, including providing reference services and collection development, and/or technical services such as cataloging, authority control, serials and circulation; or substituting five or more years of direct library experience in reference, collection or technical services for the Bachelor's Degree; or substituting course work or training in library operations or procedures for up to six months of the library experience; or any equivalent combination of experience and training.

Disclaimers

The duties listed above are intended only as illustrations of the various types of work that may be performed. The omission of specific statements of duties does not exclude them from the position if the work is similar, related or a logical assignment to the position.

The job description does not constitute an employment agreement between the employer and employee and is subject to change by the employer as the needs of the employer and requirements of the job change.

6.1.2 Library Specialist

Library Name: Mission Viejo Public Library
Library Location: Mission Viejo, California
Population Served: 98,000
Number of Volumes: 133,664
Number of Titles: N/A
Number of Periodical Subscriptions: 271

CORE VALUES:

Incumbents in all City positions are expected to exhibit the behavior characteristics reflected in the City's Values Statement in the performance of their duties: The City of Mission Viejo is committed to the community it serves: "We are dedicated providers of municipal services and stewards of the public trust. We promote the well-being of a community where caring people are the difference. Through Public Service, Integrity, Teamwork, Innovation, and Excellence, we are committed to preserving and enhancing the quality of life within Mission Viejo."

Note: All employees of the City of Mission Viejo are designated by both State law and City ordinance to be "Disaster Service Workers." In the event of a declared emergency or any undeclared emergency or natural disaster that threatens the life,

health and/or safety of the public, employees may be assigned to assist rescue and relief workers. Such assignments may be in locations, during hours and performing work significantly different from the employees' normal work assignments and may continue through the recovery phase of the emergency.

General Summary

JOB OBJECTIVE:

Under general supervision, perform complex para-professional library work; participate in the activities of a specialized library function such as circulation, technical services, and community relations; provide general information and assistance to the public, including at the Adult and Children's Reference Desks; and perform other related work as necessary.

DISTINGUISHING CHARACTERISTICS:

None.

Essential Functions and Responsibilities

Management reserves the right to add, modify, change or rescind the work assignments of different positions and to make reasonable accommodations so that qualified employees can perform the essential functions of the job.

Interpret and apply library policies and procedures for customers and staff.

Access and retrieve information for library customers and staff as requested.

Advise and assist library customers in the making most effective use of library services including accessing and retrieving information using traditional and electronic library resources, including the Internet and CD-ROM products.

Research and respond to difficult or technical questions; refer questions as appropriate.

Perform a variety of detail and advance clerical work including maintaining accurate and detailed records, verifying accuracy of information, researching discrepancies and recording information.

Additional Job Duties

Perform related duties and responsibilities as assigned.

Knowledge, Skills, and Abilities

Knowledge of:

Principles and practices of professional library work, including methods, practices, and techniques of adult reference services.

Application of automated library system.

Internet, library related technology, and computer software applications.

Library terminology and practices.

General principles of public library services and programs.

Library classification and cataloging, and bibliographic terminology.

Modern office procedures, methods and computer equipment.

Basic principles and practices of data collection and report preparation.

Principles and procedures of record keeping.

Effective public relations skills.

English usage, spelling, vocabulary, grammar and punctuation.

General principles of risk management related to the functions of the assigned area.

Safe driving principles and practices.

Safe work practices.

Skill to:

Operate modern office equipment, including computer equipment and cash register.

Operate a motor vehicle safely.

Ability to:

Organize work; schedule and coordinate projects; set priorities; adapt to changing priorities.

Interpret and apply Federal, State, and local, administrative and departmental laws, codes, regulations, policies, and procedures.

Perform varied library work accurately and under minimal supervision.

Access, retrieve, enter, and update information using a computer terminal.

Compile and maintain a variety of records and files; prepare routine reports.

Deal courteously and effectively with the public.

Work weekend and evening shifts.

Communicate clearly and concisely, both orally and in writing.

Understand and carry out oral and written instructions.

Establish, maintain and foster positive and harmonious working relationships with those contacted in the course of work.

Physical and Mental Requirements

Physical and Sensory Elements:

The sensory demands of the job typically require speaking, hearing, touching and seeing. This is primarily a sedentary office classification although standing in work areas and walking between work areas is required. Finger dexterity is needed to access, enter and retrieve data using a computer keyboard, typewriter keyboard or calculator and to operate standard office equipment. Positions in this classification occasionally bend, stoop, kneel, and reach, as well as push and pull book carts and drawers open and closed to retrieve and file information. Positions in this classification occasionally lift and carry library materials that typically weigh less than 20 pounds.

Work Environment

Environmental Elements:

Employees work in an office environment with moderate noise levels, controlled temperature conditions and no direct exposure to hazardous physical substances. Employees may interact with upset staff and/or public and private representatives in interpreting and enforcing departmental policies and procedures.

Supervisory Responsibilities

SUPERVISION EXERCISED:

May exercise functional and technical supervision over assigned library clerical, part-time, and volunteer personnel.

Education, Experience, and Training

Any combination equivalent to experience and training that would provide the required knowledge, skills, and abilities would be qualifying. A typical way to obtain the knowledge, skill, and abilities would be:

Experience:

Three (3) or more years of increasingly responsible clerical library experience.

Training: Equivalent to the completion of the twelfth (12th) grade supplemented with college course work in Library Technology, Social Science, Humanities, Liberal Arts, Business, Graphic Arts or a related field.

License and Certification Requirements

LICENSE AND/OR CERTIFICATE:

Possession of, or ability to obtain, and maintain, a valid California Driver's License may be required.

7.0 TECHNICIAN

7.1 LIBRARY TECHNICIAN

> ### 7.1.1 Library Technician
>
> **Library Name:** Brentwood Library and Center for Fine Arts
> **Library Location:** Brentwood, Tennessee
> **Population Served:** 37,000
> **Number of Volumes:** 81,926
> **Number of Titles:** N/A
> **Number of Periodical Subscriptions:** 205

Reports to

Public Services Librarian II

General Summary

JOB OBJECTIVE:

The purpose of this job is to perform technical/clerical functions and to provide general support to the Library Department. Duties and responsibilities include charging/discharging library materials; shelving materials; keeping library in neat order; processing library card applications; repairing/maintaining library materials; and providing information, guidance and assistance to patrons.

Essential Functions and Responsibilities

The following duties are normal for this job. These are not to be construed as exclusive or all-inclusive. Other duties may be required and assigned.

Performs data entry functions associated with on-line catalog maintenance.

Checks library materials in/out; shelves returned library materials.

Maintains shelving areas; reads shelves to ensure proper placement.

Receives fine/fee moneys; issues receipts; accounts for incoming fines/fees.

Issues/processes library card applications; acquaints new patrons with library and procedures.

Locates materials requested by patrons; notifies patrons of status of requests.

Assists patrons with use of library equipment.

Registers patrons for library programs and use of facilities (including use of seminar rooms, computer/typewriter center, etc.).

Performs tasks associated with facility opening/closing.

Prepares and/or generates routine correspondence, letters, memoranda, forms, reports and other documents via computer and/or typewriter.

Answers the telephone; provides information; takes and relays messages and/or directs calls to appropriate personnel; returns calls as necessary.

Responds to patron complaints/concerns; attempts to resolve problems.

Responds to routine requests for information from officials, employees, members of the staff, the public or other individuals.

Greets patrons; assists and/or directs patrons to appropriate person.

Uses knowledge of various software programs to operate a computer in an effective and efficient manner.

Additional Job Duties

Performs other duties as required.

Knowledge, Skills, and Abilities

Has general knowledge of the policies, procedures, and activities of the City and Library Department practices as they pertain to the performance of duties relating to the job of Public Services Library Technician I. Has general knowledge of Library Department practices as necessary in the completion of daily responsibilities. Assists in defining objectives for the expedience and effectiveness of specific duties of the department. Knows how to keep abreast of any changes in policy, methods, computer operations, equipment needs, etc. as they pertain to departmental operations and activities. Is able to effectively communicate and interact with supervisors, members of the general public and all other groups involved in the activities of the department. Is able to assemble information and make written reports and documents in a concise, clear and effective manner. Has good organizational, human relations, and technical skills. Is able to use independent judgment and work with little direct supervision when necessary. Has the ability to comprehend, interpret, and apply regulations, procedures, and related information. Has general knowledge of the terminology, principles, and methods utilized within the department. Has the

mathematical ability to handle required calculations. Is knowledgeable about computers.

Physical and Mental Requirements

(ADA) MINIMUM QUALIFICATIONS OR STANDARDS REQUIRED TO PERFORM ESSENTIAL JOB FUNCTIONS

PHYSICAL REQUIREMENTS: Must be physically able to operate a variety of automated office machines which includes a computer, printer, typewriter, facsimile machine, copy machine, microform reader/printer, calculator, telephone, etc. Must be able to use body members to work, move or carry objects or materials. Must be able to exert up to fifty pounds of force occasionally, and/or up to twenty-five pounds of force frequently. Physical demand requirements are at levels of those for sedentary to medium work.

DATA CONCEPTION: Requires the ability to compare and or judge the readily observable functional, technical, structural, or compositional characteristics (whether similar to or divergent from obvious standards) of data, people, or things.

INTERPERSONAL COMMUNICATION: Requires the ability of speaking and/or signaling people to convey or exchange administrative information. Includes giving assignments and/or directions to co-workers or assistants.

LANGUAGE ABILITY: Requires the ability to read a variety of informational documentation, directions, instructions, and methods and procedures related to the job of Public Services Library Technician I. Requires the ability to write reports with proper format, punctuation, spelling and grammar, using all parts of speech. Requires the ability to speak with and before others with poise, voice control, and confidence using correct English and a well-modulated voice.

INTELLIGENCE: Requires the ability to learn and understand basic to complex principles and techniques; to make independent judgments in absence of supervision; to acquire knowledge of topics related to the job of Public Services Library Technician I.

VERBAL APTITUDE: Requires the ability to record and deliver information to supervisors and officials; to explain procedures and policies; and to follow verbal and written instructions, guidelines and objectives.

NUMERICAL APTITUDE: Requires the ability to utilize mathematical formulas; add and subtract totals; multiply and divide; determine percentages; determine time and weight; and utilize statistical inference.

FORM/SPATIAL APTITUDE: Requires the ability to inspect items for proper length, width, and shape, visually with office equipment.

MOTOR COORDINATION: Requires the ability to coordinate hands and eyes in using automated office equipment.

MANUAL DEXTERITY: Requires the ability to handle a variety of items, office equipment, control knobs, switches, etc. Must have the ability to use one hand for twisting or turning motion while coordinating other hand with different activities. Must have minimal levels of eye/hand/foot coordination.

COLOR DISCRIMINATION: May require the ability to differentiate colors and shades of color.

INTERPERSONAL TEMPERAMENT: Requires the ability to deal with people (i.e. staff, supervisors, general public, and officials) beyond giving and receiving instructions such as in interpreting departmental policies and procedures. Must be adaptable to performing under minimal stress when confronted with an emergency related to the job of Public Services Library Technician I.

PHYSICAL COMMUNICATION: Requires the ability to talk and/or hear: (talking—expressing or exchanging ideas by means of spoken words). (Hearing—perceiving nature of sounds by ear).

Education, Experience, and Training

Minimum Training and Experience Required to Perform Essential Job Functions

High school diploma (or GED) required or will consider high school student with excellent grades (college degree preferred), with library experience (or related); or any equivalent combination of education, training, and experience which provides the requisite knowledge, skills, and abilities for this job.

7.1.2 Library Technician

Library Name: Neill Public Library
Library Location: Pullman, Washington
Population Served: 24,675
Number of Volumes: 60,247
Number of Titles: N/A
Number of Periodical Subscriptions: 145

General Summary

JOB OBJECTIVE:

Performs general library work in a functional area or supervises a specific area of library operations or collections such as circulation, materials shelving, or audio-visual materials cataloging, processing and maintenance.

CLASSIFICATION SUMMARY:

Depending upon the divisional assignment, the principal function of an employee in this class is to lead and direct the work of subordinate library workers involved in circulation or shelving activities or have prime responsibility for original cataloging and processing of audio-visual materials. As a supervisor, the employee performs much of the same work as subordinate staff. In any case, the Library Technician has sole responsibility within the assigned area, for planning a variety of special projects, determining and documenting procedures and training other staff. The work in this class differs from that of Library Assistants with the responsibility for a functional area of library operations which may include supervision of staff. The position requires excellent public service skills and strong organizational skills to ensure proper staff scheduling, accuracy of records, fair and consistent application of policies and procedures and efficient shelving of materials. The work is performed under the general direction of a Library Division Manager with much independence granted to perform the assigned function. The principal duties of the class are performed in a general office or library environment.

Essential Functions and Responsibilities

Circulation Supervisor

Interviews, trains, schedules, and evaluates library staff and volunteers; ensures that circulation procedures are implemented; coordinates service area with other library service areas; directs and participates in the work of library assistants at the circulation desk; provides patron services, explaining circulation procedures, fines and fees and refers patrons to various locations and services in the library; identifies changes in procedures, prepares modifications, and implements modifications after conferring with a Library Division Manager; creates and maintains various public information brochures/flyers; prepares annual work plan and report for functional area.

Shelving Supervisor

Interviews, trains, schedules and evaluates library staff and volunteers; ensures that shelving procedures are implemented; coordinates service area with other library service areas; directs and participates in the work of library staff and volunteers involved in proper shelving of library materials; maintains records on shelver productivity and accuracy; identifies changes in procedures, prepares modifications, and implements modifications after conferring with a Library Division Manager; provides patron services at the circulation desk as needed; prepares annual work plan and report for functional area.

Technical Services

Performs classification and original cataloging of library materials, serials, and audio-visual materials; performs bibliographic maintenance and authority control including classifying, cataloging, and assigning subjects; develops, implements and documents audio-visual cataloging policies and procedures; generates collection development and circulation reports; researches, generates and updates online best seller lists for public access catalog; plans and implements special projects as needed; trains staff to search and download existing bibliographic records.

Attends work on a regular and dependable basis.

Interacts in a professional and respectful manner with city staff and the public.

Knowledge, Skills, and Abilities

Knowledge of:

The procedures used in technical or public service programs of a library;

Supervisory techniques;

Dewey, AACR2, LCSH, MARC and Subject Authority techniques;

Cataloging and classification rules and procedures.

Ability to:

Recruit, train, schedule, motivate and review the work of subordinate staff;

Effectively identify problems and modify procedures to improve service to the public;

Learn, and develop proficiency in, the operation and maintenance of the library's computer software programs and hardware;

Perform original cataloging and classifying according to standard procedures;

Analyze statistics and productivity and adjust work flows;

Document policies and procedures in a systematic manner;

Maintain highly accurate and detail-oriented systems for patron and library collection databases;

Provide quality library services and to meet and deal with library patrons in a calm, pleasant, and courteous manner;

Work independently;

Communicate effectively;

Establish and maintain effective working relationships with supervisor, co-workers, and the general public;

Work a flexible schedule that includes evenings and weekends;

Provide quality services in a cost-effective manner and to recommend improved methods of performing the work;

Physically perform the essential functions of the job.

Tools and Equipment Used

Personal computer, Computerized library information system, copy machine, typewriter, telephone, modem, fax machine.

Work Environment

(The work environment characteristics described here are representative of those an employee encounters while performing the essential functions of this job. Reasonable accommodations may be made to enable individuals with disabilities to perform the essential functions.)

Work is performed primarily in a library environment while sitting at a desk or computer terminal or while standing at a counter for extended periods of time. Physical exertion may be required to replace or retrieve materials from shelves, high and low. Sufficient vision or other powers of observation are essential to permit the employee to read and sort library materials and observe and review the work of others.

Education, Experience, and Training

MINIMUM QUALIFICATIONS:

Two years of library experience in circulation or technical services, preferably with one year of supervisory experience, or substituting course work or training in library operations or procedures for up to six months of the library experience; or any equivalent combination of experience and training.

Disclaimers

The duties listed above are intended only as illustrations of the various types of work that may be performed. The omission of specific statements of duties does not exclude them from the position if the work is similar, related or a logical assignment to the position.

The job description does not constitute an employment agreement between the employer and employee and is subject to change by the employer as the needs of the employer and requirements of the job change.

III. ARCHIVES AND SPECIAL COLLECTIONS

Included in this section are archivists, genealogists, local history librarians, and map, manuscript, and museum curators.

1.0 ARCHIVIST

1.1 ARCHIVIST

1.1.1 Archivist

Library Name: Vigo County Public Library
Library Location: Terre Haute, Indiana
Population Served: 106,107
Number of Volumes: 322,960
Number of Titles: 133,374
Number of Periodical Subscriptions: 850

General Summary

Responsible for the overall management of the Archives department which includes establishing policy standards for the acquisition, processing, arrangement, description, and accessibility of archival materials with emphasis on Vigo County and Indiana, coordination of workflow for reduction of collection backlogs, pursuit of grants in support of archival digitization and access initiatives, planning and coordination of community programs, and supervision of Archives staff.

Essential Functions and Responsibilities

Ability to read and understand written and verbal instructions;
Ability to perform close vision tasks;
Ability to work in environment containing airborne particles (mold or mildew);
Ability to communicate clearly and speak knowledgeably and effectively before groups;
High degree of mental acuity;
Ability to perform work requiring accuracy and attention to detail;
Ability to supervise; requires manual dexterity and ability to utilize a computer keyboard;
Ability to file using alphabetic and numerical systems.

Education, Experience, and Training

Qualifications: B.A., M.A. in history, historic preservation, or archival management, and/or ALA accredited MLS with course work or concentration in archival procedures, management, and preservation required; two years experience in archives collection processing and management or experience in a related field of information management preferred; knowledge of MARC format, XML, EAD, and Web page development; familiarity with computer systems in general, db management and electronic record keeping; previous supervisory and/or management skills preferred; excellent communication skills, interest and enthusiasm for working with the public, excellent group presentation skills, and ability to work well with others.

Position Hours

A full time 40 hours per week salaried position in the Archives Department of the Vigo County Public Library.
Work Schedule: 8:00 AM to 5:00 PM or 9:00 AM to 6:00 PM four days per week M-F
1:00 PM to 9:00 PM one night per week
One Saturday per month 8:00 AM to 5:00 PM
One Sunday per month 1:00 PM to 4:00 PM.
Sunday hours apply from Labor Day to Memorial Day.

1.2 GENEALOGY/LOCAL HISTORY ARCHIVIST

1.2.1 Genealogy/Local History Archivist

Library Name: Henderson County Public Library District
Library Location: Henderson, Kentucky
Population Served: 44,000
Number of Volumes: 87,582
Number of Titles: N/A
Number of Periodical Subscriptions: 149

Reports to

SUPERVISORS:
Library Director and Assistant Director

General Summary

The Genealogy/Local History Archivist is responsible for the acquisition, organization, maintenance and preservation of the library's archival collections including all books, papers, maps, photographs, machine-readable materials, or other documentary materials, regardless of physical form or characteristics. The Genealogy/Local History Archivist provides reference service for the local history and genealogy collections and assists patrons in a friendly and timely manner in person, by telephone, mail, and electronic mail.

Essential Functions and Responsibilities

Assist patrons in finding appropriate research materials as needed.

Provide basic instruction to patrons in how to begin genealogy research and trace family history.

Provide basic instruction to patrons in how to use genealogy resources such as census records, telephone directories, military service records, newspapers, birth, death, marriage and divorce records, wills, tax records, property deeds, etc.

Provide basic instruction to patrons in how to use online genealogy databases offered by the library.

Assist patrons with genealogy research using all available print, nonprint, and electronic resources.

Arrange, store, preserve and safeguard all archival records, and provide reference service on such records.

Assist in the creation and application of records management policies pertaining to the library's archival collection.

Participate in the processing of additions to the archives including accessing, arranging, describing, preserving, classifying, and referencing.

Conduct research activities as directed.

Analyze and appraise items to determine value to the collection.

Actively seek items to add to the collection based on significance to local history.

Sort, alphabetize, shelve, file, and retrieve library materials.

Maintain order and neatness in the collection.

Prepare finding aids such as indexes, guides, and bibliographies in both print and electronic formats.

File and cross-index documents in alphabetical and chronological order.

Preserve, repair, and store items in the collection in accordance with professionally accepted standards and practices.

Develop and deliver presentations to community groups and organizations as needed to promote the use of the local history collection.

Develop and present workshops dealing with local history research issues as needed.

Establish good relationships with local historical societies and other genealogical groups.

Analyze and consider different mediums for storage of archival material.

Maintain good relations with public and staff.

Alphabetize, file, and perform clerical tasks with neatness and precision.

Follow procedures consistently.

Provide users with general information about library services directing them to other personnel as needed.

Answer directional and basic reference questions.

Apply library rules and regulations.

Operate office and automated equipment.

Assist patrons with library equipment and related software (i.e. Copier, Microfilm Reader/Printer, Computers, Internet, etc.).

Assist with opening and closing procedures of the library as needed.

Maintain neat and orderly public areas throughout the library.

Assist library users who may have disabilities.

Participate in meetings as required.

Attend in-service workshops, meetings and conferences as appropriate.

Perform other duties as assigned.

Knowledge, Skills, and Abilities

Knowledge of common genealogical sources such as census records, telephone directories, military service records, newspapers, birth, death, marriage and divorce records, wills, tax records, property deeds, etc.

Knowledge of and ability to proficiently use online sources of genealogy data.

Ability to develop and administer a comprehensive archival program.

Knowledge of and ability to apply standard preservation techniques.

Knowledge of digital imaging and scanning technology.

Ability to decipher deteriorated or poor quality printed matter, handwritten manuscripts, or photographs and films.

Ability to instruct others on the retrieval and use of archival materials.

Ability to learn and operate library automated system with high degree of efficiency.

Must be meticulous and detail-oriented.

Must have an inquiring mind, interest in history, patience, and thoroughness.

Ability to organize work, set priorities, use time effectively, work independently, and meet deadlines.

Excellent written and verbal communication skills are required.

Ability to work with frequent interruptions.

Ability to interact with people of varying personalities and ages in a variety of situations.

Must have desire to serve the public with friendliness, tact, and diplomacy.

Ability to maintain composure while handling complaints from the public.

Ability to follow through on numerous details, maintain records in a standard, orderly, systematic fashion, and work well under pressure.

Ability to analyze and to creatively solve problems related to the position.

Accuracy in clerical skills, including typing and filing, is required.

Ability to work with enthusiasm and initiative.

Ability to make decisions within stated guidelines and to work independently in a wide variety of situations.

Ability to communicate and deal with public and staff effectively in person, in writing and by telephone.

Ability to work under broad supervision using established procedures and oral instructions from supervisor.

Ability to work unsupervised and be able to solve problems and serve library users independently.

Cross-training in order to perform other duties and responsibilities in other departments is required.

Physical and Mental Requirements

The employee must regularly lift and/or move up to 10 pounds, frequently lift and/or move up to 25 pounds, and occasionally lift and/or move up to 60 pounds.

Specific vision abilities required by this job include close vision, distance vision, peripheral vision, and the ability to adjust focus.

The employee is regularly required for the majority of the day to stand; sit; walk; use hands to finger, handle, or feel objects, tools or controls; reach with hands and arms; and talk and hear.

The employee is occasionally required to climb or balance and stoop, kneel, crouch, or crawl.

Education, Experience, and Training

Bachelor's degree in an appropriate field required. Archival management experience or equivalent education required. Public service experience required. Computer skills and the ability to work with electronic records and databases is required. Strongly prefer master's degree in library science or related field.

Additional Qualifications

Requires obtaining the appropriate certification from the Kentucky Board for the Certification of Librarians.

Position Hours

This is a full-time position that requires 40 hours per week. Varied schedules may include mornings, afternoons, evenings and weekends. Dependability and diligent attendance are required.

1.3. ARCHIVIST/LIBRARIAN

1.3.1 Archivist/Librarian

Library Name: Escondido Public Library
Library Location: Escondido, California
Population Served: 136,956
Number of Volumes: N/A
Number of Titles: 281,548
Number of Periodical Subscriptions: 320

General Summary

Under general supervision, manages the Escondido Public Library Pioneer Room; performs routine to complex professional librarian/archivist work involving the selection, organization and reference use of print and non-print materials and resources related to local and family history; and provides library services and instruction to all age groups.

Essential Functions and Responsibilities

The following duties are typical for this classification. Incumbents may not perform all of the listed duties and/or may be required to perform additional or different duties from those set forth below to address business needs and changing business practices.

Assesses user needs, assists them in making effective use of the collection, and answers reference questions.

Assists in developing policies and procedures to maintain the collection and provide effective service.

Interprets library policies and procedures to the public.

Supervises and directs paraprofessional staff and volunteers.

Operates and assists with maintenance of computer, microform and other equipment.

Plans, coordinates and conducts public awareness events, programs, tours and classes for the public.

Acts as principal liaison with the Friends of the Pioneer Room and other local history and genealogy groups.

Assists in preparation, monitoring and administration of program budget.

Prepares a variety of oral and written reports and materials.

Represents the Library in meetings with citizens, special interest groups and other City department committees as assigned.

Assists with the classification and cataloging of print, media, software and other materials.

Develops and maintains special files, bibliographies, collections and resources, both print and non-print.

Participates in the development of overall strategic and technology planning for library systems and services.

Depending on area of assignment, duties may also include :

Participates in community outreach and services, and related programs as assigned.

Prepares grant applications.

Monitors the developments in the library and archival professions and participates in activities of professional associations as time permits.

Performs related work as required.

Knowledge, Skills, and Abilities

The following generally describes the knowledge and ability required to enter the job and/or be learned within a short period of time in order to successfully perform the assigned duties.

Knowledge of:

Collection development principles for archival, local history and family history management.

Principles and practices of archival and local history cataloging, preservation, and organization.

Theory, principles and practices of library services, organization and procedures.

Reference sources and research techniques in archival and local history materials using print, media, electronic databases and the Internet.

Principles and practices of positive and effective public relations and customer service.

Supervisory principles and practices.

Grant and report writing techniques.

Principles and practices of budget management.

Ability to:

Plan, organize, implement and evaluate archival and local history reference, services and activities.

Classify and catalog books, maps, special collections and electronic resources using both manual and automated systems.

Assess customer needs and provide accurate reference information.

Establish and maintain effective working relationships with library staff, volunteers, support groups, and the local school districts.

Effectively train, plan, direct and evaluate the work of staff and volunteers.

Prepare clear and concise reports and maintain accurate records and statistics.

Operate a personal computer and efficiently utilize software programs used by the City and the Library.

Prepare specialized programs and conduct tours and classes in related subjects for the public.

Learn new technologies applicable to archival and public library services and operations and implement them in the workplace.

Contribute to a successful team effort.

Demonstrate an awareness and appreciation of the cultural diversity of the community.

Communicate effectively with people from various backgrounds, both individually and in groups.

Physical and Mental Requirements

CONTINUOUS walking; lifting objects weighing up to 10 lbs. From below the waist to above the shoulder level and transporting distances up to 500 yards; fine finger dexterity and light pressure to operate keyboards, calculators, telephones; pinch grasp to hold books, writing materials.

FREQUENT standing, sitting, bending and stooping, squatting, reaching above and at shoulder level, pushing/pulling, twisting at waist, upward and downward flexion of neck, side-to-side turning of neck; lifting objects weighing 11-15 lbs. From below the waist to waist level with or without assistance, and transporting distances up to 10 feet.

INFREQUENT crawling, balancing above ground, lifting objects weighing 26-50 lbs., with or without assistance, and transporting distances up to 10 feet; strong grasp to lift equipment or boxes of books and other materials.

Communication:

VISION (may be correctable) to see computer screens, books and observe customers and situations.

HEARING of telephone and personal conversations with customers, fire and security alarms, sound equipment.

SPEAKING clearly to converse with customers.

WRITING to complete forms and notes to assist customers. Incumbents must occasionally deal with difficult customers in library facilities, including impaired persons or people attempting to steal items.

Work Environment

The conditions herein are representative of those that must be met by an employee to successfully perform the essential functions of this job. Reasonable accommodations may be made to enable individuals with disabilities to perform the essential job functions.

Environment: Exposure to heat and humidity working outdoors at special events; noise of crowds and groups of people; temperature variations within the building and from indoors to outdoors; possible mechanical hazards of equipment and large quantities of books and papers. Work is performed in 60-hour work periods, with unscheduled breaks. Occasional overtime may be required for adequate staffing of library facilities, and incumbents may be required to work weekends, nights and holidays. Work is performed primarily indoors at library facilities. Work setting is formal, team oriented, having both routine and variable tasks. Work pace and pressure is variable, but frequently fast-paced and high pressure.

Education, Experience, and Training

Education and Experience Guidelines – Any combination of education and experience that would likely provide the required knowledge and abilities is qualifying. A typical way to obtain the knowledge and abilities would be:

Graduation from an accredited college or university with a Master's Degree in Library Science or Master's of Arts in Archival Management or History and two years experience in reference, local history, or archival management in a public, special or academic library.

Alternate education and experience may be a Bachelor's degree in archival management or a related discipline and four years experience in reference and archival management in a public, special or academic library.

License and Other Requirements – Must possess a valid Class C California driver's license.

Position Hours

Must be willing to work evenings and weekends.

Disclaimers

Class specifications are intended to present a descriptive list of the range of duties performed by employees in the class. Specifications are not intended to reflect all duties performed within the job.

2.0 CURATOR

2.1 MANUSCRIPT CURATOR

> ### 2.1.1 Manuscript Curator
>
> **Library Name:** Nebraska State Historical Society Library/Archives
> **Library Location:** Lincoln, Nebraska
> **Population Served:** N/A
> **Number of Volumes:** 80,000
> **Number of Titles:** N/A
> **Number of Periodical Subscriptions:** 116

Essential Functions and Responsibilities

Description of Essential Duties (Purpose or Objective of Job):

Performs tasks related to collection development, acquisition, appraisal, preservation and storage of manuscript materials of enduring historical value.

Maintains collections management records.

Develops collection acquisition leads; confers with potential and actual donors.

Processes archival materials and produces formal inventories and other descriptive finding aids for manuscript collections;

Supervises others doing this work.

Works with other Agency curators on management of cross-format materials from private sources, and in developing and implementing collections management procedures.

Develops procedures for electronic records and their management, storage, and retrieval.

Provides reference services and public outreach as needed.

Initiates and/or participates in Division and Agency projects as needed.

Supervises one assistant curator and volunteers, work/study students, and interns as available.

May have occasional overnight stays and traveling.

Knowledge, Skills, and Abilities

Knowledge of archival collections management and preservation principles and methodologies.

Ability to analyze, arrange, and describe complex and significant private archival collections.

Knowledge of current information technologies and trends, and the collection, retrieval, and preservation of same. Knowledge of database management systems such as Microsoft Access.

Ability to establish and maintain effective relationships with staff, potential and actual donors, and the public.

Ability to creatively use automation technologies in the performance of the job.

Ability to operate Society motor vehicles or provide independent transportation.

Ability to lift and carry up to 50 pounds.

Education, Experience, and Training

Bachelor's degree, and at least two (2) years of archival collections management experience and supervisory experience required; Master's degree or post bachelor's coursework/training in Archives Administration, Library Science, History, Museum Studies or Records Management preferred. Must pass background checks.

2.2 MAP CURATOR

> ### 2.2.1 Map Curator
>
> **Library Name:** Boston Public Library
> **Library Location:** Boston, Massachusetts
> **Population Served:** 574,283
> **Number of Titles:** N/A
> **Number of Volumes:** 7,954,358
> **Number of Periodical Subscriptions:** 29,026

Essential Functions and Responsibilities

JOB OBJECTIVE:

Under the direction of the Library President or designee, the Curator of Maps is responsible for the maintenance, development and services of the map collections of the Boston Public Library both for the general public and the scholarly community. To that effect, he/she:

Plans and supervises the organization, access, services, preservation, and acquisitions of the collection of maps and atlases in the Boston Public Library Map Center and throughout the Boston Public Library system.

Initiates and implements the acquisition of new maps and related materials to strengthen existing library resources, including overseeing a budget for purchase of these materials and seeking opportunities for external funding for ongoing acquisition needs.

Promotes understanding of the importance and relevance of maps in the public library setting.

Supervises the organization and cataloging of the collections including the applications of new technologies in order to facilitate the use of the map collection resources.

Advises the library administration and other staff in the general field of maps.

Additional Job Duties

Administers the daily operations of the Boston Public Library Map Center.

Assumes responsibility for training of the Map Center staff in the specialized knowledge of the field.

Organizes the collections of the Map Center and plans and carries out the development of a variety of interactive access applications including both printing and electronics to facilitate use of the collections.

Applies digital scanning and other "virtual" technologies in order to facilitate the collection, organization, preservation and sharing of Map Center resources.

Initiates and implements activities which enhance the appreciation and understanding of maps both within and outside the library including coordination, planning, preparation and mounting of exhibitions, public programs, educational activities, publications, lectures and other collaborative and cooperative programs.

Creates opportunities to educate the public in the significant importance and necessity of map collections.

Provides direction for the cataloging and retro-conversion of maps.

Assesses the needs and resources of the Map Center and strengthens the collections through purchases and gifts.

Advises the library administration in the field of maps.

Maintains professional contacts in the field to further the objectives of the library.

Organizes and implements activities to enhance understanding of Map Center resources by children and youth.

Cooperates with scholars and institutions to maximize use and expand the appreciation of Map Center resources in the greater community.

Creates, nurtures and supports an active Friends of the Map Center organization.

Knowledge, Skills, and Abilities

Ability to execute library policy; ability to plan and supervise the work of others.

Initiative in generating new ideas and proven ability to improve existing work techniques and procedures; broad knowledge of library collections.

Excellent knowledge of maps and/or professional activity including pertinent literature and technology.

Ability to work well with staff and public alike; effective communicator.

Specific knowledge of maps, mapmaking, and current map technologies, including application of geographic information service technologies.

Broad acquaintance with the Antiquarian Map Book Dealers and Collectors.

Demonstrated ability to enlist the interest and support of friends and donors in the development of collections; superior communication skills including oral and written presentation skills.

Demonstration of contributions to the field of maps through participation in conferences and publications of original work.

Ability to work with the various world languages representing the collections; willingness to use and foster a variety of approaches to create enthusiasm and support for maps in widely varying constituencies; ability to work collaboratively.

Knowledge of U.S. federal government mapping and depository program administered by the U.S. Government Printing Office.

Ability to interpret and execute library policy.

Understanding and interest in the total development of library resources and services; including the ability to define the role of the Map Center in the total development.

Supervisory and administrative ability; experience in training and supervision of staff and broad professional outlook.

Ability to participate in the management of a large and complex organization.

Desired Attributes:

Proven skills in oral and written communications.

Superior ability and willingness to assume responsibility.

Initiative in generating new ideas.

Proven ability to plan and supervise the work of others.

Continuing interest in and ability to improve existing work techniques and procedures; demonstrated ability to work successfully with staff and public alike.

Commitment to library leadership; resourcefulness; willingness and proven ability to work with patrons of all age groups; professional demeanor; tact, dependability, enthusiasm, good judgment and courtesy.

Education, Experience, and Training

Masters Degree from an accredited college or university and a Master's Degree in Library and Information Science from an ALA accredited library school. Subject knowledge and professional experience in maps and allied fields and demonstrated abilities in map collection work including preservation and access. Advanced degree in related field is desirable.

In exceptional instances, specialized education, training, and/or experience may be substituted for part or all of the educational requirements.

Ten years of appropriate library experience or an equivalent combination of education, experience and training sufficient to indicate ability to do the work.

Additional Qualifications

Requirements: Must be a Resident of the City of Boston upon first day of hire.

Disclaimers

Performs other related duties as required.

2.3 MUSEUM CURATOR

2.3.1 Museum Curator

Library Name: Anacortes Public Library
Library Location: Anacortes, Washington
Population Served: 14,500
Number of Volumes: N/A
Number of Titles: 55,565
Number of Periodical Subscriptions: 126

Reports to

Director
JOB OBJECTIVE:
This position is responsible for curatorial operations and interpretation of the Anacortes Museum collections, including preservation and maintenance of the W.T. PRESTON snagboat. This position is also responsible for participating in exhibit production, educational programs and general research and preservation of the Anacortes Museum collection, and supervising other staff and volunteers in collections care and interpretation work.

Level of Authority: Performs duties which greatly impact the public's impression of the museum, the quality of care for the museum's collections and the museum's mission.

Essential Functions and Responsibilities

Management of all museum collections including: acquisition, registration, organization, storage, and preservation.

Maintenance and preservation of the W.T. PRESTON snagboat, including hands-on vessel maintenance and the handling of all requests for bids and proposals for contract maintenance and repair work.

Updating policies and procedures related to collections management.

Assists the director in all aspects of site operation and is responsible for administrative and program activities in the director's absence.

Monitors, upgrades, and provides training for others on SNAP!, our computerized collections database.

Team member for exhibit production including: planning, research, writing, and construction.

Develops and refines interpretive training materials for staff and volunteers, implements training sessions.

Develops events and educational programs related to the museum's mission.

Assists with budget, financial planning and goal setting for the museum, in particular for all collections care and educational related activities.

Recruitment and training of other staff and volunteers, providing guidance and support as necessary.

Oversees daily operations onboard the W.T. PRESTON.

Requests and orders curatorial and maintenance supplies.

Coordinates the museum's Hazardous Communications Program including inventories of MSDS sheets.

Coordinates traveling exhibitions to and from the museum including shipping, condition reporting, insurance requirements and financial details.

Researches and writes articles, lectures and public programs related to the collection and interpretation of the museum's artifacts when requested.

Assists with grant writing and fund-raising as needed.

Assists with off-site museum activities and exhibits, including community special events and Museum Foundation events.

Maintains and enforces necessary security procedures to ensure the safety of the museum environment and its collections.

Ensures that all procedures are followed for museum operations and collections management.

Works with the Anacortes Museum Foundation and Advisory Board as needed, is responsible for organizing the Advisory Board Collections Committee.

Handles public inquiries regarding donations or loans of objects.

In addition, this position may include assisting with other aspects of museum work as needed, and working with other City of Anacortes departments as required.

Knowledge, Skills, and Abilities

Must have the ability to interpret the collections and to communicate that knowledge in a variety of written and oral formats.

Must have ability to establish and maintain effective work relationships and to deal effectively and courteously with other employees, volunteers, city departments, city government bureaucracy, and the public through oral and written mediums, including supervising employees and volunteers.

Must have demonstrated ability to work on the preservation and maintenance of a historic vessel and an understanding of the Secretary of the Interior's Standards for Historic Vessel Preservation Projects with Guidelines for Applying the Standards.

Must have ability to use power tools and equipment.

Must have knowledge of the techniques of selection, evaluation, preservation, restoration, and exhibition of objects, photographs and ephemera.

Must have knowledge of legal and ethical issues of collections management, of modern museum registration techniques and current scholarship including material cultural studies and social history studies.

Must have ability to access current scholarship and research sources, and a mastery of research methods.

Must be able to independently organize, develop, plan, and produce projects.

Must be knowledgeable and skilled in use of computer word processing programs.

Desirable to have broad knowledge of other computer programs: SNAP! collections management software, desktop publishing, spreadsheet, etc.

Must be detail oriented and have ability and desire to do repetitive tasks.

Must have ability to compile data and reports, create files and monitor records.

Physical and Mental Requirements

Must be able to lift and carry objects and materials up to 50 lbs.
Must be able to maneuver stairs without difficulty.
Must be able to crawl and work in confined spaces and on ladders.
Must have sufficient visual and hearing capabilities to respond to public needs and for detailed work.

Work Environment

Work is performed primarily within the Anacortes Museum's two sites and within the community. Frequent year-round outdoor work in varied weather conditions is required. Travel is required.

Education, Experience, and Training

Qualifications:
Technical
A Bachelor's Degree in history or related field, with three to five years' demonstrated experience in collections management and/or museum interpretation. A Master's Degree in Museum Studies, American Studies or a related field preferred. Experience may substitute for an advanced degree.

Additional Qualifications

Must be able to be on-call for emergencies.
Must be bondable.
Must have own vehicle for transportation between museum sites.

Disclaimers

The statements contained in this job description reflect general details as necessary to describe the principal functions of this job, the level of knowledge and skill typically required, and the scope of responsibility. It should not be considered an all inclusive listing of work requirements. Individuals may perform other duties as assigned, including work in other functional areas to cover absences or relief, to equalize peak work periods, or to otherwise balance the work load.

2.3.2 Museum Curator

Library Name: Placer County Library
Library Location: Placer County, California
Population Served: 145,500
Number of Volumes: 290,000
Number of Titles: N/A
Number of Periodical Subscriptions: 471

Reports to

Receives direction from the Senior Museum Curator.

General Summary

To perform professional museum duties in caring for and interpreting objects belonging to or lent to the County museums; and to oversee and administer specific museum program areas as assigned.

Distinguishing Characteristics

This is the journey level in the Museum Curator series. Incumbents initially perform the more routine duties assigned to positions in this series and work under close supervision. However, as experience is gained, incumbents are expected to perform the full range of duties as assigned with increasing independence.

This class is distinguished from the Senior Museum Curator in that the latter plans, organizes and coordinates museum programs and exercises direct supervision over staff.

Essential Functions and Responsibilities

Duties may include, but are not limited to, the following:

Care for and academically interpret items belonging to or on loan to the museums; research collections owned by or lent to the museums.

Disseminate information to the public; and prepare and evaluate exhibitions and maintain exhibition calendars.

Assist with budget preparation in assigned program areas; monitor revenue and expenditures; assist with recruiting, training, evaluating and overseeing volunteer staff; maintain appropriate records; assist in the maintenance and daily operation of the museums.

Build and maintain positive working relationships with co-workers, other County employees and the public using principles of good customer service.

Perform related duties as assigned.

When assigned to Archives:

Administer principles and practices of professional archives management, including conservation and preservation of historic books, documents, photos and ephemera.

Assist public with research.

Determine records and documents that are appropriate for retention in the Archives.

Administer processing and accessioning procedures.

Conduct research, analyze information and write reports for a variety of uses and develop historical context for volunteer training and presentations.

Train and supervise docents and volunteers in Placer County history, research methods, archival procedures and conservation and preservation techniques.

Assign and monitor volunteers' projects in the Archives.

Prepare for and conduct oral histories.

When assigned to Collections:

Administer the collections management programs, collect significant artifacts relating to Placer County and ensure a safe environment for their preservation.

Administer accessioning programs, donor relations and loan activities.

When assigned to Education:

Coordinate docent guild programs, visitor services, museum tours and special programs and tourism activities.

Serve as member of the Exhibit Team, performing original research on exhibit themes and providing expertise in education trends and exhibit techniques.

Prepare docent and public education materials and coordinate publicity for exhibits and programs of the museums.

When assigned to Cultural Resources:

Inventory and analyze historical cultural and paleontological resources, including archaeological sites and historically and architecturally significant structures, sites and districts.

Review the cultural resource elements of environmental impact reports and community development plans for compliance with State and Federal legislation, including CEQA, NEPA and the National Preservation Act of 1966.

Provide other technical assistance to the Planning Department and coordinate with other County departments, agencies, boards and commissions.

Knowledge, Skills, and Abilities

Knowledge of:

Principles and practices of professional museum work, including methods of interpretation and exhibit design, standards for care and preservation of collections, accessioning and cataloging of collections.

General principles of education, public relations and fiscal management.

Modern office procedures, methods and computer equipment.

Principles and practices of work safety.

English usage, spelling, grammar and punctuation.

Arithmetic and mathematical calculations.

Ability to:

On a continuous basis, know and understand all aspects of the job; intermittently analyze work papers, reports and special projects; identify and interpret technical and numerical information; observe and problem solve operational and technical policy and procedures.

On a continuous basis sit at a desk for long periods of time; intermittently twist to reach equipment surrounding desk; perform simple grasping and fine manipulation; use telephone and write or use a keyboard to communicate through written means. Intermittently walk, stand, bend or climb while cataloging, conducting tours, assisting with exhibit installation or working in the field; and lift very heavy weight.

Independently perform professional museum duties of interpretation, collection research, exhibition planning, collection cataloging and care and public education.

Independently monitor budgets and oversee volunteer staff activities. Use various graphic arts techniques.

Work with various cultural and ethnic groups in a tactful and effective manner.

Obtain information through interview and interrogation and to deal fairly and courteously with the public.

Use a computer, calculator, typewriter, telephone, facsimile machine and photocopy machine.

Communicate clearly and concisely, both orally and in writing.

Establish and maintain effective working relationships with those contacted in the course of work.

Supervisory Responsibilities

Exercises technical and functional supervision over technical and clerical staff and volunteers.

Education, Experience, and Training

Any combination of experience and training that would provide the required knowledge and abilities is qualifying. A typical way to obtain the required knowledge and abilities would be:

Experience:

Two years of responsible professional museum experience.

Training:

Equivalent to a Bachelor's degree from an accredited college or university with major course work in museum administration, art, cultural anthropology, the humanities or a related field.

License and Certification Requirements

Possession of, or ability to obtain, a valid driver's license. Proof of adequate vehicle insurance and medical clearance may also be required.

IV. Automation, Information Technology, and Web Services

Included in this section are technology and automation administrators, information system managers, assistants, technicians, Webmasters, librarians, help desk workers, and systems coordinators.

1.0 ADMINISTRATOR

1.1 AUTOMATION AND TECHNOLOGY ADMINISTRATOR

1.1.1 Automation and Technology Administrator

Library Name: Phoenix Public Library
Library Location: Phoenix, Arizona
Population Served: 1,350,435
Number of Volumes: 2,015,587
Number of Titles: 734,921
Number of Periodical Subscriptions: 4,500

General Summary

JOB OBJECTIVE:

The fundamental reason that this classification exists is to supervise the operation of one of the library's regional branches, major Central Library section, the Automation Unit of Technical Services and the library's integrated on-line computer system, or the selection of library books and other material for the library collections. Supervision is exercised over professional, clerical, and para-professional staff. The incumbent has considerable latitude in the application of professional practices in the assigned area of responsibility. Supervision over a large and multifaceted library unit or technical expertise differentiates this class from Librarian III. This class reports to the Library Extension Services Administrator, Central Library Administrator, or Library Technical Services Administrator, who evaluates work through a review of plans, budgets, programs, reports, and conferences.

Essential Functions and Responsibilities

Interviews, selects, and supervises professional, paraprofessional, technical and clerical employees, and provides effective leadership to independently performing professionals.

Demonstrates continuous effort to improve operations, decrease turnaround times, streamline work processes, and work cooperatively and jointly to provide quality seamless customer service.

Central Library and Extension Services

Formulates goals, plans, and procedures for one of the regional branch libraries or one of the two major reference centers in the Central Library;

Directs and coordinates the activities of the branch or reference center, overseeing scheduling to ensure coverage of service points, and accepting responsibility for the overall operating effectiveness of the branch or reference center;

Maintains responsibility for the total scope and quality of a regional branch collection or of a major segment of the Central Library reference and circulating collections;

Participates in library committee work;

Keeps accurate, up-to-date work records and produces written reports;

Interprets library policies, objectives, and services to community groups, business and educational leaders, and the general public.

Technical Services

Serves as manager and supervisor of the Library Automation Unit of Technical Services;

Coordinates the planning, development, implementation, and operation of the integrated on-line library system and all microcomputer systems in the library;

Formulates and recommends policy, plans, and procedures relating to automation in order to meet the needs of all divisions of the library;

Works with library supervisors and administrators to ensure the integrity of, and access to, the library's bibliographic apparatus is maintained and enhanced through the process of automating operations;

Collection Development

Formulates goals, policies, and procedures for library system-wide collection development;

Plans and implements the selection list program;

Maintains current, in-depth knowledge of publishing, book trade and review media;

Monitors the branch and Central Library selection, and the effectiveness of all library selectors, and produces written statements of problems;

Responds to citizens' requests for addition or removal of library materials;

Knowledge, Skills, and Abilities

Knowledge of:

Principles and practices of supervision, management, materials selection, reference services, and cataloging.

Professional library theories, issues, and trends.

Public library principles, materials, practices, and organization.

Professional library publications and literature of librarianship.

Leadership styles and skills.

Ability to:

Perform a broad range of supervisory responsibilities over others.

Communicate in the English language by phone or in person in a one-to-one or group setting.

Comprehend and make inferences from written material.

Produce written documents with clearly organized thoughts using proper sentence construction, punctuation, and grammar.

Learn job-related material through oral instruction, observation, structured lecture and reading, and independent study, which takes place in an on-the-job or classroom setting.

Enter data or information into a terminal, PC or other keyboard device.

Operate a variety of standard office equipment requiring continuous or repetitive arm-hand movements.

Review or check the work products of others to ensure conformance to standards.

Analyze professional problems and take appropriate actions.

Work cooperatively with other City employees and the general public.

Work safely without presenting a direct threat to self or others.

Education, Experience, and Training

Four years of progressively responsible professional library experience, including three years supervisory experience, and a master's degree in library science from an American Library Association (ALA) accredited institution or a related field. Other combinations of experience and education that meet the minimum requirements may be substituted.

Additional Qualifications

Some positions require the use of personal or City vehicles on City business. Individuals must be physically capable of operating the vehicles safely, possess a valid driver's license and have an acceptable driving record. Use of a personal vehicle for City business will be prohibited if the employee is not authorized to drive a City vehicle or if the employee does not have personal insurance coverage.

Some positions will require the performance of other essential and marginal functions.

1.2 TECHNOLOGY ADMINISTRATOR

1.2.1 Technology Administrator

Library Name: Des Moines Public Library
Library Location: Des Moines, Iowa
Population Served: 198,682
Number of Volumes: 427,008
Number of Titles: N/A
Number of Periodical Subscriptions: 1,051

General Summary

JOB OBJECTIVE:

Under the supervision of the director, is the manager of the Library Technology Department. Manages, plans, and administers the work of the department. Responsible for the development, design, and coordination of computer-based systems within the library, and for strategic planning which anticipates the systems needs of public and staff.

Essential Functions and Responsibilities

Manages technology budget and prepares the library's short- and long-range technology plans.

Oversees selection, installation, and maintenance of hardware and software.

Develops and maintains system-wide replacement plan for hardware and software.

Selects, purchases, and maintains all electronic systems, including telephones, security systems, printers, copiers, faxes, and other peripherals.

Motivates, coaches, and develops technology support staff, and reviews individual performance.

Writes systems specifications.

Keeps library administration informed on current technology trends in administration systems.

Acts as backup to systems administrator.

Reads professional literature and attends conferences to keep informed of developing library technology practices and issues.

Knowledge, Skills, and Abilities

Knowledge of design and implementation of information storage and retrieval systems.

Knowledge of the functions and appropriateness of a variety of modern telecommunications systems.

Knowledge of the philosophy and objectives of public library service and its support systems.

Ability to analyze, comprehend, and resolve complex problems related to integrated systems and networks.

Ability to effectively train and supervise staff.

Ability to present clear and precise oral, graphic, and written reports.

Ability to convey technical information in terms that are understandable to any audience.

Ability to establish and maintain effective working relationships with staff, city departments, consultants, contractors and the public.

Physical and Mental Requirements

Sufficient clarity of speech and hearing to be able to communicate effectively.

Sufficient vision to be able to produce and review a wide variety of reports and related materials in both electronic and hard copy form.

Sufficient manual dexterity to be able to access relevant library materials and operate a keyboard.

Sufficient mobility to be able to transport materials and equipment.

Education, Experience, and Training

Minimum of three years experience with a variety of integrated systems. BA degree in Computer Science or related field. Master's degree preferred.

1.3 HEAD OF TECHNOLOGY SERVICES/ ASSISTANT COUNTY LIBRARIAN

1.3.1 Head of Technology Services/ Assistant County Librarian

Library Name: Sussex County Department of Libraries
Library Location: Georgetown, Delaware
Population Served: N/A
Number of Volumes: 4,910
Number of Titles: N/A
Number of Periodical Subscriptions: 42

General Summary

JOB OBJECTIVE:

Assistant County Librarian and administrative head of the Technology Services Division of the Department of Libraries. Incumbent is responsible for all aspects of technology services, covering acquisitions, automation, cataloging, processing, interlibrary loans, circulation, and serials for the department, bookmobile, three branch libraries, plus any consortia member library with which the department has contracted for technical services. Duties are carried out with considerable independence within the framework of established policies, procedures and a strategic plan. Work requires the exercise of initiative, independent judgment, and discretion in handling administrative duties. Technical supervision or direction is exercised over subordinate personnel. Administrative supervision is received from the County Librarian and is generally in the form of a review of plans and programs, and by periodic consultations and conferences. Incumbent works closely with the County Librarian in overall planning for county-wide library services. Incumbent is required to attend continuing education opportunities to stay current in the field. Incumbent must acquire knowledge, skills, and abilities to complete assignments accurately and efficiently. Incumbent will work closely with staff to facilitate prompt delivery of materials and services to county and consortia member libraries. Work requires sustained operation of a computer terminal and is subject to inflexible deadlines.

Essential Functions and Responsibilities

(Note: The following functions represent the essential duties and outputs of the position. Duties listed are not intended to be all inclusive or to limit duties that might reasonably be assigned.)

Specific

Ensure the efficient, accurate purchasing, cataloging, and processing of all material collections of the library system

Collect, compile, publish, and distribute all library statistics into a monthly, as well as an annual report of:

Circulation of materials

Volumes added and deleted

Patrons added and deleted

Recommend, train, supervise, and evaluate Technical Services staff

Develop, implement, and evaluate policies and procedures for Technical Services and system-wide activities

Serve as a resource person to other librarians and staff in matters relating to technical services and methods of access to electronic resources

May record minutes for consortium and staff meetings

May maintain department web site

Assist in planning, coordinating, and organizing specific aspects of technical services

Maintain an awareness of current library issues and trends affecting all libraries; read professional literature and attend continuing education workshops and meetings

Manage department operation in the absence of the County Librarian

Maintain security and password clearances when necessary

May assist with virtual reference

Participate in professional organizations

Assist in preparing the annual budget as it relates to technical services and administer the approved budget for technical services division

Establish, monitor, and evaluate overall program of service for Technical Services division

Research, plan, and coordinate new and on-going projects

Analyze and report data from Technical Services Division to measure cost and workflow effectiveness. Research, plan, and implement systems and routines to increase efficiency and lower costs and turnaround times

Conduct regular meetings with Technical Services staff to communicate administrative policy and to coordinate divisional activities

Other duties as assigned

General

Prepare monthly reports for the County Librarian

Plan work according to established procedures

Prepare documents using a professional software suite

Attend job related workshops and training sessions

Conduct training of consortia member library staff when necessary

Share answering the telephone for the department and route calls to the appropriate person

Maintain procedural manuals

Knowledge, Skills, and Abilities

(The following knowledge, abilities, and skills represent those needed at time of appointment to perform Essential Duties and Responsibilities.)

Knowledge of -

Principles, theories, and concepts of all aspects of library science

Principles and practices of ordering, cataloging, and processing library materials and library automation

Administrative, secretarial, and office management skills, including fast and accurate word processing (65 wpm) and data entry. Experience with applications of Microsoft software, Windows, and the Internet.

MARC (Machine Readable Cataloging) and/or any current and emerging formats

Ability to -

Organize and direct ordering, cataloging, processing, and computer operations

Evaluate operations and procedures and recommend improvements

Supervise professional and support staff

Make decisions in an environment of limited resources and competing claims

Administer the bibliographic maintenance function and supervise staff in technical and circulation operations

Load and troubleshoot software and provide equipment maintenance at an intermediate level

Produce written documentation

Prioritize work

Grasp or manipulate books and other forms of media. Manipulate stacks of books and similar materials weighing up to 60 pounds and loaded book carts weighing up to 100 pounds

Maintain records, prepare reports, maintain databases, and create spreadsheets

Communicate using e-mail with ability to send and receive attachments

Establish and maintain effective working relationships with superiors, subordinates, associates, officials of other agencies, and the general public

Follow procedures consistently and pay close attention to detail

Type or input accurately at approximately 65 words per minute

Handle multiple tasks/projects

Concentrate on task at hand regardless of environment

Education, Experience, and Training

Graduate degree in Library Science from an ALA accredited college or university, five years of progressively responsible library administration experience, including three years as a supervisor, plus two to three years cataloging experience working in a public library, OR, an equivalent combination of education and experience that provides the required knowledge, skills, and abilities.

Candidate must have a thorough knowledge of library issues and techniques, a working knowledge of bibliographic database management and Technical Services operations, and must be able to work independently and accurately. In addition, the Head of Technology Services must possess the interpersonal and communication skills that will enable him or her to represent the department to vendors and library consortia.

Available Resources:

(The following resources represent what is currently in use. Resources listed are subject to change.)

Dynix database and documentation
IPAC database and documentation
Dynix Cataloging for Windows
Online resources
Microsoft Office
County Librarian
Professional collection
Delaware Division of Libraries
Cataloging & Acquisitions online utilities (ITS for Windows, Title Source II)
Web building utilities (Dreamweaver or Front Page)

1.4 TECHNOLOGY AND AUTOMATED CIRCULATION SYSTEMS ADMINISTRATOR

1.4.1 Technology and Automated Circulation Systems Administrator

Library Name: Brand Library and Art Center, Glendale Public Library
Library Location: Glendale, California
Population Served: 199,022
Number of Volumes: 709,044
Number of Titles: N/A
Number of Periodical Subscriptions: 737

General Summary

JOB OBJECTIVE:

Under the direction of the Library Director, administers all applications of the library automation system with particular attention paid to the circulation function. Supervises the Circulation staff of one full time and up to five part time positions. Provides basic library services including assistance in location and use of library materials, reader's advisory, and program activities.

Essential Functions and Responsibilities

*— Insures the efficient operation of all library automation modules including circulation, cataloging, on-line public access catalog (OPAC), report generator, TAP, Dial-Pac, and e-mail.

*— Serves as the authorized contact person with the library automation vendor for hardware and software installation and operation. Coordinates all system upgrades, "patches", and "fixes".

*— Performs all routine repairs, daily troubleshooting, and preventive maintenance; conducts annual system hardware and software inventory to insure coverage under the maintenance agreement contract.

*— Trains staff and the public in the effective use of the automated library system.

— Assists library patrons, in person and on the telephone, with circulation and OPAC functions.

— Serves as the library's voting representative at the Customers of Dynix (CODI) national users group meetings.

*— Develops procedures and recommends policies related to the circulation of library materials; hires trains, schedules and evaluates Circulation staff. Establishes work priorities and delegates duties.

— Provides public service at the Circulation Desk, including patron registration, fine collection, and the check-in and out of materials; uses library resources to assist patrons with information and reader's advisory questions.

— Performs other duties as assigned.

*Essential functions of the job.

Additional Job Duties

— Approximately half of the work schedule is spent on automated library system responsibilities and half supervising public service staff at the Circulation Desk.

Knowledge, Skills, and Abilities

— Fundamental knowledge of automated library circulation systems including terminal and system printer installation and operation.

— Knowledge of library catalog organization, indexing, and filing; standard library operating procedures and terminology, related specifically to patron registration and materials circulation.

— Ability to quickly learn technical procedures using documentation, training, and customer service support and provide understandable interpretations of procedures and policies.

— Ability to analyze, research, and solve technical problems, using self initiative and vendor technical support.

— Ability to assess, organize, and resolve training needs and to explain complex technical procedures to unsophisticated staff and public with patience, thoroughness, and reinforcement.

— Ability to resolve public concerns and difficulties related to the operation of an automated library system with tact, courtesy, and good judgement.

— Ability to communicate library concerns and needs to automation vendors.

— Ability to supervise and schedule the work of others and to establish and maintain effective working relationships.

— Superior technical skills and aptitude.

— Outstanding human relations and communication skills.

Physical and Mental Requirements

The physical demands described here are representative of those that must be met by an employee to successfully perform the essential functions of this job. Reasonable accommodations may be made to enable individuals with disabilities to perform the essential functions.

— While performing the duties of this job, the employee is frequently required to walk, sit and talk or hear. The employee is occasionally required to use hands to finger, handle, feel or operate objects, tools, or controls; and reach with hands and arms. The employee is occasionally required to climb or balance; stoop, kneel, crouch, or crawl.

— The employee must occasionally lift and/or move up to 25 pounds. Specific vision abilities required by this job include close vision, distance vision, color vision, peripheral vision, depth perception, and the ability to adjust focus to both print and electronic text.

Tools and Equipment Used

— Library computer system; personal computer, including world wide web search engines and the library's web site, word processing and database management software; calculator; copy and fax machine; phone.

Work Environment

The work environment characteristics described here are representative of those an employee encounters while performing the essential functions of this job. Reasonable accommodations may be made to enable individuals with disabilities to perform the essential functions.

— Work is performed primarily in an office setting. The noise level in the work environment is generally quiet.

Education, Experience, and Training

MINIMUM QUALIFICATIONS

— Completion of a Bachelor's Degree and related public service experience, or previous public library experience with at least one (1) year of automated system and staff supervisory experience, or an equivalent combination of education and/or experience which provides the required knowledge and abilities.

Position Hours

— Must be willing to work evenings and Saturdays and must be able to attend to occasional, unscheduled, after hours system malfunctions.

2.0 ASSISTANT

2.1 AUTOMATION ASSISTANT

2.1.1 Automation Assistant

Library Name: Rochester Public Library
Library Location: Rochester, Minnesota
Population Served: 114,991
Number of Volumes: 343,031
Number of Titles: N/A
Number of Periodical Subscriptions: 588

General Summary

JOB OBJECTIVE:

The Automation Services Assistant provides standard, routine technical services for personal computer hardware and software including hardware installation, problem determination, hardware maintenance, operating systems installation, and application software installation. Responsible for basic troubleshooting Rochester Public Library computer equipment and related equipment including personal computers and printers and implementing appropriate solutions; installing and maintaining personal computer hardware and related equipment, application and system software; and performing related duties as required. Work requires general working knowledge of computer system operations and equipment and is performed under the supervision of the Automation Services Manager. The position requires evening, weekend and on-call work.

Essential Functions and Responsibilities

A. Respond to user problems with hardware and related equipment including printers, scanners, and software, troubleshoot and handle minor repairs; refer users to appropriate personnel for additional assistance when necessary

B. Install personal computer systems and related equipment and application and operating system software and upgrades

C. Provide basic instruction to users on equipment operation and general software use

D. Monitor and maintain printer supplies inventory and maintain inventory of hardware

E. Ensure security of software in accordance with established procedure

F. Perform related work as assigned

Knowledge, Skills, and Abilities

Knowledge of personal computer hardware and related software.

Knowledge of the techniques, procedures and methods of installing personal computer hardware and software.

Knowledge of personal computer related applications software packages including word processing, spreadsheets and emulation software.

Ability to analyze and resolve computer problems.

Ability to establish work priorities and handle multiple tasks.

Commitment to the standards and objectives of the library.

Ability to maintain accuracy and work steadily, and to organize and carry through assigned tasks.

Ability to communicate effectively both verbally and in writing and maintain effective working relationships.

Skill in the use of personal computer related hardware and software.

Skill in accomplishing work in a timely and effective manner.

Physical and Mental Requirements

COMPLIANCE WITH THE AMERICANS WITH DISABILITIES ACT THE FOLLOWING REPRESENTS THE PHYSICAL AND ENVIRONMENTAL DEMANDS

This position requires an equal amount of time spent standing, walking, and sitting.

Lifting, pushing/pulling, or carrying of objects weighing up to twenty-five (25) pounds is sometimes required, with a maximum of seventy-five (75) pounds infrequently required.

Climbing, stooping, kneeling, crouching, crawling, twisting, and bending are sometimes required.

Repetitive movements of the hands are sometimes required.

Audio, visual, and verbal functions are essential functions to performing this position.

Work Environment

The work is performed indoors. (A breakdown of the physical and environmental demands is available on the "Job Analysis of Physical and Environmental Demands" in the Human Resources Department)

Education, Experience, and Training

MINIMUM QUALIFICATIONS

Education High school diploma and one year computer technical training.

Experience One year computer technical customer service experience including experience with operating systems and various application software programs, and installing and maintaining hardware and software

Additional Qualifications

Experience with Microsoft Windows operating systems.
Public service experience.
Basic knowledge of library operations and policies.

3.0 MANAGER

3.1 INFORMATION SYSTEMS MANAGER

3.1.1 Information Systems Manager

Library Name: Hartford Public Library
Library Location: Hartford, Connecticut
Population Served: 133,280
Number of Volumes: 485,000
Number of Titles: 255,000
Number of Periodical Subscriptions: 805

General Summary

JOB OBJECTIVE: The Information Systems Manager works to develop information technology system wide that is responsive to community needs, with responsibility for the planning, assessment, implementation and maintenance of the Library's technology-related policy, services and technical infrastructure. The Information Systems Manager provides effective access to resources, information and ideas, and supports the Mission and Core Values of the Hartford Public Library.

Essential Functions and Responsibilities

Strategic, tactical and operational leadership of all aspects of Information Technology, including but not limited to hardware, software, the network, applications, data, connections, security and recovery.

Collaborate with Metro Hartford Information Services in the development of citywide technology as it relates to the library system.

Oversee management of the integrated library system database; the Community Information database, and the Hartford Info database; the coordination of the overall web environment, including the Hartford Public Library web site and City of Hartford web site, and the system-wide application of media-based technology.

Evaluate and update a comprehensive, innovative and advanced technology plan.

Serve on various committees and teams to recommend and support the Library's goals and objectives.

Keep library administration informed of system-wide needs and concerns.

Stay abreast of developments in the information technology profession and recommend and implement technology as appropriate. Attend one – two industry conventions each year.

Oversee budgets and expenditures.

Responsible for supervising, coaching and evaluating staff. Assign duties and work schedules.

Perform other duties as required.

Knowledge, Skills, and Abilities

Thorough knowledge of the resources, procedures, and practices of the information technology field.

Technical knowledge of computers, networks, system design and implementation; IS systems architecture, security, anti-virus, firewalls, backup procedures and disaster recovery methods.

Knowledge of switches, hubs and Ethernet technology; LAN/WANs including Cisco router technology; network and telecommunications systems design; and Microsoft operating systems and server technology.

Ability to prioritize and organize with focus on task completion.

Ability to conceptualize the nature of technical problems and determine ways to implement innovative and cost-effective solutions.

Demonstrated commitment to internal and external customer service.

Ability to plan and develop programs and services to achieve positive outcomes.

Ability to work independently and also in a team environment.

Ability to interact with a diverse population.

Ability to present ideas effectively, orally and in writing.

Ability to establish and maintain effective working relationships with customers, staff, and community groups.

Education, Experience, and Training

MINIMUM REQUIREMENTS:

Education: Bachelor of Science in Management Information Science, Computer Science or related discipline or an equivalent combination of education, training and experience. MSCA or equivalent experience; or CCNP or equivalent experience; or CCNA or equivalent experience.

Experience: Minimum eight years of progressively responsible experience in the Information Technology field including a minimum of three years in a management role.

Additional Qualifications

License: Valid Motor Vehicle's Operator's License.

Position Hours

Schedule: The normal workweek includes day, evening and weekend hours.

4.0 INTERNET AND INTRANET

4.1 WEBMASTER

4.1.1 Webmaster

Library Name: Phoenix Public Library
Library Location: Phoenix, Arizona
Population Served: 1,350,435
Number of Volumes: 2,015,587
Number of Titles: 734,921
Number of Periodical Subscriptions: 4,500

Essential Functions and Responsibilities

Manages and supervises the Library Web Team responsible for administering public and staff Web services and Web-based subscription services.

Communicates with designated content providers to identify needs and expectations for growth and expansion of Web services.

Designs and/or participates in the design of Web pages, and performs layout work, linking, and all the other tasks required to create, develop, and expand Web pages and services.

Responsible for evaluating, electing, and upon approval, ordering, installing, integrating, and testing Web server hardware and software to accomplish effective Web services and management including effective security measures, online surveys and other interactive services, document management, search engines, monitoring and production of statistical reports of Web site usage, and simplified means for Library staff to place content into the Web environment with a minimum of effort and training.

Participates in the quality assurance review of all new Web development activity, and is responsible for technical troubleshooting and correcting of technical problems.

Additional Job Duties

Employees in this class who are skilled in a second language may be called upon to utilize that skill in the routine performance of their duties.

Physical and Mental Requirements

Moving objects weighing up to 50 pounds may be required.

Education, Experience, and Training

Requires one-year managing staff or serving as a project manager of a web division, and two years of experience developing and maintaining web pages and services, including one year of experience in an enterprise technical support role.

This experience must include strong skills in Relational Databases (SQL).

Knowledge of XML,HTML, WebPro, JSP, CGI scripting/programming, embedded web page scripting (JavaScript, ASP, or PHP), systems management experience with Unix or NT, experience configuring and maintaining Apache, Tomcat, Jboss, or Microsoft IIS (latest releases) web server, and programming languages (C++, Visual Basic).

Training and experience with web-database integration, E-commerce, SQL, and Perl are highly desirable.

Training and experience with XML, Java (applets), database administration and/or TCP/IP are desirable.

A Bachelor's degree in computer science, math, or a related field is also required.

Other combinations of experience and education that meet the minimum qualifications may be substituted.

Additional Qualifications

Excellent writing skills are essential, as is the ability to communicate effectively with both technical and non-technical audiences.

Position Hours

Working irregular hours, shifts, weekends, holidays and evenings may be required.

4.2 INTRANET AND INTERNET ADMINISTRATOR

4.2.1 Intranet and Internet Administrator

Library Name: Bellevue Regional Library
Library Location: Bellevue, Washington
Population Served: N/A
Number of Volumes: N/A
Number of Titles: 372,167
Number of Periodical Subscriptions: 1,061

Reports to

Works under the general supervision of the Information Services Manager (Applications).

General Summary

JOB OBJECTIVE: Responsible for the organization's Internet and or Intranet technical functions. Based on marketing and business plans, will analyze, design, and implement technical solutions via the organization's Internet/Intranet system. Will coordinate the content and organization of data with various departments but it is typically not responsible for content development. Will advise personnel or departments on the proper production, technical and design technique specific to Internet/Intranet development. Has experience and skill with dominant applications to maintain and modify the organization's Internet/Intranet efforts including content, graphical and multimedia displays, and communications. Typically works in set production schedules and under very tight deadlines. Has extensive experience in one or more of the following: C, C++, JAVA, Visual Basic, PERL, on-line services, and multimedia applications. Incumbents in this position may be single contributors or part of a team effort.

Essential Functions and Responsibilities

Manages the City's Internet/Intranet Web Servers.

Managers and coordinates Internet/Intranet Web applications and projects

Designs, maintains and documents the development of web pages according to agency specifications; creates web pages; reviews work for quality control and consistency.

Meets with representatives from City departments to discuss web site project requests; provides assistance to clients as necessary.

Interfaces with graphic designers to develop complex graphics.

Implements time-sensitive updates to web site information from numerous agencies.

Designs and recommends technical solutions based on Internet technologies.

Researches new technologies for web site enhancements in HyperText Markup Language (HTML), sound, video, animations, and other related features.

Writes and develops information as needed for placement on the web site.

Supervises the work of Web site developers, contractors and volunteers.

Knowledge, Skills, and Abilities

Considerable knowledge of computer programming theory, principles, and practices.

Considerable knowledge of current Web related programming languages.

Working knowledge of office automation and computerization.

Working knowledge of local area networks (LANs).

Ability to successfully supervise the development of complex software programs;

Ability to maintain existing software programs and computer systems;

Ability to troubleshoot software programs;

Ability to train Web software developers;

Ability to meet project deadlines;

Ability to effectively supervise Web development staff;

Ability to establish and maintain effective working relationships with supervisors and employees;

Ability to communicate effectively orally and in writing.

Physical and Mental Requirements

The physical demands and work environment described here are representative of those that must be met by an employee to successfully perform the essential functions of this job.

Reasonable accommodations may be made to enable individuals with disabilities to perform the essential functions.

Work involves walking, talking, hearing, using hands to handle, feel or operate objects, tools, or controls and reach with hands and arms.

Vision abilities required by this job include close vision, distance vision, peripheral vision, depth perception, and the ability to adjust focus.

The employee may be required to push, pull, lift, and/or carry up to 40 pounds.

The noise level in the work environment is usually moderately quiet.

Supervisory Responsibilities

May supervise Web site developers, contractors and volunteers, as assigned.

Supervises the work of Web site developers, contractors and volunteers.

Education, Experience, and Training

Graduation from an accredited four-year college or university with a degree in Computer Science or related field.

Four or more years of progressively responsible related experience in web design and software development.

Or any equivalent combination of education, experience and training that provides the required knowledge, skills, and abilities.

Microsoft Certified Professional training and Microsoft Certified Systems Engineer training preferred.

5.0 LIBRARIAN

5.1 TECHNOLOGY LIBRARIAN

5.1.1 Technology Librarian

Library Name: Saline County Public Library
Library Location: Benton, Arkansas
Population Served: 83,529
Number of Volumes: N/A
Number of Titles: 60,000
Number of Periodical Subscriptions: 105

General Summary

JOB OBJECTIVE: The Reference and Technology Librarian will serve the public at the reference desk and maintain and troubleshoot all computer systems within the library.

Essential Functions and Responsibilities

Friendly with people who use the library, both patrons coming through the front door and staff.

Keeps informed of new developments in information technology.

Assists and instructs patrons in the use of library materials, including online databases, Internet sources, and the PAC.

Maintains and troubleshoots computer workstations and peripherals.

Maintains 6 Win 2000 servers, including Horizon automation software and hardware.

Works regular assignments at the reference desk and circulation desk as well as provide backup when needed.

Installs new hardware and software updates.

Consults and requests computer-related purchases through Department Head.

Assists and recommends to the Department Head policies and procedures relating to reference and information services.

Participates in professional activities, some of which may be out of state.

Assists in departmental computer classes offered to the public.

Ability to assume more difficult duties as experience increases.

Knowledge, Skills, and Abilities

Candidate should be conversant with the library's resources, services, classification system, policies and procedures.

Candidate must like people, libraries, computers, innovation, and change.

Candidate must demonstrate ability to use the internet and online databases; confidence in using pc applications, including Microsoft Office 2000, and other computer resources.

Familiarity with Dynix's Horizon automation software is a plus; willingness and ability to learn SQL Sybase 12) is essential.

Education, Experience, and Training

QUALIFICATIONS:

Bachelor's degree with prior public library experience or Master's degree from an ALA accredited library school.

Position Hours

This is a full-time, 40 hour per week position that includes one night per week and alternating Fridays/Saturdays (off on Friday when working Saturday).

Disclaimers

Other duties as assigned.

6.0 SYSTEMS

6.1 SYSTEMS COORDINATOR

6.1.1 Systems Coordinator

Library Name: Neill Public Library
Library Location: Pullman, Washington
Population Served: 24,675
Number of Volumes: 60,247
Number of Titles: N/A
Number of Periodical Subscriptions: 145

General Summary

Plans, coordinates, and manages the systems operations of Neill Public Library and the Whitman County Library District. Responsible for the development and delivery of library technology plans and the operations and maintenance of automated library systems, computers and Internet services. Performs related duties as assigned.

CLASSIFICATION SUMMARY

The Library Division Manager–Systems Administrator serves as the Systems Manager for library computer systems, hardware and software. Librarians serve as members of the management team of both libraries. As such, librarians work closely with each other, the Library Directors, area supervisors and staff work groups, as well as with the Boards of Trustees of both libraries and with local institutions to cooperatively develop goals consistent with the overall mission of the libraries. Computer system development, management, operation, and maintenance work is performed independently based on knowledge and research conducted. The employee in this class plans, directs and coordinates the work of library personnel in the systems units and participates in the work as required. The work is performed independently under the broad direction and guidance of the respective Library Directors.

Essential Functions and Responsibilities

Identifies and analyzes emerging community issues and needs to determine directions for related library services and collections.

Evaluates library services in order to improve them; determines the activities required to achieve objectives.

Organizes equipment, facilities and staffing needed to accomplish activities.

Develops annual work plans.

Establishes standards and implements procedures for technology plans and systems management.

Supervises systems staff at each library.

Plans, develops, and revises procedures for the unit.

Interviews and selects subordinate personnel.

Schedules and assigns activities to staff.

Evaluates staff performance.

Develops and updates training materials and procedures manual.

Provides orientation and work-related instructions.

Resolves personnel issues.

Establishes standards for data entry and authority control to ensure accuracy and accessibility.

Encourages staff development through training, workshops and conferences.

Schedules and conducts staff meetings to provide information and seek input on policies and procedures.

Provides leadership in community partnerships and serves on select committees working to provide optimal library services.

Collaborates with the school districts, libraries, Friends of the Library groups, Boards of Trustees, higher education institutions, city and county departments, and a variety of other service groups and organizations as needs and opportunities arise.

Plans, develops and implements short- and long-range plans for automation for the libraries.

Develops hardware and software needs, reviews proposals received from vendors, and recommends hardware-software configurations to meet the needs of the libraries.

Implements library automated system upgrades, enhancements, and additions.

Develops and coordinates training on the automated systems for staff and the public.

Serves as automation coordinator for interlibrary and other projects, establishes and maintains system policies and procedures.

Serves as systems manager for the libraries' online cataloging and circulation system, web and email services, local area network and related hardware and software.

Troubleshoots problems with hardware and software and confers with vendors or computer technicians as needed to resolve major problems.

Performs system backups; monitors system performance and takes appropriate action to resolve problems.

Loads software upgrades, sets up and installs equipment.

Maintains operational and maintenance logs, system parameters and documentation.

Represents the library to the public in a helpful, courteous, and resourceful manner by assisting patrons.

Assists with other work as needed for the smooth operation of the libraries.

Attends work on a regular and dependable basis.

Interacts in a professional and respectful manner with city staff and the public.

Additional Job Duties

Performs other tasks as assigned.

Knowledge, Skills, and Abilities

SELECTION FACTORS

(Applicants should describe their previous experience and training for each of the following factors. These factors will be the basis for selecting the most qualified applicants to be interviewed. Candidates selected for employment must satisfactorily demonstrate possession of these factors during a prescribed probationary period, and afterwards, for continued employment.)

Knowledge of:

Current developments, trends, practices and philosophy in library services;

Management theory and supervisory techniques;

LANS, WANS, network and PC security; operating systems including UNIX, NT, Website management and HTML; online reference resources and office applications;

Library automation software and technology;

Operation and maintenance requirements of computers and peripheral equipment related to library services.

Ability to:

Effectively analyze program services, identify and write objectives, and determine implementation methods and resources;

Assess needs and develop short- and long-range plans for library programs;

Effectively supervise the work of subordinate staff;

Effectively operate and maintain library computerized information systems, both hardware and software;

Meet and deal with the public in a pleasant and courteous manner;

Communicate effectively;

Establish and maintain effective working relationships with staff, co-workers, vendors, community agencies and the general public;

Define problems, collect data, establish facts and draw valid conclusions;

Maintain flexibility in scheduling, including being "on-call" as needed;

Apply common sense understanding to solve practical problems and deal with a variety of situations;

Learn computer software packages and adapt them for specific user applications;

Troubleshoot and repair computer systems;

Read and interpret technical journals, financial reports, operating and procedures manuals;

Represent the libraries' interests effectively and efficiently with vendors;

Work independently on many tasks at one time;

Physically perform the essential functions of the job;

Determine budgets and allocate resources.

Tools and Equipment Used

Variety of computer equipment, hardware and software, including the libraries' catalog and web servers, routers, switches, peripherals; copy machine, telephone, 10-key calculator, VCR, tape players, motor vehicle.

Work Environment

(The work environment characteristics described here are representative of those an employee encounters while performing the essential functions of this job. Reasonable accommodations may be made to enable individuals with disabilities to perform the essential functions.)

Work is performed primarily in an office environment in Colfax and Pullman while sitting at a desk or computer terminal or while standing at a counter for extended periods of time.

Travel between both locations is a necessity, requiring uncompensated use of the employee's own motor vehicle.

Physical exertion is required to service and lift office supplies; library materials and computer equipment.

Sufficient vision or other powers of observation are essential to permit the employee to read and sort library materials, repair and maintain computer equipment and supervise subordinate staff.

Education, Experience, and Training

MINIMUM QUALIFICATIONS

(Persons applying for a position of this class should have any combination of the following experience and training.)

Master's of Library Science Degree with three years of professional library experience in systems and technical services, with at least one year of supervisory experience.

or, a Bachelor's degree and five years of library experience, including three years working with automated library systems and technical services activities and one year in a supervisory capacity.

or at least five years of library management experience and three years experience in systems management with the operation of a library computer system.

or any equivalent combination of experience and training.

Disclaimers

The duties listed above are intended only as illustrations of the various types of work that may be performed. The omission of specific statements of duties does not exclude them from the position if the work is similar, related or a logical assignment to the position.

The job description does not constitute an employment agreement between the employer and employee and is subject to change by the employer as the needs of the employer and requirements of the job change.

6.1.2 Systems Coordinator

Library Name: Manitowoc-Calumet Library System
Library Location: Manitowoc, Wisconsin
Population Served: 58,213
Number of Volumes: 195,166
Number of Titles: N/A
Number of Periodical Subscriptions: 395

General Summary

JOB OBJECTIVE:

Under general direction from the System Director, plans, develops, manages, and evaluates the overall activities of the Manitowoc-Calumet Library System and oversees or performs the day to day operations of the System.

Administers and manages the System's service programs; develops and manages the System budge.

Supervises System staff. Develops and prepares System plans, reports, compliance documentation, and library agreements.

Monitors and maintains compliance with all statutory requirements for Wisconsin public library systems.

Writes and implements grants.

Participates on the MPL/MCLS management team and coordinates activities of the System with those of other units of the Resource Library and other libraries within the System area.

The Manitowoc-Calumet Library System (MCLS) is comprised of the six public libraries in Manitowoc and Calumet Counties. Manitowoc Public Library (MPL) is the resource library. Other MCLS libraries include the Brillion Public Library, Chilton Public Library, Kiel Public Library, Lester Public Library in Two Rivers, and New Holstein Public Library. MCLS and its six member libraries have formed the Manitowoc-Calumet Library Automated Resource Sharing Consortium (LARS) for the purpose of maintaining an integrated library system. Headquartered in MPL, MCLS shares a director with the resource library. MCLS staff are employed by MPL and provided by contract to MCLS.

MPL refers to the Manitowoc Public Library; MCLS refers to the Manitowoc-Calumet Library System; LARS is an integrated library system shared by the six public libraries in MCLS.

Essential Functions and Responsibilities

The following list identifies principal duties and responsibilities of the job. It is not a definitive list and other similar duties may be assigned. An asterisk (*) before any of the following items indicates duties and responsibilities which are not "essential functions" of the job as defined by the Americans with Disabilities Act.

Plans, develops, manages and evaluates the overall activities of the Manitowoc-Calumet Library System, and works to assure that MCLS complies with all statutory requirements for Wisconsin public library systems.

Coordinates and maintains service programs for backup reference and interlibrary loan, referral of reference and interlibrary loan requests, "sames services" from member libraries, in-service training, delivery and communications, agreements with adjacent systems, professional consultation, users with special needs, cooperation with other types of libraries, library technology and resource sharing, collection development, services to youth, and any other service programs included in the System plan.

Provides and performs administrative support services to facilitate the functioning of the System board, System Director, System office routines, and the System in general.

Makes recommendations to the System Director for the improvement of the operations of the Manitowoc-Calumet Library System.

Coordinates activities of the System with those of other units of the System Resource Library (MPL) and other libraries within the System area.

Assists the System Director and functions in the Director's absence, if assigned.

Develops and writes the System's annual plan, annual report, and other required plans and reports, with input and review by the System Director and MCLS member librarians as appropriate.

Plans, writes, administers, and implements grants and other proposals for the System.

Compiles, maintains, reports, and interprets statistics relevant to the System's service programs.

Prepares and administers the budget for each System service program and the System as a whole, subject to the review of the System Director.

Performs managerial and technical duties related to budgetary control such as authorizing invoices for payment, receiving and allocating revenues, scheduling and preparing for an annual audit, etc.

Negotiates, writes, implements, and monitors agreements with the System's member counties and libraries; the System Resource Library; and other libraries, library systems, and library organizations.

Develops and administers any budget processes necessary to maintain specific agreements.

Supervises and schedules MCLS staff. Evaluates MCLS staff in conjunction with the System Director.

Team interviews and makes hiring recommendations to the System Director. Develops and implements plans for training of MCLS staff, and involves staff from member libraries, as appropriate.

Interprets management decisions, directives, policies and regulations to staff; communicates staff needs and suggestions to the Director.

When necessary, handles progressive discipline of staff through the level of written warnings and makes recommendations for further discipline up to and including firing to the System Director.

Keeps informed on current trends and developments affecting libraries, and disseminates such information to System staff, member libraries, and the System Board.

Serves as a general consultant for member libraries.

Monitors legislative developments affecting libraries, maintains contacts with legislators and officials, and advocates for libraries and library systems.

Organizes and conducts meetings.

Represents MCLS at regional and state meetings relevant to system services and attends other library-related meetings, workshops, in-service programs, etc., as necessary.

Serves as continuing education validator for recertification of public librarians in the System.

Provides public relations for the System.

Confers with the MPL Public Relations Supervisor regarding publicity and public relations.

Encourages the use of system services and resources by other area libraries and the public.

Provides professional back-up to System interlibrary loan staff. Assists with difficult reference questions, verification, etc.

Drives system van, as needed.

Assists with the other work of MCLS and performs work of other MCLS staff, as needed.

May perform work of another member of the MCLS/MPL management team, as assigned.

Serves on the Participants Council of the Manitowoc-Calumet Library Automated Resource Sharing Consortium (LARS). May provide supportive services in assistance to the operation of LARS.

Selects materials purchased by the System. May assist in the selection of materials for Manitowoc Public Library.

Acts as a cooperative member of the MCLS/MPL management team.

Cooperates with MPL Public Services Coordinator in coordinating the public services and collection management efforts of the library and with MPL Automation & Technology Coordinator in collection maintenance, automation efforts, and LARS.

Confers with the MPL Circulation Services Supervisor and MPL Technical Services Department Head about automation and support services; with MPL Information & Adult Services Department Head, and MPL Youth Services Department Head about public service needs and collection management issues; and with MPL Business Office Supervisor about personnel and financial issues.

Deals with problem patrons in the System Resource Library (MPL), particularly those who disrupt normal use or operation of the Library, or attempt to unlawfully remove library materials from premises.

Assists with maintenance of building security.

For example: enforces library policies for patron behavior; responds to alarms; completes Incident

Reports and calls police or other official assistance, when necessary.

Knowledge, Skills, and Abilities

Thorough knowledge of the principles and practices of modern library administration and management as well as current library system/consortium practices, and ability to apply these to library system setting.

Willingness and ability to contribute to and lead on-going development of System-wide philosophy, mission and services, and ability to provide consultation on the development of library philosophy, goals and services.

Thorough knowledge of public library planning practices and their application to system services.

Ability to analyze and evaluate current conditions and make logical evaluations of future needs.

Ability to develop and execute short-range plans.

Ability to synthesize and creatively adapt trends in technology, publishing, information retrieval and library science to planning for the System.

Ability and willingness to assume a leadership role in a group setting.

Ability to establish and maintain effective working relationships with the System Director and Trustees, directors and trustees of other member libraries, MPL Management Team members, other member library staff members, sales representatives, community and state officials, agency representatives, and the public.

Ability to work in the MCLS/MPL/LARS team setting.

Willingness to assist and support coworkers, contribute ideas, and maintain flexibility.

Ability to adapt to a rapidly changing environment.

Ability to make realistic budget proposals, to operate within established budgetary guidelines, and to identify and analyze budgetary impact of services.

Commitment to and skill in supervising people.

Thorough knowledge of supervisory and training techniques.

Willingness and ability to provide a positive managerial example.

Willingness and ability to foster an environment in which employees are self-motivated and can exhibit high morale.

Capacity to recognize and utilize talents of others.

Fairness when distributing workload, responsibility, and authority.

Ability to identify proper work assignments for subordinates and willingness to follow-up to ensure proper completion.

Ability to set realistic standards for employees and to encourage productive and efficient performance.

Conscientiousness when appraising performance, counseling employees, writing and administering performance appraisals, and making personnel recommendations.

Skill in managing departmental workflow, including ability to identify, negotiate, establish, communicate, and apply priorities.

Skill in performing and supervising routine and non-routine procedures involving many steps.

Ability to give and follow complex written and/or verbal instructions and to pay close attention to detail.

Willingness to provide professional and managerial support to the System Director.

Ability to accept delegation and to work under general supervisory direction.

Ability to communicate effectively.

Skill in interpersonal communication and public speaking.

Capacity to be easily understood on voice telephone.

Ability to do technical writing for procedures, proposals, reports, etc.

Ability to interact effectively with the MCLS/MPL/LARS automated systems.

Skill in using microcomputers and related software.

Knowledge of database, spreadsheet and word processing software programs.

Knowledge of or ability to quickly learn current software programs as these apply to job responsibilities.

Knowledge of and ability to use modern library technology. Interest in emerging technologies.

Knowledge of reference practices and collection development tools and theory.

Ability to apply this knowledge as a consultant, as requested by member libraries.

Possession of or ability to obtain a valid Wisconsin driver's license, and good driving record with no accidents or citations for major violations within the last three years, and ability to obtain other appropriate licenses if required.

Willingness, physical capacity and mechanical aptitude to drive a large cargo-type van, truck and/or other System vehicles or personal vehicle in normal Wisconsin weather conditions.

Must comply at all times with the System's "Drug-Free Workplace" policy and be willing to submit to drug and alcohol testing if involved in any traffic accident while operating any System vehicle.

Initiative and resourcefulness to take acceptable risks, make appropriate decisions, and exercise proper authority.

Ability to present clear explanations of established policies and procedures.

Ability to think and act appropriately under pressure.

Willingness and ability to grant logical exceptions to policies and procedures when warranted.

Willingness to maintain confidentiality when appropriate and to be held accountable.

Ability to develop work-related goals and objectives.

Willingness to develop job-related abilities, skills and knowledge.

Willingness and ability to keep abreast of changing technologies and procedures, and to assume responsibilities required by introduction of different services and equipment.

Willingness and ability to understand and support the fundamental principles of library services, such as offering open access to library materials in any format for people of all ages; providing materials representing as many points of view as possible; and protecting a patron's right to privacy in dealings with MCLS and with respect to records maintained by the System.

Work Environment

Usually (up to 100% of work time) works in shared office environment with considerable staff contact, both in person and via phone, fax and email.

Occasionally (up to 10% of work time) has direct contact with the public.

Usually (up to 100% of work time) works in close proximity with terminals and other similar electronic equipment.

Usually (up to 100% of work time) maintains work environment.

For example: vacuuming computer areas, dusting, recycling paper; cleaning up after programs. Infrequently (as situation requires) assists with building emergencies which may involve cleaning up snow, bodily fluids, etc.

Sometimes (up to 25% of work time) lifts and/or transports objects weighing 5 to 35 pounds; pushes or pulls carts loaded with materials weighing more than 150 pounds.

Sometimes (up to 25% of work time) works with equipment and performs procedures where carelessness may result in minor cuts, bruises, or muscle strains.

Occasionally (up to 10% of work time) works in bookstack areas where there is exposure to dust, newsprint, etc.

Occasionally (up to 10% of work time) retrieves and/or shelves objects weighing 5 to 20 pounds from all shelving levels.

Occasionally (up to 10% of work time) works with vehicles and equipment, and performs procedures where carelessness may result in traffic accident and/or cuts, bruises, muscle strains, or other injuries.

Occasionally (up to 10% of work time) drives full-size cargo-type van, truck, and/or other System vehicle up to 120 miles per trip in all types of weather, getting in and out of van at least 20 times per trip.

Education, Experience, and Training

MINIMUM QUALIFICATIONS:

Master's degree in library science from an A.L.A.-accredited school.

Eligibility for Grade 1 Wisconsin Library Certificate.

3 years post-M.L.S. managerial experience in a library system, consortium, or public library setting, 1 year in a supervisory role, and one year in administration; or, equivalent education / experience mix as determined by the System Director.

Demonstrated ability to supervise staff, preferably in a union environment.

Possession of or ability to attain a valid Wisconsin driver's license and good driving record with no accidents or citations for major violations within the last three years, and ability to obtain other appropriate licenses if required.

Ability to maintain a valid Wisconsin driver's license and a good driving record with no accidents or citations for major violations either on or off the job.

Demonstrable possession of knowledge, skills, abilities, and capacities identified in "Job Specifications" section, above.

Capacity to work under conditions described in "Working Conditions" section, above.

Position Hours

Salaried full-time, typically working at least 80 hours per two-week pay period on a flexible schedule which may vary from day to day. May be scheduled to work days, evenings, Saturdays, and Sundays.

7.0 TECHNICIAN

7.1 AUTOMATION AND TECHNOLOGY TECHNICIAN

7.1.1 Automation and Technology Technician

Library Name: Manitowoc-Calumet Library System
Library Location: Manitowoc, Wisconsin
Population Served: 58,213
Number of Volumes: 195,166
Number of Titles: N/A
Number of Periodical Subscriptions: 395

General Summary

JOB OBJECTIVE: Works with the Library's array of PCs. Assists in administration of the integrated library system and LAN/WAN and functions as system administrator in the absence of the A&TS Coordinator. Trains MPL and MCLS staff on use of PC's, software, local area network, email, and Internet access. Routinely scheduled to work in the Circulation Department for an average of twenty hours per week. Provides clerical and semi-professional support to A&TS Coordinator and assumes responsibility for projects, as delegated or assigned. May assist webmaster in maintenance of Website, or act as webmaster in the absence of the PR Supervisor. May train or assist in training of MPL staff, MCLS staff and staff at other LARS libraries on the integrated library system.

Essential Functions and Responsibilities

The following list identifies principal duties and responsibilities of the job. It is not a definitive list and other similar duties may be assigned. An asterisk (*) before any of the following items indicates duties and responsibilities which are not "essential functions" of the job as defined by the Americans with Disabilities Act.

Works with the Library's array of PCs.

For example: Uncrates, sets up, installs, and configures new PCs for use on the local area network; attaches cables and peripherals; installs components, e.g. network interface cards, CD drives, hard drives, DVD drives; partitions hard drives, as specified or necessary; loads operating system and network software and/or updates; downloads and/or loads software; adjusts settings; places icons on desktop; confirms proper functioning; maintains or assists in maintenance of the documentation of the Library's PCs; cleans components; troubleshoots problems with PCs.

Assists in administration of the integrated library system and LAN/WAN and functions as system administrator in the absence of the A&TS Coordinator.

For example: helps to plan, develop, implement and evaluate the Library's program of technology and automation services for the community; establishes new accounts; sets passwords; grants permissions; loads CD-ROMs and other software onto LAN; sets up and runs reports; maintains or assists in maintenance of the documentation of the networks; schedules and runs batch processes; rebuilds indexes; is available on call, and must return to work, if needed, to operate and monitor the Library's automated systems; reboots, backs up, and troubleshoots hardware and software problems; contacts system administrator at ESLS and/or calls for other technical assistance; maintains logs of backups, batch programs and maintenance programs; maintains logs of system problems; assists in the installation of new software releases, new hardware, etc. May be assigned to pull cable, install hubs, etc.

Assists with the planning, development, implementation and evaluation of staff technology training for MPL, MCLS, and other LARS libraries. (MPL refers to the Manitowoc Public Library; MCLS refers to the Manitowoc-Calumet Library System; LARS is an integrated library system shared by the six public libraries in MCLS.) In particular, trains MPL and MCLS staff on use of PC's, software, local area network, email, and Internet access.

For example: develops training modules; maintains checklist of training milestones; works with staff members and supervisors to establish and reach training goals; provides end user support for the integrated library system and LAN/WAN to staff at MPL, MCLS, and other LARS libraries.

Routinely scheduled to work in the Circulation Department for an average of twenty hours per week.

For example: Assists patrons at service desk and over telephone by performing procedures related to circulation of materials. Performs other procedures related to circulation of materials.

Answers central switchboard. Takes messages. Routes patrons and telephone calls to appropriate destinations. Prepares materials for shelving or filing. Sensitizes, inspects, cleans as necessary, and sorts materials onto sorting shelves. May direct routine tasks of Circulation Page.

Provides clerical and semi-professional support to A&TS Coordinator and assumes responsibility for projects, as delegated or assigned.

Performs a variety of clerical tasks.

For example: Maintains inventory of supplies for the computer room and orders new stock as assigned; assists in selection and purchase of computer and other equipment; maintains inventory of computer and technology-related equipment; prepares equipment to be returned.

Deals with problem patrons, particularly those who disrupt normal use or operation of the Library, or attempt to unlawfully remove library materials from premises.

Assists with maintenance of building security.

For example: enforces library policies for patron behavior; responds to alarms; provides policy interpretation for public and staff, particularly Circulation staff, as required or requested; completes Incident Reports and calls police or other official assistance, when necessary.

May assist webmaster in maintenance of Web site, or act as webmaster in the absence of the PR Supervisor.

For example: uploads pages and links; checks for dead links and updates; may develop pages from content developed by the Web Committee.

May train or assist in training of MPL staff, MCLS staff and staff at other LARS libraries on the integrated library system.

Knowledge, Skills, and Abilities

Skill at setting up, configuring, installing and maintaining microcomputer software, hardware and peripherals.

Working knowledge of PCs operating in various Windows environments and skill at maintaining them.

Ability to acquire and demonstrate knowledge of other operating systems or updates of current versions operation systems, as necessary.

Skill at installing, downloading, and configuring network and desktop operating system software as well as software packages and updates, and ability to perform these tasks within a reasonable period of time.

Knowledge of and ability to employ documentation techniques and practices.

Skill at functioning as system administrator with the Library's automated systems.

Minimum skill level: Working knowledge and skill at using administrator modes in various Windows versions at client and server levels, anti-virus, and security software.

Working knowledge of databases and ability to quickly acquire skill in using the administrator mode in the integrated library system.

Working knowledge of query languages and ability to quickly acquire skill to generate customized reports from the integrated library system.

Working knowledge of telnet programs and ability to quickly acquire skill in using Anzio. Working knowledge of on-line scheduling managers and ability to quickly acquire skill in using SAM (Smart Access Manager).

Ability to acquire and demonstrate knowledge of other software packages and operating systems, as necessary.

Working knowledge and skill at using Microsoft and Corel software products.

Ability to acquire and demonstrate working knowledge of other software packages or updates of current versions, as necessary.

Minimum skill level: Ability to generate effective documents using Word and WordPerfect.

Ability to design user-friendly spreadsheets in Excel and Quattro Pro.

Skill at automating word processing operations using macros and programming techniques.

Ability to design effective presentations using PowerPoint.

Ability to implement customized relational database systems using Access.

Ability to use FrontPage as a webmaster and Web page designer.

Initiative and ability to apply problem-solving skills when troubleshooting equipment software or hardware issues.

Skill at providing training and support for end users, particularly newly hired Library staff and those who require refresher training.

Ability to develop user-friendly training modules.

Ability to communicate technical information effectively

Skill in performing routine and non-routine procedures involving many steps.

Ability to follow complex written and/or verbal instructions and to pay close attention to detail.

Ability to work with limited direct supervision.

Ability to provide courteous public service and to present clear explanations of established policies and procedures.

Ability to think and act appropriately under pressure.

Willingness and ability to grant logical exceptions to Library policies and procedures when warranted.

Capacity to be easily understood on voice telephone and public address systems.

Minimum skill level: Demonstrated knowledge of proper telephone etiquette; ability to use public address and phone systems; ability to take messages and identify appropriate destinations.

Ability to interact effectively with the Library's automated system.

Minimum skill level: accurate keyboarding at a minimum of 25 words per minute.

Ability to acquire and demonstrate knowledge of all parts of the circulation module at security level 3.

Skill at accurately and efficiently sorting and shelving materials in alphanumeric order.

Physical capacity to place materials on shelves at all shelving heights.

Must comply at all times with the Library's "Drug-Free Workplace" policy

Ability to work in a team setting.

Willingness to assist and support coworkers, contribute ideas, maintain flexibility, and be able to adapt to a rapidly changing environment.

Ability to develop work-related goals and objectives.

Willingness to develop job-related abilities, skills and knowledge.

Willingness and ability to keep abreast of changing technologies and procedures and to assume responsibilities required by introduction of different services and equipment.

Willingness and ability to understand and support the fundamental principles of library services, such as: open access to library materials for people of all ages; the library's obligation to provide materials representing as many points of view as possible; and a patron's right to privacy in dealings with the library and with respect to records maintained by library.

Physical and Mental Requirements

Physical capacity and skill at installing and maintaining equipment.

Minimum skill level: Physical capacity to lift and maneuver monitors, servers, and other equipment often weighing up to 50 lbs.

Physical capacity to crawl beneath desks and to reach up behind desks to attach cables, plug in computers, etc.

Physical capacity to climb ladders to reach cable raceways in ceiling.

Physical capacity to pull cable.

Manual dexterity to install cable ends, network cards, modems, etc.

Work Environment

Usually (up to 100% of work time) works in environment with considerable contact with other staff members.

Usually (up to 100% of work time) performs routines with many rapid, repeated motions.

Usually (up to 100% of work time) lifts and/or transports objects weighing 40 to 50 pounds.

Usually (up to 100% of work time) works in close proximity with computers and other similar electronic equipment.

Usually (up to 100% of work time) maintains work environment. For example: vacuuming computer areas, dusting, recycling paper.

Often (up to 50% of work time) works with equipment and performs procedures where carelessness may result in minor cuts, bruises, or muscle strains.

Often (up to 50% of work time) works at service counter where seating cannot be provided.

Often (up to 50% of work time) pushes or pulls carts loaded with materials weighing more than 150 pounds.

Sometimes (up to 25% of work time) works in bookstack areas where there is exposure to dust, newsprint, etc.

Education, Experience, and Training

MINIMUM QUALIFICATIONS:

General educational development at a level normally acquired through completion of an associate degree at an accredited technical college as a Microcomputer Specialist, Network Specialist, or similar degree.

3 months previous on the job, volunteer, or life experience in a public services setting.

Demonstrable possession of knowledge, skills, abilities, and capacities identified in "Job Specifications" section, above.

Capacity to work under conditions described in "Working Conditions" section, above.

Position Hours

Full-time, typically working 80 hours per two-week pay period on a flexible schedule which varies from week to week. May be scheduled to work days, evenings, Saturdays, and Sundays.

Disclaimers

Performs Assistant-level work in other departments, as assigned.

7.2 COMPUTER TECHNICIAN

7.2.1 Computer Technician

Library Name: Mount Prospect Public Library
Library Location: Mount Prospect, Illinois
Population Served: 56,265
Number of Volumes: 332,413
Number of Titles: N/A
Number of Periodical Subscriptions: 450

Reports to

SUPERVISION:

Under direct supervision of the Network Manager.

General Summary

JOB OBJECTIVE: The Computer Technician is responsible for installation, preventative maintenance and minor repair of all computers and their peripherals, and miscellaneous office equipment.

In addition, the position performs on-call computer help desk duties for Library staff and patrons involving computer hardware, applications, and office equipment. It requires the ability to access, input and retrieve data from the computer; ability to perform light to medium work; ability to use phone effectively.

Essential Functions and Responsibilities

Assists in diagnosing computer and local area network problems.

Assists with maintaining computer and various office equipment supplies.

Assists with network and Internet maintenance duties.

Generates system reports from the Integrated Library System.

Installs communication and computer cabling including but not limited to

Ethernet cat5 and telephone.

Installs, configures and tests computer software and updates.

Monitors server logs and events.

Performs all necessary housekeeping and updating tasks at the mainframe console.

Performs on-call help desk duties for Library staff and patrons involving computer hardware, applications, and office equipment.

Performs physical maintenance on all computers, keyboards, monitors, disk drives, printers, peripherals, terminals and various office equipment (i.e. copy machines, typewriters, etc.) according to a schedule developed and maintained by the Network Manager.

Performs routine maintenance of computers, terminals, peripherals and upgrades including but not limited to network adapter cards, video cards, disk drives, and various interface cards.

Prepares, delivers and picks up equipment that is sent out of the building for repair.

Provides assistance in use of equipment and software to both patrons and staff.

Remains aware of new technologies which have application to library operation.

Attends appropriate meetings, workshops and seminars.

Serves on committees as assigned.

Other duties as assigned.

Knowledge, Skills, and Abilities

Ability to climb, stoop, kneel, crouch and crawl.

Ability to deal with multiple tasks effectively and efficiently.

Ability to drive Library van, have valid Illinois driver's license.

Ability to follow directions.

Ability to interact with patrons/staff courteously, skillfully and accurately.

Ability to interpret and communicate computer problems.

Ability to lift and handle a minimum of 50 lbs.

Ability to train/assist others in use of equipment/software.

Ability to use phone effectively.

Ability to work as a member of a team.

Ability to work effectively and courteously with staff.

Ability to work independently with little supervision.

Knowledge necessary to be able to provide general preventative maintenance and repair of Library computer equipment and peripherals.

Knowledge of computer networking concepts.

Knowledge of internet and online computer services.

Knowledge of standard office and internet application software.

Knowledge of Windows, and Linux/Unix operating systems.

Skill in working with electrical and mechanical equipment.

Thorough knowledge of personal computer hardware.

Verbal and written communication skills.

Education, Experience, and Training

High school Diploma required.

A minimum of two years experience in computer maintenance.

College/technical training in computer science highly desirable.

7.2.2 Computer Technician

Library Name: Williamsburg Regional Library System
Library Location: Williamsburg, Virginia
Population Served: 60,100
Number of Volumes: 261,243
Number of Titles: N/A
Number of Periodical Subscriptions: 562

Reports to

Under the supervision of the Assistant Library Director, the Automated Systems Specialist

General Summary

JOB OBJECTIVE: Computer Technician is responsible for the installation, troubleshooting, and maintenance of personal computer hardware, software, and peripherals throughout the library system, assisting staff as needed. Assists in purchasing hardware, software, and peripherals. Assists with managing integrated library system (Dynix), and library network. Participates in the analysis and planning of automated services operations within the Support Services department.

Essential Functions and Responsibilities

Sets up and configures PC workstations to meet users' functional specifications.

Installs new PC software and performs PC system upgrades.

Trains library staff on software applications.

Addresses problems with PC hardware and software through the use of troubleshooting techniques.

Makes repairs onsite when possible.

Tracks equipment sent offsite for repairs.

Contributes to library's hardware/software inventories and repair records.

Prioritizes requests for computer assistance and responds accordingly.

Develops and maintains knowledge of the PC industry.

Uses this knowledge to help assess the need for and make recommendations on the purchase, repair, and replacement of library PC hardware, software, and peripherals.

Assists with Dynix and library network support including backups, upgrade installations, troubleshooting, and emergency shutdown.

May participate in library-wide committees or projects.

Performs other duties as assigned by supervisor.

Knowledge, Skills, and Abilities

Proficiency with PC workstation set up and configuration, software and peripheral installation, troubleshooting techniques, and PC repair.

Understanding of library automation desirable, UNIX and Microsoft networking knowledge helpful.

Ability to organize work, set priorities, use time effectively, work independently, and meet deadlines.

Ability to communicate well with supervisor, colleagues, vendors, and the general public.

Ability to analyze and creatively solve problems related to the position.

Ability to work with enthusiasm and initiative.

Work Environment

This job is based at the Williamsburg Library, requiring work at both the Williamsburg and the James City County Libraries.

Administers work typically sitting in an office, in the computer room, and at library computer workstations.

Requires frequent walking, light to medium lifting, working with cabling, and the use of hand tools and some office equipment.

Regular contact is made with vendors, technicians, community groups, employees, and the general public.

Education, Experience, and Training

MINIMUM QUALIFICATIONS:

College degree in the field of computer technology, or equivalent education and experience. Previous library and/or public service experience preferred.

Additional Qualifications

Requires the ability to travel among various library sites.

7.3 HELP DESK TECHNICIAN

7.3.1 Help Desk Technician

Library Name: St. Clair County Library
Library Location: Port Huron, Michigan
Population Served: 160,708
Number of Volumes: 432,880
Number of Titles: 206,173
Periodical Subscriptions: 56

Reports to

SUPERVISION RECEIVED: Reports to Computer Systems Coordinator.

General Summary

General Duties: To perform regular maintenance, troubleshooting and repair of PC's at all locations in the Library system.

Essential Functions and Responsibilities

Typical Work: (An employee in this classification may be called upon to perform the following tasks which are illustrative and not exhaustive in nature.)

Regular maintenance, troubleshooting and repair of PC's at all locations in the Library system.

Setup and installation of computer hardware and software and assisting with software upgrades.

Informal training and support of Library staff in basic computer applications.

Assisting staff with day to day computer questions.

Assisting in the handling of computer crises.

Knowledge, Skills, and Abilities

Knowledge of PC hardware and software installation and troubleshooting, MS-DOS, Windows 3.1 & 95, CD-ROM software, LAN's, Internet & TCP/IP, security software and various other computer applications.

Possess a proactive, public service initiative; strong communication skills and demonstrated aptitude for performing informal training and user support.

Valid driver's license as regular travel is required.

Education, Experience, and Training

High school diploma; some college course work in computer related field desired.

Experience and proven skills in various computer applications.

Disclaimers

Additional duties as required.

V. CHILDREN'S AND YOUTH SERVICES

Included in this section are administrators, supervisors, managers, program coordinators, summer reading assistants, young adult and children's librarians, early childhood specialists. and children's specialists.

1.0 ADMINISTRATOR
1.1 YOUTH AND COMMUNITY ADMINISTRATOR

1.1.1 Youth and Community Administrator

Library Name: Neill Public Library
Library Location: Pullman, Washington
Population Served: 24,675
Number of Volumes: 60,247
Number of Titles: N/A
Number of Periodical Subscriptions: 145

General Summary

JOB OBJECTIVE:

As a Library Division Manager in Community Services or Youth Services, provides professional library work in the development and delivery of quality library programs and collections for all age groups in the community. Performs related duties as assigned.

CLASSIFICATION SUMMARY:

Library Division Managers serve as members of the library's management team. As such, the Division Managers work closely with one another, the Library Director, area supervisors and staff work groups, as well as with the Library Board and local institutions to cooperatively develop library and divisional goals consistent with the overall mission of the Library. Employees in this class analyze and evaluate the needs of the community to provide library services that meet educational, informational and recreational needs. The primary function of the Library Division Manager includes planning and implementing services, managing collections and allocating resources. A position can specialize in youth services or community services. Work is performed independently under the broad direction and guidance of the Library Director, who reviews work for the quality of program implementation, services provided to patrons, and professional library standards.

Essential Functions and Responsibilities

Identifies and analyzes emerging community issues and needs to determine directions for related library services and collections;

Evaluates library services provided by the division and the library as a whole in order to improve services;

Determines the activities required to achieve objectives;

Organizes equipment, facilities and staffing needed to accomplish activities;

Develops annual work plan;

Establishes standards and implements procedures for reference and reader's advisory services and collection development;

Secures and allocates alternative funding sources such as gifts or grants;

May serve as Library Director in the Director's absence.

Supervises division staff;

Plans, develops, and revises procedures for the unit;

Interviews and selects subordinate personnel;

Schedules and assigns activities to staff;

Evaluates staff performance;

Develops and updates training materials and procedures manual;

Provides orientation and work-related instructions;

Resolves personnel issues;

Establishes standards for library services;

Encourages staff development through training, workshops and conferences;

Schedules and conducts staff meetings to provide information and seek input on policies and procedures.

Provides leadership in community partnerships and serves on select committees working to provide optimal library services; collaborates with the school district, area daycare and preschool facilities, libraries, senior centers, Friends of the Library, Board of Trustees, higher education institutions, other City departments and a variety of other service groups and organizations as needs and opportunities arise.

Provides reference and reader advisory services to patrons; assists patrons in identifying and clarifying needs by asking questions in an enthusiastic and helpful manner; uses knowledge of library resources to obtain the appropriate resource which is understandable, useable, and acceptable; listens attentively to the child's expressed subject interests and needs, and selects materials which are appropriate in format and interest..

LIBRARY DIVISION MANAGER 1309

Comprehension level; delivers library services at various locations in the community. Plans, prepares, presents, and evaluates program activities for adult and youth groups; serves as liaison or resource support to others in program presentations; performs program publicity and public relations duties involving scheduling, developing, writing newspaper articles, and involving public presentations.

Selects, reviews, evaluates, replaces, and withdraws print and non-print materials as appropriate to maintain a collection which meets the needs of the community; identifies community needs by listening to problems as well as applying professional expertise; identifies resources available and purchases resources within assigned budget.

Attends work on a regular and dependable basis.

Interacts in a professional and respectful manner with city staff and the public.

Additional Job Duties

Performs other tasks as assigned.

Knowledge, Skills, and Abilities

Knowledge of:

The principles and practices of library and information science in the areas of reference, collection development, information delivery systems, cataloging and adult and youth services;

The techniques used to plan, develop, implement, and evaluate library service programs;

Management theory and supervisory techniques;

Current reference materials and sources available for a small-medium sized public library.

Ability to:

Effectively analyze program services, identify and write objectives, and determine implementation methods and resources;

Assess needs and develop short- and long-range plans for library programs;

Understand and abide by legal parameters in dealing with issues such as censorship, library use policies, fund raising and public relations;

Effectively supervise the work of subordinate staff;

Evaluate adult or youth library needs and to develop programs and collections to meet those needs;

Listen actively and respond sensitively to elicit confidence and trust from those seeking reference/readers' advisory assistance;

Develop, plan, implement and evaluate library projects, programs, services and collections;

Determine budgets and allocate resources;

Deal with the public in a calm, pleasant, and courteous manner;

Communicate effectively and make effective presentations to small and large groups;

Provide quality services in a cost-effective manner and to recommend improved methods of performing the work;

Establish and maintain effective working relationships with the public, library personnel and community organizations;.

Work independently on many tasks at one time;

Maintain flexibility in scheduling;

Represent the library and provide leadership for professional, educational and community organizations;

Physically perform the essential functions of the job.

Tools and Equipment Used

Personal computer, computerized library information systems, multiple online databases and systems, copy machine, telephone, 10-key calculator, VCR, tape player, puppet theater.

Work Environment

(The work environment characteristics described here are representative of those an employee encounters while performing the essential functions of this job. Reasonable accommodations may be made to enable individuals with disabilities to perform the essential functions.)

Work is performed primarily in an office environment while sitting at a desk or computer terminal or while standing at a counter for extended periods of time. However, some travel to a variety of locations to perform work and/or attend meetings is required. Some physical exertion may be required to lift office supplies and library materials from overhead and from the floor. Sufficient vision or other powers of observation are essential to permit the employee to read and sort library materials, and supervise and evaluate the work of subordinate staff.

Education, Experience, and Training

MINIMUM QUALIFICATIONS:

Required to have certification by the State Board for Certification, or the ability to obtain certification at the time of appointment, as required by R.C.W. 27.04.030. Certification may be obtained by 1) having a Masters of Library Science from an ALA accredited school, or 2) passing an examination given by the M.L.S. Three years of progressively responsible experience utilizing independent judgment in one or more of the following areas: collection management, cataloging, reference, supervision and programming for adults or children.

Disclaimers

The duties listed above are intended only as illustrations of the various types of work that may be performed. The omission of specific statements of duties does not exclude them from the position if the work is similar, related or a logical assignment to the position.

The job description does not constitute an employment agreement between the employer and employee and is subject to change by the employer as the needs of the employer and requirements of the job change.

1.2 CHILDREN'S COLLECTIONS AND COMMUNITY PROGRAMS ADMINISTRATOR

> ### 1.2.1 Children's Collections and Community Programs Administrator
>
> **Library Name:** Anacortes Public Library
> **Library Location:** Anacortes, Washington
> **Population Served:** 14,500
> **Number of Volumes:** N/A
> **Number of Titles:** 55,565
> **Number of Periodical Subscriptions:** 126

Reports to

Library Director

General Summary

JOB OBJECTIVE: This is a full-time, exempt professional position responsible for the development of the library's children's collection.. This position also coordinates community programs and is responsible for the technical-service functions of the library.

LEVEL OF AUTHORITY: Performs duties with only general direction and defined latitude for independent action and decisions commensurate with demonstrated ability. Errors in judgment could have substantial impact on library's fiscal condition and the public's acceptance of programs, personnel and facilities.

Essential Functions and Responsibilities

Research and recommend children's Library programs to the Director. Contact various agencies, as necessary and as directed, for assistance in such programs. Assist in the preparation of appropriate supporting materials for financial assistance.

Hire and, in turn, plan, schedule, supervise and evaluate the work of the assistant to the children's librarian and the technical services supervisor.

As directed, review and select books and other informational materials for purchase and distribution in the Library's children's collection. Catalog and classify incoming materials.

Provide reference services as scheduled or as time permits.

Respond to public inquiries in a courteous manner. Provide information within scope of knowledge or refer to other staff as appropriate.

Coordinate programs to stimulate interest in reading for all age groups, including the summer reading program, story times, family literacy programs and adult book clubs.

Write news releases and prepare articles relative to areas of responsibility. Oversee and develop promotional materials for the library.

Serve as liaison with school librarians.

Maintain records and statistics related to the Library's children's collection and patronage.

Prepare and monitor budget for areas of responsibility, generating budget reports and analyses as required.

Serve as systems administrator for Dynix and Local Area Network systems.

Act as Director in his/her absence.

Additional Job Duties

Attend staff and community meetings as required, often outside regular working hours.

Work with technical-service coordinator in reviewing the performance of technical-service clerks and pages.

May perform portions of the work of higher classified positions, as assigned.

May perform portions of the work of lower classified positions, as needed.

Must be able to drive an automobile in the course of Library business

Knowledge, Skills, and Abilities

Attention to detail and accuracy.

Ability to communicate effectively, patiently and courteously with City employees, patrons and other community members.

Ability to handle multiple activities or interruptions at once and to work positively and effectively within a team model.

Must like children and be comfortable working with children both individually and in groups.

Ability to work a schedule including evenings, weekends and mornings.

Ability to supervise staff .

Ability to enforce Library rules.

Physical and Mental Requirements

Strength, for example, to push loaded book cart weighing approximately 300 pounds on level floor and up ramp, to lift or maneuver onto cart loads up to 50 pounds and to carry cartons of books up and down stairs.

Ability to bend, stoop and lift for prolonged periods in cramped spaces.

Stamina, for example, to stand for prolonged periods up to six hours in a shift. High energy to deal with the public for sustained periods while maintaining positive and enthusiastic communication.

Ability to sit and use computer workstation, including keyboard and visual display terminal, for extended periods of time.

Tools and Equipment Used

Audio-visual equipment, such as; cassette recorder, VCR and film and slide projectors; Office equipment, such as; computer, modem, typewriter, adding machine, microfiche reader, paper cutter, fax, copier, telephone and postage meter.

Work Environment

Work is performed primarily in indoor office setting, in community meeting rooms and at the library, in frequently dusty atmosphere with potential exposure to airborne pathogens.

Education, Experience, and Training

Technical

Must have a master's degree in Library or Information Science from an American Library Association-accredited college or university.

Must have previous related experience sufficient to demonstrate thorough competency and extensive knowledge of the principles and practices of Library management.

Must have ability to plan, schedule, supervise and evaluate the work of assigned staff for proficient performance and high morale.

Must be bondable.

Must possess a valid Washington State driver's license.

Must have computer ability to adequately utilize automated library cataloging, circulation and other systems.

Must maintain professional and technical expertise through participation in continuing education.

Disclaimers

OTHER

As an absolute condition of employment, employees are required upon hire to sign a drug-free workplace agreement and an agreement not to use tobacco products of any kind while on the job.

The statements contained in this job description reflect general details as necessary to describe the principal functions of this job, the level of knowledge and skill typically required and the scope of responsibility. It should not be considered an all-inclusive listing of work requirements. Individuals may perform other duties as assigned, including work in other functional areas to cover absences or provide relief, to equalize peak work periods or otherwise to balance the workload.

2.0 LIBRARY ASSISTANT

2.1 CHILDREN'S LIBRARY ASSISTANT

2.1.1 Children's Library Assistant

Library Name: Anacortes Public Library
Library Location: Anacortes, Washington
Population Served: 14,500
Number of Volumes: N/A
Number of Titles: 55,565
Number of Periodical Subscriptions: 126

Reports to

Assistant Director, Children's Collection and Community Programs

General Summary

JOB OBJECTIVE: This position is in the Children's Library. Responsibilities range from routine clerical and customer-service activities to program implementation requiring creativity and strong organizational skills.

LEVEL OF AUTHORITY: Performs routine and repetitive duties independently with only general supervision and according to well-know practices and procedures. Performs relatively more complex assignments and specialized functions under closer supervision. Responsibility for accuracy and courtesy is important due to potential adverse Library patron relationships.

Essential Functions and Responsibilities

Assist the children's librarian, as assigned.

Assist in the development and implementation of children's reading, craft and story time programs.

Coordinate displays for all library display cases.

Respond to public inquiries, including Children's Library reference questions, in a courteous manner; provide information within scope of knowledge and refer to employee of higher classification as appropriate.

Responsible for the general appearance of the Children's Library.

Supervise volunteers and pages working in the Children's Library.

Enforce Library rules.

Produce library promotional materials.

Collection responsibilities, as assigned.

Monitor Library security, safety and health conditions.

Additional Job Duties

May perform portions of the work of higher or lower classified positions, as required.

Must be able to drive in the course of Library business.

Physical and Mental Requirements

Strength, for example, to push loaded book cart weighing approximately 300 pounds on level floor and up ramp, to lift or maneuver onto cart loads up to 50 pounds and to carry cartons of books up and down stairs.

Ability to bend, stoop and lift for prolonged periods in cramped spaces.

Ability to sit and use computer workstation, including keyboard and visual display terminal, for extended periods of time.

Tools and Equipment Used

Office equipment, such as; computer, modem, typewriter, adding machine, microfiche reader, paper cutter, fax, copier, telephone and postage meter. Various tools for book repair and glue guns and lamination equipment.

Work Environment

Work is performed primarily in an indoor office setting, in community meeting rooms and at the library, in frequently dusty atmosphere with potential exposure to airborne pathogens. There may be some work performed out-of-doors or in other community buildings.

Education, Experience, and Training

Technical

Must have a four-year college degree or equivalent experience.

Must have computer ability to adequately utilize automated library cataloging and circulation systems, as well as word processing, data base and spreadsheet programs.

Must have ability to work with numbers accurately and understand verbal and written instructions.

Prior library experience preferred.

Must have excellent verbal and non-verbal communication skills, including the ability to give coherent directions.

Must be bondable.

Additional Qualifications

Attention to detail and accuracy.

Ability to communicate effectively, patiently and courteously with City employees, patrons and other community members.

Ability to handle multiple activities or interruptions at once and to work positively and effectively within a team model.

Must like children and be comfortable working with children individually and in groups.

As an absolute condition of employment, employees are required upon hire to sign a drug-free workplace agreement and an agreement not to use tobacco products of any kind while on the job.

Position Hours

Ability to work weekday, evening, weekend and morning hours.

Disclaimers

The statements contained in this job description reflect general details as necessary to describe the principal functions of this job, the level of knowledge and skill typically required and the scope of responsibility. It should not be considered an all-inclusive listing of work requirements. Individuals may perform other duties as assigned, including work in other functional areas to cover absences or provide relief, to equalize peak work periods or otherwise to balance the workload.

Following an offer of employment, and prior to starting work, individuals may be required to have a pre-employment physical examination by a physician designated by the City of Anacortes. The examination will be paid for the by the City. Satisfactory clearance to perform essential job functions will be required for employment.

2.1.2 Children's Assistant

Library Name: York County Public Library
Library Location: Yorktown, Virginia
Population Served: 57,900
Number of Volumes: 143,353
Number of Titles: 84,290
Number of Periodical Subscriptions: 450

General Summary

JOB OBJECTIVE: Responsible for providing assistance with children's library programs in addition to providing technical and reference assistance to children, parents, teachers, and other patrons. Assists in planning, organizing, and performing scheduled programs and events. Work is performed under regular supervision.

Essential Functions and Responsibilities

Assists in scheduling, planning, and presenting Children's Services programs for pre-school and school-aged library patrons; organizes, schedules and promotes special exhibits and programs.

Assists in planning, publicizing and conducting Summer Reading Program and Pre-school Story Hour Programs and contests such as Battle of the Books.

Provides reference assistance for children, parents, teachers, and patrons; locates materials; suggests resources in other libraries.

Advises patrons concerning choice of books or materials for themselves or for their children.

Attends seminars, conferences, workshops, classes or lectures to enhance and maintain knowledge of trends and developments in library services for pre-school and school-aged children.

Additional Job Duties

Prepares bulletin boards, banners and reading lists.
Conducts library tours.
Performs other related work as required.

Knowledge, Skills, and Abilities

General knowledge of resource and reference materials, particularly those pertaining to children.

General knowledge of children's books and authors.

General knowledge of the Anglo-American Cataloging Rules.

General knowledge of the Dewey Decimal Classification System and Library of Congress subject headings.

Ability to analyze and evaluate work procedures and to exercise appropriate judgement in establishing priorities and work methods.

Ability to communicate effectively.

Ability to deal effectively and courteously with the general public and other employees.

Ability to train others in assigned area.

Ability to use a personal computer with reasonable speed and accuracy.

Physical and Mental Requirements

Must be physically able to operate a variety of machinery and equipment including office equipment such as computers, calculators, copiers, facsimile machines, microfiche machines, etc.

Work involves some lifting of boxes of books and/or periodicals, and pushing, and pulling of a handcart or other type of cart.

Data Conception: Requires the ability to compare and/or judge the readily observable, functional, structural or compositional characteristics (whether similar or divergent from obvious standards) of data, people or things.

Interpersonal Communication: Requires the ability of speaking and/or signaling people to convey or exchange information. Includes receiving instructions, assignments or directions from supervisors, and giving instructions, assignments and directions to employees.

Language Ability: Requires the ability to read a variety of reports, requests, forms, manuals, lists, etc.

Requires the ability to prepare reports, forms, requests, etc., using prescribed formats.

Intelligence: Ability to apply principles of logical or scientific thinking to define problems, collect data, establish facts, and draw valid conclusions; to interpret an extensive variety of technical instructions in mathematical or diagrammatic form; deal with several abstract and concrete variables.

Verbal Aptitude: Requires the ability to record and deliver information, to explain procedures, to follow oral and written instructions. Must be able to communicate effectively and efficiently.

Numerical Aptitude: Requires the ability to utilize mathematical formulas; to add and subtract; multiply and divide; utilize decimals and percentages.

Form/Spatial Aptitude: Requires the ability to inspect items for proper length, width and shape.

Motor Coordination: Requires the ability coordinate hands and eyes rapidly and accurately in using office equipment.

Manual Dexterity: Requires the ability to handle a variety of items such as office equipment. Must have minimal levels of eye/hand/foot coordination.

Physical Communication: Requires the ability to talk and hear.

Education, Experience, and Training

Bachelor's degree in Library Science, or liberal arts, or any equivalent combination of training and experience which provides the required knowledge, skills, and abilities.

2.2 CHILDREN'S SUMMER READING ASSISTANT

2.2.1 Children's Summer Reading Assistant

Library Name: Williamsburg Regional Library System
Library Location: Williamsburg, Virginia
Population Served: 60,100
Number of Volumes: 261,243
Number of Titles: N/A
Number of Periodical Subscriptions: 562

General Summary

JOB OBJECTIVE:

Under the supervision of the Senior Library Services Director (Youth Services), the Summer Reading Assistant does story times and summer reading at both libraries, and occasionally at various recreation sites, at bookmobile sites, and other outreach locations for pre-school to middle school children.

Essential Functions and Responsibilities

Performs all aspects of summer reading, including talking with children, awarding incentives, and maintaining records of progress.

Prepares and performs age-appropriate story times.

Collects, records, and reports appropriate statistics.

Maintains appropriate supplies of summer reading materials.

Assists with other summer programs including the Wheel of Reading Auction.

Assists with general library duties as needed.

Work Environment

Computer, copier, audiovisual equipment, and other office equipment as required.

The job is performed throughout the Williamsburg/James City County area and at the libraries in Williamsburg and James City County.

Frequent walking, light to medium lifting, bending, and other limited physical activities.

Regular contact is made with employees and the general public.

Knowledge, Skills, and Abilities

General knowledge of children's literature.

Ability to use the literature in creative ways for storytime and programs.

Ability to interact and communicate with children, teenagers, and adults in a pleasant and effective manner.

Ability to plan and organize daily work and special projects.

Ability to work independently. Problem-solving skills, and demonstrated creativity, initiative, and enthusiasm.

Education, Experience, and Training

MINIMUM QUALIFICATIONS:

High school diploma or equivalent.

Some college and/or public library experience desirable.

Experience working with children required.

Additional Qualifications

NECESSARY SPECIAL QUALIFICATIONS:

Requires the ability to travel among various library sites.

2.3 YOUTH LIBRARY ASSISTANT

2.3.1 Youth Library Assistant

Library Name: Anacortes Public Library
Library Location: Anacortes, Washington
Population Served: 14,500
Number of Volumes: N/A
Number of Titles: 55,565
Periodical Subscriptions: 126

Reports to

Assistant Director, Children's Collection and Community Programs

General Summary

JOB OBJECTIVE:

This position is in the Children's Library. Responsibilities range from routine clerical and customer-service activities to program implementation requiring creativity and strong organizational skills.

LEVEL OF AUTHORITY: Performs routine and repetitive duties independently with only general supervision and according to well-know practices and procedures. Performs relatively more complex assignments and specialized functions under closer supervision. Responsibility for accuracy and courtesy is important due to potential adverse Library patron relationships.

Essential Functions and Responsibilities

Assist the children's librarian, as assigned.

Assist in the development and implementation of children's reading, craft and story time programs.

Coordinate displays for all library display cases.

Respond to public inquiries, including Children's Library reference questions, in a courteous manner; provide information within scope of knowledge and refer to employee of higher classification as appropriate.

Responsible for the general appearance of the Children's Library.

Supervise volunteers and pages working in the Children's Library.

Enforce Library rules.

Produce library promotional materials.

Collection responsibilities, as assigned.

Monitor Library security, safety and health conditions.

Additional Job Duties

May perform portions of the work of higher or lower classified positions, as required.

Must be able to drive in the course of Library business.

Knowledge, Skills, and Abilities

Attention to detail and accuracy.

Ability to communicate effectively, patiently and courteously with City employees, patrons and other community members.

Ability to handle multiple activities or interruptions at once and to work positively and effectively within a team model.

Must like children and be comfortable working with children individually and in groups.

Ability to work weekday, evening, weekend and morning hours.

Physical and Mental Requirements

Strength, for example, to push loaded book cart weighing approximately 300 pounds on level floor and up ramp, to lift or maneuver onto cart loads up to 50 pounds and to carry cartons of books up and down stairs.

Ability to bend, stoop and lift for prolonged periods in cramped spaces.

Ability to sit and use computer workstation, including keyboard and visual display terminal, for extended periods of time.

Tools and Equipment Used

Use of Tools and Equipment

Office equipment, such as; computer, modem, typewriter, adding machine, microfiche reader, paper cutter, fax, copier, telephone and postage meter. Various tools for book repair and glue guns and lamination equipment.

Work Environment

Work is performed primarily in an indoor office setting, in community meeting rooms and at the library, in frequently dusty atmosphere with potential exposure to airborne pathogens. There may be some work performed out-of-doors or in other community buildings.

Education, Experience, and Training

QUALIFICATIONS

Technical

Must have a four-year college degree or equivalent experience.

Must have computer ability to adequately utilize automated library cataloging and circulation systems, as well as word processing, data base and spreadsheet programs.

Must have ability to work with numbers accurately and understand verbal and written instructions.

Prior library experience preferred.

Must have excellent verbal and non-verbal communication skills, including the ability to give coherent directions.

Must be bondable.

Additional Qualifications

OTHER

As an absolute condition of employment, employees are required upon hire to sign a drug-free workplace agreement and an agreement not to use tobacco products of any kind while on the job.

The statements contained in this job description reflect general details as necessary to describe the principal functions of this job, the level of knowledge and skill typically required and the scope of responsibility. It should not be considered an all-inclusive listing of work requirements. Individuals may perform other duties as assigned, including work in other functional areas to cover absences or provide relief, to equalize peak work periods or otherwise to balance the workload.

2.4 YOUNG ADULT LIBRARY ASSISTANT

2.4.1 Young Adult Library Assistant

Library Name: Albany County Public Library
Library Location: Laramie, Wyoming
Population Served: 31,000
Number of Volumes: 117,749
Number of Titles: N/A
Number of Periodical Subscriptions: 214

General Summary

JOB OBJECTIVE: The Young Adult Assistant is responsible for selection, outreach, and programming for young adults.

DISTINGUISHING FEATURES OF THE POSITION: Coordinates young adult collection development and programming. Reports to the Adult Services Librarian.

Essential Functions and Responsibilities

Develops, selects, and maintains the young adult collection, including books and nonprint media and periodicals for circulation and reference

Plans and conducts young adult programming, with the help of the Teen Advisory Board where appropriate, such as book clubs, displays, summer reading and special events such as poetry slams, parties, etc. Coordinates YA programming and helpers with the children's department.

Consults with branch librarians and local teachers on young adult collection development and programming.

Maintains young adult portion of the library's web site. Creates public relations materialssuch as flyers, reminder mailings (and phone calls), "Ask a Librarian" column, and produces monthly report. Writes and maintains bibliographies on a variety of topics.

Participates on library committees, attends continuing education training, and keeps up with literature on young adults in the library.

Responsible for maintaining appropriate library atmosphere and encouraging young adult participation in library activities

Additional Job Duties

Knows and follows library policy and procedures and can operate technology/software, pointing out problem areas and suggesting improvements.

Turns time sheets in on time.

Keeps work and break area clean.

Knows and follows safety procedures, pointing out problems and keeping equipment in satisfactory condition.

Keeps informed on library issues: attends at least one or more continuing education sessions per year, in addition to staff meetings, reading and initialing the log, and reading e-mail.

Works well with others, including public, volunteers, and fellow staff: is flexible, has a good sense of humor about the irritations of daily work life, and respects the feelings and needs of co-workers.

Is sensitive to patron privacy and intellectual freedom issues.

Is committed to public service values: is patient and helpful with all patrons and staff; seeks appropriate referrals (in-house or outside) and does not value library rules above patron satisfaction.

Understands that change and evolving procedures are constants in library work.

Knowledge, Skills, and Abilities

Good communication skills. At least one year of library experience or work in education, with corresponding skills with software, databases, etc. Experience with and genuine enjoyment

of working with young adults. A strong sense of humor, high energy level, flexibility, persistence, and understanding of teens' irregular attendance or response. Willingness to read young ad literature on a regular basis.

Education, Experience, and Training

Class work in collection development or child development. Preference given to applicants with demonstrated ability to work with young adults in a library, school, or social service setting. Working knowledge of the Internet, current Microsoft Office programs, and office equipment (projectors, printers, copiers, fax machines, microform readers).

3.0 ASSOCIATE

3.1 ASSOCIATE CHILDREN'S

3.1.1 Children's Associate

Library Name: Cecil County Public Library
Library Location: Elkton, Maryland
Population Served: 80,600
Number of Volumes: 224,182
Number of Titles: 94,293
Number of Periodical Subscriptions: 201

Reports to

Reports to Children's Librarian

General Summary

Under direct supervision of the children's librarian provides information services and reader's advisory to children; develops and conducts library and reading related programs for children.

Essential Functions and Responsibilities

Provides reader guidance and homework help for children.

Manages one or more projects in Children's Department.

Helps plan and conducts story times for babies, toddlers and preschoolers.

Helps plan and conducts programming for school age children.

Helps plan and conducts craft programs.

Circulates materials and registers borrowers.

Monitors and maintains collections.

Markets materials and services. Merchandises collections.

Helps children and parents use computers and technology.

May lead book discussions, conduct book-talks, prepare age related booklists and brochures or conduct other creative programs designed to encourage reading.

Maintains accurate circulation, attendance and patron statistics.

Performs ongoing assignments of moderate to high difficulty.

Additional Job Duties

Maintains positive relations with the public and staff.

Promotes and maintains high standard of customer service.

Performs job in keeping with the policies and procedures of the Cecil County Public Library.

Tools and Equipment Used

Desktop computer system, laptop computer and projection equipment, library computer system, copy machine.

Work Environment

Works in normal heat and light conditions, with exposure to seasonal conditions.

Travels to outreach locations on a rotating basis.

Some stress from public contact.

Education, Experience, and Training

Baccalaureate degree from an accredited college.

Within two years of appointment, each Library Associate II shall have successfully completed Library Associates' in service training or six credit hours of formal academic coursework in library science. Such training may have been received prior to the date of appointment. Training provided by CCPL on and off-site in Maryland.

Excellent written and verbal communication skills.

Excellent customer service skills.

Previous experience working with children, babies through age 12.

Good knowledge of personal computers and the Internet and willingness and ability to acquire knowledge of advanced library computer applications.

Ability of analyze and perform and/or manage a wide variety of library projects.

Ability to reach, bend, and lift up to 20 lbs.

Ability to push/pull library book carts.

Additional Qualifications

Knowledge of literature for children.

Knowledge of child development and reading readiness.

Experience working in the public library.

License and Certification Requirements

Valid driver's license and good driving record.

Position Hours

19 hours per week. Includes one regular evening and every other Saturday.

Disclaimers

Performs other job related tasks as needed.

May substitute in Outreach Services

NOTE: Certain conditions, e.g. economic constraints, staffing patterns, may necessitate change in job description.

4.0 CLERK

4.1 YOUTH CLERK

4.1.1 Youth Clerk

Library Name: Westminster Public Library
Library Location: Westminster, Colorado
Population Served: 103,000
Volumes: 221,000
Titles: N/A
Periodical Subscriptions: 300

General Summary

JOB OBJECTIVE:

This is paraprofessional library work assisting the Youth Services Coordinator in the operation of the Youth Services area, assisting with services and programs for children and young adults, performing technical and complex library duties, and reporting to the Youth Services Coordinator. Some evenings and weekends required.

Essential Functions and Responsibilities

Provides assistance to library patrons at the Children's Services Desk. Plans, organizes, publicizes, and presents story time for the Westminster Public Libraries. Gives tours of library facilities and provides programs, readers' advisory/reference services and library instruction for classes or groups of children visiting the library and outreach programs for various Westminster community groups and organizations. Supervises volunteers working in the Youth Services area when the Youth Service librarians are not available. Assists the Youth Services Coordinator and librarians in providing readers' advisory and reference service. Participates in planning/implementation of the annual Summer Reading Program and other special community programs. May assist the Youth Services Coordinator and librarians in weeding, mending, and ordering of books and materials.

Additional Job Duties

Prepares bulletin boards, book displays and provides clerical assistance in the preparation of bibliographies and reports. Performs other duties as assigned.

Knowledge, Skills, and Abilities

Basic knowledge of books and authors.

Ability to plan, organize, publicize and present a story time, give tours and provide special programs for children.

Ability to assist patrons in finding materials and resources in the library.

Knowledge of the Dewey Decimal system.

Knowledge of basic library procedures, methods and techniques. Ability to effectively and courteously work with the public, supervisors, and coworkers.

Good oral and written communication skills. Ability to interpret manuals and written instructions.

Physical and Mental Requirements

This position involves bending, stooping, reaching, standing, walking and sitting. Must be able to prepare detailed arts and crafts materials for programs and library displays. Must be able to reach high and low shelves to retrieve books and other materials and equipment. Must be able to climb stairs and drive an automobile. Must be able to transport boxes of books and materials, audiovisual and other equipment to various locations.

Tools and Equipment Used

MATERIAL AND EQUIPMENT DIRECTLY USED

This position requires the use of telephone, computer terminals, photocopiers, FAX machines and various electronic and audiovisual equipment such as slide, overhead, video projectors, cassette and CD players. Regular use of personal transportation to the library's various facilities and other locations in the provision of library services and programs.

Education, Experience, and Training

High school diploma required. Graduation from a four-year college or university preferred. Experience working with children in a day care, preschool, elementary school or Children's Department of a public or school library preferred. Experience in adult reference service or general library experience preferred. Advancement to the Library Associate II level requires a minimum of three years experience as a Library Associate I and demonstrated proficiency in all duties and responsibilities of the Library Associate I classification. Employees at the Library Associate II level must also demonstrate the following skills and abilities: demonstrated ability to supervise Youth Services in the absence of a library Supervisor: experience in development of policies and procedures; ability to work independently; working knowledge of children's and young adult literature and experience in planning and executing programs for children and young adults.

Additional Qualifications

Successful candidates will be required to complete a pre-placement physical and a substance screen prior to employment. Background investigations may be done prior to employment.

5.0 COORDINATOR

5.1 PROGRAM COORDINATOR

5.1.1 Program Coordinator

Library Name: Santa Clara City Library
Library Location: Santa Clara, California
Population Serve: 104,301
Number of Volumes: N/A
Number of Titles: 307,803
Periodical Subscriptions: 739

Reports to

Supervision Received

Works under the general direction of the Library Division Manager.

General Summary

Distinguishing Characteristics

The library program coordinator is a professional position in the classified service responsible for a specialized program area, coordinating staff activities, collections, or computer services, assigning, reviewing, and supervising the work of library staff, and is part of the Library Program Coordinators' Team. Specific knowledge of a program area is required.

Essential Functions and Responsibilities

Typical Duties

Under general direction coordinates and schedules work of children's services staff; coordinates unit projects.

Supervises provision of a full range of reference and information services to children, young adults, their teachers and families, both in person and by telephone using a full range of print, online, and electronic resources.

Responsible for services for children and young adults and their families and teachers; participates actively and personally in story hour and school visits.

Plans, develops, coordinates, and evaluates the activities of a library program unit; coordinates activities of program unit with other divisions in the library.

Participates in the development and implementation of written library and program unit goals and objectives, budgets, policies and procedures, and interprets them to the staff and public.

Participates in the development of individual and program unit work plans.

Analyzes library operational procedures related to activities of a program unit and makes recommendations for improvements

Responds to community information needs.

Participates in the selection of personnel.

Schedules, trains, supervises, and evaluates staff assigned to the program unit.

Assigns work activities, projects, and programs, and monitors work flow.

Fosters an environment of teamwork within the division and throughout the library.

Oversees tasks performed by the team; ensures consistency of service standards.

Resolves conflict among team members.

Assists in setting individual and team goals.

Works with employees to improve performance.

Participates in budget preparation and administration.

Prepares cost estimates for budget recommendations.

Submits justifications for budget items, monitors and controls expenditures.

Coordinates with other library staff to plan for the best use of resources.

Maintains records and prepares reports, computer data, special studies and correspondence as directed.

Performs professional library duties including reference and reader's advisory, cataloging, collection development, and programming for library patrons of all ages.

Responsible for selection and deselection of materials in juvenile collections.

Prepares publicity, displays, and bibliographies.

Serves as a member of the Division and Library Program Coordinators' teams; represents the library with groups, organizations, committees, and at professional meetings and workshops.

Plans and conducts regular staff and/or committee meetings; and performs other, related duties as assigned.

Knowledge, Skills, and Abilities

Knowledge of:

Current practices of children's and young adult library service; children's and young adult literature and materials;

Storytelling, book talking, and other public performance techniques;

Childhood development and learning stages.

Community information and recreation needs for library materials.

Public library principles, organization, objectives, trends, materials, services, and practices.

Role of computerized bibliographic databases and searching techniques, online public access catalogs, and integrated library systems.

Reference interviewing techniques, strategy, and tools; adult, children's and young adult literature and materials.

Principles of selection, deselection, and evaluation of library collections.

Principles and practices of team building and principles and practices of participative management.

Ability to:

Develop and apply library procedures and policies and other professional knowledge to the practical problems of the job.

Establish and maintain courteous and effective working relationships.

Analyze and respond to community interests and concerns regarding library collections and services.

Prioritize work and exercise independent, sound judgment particularly in stressful situations.

Communicate clearly, both orally and in writing.

Plan, organize, and supervise the work of professional, paraprofessional, page, and volunteer staff; assign, train, and evaluate the work of professional, paraprofessional, page and volunteer staff; exercise leadership.

Listen

Understand budgeting procedures, accounting practices, and computerized financial systems; plan and create library programming and promotional materials.

Use computer applications in a library setting.

Foster an environment of cooperation and shared responsibility.

Physical and Mental Requirements

Other Requirements

Performs physical tasks, such as lifting and moving library materials and equipment weighing up to 10 lbs., stooping, reaching, kneeling, and walking up and down stairs. Must be able to perform all the essential functions of the job assignment.

Supervisory Responsibilities

Supervision Exercised

Coordinates, evaluates, and supervises the work of professional, paraprofessional, clerical, page, or volunteer staff as assigned. May act as Library Division Manager in his/her absence.

Education, Experience, and Training

Possession of a Masters Degree in Library/Information Science from an American Library Association accredited library school, plus three years of increasingly responsible professional library experience.

Knowledge of literature for children and young adults is required.

Successful professional library experience serving children, young adults, and families, including materials selection, reference and reader's advisory, planning and producing programs, and publicity materials, is required.

Experience scheduling staff, coordinating the work of others, and management of a significant project is desirable.

Supervisory experience of professional, paraprofessional, page, or volunteer staff is desirable.

License and Certification Requirements

Possession of an appropriate, valid California driver's license is required.

Position Hours

Special Conditions
May be required to work evenings and weekends.

6.0 LIBRARIAN

6.1 CHILDREN'S LIBRARIAN

6.1.1 Children's Librarian

Library Name: Newport Beach Public Library
Library Location: Newport Beach, California
Population Served: 70,100
Number of Volumes: 374,361
Number of Titles: 280,758
Number of Periodical Subscriptions: 905

General Summary

JOB OBJECTIVE:

This is a full time professional position located in the Newport Beach Public Library which was named in American Libraries as among the best libraries in America. The library has a strong commitment to youth services. The library is looking for a creative, energetic individual to work with staff to enhance already excellent children's services through planning, conducting and advocating services that meet the needs of the children in the community. In addition, this position will be asked to support the delivery of young adult and reference services and to participate in the selection and acquisition of library materials for children.

Essential Functions and Responsibilities

The appointee must be able to perform essential job functions, with or without reasonable accommodation, which include but are not limited to: interpret and apply general Library policies and procedures for patrons and staff; advise children in locating and choosing appropriate materials; advise children and teachers in choosing materials for children of all ages; develop and implement a variety of library-related educational programs and activities for children including story hour, library tours, and instructional classes in library use; prepare reading lists and bibliographies; develop and prepare promotional materials and publicity for the Children's section; make school visits to promote library; select and deliver materials for school loans; access and retrieve information for Library patrons and staff as requested; research and respond to difficult or technical reference questions; refer questions as appropriate; advise and assist Library patrons in the use of Library services and tools; participate in the acquisition, retention, discarding or special handling of Library materials; participate in the preparation and presentation of, and attend workshops and training for staff develop-

ment; direct and train assigned staff; process interbranch and interlibrary loans; receive and process reserve requests; search owned materials; notify patrons when materials are available; perform related duties as assigned.

Knowledge, Skills, and Abilities

Knowledge of:

Principles and practices of professional library work including methods, practices and techniques of library reference, technical services or children's services; general reference methods, techniques and sources used in library work; principles, techniques and procedures in cataloging, indexing, classifying & organizing library materials; principles and techniques used in bibliographic research; record keeping and reporting procedures; and library materials selection standards.

Ability to:

Interpret reference sources and methods; compile and classify informational material; apply City Library materials selection standards and policies, develop and implement library programs and services for children, families, and school personnel; perform technical and complex professional library tasks; plan and conduct the activities and operations of a specialized library function; direct and train assigned staff; and lift up to 20 pounds.

Education, Experience, and Training

MINIMUM JOB QUALIFICATIONS

Experience: Some library experience is highly desirable.

Education: Possession of a Master of Library Science degree from an ALA accredited college or university.

License and Certificate: Possession of, or ability to obtain a valid California Class "C" driver's license.

6.1.2 Children's Librarian

Library Name: Needham Free Public Library
Library Location: Town of Needham, Massachusetts
Population Served: 28,949
Number of Volumes: 135,436
Number of Titles: N/A
Number of Periodical Subscriptions: 268

General Summary

JOB OBJECTIVE:

Under general supervision of the Children's Librarian, performs circulation, reference and technical services functions and assists in cataloging activities in support of the Children's Room of the library; and in the absence of the Children's Librarian, provides operational guidance for the Children's Room, assigned staff and volunteers.

Essential Functions and Responsibilities

Interacts with Children's Room patrons, answers phones, assists patrons and callers with routing questions and directs them to appropriate areas or staff. Explains routine library policies.

Processes Children's Room withdrawals, renewals, returns, overdue notices, reserves and registrations, utilizing inter-library network computerized circulation system. Checks availability of items on computer; may assist in physically locating the item for the patron and/or placing it on hold for later pick-up. Calculates bills and collects fines for overdue, lost, or damaged materials. Opens and closes Children's Room circulation desk.

Provides assistance to Children's Room patrons. Identifies location of materials in the Children's Room; in the absence of the Children's Room Librarian, searches for information and responds to basic reference questions using print and electronic sources; and assists in the selection of reading or other materials that meet children's needs; and instructs in the use of library technology and equipment; processes interlibrary loan requests.

Provides assistance in cataloging activities related to Children's Room materials. Searches database for correct item record and matches shelf list information to record; enters related data (codes, circulation status, shelf list information, volume number, item notes when applicable, etc.)

Edits pre-existing item records when needed.

Performs technical services functions related to Children's Room materials. Types shelf list cards and pockets; labels book spines and other materials; stamps and pastes pockets; plasti-coats paperback covers; repairs books and other collection materials, etc.

Monitors and maintains orderliness of Children's Room shelves and other collection materials; collects and moves books and other materials as required. Assists in weeding activities, removing materials for potential discard, subject to final determination by the Children's Librarian.

Assists in supervision of Children's Room operations to ensure reasonable quiet, orderliness and patron compliance with Library policies.

Additional Job Duties

Prepares and conducts Children's Room story hours and craft programs for various age ranges, utilizing a variety of approaches (books, puppets, songs, etc.)

Produces brochures and bookmarks for promotion of library events.

Provides typing and other clerical assistance for the Children's Room, utilizing word processing skills.

Compiles department statistics.

Knowledge, Skills, and Abilities

MINIMUM QUALIFICATIONS

Knowledge of library and Children's Room operations, policies and procedures.

Knowledge of current library technology, its application within a regional library network, and adaptability to its frequent change.

Ability to communicate effectively to establish positive public relations for the Town, department and/or division; and to interact effectively with a wide variety of people.

Ability to fairly and tactfully enforce library and Children's Room policies with patrons as required.

Education, Experience, and Training

Duties require knowledge or computerized circulation systems, basic print and electronic reference materials, and children's literature equivalent to two years of college, plus 2-3 years of experience in general and children's library operations.

Supervisory Responsibilities

Provides guidance to Children's Room operations, staff and volunteers in the absence of the Children's Librarian.

Physical and Mental Requirements

Substantial periods of standing.

Substantial lifting of books and related library materials; some lifting of young children.

Regularly uses computer keyboards requiring eye-hand coordination and finger dexterity.

Work subject to regular interruptions, noise from children's activities, and odors associated with young children, drafts, fumes, and wide temperature variations.

6.2 CHILDREN'S LIBRARIAN, BRANCH SUPERVISOR

6.2.1 Children's Librarian, Branch Supervisor

Library Name: Public Library of Cincinnati and Hamilton County
Library Location: Cincinnati, Ohio
Population Served: 840,443
Number of Volumes: 4,799,527
Number of Titles: 1,239,511
Number of Periodical Subscriptions: 6782

Reports to

Branch Manager

General Summary

JOB OBJECTIVE:

Creates, implements, and presents agency and community programs for children ages 1-12 years of age and child related programs for parents, caregivers and teachers. Provides reference and reader's advisory services and interprets the Library's policies and procedures. Develops and maintains a reference and circulating collection for juvenile patrons.

Responsibilities (not all-inclusive) all of the duties listed below are essential job functions for which reasonable accommodations will be made. All job requirements listed indicate the minimum level knowledge, skills and/or ability deemed necessary to perform the job proficiently. This job description is not to be construed as an exhaustive statement of duties, responsibilities or requirements. Employees may be required to perform any other job-related instructions as requested by their supervisor subject to reasonable accommodations.

Essential Functions and Responsibilities

Plans and conducts programs for children to encourage reading, viewing, and listening of library materials in an effort to create lifelong readers.

Evaluates and selects materials of interest to children for purchase be the Branch.

Performs reference and reader's advisory services in person, by telephone and by e-mail, using materials in a variety of formats.

Provides service to the community and schools through programming, teacher collection services, and other Library services.

Supervises the operation of the Branch in the absence of the Branch Manager.

Interprets the Library's policies and procedures to the public in a customer friendly manner.

Maintains knowledge of circulation system in order to assist at circulation desk.

Uses computers and the Internet effectively for providing Library service.

Identifies reading trends among juvenile patrons.

Creates displays to enhance the Library collection and to promote reading.

Attends workshops, conferences, and meetings and reads professional literature to stay current in the field.

Serves on committees, as requested, to enhance the profession.

Assists patrons in the use of online catalog and other electronic tools.

Compiles bibliographies and develops library user guides.

Participates in the Branch routines including, but not limited to, desk set up, shelf reading, banking and filling interagency requests.

Additional Job Duties

Specific Requirements:

Demonstrates creativity through a variety of programs and storytelling techniques.

Establishes and maintains an effective working relationship with persons of all ages.

Is self-motivated.

Provides good customer service.

Is able to train, direct and supervise staff.

Maintains composure while handling a variety of duties, deadlines, and complaints from the public.

Knows reference sources in a variety of formats.

Skilled in the use of computers and search techniques.

Demonstrates problem-solving and decision-making techniques. Computer literacy.

Must be able to read, write, speak and understand the English language.

Valid driver's license.

Must be able to effectively communicate with the public.

Must be able to communicate clearly and concisely, orally and in writing, including formal communications and making presentations.

Must possess the ability to make independent decisions when circumstances warrant.

Must be able to operate office equipment including information management tools (Windows applications, database, etc.).

Must possess the ability to deal tactfully with personnel, visitors, government agencies/personnel, and the general public.

Must possess ability and willingness to work harmoniously with other personnel.

Must be willing to seek out new methods and principles and be willing to incorporate them into existing practices.

Must have patience, tact, a cheerful disposition and enthusiasm as well as the willingness to handle difficult staff and situations.

Must not pose a direct threat to the health or safety of other individuals in the workplace.

Physical And Sensory Requirements (with or without the aid of mechanical devices):

Must be able to move intermittently throughout the workday.

Must be able to cope with the mental and emotional stress of the position.

Must be able to see and hear, or use prosthetics that will enable these senses to function adequately to assure that the requirements of this position can be fully met.

Must function independently and have flexibility, personal integrity, and the ability to work effectively with personnel, visitors, government agencies, and general public, etc.

Attends and participates in continuing educational programs designed to keep you abreast of changes in your profession.

Position may require out of town travel.

Knowledge, Skills, and Abilities

Minimum Qualifications:

Knowledge of the basic elements of library administration and the ability to apply such knowledge to work performed.

Knowledge of the Library's policies and procedures.

Analytical abilities sufficient to perform reference searches quickly and accurately with material at the appropriate age level.

Independent judgment in order to set priorities and work independently.

Interpersonal skills to deal effectively with the public and staff.

Effective verbal and written communication skills.

Manual dexterity to operate office equipment.

Concentrates on a task despite frequent distractions.

Physical and Mental Requirements

Must meet the general health requirements set forth by the policies of the Public Library, which may include a physical examination.

Must be able to push, pull, move and/or lift a minimum of 15 lbs. to a minimum height of 2 feet and be able to push, pull, move and/or carry such weight a minimum of 5 feet.

Acknowledgment

Work Environment

Works in assigned area, including office areas, training rooms, library, etc., as necessary.

Moves intermittently during working hours.

Is subject to frequent interruptions.

Supervisory Responsibilities

Entire Branch Staff

Education, Experience, and Training

Minimum Qualifications:

Master's Degree in Library Science from an ALA-accredited library school.

Experience working with children

Strong background in children's literature and knowledge of children's behaviors

Position Hours

Must be able to work evenings and weekends

Is subject to work beyond normal working hours, evenings, weekends and holidays when necessary.

Works flexible hours.

6.3 CHILDREN'S SERVICES MANAGER

6.3.1 Children's Services Manager

Library Name: Cuyahoga County Public Library

Library Location: Parma, Ohio

Population Served: 607,909

Number of Volumes: 3,297,420

Number of Titles: N/A

Number of Periodical Subscriptions: 8,502

General Summary

Under general direction, coordinates and directs programs of service to children and provides support to those working with children; develops and proposes service programming, policies and procedures; monitors the quality and effectiveness of existing programs and practices; and maintains close contact with all CCPL leadership involved with children's collections and services to ensure administration of quality service.

Essential Functions and Responsibilities

A. Complies with work scheduling and attendance requirements according to reasonable policy and practices. Staffing for branch and regional libraries and some Administration (ADM) departments requires rotational scheduling, which includes evening and weekend (Saturday and Sunday) hours. Most ADM departments are weekday operations.

B. Consistently presents Cuyahoga County Public Library and its services in a positive manner and adheres to customer service guidelines and procedures as established by the Library.

C. Complies with the established rules of operation, procedures, and policies when using library computers, peripheral hardware, and software. Individual passwords and any other confidential information regarding library records shall be kept confidential.

Provides advisement, general information, support, training and development to branch/regional managers and Children's Staff.

Develops and proposes departmental programming including collections development, policies and procedures for effectively administering children's services, materials selection, special events, etc.

Prepares related progress reports and submits recommendations to supervisor for new and revised programming.

Performs necessary functions to ensure the quality and effectiveness of children's services to the public.

Ensures established program and policy guidelines are maintained by departmental personnel.

Monitors and evaluates work performance as directed by supervisor and provides adequate training and development for Branch/Regional Managers, Children's Librarians and staff as delegated.

Monitors effectiveness of departmental services such as materials examination meetings, central selection of materials, Project LEAP, the Puppet Center, etc.

Consults with Regional Children's Services Managers, Children's Librarians, their Managers and ADM Directors and Managers to ensure administration of quality service to the public.

Prepares, implements and monitors Children's Services Department budget.

Completes various reports, documentation and records related to departmental operations including payroll and personnel records, grant proposals and related documents.

Participates in professional organizations at the national level.

Knowledge, Skills, and Abilities

Thorough knowledge of principles, theories and concepts of library science.

Comprehensive knowledge of children's services program development and implementation including materials selection, collection development and public needs.

Knowledge of CCPL policies and procedures particularly those applying to child services.

Basic knowledge of contemporary concepts and practices of library administration.

Excellent supervisory skills including ability to monitor and evaluate job performance and provide training and development to staff.

Strong communication, interpersonal and public speaking skills.

Strong analytical and problem solving skills.

Ability to analyze, prepare and monitor budget data.

Computer literate with ability to utilize library software systems and equipment.

Summary Minimum Education & Experience Required

Work Environment

PHYSICAL DEMANDS AND WORKING CONDITIONS

Occasional exposure to minor discomforts of outside weather conditions when traveling between various branches of CCPL.

Supervisory Responsibilities

Positions Supervised: Children's Services Assistant Manager, Early Childhood Specialist, Puppeteer, Children's Services Lead Clerk, Children's Services Clerk

Education, Experience, and Training

Master's degree in Library Science.

Four to six years of professional library experience including a background in children's services and three years of supervisory experience.

License and Certification Requirements

License

Requires a valid State driver's license and own vehicle preferred, for visiting branches and area functions.

A criminal background check is required.

Disclaimers

The intent of this position description is to provide a representative summary of the major duties and responsibilities performed by incumbents of this job. Incumbents may be requested to perform job-related tasks other than those specifically presented in this description.

6.3.2 Children's Services Manager

Library Name: Woodland Public Library
Library Location: Woodland, California
Population Served: 46,300
Number of Volumes: 95,372
Number of Titles: N/A
Number of Periodical Subscriptions: 237

Reports to

SUPERVISION RECEIVED AND EXERCISED

Direction is provided by the Library Services Director; responsibilities may include functional supervision over lower level library personnel.

General Summary

To perform a variety of professional librarian duties related to children's services at the Woodland Public Library; to plan, organize and direct children's programs; and to oversee activities in the children's section of the library.

DISTINGUISHING CHARACTERISTICS

This is a journey level class in the professional library services class series. The position specializes in children's services, develops programs and makes policies for children's library services, and has substantial contact with schools, parents, and other community groups concerned with these services.

Essential Functions and Responsibilities

The following are typical illustrations of duties encompassed by the job class, not an all inclusive or limiting list:

Oversee Young People's Library; maintain books and materials, displays, and bulletin boards; supervise children.

Plan, organize and present children's programs including storytelling, book readings, film showings, crafts, and puppet shows.

Select materials for the Young People's Library; order books, paperbacks, and periodicals; screen material coming into library; select toys for library.

Present programs to patrons visiting the library; visit City schools to inform children of programs available.

Respond to public inquiries and complaints regarding library materials and services.

Participate in the selection of library operational equipment and furniture.

Perform various administrative and procedural tasks such as supervising and implementing the automated circulation system, running daily computer logs and reports, shelving books, and repairing damaged materials.

As needed, train and supervise subordinate library positions.

Regularly participate in adult reference activities.

Represent the library at City and community meetings as necessary.

Perform related duties as assigned.

Knowledge, Skills, and Abilities

Knowledge of:

Principles and practices of library science.

Children's services as a specialized part of the library field; children's literature.

Modern office procedures and methods including automated library systems.

Principles of personnel training and supervision.

Skill to:

Take complete responsibility for a major functional area in the library (Children's Services).

Relate well to children; present and perform programs.

Exercise creativity in program development.

Learn the operation of a computer for various structured library applications.

Communicate effectively, both orally and in writing.

Establish and maintain effective work relationships with those contacted in the performance of required duties.

Education, Experience, and Training

Any combination of education and experience that would likely provide the required knowledge and abilities is qualifying. A typical way to obtain the knowledge and abilities would be:

Education:

Possession of a Master of Library Science Degree from an accredited college or university.

Experience:

Two years of experience as a professional librarian, one of which involved children's services.

6.4 YOUTH LIBRARIAN

6.4.1 Youth Librarian

Library Name: Kettleson Memorial Library
Library Location: Sitka, Alaska
Population Served: 8,835
Number of Volumes: 57,448
Number of Titles: 54,733
Number of Periodical Subscriptions: 279

General Summary

JOB OBJECTIVE:

Oversees the functions and operations of the Children's section of the Library; performs related work as required.

Distinguishing Features of the Class

The principal function of an employee in this class is to develop, maintain and provide youth services for the City and Borough of Sitka through the Library. The work is performed under the direct supervision of the Library Director but consid-erable leeway is granted for the exercise of independent judge-ment and initiative. Direct supervision is exercised over the work of employees in the class of Library Pages and volunteers. An employee in this class performs the duties of other employees in the Library as required or as assigned by supervisory personnel. The nature of the work performed requires that an employee in this class establish and maintain effective working relationships with other Department and City employees, school officials, business and community groups and the public. The principal duties of this class are performed in a public Library environ-ment. An employee in this class may perform any one or more or any additional duties as assigned.

Essential Functions and Responsibilities

Plans, schedules, produces and publicizes activities for chil-dren and adults, including story hours, day care programs, Head Start, Reading Buddy programs, Parent Support programs, sum-mer reading schedules and other related youth services;

Coordinates activities with local schools to promote an inter-est in programs and disseminate information to the largest group of youth possible;

Maintains a knowledge of reference services within the library and provides reference services to patrons on a wide variety of subjects and educational levels;

Maintains a safe and secure library environment through monitoring patrons adherence to library procedures and guide-lines and maintaining an awareness of all persons within the facility;

Maintains and develops Library collections for children, including selecting and ordering quality age appropriate books and related materials;

Monitors literary journals, reviews and related information sources to identify and select material which will be of interest and use to youth readers;

Monitors use within the youth area of the Library for the pur-pose of ordering replacement titles to ensure a current and com-plete collection;

Provides reader advisory services for children and adults and makes recommendations to patrons in locating age appropriate materials;

Reviews new material as it arrives to determine which area of the library it should be located in;

Analyzes and recommends policy development/changes as they relate to youth services;

Develops and implements public relations campaigns of vari-ous forms, including coordination with schools and community groups, to solicit and maintain an interest level in Library youth services and reading development;

Manages the budget for the Children's section of the Library;

Provides information to other Library personnel in the func-tion of the youth services section;

Evaluates donated materials to determine if they warrant an addition to the collection;

Solicits funds, promotes donations and compiles reports on all charitable activities involving youth services;

Maintains data and compiles reports on all activities and functions within the youth services section of the Library;

Manages the telephone Dial-A-Story service;

Provides direct services to Library patrons, including answering patron questions regarding the use of Library resources and general questions relating to a wide variety of academic and related areas;

Explores all possible information sources for inquiring patrons, including all materials within the Library consortium of Sitka, other contributing Libraries in the inter-library loan program and other related sources as necessary;

Checks books, videos, cassettes, CD's and other materials in and out of the Library, renews materials, places books on hold, notifies patrons the arrival of held books and collects overdue fines;

Registers new patrons, including advising all individuals of the requirements for obtaining a

Library card and the responsibilities entailed;

Performs other duties of Library Assistants as necessary;

Provides needed information and demonstrations concerning how to perform certain work tasks to new employees in the same or similar class of positions;

Keeps immediate supervisor and designated others fully and accurately informed concerning work progress, including present and potential work problems and suggestions for new or improved ways of addressing such problems;

Attends meetings, conferences, workshops and training sessions and reviews publications and audio-visual materials to become and remain current on the principles, practices and new developments in assigned work areas;

Responds to citizens' questions and comments in a courteous and timely manner;

Trains, assigns, prioritizes, supervises, motivates and evaluates the work of assigned employees;

Communicates and coordinates regularly with appropriate others to maximize the effectiveness and efficiency of interdepartmental operations and activities;

Performs other related duties as assigned.

Knowledge, Skills, and Abilities

Comprehensive knowledge of youth services programs;

Comprehensive knowledge of literature written for children and youth;

Thorough knowledge of standard library practices and procedures;

Thorough knowledge of equipment used in library operations, including microfilm, microfiche, video and related communications equipment, CD Rom, Library computer systems and Internet services;

Ability to ascertain the needs of Library patrons and direct them to the needed resource within the Library or contact outside services to ensure all available information is obtainable to the patron;

Ability to use child psychology or related skills to understand and interpret the interest of children;

Ability in basic math computations and alphabetic filing systems;

Ability to communicate well with others, both orally and in writing, using both technical and non-technical language;

Ability to understand and follow oral and/or written policies, procedures and instructions;

Ability to prepare and present accurate and reliable reports containing findings and recommendations;

Ability to operate or quickly learn to operate a personal computer using standard or customized software applications appropriate to assigned tasks;

Ability to use logical and creative thought processes to develop solutions according to written specifications and/or oral instructions;

Ability to perform a wide variety of duties and responsibilities with accuracy and speed under the pressure of time-sensitive deadlines;

Ability and willingness to quickly learn and put to use new skills and knowledge brought about by rapidly changing information and/or technology;

Integrity, ingenuity and inventiveness in the performance of assigned tasks.

Physical and Mental Requirements

Essential Physical Abilities

Sufficient clarity of speech and hearing or other communication capabilities, with or without reasonable accommodation, which permits the employee to communicate effectively;

Sufficient vision or other powers of observation, with or without reasonable accommodation, which permits the employee to read books and patron requests;

Sufficient manual dexterity with or without reasonable accommodation, which permits the employee to type and record library files;

Sufficient personal mobility and physical reflexes, with or without reasonable accommodation, which permits the employee to reshelve library materials.

Education, Experience, and Training

Graduation from an accredited college or university with a Bachelor's Degree in a related field, M.L.S. preferred; and

Considerable experience using basic research techniques and library sciences directed at children's and youth services; or

Any equivalent combination of experience, education and training which provides the knowledge, skills and abilities necessary to perform the work.

Additional Qualifications

Required Special Qualifications

None

6.4.2 Youth Librarian

Library Name: Tippecanoe County Public Library
Library Location: La Fayette, Indiana
Population Served: 104,310
Number of Volumes: 297,091
Number of Titles: N/A
Number of Periodical Subscriptions: 1,947

Reports to

SUPERVISOR: Managing Librarian
SALARY SCHEDULE CLASSIFICATION: Professional Librarian

General Summary

JOB OBJECTIVE:
Participate in activities which support the daily operation of the campus library, with emphasis on planning and providing library services, programs and materials to youth and young adult customers.

Essential Functions and Responsibilities

Support and contribute to overall library mission
Know and apply professional codes and library policies
Understand the necessity of, and maintain, confidentiality of library use
Deal with disturbances and problem users
Act as staff member in charge of library as needed
Provide assistance at any public service desk as needed
Participate in developing policies and procedures
Assume responsibility for collection management in specific areas of the circulating, reference, and any special collections.
Assist and instruct customers in the use of library resources
Provide reference and readers' advisory services
Conduct library tours and instructional training
In consultation with the Managing Librarian, assist in the supervision and training of library staff and volunteers.
Maintain professional and technical knowledge by attending workshops, reading professional publications, and participating in individual and departmental training
Research and apply for grant funding
Maintain effective communication with library staff and all library constituents
Participate on library committees
In consultation with the Managing Librarian, carry out special projects and programs
Actively participate in professional organizations or activities
Assist in the creation of all forms of promotional materials and materials displays
Serve as a resource to adults who work with children and young adults
Work evenings and weekends

Other duties as assigned and/or required

Knowledge, Skills, and Abilities

Skills:
Must have good problem solving skills and be able to make independent decisions
Must be dedicated to quality customer service
Must be able to effectively juggle multiple projects and deadlines
Must be able to prioritize tasks and responsibilities
Must be cooperative and amiable with public and staff
Must have effective communication skills with public and staff; Proficiency in English required and the ability to communicate in other languages highly desirable
Must be dependable
Must have good memory for facts and routines
Must be able to efficiently utilize word processing software and troubleshoot simple equipment problems
Must have up-to-date knowledge/training with electronic resources
Must have good supervisory skills
Must be able to efficiently ascertain and handle problematic situations
Must be able to apply latest trends in technology and library services
Must have up-to-date knowledge of children's and young adult materials
Must have up-to-date knowledge of child and adolescent development and related issues, and the ability to translate that knowledge into appropriate library services
Must have empathy with children and young adults; their interests, activities and problems
Must have flexibility to work in different service areas of the library
Must be able to organize work

Physical and Mental Requirements

Must be able to:
adapt to various locations of programs
tolerate some sustained walking
bend and stoop
sit in a confined position
lift and carry bags of materials up to 40 pounds
maneuver a loaded book cart weighing up to 200 pounds

Tools and Equipment Used

Able to use, replenish supplies and correct normal problems on general office aids including:
Personal computers
Telephone
Projectors
VCR equipment
Cassette player/recorder
Photo copier
FAX Machines

General office aids

Education, Experience, and Training

QUALIFICATIONS:
Education:
MLS from an ALA accredited library school
Previous experience:
Experience in Youth Services desired.

License and Certification Requirements

License/certification:
Indiana Librarian III certification

Disclaimers

Note: This job description contains the facts necessary to evaluate and distinguish it from other TCPL positions. It is not, however, a detailed description of every task, duty or responsibility.

6.5 YOUTH LIBRARIAN MANAGER/DEPARTMENT HEAD

6.5.1 Youth Librarian Manager/Department Head

Library Name: Bemis Public Library
Library Location: Littleton, Colorado
Population Served: 42,000
Number of Volumes: 135,000
Number of Titles: N/A
Periodical Subscriptions: 304

Essential Functions and Responsibilities

Oversees the daily activities of the division and the division staff. Plans activities and evaluates staff through weekly scheduling, oral and written communications and oral and written evaluations.

Actively participates in library management team, including long-range planning, problem solving and policy development. Plans, produces and coordinates programs for children, age 0-11 (fifth grade), including family-oriented activities. This includes selection of program theme, related books and materials, fingerplays, poems, music, puppets, games and crafts that are age and ability appropriate.

Coordinates the development of the division's collection development plan. Evaluates the library collection in the light of the collection development plan and by listening to customer requests, knowing and considering the community needs, maintaining an awareness of curriculum, checking dates for currency of information and checking standard recommended lists to determine in what areas materials need to be ordered.

Selects print and non-print collection materials by reading reviews and taking into consideration the collection development plan, community needs and issues and school curriculum. Sends ordering information to the Technical Services Division. Responsible for selecting materials within approved budget. Serves as a resource person for intellectual freedom trends, issues and policies. Provides library staff, library board and community with awareness programs of these issues. Handles challenges for all children's materials according to library policies and procedures.

Through thoughtful and tactful questioning, determines customers' needs. Assists customers in locating information or books through the use of the public catalog, the Internet, standard reference materials or other resources. Information and assistance is provided in-person and by telephone or computer. Trains and otherwise assists children and adults visiting the children's area in the use of computers to locate desired information and materials. This computer use includes the public catalog, software programs and the Internet. Reads professional journals to increase knowledge of issues and resources to help with future plans for the division. Stays abreast of community needs, programs and issues.

Visits schools, day care centers and other locations. Gives presentations regarding the library and tours of the library in order to promote reading and literacy and make others aware of what the library has to offer.

Maintains daily order and safety of the children's library section by observing customers' behavior and activities. Communicates with customers to enforce general library standards and rules of safety and conduct. Helps to maintain a safe environment by picking up books, pushing in chairs and observing activities in the area.

Plans for staff development and future division needs by finding out about new programs, attending meetings and networking with other staff and librarians elsewhere.

Provides expertise in children's literature to children, parents and teachers or anyone else who needs help in selecting good children's materials.

Plans and prepares budget requests. Determines manner in which the division's collection materials and supplies funds should be allocated to its staff members.

Observes and follows established city and department policies and procedures in the daily conduct of job.

Plans and arranges workload and establishes priorities to complete scheduled assigned work within parameters and deadlines assigned by supervisor.

Delivers work products and services to customers within assigned work schedule that averages 40 hours per week, including evening and weekend hours, including Sundays.

Delivers work product and services with responsiveness, courtesy and tact in personal interactions with customers and staff.

Knowledge, Skills, and Abilities

Requires solid knowledge of the general principles and specific details of: public library management; child development; cataloging of materials; and supervision of personnel and the ability to apply that knowledge to perform the essential duties and responsibilities of the position. Requires a strong knowledge and sense of the community's needs and desires for youth library services.

Requires expert knowledge of the principles of children's literature and collection development and the ability to apply that knowledge to perform the essential duties and responsibilities of the position.

Requires expert knowledge of the principles and issues/policies of intellectual freedom and the ability to apply that knowledge in a library setting. Requires solid keyboarding/data entry skills and abilities and a solid ability to use and teach customers to use the following computer applications: CARL searching techniques, including limiting search; word processing, databases and spreadsheets; Internet searches, including use of search engines and limiting searches.

Requires a working knowledge of children's behavior, intellectual level and interest level; and the ability to apply general principles of children's library service.

Requires solid written and verbal communication and customer service skills, including the skill and ability to: effectively listen, ask and answer questions; communicate with adults and children; effectively interact with staff; effectively read, write and speak; effectively organize and give presentations to groups of listeners, including story telling, read aloud, drama and puppetry; prepare press releases and monthly reports; and prepare written materials for programs, flyers, tickets, and game boards.

Requires solid analytical skills, including the ability to: gather and analyze data, identify problems, compare results and consider options for solutions. Requires solid project management skills and abilities, including the ability to: determine overall plans, outline tasks, delegate responsibilities, set deadlines, get feedback, review and report results.

Requires solid supervisory skills and abilities; the ability to read, understand and apply personnel policies and procedures; requires a knowledge of library standards and rules of safety and conduct and the ability to communicate and enforce these standards and rules.

Requires solid general management skills and abilities; knowledge of basic budgeting; the ability to compare policies of other libraries and consider them when implementing new policies.

Requires the ability to provide user maintenance on computer hardware: change printer toner; check for paper jams and correct them. Requires the ability to use cassette and CD players and set-up public address systems. Requires creative skills and a knowledge of arts and crafts; the ability to incorporate songs and rhymes into a story time; the ability to conduct public performances (drama), including puppet shows and plays.

Requires a genuine liking and understanding of children of all ages; enthusiasm, optimism, resourcefulness, flexibility and creativity; excellent interpersonal skills; knowledge of public library issues, especially those related to intellectual freedom and Internet access; ability to work effectively with children of all ages and their families; expert knowledge of children's literature and trends; story-telling or drama ability; computer skills, including

word processing, Internet searching, online library catalog searching and knowledge of age-appropriate software for children.

Supervisory Responsibilities

Serves as the supervisory authority for subordinate employees assigned to the division. Responsible for the daily supervision of assigned employees.

Supervisory responsibilities include: planning, directing and supervising the work activities of subordinates; evaluating and reviewing the work products and work performance of subordinates; making recommendations for hiring, terminations, promotions, demotions and transfers of subordinates; conducting performance evaluations and making merit pay salary adjustment recommendations; taking disciplinary actions (excluding terminations) as required; scheduling and assigning work; allocating equipment and resources necessary to accomplish assigned work; and assisting in the training and professional development of subordinate employees.

Education, Experience, and Training

Requires a Master's degree in Library Science; additional coursework in child development, general management and personnel management is desired; and requires a minimum of five years work experience in children's services in a public library. At least two years experience in a supervisory role in children's services in a public library is preferred. Previous experience in public performance in storytelling, drama, puppetry and related activities is preferred; or Requires an equivalent combination of education, formal training and work experience that produces the knowledge, skill and ability to perform the essential duties and responsibilities of the position.

6.5.2 Youth Services Manager/Department Head

Library Name: Seminole County Public Library
Library Location: Sanford, Florida
Population Served: 350,000
Number of Volumes: N/A
Number of Titles: 175,000
Periodical Subscriptions: 742

General Summary

Function: Professional and supervisory work assigned as coordinator for Youth Services Programs.

Essential Functions and Responsibilities

Plans, directs, evaluates, schedules, and coordinates systemwide children's and young adult programs to include development and maintenance of children's and young adult books and materials collection.

Provides reader advisory service, reference assistance, and programming resource collection and files.

Develops recommendations for programs, policies, and procedures to improve children's and young adult library services.

Plans meetings and workshops to enhance staff skills system wide and improve services system wide.

Provides technical guidance and on-the-job training for staff engaged in providing children's and young adult services at all branches.

Supervises, trains and provides guidance to personnel assigned to children's and young adult services.

Initiates and recommends, for final approval by the Department Director, hiring, termination, performance evaluation, disciplinary and/or commendatory action of personnel assigned to children's and young adult services.

Monitors expenditures of the budget related to children's and young adult services and programs. Selects and submits orders for books and other library materials for processing and approval by collection development staff.

Performs professional librarian work in the promotion, circulation, and reference use of library materials specializing in children's and young adult services.

Prepares and submits regular and special statistical, management, and other reports as required. Resolves or initiates action to resolve complaints of library patrons related to children's and young adult services and library materials.

Cooperates with public and private schools, day care centers, and other community groups serving youth.

Performs other duties as assigned or as may be necessary.

Knowledge, Skills, and Abilities

Qualifications:

Considerable knowledge of established principles, practices, and methods of library science and administration specializing in children's and young adult services and programs to include classification, cataloging, circulation, selection of appropriate materials, and development of collections.

Considerable ability to plan, direct, and organize the activities of subordinate staff.

Ability to establish and maintain effective working relationships with others.

Ability to prepare comprehensive reports and present ideas clearly and concisely.

Ability to communicate effectively both orally and in writing.

Skilled in the use of library automated and cataloging systems.

Work Environment

The work environment for this position is in an office setting. Most duties are performed sitting at a desk, table or workstation. Incumbents are required to shelve books and perform some heavy lifting. Incumbents in this classification have regular exposure to radiant and electrical energy found in an office environment.

Education, Experience, and Training

Master's degree in Library Science from an accredited American Library Association College or university and three (3) years' professional library experience as a Children's Librarian in a public library. A valid Florida driver's license is required. A comparable amount of education, training, or experience may be substituted for the minimum qualifications.

Disclaimers

These are intended only as illustrations of the various types of work performed. The omission of specific duties does not exclude them from the position if the work is a logical assignment to the position.

6.6 YOUTH LIBRARIAN WITH SUPERVISORY RESPONSIBILITIES

6.6.1 Youth Librarian with Supervisory Responsibilities

Library Name: Williamsburg Regional Library System
Library Location: Williamsburg, Virginia
Population Served: 60,100
Number of Volumes: 261,243
Number of Titles: N/A
Number of Periodical Subscriptions: 562

Reports to

DEPARTMENT: Youth Services
SUPERVISOR: Youth Services Director

General Summary

DEPARTMENT: Williamsburg Regional Library/Youth Services

JOB OBJECTIVE:

Under the supervision of the Youth Services Director, the Youth Services Librarian II provides reference and readers' advisory services to the public; organizes the department's special services in at least one area; assists with departmental operations; and promotes library services to the community.

Essential Functions and Responsibilities

Provides the public with the information and materials from the library's collections and from other sources by researching and interpreting print, online, and other sources; locating and recommending materials appropriate for patrons' interest and reading levels; evaluating the accuracy, currency, and usefulness of the information or materials; teaching individuals and groups how to use library resources and research methods; recommending materials to read, view, or hear; recommending topics for reports and other assignments; and preparing booklists, library guides, and displays.

Organizes the department's special services in one or more of the following areas: electronic resources; print sources; summer reading programs; volunteers; outreach; school partnerships; etc.

Develops and implements training for individuals and groups; researches in-depth reference questions; develops specialized collections, including electronic and online resources; creates instructional materials to inform and promote resources; keeps the community and local officials informed of relevant new information and materials; and serves as a library liaison to these segments of the community.

Assists with departmental operations, including supervision of staff and volunteers; maintaining, updating, and interpreting departmental and library policies and procedures; scheduling; and solving staff, patron, equipment, and building problems as needed.

Develops, supports, and presents library programs.

Improves the quality of library services through individual and general staff development, including attendance at workshops and conferences; serves on library committees; trains other staff as appropriate.

Monitors patron activities in the library, handling problems as they occur.

Supervises volunteer projects.

Performs other related duties as required.

Knowledge, Skills, and Abilities

Extensive knowledge of electronic sources and personal computers.

Extensive knowledge of the principles, practices, and techniques of library services, including reference, readers' advisory, collection development, and programming.

Extensive knowledge of children's literature and of reference sources and research techniques.

Excellent oral and written communication skills.

Knowledge of supervisory principles and skills.

Experience in and commitment to public service.

Ability to work effectively with the public of all ages and other library personnel.

Ability to plan and organize daily work and special projects.

Work Environment

The job is located in both library buildings. Administers work in both an office and at a public service desk. At least 50% of time requires walking, light to medium lifting, reaching, bending, and other limited physical activity; operation of computers is required; other office and library equipment as required. Regular contact is made with library staff, vendors, and the general public.

Education, Experience, and Training

MINIMUM QUALIFICATIONS:

American Library Association (ALA) accredited Master of Library Science (MLS) degree required. Two years public library experience preferred.

Additional Qualifications

NECESSARY SPECIAL QUALIFICATIONS:

Ability to travel among the various job sites.

Position Hours

WORK SCHEDULE: Full-time, exempt position is 40 hours per week. Schedules include some nights and weekends.

7.0 SPECIALIST

7.1 YOUTH SPECIALIST

> ### 7.1.1 Youth Specialist
>
> **Library Name:** Clermont County Public Library
> **Library Location:** Batavia, Ohio
> **Population Served:** 178,749
> **Number of Volumes:** 534,527
> **Number of Titles:** 151,295
> **Number of Periodical Subscriptions:** 547

Reports to

Immediate Supervisor: Branch Manager

General Summary

JOB OBJECTIVE:

Shares responsibility with the Youth Services Librarian for providing direct library service to people of all ages, especially children from birth through late teens.

Essential Functions and Responsibilities

Answers library users' reference questions in person and over telephone, using materials in variety of formats (i.e. books, periodicals, newspapers, microfilm, indexes). This would include utilizing the Online Public Service Catalog (OPAQ) and Internet.

Assists in the planning, preparation and presentation of story times, summer reading activities and special programs for youth. Outreach in community includes storytelling.

Presents information about library services and programs to individuals and groups.

Develops displays and public relations materials (such as bibliographies and program fliers).

Assists in the development and de-selection of children's and/or young adult material collections.

Maintains working knowledge of materials collections, services available and trends in library services to people of all ages, primarily youth.

Assists with system wide decision-making by serving on committees.

Interprets CCPL policy and procedures to public in a customer-responsive manner.

Assists with monitoring youth supply budget.

Assists with monitoring youth collection budget.

Assists in maintaining youth service records and files.

Assists customers using the OPAC.

Attends meetings and workshops as required.

Reserves library materials for customers using computerized holds management technique and interlibrary loan.

Maintains knowledge of circulation system in order to assist at circulation desk.

Additional Job Duties

Additional Examples of Work Performed:

Assists in preparation of branch public services monthly report.

Supervises the activities of branch page staff.

Maintains branch vertical files and vacation files.

Knowledge, Skills, and Abilities

Effective verbal and written communication skills.

Knowledge of children's materials both current and classic.

Analytical ability to understand and solve reference questions.

Knowledge of and ability to explain available library services.

Ability to work independently.

Establishes and maintains an effective working relationship with people of all ages, especially children and young adults.

Provides good customer services as defined by system guidelines.

Maintains composure while handling complaints from the public.

Demonstrates problem-solving and decision-making techniques.

Must be self-motivated.

Must have some agility to stoop, stretch and climb to retrieve materials and conduct programs.

Must learn to use a computer to aid in reference work, programming and word processing.

Maintains working relationship with other community leaders.

Stands for extended periods of times, lifts and carries books and other library materials.

Assists in setting long and short range goals, objectives and priorities.

Moderate strength to rearrange furniture, shovel snow and clean up library clutter.

Must have reliable transportation for travel to agencies within system and out.

Education, Experience, and Training

Qualifications: A broad range of knowledge of a wide variety of subjects usually acquired through a four-year college program or associate degree and appropriate library experience.

Position Hours

Must be able to work evenings and weekends.

Disclaimers

Note: This job analysis describes the nature and level of assignments normally given in this position; they are not an exhaustive list of duties. Additional related duties may be assigned.

7.2 EARLY CHILDHOOD SPECIALIST

7.2.1 Early Childhood Specialist

Library Name: Cuyahoga County Public Library
Library Location: Parma, Ohio
Population Served: 607,909
Number of Volumes: 3,297,420
Number of Titles: N/A
Number of Periodical Subscriptions: 8,502

Reports to

Supervisor's Title: Children's Service Manager

Positions Supervised: N/A

General Summary

Under general direction, works from established policies and procedures, and participates in setting early childhood program objectives. Provides comprehensive library services to the library system, patrons and community agencies specializing in early childhood.

Essential Functions and Responsibilities

Complies with work scheduling and attendance requirements according to reasonable policy and practices. Staffing for branch and regional libraries and some Administration (ADM) departments requires rotational scheduling, which includes evening and weekend (Saturday and Sunday) hours. Most ADM departments are weekday operations.

Consistently presents Cuyahoga County Public Library and its services in a positive manner and adheres to customer service guidelines and procedures as established by the Library.

Complies with the established rules of operation, procedures, and policies when using library computers, peripheral hardware, and software. Individual passwords and any other confidential information regarding library records shall be kept confidential.

Promotes project LEAP, literacy and library resources to community, parent and educational groups.

Creates and updates project LEAP story-time kits.

Provides information and training regarding developmentally appropriate materials and programming targeting early childhood.

Evaluates all materials for children birth to age five, and makes recommendations for purchase.

Plans and provides additional training in the form of workshops and in-service training for staff, care providers and parents to augment their knowledge of early childhood literature and programming.

Supports literacy development through the publication of a quarterly newsletter, and creation of bibliographies and other informational materials.

Provides collection development guidance for children's services staff, adult staff, parents and care providers.

Shares resources and information with other libraries, educational organizations and social service agencies.

Supervises development of Project LEAP mailing list, mailings, statistical reports and files.

Works with other Children's Services staff in the creation of new programs, projects and materials.

The intent of this position description is to provide a representative summary of the major duties and responsibilities performed by incumbents of this job. Incumbents may be requested to perform job-related tasks other than those specifically presented in this description.

Knowledge, Skills, and Abilities

Comprehensive knowledge of early childhood development theory, practice and programming.

Comprehensive knowledge of early childhood literature and developmental materials and programming.

Strong organizational skills.

Ability to develop and implement programming appropriate for target groups associated with children birth to age five.

Writing skills necessary to create TIP sheets, bibliographies, newsletters, and reviews.

Strong communication, interpersonal and oral presentation skills for creating and presenting developmental programming to various groups.

Computer literate.

Physical and Mental Requirements

May require moderate physical effort such as stooping, bending, lifting boxes weighing approximately 30 pounds.

Work Environment

PHYSICAL DEMANDS AND WORKING CONDITIONS
Job is physically comfortable.

Education, Experience, and Training

Master's degree in Library Science and undergraduate work specializing in early childhood development.

Two to four years of early childhood development experience in a library setting.

License and Certification Requirement

Requires a valid State Driver's license and own vehicle preferred, for visiting branches and area functions.

A criminal background check is required.

VI. CIRCULATION SERVICES

Included in this section are circulation administrators, managers, coordinators, clerks, pages, and midrange positions at the library associate, assistant, and specialist level.

1.0 ADMINISTRATOR

1.1. CIRCULATION ADMINISTRATOR

1.1.1 Circulation Administrator

Library Name: Williamsburg Regional Library System
Library Location: Williamsburg, Virginia
Population Served: 60,100
Number of Volumes: 261,243
Number of Titles: N/A
Number of Periodical Subscriptions: 562

General Summary

JOB OBJECTIVE:

Under the supervision of the Library Director, the Library Services Director (Circulation Services) is responsible for all circulation services department operations and staff. Performs complex tasks involved with the computerized transactions of library materials to the public. Participates in the planning and evaluation of programs, services, and goals for the entire library through the management team.

Essential Functions and Responsibilities

Administers all functions of the circulation services department.

Oversees all circulation services staff procedures including hiring, training, scheduling, and evaluating.

Conducts staff meetings and training sessions; monitors workload of staff and facilitates completion of tasks.

Prepares budget requests, written reports and plans for the circulation services department.

Designates goals for overall efficiency of the circulation services department and its individual staff development; drafts various procedures/forms to accommodate new and revised department procedures.

Uses library automated system efficiently for transactions in the checking in and charging out of library materials, processing patron records, and determining materials status.

Monitors patron activities in the library, handling problems as they occur.

Oversees opening and closing procedures of library; responsible for bookdrop schedule when library is closed.

Participates in library-wide planning and decision making as a member of the library management team to improve the quality of library services.

Performs other related duties as required.

Knowledge, Skills, and Abilities

Ability to plan, organize and administer a department.
Demonstrated management and supervisory skills.

Ability to learn and use the library computer system with high degree of efficiency.

Desire and ability to serve the public with friendliness, tact, and diplomacy.

Excellent written and oral communication skills.

Ability to work well under pressure, paying close attention to detail.

Ability to delegate work effectively.

Ability to set own priorities for work to be done, and meet deadlines.

Ability to establish and maintain effective working relationships with staff members, government officials and staff, and the general public.

Work Environment

Administers work typically sitting in an office and standing at a public service desk, with occasional walking, light lifting and other limited physical activities. Frequent sustained operation of computer and other office equipment is required. Regular contact is made with staff members, government officials and staff, vendors, and the general public. The job is located in the library buildings.

Education, Experience, and Training

MINIMUM QUALIFICATIONS:

Bachelor's degree from an accredited four-year college or combination of higher education and experience in related fields to provide the necessary expertise. Minimum of three years of library experience, preferably including library automated systems experience. Supervisory experience required.

Additional Qualifications

Requires the ability to travel among various library sites.

2.0 LIBRARY ASSISTANT

2.1 RECEPTION AND INFORMATION ASSISTANT

2.1.1 Reception and Information Assistant

Library Name: Mount Prospect Public Library
Library Location: Mount Prospect, Illinois
Population Served: 56,265
Number of Volumes: 332,413
Number of Titles: N/A
Number of Periodical Subscriptions: 450

Reports To

SUPERVISOR: Under the direct supervision of Registration Desk Department Head.

General Summary

JOB OBJECTIVE:

The Registration Desk Assistant performs general reception duties including fielding in-person and on the telephone informational and directional questions from patrons. This position operates the telephone switchboard.

Extensive contact with the public and with other departments occurs within the library. In addition, a variety of major and minor clerical duties are performed. The position requires accessing, inputting and retrieving information from computer; effectively using telephone; effectively receiving and providing information about Library; exercising judgment in non-routine situations; requires ability to perform light to medium work; ability to use a multi-line switchboard; ability to perform several jobs simultaneously.

Essential Functions and Responsibilities

Answers patron informational and directional questions.

Assists with various clerical duties including photocopying for other departments when assigned.

Contacts patrons for reserve books, ILL material, lost & found materials, in-house program calls, etc. as assigned.

Faxing when assigned.

Generates Dynix Horizon reports as assigned.

Maintains accurate and up-to-date patron database.

Maintains department files as assigned.

Maintains department supplies as assigned.

Maintains lost and found and materials pick-up-file.

Maintains online website activity calendar.

Maintains sign out & issue keys for Friends, meeting room & elevator.

Maintains supply of printed material (brochures, bus schedules, etc.) for public distribution.

Maintains weekly Registration Desk staff schedule when assigned.

Participates in special projects when assigned.

Performs data entry.

Performs duties and tasks associated with the operation of the registration desk and switchboard.

Performs responsibility as voter registrar.

Prepares reports and compiles statistics as assigned.

Processes postage for outgoing library mail & UPS for pick-up.

Processes registration for Library sponsored programs.

Processes work from other departments when assigned.

Registers patrons for Library cards.

Registers voters.

Responsible for switchboard operation, routing incoming calls, taking messages and relaying same.

Responsible for display case sign ups.

Screening visitors & issuing visitor passes.

Serves on committees as assigned.

Supervises staff when assigned.

Supervises volunteers when assigned.

Types supply orders for Bookkeeper.

Updates public bulletin board as assigned.

Attends meetings, workshops and seminars.

Other duties as assigned.

Knowledge, Skills, and Abilities

Ability to alphabetize correctly and to understand numerical arrangements utilizing the decimal point.

Ability to carry books weighing 5–10 lbs.

Ability to communicate skillfully, accurately and pleasantly with patrons in person and on the telephone.

Ability to exercise judgment in non-routine situations.

Ability to efficiently organize work.

Ability to perform light to medium work.

Ability to perform several tasks simultaneously.

Ability to sit for varied lengths of time.

Ability to stoop, reach, lift, kneel, crouch, stand and grasp.

Ability to work efficiently, effectively and courteously with patrons and staff.

Ability to work as a member of a team.

Ability to work independently.

Ability to type and to file.

Knowledge of Library policies and procedures.

Knowledge of general office work.

Knowledge of materials/services available at the Library as well as activities and current programs.

Knowledge of physical organization of the building & functions of the various Departments within the library.

Knowledge/skill in use of the library automation system.

Knowledge/skill with word processing and basic spreadsheets.

General office skills.

Education, Experience, and Training

High School diploma.

Keyboarding skill required. Computer experience required.

Phone and office work experience required.

Current voter registrar status.

2.2 CIRCULATION ASSISTANT

2.2.1 Circulation Assistant

Library Name: Manitowoc-Calumet Library System
Library Location: Manitowoc, Wisconsin
Population Served: 58,213
Number of Volumes: 195,166
Number of Titles: N/A
Periodical Subscriptions: 395

Reports To

Circulation Services Supervisor

General Summary

JOB OBJECTIVE:

Working under general supervision of Circulation Supervisor, assists patrons and performs procedures related to circulation of materials; also routes patrons and telephone calls to appropriate destinations. May perform work of and/or direct routine tasks of the Circulation pages. May perform Assistant-level work in other departments.

Essential Functions and Responsibilities

The following list identifies principal duties and responsibilities of the job. It is not a definitive list and other similar duties may be assigned. An asterisk (*) before any of the following items indicates duties and responsibilities which are not "essential functions" of the job as defined by the Americans with Disabilities Act.

Assists patrons at service desk and over telephone by performing procedures related to circulation of materials. For example: checking out and renewing materials; placing holds; collecting fees and fines; registering borrowers; explaining policies and procedures and granting exceptions when necessary.

Deals with problem patrons, particularly those who disrupt normal use or operation of the Library, or attempt to unlawfully remove library materials from premises. Assists with maintenance of building security. For example: enforcing library policies for patron behavior; participating in disaster and emergency procedures, responding to materials theft detection system and other alarms; completing Incident Reports and calling police or other official assistance, when necessary.

Performs other procedures related to circulation of materials. For example: checking in materials; processing holds; processing overdue and other notices; emptying materials return bins; maintaining inventories, statistics, etc. May assist with processing lost/damaged materials, City Attorney letters collection agency, and other retrieval procedures.

Answers central switchboard. Takes messages. Routes patrons and telephone calls to appropriate destinations.

Prepares materials for shelving or filing.

Sensitizes, inspects, cleans as necessary, and sorts materials onto sorting shelves.

Searches stacks and other areas for claimed returned, traced, lost, missing, or other items, as assigned.

Makes closing and other necessary announcements over the public address system.*

Performs work of Circulation Page, as needed or assigned. May direct routine tasks of Circulation Page.

Performs Assistant-level work in other departments, as assigned.*

Knowledge, Skills, and Abilities

Ability to provide courteous public service and to present clear explanations of established policies and procedures. Ability to think and act appropriately under pressure. Willingness and ability to grant logical exceptions to Library policies and procedures when warranted.

Skill in performing routine and non-routine procedures involving many steps. Ability to follow complex written and/or verbal instructions and to pay close attention to detail. Ability to work with limited direct supervision.

Ability to interact effectively with the Library's automated system. Minimum skill level: accurate keyboarding at a minimum of 25 words per minute; ability to acquire and demonstrate knowledge of all parts of the circulation module at security level 3.

Capacity to be easily understood on voice telephone and public address systems. Minimum skill level : Demonstrated knowledge of proper telephone etiquette; ability to use public address and phone systems; ability to take messages and identify appropriate destinations.

Skill at accurately and efficiently sorting and shelving materials in alphanumeric order. Minimum skill level: ability to accurately shelve at a consistent rate of at least 100 items per hour; shelf read at 500 items per hour. Physical capacity to place materials on shelves at all shelving heights.

Ability to work in a team setting. Willingness to assist and support coworkers, contribute ideas, maintain flexibility, and be able to adapt to a rapidly changing environment.

Position Hours

Full-time, typically working 80 hours per two-week pay period on a flexible schedule which varies from week to week. May be scheduled to work days, evenings, Saturdays, and Sundays.

Part-time, typically working 20, 30, 40, 48, or 64 hours per two-week pay period (depending on position) on a flexible schedule which varies from week to week. May be scheduled to work days, evenings, Saturdays, and Sundays.

2.2.2 Circulation Assistant

Library Name: Rowan Public Library
Library Location: Salisbury, North Carolina
Population Served: 125,800
Number of Volumes: 198,050
Number of Titles: N/A
Number of Periodical Subscriptions: 548

General Summary

HUMAN RESOURCES JOB DESCRIPTION
JOB OBJECTIVE:

Varied clerical work of moderate responsibility within the Public Library system.

Supervision is received from a Library Associate or Librarian, who reviews work through periodic conferences, observation, and analysis of work performed.

Essential Functions and Responsibilities

(Any one position may not include all of the duties listed, nor do the listed examples include all tasks which may be found in positions of this class.)

Charges and discharges materials and equipment to the public;

Registers the public as library users

Handles reserves for specific library materials

Notifies users of fines and collects fines for overdue library materials.

Waits on the public in person and by telephone; gives out specific information and instructions.

Types labels and file cards.

Maintains and/or processes a variety of departmental records, forms, reports, logs, and files.

Processes incoming and outgoing mail; routes documents to the proper source.

Assists in the maintenance of library database; operates the library automated retrieval system for the variety of tasks.

Additional Job Duties

Shelves books as necessary.

Performs related duties as required.

Management reserves the right to add or amend duties at any time.

Knowledge, Skills, and Abilities

Ability to process incoming mail independently or route to proper source.

General knowledge of office practices and procedures.

Working knowledge of arithmetic and its uses in general office work.

Ability to compile information based on general instructions.

Ability to record information and to alphabetize.

Ability to type with accuracy at no specified speed.

Ability to gather and give basic information and instructions regarding the operation of the library.

Ability to communicate effectively both orally and in writing.

Ability to establish and maintain effective working relationships with the public and with fellow employees.

Ability to learn and follow varied procedures involved in office work, technical support, and circulation services.

Ability to maintain and work with a variety of records.

Physical and Mental Requirements

Work is primarily sedentary in nature. Physical requirements include sitting for extended periods of time, walking, bending, stooping, and lifting books and files of approximately 35 lbs or less.

Work may include extended periods of time viewing a computer video monitor and/or operating a keyboard. Work may include operation of a motor vehicle.

Work Environment

EXPOSURE CONTROL

Work activity does not entail predictable or unpredictable exposure to blood or body fluids.

Education, Experience, and Training

MINIMUM EXPERIENCE AND TRAINING

High school graduation and one year of experience working in a library, office environment, or public service setting. Secretarial school preferred.

3.0 ASSOCIATE

3.1 CIRCULATION ASSOCIATE

3.1.1 Circulation Associate

Library Name: Ellensburg Public Library

Library Location: Ellensburg, Washington

Population Served: 15,400

Number of Volumes: 59,000

Number of Titles: 53,000

Number of Periodical Subscriptions: 188

Reports To

LIBRARY DIRECTOR

TYPE OF SUPERVISION RECEIVED:

Employee is under the general supervision of the Library Director.

General Summary

JOB OBJECTIVE:

Supervise circulation services and organization of library collection; coordinate activities with other principal library divisions; assist Director in achieving goals and objectives of quality library service.

SUMMARY:

Responsible for planning, supervision, and coordination of activities of a principal division or function within the library. In this position, all activities having to do with circulation of materials and related services, patron registration and record keeping, collection of library revenues, keeping library materials in order on the shelves, handling rotating collections and inter-library loan services. Shares responsibility for automation system administration with Library Director and Head of Support Services. Responsible for training and supervision of all staff, trainees, and volunteers working in circulation.

Essential Functions and Responsibilities

All of the following are to be performed while adhering to City of Ellensburg operational policies, safety rules, and procedures.

Circulation Supervision:

Assist in policy development; implement policies for registration, lending; fine/fees, etc.

Develop procedures for circulation staff to accomplish division work

Provide reasonably close supervision on quality and quantity of circulation staff work

Plan work schedule for circulation staff, review and approve time sheets and maintain calendar

Participate in interview and hiring process to fill vacant circulation positions; provide orientation and training for new hires; assist in performance appraisals of supervised staff as requested by Director

Implement use of automation system for circulation services; provide staff training and supervision; perform automated system administration duties; prepare reports for Director and staff as needed

Provide annual system maintenance procedures; i.e. purging inactive patrons

Resolve problems with overdues, fines, registration, etc. for patrons and staff

Develop procedures for inter-library loan service; supervise and train staff; supervise interlibrary cooperative services

Generate system notices for overdues and oversee notification process

Assure staff maintains confidentiality of patron records

Reconcile cash register, prepare deposits in absence of Office Specialist

Ensure that desks, cabinets, supplies and equipment are orderly for shared staff use

Report major problems with equipment or building systems to director/city maintenance

Patron Service:

Perform registration and check out duties as needed

Demonstrate use of computer catalog and assist patrons in use

Locate items in catalog and on shelves for patrons as needed; Assist patrons with holds

Collect and record fines and fees; determine damage/loss fees; resolve problems; locate information for patrons using standard reference sources in books and CD ROM databases to answer questions; refer to reference staff as needed

Provide information about library programs and services, orally and with flyers

Answer inquiries made by telephone

Enforce library rules of behavior; take appropriate action in case of misbehavior; keep Director informed

Miscellaneous:

Is person in charge of the library in absence of the Director

Attend city staff meetings in absence of the Director

Attend workshops, conferences, training

Attend weekly and monthly library staff meetings

Conduct monthly meeting for circulation staff

Prepare forms for use by staff

Other duties may be assigned.

This is a representative sample—not to imply a complete listing of responsibilities and tasks.

Additional Job Duties

The key relationships described here are representative of those an employee encounters while performing the essential functions of this job.

While performing the duties of this job, the employee will provide information to and collect information from the public, and other libraries. Children are a significant proportion of the public. Contact will be made by telephone and in person and in writing.

The employee will coordinate projects and activities with the patrons and other libraries, by telephone, in person, or in writing.

The employee will solve problems and negotiate solutions within policy guidelines with the public, and other libraries by telephone, in person, or in writing.

Knowledge, Skills, and Abilities

A) Knowledge of general office practice and procedures; knowledge of basic principles of library practices and procedures, considerable knowledge of library circulation practices and classification systems; working knowledge of principles of supervision and personnel practices; knowledge of basic reference resources; some knowledge of personal computer software and equipment

B) Interviewing skills to determine patron needs; Skill in using automated library systems; skill in keyboard and computer data entry; skill in library data base searching; operation and maintenance of listed tools and equipment; skill in public relations; Periodically accesses sensitive information required to perform job tasks, requiring the ability to maintain confidentiality.

C) Ability to be courteous and tactful with the general public; Ability to communicate effectively, verbally and in writing; to implement policy and procedure; to exercise initiative and judgment in completing tasks; to organize various activities; Ability to work independently, exercising initiative and judgment in directing the work of others; ability to establish and maintain effective working relationships with patrons, employees, supervisors, and the general public.

Physical and Mental Requirements

The physical demands described here are representative of those that must be met by an employee to successfully perform the essential functions of this job. Reasonable accommodations may be made to enable individuals with disabilities to perform the essential functions.

While performing the duties of this job, the employee is regularly required to stand; walk; sit; use hands to finger, handle, or feel objects, tools, or controls; The employee is frequently required to reach with hands and arms; climb or balance; stoop, kneel, crouch, or crawl; and talk or hear. The employee is occasionally required to taste or smell.

The employee must regularly lift and/or move up to 25 pounds and occasionally lift and/or move more than 50 pounds. Specific vision abilities required by this job include close vision, distance vision, color vision, peripheral vision, depth perception, and the ability to adjust focus. Tasks affected include, computer work, watching patrons while working, supervision of staff.

Tools and Equipment Used

Automated library system; personal computer, printer, software programs, cash register, calculator, adding machine, typewriter, copier; phone and fax; postage machines; audio-visual equipment, microfilm reader/printer, Kurzweil reading machine, book carts

Work Environment

The work environment characteristics described here are representative of those an employee encounters while performing the essential functions of this job. Reasonable accommodations may be made to enable individuals with disabilities to perform the essential functions.

While performing the duties of this job, the employee is regularly exposed to airborne particles. The employee occasionally works in outside weather conditions for brief periods and is exposed to wet and/or humid conditions or extreme heat, and risk of electrical shock.

The noise level in the work environment is usually moderate.

Supervisory Responsibilities

Supervises Library Assistants (5-6), CWU Work Study (2-3) and Community service volunteers in circulation duties. Plan, assign, and direct work; train and supervise as to quality and quantity; promotes proper staff discipline and work productivity; address complaints and problems; Coordinate activities of circulation with other public service units of reference, children's services, and collection support services.

Education, Experience, and Training

QUALIFICATION REQUIREMENTS:

To perform this job successfully, an individual must be able to perform each essential duty satisfactorily. The requirements listed below are representative of the knowledge, skill, and/or ability required. Reasonable accommodations may be made to enable individuals with disabilities to perform the essential functions.

EDUCATION and/or EXPERIENCE:

Bachelor's degree (B.A.) from four year college or university; and one to two years of related experience and/or training; or equivalent combination of education and experience.

LANGUAGE SKILLS:

Ability to read, analyze and interpret general business periodicals, professional journals, technical procedures, or governmental regulations. Ability to write reports, business correspondence, and procedure manuals. Ability to effectively present information and respond to questions from groups of managers, clients, customers, and the general public.

MATHEMATICAL SKILLS:

Ability to calculate figures and amounts such as interest, percentages, area, circumference, and volume. Ability to apply concepts of basic algebra and geometry.

Additional Qualifications

SPECIAL REQUIREMENTS:

Certification in First Aid and CPR

License and Certification Requirements

First aid and CPR certification

Disclaimers

NOTICE: The above job profile does not include all essential and nonessential duties of this job. All employees with disabilities are encouraged to contact the Personnel Department to review and discuss the essential and nonessential functions of the job. An employee with a disability can evaluate the job in greater detail to determine if she/he can safely perform the essential function of this job with or without reasonable accommodation.

DISCLAIMERS: Job profiles are not intended, nor should they be construed to be, an exhaustive list of all responsibilities, tasks, skills, efforts, working conditions or similar behaviors, attributes or requirements associated with a job. A job profile is not a comprehensive job description. It is intended for the sole purpose of acquainting a person who is unfamiliar with such position with a brief overview of the position's general direction and scope. This position profile is confidential, is intended for internal use only and may not be copied or reproduced by anyone for any purpose without written permission from the Director of Personnel or the City Manager.

4.0 CLERK

4.1 CIRCULATION CLERK

> **4.1.1 Circulation Clerk**
>
> **Library Name:** West Chicago Public Library District
> **Library Location:** West Chicago, Illinois
> **Population Served:** 22,337
> **Number of Volumes:** 81,851
> **Number of Titles:** N/A
> **Number of Periodical Subscriptions:** 238

General Summary

JOB SUMMARY:

The Circulation Clerk greets and directs library patrons, and charges and discharges library materials in accordance with established library policies and procedures.

Essential Functions and Responsibilities

Performs opening and closing procedures.

Checks out, discharges, and renews all library materials.

Registers patrons for library cards, issues and renews cards.

Creates and updates patron records regarding Internet, expiration dates, fines, etc.

Pulls and sends out Pick List Materials.

Checks in DLS book bag materials and calls patrons when requested materials arrive.

Answers patron questions and solves problems regarding circulation of library materials.

Answers incoming calls, handles patron requests or problems and/or directs calls to correct extensions.

Sorts and distributes daily mail. Checks in and distributes newspapers, magazines, and periodicals to appropriate departments.

Performs other duties as requested.

Additional Job Duties

Investigates, edits, prints, and mails overdue notices and bills to patrons.

Handles interlibrary loans:

Pulls requested materials, logs, and sends to requested libraries

Receives requested materials, logs, check out to patron, then returns to owning library.

Knowledge, Skills, and Abilities

Skills:

Knowledge of computerized library systems.

Ability to operate basic office equipment including computers, keyboard, copier, fax machine, and calculator.

Ability to count money and make change.

Must have demonstrated interpersonal and communication skills.

Ability to prioritize work.

Physical and Mental Requirements

Requires sitting, standing, stooping, bending, and lifting/moving books and carts up to 40 pounds.

Must be able to communicate effectively in English, both orally and in writing.

Must be able to hear, comprehend and respond to library patrons both in person and in telephone conversations.

Must have visual ability to see computer screens.

Requires good hand dexterity for computer.

Requires mental alertness, focus, and attention to details.

Requires ability to operate basic business machinery (computer, printer, copier, telephone, FAX machine, paper cutter, laminating machine, and die cut machine).

Work Environment

Indoor conditions

Must maintain professional manner when dealing with patrons, including teens, young children, staff and others.

Must be able to work independently as well as with a team.

Must be flexible, creative, patient, and have a sense of humor.

May be required to work evenings and weekends.

Education, Experience, and Training

MINIMUM QUALIFICATIONS REQUIRED:

Education: High School diploma or equivalent.

Experience: Demonstrated customer service experience.

Strong interest in reading and library services.

4.2 PUBLIC SERVICES CLERK

4.2.1 Public Services Clerk

Library Name: Anacortes Public Library

Library Location: Anacortes, Washington

Population Served: 14,500

Number of Volumes: N/A

Number of Titles: 55,565

Number of Periodical Subscriptions: 126

Reports To

Public Services Supervisor

General Summary

JOB OBJECTIVE:

This position performs a variety of clerical and technical duties. Assignments typically involve checking out and receiving materials; receiving payments; providing general information to patrons and maintaining the Library in an orderly fashion.

LEVEL OF AUTHORITY: Performs routine and repetitive duties independently with only general supervision and according to well-known practices and procedures. Performs relatively more complex assignments and specialized functions under close and frequent supervision. Responsibility for accuracy and courtesy is important due to potential adverse Library patron relationships.

Essential Functions and Responsibilities

Check out to patron and receive Library print and non-print materials.

Calculate and collect funds due from the public.

Record receipt of returned materials and reintroduce materials into circulation system.

Process new and replacement patron cards.

Respond to public inquiries in a courteous manner; provide information within scope of knowledge and refer to employee of higher classification as appropriate.

Enforce Library rules.

If scheduled, open or close the library, following established procedures.

Monitor library security, safety and health conditions.

Maintain Library in a neat and orderly fashion.

Additional Job Duties

May perform portions of the work of higher or lower classified positions, as required.

Knowledge, Skills, and Abilities

Ability to bend, stoop and lift for prolonged periods in cramped spaces.

Ability to sit and use computer workstation, including keyboard and visual display terminal, for extended periods of time.

Ability to stand for extended periods of time.

Other

Attention to detail and accuracy.

Ability to communicate effectively, patiently and courteously with City employees, patrons and other community members.

Ability to handle multiple activities or interruptions at once and to work positively and effectively within a team model.

Ability to work a schedule that includes weekday, evening and weekend hours.

Physical and Mental Requirements

Strength, for example, to push loaded book cart weighing approximately 300 pounds on level floor and up ramp, to lift or maneuver onto cart loads up to 50 pounds and to carry cartons of books up and down stairs.

Tools and Equipment Used

Office equipment, such as; computer, modem, typewriter, adding machine, microfiche reader, paper cutter, fax, copier, telephone and postage meter. Might use various tools such as glue guns and lamination equipment.

Work Environment

Work is performed primarily in an indoor office setting at the library, in frequently dusty atmosphere with potential exposure to airborne pathogens.

Education, Experience, and Training

QUALIFICATIONS

Technical

Must have computer ability to adequately utilize automated library circulation systems.

Must possess a two-year college degree or have equivalent work experience.

Prior library experience preferred.

Must have excellent verbal and non-verbal communication skills.

Must be bondable.

Additional Qualifications

OTHER

As an absolute condition of employment, employees are required upon hire to sign a drug-free workplace agreement and an agreement not to use tobacco products of any kind while on the job.

Disclaimers

The statements contained in this job description reflect general details as necessary to describe the principal functions of this job, the level of knowledge and skill typically required and the scope of responsibility. It should not be considered an all-inclusive listing of work requirements. Individuals may perform other duties as assigned, including work in other functional areas to cover absences or provide relief, to equalize peak work periods or otherwise to balance the workload.

4.3 CLERK WITH SUPERVISORY RESPONSIBILITIES

4.3.1 Clerk with Supervisory Responsibilities

Library Name: Williamsburg Regional Library System
Library Location: Williamsburg, Virginia
Population Served: 60,100
Number of Volumes: 261,243
Number of Titles: N/A
Number of Periodical Subscriptions: 562

General Summary

JOB OBJECTIVE:

Under the supervision of the Circulation Services Director, the Circulation Services Senior Clerk is responsible for processing the incoming library materials on an automated system; keeping the library shelves in order; retrieving reference materials; handling simple clerical duties; changing the status of items needing mending; and performing other duties as requested by supervisor.

Essential Functions and Responsibilities

ESSENTIAL FUNCTIONS OF THE JOB:

Checks in library materials on automated system; changes the status of items on computer as needed.

Checks and empties all book and video drops.

Sorts and shelves library materials; shelf reads daily to maintain shelf order. Adjusts Circulation as needed to relieve overcrowding.

Assists in the opening and closing of the library.

Assists in maintaining neatness, order and repair of periodical collection.

Assists in maintaining neatness and order of CD collection.

Assists the reference department by checking in, taping, stamping, and routing periodicals.

Assists with implementing new procedures.

Assists Circulation Services Director with training of new shelver/clerks.

Assists in maintaining neatness of public areas of the library.

Assists in processing incoming mail.

Assists bookmobile staff with story times, shelving, and checking out library materials.

Performs general clerical duty such as making copies of handouts and other materials as needed.

Assists administration staff with copier maintenance.

May participate in library-wide committees or projects.

Perform other duties as needed.

Knowledge, Skills, and Abilities

Ability to compare names and numbers quickly, resulting in a working knowledge of the Dewey Decimal System.

Ability and willingness to understand and carry out oral and written instructions efficiently.

Ability to work under minimal supervision.

Ability to work well with other employees and maintain good work habits in an open space.

Ability to follow through on numerous details and work well under pressure.

Ability to learn and work with the library's automated system.

Ability to lift up to 25 pounds.

Work Environment

The job is located in two libraries; also in the bookmobile as needed. Work involves bending, lifting up to 25 pounds, and pushing and maneuvering book carts filled with library materials. Administers work typically standing at a counter with regular walking, light to medium lifting and other limited physical activities, regular operation of computer and scanning equipment is required; other office equipment as required. Regular contact is made with employees and the general public.

Education, Experience, and Training

MINIMUM QUALIFICATIONS:

High school diploma or equivalent preferred. Experience as a shelver/clerk.

Additional Qualifications

NECESSARY SPECIAL QUALIFICATIONS:

Requires the ability to travel among various library sites.

5.0 COORDINATOR

5.1 CIRCULATION COORDINATOR

> ### 5.1.1 Circulation Coordinator
>
> **Library Name:** Palo Alto City Library
> **Library Location:** Palo Alto, California
> **Population Served:** 238,636
> **Number of Volumes:** N/A
> **Number of Titles:** 166,858
> **Number of Periodical Subscriptions:** 952

Reports To

Manager, Main Library Services

General Summary

JOB OBJECTIVE:

The Coordinator, Library Circulation is a one-position, first-level management position in the Library Division of the Community Services Department. It has responsibility for implementing circulation services as well as development, coordination, and supervision of system wide activities for library circulation services library-wide. It differs from the Coordinator, Library Programs classification in that it includes direct supervision of staff. It is a distinguished from the higher level of Supervising Librarian in that the latter position supervises professional staff.

Essential Functions and Responsibilities

Essential and other important responsibilities and duties may include, but are not limited to, the following:

Essential Functions:

-Manages library-wide circulation services, including supervision of Main Library circulation activities and staff on a day-to-day basis.

-Develops, coordinates and interprets system-wide circulation policies and procedures.

-Interprets circulation services for the public, handles patron relations concerning library-wide circulation activities, and evaluates patron needs and references for circulation services.

-Develops and implements training program for circulation services for all library employees, with an emphasis on the computerized circulation system.

-Participates in planning for and implementation of computer system hardware and software, analyzes the effect of computer system software on circulation routines, troubleshoots computer system problems, and maintains system hardware peripherals.

Essential Functions:

-Develops and supervises library cash handling policies and procedures in accordance with City regulation and recommends appropriate user fees for circulation services.

-Prepares budget requests and monitors funds in program area.

-Prepares, maintains, and analyzes computer-based circulation statistical reports.

-Selects and deselects library material.

-Provides assistance at public service desks.

Related Functions:

-Chairs or participates in library, City, and cooperative library system committees.

-Performs related duties and responsibilities as required.

Knowledge, Skills and Abilities:

-Extensive knowledge of public library processes, particularly circulation, and application of state-of-the-art library computer systems.

-Knowledge of principles and practices of library administration.

-Ability to supervise personnel and programs to achieve goals.

Knowledge, Skills and Abilities:

-Ability to communicate with a wide variety of people.

-Ability to use computer terminal effectively, and to train others in use of library computer systems.

-Ability to work effectively with the public and staff in a variety of circumstances including stressful situations.

-Ability to use independent and sound judgement to organize, plan, and direct a section of library activities.

-Ability to communicate effectively orally and in writing in English to a variety of audiences.

-Ability to trouble-shoot minor equipment failures and make minor repairs.

-Ability to develop, prepare, and monitor budget.

-Ability to work evenings and weekends as required.

-Ability to maintain physical condition appropriate to the performance of assigned duties and responsibilities which may include sitting for extended periods of time and operating assigned office equipment.

-Ability to communicate with others and to assimilate and understand information, in a manner consistent with the essential job functions.

-Ability to operate assigned equipment.

-Ability to make sound decisions in a manner consistent with the essential job functions.

Physical and Mental Requirements

WORKING CONDITIONS:

Work in a library environment directly with the public; sustained posture in a standing or seated position for prolonged periods of time; perform lifting, crouching and pushing; may travel to other library facilities; some positions may include prolonged usage of computer equipment.

Supervisory Responsibilities

SUPERVISES: Library Specialists Library Assistants Hourly and volunteer employees

Education, Experience, and Training

MINIMUM QUALIFICATIONS:

Sufficient education, training and/or work experience to demonstrate possession of the following knowledge, skills, and abilities which would typically be acquired through:

-College degree or a combination of related experience and training substantially equivalent to graduation from a college or university.

and

-Three years of library experience in areas of job responsibility including at least one year of experience with a computerized library system.

5.2 STAFFING COORDINATOR

5.2.1 Staffing Coordinator

Library Name: Williamsburg Regional Library System

Library Location: Williamsburg, Virginia

Population Served: 60,100

Number of Volumes: 261,243

Number of Titles: N/A

Number of Periodical Subscriptions: 562

General Summary

NATURE OF WORK:

Under the supervision of the Circulation Services Director, the Circulation Staff Coordinator performs a variety of administrative and public service tasks to support the activities of the circulation services departments, including overseeing its scheduling, timesheets, and leave records. Other essential duties include complex procedures involved with the computerized transactions of library materials to the public. Also answers circulation and directional questions, collects money for late and lost library materials and sale items, and assists in opening and closing of the library. The Circulation Staff Coordinator is in charge of the department, as needed, in the absence of the Circulation Services Director.

Essential Functions and Responsibilities

Prepares and maintains the department's monthly work schedules and the weekly desk schedules for both the senior library assistants (circulation) and the shelver/clerks.

Balances and verifies the department's timesheets in preparation for payroll transactions.

Balances and verifies the department's leave records.

Works at the circulation desk on a regular basis, performing all related tasks.

Uses library automated system for transactions in the charging out of library materials, processing patron records, determining materials status, locating resources within the system, arranging for transfers of library materials, placing reserves, registering new patrons, and performing additional procedures as needed.

Learns new computer procedures for each upgrade and software release in a timely manner; runs computer reports as required.

Answers circulation and directional questions; refers other questions to appropriate person or department.

Oversees the tally and transfer of funds from the cash register to the safe.

Verifies and sends overdue notices; resolves problem files; receives and records overdue fines; sends related correspondence as needed; processes lost/damaged library materials to technical services; resolves patron records; and processes patron refunds.

Assists in opening and closing procedures of library.

Assists in checking in library materials as needed.

Assists in training new employees; may schedule and supervise department volunteers.

Monitors patron activities in the library, and may handle problems as they occur.

May participate in library-wide committees or projects.

Performs other duties are required.

Knowledge, Skills, and Abilities

Ability to plan and organize work schedules.

Ability to learn and operate library automated system with high degree of efficiency.

Ability to organize work, set priorities, use time effectively, work independently, and meet deadlines.

Excellent written and verbal communication skills.

Must have desire to serve the public with friendliness, tact, and diplomacy.

Ability to follow through on numerous details and maintain records in a standard, orderly, systematic fashion, and work well under pressure.

Ability to analyze and to creatively solve problems related to the position.

Accuracy in clerical skills, including typing and filing.

Desire and ability to work with enthusiasm and initiative.

Work Environment

This job is located in two library buildings. Administers work typically standing at a counter or public service desk. Work involves bending, reaching, lifting up to 25 pounds, walking and other limited physical activities.

Frequent operation of computer keyboard, bar code scanner, and cash register is required; other office equipment as needed. Regular contact is made with employees and the general public.

Education, Experience, and Training

MINIMUM QUALIFICATIONS:

Must have been in a full-time Circulation Assistant position with the Williamsburg Regional Library for a minimum of one year.

Additional Qualifications

NECESSARY SPECIAL QUALIFICATIONS:

Requires the ability to travel among various library sites.

6.0 MANAGER

6.1 CIRCULATION MANAGER

6.1.1 Circulation Manager

Library Name: West Chicago Public Library District
Library Location: West Chicago, Illinois
Population Served: 22,337
Number of Volumes: 81,851
Number of Titles: N/A
Number of Periodical Subscriptions: 238

General Summary

JOB SUMMARY:

The Circulation Supervisor serves as a member of the library management team. He/she is responsible for all activities dealing with the circulation of materials and related services, patron registration, record keeping and collection of library revenue.

Essential Functions and Responsibilities

Prepares recommendations for the Circulation Department's budget and submits them to the Administrative Librarian.

Prepares Long Range Plans and Goal Assessments for the Circulation Department.

Works with other department managers to develop programs and procedures for the library.

Prepares monthly statistical reports for the Administrative Librarian and the Board of Directors.

Represents the library at professional meetings and activities.

Interfaces with other LINC libraries in determining and developing circulation system parameters.

Monitors the behavior and conduct of library patrons to ensure an atmosphere conducive to use of library facilities for all patrons.

Assumes other responsibilities as requested.

DEPARTMENT RESPONSIBILITIES:

Plans and implements department procedures that address the needs of all library patrons.

Selects, supervises, schedules, trains, and evaluates the staff assigned to the Circulation department.

Ensures the proper charge and discharge of materials using the library's automated system.

Implements corrections and changes in the circulation mode of the computer system and informs the Administrative Librarian of changes made.

Maintains circulation statistics and borrower records.

Compiles statistics and annual reports for the library Board of Directors and the State of Illinois.

Responsible for all patron records. Registers patron cards, renews and/or pulls expired cards.

Distributes mail, logs in and distributes magazines, newspapers, and periodicals.

Responsible for all patron material requests and reserves. Ensures that requested materials from member libraries are prepared and routed on a daily basis.

Responsible for promoting all library programs and program registration.

Performs all duties outlined in the job functions of the Circulation Clerks on a daily basis.

Additional Job Duties

Troubleshoots problems with the library telephone system, other equipment, and the security alarm system. Repairs the problem or arranges appropriate service.

Knowledge, Skills, and Abilities

Skills:

Knowledge of computerized library systems.

Basic office equipment including computer, keyboard, copier, fax machine, and calculator.

Must have demonstrated interpersonal and communication skills.

Ability to prioritize work.

Management skills.

Strong interpersonal skills.

A strong interest in reading is preferred.

Bilingual a plus.

Physical and Mental Requirements

Requires sitting, standing, stooping, bending, and lifting/moving books and carts up to 40 pounds.

Must be able to communicate effectively in English, both orally and in writing.

Must be able to hear, comprehend and respond to library patrons both in person and in telephone conversations.

Must have visual ability to see computer screens.

Requires good hand dexterity for computer.

Requires mental alertness, focus, and attention to details.

Requires ability to operate basic business machinery (computer, printer, copier, telephone, FAX machine, paper cutter, laminating machine, die cut machine).

Work Environment

Indoor conditions

Must maintain professional manner when dealing with patrons, including teens, young children, staff and others.

Must be able to work independently as well as with a team.

Must be flexible, creative, patient, and have a sense of humor.

May be required to work evenings and weekends.

Supervisory Responsibilities

SUPERVISORY RESPONSIBILITIES

Supervises the Senior Circulation Clerk, the Circulation Clerks, the Pages and Volunteers.

Education, Experience, and Training

MINIMUM QUALIFICATIONS REQUIRED:

Education: Library Technical Assistant Certification (LTA) or Bachelor's degree required.

Experience: Three years of office or library experience including customer service experience.

7.0 PAGE, SHELVER, AND AIDE

7.1 AIDE

7.1.1 Aide

Library Name: Milwaukee Public Library
Library Location: Milwaukee, Wisconsin
Population Served: 608,150
Number of Volumes: 2,553,934
Number of Titles: N/A
Number of Periodical Subscriptions: 9,719

General Summary

Library Circulation Aides are employed 20 hours per week, primarily during evenings and weekends, on a year round basis. Persons employed as Library Circulation Aides must be available to work the schedule of hours required by the Library's public service needs. Library Circulation Aides work at the Milwaukee Public Central Library and Neighborhood Libraries.

NOTE: The eligible list resulting from this examination may be used to fill similar positions, but will not be used to fill full-time Clerk positions for the Milwaukee Public Library.

Essential Functions and Responsibilities

Circulation Services—shelving; shelf reading; arranging and handling books, periodicals, microfilm and other library materials.

Service Desk—registering borrowers for library cards using a CRT; answering phone and in person inquiries; checking library materials in and out of the library.

Performing other duties as assigned.

Reasonable accommodations requested by qualified individuals with disabilities will be made in accordance with the Americans with Disabilities Act (ADA) of 1990.

Knowledge, Skills, and Abilities

Ability to communicate with people in a tactful manner.

Ability to relate well with other employees and the general public.

Ability to follow directions.

Ability to be punctual.

Education, Experience, and Training

THE REQUIREMENTS:

At least 16 years of age at time of application.

Current enrollment as a high school student OR college or technical school student for a minimum of 3 credits.

NOTE: Proof of student status (grade report and/or fee receipt) will be required before appointment to this position and status will be monitored on a semester basis after hire. Individuals who do not maintain student status will no longer be eligible for employment as Circulation Aides.

Additional Qualifications

Residence in the City of Milwaukee at time of application and throughout employment.

Note: All library fines must be paid in full before any candidate will be hired.

DESIRABLE QUALIFICATIONS:

Typing or keyboarding skills.

7.1.2 Library Aide

Library Name: Columbus Metropolitan Library
Library Location: Columbus, Ohio
Population Served: 762,235
Volumes: 780,849
Titles: N/A
Periodical Subscriptions: 2195

General Summary

PURPOSE OF JOB: Performs various support duties at branch and division locations.

Essential Functions and Responsibilities

Sorts mail and books, prepares delivery.

Performs backroom support duties such as processing delivery, clearing bookdrop.

Performs bulk photo copying.

Performs "finishing" tasks on printed materials such as folding, counting, cutting, collating, stitching/stapling.

Additional Job Duties

SECONDARY DUTIES AND RESPONSIBILITIES:

Performs other duties as assigned.

Work Environment

INTER-ACTION:

Library staff.

Supervisory Responsibilities

SUPERVISORY/MANAGEMENT RESPONSIBILITIES:

No direct reports

Education, Experience and Training:

QUALIFICATION REQUIREMENTS:

Minimum Requirements:

16 years of age (work permit required for minors).

Ability to perform alphabetic and numeric sorting and filing.

Highly Preferred Requirements:

Ability to operate CML technology systems, in addition to personal computer, software programs and other job related equipment.

Additional Qualifications

TRAVEL REQUIREMENTS:

Periodic

Position Hours

SPECIAL REQUIREMENTS:

Location will determine work schedule; may be required to work evenings or weekends.

7.1.3 Library Aide

Library Name: Mesquite Public Library
Library Location: Mesquite, Texas
Population Served: 126,570
Number of Volumes: 140,968
Number of Titles: 105,726
Number of Periodical Subscriptions: 324

Reports To

SUPERVISION

General supervision is provided by the Manager of Branch Library Services.

General Summary

GENERAL SUMMARY To perform a variety of tasks involved in the arrangement and order of library materials in the general maintenance and upkeep of the library.

Essential Functions and Responsibilities

All behaviors comply with the Code of Conduct & Rules of Behavior outlined in chapter 8 of the General Government Policies and Procedures Manual.

Perform a variety of tasks involved in ensuring that books and other library material are shelved including clearing the book drop, clearing books from tables, and shifting books to ensure they are in their proper shelf order.

Arrange and shelve library materials by a numerical filing system.

Assist in setting up for library programs; move furniture.

Perform minor library maintenance including changing light bulbs and assembling displays; assist in removing displays.

Assist with the Friends of the Library book sale; move and lift book donation boxes.

Provide daily count for in-house use of materials. Work as a cooperative and supportive member of the Library team. Provide the best possible customer service to the public.

Additional Job Duties

Assist in repairing books with broken binding or ripped pages.

Assist in maintaining the copy machine including adding paper and changing toner; direct material needs to appropriate staff person. May assist in sorting and distributing mail. May pick up and deliver material to and from the Branch and the Main Library. Prepare book spine labels; label books. Perform other duties as assigned.

Knowledge, Skills, and Abilities

COMPETENCIES

An employee's performance will be evaluated based on five competencies: Job knowledge; Teamwork; Customer Service; Flexibility; Work Ethic.

Knowledge of: Safe work practices. Modern office procedures, practices, methods and equipment.

Skill in: Operating modern office equipment.

Ability to: Work varied shifts. Shelve books. Learn the Dewey Decimal Classification System. Learn alphabetical and numerical filing.

Physical and Mental Requirements

Maintain effective audio-visual discrimination and perception needed for making observations, communicating with others operating assigned equipment. Maintain physical condition appropriate to the performance of assigned duties and responsibilities which may include the following: standing, kneeling, walking, stooping, bending, twisting or otherwise moving around the facility to file, assist patrons, distribute or shelve library materials and perform related duties. Frequently pushing or pulling book trucks that requires the exertion of 30 lbs. of force to move.

Education, Experience and Training:

MINIMUM JOB REQUIREMENTS EDUCATION

Formal or informal education or training which ensures the ability to read and write at a level necessary for successful job performance.

EXPERIENCE No experience required.

Additional Qualifications

Perform heavy manual labor. Work in a team environment. Tactfully respond to requests and inquiries from the public. Establish and maintain effective working relationship with those contacted in the course of work. Flexibly adapt to a variety of work situations and interruptions. Readily adapt to changes in policies or work methods Pass a medical physical examination and drug test. Meet the City's driving standards.

License and Certification Requirements

Possession of a valid Class C Texas driver's license depending upon assignment.

Disclaimers

Job description statements are intended to describe the general nature and level of work being performed by employees assigned to this job title. They are not intended to be construed as an exhaustive list of all responsibilities, duties and skills required.

7.2 CIRCULATION PAGE/SHELVER

7.2.1 Circulation Page/Shelver

Library Name: West Chicago Public Library District
Library Location: West Chicago, Illinois
Population Served: 22,337
Number of Volumes: 81,851
Number of Titles: N/A
Number of Periodical Subscriptions: 238

General Summary

JOB SUMMARY:

The Page shelves library materials and maintains the library shelving areas so patrons and staff can locate materials.

Essential Functions and Responsibilities

Sorts material by call number prior to shelving.

Resensitizes returned material.

Shelves materials in correct location.

Straightens shelves and cleans as needed.

Brings materials in poor condition to the attention of the Circulation or Youth Services staff.

Shifts and discards old issues of magazines and newspapers.

Answers simple directional questions.

Performs other tasks as needed by Circulation staff.

Knowledge, Skills, and Abilities

Skills:

Knowledge of the purpose and function of public libraries.

Ability to use the alphabet and numbers as applied to the Dewey Decimal Classification System.

Must have demonstrated interpersonal and communication skills.

Ability to prioritize work.

A strong interest in reading is preferred.

Physical and Mental Requirements

Extensive standing, stooping, bending, and lifting/moving books and carts up to 40 pounds.

Ability to understand and follow oral and written instructions.

Good vision and hearing.

Mental alertness, focus, and attention to details.

Work Environment

Indoor conditions

Must maintain professional manner when dealing with patrons, including teens, young children, staff and others.

Must be dependable, accurate, and responsible in his/her work.

Must be able to work independently as well as with a team.

May be required to work evenings and weekends.

Education, Experience, and Training

MINIMUM QUALIFICATIONS REQUIRED:

Education: Fourteen years of age (with a work permit if less than sixteen years old) and completion of the eight grade.

Experience: No experience required. Prior experience as a School Library Aide or community library volunteer preferred.

7.2.2 Circulation Page

Library Name: Manitowoc-Calumet Library System

Library Location: Manitowoc, Wisconsin

Population Served: 58,213

Number of Volumes: 195,166

Number of Titles: N/A

Periodical Subscriptions: 395

General Summary

BROAD SCOPE OF POSITION: Working under direct supervision of Circulation Supervisor, maintains order of collections throughout Library by means of shelving, shelfreading, inspecting, sorting, book pick-up, searching, etc.; also routes patrons and telephone calls to appropriate destinations. Assists in the maintenance of building security; assists in securing the building at closing time Routine tasks may be directed by other departmental staff. May perform Page-level work in other departments.

Essential Functions and Responsibilities

The following list identifies principal duties and responsibilities of the job. It is not a definitive list and other similar duties may be assigned. An asterisk (*) before any of the following items indicates duties and responsibilities which are not "essential functions" of the job as defined by the Americans with Disabilities Act.

1. Prepares materials for shelving or filing, and shelves or files materials in alphanumeric order. Shifts materials, as assigned or as necessary. Shelf reads to ensure that materials are in alphanumeric order.

2. Assists Circulation and other staff in dealing with problem patrons, particularly those who disrupt normal use or operation of the Library, or attempt to unlawfully remove library materials from premises. Completes Incident Reports, when necessary, and reports informally about other security and/or public behavior problems.

3. Participates in sweep of the building at closing time. Cooperates with Guard/Custodians while conducting closing procedures. Communicates effectively with the public regarding closing procedures and escorts patrons to appropriate service desks.

4. Maintains appearance of collections by aligning materials, and through use of supports, dividers and dust cloths. Retrieves and discards litter from stack areas, etc.

5. Answers central switchboard. Takes messages. Routes patrons and telephone calls to appropriate destinations.

6. Assists with the work of the Circulation Department. Retrieves unshelved materials from stack areas, etc. Empties materials from return bins, as assigned. Sensitizes, inspects, cleans when necessary, and sorts materials, as assigned. Searches stacks and other areas for claimed returned, traced, lost, missing, shared catalog use ("pick list"), or other items, as assigned.

7. Sorts, bundles and removes outdated issues of newspapers, as assigned.

*8. Makes closing and other necessary announcements over the public address system, as assigned.

*9. Performs Page-level work in other departments, as assigned.

Knowledge, Skills, and Abilities

1. Skill at sorting and shelving materials in alphanumeric order. Minimum skill level: ability to accurately shelve at a consistent rate of at least 100 items per hour; shelf read at 500 items per hour. Physical capacity to place materials on shelves at all shelving heights.

2. Ability to follow multi-step written and/or verbal instructions and to perform routine procedures involving several steps. Ability to exercise valid judgment in evaluating situations and making decisions. Ability to work with limited direct supervision.

3. Ability to establish and maintain effective working relationships with Library staff members and the public. Ability to work in a team setting. Willingness to assist and support coworkers,

contribute ideas, and maintain flexibility. Ability to adapt to a rapidly changing environment.

4. Ability to communicate effectively.

5. Capacity to be easily understood on voice telephone and public address systems. Minimum skill level: Demonstrated knowledge of proper telephone etiquette; ability to use public address and phone systems; ability to take messages and route them to the appropriate staff member or department.

6. Must comply at all times with the Library's "Drug-Free Workplace" policy.

7. Willingness and ability to understand and support the fundamental principles of library services, such as: open access to library materials in any format for people of all ages; the library's obligation to provide materials representing as many points of view as possible; and a patron's absolute right to privacy in dealings with the library and with respect to records maintained by library.

Physical and Mental Requirements

WORKING CONDITIONS:

1. Usually (up to 100% of work time) lifts and/or transports objects weighing 5 to 20 pounds; pushes or pulls carts loaded with materials weighing more than 150 pounds.

2. Usually (up to 100% of work time) places books and other materials in proper alpha-numeric order on shelves at various heights, ranging from floor level up to 90" high. May need to use step stool.

2. Usually (up to 100% of work time) performs job in areas where seating cannot be provided.

3. Regularly (up to 75% of work time) works in bookstack areas where there is exposure to dust, newsprint, etc.

4. Regularly (up to 75% of work time) works with equipment and performs procedures where carelessness may result in minor cuts, bruises, or muscle strains.

5. Regularly (up to 75% of work time) uses cleaning solutions to dust shelves.

Education, Experience, and Training

MINIMUM QUALIFICATIONS:

1. Educational development at a level normally acquired through completion of the 8th grade in the United States.

2. Must have work permit, if required by law.

3. Demonstrable possession of knowledge, skills, abilities, and capacities identified in "Job Specifications" section, above.

4. Capacity to work under conditions described in "Working Conditions" section, above.

Position Hours

Part-time, typically working 20 hours per two-week pay period on a flexible schedule which varies from week to week. May be scheduled to work days, evenings, Saturdays, and Sundays.

7.2.3 Page

Library Name: Omaha Public Library
Library Location: Omaha, Nebraska
Population Served: 437,431
Volumes: 1,012,761
Titles: 370,807
Periodical Subscriptions: 2508

General Summary

NATURE OF WORK

This work involves assisting in the daily operations of the Omaha Public Library.

Essential Functions and Responsibilities

(Any one position may not perform all of the duties listed, nor do the listed examples include all of the duties that may be performed in positions allocated to this class. Also, the duties are not necessarily listed in order of importance or frequency of performance.)

Places books and other library materials in their rightful places and keeps shelves in order.

Labels, covers, and stamps books.

Assists in the operation of the circulation desk including checking books in and out and other related tasks.

Clips articles and pictures from newspaper and periodical files and makes photocopies for distribution.

Types and files routine correspondence and other documents.

Processes correspondence and books to be sent by mail and packages non-print media.

Sorts and distributes incoming materials.

Processes reserved library items.

Delivers items to City facilities throughout the City.

Shovels snow from sidewalks.

Performs other duties as assigned or as the situation dictates within the scope of this classification.

Knowledge, Skills, and Abilities

Knowledge of the Dewey Decimal system.

Ability to file books, periodicals, and other materials.

Ability to communicate effectively with workmates and the public.

Ability to understand oral and written instructions.

Ability to use up to one hundred (100) pounds of force occasionally and lesser amounts of force more frequently to move objects.

Position Hours

SPECIAL QUALIFICATIONS

Must be able to work varied times, including evenings and weekends.

Tools and Equipment Used

EQUIPMENT OPERATION (Any one position may not use all of the tools and equipment listed, nor do the listed examples comprise all of the tools and equipment that may be used in positions allocated to this classification.)

Computer, Copier, Checkout Equipment, Microfilm Reader-Printer, Typewriter, Telephone, Laminator

7.2.4 Shelver

Library Name: Walla Walla Public Library
Library Location: Walla Walla, Washington
Population Served: 30,000
Number of Volumes: 114,540
Number of Titles: N/A
Number of Periodical Subscriptions: 253

General Summary

Under the direction of an assigned supervisor, perform a variety of shelving duties within the Public Library; exercise judgment and ingenuity to analyze situations and select appropriate solution strategy.

Essential Functions and Responsibilities

REPRESENTATIVE DUTIES:

Maintain books and materials in proper alphabetical or numerical order.

Reshelve books, periodicals and other materials to the proper locations in the library.

Clean and store phonograph records.

File legislative bills and newspapers.

Maintain assigned area in a neat and orderly condition.

Discard magazines that are out of circulation; stamp in new or donated books.

Perform related duties as assigned.

Knowledge, Skills, and Abilities

KNOWLEDGE OF:

Basic functions, operations and maintenance of a City library.

Alpha and numeric filing systems.

ABILITY TO:

Work cooperatively with others.

Utilize alpha and numeric filing systems.

Maintain library in a neat and orderly condition.

Work courteously and tactfully with customers and employees.

Education, Experience and Training:

Any combination equivalent to: sufficient training and experience to demonstrate the knowledge and abilities listed above.

Work Environment

Indoor work environment.

Physical and Mental Requirements

Reaching overhead, above the shoulders and horizontally; sitting for extended periods of time; standing for extended periods of time; bending at the waist; kneeling or crouching; hearing and speaking to exchange information; seeing to read; carrying, pushing or pulling; lifting heavy objects.

HAZARDS:

Working at heights while shelving books.

7.2.5 Shelver

Library Name: Richland County Public Library
Library Location: Columbia, South Carolina
Population Served: 320,700
Number of Volumes: 1,059,806
Number of Titles: N/A
Number of Periodical Subscriptions: 2840

Essential Functions and Responsibilities

EXAMPLES OF WORK: (illustrative only)

Essential Functions of the Job:

Shelves library materials.

Empties bookdrops and video drops and brings materials into the building.

Reads shelves.

Searches for materials on shelves from printouts and lists.

Shifts collection when needed.

Additional Job Duties

Other Important Responsibilities:

Performs opening and closing procedures.

Sorts and stamps date cards.

May perform inside and outside duties related to housekeeping (e. g., dusting, moves hoses, etc.).

May assist patrons in use of copiers, PAC terminals, and other equipment.

Performs other associated duties as required or assigned.

Education, Experience and Training:

MINIMUM QUALIFICATIONS:

Completion of at least two years of high school.

Ability to perform job responsibilities.

7.3 LEAD PAGE

7.3.1 Lead Page

Library Name: Mission Viejo Public Library
Library Location: Mission Viejo, California
Population Served: 98,000
Number of Volumes: 133,664
Number of Titles: N/A
Number of Periodical Subscriptions: 271

General Summary

DEFINITION: Under moderate supervision, perform manual and clerical duties according to defined procedures; store and retrieve library materials; process library materials for public use; and perform other related work as necessary.

DISTINGUISHING CHARACTERISTICS: This is the advanced level in the Library Page class series. Positions at this level are distinguished from the Library Page level by the level of responsibility assumed and the complexity of duties assigned. Incumbents perform the most difficult and responsible types of duties assigned including training and technical and functional oversight duties. Positions at this level receive only occasional instruction or assistance as new or unusual situations arise, and are fully aware of the operating procedures and policies of the work unit.

Essential Functions and Responsibilities

These functions may not be present in all positions in this class. When a position is to be filled, the essential functions will be noted in the announcement of position availability. Management reserves the right to add, modify, change or rescind the work assignments of different positions and to make reasonable accommodations so that qualified employees can perform the essential functions of the job.

Provide training and orientation to new Library Pages and Volunteer Shelvers.

Provide oversight, assignments, and follow-up to Library Pages during the weekend and evening hours.

Shelve and file all library materials using different filing systems.

Clean, maintain, operate and instruct the public on how to use microfilm and copy machines. Receive new materials, verify with order, and inform staff of discrepancies

Repair library materials.

Collect, sort and file any materials used in the library.

Retrieve magazines and answer questions from the public about the magazine collection.

Keep library in good order.

Process new and gift materials for public use.

Additional Job Duties

Moves furniture, equipment and supplies as assigned to set-up facilities and meeting rooms; assist groups using facilities;

May explain or enforce facility rules; monitor facility use; open, close, and secure building for events and provide assistance at special events.

Perform related duties and responsibilities as assigned.

Knowledge, Skills, and Abilities

Knowledge of:

Alphabetical and decimal numeric filing system.

Purpose and functions of the library.

Effective public relations.

General principles of risk management related to the functions of the assigned area.

Safe work practices.

Skill to: Operate modern office equipment including computer equipment, software programs, microfilm and copy machines.

Ability to:

Work with minimum supervision.

Oversee the work of others.

Respond to requests and inquiries from the general public.

Deal courteously and effectively with the general public.

Communicate clearly and concisely, both orally and in writing.

Work weekends, evenings and holidays.

Understand and carry out oral and written instructions.

Establish, maintain and foster positive and harmonious working relationships with those contacted in the course of work.

Physical and Mental Requirements

Physical and Sensory Elements:

The sensory demands of the job typically require speaking, hearing, touching and seeing. This is primarily a sedentary office classification although standing in work areas and walking between work areas is required. Finger dexterity is needed to access, enter and retrieve data using a computer keyboard, typewriter keyboard or calculator and to operate standard office equipment.

Positions in this classification occasionally bend, stoop, kneel, and reach, as well as push and pull up to 250 pounds with heavy book carts and drawers open and closed to retrieve and file information. Positions in this classification occasionally lift and carry library materials that typically weigh less than 20 pounds.

Work Environment

Environmental Elements: Employees work in an office environment with moderate noise levels, controlled temperature conditions and no direct exposure to hazardous physical substances. Employees may interact with upset staff and/or public and private representatives in interpreting and enforcing departmental policies and procedures.

Supervisory Responsibilities

SUPERVISION EXERCISED: Exercises technical and functional supervision over Library Pages.

Education, Experience and Training:

Any combination equivalent to experience and training that would provide the required knowledge, skills, and abilities would be qualifying. A typical way to obtain the knowledge, skill, and abilities would be: Experience: Equivalent to the completion of two (2) years as a Library Page. Training: Equivalent to the completion of the eleventh (11th) grade.

License and Certification Requirements

Applicants must be fifteen (15) years of age or older. Applicants under the age of eighteen (18) who are required to attend school must provide a valid California Worker's Permit prior to appointment.

Position Hours

Employees must be able to work evenings and weekends.

7.4 FILM PAGE AND RECORDING SHELVER

7.4.1 Film Page and Recording Shelver

Library Name: Richland County Public Library
Library Location: Columbia, South Carolina
Population Served: 320,700
Number of Volumes: 1,059,806
Number of Titles: N/A
Periodical Subscriptions: 2,840

Essential Functions and Responsibilities

EXAMPLES OF WORK: (illustrative only)
Shelves Film and Sound materials.
Maintains service area in neat and proper order.
Maintains shelves in correct numerical order.

Additional Job Duties

Other Important Responsibilities:
Searches for materials on shelves from printouts and lists.
Retrieves returned non-print material from circulation and receiving.
Assists with placing holds in circulation workroom for patron pickup.

May assist patrons in the use of equipment and in locating specified materials.
Performs other associated duties as required.

Education, Experience, and Training

MINIMUM QUALIFICATIONS:
Completion of at least two years of high school.
Ability to perform job responsibilities.

8.0 SPECIALIST

8.1 CIRCULATION SPECIALIST

8.1.1 Circulation Specialist

Library Name: Palo Alto City Library
Library Location: Palo Alto, California
Population Served: 60,800
Number of Volumes: 238,636
Number of Titles: 166,858
Number of Periodical Subscriptions: 952

Reports To

Various Library Managers or Supervisors

General Summary

DEFINITION:

Under general supervision performs routine and specialized circulation activities involving library materials, files and equipment, using library computer system or technical tasks involved in preparation and/or repair of library collection records and materials.

DISTINGUISHING FEATURES:

Library Specialist is a classification found in the Library Division within the Department of Social and Community Services and is distinguished by the performance of a variety of complex clerical and coordinate tasks under minimal supervision. Incumbents are assigned to a particular unit with defined tasks and are required to have a detailed working knowledge of program areas. Significant portion of day may include direct public contact.

Essential Functions and Responsibilities

Essential and other important responsibilities and duties may include, but are not limited to, the following:

-Performs all duties required to effectively operate circulation computer such as maintenance activities for hardware and software, telephone communication with computer engineers, interpretation of computer to staff, running and monitoring daily reports, library-wide supervision of computer downtime activity, building and maintaining required computer records and files.

-Performs routine circulation tasks required to serve public such as registering and updating files of borrowers; interpreting status of patron accounts, checking in and out library materials via computerized equipment, accepting payments for fines, bills, fees, assisting patrons with inquiries regarding availability and status of items in collections, and assisting users regarding circulation services.

-Collects, records, tabulates and deposits monies received daily from all library facilities, complying with cash handling procedures.

-Under direction of supervisor, develops, organizes and monitors procedures for circulation of all collections and maintenance of library equipment.

Essential Functions:

-Maintains up-to-date reservations system including (coordinating requests city-wide,) utilizing the library computer as appropriate.

- Monitors total overdue processes.

-Schedules, trains, and coordinates work of clerical, temporary and volunteer staff in variety of routines.

- Coordinates daily processing activities.

-Responsible for the manual preparation of all materials for circulation. Uses specialized tools and equipment to prepare materials for public use.

-Responsible for the manual preparation and restoration of all items needing repair, including book and non-book items using specialized tools and equipment to reback, rebind, recover, reglue, relabel, resew, laminate and otherwise repair materials for public use.

-Responsible for manual preparation, preservation, and restoration of valuable, historical materials in the library collection.

-Builds and maintains on-line computer files of bibliographic data for all new items.

- Gathers and compiles statistical data.

Additional Job Duties

-Selects, orders, and maintains supplies. Interacts directly with vendors to resolve ordering problems.

- May serve on library, City or cooperative library system committees.

- May select and deselect materials in a limited area.

-Performs related duties and responsibilities as required.

Supervisory Responsibilities

SUPERVISES: Non-supervisory position, may assign work to clerical, temporary and/or volunteer staff.

Education, Experience, and Training

MINIMUM QUALIFICATIONS:

Sufficient education, training and/or work experience to demonstrate possession of the following knowledge, skills, and abilities, which would typically be acquired through:

- High school diploma or equivalent and Two years of work experience.

Knowledge, Skills and Abilities:

-Ability to communicate with a wide variety of people.

-Ability to type and use computer terminal effectively and to learn operation of computerized system used in library.

-Ability to work effectively with public and co-workers in variety of circumstances ranging from pleasant to stressful.

- Ability to interpret and apply procedures and policies of the library.

-Ability to organize work assignments, recognize priorities, understand and follow written and oral directions.

- Ability to use independent and sound judgment to resolve problems.

-Possesses manual dexterity and ability to manipulate small and large computer components and/or hand-eye coordination to use small tools.

-Ability to effectively communicate complex data both orally and in writing to public and staff.

-Ability to train and direct work of temporary and/or volunteer employees.

-Ability to work varied schedule including early mornings, evenings and weekends may be required.

-Ability to maintain physical condition appropriate to the performance of assigned duties and responsibilities which may include standing or sitting for extended periods of time and operating assigned office equipment.

-Ability to communicate with others and to assimilate and understand information, in a manner consistent with the essential job functions.

-Ability to operate assigned equipment.

-Ability to make sound decisions in a manner consistent with the essential job functions.

-Ability to speak and be understood in the English language.

Work Environment

Work in an library environment directly with the public; sustained posture in a standing or seated position for prolonged periods of time; perform lifting, crouching and pushing; may travel to other library facilities; some positions may include prolonged usage of computer equipment.

VII. COMMUNITY RELATIONS AND MARKETING

Included in this section are community development, marketing, and public relations coordinators and librarians;, marketing assistants and managers; and communication specialists.

1.0 COMMUNITY RELATIONS AND DEVELOPMENT COORDINATOR

1.1 COMMUNITY RELATIONS COORDINATOR

1.1.1 Community Relations Coordinator

Library Name: Hurt-Battelle Memorial Library of West Jefferson
Library Location: West Jefferson, Ohio
Population Served: 5,600
Number of Volumes: N/A
Number of Titles: 44,768
Number of Periodical Subscriptions: 85

Reports To

Director

Essential Functions and Responsibilities

Promotes community awareness of library services and programs with the Director through planning and appropriate communication with media, area organizations, and local businesses.

Works closely with the Director to develop an annual plan of library objectives and activities for community relations based on the Library's goals and objectives.

Works closely with the Director and staff to plan and implement special promotions and coordinate participation in community events.

Keeps informed of local developments and activities through the local press and maintains contact with as many community and business groups as possible.

Works with the Friends of the Library and their staff liaisons to promote projects and activities.

Shares duties at the circulation desk on assigned evenings and Saturdays.

Responsible for readers advisory services and reference services to adults and provides instruction to patrons wishing to use OPLIN and other computer programs in the computer center.

Works with the Director to plan and implement adult programming.

Participates with the other staff members in the selection and merchandising of materials which reflect the interests and needs of Library patrons and the community.

Shares responsibility for building supervision, opening and closing procedures.

Attends library conferences and workshops which relate to duties as authorized or recommended by the Director.

Prepares bibliographies, booklists, etc., as needed.

Works closely with NRG and the Director in monitoring and maintaining computer hardware and software.

Performs other duties as assigned by the Director.

Knowledge, Skills, and Abilities

Required Competencies:

Familiarity with the Library's automated system.

Experience with word processing and desktop publishing software.

Ability to exercise initiative and good judgment.

Ability to communicate effectively with staff, patrons, the press, and members of the community.

Ability to plan and present programs to Library patrons and community groups.

Physical Demands:

Ability to read titles on shelves and print on-computer screens.

Ability to work with keyboard and terminal for extended periods of time.

Education, Experience and Training:

Minimum Qualifications:

College degree in journalism, communications or library science; or relevant library or public relations experience desirable.

1.1.2 Community Relations Coordinator

Library Name: St. Clair County Library System
Library Location: Port Hudson, Michigan
Population Served: 160,708
Number of Volumes: 432,880
Number of Titles: 206,173
Periodical Subscriptions: 560

General Summary

General Duties: The Community Relations Coordinator identifies, develops and implements all marketing and promotional strategies for the St. Clair County Library System and works closely with Library personnel to promote events at all branches of the library.

Reports To

SUPERVISION RECEIVED: Work is performed under the direct supervision of the Executive Director of the Library.

Knowledge, Skills, and Abilities

The ability to apply marketing, public relations, and/or communications methodologies and techniques to a library environment.

Thorough understanding of various news media and their requirements for effective communications.

The ability to establish and maintain effective working relationships with media representatives, community groups, public officials employees and the general public.

Exceptional verbal and written communication skills.

A thorough knowledge of or a willingness to learn the culture of the surrounding communities. Exceptional organizational skills.

Initiative, energy and imagination necessary to perform job functions with a minimum of direction. A clear understanding of the public service mission of the District Library and a forward thinking vision regarding the District's dynamic role in the community.

Essential Functions and Responsibilities

Assists the Executive Director in the development and implementation of policies subject to Library Board approval.

Takes a proactive approach with local media to stimulate and anticipate coverage about the District and its services, events, and proposed projects.

Coordinates media relations for the District.

Identifies library products, e.g. services, resources and programs for marketing and promotional opportunities in consultation with administration, management and staff. Identifies and assesses target markets.

Plans and organizes District public relations campaigns, receptions and special events. Manages communications with collaborating or co-sponsoring organizations as required.

Oversees the creation and distribution of a wide range of District communications and publications, e.g. brochures, flyers, posters and calendars.

Ensures the maintenance of an archive of articles pertaining to the Library that appear in various written media.

Supervisory Responsibilities

SUPERVISION EXERCISED: Technical/Graphics Specialist and Library Page (when required).

Education, Experience and Training:

Desired Qualifications:

Experience Needed:

Masters Degree in Library Science from an ALA accredited institution. Undergraduate degree in Marketing, Public Relations, Journalism or Communications or a minimum of three to five years experience in marketing or an associated field preferred.

Disclaimers

Performs other related duties as assigned or required by Supervisor.

2.0 LIBRARIAN

2.1 COMMUNITY DEVELOPMENT LIBRARIAN

2.1.1 Community Development Librarian

Library Name: Williamsburg Regional Library System
Library Location: Williamsburg, Virginia
Population Served: 60,100
Number of Volumes: 261,243
Number of Titles: N/A
Number of Periodical Subscriptions: 562

General Summary

NATURE OF WORK:

Under the supervision of the Library Director, the Community Partnership Development Librarian (CPDL) directs library-community partnerships to extend awareness of the library's resources and services within the community, to access new users through partnering, to expand library resources and to further the goals shared by the library and a partner. The CPDL is also a member of the library's management ensemble.

Essential Functions and Responsibilities

Initiates, coordinates, and manages alliances between library departments and strategic community partners to extend awareness of the library's resources and services within the community, to expand library resources, to access new users through partnering and to further shared library-community partner goals. Strategic community partners may include association, organizations, agencies, and businesses.

Evaluates effectiveness of library-community partnerships in light of specific project goals, department goals and the Library's long-range plan. Serves as resource to departments in incorporating initiatives into the library's annual long-range planning process.

In collaboration with the director of development, develop grant and award applications to secure funding for community partnership initiatives and to publicize same.

Manages the partnership between the Williamsburg Community Hospital and the library for continuous development of the Phillip West Memorial Cancer Resource Center and other consumer health initiatives with the hospital.

Collaborates with WRL departments to involve library staff in the development and management of community partnership initiatives.

Chairs the library's Community Partnership Development Group.

Participates in library-wide planning and decision making as a member of the library management team.

Performs other duties as required.

Knowledge, Skills, and Abilities

Ability to establish and maintain effective working relationships with employees, community administrators, and staff, and the general public.

Ability to develop, implement, oversee, and evaluate effective library partnership programs throughout the community.

Excellent negotiation skills.

Excellent writing and oral communication skills.

Excellent research skills.

Knowledge of public library resources, collections, and processes.

Expertise in word processing, databases, and other computer software.

Ability to compile and analyze information.

Ability to set own priorities for work to be done and meet deadlines.

Work Environment

Administers work both in an office and within the community at large. Operation of computers is required.

Frequent contact is made with employees, community administrators, and staff, and the general public.

Education, Experience and Training:

MINIMUM QUALIFICATIONS:

Master of Library Sciences degree, or equivalent training and experience. Public library experience preferred.

Additional Qualifications

NECESSARY SPECIAL QUALIFICATIONS:

Requires the ability to travel among various community sites.

3.0 MARKETING RESEARCH ASSISTANT

3.1 ASSISTANT

3.1.1 Assistant

Library Name: Fort Collins Public Library
Library Location: Fort Collins, Colorado
Population Served: 138,974
Number of Volumes: 360,000
Number of Titles: 236,688
Number of Periodical Subscriptions: 454

General Summary

SUMMARY

Under the general direction of the Library Director, performs various marketing research activities and statistical analyses for the Public library.

Essential Functions and Responsibilities

The following duties and responsibilities are illustrative of the primary functions of this position and are not intended to be all-inclusive.

Researches and analyzes information to help formulate policies, procedures and programs in support of Library goals and objectives.

Prepares and presents analysis of library performance measures, budget statistics and trend indicators.

Participates in and responds to surveys conducted by other organizations and jurisdictions; coordinates responses by other departments.

Identifies grant opportunities and assists in the preparation and administration of grant proposals.

Drafts or coordinates the preparation of press releases, newsletters, feature stories and official letters.

Coordinates special events, fundraising and publicity activities, and assists the Library Director with special projects.

Performs other related duties as assigned.

Knowledge, Skills, and Abilities

QUALIFICATIONS

The requirements listed below are representative of the knowledge, skills and abilities required to perform the necessary functions of this position.

Demonstrated knowledge of word processing, desktop publishing, spreadsheets, graphic and data base applications. Strong verbal and written communication skills. Knowledge of program evaluation techniques, statistical and research methodologies. Ability to multi-task, meet strict deadlines, and work effectively with a variety of people and situations. Grant writing skills preferred. Experience using the Internet preferred.

Work Environment

Work is performed indoors in a standard library environment and involves extended periods of sitting, working on a personal computer, answering the telephone, and reaching. May require lifting and carrying office supplies and equipment weighing up to 25 lbs. May require some travel.

Education, Experience, and Training

BA degree in marketing, public relations, or related field, plus three years related public sector work experience. Grant writing experience preferred. An equivalent combination of education and experience will be accepted.

4.0 MARKETING MANAGER
4.1 MARKETING MANAGER

4.1.1 Marketing Manager

Library Name: Clermont County Public Library System
Library Location: Batavia, Ohio
Population Served: 178,749
Number of Volumes: 534,527
Number of Titles: 151,295
Number of Periodical Subscriptions: 547

General Summary

Position Description: Plans and facilitates a system approach to community relations through graphic displays, publicity and marketing techniques. Decisions made will affect public's perception of the library.

Essential Functions and Responsibilities

Through the effective management and operation of the Resource Area, produces publicity materials for the system, including but not limited to signage, flyers and press releases.

Develops, conducts and evaluates effectiveness of marketing plan and reports quarterly.

Participates in the personnel process for department staff, including, but not limited to hiring, supervision and evaluation of staff performance and identification of staff training needs.

In cooperation with staff, coordinates promotion of library programs and events to area media through a variety of means.

Educates personnel to the value and library applications of marketing and provides guidance and encouragement for initiative in this area.

Develops a method to periodically survey the library's customers and non customers concerning attitudes towards the library's current services and determine needs for new services.

Refers media inquiries to library director and other staff when appropriate.

Additional Job Duties

Additional Examples of Work Performed:

Oversees system wide signage and graphic displays to ensure quality and consistency of presentation.

Assists Adult Services Coordinator and Youth Services Coordinator in identifying unserved library needs.

Networks with other agencies and organizations to facilitate cooperative projects.

Knowledge, Skills, and Abilities

Able to work independently, conceptualize projects and manage multiple priorities.

Broad knowledge of public library policy, services, practices, plans and problems.

Familiarity with word processing, desktop publishing, database and graphics software.

Analytical ability required to interpret sensitive issues affecting the library's image.

Supervision of design, layout, production and distribution functions.

Effective written and oral communication with staff, community, library board of trustees and media representatives.

Must have reliable transportation for travel to agencies within system and out.

Education, Experience, and Training

Qualifications:

Bachelors degree and/or other education and experience supportive of public relations and marketing assignments. Skills include writing, public speaking, planning, graphic design and layout, desktop publishing, knowledge of software for word processing and graphic design, coordination and supervision of project production.

Position Hours

Must be able to work evenings and weekends.

Disclaimers

NOTE: This job analysis describes the nature and level of assignments normally given in this position. They are not an exhaustive list of duties. Additional related duties may be assigned.

4.2 MARKETING AND COMMUNICATIONS MANAGER

4.2.1 Marketing and Communications Manager

Library Name: Milwaukee Public Library
Library Location: Milwaukee, Wisconsin
Population Served: 608,150
Number of Volumes: 2,553,934
Number of Titles: N/A
Number of Periodical Subscriptions: 9,719

Reports To

SUPERVISION RECEIVED: (Indicate the extent to which work assignments and methods are outlined, reviewed, and approved by others.)

Under general administrative direction, With general review of results and approval of policies by the City Librarian.

General Summary

BASIC FUNCTION OF POSITION:

The incumbent is responsible for coordinating the library's communications and marketing program through use of appropriate media, including print and electronic media. This position is further responsible for the development of a marketing program based upon analyses of community needs to further improve public use of library facilities and resources.

The Milwaukee Public Library is committed to providing the highest quality of service to internal and external customers. In meeting this commitment, employees are expected to be knowledgeable, competent, dependable and courteous in the performance of their job responsibilities, and to work cooperatively as part of a team.

Essential Functions and Responsibilities

DESCRIPTION OF JOB: (Describe the specific duties and responsibilities of the job as accurately and completely as possible. Use additional sheet if necessary.)

DUTIES AND RESPONSIBILITIES: (Break job into component parts as you would describe it to the incumbent. Indicate the approximate percentage of time devoted to each major task or group of related tasks. List the most important duties and responsibilities first. Include responsibilities related to employee safety and affirmative action goals for management positions.)

30% 1. EDITORIAL WORK: Coordinates, assembles, prepares and supervises preparation of information, illustrative material, and other data relating to the library's resources and services for the library's print and electronic publications, the press, television and radio. Exercises overall coordinating and supervisory judgment to insure effective paralleling of the various media.

Maintains contacts and coordinates with other city and community agencies which can supplement the library's programs and goals.

a) Prepares and supervises preparation of releases for the daily and community newspapers; contacts members of the press, directing them to the proper officers of the library when necessary or desirable; edits press releases or articles written by other members of the staff; prepares and supervises preparation of copy for house organs, industrial publications and other publishing outlets.

b) Supervises and helps in preparation of library's own publications including the "Milwaukee Reader," booklists, exhibit catalogs, directories and schedules. Supervises the establishment of mailing lists to be used in distribution of library material, and contacts staff of various divisions to secure material.

c) Edits for publication lists of books, which are selected and annotated by librarians, such as lists on special subjects and the annual list of children's books.

d) Edits statistical information and reports for the library's annual report.

e) Provides information about the Milwaukee Public Library for professional library publications.

25% 2. MARKETING: Develops and implements an effective marketing plan for the Library's services, resources and facilities.

a) Through analysis of community needs and trends in the public library field, develops a comprehensive marketing plan to make greater use of library services, resources and facilities.

b) Implements the library's marketing plan through effective use of the institution's resources.

c) Represents the library on various committees planning cooperative marketing projects with outside sponsorship.

20% 3. LIBRARY PROGRAMS AND EVENTS: Works with the City Librarian, Deputy City Librarian, Assistant City Librarian, Library Coordinators of Extension Services, Children's Services, Art, Music and Recreation, Humanities and Science, Business & Technology, and with the Library Foundation Director in planning and coordinating programs and events.

a) Represents the library on various committees of community groups and in planning community events.

b) Represents the library in the solicitation of gifts for the library collections and events.

c) Coordinates the annual Dr. Martin Luther King Jr. Read-In.

10% 4. TELEVISION AND RADIO: Coordinates radio and television activities to effectively take the library into the homes of the community. Plans a balanced program to reach the various publics of the library.

a) Arranges for public service announcements with radio and television stations.

b) Arranges for guests on station-produced programs. Arranges coverage of library events by television news departments.

c) Selects librarians for radio and television programs who can most effectively present library information.

d) Writes and supervises preparation of a regular schedule of public service announcements.

e) Engages free-lance talent for production and for on-the-air appearances.

f) Maintains effective contacts with radio and television stations.

10% 5. EXHIBITS AND SIGNS: Works with Assistant City Librarian and Deputy City Librarian to plan and show displays which introduce and relate library materials to events, current topics of interest. Coordinates exhibits by community organizations for showing in the libraries. Arranges for showing of traveling exhibits, which supplement the library's overall program.

a) Arranges for and organizes exhibits for local conferences, conventions, exhibitions, etc.

b) Plans posters with library artist for Central and Neighborhood library displays, informational signs for the daily conduct of the library's activities and posters for distribution to outside agencies calling attention to particular activities.

5% 6. Performs other related duties as assigned.

Name and title of Immediate Supervisor: City Librarian

Knowledge, Skills, and Abilities

1. Strong customer service orientation;

2. Ability to write and edit copy informing the public about library resources and activities and ability to arrange exhibits and displays;

3. Thorough knowledge and understanding of modem library organization, procedures, policies, aims and services;

4. Ability to develop and maintain effective community contacts;

5. Supervisory ability.

Physical and Mental Requirements

List the physical demands which are representative of those that must be met to successfully perform the essential function of the job. Reasonable accommodations may be made to enable individuals with disabilities to perform the essential functions.

1. Frequently sitting simultaneously using hand, wrist and fingers;

2. Sometimes standing, walking, stooping, bending, squatting, reaching overhead or in front of body, and traveling to outside meetings and engagements.

3. On occasion kneeling, crouching, twisting, climbing ladders and stairs

4. Sometimes lifting up to 10 pounds and on occasion up to 50 pounds. Maximum weight lifted to hip height: 20 pounds, to shoulder height or above shoulders: 10 pounds. Maximum weight lifted and carried without assistance: 20 pounds.

5. Sometimes pushing/pulling up to 10 pounds and on occasion up to 50 pounds. Maximum weight pushed/pulled without wheels or assistance: 10 pounds.

6. Frequently talking and hearing ordinary conversation in person or by phone in a quiet but sometimes noisy environment.

7. Usual need for near vision at 20" or less (reading, computer work etc.)

8. Occasional need for far vision at 20" or more (driving, etc.)

List the mental requirements, which are representative of those that must be met to successfully perform the essential function of the job. Reasonable accommodations may be made to enable individuals with disabilities to perform the essential functions.

1. Communication Skills: effectively communicate ideas and information both in written and oral form to a very high degree;

2. Reading Ability: effectively read and understand information contained in procedure manuals, reports, etc.;

3. Time Management: set priorities in order to meet assignment deadlines;

4. Problem Solving: develop feasible, realistic solutions to problems, recommend actions designed to prevent problems from occurring;

5. Planning and Organizing: develop long-range plans to solve complex problems or take advantage of opportunities; establish systematic methods of accomplishing goals;

6. Analytical Ability: identify problems and opportunities; review possible alternative courses of action before selection; utilize available information resources in decision making;

6. Creative Decision Making: effectively evaluates or makes independent decisions based upon experience, knowledge or training, without supervision.

Tools and Equipment Used

List equipment, which is representative of that which would be used to successfully perform the essential functions of the job. Reasonable accommodations may be made to enable individuals with disabilities to perform the essential functions.

Computer terminal or networked personal computer and peripheral equipment including printer(s), telephone, typewriter, photocopier, fax machine, TV NCR, book truck.

Work Environment

ENVIRONMENTAL/WORKING CONDITIONS list the conditions, which are, representative of those that must be met to successfully perform the essential function of the job. Reasonable accommodations may be made to enable individuals with disabilities to perform the essential functions.

1. Inside work environment;

2. Flexible work hours; some evening and weekend hours as needed;

3. Work in excess of 40 hours/week as needed.

Supervisory Responsibilities

SUPERVISION EXERCISED:

1. Total number of employees for whom responsible, either directly or indirectly.

Direct Supervision. List the number and titles of personnel directly supervised. Specify the kind and extent of supervision exercised by indicating one or more of the following: (a) assign duties; (b) outline methods; (c) direct work in process; (d) check or inspect completed work; (e) sign or approve work; (f) make hiring recommendations; (g) prepare performance appraisals; (h) take disciplinary action or effectively recommend such.

Supervises the work of one Administrative Specialist Sr., one Program Assistant II, one Graphic Designer II and one Printer by making hiring recommendations, assigning duties, outlining methods, directing work in progress, checking completed work, evaluating job performance, taking disciplinary action as needed, issuing commendations as warranted, and being available for consultation on problems that arise.

Education, Experience, and Training

1. Bachelor's degree from an accredited college or university with a major in journalism or communications, or closely related field.

2. Significant experience in communication/publications involving approximately seven years in any combination of the following: radio and television writing, production and/or creating

programs, coordinating an information program, public relations, advertising, publishing, news reporting or editing.

5.0 PUBLIC RELATIONS

5.1 PUBLIC RELATIONS SUPERVISOR

5.1.1 Public Relations Supervisor

Library Name: Manitowoc-Calumet Public Library
Library Location: Manitowoc, Wisconsin
Population Served: 58,213
Number of Volumes: 195,166
Number of Titles: N/A
Periodical Subscriptions: 395

General Summary

BROAD SCOPE OF POSITION: Plans, develops, implements and evaluates the Library's program of publicity and public relations. Guides overall functions and direction of the department. Supervises and evaluates the Public Relations Assistant. Participates on the Library's management team and assists in administration of the Library. Serves as liaison to the Friends of the Manitowoc Public Library, Manitowoc Public Library Foundation, and other groups, as assigned. Administers the Library's volunteer program. Handles large-scale, on-going projects for the Library, as assigned. Books and coordinates use of the Library's meeting rooms. Performs work of other departmental staff or of another member of the Library's management team, as needed or assigned.

Essential Functions and Responsibilities

The following list identifies principal duties and responsibilities of the job. It is not a definitive list and other similar duties may be assigned. An asterisk (*) before any of the following items indicates duties and responsibilities which are not "essential functionsî of the job as defined by the Americans with Disabilities Act.

1. Plans, develops, implements and evaluates the Library's program of publicity and public relations by: budgeting and expending resources (personnel, space, money, etc.); developing, coordinating and administering a marketing plan for the Library. Establishes departmental priorities. Analyzes technological advances and recommends appropriate applications. Works with rest of Management Team and Director on short- and long-range planning and coordinates departmental plans within Library's goals, objectives and policies.

2. Participates on the Library's management team and assists in administration of the Library. Attends meetings and communicates decisions with staff, as appropriate. Provides professional and managerial support to Library Director and other members of the management team. Assists in establishing and meeting goals and objectives for the Library. Recommends policies and administrative actions to Coordinators and Library Director. Communicates with other members of the management team about departmental issues and priorities. Acts as consultant for MCLS and other libraries, as delegated or assigned.

3. Guides overall functions and direction of the department. Administers and manages departmental budget and plan of departmental services. Directs development and implementation of departmental procedures and routines. Writes (or supervises writing by other staff) project proposals and grants, and implements programs.

4. Supervises and evaluates the Public Relations Assistant. Team interviews and makes hiring recommendations to Library Director. Develops and implements plans for training of departmental staff, and involves staff from other departments, as appropriate. When necessary, handles progressive discipline of staff through the level of written warnings and makes recommendations for further discipline up to and including firing to the Library Director.

5. Serves as liaison to the Friends of the Manitowoc Public Library, Manitowoc Public Library Foundation, and other library-related groups, as assigned. Assists these groups with fund-raising, events and public relations, as assigned. Acts as liaison between the Library and non-library community groups. Maintains area in Library reserved for distribution of brochures, posters and similar materials advertising events sponsored by area non-profit organizations. Books and coordinates use of the Library's meeting rooms. Responsible for communicating issues, needs and concerns of various groups to the Director and other members of Management Team, as appropriate.

6. Administers a volunteer program for the Library. Coordinates recruitment and use of volunteers with other members of the Management Team.

7. Promotes services, resources and special events of the Library through public appearances, news articles, feature stories, radio and television releases, and other forms of publicity and public relations. Gives library-related promotional talks to community groups, as assigned. Supervises and coordinates the production of flyers, booklists, bookmarks, signs, and other promotional materials. Produces the monthly newsletter, as assigned. Maintains information on the Library electronic kiosks. May serve as webmaster for the library, as needed or assigned. Handles photography for the Library. Provides support to other staff members in their efforts at marketing the Library and its services. Maintains scrapbooks, photo files, and other records of Library history.

8. Handles large-scale, on-going projects for the Library, as assigned. Conceives, plans, promotes, coordinates and conducts special events in conjunction with other departments.

*9. Uses personal vehicle in City and surrounding areas, as needed or assigned. Attends meetings, picks up and delivers printing jobs, etc.

*10. May perform work of another member of the Library's management team, as assigned.

11. Performs work of other departmental staff, as needed.

Knowledge, Skills, and Abilities

1. Knowledge of marketing, public relations, fundraising, publicity and ways of promoting an organization and its services. Ability to apply this knowledge in a public library setting. General knowledge of library organization, operations, services, resources, and user interest levels. Willingness to contribute to on-going development of Library-wide philosophy, mission and services, and ability to lead development of departmental philosophy, goals and services.

2. Ability to assume a leadership role in a group setting. Ability to establish and maintain effective working relationships with the Library Director, Management Team members, other library staff members, sales representatives, community officials, agency representatives, and the public. Ability to work in the Library's team setting. Willingness to assist and support coworkers, to contribute ideas, and to maintain flexibility. Ability to adapt to a rapidly changing environment.

3. Ability to analyze and evaluate current conditions and to make logical evaluations of future needs. Ability to plan and execute short-range plans. Ability to synthesize and creatively adapt trends in technology, marketing, public relations and publicity to planning for the department and the organization. Skill in negotiating for resources to meet departmental needs.

4. Commitment to and skill in supervising people. Knowledge of supervisory and training techniques. Willingness and ability to provide positive managerial example. Willingness and ability to foster environment in which employees and volunteers are self-motivated and can exhibit high morale. Capacity to recognize and utilize talents of others. Fairness when distributing workload, responsibility, and authority. Ability to identify proper work assignments for subordinates and willingness to follow-up to ensure proper completion.

5. Ability to set realistic standards for employees and volunteers, and to encourage productive and efficient performance. Conscientiousness when appraising performance, counseling employees, writing and administering performance appraisals, and making personnel recommendations.

6. Skill in managing departmental workflow, including ability to identify, negotiate, establish, communicate, and apply priorities. Skill in performing and supervising routine and non-routine procedures involving many steps. Ability to give and follow complex written and/or verbal instructions and to pay close attention to detail. Willingness to provide professional and managerial support to supervisor. Ability to accept delegation and to work under general supervisory direction.

7. Ability to make realistic budget proposals, to operate within established budgetary guidelines, and to identify and analyze budgetary impact of services.

8. Initiative and resourcefulness to take acceptable risks, make appropriate decisions, and exercise proper authority. Ability to present clear explanations of established policies and procedures. Ability to think and act appropriately under pressure. Willingness and ability to grant logical exceptions to policies and procedures when warranted. Willingness to maintain confidentiality when appropriate and to be held accountable.

9. Ability to communicate effectively. Skill in interpersonal communication. Ability to do journalistic writing for press releases, news articles, feature stories, etc. as well as technical writing for procedures, proposals, reports, etc. Ability to write speeches and to speak effectively in front of groups. Capacity to be easily understood on voice telephone. Must be accurate and possess excellent grammar, spelling and proofreading skills.

10. Ability to interact effectively with the Library's automated systems. Skill in using microcomputers and related software. Basic knowledge of database, spreadsheet, word-processing, and fundraising software programs. Knowledge of or ability to quickly learn Library's current software programs as these apply to job responsibilities.

11. Skill in layout and graphic design. Ability to utilize desktop publishing and web production hardware and software. Ability to use other equipment associated with production and distribution of promotional materials, including photocopier, postage meter, cameras, letter press, opaque projector, staplers, and paper cutter.

12. Willingness and ability to set and apply departmental artistic, graphic and technical standards. Ability to create acceptable products in a time-efficient manner, and to do so by deadlines. Ability to work cooperatively and contribute to projects being developed by a group.

13. Ability to explain and promote library services and to work with a diversity of individuals and community groups. Skill at exercising diplomacy when needed. Possession of an outgoing personality.

14. Skill at conceiving, scheduling, organizing, coordinating and orchestrating special events. Ability to use audio, video and computer equipment found in the Library's meeting rooms. Ability to train the public in use of this equipment.

15. Possession of valid Wisconsin driver's license and good driving record. Willingness to use personal vehicle for semi-weekly trips in City and surrounding areas in all weather conditions for distances at least 25 miles per trip (under 5 miles usually). May make 10 or more stops per trip. Routine trips are usually 1 stop and under 1 mile. Mileage is reimbursed.

16. Physical capacity to lift, maneuver, and carry boxes of paper and other similar containers, weighing up to 25 pounds.

17. Ability to enforce the library's established policies, procedures and standards of public behavior in nondiscriminatory fashion. Ability to present clear explanations of these rules to members of public.

18. Ability to develop work-related goals and objectives. Willingness to develop job-related abilities, skills and knowledge. Willingness and ability to keep abreast of changing technologies

and procedures, and to assume responsibilities required by introduction of different services and equipment.

19. Willingness and ability to understand and support the fundamental principles of library services, such as offering open access to library materials in any format for people of all ages; providing materials representing as many points of view as possible; and protecting a patron's right to privacy in dealings with the library and with respect to records maintained by library.

Work Environment

Usually (up to 100% of work time) works in shared-office environment with considerable staff and public contact.

Usually (up to 100% of work time) performs routines with many rapid, repeated motions.

Usually (up to 100% of work time) works in close proximity with terminals and other similar electronic equipment.

Usually (up to 100% of work time) maintains work environment. For example: vacuuming computer areas, dusting, recycling paper; cleaning up after special events. Infrequently (as situation requires) assists with building emergencies which may involve cleaning up bodily fluids.

Physical and Mental Requirements

Sometimes (up to 25% of work time) lifts and/or transports objects weighing 5 to 25 pounds; pushes or pulls carts loaded with objects weighing more than 150 pounds.

Sometimes (up to 25% of work time) works with equipment and performs procedures where carelessness may result in minor cuts, bruises, or muscle strains.

Infrequently (as situation requires) climbs ladder to put up and take down displays.

Education, Experience and Training:

MINIMUM QUALIFICATIONS:

1. Bachelor's degree in journalism, communications or related field from a college or university accredited by a nationally recognized agency, such as North Central Association of Colleges & Schools.

2. 1–2 years experience in public relations or similar setting.

3. Demonstrated ability to supervise staff, preferably in a union environment.

4. Demonstrable possession of knowledge, skills, abilities, and capacities identified in "Job Specificationsî section, above.

5. Capacity to work under conditions described in "Working Conditions" section, above.

Position Hours

Salaried full-time, typically working at least 80 hours per two-week pay period on a flexible schedule which may vary from week to week. May be scheduled to work days, evenings, Saturdays, and Sundays.

5.2 PUBLIC RELATIONS OFFICER

5.2.1 Public Relations Officer

Library Name: Lorain Public Library System
Library Location: Lorain, Ohio
Population Served: 120,132
Number of Volumes: 497,959
Number of Titles: 254,987
Number of Periodical Subscriptions: 1,594

General Summary

Basic Function:

Plans and directs continuous development and execution of the Library publicity, public relations and graphics program.

Distinguishing Features of the Class:

This classification directs and performs responsible advisory work in connection with the public relations program for the Library, including extensive contact with private and public agencies in the community, and department heads and librarian supervisors within the Library. The employee in this class must be creative, an effective communicator, and a capable representative for the Library in public relations. The work is performed at the direction of the Library Director.

Essential Functions and Responsibilities

Manages the operation of public relations office, training and evaluation employees, written reports, ordering supplies, assisting in budget preparation for the unit.

Develops on-going relationships with local media to ensure fair library coverage as means of informing public.

Oversees design and printing of newsletter, fliers, brochures, annual report and other publication or promotional materials.

Serves as library liaison for Lorain Friends Group and in an advisory role for branch Friends Group, levy campaign committees, and other citizen groups affiliated with the library.

Plans and oversees special library events system-wide.

Maintains personal contact with government officials, community leaders and community organizations.

Designs and implements surveys and focus groups, patron suggestion boxes, etc. to monitor community interests, opinions and needs.

Plans and implements publicity and promotions for library programs and services.

Advises units on public relations and marketing activities.

Advises board members, administration, Friends group and library committees on public relations and communications matters; may serve as official spokesperson for the library.

Participates in planning and implementing county or state-wide cooperative public relations activities.

Prepares direct responses to requests by telephone, mail and other media for general information about the library; plans and schedules exhibits and displays.

Prepares, edits, and places news releases and other written publicity for newspapers, radio and television; originates production of library sponsored radio and television programs.

Confers with staff and miscellaneous groups regarding public relations and represents the library to outside organizations and firms in conducting public relations.

Serves as a member of planning committees and administrative staff, and attends Board meetings.

Attends meetings and continuing education programs to keep informed and current about trends, issues, and methods of implementing public relations in the public library.

Serves as member of the Library System's Management Team.

Knowledge, Skills and Abilities:

Thorough knowledge of modern principles and practices of public relations and publicity for libraries

Thorough knowledge of graphics

Ability to plan and supervise the work of others

Ability to speak effectively in public

Excellent writing ability

Ability to use office productivity and communications software applications in a computerized networked environment

Creativity; tact and courtesy

Ability to work in a team environment

Sound judgment

Education, Experience and Training:

Bachelor's degree in public relations or related field and three to four years of related experience or any equivalent combination of experience and training which provides the required knowledge, skills and abilities.

Disclaimers

The intent of this summary is to characterize the typical duties and responsibilities that will be required of individual positions assigned to this classification and should not be construed as representing the specific duties and responsibilities of any particular position. Employees may be expected to perform their related duties which are specific to their area that may not be reflected in this class summary.

5.3 PUBLIC RELATIONS ASSISTANT

5.3.1 Public Relations Assistant

Library Name: Clermont County Public Library
Library Location: Batavia, Ohio
Population Served: 178,749
Number of Volumes: 534,527
Number of Titles: 151,295
Number of Periodical Subscriptions: 547

Reports To

Immediate Supervisor: Communications Manager

Education, Experience, and Training

Qualifications: High school diploma or G.E.D. equivalency. Word processing and database skills required; arts and crafts skills desirable.

Position Hours

Must be able to work evenings and weekends.

General Summary

Position Description: Performs the various clerical tasks dealing primarily with the production, duplication and distribution of program and publicity materials for the library's agencies.

Essential Functions and Responsibilities

Writes, processes and distributes standard program news releases.

Orders promotion-related material, including catalog research; completing, processing and filing of purchase requisitions.

Enters statistical information into appropriate database.

Prints system-wide forms.

Constructs signs, file various materials.

Assists with mailings and other distribution of system-level projects.

Assists with miscellaneous tasks related to the newsletter and website such as proofreading.

Locates materials for placement in shuttle delivery and file materials when returned including browsers and book display art.

Additional Job Duties

Additional Examples of Work Performed:

Produces craft pieces and creates programming pieces.

Searches for graphics used in production of program materials.

Assists in creation of browsers per branch requests.

Assists in creation and maintenance of program materials as time permits.

Runs errands when necessary.

Knowledge, Skills, and Abilities

Operates computer using word processing, database and/or e-mail software.

Understands basics of English composition.

Writes simple news releases utilizing existing format.

Retrieves, organizes and inputs computer data.

Operates copier, laminator and other office equipment.

Uses basic art department equipment such as T-square, exacto knife, etc.

Ability to interact with people of varying personalities and ages in a variety of situations.

Grasps materials/equipment.

Communicates in oral and written forms.

Stands and uses hand to perform tasks for the majority of the workday.

Handles multiple projects and assigns priorities.

Works independently.

Disclaimers

Note: This job analysis describes the nature and level of assignments normally given in this position; they are not an exhaustive list of duties. Additional related duties may be assigned.

6.0 SENIOR SPECIALIST

6.1 COMMUNICATIONS AND MARKETING SENIOR SPECIALIST

> ### 6.1.1 Communications and Marketing Senior Specialist
>
> **Library Name:** Milwaukee Public Library
> **Library Location:** Milwaukee, Wisconsin
> **Population Served:** 608,150
> **Number of Volumes:** 2,553,934
> **Number of Titles:** N/A
> **Number of Periodical Subscriptions:** 9,719

Reports To

SUPERVISION RECEIVED: (Indicate the extent to which work assignments and methods are outlined, reviewed, and approved by others.

Under general supervision of Librarian V who is available for consultation on difficult problems. Is expected to be self-directed.

General Summary

BASIC FUNCTION OF POSITION:

The incumbent of this position is responsible for promoting the library's services and resources by editing and writing library publications, developing and maintaining electronic media, and assisting in developing and coordinating public relations, marketing programs, and special events planning for the library system, in order to assure continued good public relations for the library and customer satisfaction with its services.

The Milwaukee Public Library is committed to providing the highest quality of service to internal and external customers. In meeting this commitment, employees are expected to be knowledgeable, competent, dependable and courteous in the performance of their job responsibilities, and to work cooperatively as part of a team.

Essential Functions and Responsibilities

DESCRIPTION OF JOB: (Describe the specific duties and responsibilities of the job as accurately and completely as possible. Use additional sheet if necessary.)

DUTIES AND RESPONSIBILITIES: (Break job into component parts as you would describe it to the incumbent. Indicate the approximate percentage of time devoted to each major task or group of related tasks. List the most important duties and responsibilities first. Include responsibilities related to employee safety and affirmative action goals for management positions.)

25% 1. Responsible for production of library publications, including Milwaukee Reader newsletter. Identifies needs for printed materials and edits copy. Prepares information on events for printed and electronic calendars. Arranges for photographers and other free-lance help as needed for various projects and events. 25%

25%. 2. Responsible for the library's Web site. Develops new pages, maintains calendars and performs routine updates. Assists committees in developing content for web pages. Works with technical support staff in the maintenance of the library's web software

15% 3. Performs full range of media relation's activities for the Central Library, neighborhood libraries, Foundation and library support groups. Contacts and responds to media representatives, identifies opportunities for media coverage, writes news releases, works with print and broadcast representatives, works with media representatives on media sponsorships of library projects.

15%. 4. Serves as the library's public relations representative on various departmental, citywide and community committees and/or projects as assigned (i.e. Combined Giving, Caring & Sharing, King Celebration). Works closely with Library Foundation Executive Director to promote the foundation and its events.

10%. 5. Assists in the development and implementation of public relations/marketing campaigns for the library system. Coordinates implementation of strategies to increase public awareness and use of library services, resources and activities.

5% 6. Assists in developing and conducting marketing research, analyzing findings and writing reports on findings for various audiences.

5%. 7. Performs other related duties as assigned.

Name and title of Immediate Supervisor: Communication and Marketing Director

Knowledge, Skills, and Abilities

1. Strong customer service orientation. Team player with ability to work successfully with others, to maintain cordial and professional relations with staff, volunteers, donors, and various publics.

2. Strong background in journalism and writing. Ability to deal with print and electronic media representatives in a professional manner.

3. Demonstrated strong ability to write clearly and interestingly for a variety of audiences.

4. Knowledge of Web site software and ability to design pages for electronic media.

5. Knowledge of graphics and printing production.

6. Initiative, tact, resourcefulness, creativity and common sense.

7. Knowledge and understanding of modem library and its services preferred.

Physical and Mental Requirements

List the physical demands which are representative of those that must be met to ~ perform the essential function of the job. Reasonable accommodations may be made to enable individuals with disabilities to essential functions.

1. Usually sitting and simultaneously using hand, wrist and fingers (i.e.: computer entry)

2. Sometimes standing, walking, stooping, twisting, bending and reaching in front of body

3. On occasion crouching, reaching overhead, and traveling to outside meetings and engagements

4. Sometimes lifting up to 10 pounds and on occasion up to 20 pounds. Maximum weight lifted to hip height: 20 pounds; to or above shoulders: 10 pounds. Maximum weight lifted and carried without assistance: 20 pounds.

5. Sometimes pushing/pulling loads weighing up to 10 pounds and on occasion up to 50 pounds. Maximum weight pushed/pulled with wheels or assistance: 10 pounds.

6. Frequently talking and hearing ordinary conversation, in person or by phone in a quiet but sometimes noisy environment

7. Usual need for near vision at 20" or less (proofing, editing, computer work)

8. Occasional need for far vision at 20" or more (driving)

MENTAL REQUIREMENTS: List the mental requirements, which are, representative of those that must be met to successfully perform the essential function of the job. Reasonable accommodations may be made to enable individuals with disabilities to perform 1 functions.

1. Communication Skills: effectively communicate ideas and information both in written and oral form.

2. Reading Ability: effectively read and understand information contained in procedure manuals, reports, etc.

3. Time Management: set priorities in order to meet assignment deadlines. Ability to work on various projects at the same 1 interruptions and maintain composure

4. Problem Solving: develop feasible, realistic solutions to problems, recommend actions designed to prevent problems from

5. Planning and Organizing: develop long-range plans to solve complex problems or take advantage of opportunities; establish methods of accomplishing goals.

6. Analytical Ability: identify problems and opportunities; review possible alternative courses of action before selection; utilize information resources in decision making.

7. Creative Decision Making: effectively evaluates or makes independent decisions based upon experience, knowledge or training with minimal supervision.

Tools and Equipment Used

List equipment which is representative of that which would be used to successfully perform the essential functions of the job. Reasonable accommodations may be made to enable individuals with disabilities to perform the essential functions.

Computer terminal or networked personal computer, printer, telephone, photocopier, fax machine paper/poster board cutter

Work Environment

List the conditions which are representative of those that must be met to perform the essential function of the job. Reasonable accommodations may be made to enable individuals with disabilities to essential functions.

1. Inside work environment

2. Flexible work hours; some evening and weekend hours

3. Occasional work in excess of 40 hours per week (i.e.: special projects and programs.)

4. Sometime working with glare/improper illumination.

Supervisory Responsibilities

SUPERVISION EXERCISED:

Total number of employees for whom responsible, either directly or indirectly.

Direct Supervision. List the number and titles of personnel directly supervised. Specify the kind and extent of supervision exercised by indicating one or more of the following: (a) assign duties; (b) outline methods; (c) direct work in process; (d) check or inspect completed work; (e) sign or approve work; (f) make hiring recommendations; (g) prepare performance appraisals; (h) take disciplinary action or effectively recommend such.

Responsible for efficient operation of the Communications & Marketing section in the absence of Librarian V. May give directives to other members of the staff. Supervises volunteers for special projects as required.

Education, Experience, and Training

1. Graduation from accredited college or university with major in public relations/marketing/ communications or closely related field.

2. Two years of significant experience in public relations and marketing, including special events.

3. Other combinations of education and experience may also be considered.

VIII. Design and Graphic Services

Included in this section are desktop publishing specialists and graphic designers.

1.0 DESKTOP PUBLISHING

1.1 DESKTOP PUBLISHING SPECIALIST

1.1.1 Desktop Publishing Specialist

Library Name: Clermont County Public Library System
Library Location: Batavia, Ohio
Population Served: 178,749
Number of Volumes: 534,527
Number of Titles: 151,295
Number of Periodical Subscriptions: 547
Department: Communications and Resource Area

Reports To

Immediate Supervisor: Communications Manager

General Summary

Position Description: Produces system-wide communication tools and program publicity.

Essential Functions and Responsibilities

Creates branch-specific and system-wide program publicity and other communications tools.

Maintains and produces system catalogs, manuals, files, and lists.

Responsible for maintaining paper inventory which requires a knowledge of the various papers used in the department.

Utilizes drawing and page layout computer programs to complete projects.

Additional Job Duties

Examples of Work Performed:

Orders supplies for Resource Area.

Assists in production of programming materials.

Assists with other functions of department as needed.

Knowledge, Skills, and Abilities

Knowledge of basic computer software maintenance for Macintosh system.

Problem solving skills.

Understanding of graphic design concepts including lay-out, type specification, paste-up, art creation, manipulation and selection.

Handles multiple projects.

Meets deadlines.

Works independently.

Follows oral and written instructions.

Manual dexterity to operate computer and other office equipment.

Education, Experience, and Training

Qualifications: A broad range of knowledge of a wide variety of subjects usually acquired through a four-year college program or appropriate experience.

Basic skills in graphic design and desktop publishing.

Accurate keyboarding skills, basic knowledge of computer operation, page layout, drawing, and word-processing software.

Artistic talent desired. Must be able to work evenings and weekends.

Disclaimers

Note: This job analysis describes the nature and level of assignments normally given in this position; they are not an exhaustive list of duties. Additional related duties may be assigned.

2.0 GRAPHIC DESIGN

2.1 GRAPHICS DESIGNER

2.1.1 Graphics Designer

Library Name: Cuyahoga County Public Library
Library Location: Parma, Ohio
Population Served: 607,909
Number of Volumes: 3,297,420
Number of Titles: N/A
Number of Periodical Subscriptions: 8,502

Reports To

Supervisor's Title: Graphics Manager

General Summary

Under limited supervision with alternating periods of relative autonomy and general review, creates visual graphics on various software through a PC-based network to fulfill the library's promotional and publicity needs.

Essential Functions and Responsibilities

Complies with work scheduling and attendance requirements according to reasonable policy and practices.

Staffing for branch and regional libraries and some Administration (ADM) departments requires rotational scheduling, which includes evening and weekend (Saturday and Sunday) hours.

Most ADM departments are weekday operations.

Consistently presents Cuyahoga County Public Library and its services in a positive manner and adheres to customer service guidelines and procedures as established by the Library.

Complies with the established rules of operation, procedures, and policies when using library computers, peripheral hardware, and software. Individual passwords and any other confidential information regarding library records shall be kept confidential.

Provides graphic design concepts, layouts and camera-ready copy to support the production of various one color and multi-color printed materials including program and promotional flyers, brochures, booklists, posters, bookmarks and other printed materials.

Creates layout and design for weekly, quarterly, and various branch newsletters.

Provides input on the design, layout and production of other graphics projects including signs and banners.

Communicates directly with CCPL staff and Friends groups to offer advise/suggestions on design and artistic layout of requested materials.

Maintains digital art and project files to support the operation of departmental PC-network in accordance with the departmental standards.

Design graphics for Library related presentations, conferences and display ads as directed.

Serves on various library committees to represent the Graphics Department.

The intent of this position description is to provide a representative summary of the major duties and responsibilities performed by incumbents of this job. Incumbents may be requested to perform job-related tasks other than those specifically presented in this description.

Knowledge, Skills and Abilities:

Thorough knowledge of design, layout and graphic presentation concepts.

Thorough knowledge of rules of grammar, punctuation and spelling, and their use in effective copy composition.

Knowledge of various design and layout software, such as QuarkXpress, Photoshop, Illustrator, etc., and working in a local area network (LAN).

Computer literate with ability to utilize design software and CD-ROM products.

Strong visual and artistic design skills.

Strong oral and written communication skills.

Ability to use scanner, laser printers and other graphics related equipment.

Physical and Mental Requirements

Light physical effort required involving bending and stooping.

Routine discomforts associated with near continuous use of video display terminals.

Education, Experience, and Training

Summary Minimum Education & Experience Required

Associate's degree or completion of technical specialty program of over eighteen months and up to three years duration in Graphic Design.

Two to four years of desktop publishing experience using graphic design software.

License and Certification Requirement:
A criminal background check is required.

2.1.2 Graphics Designer

Library Name: Clermont County Public Library System
Library Location: Batavia, Ohio
Population Served: 178,749
Number of Volumes: 534,527
Number of Titles: 151,295
Number of Periodical Subscriptions: 547

General Summary

Position Description: Under the direction of the Communications Manager, designs and creates promotional materials for the library system. Must be able to work evenings and weekends.

Reports To

Immediate Supervisor: Communications Manager

Essential Functions and Responsibilities

Creates and produces original display signage and materials, e.g., one of a kind display signs, book browser signs, book display props.

Assists in preparation and set up of displays and other visuals, e.g., freestanding displays at branches, fairs; wall hangings.

Assists in creation and production of a variety of printed items including bookmarks, system brochures, program materials (such as items used for summer reading program) and as of yet undetermined projects.

Maintains bulletin board updates in branches that have bulletin boards.

Other projects associated with the visual enhancement of the library.

Additional Examples of Work Performed:

Assists with other C&R department functions.

Knowledge, Skills, and Abilities

Solves visual problems using knowledge of basic graphic design skills.

Completes projects using appropriate tools: traditional and computer methods.

Works independently with little direct supervision.

Communicates with others in person or by telephone.

Understand oral and/or written instructions from supervisor.

Grasps materials/equipment used in an art department.

Reaches up and down to place and/or retrieve materials.

Physical and Mental Requirements

Climbs ladder.

Lifts items weighing up to 60 pounds.

Manipulates loaded roller bins or dollies to various locations (department or outside sites).

Operates department equipment.

Exercises safety precautions in the use of department equipment and materials.

Education, Experience, and Training

Qualifications: Associate degree and/or equivalent experience in art, graphic design. Must be able to work evenings and weekends. Skills include graphic design and layout, and knowledge of software for graphic design.

Additional Qualifications

Must have reliable transportation for travel to agencies within system and out.

Disclaimers

NOTE: This job analysis describes the nature and level of assignments normally given in this position. They are not an exhaustive list of duties. Additional related duties may be assigned.

3.0 GRAPHIC DESIGN II

3.1 GRAPHIC DESIGNER II

3.1.1 Graphic Designer II

Library Name: Milwaukee Public Library
Library Location: Milwaukee, Wisconsin
Population Served: 608,150
Number of Volumes: 2,553,934
Number of Titles: N/A
Number of Periodical Subscriptions: 9,719

Reports To

Name and title of Immediate Supervisor: Director of Communications & Marketing

SUPERVISION RECEIVED: (Indicate the extent to which work assignments and methods are outlined, reviewed, and approved by others.)

Reports to the Director of Communications & Marketing. Under the supervision of the Director who supervises day-to-day operations, assigns deadlines, oversees workflow, checks completed work, and is available for consultation on problems that arise. Also receives assignments from the Administrative Specialist Sr. Many assignments are carried out by the Graphic Designer II with a high degree of independence

General Summary

BASIC FUNCTION OF POSITION:

The Graphic Designer II has major responsibility for developing artwork for printed publications. The designer works closely with the print shop and communications and marketing staff to assure timely production of quality printed and electronic materials which educate and inform the public of library services, programs and resources.

The Milwaukee Public Library is committed to providing the highest quality of service to internal and external customers. In meeting this commitment, employees are expected to be knowledgeable, competent, dependable and courteous in the performance of their job responsibilities, and to work cooperatively as part of a team.

Essential Functions and Responsibilities

Designs layouts, original art and camera-ready art for print and electronic materials for 13 library locations as well as additional units within the Milwaukee Public Library system based on written work requests. Designs continuing publications such as the Milwaukee Reader newsletter and the Staff News. Creates camera-ready advertisements for newspapers and magazines. Fits copy and assists with copy proofing.

Works closely with the print shop in producing printed materials, including pamphlets, brochures, invitations, flyers, and bookmarks. Prepares color separations and pre-press layout for plate making by printer. Reviews, updates and recommends standing orders for paper and selects paper for special projects.

Assists Administrative Specialist Sr. with web page design, including developing graphic images and creating templates. Along with Administrative Specialist Sr. and Program Assistant II develops templates for creation of stationery, signs and brochures used on library network system.

Assists in developing marketing strategies and promotional ideas and materials for library marketing and public relations campaigns.

Designs and implements the creation of point-of-purchase style posters and signs for the library system which are produced on computer or press in-house or by outside vendors. Designs special signs for changing book displays at Central Library and coordinates production with outside vendors. Sets standards for in-house signs to be created by other library staff. Consults with library staff on displays, exhibits and sign placement. Schedules and designs promotional signs for the Central Library Wisconsin Avenue kiosk.

Acts as art director, organizing and coordinating photo shoots, selecting photos for use in press releases, Staff News, Milwaukee Reader and other print/electronic publications. Maintains photo files. Takes photos with digital or 35 mm camera. Prepares photo images for print or electronic publication.

Coordinates and oversees work of outside vendors of specialty items such as book bags, pencils, etc. Plays an active role is ensuring quality of products produced by outside vendors. Negotiates with outside vendors for best price and results.

Participates on system-wide committees and/or joint projects with outside organizations, which require graphic support as assigned. Maintains files on all printed publicity.

Additional Job Duties

Miscellaneous

Assists with creation of forms as needed.

Performs routine maintenance on computer and printer.

Knowledge, Skills, and Abilities

Strong customer service orientation

Basic knowledge of and ability in the areas of illustration, layout, composition, design and typography is required.

Ability to work with library network applications.

Working knowledge of web design software.

Competence in using all standard art instruments and materials.

Knowledge of paper purchasing as regards to printing, economical use and cost effectiveness for print projects.

Knowledge of computer color separation in pre-press preparation.

A high degree of creative imagination and originality; a feeling for color, design and form.

Ability to work effectively and harmoniously with others. Ability to interpret the ideas of others.

Ability to meet ever changing deadlines

Physical and Mental Requirements

List the physical demands which are representative of those that must be met to successfully perform the essential function of the job. Reasonable accommodations may be made to enable individuals with disabilities to perform the essential functions.

Usually using hand, wrist and fingers simultaneously;

Frequently sitting;

Sometimes standing, walking, squatting, and reaching overhead;

On occasion stooping, twisting, bending, and using feet/legs to control equipment;

Frequently talking and hearing ordinary conversation in person or by phone in a frequently quiet but sometimes noisy environment

Usual need for near vision at 20" or less (i.e.: computer entry)

Sometimes need for far vision at 20" or more (everyday activities).

MENTAL REQUIREMENTS: List the mental requirements, which are, representative of those that must be met to successfully perform the essential function of the job. Reasonable accommodations may be made to enable individuals with disabilities to perform the essential functions

Communication Skills: effectively communicate ideas and information both in written and oral form;

Reading Ability: effectively read and understand information contained in manuals, reports, etc.

Time Management: set priorities in order to meet assignment deadlines;

Problem Solving: develop feasible, realistic solutions to problems, recommend actions designed to prevent problems from occurring;

Planning and Organizing: develop plans to solve complex problems or take advantage of opportunities; establish systematic methods of accomplishing goals;

Analytical Ability: identify problems and opportunities; review possible alternative courses of action before selection; utilize available information resources in decision making;

Creative Decision Making: effectively evaluates or makes independent decisions based upon experience, knowledge or training, with minimal or no supervision;

Ability to Comprehend and Follow Instructions: effectively follow instructions from supervisor, verbally and in written form.

Tools and Equipment Used

List equipment, which is representative of that which would be used to successfully perform the essential function of the job. Reasonable accommodations may be made to enable individuals with disabilities to perform the essential functions.

Personal computer, telephone, printer, photocopier, fax machine, light table, large paper cutter, drawing board, photostat machine, and booktruck.

Work Environment

List the conditions that are representative of those that must be met to successfully perform the essential function of the job. Reasonable accommodations may be made to enable individuals with disabilities to perform the essential functions.

Frequent encounters with hazardous toxic materials and loud noises;

Sometimes working in dusty conditions or with equipment vibrations;

Occasional conditions of glare/improper illumination, electrical hazards, confirmed spaces, extreme heat/cold, sudden temperature changes, limited access to restroom facilities, and equipment with moveable parts;

Frequent exposure to recurring noise from printing press, and other equipment located in adjacent work area

Supervisory Responsibilities

Supervises field students as needed.

Provides training on Macintosh system basics to Program Assistant II who serves as back up to graphic designer.

Education, Experience, and Training

MFA degree (or related) from an accredited school of art, or from an accredited college or university, or the equivalent art experience, or equivalent combination of education and experience.

Working experience with Macintosh desktop publishing using QuarkXpress, Adobe Illustrator, Photoshop, and other software applications.

Disclaimers

Performs other related duties as assigned.

4.0 GRAPHICS SPECIALIST

4.1 SPECIALIST

4.1.1 Specialist

Library Name: Lorain Public Library System
Library Location: Lorain, Ohio
Population Served: 120,132
Number of Volumes: 497,959
Number of Titles: 254,987
Number of Periodical Subscriptions: 1,594

General Summary

Basic Function:

Performs varied desktop publishing graphic-related and secretarial tasks.

Distinguishing Features of the Class:

This classification is responsible for technical and clerical work. The work requires the application of design software and graphic design methods, considerable judgment in planning and organizing the work of the printing unit. Employees in this class work under general supervision and the work is checked by the Public Relations Officer.

Essential Functions and Responsibilities

Characteristic Duties and Responsibilities:

Plans, composes and produces graphics and other printed materials under direction.

Maintains files within the Macintosh computer system by adding, deleting, storing, and enhancing data files.

Operates and maintains printing equipment, including lettering machines, offset press, platemaker, plate converter, postage meter, paper folder, electric paper cutter and Macintosh computer systems.

Maintains community bulletin boards, and maintains and creates display board graphics, and other exhibits.

Performs wide variety of secretarial functions, including preparation of letters, memoranda, reports, press releases and filing.

Serves as receptionist of the unit including answering the telephone and giving general information in response to public inquiries.

Trains and oversees Clerk in production of in-house system forms, filing and operations of computers and printing equipment.

Assists in research and purchase of equipment and software.

Coordinates bulk mailing of newsletters and direct mail pieces.

Responsible for maintaining in-house forms.

Knowledge, Skills and Abilities:

Good knowledge of desktop publishing and graphic design software and equipment including Macintosh; good knowledge of advanced graphic principles including layout and design; good knowledge of printing methods; analytical ability sufficient to perform routine maintenance and correct malfunctions of unit equipment and machinery; good knowledge of the work of the library public relations office; ability to maintain clerical records and prepare reports; ability to make minor decisions in accordance with regulations and established policies; clerical aptitude; tact and courtesy; ability to work in a team environment; good judgment.

Education, Experience and Training:

Requires an associate's degree or completion of a technical specialty program in graphic design or related area and up to six months of related experience or any equivalent combination of experience and training which provides the required knowledge, skills and abilities.

Disclaimers

The intent of this summary is to characterize the typical duties and responsibilities that will be required of individual positions assigned to this classification and should not be construed as representing the specific duties and responsibilities of any particular position. Employees may be expected to perform their related duties, which are specific to their area that may not be reflected in this class summary.

IX. FACILITIES AND MAINTENANCE SERVICES

Included in this section are facilities managers, custodial and building assistants, and maintenance personnel.

1.0 BUILDING MAINTENANCE

1.1 BUILDING MAINTENANCE AND CUSTODIAL SPECIALIST

1.1.1 Building Maintenance and Custodial Specialist

Library Name: Williamsburg Regional Library System
Library Location: Williamsburg, Virginia
Population Served: 60,100
Number of Volumes: 261,243
Number of Titles: N/A
Number of Periodical Subscriptions: 562

General Summary

NATURE OF WORK:

Under the supervision of the Director of Maintenance and Audiovisual Services, the Building Maintenance Specialist II performs custodial and maintenance services at library buildings. Work includes custodial, carpentry, plumbing, painting, and mechanical.

Essential Functions and Responsibilities

Leads assigned personnel in the accomplishment of maintenance repair and construction activities.

Performs preventive and corrective maintenance on all library buildings and equipment.

Paints interior walls and miscellaneous components.

Operates vehicles, power tools, and hand tools.

Performs basic carpentry work.

Performs basic plumbing work.

Performs custodial work. This includes but is not limited to sweeping, mopping, buffing floors; vacuuming carpets; dusting and cleaning furniture and shelves and equipment; washing windows; cleaning and supplying restrooms; removing trash.

Responsible for inventories of custodial supplies; works with supervisor to record needed supplies.

Perform job safely in accordance with library safety procedures.

Administers work typically moving, using, and adjusting a variety of heavy equipment and materials.

Regular contact is made with employees, vendors, outside building maintenance services personnel, and the general public.

Tools and Equipment Used

Cleaning chemicals, repair tools, custodial and other equipment and materials is required. Also, computer and other office equipment are required. The job is located in two libraries.

Knowledge, Skills, and Abilities

Ability to learn and use the library's custodial and maintenance equipment, materials, repair tools, computer, and office equipment.

Ability to work under minimum supervision.

Ability to follow emergency procedures to provide security for the libraries, patrons, and staff.

Ability to establish and maintain effective working relationships with fellow staff members, vendors, government personnel, and other service providers.

Ability to work effectively as a team member.

Education, Experience, and Training

MINIMUM QUALIFICATIONS:

High school diploma or equivalent preferred supplemented by vocational, technical, or trade school training in building trades; and considerable experience in general building maintenance and repair or any equivalent combination of acceptable education and experience providing the knowledge, abilities, and duties cited above.

Licenses and Certification Requirements:

Must possess a valid Virginia driver's license and have an acceptable driving record based upon James City County's criteria

Additional Qualifications

A police criminal history record check is required.

1.2 CUSTODIAL AND MAINTENANCE ASSISTANT

1.2.1 Custodial and Maintenance Assistant

Library Name: Williamsburg Regional Library System
Library Location: Williamsburg, Virginia
Population Served: 60,100
Number of Volumes: 261,243
Number of Titles: N/A
Number of Periodical Subscriptions: 562

General Summary

NATURE OF WORK:

Under the supervision of the Library Facilities Director, the Building Maintenance Assistant provides a comprehensive program of custodial services for two libraries, including preventative maintenance and light repair of custodial equipment and keeping track of supplies. Also trains and supervises volunteers; assists the Delivery Service Manager as needed.

Essential Functions and Responsibilities

Maintains overall order and cleanliness of two libraries. This includes, but is not limited to, sweeping, mopping, and buffing floors; vacuuming carpets; dusting and cleaning furniture, shelves, and equipment; washing windows; cleaning and supplying restrooms; removing trash.

Maintains order and cleanliness of storage areas.

Provides preventative maintenance, cleaning, and light repair of custodial equipment on a regular basis.

Includes emptying and/or cleaning filters of cleaning equipment after each use, if necessary.

Returns supplies, equipment, and tools to their designated places after each use.

Tracks and keeps inventories of custodial supplies; submits reordering requests to supervisor in a timely manner.

Provides assistance to staff in moving furniture; and in moving and reassembling modular office furniture.

Assists the Delivery Services Manager; loads and unloads library materials, supplies, equipment, etc., to and from the van; assists in transporting items by hand or cart inside and/or outside the buildings.

Trains new custodial staff; trains and supervises volunteers from the District Court Community Services

Program as needed.

May participate in library-wide committees or projects.

Performs other tasks as needed.

Tools and Equipment Used

Administers work typically moving, using, and adjusting a variety of heavy equipment and materials.

Heavy lifting up to 100 pounds and other strenuous physical activities, and frequent sustained operation of building and custodial equipment required.

Work includes exposure to chemicals and vapors, debris and dust, and other uncomfortable conditions.

Regular contact is made with employees, vendors, outside building maintenance services personnel, and the general public.

Cleaning chemicals, repair tools, custodial and other equipment and materials as required. Also, computer and other office equipment as required. The job is located in two libraries.

Knowledge, Skills, and Abilities

Ability to learn and use the library's custodial equipment, materials, repair tools, computer, and office equipment.

Ability and willingness to understand and efficiently carry out oral and written instructions, and to follow through on numerous details in an orderly, systematic fashion.

Ability to work under minimum supervision.

Ability to follow emergency procedures to provide security for the libraries, patrons, and staff.

Ability to establish and maintain effective working relationships with fellow staff members, vendors, government personnel, and other service providers.

Ability to maintain good work habits.

Education, Experience, and Training

MINIMUM QUALIFICATIONS:

High school diploma or equivalent preferred.

Experience in custodial services preferred.

License and Certification Requirements

NECESSARY SPECIAL QUALIFICATIONS:

Requires the ability to travel among various library sites.

Additional Qualifications

A police criminal history record check is required.

2.0 MANAGERS

2.1 FACILITIES MANAGER

2.1.1 Facilities Manager

Library Name: Hartford Public Library
Library Location: Hartford, Connecticut
Population Served: 133,280
Number of Volumes: 485,000
Number of Titles: 255,000
Number of Periodical Subscriptions: 805

General Summary

The Facilities Manager ensures that the physical facilities and grounds of the Hartford Public

Library support the delivery of responsive community service and are adequate, safe, and hospitable for customers and staff. Manages and directs the operations of the Facility Services

Department of the Hartford Public Library; participates in the planning and construction of new facilities and renovations of existing facilities; manages the daily and major maintenance of all facilities, maintenance of all Library vehicles, and the safety program, including security.

Advocates for the public and Library staff to ensure safe and fully adequate facilities.

Essential Functions and Responsibilities

Provides leadership to a staff of 18 FTE, 10 facilities, and four vehicles.

Participates in planning for new facilities and renovations of existing facilities. Oversees layout and construction of new interior workspaces and/or leased facilities.

Coordinates and supervises the moving of materials and/or furnishings involved in all relocation or storage.

Serves as liaison with outside agencies, negotiating and resolving facilities issues.

Oversees the operation of electrical, HVAC, and plumbing systems as well as the physical maintenance of facilities.

Develops and implements a schedule for regular preventive maintenance of all systems and equipment.

Develops and maintains periodic schedules for upkeep/improvement of lawns, trees, shrubs, plants, parking areas and other exterior landscaping of all Library facilities.

Develops and oversees maintenance schedule for all Library vehicles, including the 40-ft. Library on Wheels. Recommend replacements as needed. Develops and oversees policies for all drivers of vehicles.

Operates computer programs for building systems, facilities planning and reporting.

Oversees the receipt and installation of all furnishings and equipment.

Develops and recommends policies and procedures relevant to security of all facilities. Has oversight for the hiring, training and supervision of security guards. Responds to disturbances in the Library system.

Manages safety program. Ensures compliance with health, fire, building codes and OSHA regulations.

Prepares and administers department operating budget and capital improvement budget.

Approves accounts payable and spending limits.

Attends and participates in outside meetings related to facilities services. Stays abreast of new trends in facilities and fleet management.

Collects and compiles data on a quarterly and annual basis on the physical condition of all facilities. Submits quarterly reports on department activities.

Knowledge, Skills, and Abilities

MINIMUM JOB QUALIFICATION STANDARDS:

Knowledge of:

Operational characteristics, services and activities of a multi-faceted maintenance and construction program.

Modern and complex principles and practice of construction, maintenance and repair activities related to building, grounds, equipment and vehicles.

Principles and practices of budget management.

Operation of mechanical systems.

Federal, state and local regulations and building codes, including OSHA and ADA.

Management and supervision practices.

Ability to:

Provide professional leadership and direction for the Facility Services Department

Read, interpret and draw plans for building construction, renovations, equipment and furnishings.

Analyze complex problems and develop reasonable solutions.

Operate computers and relevant software.

Work independently in a team environment.

Train, motivate and supervise employees.

Present ideas effectively, orally and in writing.

Establish and maintain effective working relationships.

Maintain confidentiality related to the area of work.

Education, Experience, and Training

MINIMUM REQUIREMENTS:

Education: Bachelor's degree in Engineering, Architecture, Business Administration or a closely related field.

Experience: 5–7 years of increasingly responsible management experience in an organization with multiple locations. Supervisory experience required; experience in union environment preferred.

License and Certification Requirements

License: Valid CT Motor Vehicle Operator's license during term of employment.

Position Hours

Schedule: The normal work schedule includes day, evening and weekend hours.

2.1.2 Facilities Manager

Library Name: Anacortes Public Library
Library Location: Anacortes, Washington
Population Served: 14,500
Number of Volumes: N/A
Number of Titles: 55,565
Number of Periodical Subscriptions: 126

Reports To

Director

General Summary

PRINCIPAL PURPOSE OF JOB: Responsible for planning, organizing, directing and performing the activities related to maintenance, repairs and improvements to the following City facilities (Municipal Building, Fidalgo Center, Police Buildings, Fire Buildings, Museum Buildings, Library and others as assigned) in compliance with established local, state, and federal standards. Participate in short-term and long-range planning for the department and responsible for day to day supervision of assigned employees to make the most effective and efficient use of skills, facilities, and equipment available.

LEVEL OF AUTHORITY: Performs duties with only general direction and defined latitude for independent judgment within established guidelines and policies. Errors in judgment could have substantial impact on public acceptance of programs and efficient operations of the department.

Work Environment

Some work is performed outdoors in all kinds of weather conditions and may involve potential exposure to hazards such as chemicals. Other work is performed indoors at the above-listed City facilities. Work performed in this job may place the employee at risk of occupational exposure to blood borne pathogens.

Essential Functions and Responsibilities

Participate with Director in long-range planning and establishing priorities for facilities maintenance, repairs and improvements.

Supervise assigned staff, regular and seasonal, planning, organizing, and directing work activities, participating in hiring; conducting orientation and training; preparing performance evaluations for the approval of the Director; and recommending disciplinary action to the Director.

Direct and/or perform the daily maintenance, repairs and improvements of assigned facilities.

As required, coordinate work activities with other City departments, representatives of local, state, and federal agencies, citizens, and equipment and service suppliers.

Maintain excellent public relations by assuring that public/and internal inquiries are answered in a courteous manner and that complaints are responded to promptly. Where appropriate, refer inquiries to the Director.

Negotiate, prepare, implement and administer construction and service contracts.

Prepare and coordinate bid packages necessary for the purchase of maintenance equipment, materials and supplies.

Periodically inspect all city buildings and advise as to preventative maintenance measures needed.

Establish and implement maintenance schedules for all city buildings.

Assure that all City facilities are accessible to the extent reasonably possible.

Stay informed on changing products and technology and make recommendations to the director.

As required, prepare labor, material, time, and equipment estimates for new or modified facilities.

Participate in Exposure Control Plan of the City of Anacortes in accordance with WAC 296-62-08001.

Additional Job Duties

May perform portions of the work of higher classified positions occasionally, as assigned.

May perform duties of similar complexity in any City department as required or assigned.

Physical and Mental Requirements

Physical Capabilities

Physical strength and ability to perform moderate to heavy manual labor for extended periods under dirty and uncomfortable conditions and in all types of weather, as necessary.

Ability to monitor radio messages while doing other work throughout the day.

Tools and Equipment Used

Ability to use all tools and operate all equipment necessary to perform work of the position.

Reading ability to read and interpret technical journals, manuals and other materials pertaining to facility maintenance, equipment, systems and repair.

Education, Experience, and Training

QUALIFICATIONS

Technical

Must have or acquire a working knowledge of facility maintenance and operations.

Must have sufficient experience in the field to have acquired an extensive knowledge of the methods, materials, tools, and equipment used in all phases of building maintenance, including a basic general knowledge of electricity, plumbing, carpentry and an extensive knowledge of HVAC systems.

Must have a thorough knowledge of work hazards, safety procedures, and public safety matters.

Must be bondable.

Must have ability to plan, schedule, and review the work and performance of others in a manner conducive to proficient performance and high morale.

Additional Qualifications

As an absolute condition of employment, employees are required upon hire to sign a drug-free workplace agreement and an agreement not to use tobacco products, in any form, on the job.

Must have excellent communications skills to direct employees, coordinate with other departments, answer public inquiries and enforce City facilities rules tactfully but firmly.

Ability to take initiative and apply considerable ingenuity and practical knowledge to interpret and resolve new, unusual, or particularly troublesome situations.

Flexibility to be available for emergency call-outs during off time.

Writing ability to write correspondence, memos to employees, and schedules.

Disclaimers

The statements contained in this job description reflect general details as necessary to describe the principal functions of this job, the level of knowledge and skill typically required, and the scope of responsibility. It should not be considered an all-inclusive listing of work requirements. Individuals may perform other duties as assigned, including work in other functional areas to cover absences or provide relief, to equalize peak work periods, or otherwise to balance the workload.

License and Certification Requirements

Must possess a valid Washington State driver's license.

Must be able to obtain a first-aid/CPR card.

2.2 MAINTENANCE AND CUSTODIAL MANAGER

2.2.1 Maintenance and Custodial Manager

Library Name: Cuyahoga County Public Library
Library Location: Parma, Ohio
Population Served: 607,909
Number of Volumes: 3,297,420
Number of Titles: N/A
Number of Periodical Subscriptions: 8,502

Reports To

Facilities Director

General Summary

Under limited supervision of the Facilities Director, determines needed repairs and improvements for all buildings, and plans and directs the related maintenance activities, and manages the usage and monitors all library utilities costs and energy conservation programs.

Essential Functions and Responsibilities

Complies with work scheduling and attendance requirements according to reasonable policy and practices. Staffing for branch and regional libraries and some Administration (ADM) departments requires rotational scheduling, which includes evening and weekend (Saturday and Sunday) hours. Most ADM departments are weekday operations.

Consistently presents Cuyahoga County Public Library and its services in a positive manner and adheres to customer service guidelines and procedures as established by the Library.

Complies with the established rules of operation, procedures, and policies when using library computers, peripheral hardware, and software. Individual passwords and any other confidential information regarding library records shall be kept confidential.

Coordinates and directs day-to-day operations of the maintenance shop including determining needed repairs and improvements, establishing project priorities and assigning work tasks, scheduling work to most effectively meet facility needs, etc.

Supervises and directs the maintenance staff including Maintenance Workers and Specialists by providing training and development, monitoring and evaluating work performance, interviewing and hiring adequate staff and disciplining staff as necessary.

Confers with architects, engineers, contractors, Library Directors and other staff regarding maintenance projects such as progress reports, work evaluations and project details.

Manages and oversees all CCPL utilities' usage and costs for: phones (telecommunications); electric and gas billing rates and contracts; water and sewer billing and metering; and monitors energy conservation programs.

Documents departmental activity through preparation of various reports, work orders, maintenance schedules and other incidental record keeping.

Prepares, implements and monitors departmental budget.

Reviews and analyzes project specifications, drawings and blue prints.

Develops and maintains inventory of spare and repair parts, materials and tools.

Supervises and directs various seasonal projects such as roofing maintenance and repairs, parking lot repairs and HVAC maintenance.

Plans, directs and schedules snow and ice removal and ensures adequate supplies of salt and ice melt are stocked.

Ensures all OSHA required training is administered to workers in accordance with established standards.

The intent of this position description is to provide a representative summary of the major duties and responsibilities performed by incumbents of this job. Incumbents may be requested to perform job-related tasks other than those specifically presented in this description.

Knowledge, Skills, and Abilities

Thorough knowledge of building design and construction methods, techniques and industry standards and general knowledge of various skilled trades such as HVAC, plumbing and electrical systems repair and installation.

Comprehensive knowledge of methods and techniques of buildings and grounds maintenance including program organization and implementation methods of HVAC, electronics, plumbing and electrical systems.

Knowledge of CCPL preventive maintenance, work order and related program policies and procedures.

Knowledge of OSHA safety regulations and penalties, State safety regulations, environmental polices affecting facilities maintenance.

Ability to read and comprehend blueprints and drawing specifications.

Ability to operate various maintenance equipment and tools including various hand held power tools, welding equipment, grounds maintenance and snow removal equipment, etc.

Strong supervisory skills for delegating project and task responsibilities, monitoring and evaluating work performance and maintaining an effective, trained work staff.

Ability to prepare and implement departmental budgets.

Ability to prepare materials estimates from job specifications, work orders and blueprints.

Ability to train maintenance staff in correct maintenance procedures, tool and equipment use and safety issues.

Physical and Mental Requirements

Requires incumbent to be on 24 hour on-call status for projects and facilities emergencies.

Moderate physical effort required involving long periods of standing/walking, climbing ladders and lifting moderately heavy objects (25–50 lbs) such as helping to load 50 pound bags of salt into vehicle salt spreaders.

Involves modestly unpleasant situations, as with occasional exposure to dust, fumes and outside weather conditions.

Supervisory Responsibilities

Maintenance Supervisor

Education, Experience, and Training

Associate's degree or completion of a technical specialty program of over eighteen months and up to three years beyond high school in Building Maintenance/Engineering or related field.

Over six years of building/facilities maintenance experience.

License and Certification Requirements

Due to the physical exertion required to perform the essential duties of this job, the decision to hire is contingent on job candidate passing a pre-employment medical exam through a medical provider contracted by the library.

A valid Ohio Driver's license is required to operate library owned vehicles and a clean driving record must be maintained at all times.

A criminal background check is required.

X. LIBRARY BOARD MEMBERS

Included in this section are board trustees and officers.

1.0 LIBRARY BOARD MEMBER AND TRUSTEE

1.1 PUBLIC LIBRARY TRUSTEE

1.1.1 Public Library Trustee

Library Name: Montana State Library
Name: Montana Public Library Trustee Manual
Revised 6/1993
http://msl.state.mt.us/slr/trustee.pdf

General Summary

SAMPLE POSITION DESCRIPTION
MEMBER, BOARD OF TRUSTEES
SUMMARY

Provides governance for the Public Library, establishes policy; sets goals; hires Library Director; establishes and monitors the annual budget; signs necessary contracts, exercises such other powers, not inconsistent with law, necessary for the effective use and management of the Library.

Essential Functions and Responsibilities

Participates in the ongoing responsibilities of the governing body, including establishment of library policies and planning for current and future library services and programs.

Determines and adopts written policies to govern the operation and services of the library.

Attends all regular and special meetings of the Board, and participates in committees and activities as necessary; attends appropriate library functions.

Represents the interests and needs of community members.

Lends expertise and experience to the organization.

Sets an annual budget and approves expenditure of funds; monitors budget and expenses throughout the year.

Maintains an awareness of library issues and trends and the implications for library users.

Acts as liaison with the public, interpreting and informing local government, media and public of library services and needs.

Hires, sets salary, and supervises a qualified library director to implement board decisions and directions and to carry out day-to-day provision of library services.

Establishes short and long-term goals for Library.

Understands pertinent local and state law; actively supports library legislation in the state and nation.

Ensures compliance with open meeting law.

Reviews and signs necessary contracts (e.g. contract with County).

Reports activities to City and County Commissions annually.

Knowledge, Skills, and Abilities

Is interested in the library and its services.

Has the ability to contribute adequate time for effective participation in board activities and decision making.

Has the ability to represent needs and varied interests of the community at large and the library.

Has strong interpersonal and communication skills.

Has the ability to work with governmental bodies, agencies and other libraries.

Has the ability to handle opposition and make decisions in the interest of library service.

TIME COMMITMENT

The Board of Trustees meets monthly at a time convenient for members. Meetings generally last about three hours. Meetings are generally held at the library and are usually during a weekday.

Members are appointed by the mayor with the advice and consent of the city commission to a five-year term (or to complete an unexpired term). Members shall serve no more than two full terms in succession.

Special meetings or committee meetings may be called as necessary at times convenient to members as well as complying with open meeting laws.

1.1.2 Public Library Trustee

Name: Wisconsin Department of Public Instruction Public Library Development Trustee Essential #1 January 2002
http://www.dpi.state.wi.us/dpi/dlcl/pld/te1.html
"Copyright 2002 Wisconsin Department of Public Library Instruction. Duplication and distribution for not-for-profit purposes with the copyright notice."

GENERAL FUNCTION: Participate as a member of a team (the library board) to protect and advance the interests of the broader community by effectively governing the operations and promoting the development of the local public library.

QUALIFICATIONS:

serious commitment to being a library trustee

serious commitment to the provision of library services within your community

ability to attend regularly scheduled board meetings and be an active member of the library board

willingness to become familiar with Wisconsin library law, standards for libraries, and principles and practices for ensuring that the library provides broad and equitable access to the knowledge, information, and diversity of ideas needed by community residents

commitment to freedom of expression and inquiry for all people

PRINCIPAL ACTIVITIES:

1. Prepare for and attend regular board meetings.

The library board meeting will be the primary opportunity for you to contribute to the development of your library. To get the most from the meetings, and to be able to share your skills and knowledge, you must attend each meeting after having read and thought about the issues and topics that will be discussed. While you and your fellow trustees are busy people, it is important that the full board meet on a monthly basis to conduct business. You can contribute to the library by encouraging regular meetings and assuring that the meetings are properly noticed in accordance with Wisconsin's open meetings law. (See Trustee Essential #4: Effective Board Meetings and Trustee Participation and Trustee Essential #14: The Library Board and the Open Meetings Law .)

2. Work with the municipal governing body to obtain adequate library funding. Assist in the review and approval of the annual budget and monthly expenditures as presented by the library director.

One of the library board's most important responsibilities is to work to obtain adequate financial support so that the library can provide a meaningful program of services for the residents of the area. As a trustee, your focus should be on those services and what is required to provide them to the public in the most beneficial manner. Once a determination is made as to how much money will be needed, the request must be carefully and accurately prepared and then presented to the municipal governing body (for example, the village board or the city council). Trustees should attend the governing body meetings when budget requests are presented so that they can answer questions about need and account for how previous appropriations benefited the citizens and the community. After municipal funding has been approved, the library board must monitor the use of these public funds to assure that they provide what was intended. By law, only the library board has the authority to approve expenditures made by the library. (See Trustee Essential #8: Developing the Library Budget and Trustee Essential #9: Managing the Library's Money.)

3. Participate in the development and approval of library policies. Review policies on a regular, systematic schedule.

Certainly the money is important to pay staff, buy materials, and maintain the facilities, but a library cannot operate successfully without policies that assure consistent and equitable treatment of all users while at the same time protecting the resources of the institution. Developing and adopting these policies is another important responsibility of a library board. Each trustee acts as a contact with other members of the community and has the chance to hear about concerns or desires relating to the library. The comments you receive from the public can help you and the other members of the board address the community standards through thoughtful and fair policies. Understanding the feelings of community members and the challenges the staff faces in operating the library can prepare you to participate with other board members and the director in defending policies that may provoke controversy. As needs, processes, and services change within the library, there will be a need to review, revise, and add policies. It can be helpful for the board to establish a routine procedure for reviewing policies to be sure that they remain current. This is often accomplished by the board looking at individual policies at meetings throughout the year. (See Trustee Essential #10: Developing Essential Library Policies.)

4. Help determine and advocate for reasonable staff salaries and benefits.

If the library is to offer meaningful and accessible services to the residents of your community, it must have a trained, certified library director and other capable assistants to provide those services. To attract capable employees, and to keep them once they are hired and oriented, it will be crucial that the library board offer reasonable and competitive compensation, including a meaningful wage and benefits like health insurance, retirement, sick leave, and vacation. By providing adequate compensation for staff, the library board will help local officials and the public generally to understand the importance of the library and the complexity of the tasks involved with providing good library services. (See Trustee Essential #7: The Library Board and Library Personnel.)

5. Assist in the hiring, supervising, and evaluating of the library director.

Though it is hopefully not a regular task, there may come a time when the library board must hire a new director. If this is required, deciding how the process is conducted and who is finally selected will be among the most important decisions a library board will ever make. A library director can be around for many years and have a significant impact on the tone and quality of library service. In the one-person library, the library director often becomes the personification of the entire institution. So it is important that this task be given serious consideration and that each trustee take an active role in selecting and then welcoming and orienting the new director. Finally, in order to assure that you do not have to go through this process unnecessarily, the library board needs to establish a regular procedure and schedule for assessing the performance of the director and providing suggestions for improvements. Your willingness as a trustee to participate in these processes will greatly contribute to the library's overall effectiveness. (See Trustee Essential #5: Hiring a Library Director; Trustee Essential #6: Evaluating the Director; and Trustee Essential #7: The Library Board and Library Personnel.)

6. Study the needs and interests of the community and see that they are addressed, as appropriate, by the library.

As a community liaison, you are in a unique position to survey the community, learn of its needs and wants, and include those interests in discussions relating to library development. This opportunity and responsibility is satisfied at an informal and formal level. Informally, just being visible and accessible as a library trustee and communicating with your neighbors will allow you to gather important information about how the library can help its customers. In a more formal fashion, the library board may decide to conduct a community survey and/or call together a focus group to help it pinpoint important issues. Active participation by each trustee at both levels will be invaluable to the library's progress. (See Trustee Essential #11: Planning for the Library's Future.)

7. Act as an advocate for the library through contacts with civic groups and public officials.

Gathering information on community needs will certainly put you in contact with your community; the purpose of that activity is to focus development energies. Other kinds of contacts are also important, however, and their purpose will be to raise awareness of the library and promote its services. It has been written that the core of effective politics is the building of rapport. Since local politics are personal, your contacts on behalf of the library with public officials from the municipality, the county, and the state will advance the cause of your institution. In the same way, building rapport and networking with civic and service groups will advance your cause with your customers and potential individual supporters. This is an area where an individual trustee can directly help the library in a significant way. (See Trustee Essential #13: Library Advocacy.)

8. Become familiar with principles and issues relating to intellectual freedom and equitable provision of public library services.

Public libraries in our country and state are founded on the principle that for a democracy to function properly it must have an educated electorate, and to be educated, people must have free access to the broadest possible array of information. Libraries, along with other institutions such as the press and the judiciary, have long stood as protectors of the individual's right to have the information that he or she requires to thrive in and contribute to society. Regardless of these basic rights, though, sometimes people seek to limit the access of others to certain ideas and presentations. It is a responsibility of your library board, and each member of that board, to make a commitment to the community's freedom of inquiry and expression, and to be prepared to address calmly and respectfully the challenges that may come before you. While the board must have a carefully devised process for addressing challenges and speak in a single voice on censorship issues to the public and the media, it is up to you as a trustee to take the time to become informed about the principles and issues. While it is said that a public library without something to offend everyone is not doing its job, it is not the job of the library board to offend, but rather to defend the rights of each citizen to search for the truth through his or her own journey. The nation's and the library's future relies on unrestricted access to information. (See Trustee Essential #22: Freedom of Expression and Inquiry and Trustee Essential #23: Dealing with Challenges to Materials and Policies.)

9. Assist in the formulation and adoption of a long-range plan for the library. Periodically review and revise long-range plan.

Working through the budget process, developing policies, and studying community needs and making contacts with individuals and groups prepares you for the valuable process of formulating plans for the library's future. Your library may be accomplishing great things already, but as the world changes, the library must change with it. Trustees, as the citizen representatives with detailed information about how the library functions, are in an ideal position to assist with planning. Your important role in planning will be to investigate, along with the library director, different planning options and then decide on the most appropriate process for your library. If additional resources are required to fulfill the plans, you can also help to establish the amount and identify sources. Finally, once proposed plans are approved by the full board, you can continue to participate by being active in the annual review of the library's plan, during which you can suggest revisions that will keep the library on course. A plan is a means to an end, and it will be the active participation of each trustee in the planning process that will offer ongoing strength and insight to the library board as it pursues its responsibility for library development. (See Trustee Essential #11: Planning for the Library's Future.)

10. Attend Wisconsin Library Association conferences, regional system workshops, and other training opportunities in order to expand knowledge of effective leadership, and consider membership in the Wisconsin Library Trustees Association (WLTA).

As you have probably concluded by now, the library trustee's job is complex and demanding. At the same time, though, it can be stimulating and exceedingly rewarding. One way to maintain energy and enthusiasm, as well as to increase understanding of trusteeship, is to participate in the various opportunities for education that are available to trustees. Through your director or direct mailings, you should be regularly informed of upcoming seminars, workshops, and conferences. Another method for gaining insights and ideas and also a great way to rejuvenate the spirit and not feel alone in the challenges you face is to get involved in the state library trustee association. The network of friends that can be developed through WLTA will keep you interested and vital; your participation in the association will strengthen the statewide library community, and that, in turn, will help your library as well.

1.1.3 Public Library Trustee

Library Name: Portage County Public Library
Library Location: Stevens Point, Wisconsin
Population Served: 67,378
Number of Volumes: 157,918
Number of Titles: N/A
Number of Periodical Subscriptions: N/A

Reports to

Accountable to:

The taxpayers of Portage County and the people served by the library.

Legal Responsibilities:

Members of the library board are mandated by Wisconsin law to control:

Library funds
Library property
Library expenditures
The selection and hiring of a library director

Members of the library board are required to maintain open records and hold open meetings under the requirements of Chapter 19 of the Wisconsin Statutes.

Duties:

Selects and hires a competent and qualified library director.

Determines, adopts and reviews written policies to govern the operation and program of the library, as necessary.

Attends all board meetings. Reads board meeting minutes and other materials sent out before the board meeting. Participates appropriately in board meetings.

Lends expertise to the board for the good of the library.

Serves on committees as assigned by board chair.

Assists with the development of a long-range plan for commitment of resources to meet the changing needs of the service population.

Assists with the preparation of a statement of purpose, service goals and objectives.

Adopts an annual budget adequate for the support of the library: works actively for public and official support of the budget.

Reviews monthly financial statements in the context of the annual budget, approves reasonable expenditures that are within the total approved budget, forwards approved bills for payment by Portage County.

Develops and maintains capital improvement plan.

Participates in System workshops and activities as time permits.

Promotes and advocates the library—talks about the merits of quality library service and the importance of reading.

Qualifications:

Listens to the community—acts as the library's eyes and ears.

Willingness to devote time and talents.

Ability to think clearly, question objectively, and plan creatively.

Skill in communicating and cooperating.

Awareness and appreciation of the library's past, present and future role in society.

Willingness to become more knowledgeable about library services and standards of operation.

Code of Ethics:

Ability to represent the Library Board in public forums as necessary, to act as an advocate for library services, and to reflect the concerns of the public at library board meetings.

Members of the library board are expected to follow the codes of ethics outlined in Wisconsin Statutes and the Portage County Code.

A member of the library board will:

declare any personal conflicts of interest and avoid voting on issues that appear to be conflicts of interest.

not be critical, in or outside of the board meeting, of fellow board members or their opinions.

not use position on Library Board for personal advantage or the personal advantage of friends or relatives.

observe confidential proceedings of the board and not discuss outside the board meeting.

support open discussion on any agenda item prior to a vote. Once vote is taken, support the decision of the majority.

not interfere with the day-to-day work of library staff nor interfere with the duties of the director or undermine the director's authority.

recognize that the library's and community's best interests must prevail over any individual interest.

Skills and Abilities:

Ability to work well with others.

Ability to relate to the public.

Ability to listen effectively.

2.0 OFFICER

2.1 BOARD OF LIBRARY COMMISSIONERS OFFICER

2.1.1 Board of Library Commissioners Officer

Name: Massachusetts Board of Library Commissioners, Massachusetts Library and Information Network
Location: Boston, Massachusetts
Population Served: N/A
Number of Volumes: N/A
Number of Titles: N/A
Periodical Subscriptions: N/A

Duties of Officers

All boards of trustees recognize the need for officers with clearly defined duties and powers for each office, all in writing and well understood by everyone. Board position descriptions can and should be designed to meet the specific needs of the individual library. Following are some sample position descriptions. Boards of trustees traditionally elect the following officers:

Chairperson/ President

Keeps the board operating effectively, while working well with all board members and other key contacts.

Works closely and cooperatively with the library director.

Serves as diplomatic troubleshooter to identify potential problems and issues which require advance board study and action.

Never loses sight of the fact that the chairperson is only one member of the board, not empowered alone to set policy for the board or the library.

Graciously walks a delicate line between front stage and back stage, doing and delegating, silent and speaking, pushing and pulling, persisting and praising, listening and leading.

Carrying all the workload for the board is not necessarily the mark of a good chairperson. To ensure that all board members contribute and are given due credit is a greater challenge and accomplishment.

The chairperson is the chief spokesperson representing the board both orally and in correspondence.

Plans and presides over board meetings. The chairperson is responsible for advance, written agenda; plans and conducts meetings to assure productive sessions which steadily move the board toward its internal goals and objectives as well as the library goals and objectives. The chairperson's knowledge of, and commitment to, parliamentary procedure, plus an understanding of group dynamics, can make the difference between a meeting which keeps the discussion focused on the major action issues to be considered, or a rambling, semi-social session.

Appoints committees for specific assignments. Exerts care in selecting as committee chairs, board members who have commitment and ability to lead a committee to reach the board's assigned objective within the assigned time. The wise board chairperson recognizes and utilizes any special expertise which potential committee members may have. The chairperson monitors the progress of the committee and provides help if needed, yet is careful not to dominate. Some board chairpersons serve as ex-officio members of all committees except the nominating committee.

Some boards limit the chairperson's term of office to one year, to facilitate rotation of leadership responsibilities. This creates a stronger board and lessens the potential for one person to dominate the board.

Vice Chairperson/Vice President

The commitment and leadership abilities of the person the board elects as vice chairperson should be similar to those of chairperson.

The vice chairperson automatically becomes the chairperson in the event of resignation or death unless the bylaws provide otherwise. If the vice chairperson does not want to assume the office of chairperson, he must resign unless the bylaws provide otherwise.

Presides in the absence of the chairperson or whenever the chairperson temporarily vacates the position.

In the absence of the chairperson, the vice chairperson is not an ex-officio member of any committee; cannot fill vacancies in cases in which the bylaws state that such vacancies be filled by chairperson.

Secretary

It is important for the secretary to have a general knowledge of the board's statutory authority, bylaws and operating policies as well as parliamentary procedure. The secretary should understand that minutes of a public body must be a clear, concise, factual record for possible later reference or legal evidence showing what specific action was taken, why it was taken, when and by whom.

Issues and posts for public notice advance agendas of meetings following specific legal requirements for open meetings.

Prepares the official board minutes and keeps on public file.

Keeps member attendance record.

Presides at meetings in absence of chairperson and vice-chairperson until election of a chair pro tem.

Handles all official correspondence on behalf of the board.

If the library director or a library staff member serves as board secretary, it should be mutually agreed in advance and in writing precisely which responsibilities will be, and which will not be, assumed by the library director or staff member. Without such an agreement there could be misunderstanding, conflict or board resentment that it was not in control of its own affairs.

Treasurer

Understands financial accounting.

Serves as chairperson of the board finance committee.

Works with the library director to insure that appropriate financial reports are made available to the board on a timely basis.

Assists the library director in preparing the annual budget and presenting the budget to the board for approval.

Reviews the annual audit and answers board members' questions about the audit.

Trustee Tip

The treasurer's role varies with the size of the library. In small libraries, the treasurer may keep the books, deposit funds, prepare reports and even write checks or vouchers. In larger libraries, the treasurer is legal officer named to assure that financial operations are being properly handled. Bylaws should outline the specific job.

XI. LIBRARY FOUNDATION MEMBERS

Included in this section are foundation board directors and members.

1.0 FOUNDATION DIRECTOR

1.1 FOUNDATION DIRECTOR

1.1.1 Foundation Director

Library Name: Laramie County Library System
Library Location: Cheyenne, Wyoming
Population Served: 80,000
Number of Volumes: 253,962
Number of Titles: N/A
Periodical Subscriptions: 413

General Summary

JOB SUMMARY

As chief executive officer of the Laramie County Library Foundation (LCLF), administers all aspects of LCLF in a responsible, efficient and effective manner. In conjunction with the LCLF Board of Directors, this position is responsible for raising substantial funds to further the mission of the Laramie County Library System. The Foundation Director serves as the Board of Directors' Agent to administer fundraising, investment of funds and expenditure of funds to ensure the wishes of the donor and/or contractual agreements with granting agencies are fulfilled. This position communicates in such a manner as to further the credibility of the LCLF within Laramie County and to promote trust and confidence in the Foundation Board of Directors, System Board of Directors, and the employees of Laramie County Library System. This position plans, organizes and solicits major donations, establishes and maintains contacts with individual and corporate donors, builds relationships with foundations, and coordinates affiliated support from groups as appropriate.

Essential Functions and Responsibilities

1. Provide leadership and direction for the Board of Directors and broad policy guidance for the Foundation program which includes developing and implementing a comprehensive and coordinated fundraising program that will include the identification, cultivation and solicitation of major donors, especially individuals, while targeting foundations, corporations and government sources. The program must encompass major individual and deferred gifts; bequests and other planned giving programs, and to a lesser extent, special events and grants.

2. With the County Librarian and LCLS's needs as a backdrop, work closely and effectively with the LCLF Board of Directors to establish and execute a comprehensive development plan based on the short and long-range needs of the LCLS.

3. Work independently as a self-starter to accomplish the goals that are agreed upon by the Foundation Director and the LCLF

Board of Directors. Meeting the fund raising goals is the direct responsibility of the Foundation Director.

4. Establish and administer fundraising programs for major individual donations, corporate giving, foundation support, planned giving, annual giving and special events.

5. Serves as the Foundation's representative in the community and throughout the county. Understands that the community also perceives the Foundation Director as a representative of LCLS.

6. Identify and research potential sources of gift support including individuals, corporations and foundations. Plan and administer programs designed to secure such support.

7. Participate in individual and institutional fundraising activities maintaining contact with significant donors before and after gifts are committed.

8. Develop, administer and control the expenditures of the LCLF budget to ensure the financial stability and growth of the LCLF. The LCLS Business Office Manager can provide assistance.

9. Research, identify, develop and submit proposals for grants to foundations, corporations and government agencies.

10. Ensure that LCLF database (currently using GiftMaker Pro 8.1) is kept up-to-date and accurate in terms of all appropriate aspects of Foundation business including the recording and acknowledging process for all donations submitted to the LCLF.

11. In consultation with LCLF Board members who have expertise in the area of tax law, charitable giving and other information necessary for the successful operation of a 501©3 organization, keep up-to-date to insure LCLF is in compliance with sound financial practices as well as federal and state requirements.

12. Understand the role LCLS plays in the community including its mission statement and Strategic Plan. Understand the need to uphold the current level of tax support for LCLS. Fundraising must be accomplished in a manner to ensure tax support is not jeopardized.

13. Organize, coordinate and/or conduct presentations to community groups including preparing appropriate handouts, packets, and/or audiovisual presentations.

14. Produce brochures, public press releases, newsletters, documents, etc. and submit them for review by the appropriate LCLS employee prior to their release.

15. In conjunction with LCLF's Investment Committee and investment broker, track and make recommendations concerning investments to the LCLF Board.

16. Work in conjunction with the library's Volunteer Coordinator to develop ways of using volunteers of all ages as a resource for the LCLF.

17. In conjunction with the LCLS, annually develop/revise, implement and evaluate a marketing plan for the LCLF. The LCLF Board must approve the plan. Included should be a timeline for solicitations, i.e. mailings, one-on-one visits, grants deadlines, fund-raising events, etc. The Foundation Director will implement the Foundation aspect of the plan. The Public

Relations Specialist and library management team will implement the LCLS aspect of the plan.

18. Communication is critical. To facilitate communication between the Foundation Director and LCLS, attend Management Team meetings and LCLS general staff meetings to improve communication and builds rapport. Responsible for knowing and understanding all aspects of the LCLS and the LCLF. This is necessary to accurately and adequately promote the library to the community. Communication includes being responsible for LCLF board and LCLS staff training and development within the area of foundation promotion. This includes training in library advocacy, grant writing, and fund raising where appropriate.

19. Actively advocates for the LCLF and the LCLS through a variety of media including print, TV, radio and the Internet.

20. Other duties as assigned, as needed or as opportunities arise.

MINIMUM REQUIREMENTS
• Bachelor's degree from an accredited college or university
• Professional fundraising experience required
• Capital campaign experience desirable

REQUIRED CERTIFICATIONS, SKILLS AND ABILITIES
• Must have current driver's license valid in the State of Wyoming
• Proficiency with a variety of software programs related to foundation operations including word processing, Internet, desk top publishing, donor tracking, etc.
• Ability to analyze complex issues, develop creative and innovative solutions to problems, and to convince others to take specific course of action
• Ability to work with limited supervision, with an aptitude for detailed work and proficiency in prioritizing tasks
• Ability to work with a wide variety of people

REPORTING RELATIONSHIPS
Reports to: Chair, Board of Directors of the LCLF
Supervises: Volunteers

PHYSICAL EFFORT AND WORKING ENVIRONMENT
The essential duties and responsibilities of this job require the employee to work in a normal office environment.

2.0 FOUNDATION BOARD MEMBER
2.1 BOARD MEMBER

2.2 Board Member

Library Name: Washoe County Library System
Library Location: Reno, Nevada
Population Served: N/A
Number of Volumes: 25,000
Number of Titles: N/A
Number of Periodical Subscriptions: N/A

The primary purpose of the Washoe Library Foundation is to support the library needs of the citizens of Washoe County by enhancing Washoe County Library services, programs, and resources.

The Washoe Library Foundation Board is a working Board. A Board Member should be willing to:

Become acquainted with the bylaws, strategic plan, policies and practices of the Foundation.

Regularly attend Board meetings and other functions.

Accept committee assignments.

Assist the Board in achieving fund-raising goals.

Make a two-year commitment of time, in-kind services, and/or money in order to achieve the Foundations goals.

Represent the Foundation at other community functions.

XII. Mail and Delivery Services

Included in this section are delivery drivers and shipping and receiving personnel.

1.0 DELIVERY DRIVER
1.1 DELIVERY DRIVER

1.1.1 Delivery Driver

Library Name: Clermont County Public Library
Library Location: Batavia, Ohio
Population Served: 178,749
Number of Volumes: 534,527
Number of Titles: 151,295
Number of Periodical Subscriptions: 547

General Summary

Position Description: Makes deliveries and pick-ups at all agencies of the library.

Essential Functions and Responsibilities

Loads and unloads van for deliveries to library agencies.

Drives delivery van from Technical Services department to all agencies and Administration, delivering and picking up library materials.

Makes other stops as assigned within county and out.

Keeps library vehicle fueled, clean and in good working condition. Reports any problems to Facilities Manager.

Keeps record of maintenance work for van.

Does general maintenance as required at library agencies.

Knowledge, Skills, and Abilities

Required Abilities:

Drives a commercial van.

Manipulates bins weighing up to 60 pounds.

Reads written directions.

Makes traffic-related decisions while driving.

Understands and obeys all traffic laws.

Determines course of action in the event of a breakdown of vehicle, deteriorating road conditions in poor weather or other situations where consultation with supervisor is impossible.

Possesses manual dexterity for using tools for general maintenance.

Education, Experience, and Training:

Qualifications: Must have a valid driver's license with good driving record and be in good physical condition. Must be able to work evenings and weekends.

Disclaimers

NOTE: This job analysis describes the nature and level of assignments normally given in this position. They are not an exhaustive list of duties. Additional related duties may be assigned.

1.1.2 Delivery Driver

Library Name: Williamsburg Regional Library System
Library Location: Williamsburg, Virginia
Population Served: 60,100
Number of Volumes: 261,243
Number of Titles: N/A
Number of Periodical Subscriptions: 562

General Summary

NATURE OF WORK:

Under the supervision of the Assistant Library Director, the Delivery Services Specialist performs a variety of tasks that insure the prompt, accurate, and efficient delivery of library mail, collections, equipment, and supplies. Position requires driving a delivery van and overseeing its maintenance. Participates in the analysis and planning of delivery services operations within the Support Services department.

Essential Functions and Responsibilities

Drives a delivery van, overseeing its maintenance and performing routine maintenance tasks.

Prepares, loads, and delivers mail and collection items to both library buildings and other destinations (e.g., WRL Board members' homes and offices).

Picks up and delivers library bank deposits.

Oversees all mail room operations. Duties include:

Sorting, metering, and batching outgoing mail and other deliveries.

Preparing packages and bulk materials for mailing or shipping.

Sorting and delivering intra-library mail, U.S. mail, and other shipments.

Receiving and unpacking shipments as needed.

Maintaining logs and statistics.

Monitoring U.S. Postal Service regulations and developments along with those of other carriers; recommending and implementing procedural changes accordingly.

Assessing and making recommendations on the use of vendors' services; coordinating the use of selected vendors.

Transports library supplies and equipment to and from a wide variety of sites; delivers those items to the appropriate building.

Procures library supplies and equipment (e.g., refreshments for library events). Consults with staff about their needs and exercises discretion and judgment on shopping trips.

Picks up donations of library materials from the community and delivers them to the appropriate building.

Drives official library visitors and staff on official business to and from their destinations.

May participate in library-wide committees or projects.

Performs other tasks as assigned.

Knowledge, Skills, and Abilities

Ability to load and safely drive a delivery van.

Ability to follow verbal and written instructions.

Ability to operate office equipment (including a personal computer) in the performance of duties.

Ability to perform a variety of clerical work, including accurate record-keeping, requiring the exercise of judgment.

Ability to work under pressure and to meet deadlines.

Ability to maintain and secure confidential materials.

Ability to establish and maintain effective working relationships with employees, the business community, and the general public.

Work Environment

JOB LOCATION AND EQUIPMENT OPERATED:

The job is based at the James City County Library. Duties are performed in both libraries, in a delivery van, and throughout the region between Richmond and Norfolk, Virginia. Administers works typically in an office setting and also driving a delivery van, with frequent walking, medium to heavy lifting (up to 100 pounds), and other strenuous physical activities. Operation of a delivery van is required. Postage meter, scales, personal computer, and other office equipment as required. Regular contact is made with employees, the U.S. postal service and other carriers' staff, and the general public.

Education, Experience and Training:

MINIMUM QUALIFICATIONS:

High school diploma or equivalent, and one year of experience in general clerical work; or an equivalent combination of education, training, and experience providing the knowledge, skills, and abilities cited in this job description.

License and Certification Requirements

NECESSARY SPECIAL QUALIFICATIONS:

Valid Virginia driver's license.

Acceptable driving record based on James City County's criteria to be verified annually.

Additional Qualifications

Requires the ability to travel among various library sites.

> ## 1.1.3 Delivery Driver
>
> **Library Name:** Manitowoc-Calumet Public Library
> **Library Location:** Manitowoc, Wisconsin
> **Population Served:** 58,213
> **Number of Volumes:** 195,166
> **Number of Titles:** N/A
> **Periodical Subscriptions:** 395

Position Hours

Part-time, typically working 16 hours per two-week pay period on a flexible schedule, which may vary from day to day, and which can change on short notice depending on workload, weather, road or other similar conditions. May be scheduled to work days, evenings, Saturdays, and Sundays.

General Summary

BROAD SCOPE OF POSITION: Working under general supervision of the System Coordinator and functioning as a highly visible representative of MCLS, drives cargo-type van, truck, and/or other System vehicle between libraries and agencies served by MCLS, delivering, picking up, and transferring books and other materials on a set schedule. Performs very basic vehicle maintenance and cleaning. Provides entry-level clerical support to System Coordinator and other staff, and performs other tasks as delegated or assigned.

Essential Functions and Responsibilities

The following list identifies principal duties and responsibilities of the job. It is not a definitive list and other similar duties may be assigned. An asterisk (*) before any of the following items indicates duties and responsibilities which are not "essential functions" of the job as defined by the Americans with Disabilities Act.

1. Delivers bins of books and other materials, including checks and other items of value, to libraries and agencies served by MCLS on a set schedule, which may be revised periodically to meet delivery needs. For example: drives cargo-type van, truck, and/or other System vehicle on 120-mile route throughout Manitowoc and Calumet counties making delivery stops at ten or more libraries and agencies; meets set delivery schedule under normal road and weather conditions; loads and unloads vehicle, which does not have a mechanical lift; maneuvers bins of materials and other objects, and balances and re-arranges load within vehicle; uses wheeled dolly or cart to transport loaded bins at most locations; may need to carry loaded bins and other materials up and down steps in some locations; pushes loaded dolly up and down ramp and/or through several sets of doors in some locations; sorts some materials en route; pays attention to road conditions and severe weather reports, and takes prudent action; uses mobile phone in emergencies.

2. Functions as a highly visible representative of MCLS. Makes contacts with all libraries and agencies served by the System. Communicates regularly with MCLS staff and staff at libraries and agencies, and serves as a conduit for communication between MCLS and delivery locations. May need to negotiate what will be delivered and/or picked up, as circumstances require.

3. Performs very basic maintenance on cargo-type van, truck, and/or other System vehicle. For example: pumps gas, cleans windshield, checks oil, checks air pressure on tires, and performs other routine maintenance on vehicle; cleans vehicle interior and takes vehicle to car wash, as needed or assigned; reports any maintenance or repair needed to System Coordinator; may arrange to have any maintenance and repair work done, as assigned; may deliver vehicle to shop for repairs, as assigned.

4. Reports motor vehicle accidents immediately to proper authorities and to System Coordinator and reports police citations immediately to System Coordinator. Notifies System Coordinator promptly about involvement in any motor vehicle accidents or citations that occur off the job.

5. May deliver mail to post office and perform other errands as assigned.

6. Orients substitute drivers to delivery route and delivery procedures, as assigned.

7. Assists with the System's workflow. Provides entry-level clerical support to System Coordinator and other staff, and performs other tasks, as delegated or assigned. For example: counts and records items in delivery; records and reports mileage; writes memos, brief reports related to delivery duties, etc.; assembles cardboard bins.

8. Deals with problem patrons, particularly those who disrupt normal use or operation of the Manitowoc Public Library, or attempt to unlawfully remove library materials from premises. Assists with maintenance of building security. For example: enforces library policies for patron behavior; participates in disaster and emergency procedures; completes Incident Reports; calls police or other official assistance, when necessary.

Work Environment

WORKING CONDITIONS:

1. Usually (up to 100% of work time) works with vehicles and equipment, and performs procedures where carelessness may result in traffic accident and/or cuts, bruises, muscle strains, or other injuries.

2. Often (up to 85% of work time) drives full-size cargo-type van, truck, and/or other System vehicle up to 120 miles per trip in all types of weather, getting in and out of van at least 20 times per trip.

3. Routinely (up to 30% of work time) works in delivery environment with considerable contact with personnel from MCLS and the libraries and agencies served by MCLS.

4. Routinely (up to 30% of work time) lifts and carries objects and loaded bins weighing up to 40 pounds. Maneuvers such objects and bins of materials in and out of vehicles and may carry them for distances up to 200 feet and up and down stairs. Pushes or pulls loaded dollies and carts weighing more than 150 pounds up or down ramps and/or through several sets of doors.

Education, Experience and Training:

MINIMUM QUALIFICATIONS:

1. Must be at least 21 years old (insurer's requirement).

2. General educational development at a level normally acquired through completion of the 8th grade in the United States.

3. Must possess valid Wisconsin driver's license and good driving record with no accidents or citations for major violations within the last three years. "Major violations" as defined by MCLS's insurer include but are not limited to: operating while intoxicated, speeding in excess (20 miles or more over posted limit), reckless driving, failure to report an accident, etc.

4. 3 months previous on the job, volunteer, or life experience in a public service setting.

5. Demonstrable possession of knowledge, skills, abilities, and capacities identified in "Job Specification" section, above.

6. Capacity to work under conditions described in "Working Conditions" section above.

Additional Qualifications

JOB SPECIFICATIONS:

1. Possession of valid Wisconsin driver's license and good driving record with no accidents or citations for major violations within the last three years, and ability to obtain other appropriate licenses if required. "Major violations" as defined by MCLS's insurer include but are not limited to: operating while intoxicated, speeding in excess (20 miles or more over posted limit), reckless driving, failure to report an accident, etc. (Note: As of May 2002, neither a CDL nor chauffeur's license is required for the System delivery as it currently operates.)

2. Ability to maintain a valid Wisconsin driver's license and a good driving record with no accidents or citations for major violations either on or off the job. "Major violations" as defined by MCLS's insurer include but are not limited to: Operating while intoxicated, speeding in excess (20 miles or more over posted limit), reckless driving, failure to report an accident, etc.

3. Willingness, physical capacity and mechanical aptitude to drive a large cargo-type van, truck and/or other System vehicles in normal Wisconsin weather conditions for distances up to 120 miles per trip. Ability to operate effectively using vehicle's mirrors more extensively than in a windowed passenger van.

4. Knowledge of safe driving habits and procedures, including knowledge of motor vehicle laws and regulations. Interest in defensive driving and ability to recognize and to effectively handle potentially dangerous traffic situations and hazardous road conditions.

5. Commitment to completing the delivery in a timely fashion.

6. Must comply at all times with the System's "Drug-Free Workplace" policy and be willing to submit to drug and alcohol testing if involved in any traffic accident while operating any System vehicle.

7. Physical capacity to lift and maneuver loaded bins or other items weighing up to 40 pounds, to utilize wheeled dollies and carts with loads weighing more than 150 pounds, to push loaded dolly up or down ramp and/or through several sets of doors, and to carry loaded bins and other items, if necessary, at least 200 feet and up and down at least one flight of stairs.

8. Ability to work independently without immediate supervision.

9. Ability to think and act appropriately under pressure.

10. Interest in providing courteous and efficient delivery service. Ability to establish and maintain effective working relationships with MCLS staff and personnel at delivery locations. Ability to present clear explanations of established MCLS delivery policies and procedures. Willingness and ability to grant logical exceptions to policies and procedures when warranted. Willingness and ability to serve as a conduit for communication between MCLS and delivery locations.

11. Ability to communicate effectively in English, both orally and in writing. Skill level: capacity to be easily understood on voice phone; ability to write clear and understandable short memos; ability to read, understand and interpret policy and procedure; ability to explain and demonstrate delivery procedures to substitute drivers.

12. Mechanical aptitude and motor skills to perform very basic vehicle maintenance, to use mobile phone, to assemble cardboard bins, and to perform similar activities.

13. Ability to perform entry-level clerical tasks, such as: counting, adding and subtracting, alphabetizing, and reading instructions. Ability to follow multi-step written and/or verbal instructions and to perform routine procedures involving several steps.

14. Ability to work in a team setting. Willingness to assist and support coworkers, contribute ideas, maintain flexibility, and be able to adapt to a rapidly changing environment.

15. Ability to develop work-related goals and objectives. Willingness to develop job-related abilities, skills and knowledge. Willingness and ability to keep abreast of changing technologies and procedures and to assume responsibilities required by introduction of different services and equipment.

16. Willingness and ability to understand and support the fundamental principles of library services, such as: open access to library materials for people of all ages; the library's obligation to provide materials representing as many points of view as possible; and a patron's right to privacy in dealings with the library and with respect to records maintained by library.

2.0 SHIPPING AND RECEIVING

2.1 SHIPPING AND RECEIVING MANAGER

2.1.1 Shipping and Receiving Manager

Library Name: Cuyahoga County Public Library
Library Location: Parma, Ohio
Population Served: 607,909
Number of Volumes: 3,297,420
Number of Titles: N/A
Number of Periodical Subscriptions: 8,502

General Summary

Under general direction of the Facilities Director, manages shipping and receiving, supply and delivery and mail services functions for the Library. Drives 33,000 pound flatbed truck as needed for transporting heavy equipment and furniture to and from warehouse and branches.

Essential Functions and Responsibilities

Complies with work scheduling and attendance requirements according to reasonable policy and practices. Staffing for branch and regional libraries and some Administration (ADM) departments requires rotational scheduling, which includes evening and weekend (Saturday and Sunday) hours. Most ADM departments are weekday operations.

Consistently presents Cuyahoga County Public Library and its services in a positive manner and adheres to customer service guidelines and procedures as established by the Library.

Complies with the established rules of operation, procedures, and policies when using library computers, peripheral hardware, and software. Individual passwords and any other confidential information regarding library records shall be kept confidential.

Coordinates and supervises shipping and receiving including verifying receipt of shipments with purchase orders, noting any damages incurred, maintaining related records and conducting follow up with vendors and cost center managers.

Schedules and coordinates delivery of all materials to and from branch locations and headquarters.

Supervises mailroom tasks including receipt and distribution of daily mail, preparing out-going mail for postal delivery and monitoring mail items for adherence to postal standards for delivery.

Maintains other departmental records such as carton inventories, recycling activities, courier/UPS shipments, fuel use, postage use and driver delivery and time schedules.

Monitors safety compliance for department including lifting techniques, driving records, vehicle maintenance inspection, hazardous chemicals handling and storage, tow motor operation and security of shipping/receiving area.

Prepares and implements departmental budget, monitors expenses and approves purchases of supplies and equipment.

Coordinates and directs receipt and distribution of library materials, equipment and supplies including maintaining inventories and related records, and developing distribution and storage procedures.

Organizes activities related to sale and distribution of surplus furniture and equipment such as scheduling public auctions, arranging for storage and storage security and maintaining inventory records.

Knowledge, Skills, and Abilities

Thorough knowledge of shipping and receiving procedures and practices.

Knowledge of central storeroom supply procedures including inventory maintenance and supply requisitioning.

Knowledge of U.S. and foreign postage regulations and procedures, CCPL Shipping/Receiving/Delivery procedures, common carrier over, short and damage procedures and transportation industry standards related to shipping/receiving.

Knowledge of safe work habits necessary for departmental staff to perform their duties injury free such as proper lifting techniques and inspection and maintenance of motor vehicles and equipment.

Strong organizational skills for coordinating shipping/receiving, mail and supply functions.

Ability to supervise and direct S/R staff including scheduling work, assigning job tasks and monitoring and evaluating work performance.

Physical and Mental Requirements

Considerable physical exertion required involving bending, stooping, lifting or carrying heavy items (50–75 lbs).

Routine discomforts from exposure to moderate levels of heat, cold, moisture/wetness from working in the warehouse facility.

Occasional hazards associated with handling shipments of chemicals used by Graphics and Maintenance.

Operation of tow motor and forklift required to move materials weighing 200-1,600 pounds.

Must operate a 9-speed 33,000 pound flatbed tractor-trailer to haul surplus materials to the warehouse and transport furniture and equipment among branches. Also, operates other departmental vehicles as needed.

Supervisory Responsibilities

Positions Supervised: Delivery Driver, Shipping and Receiving Clerk

Education, Experience and Training:

High school diploma or GED plus eighteen months of education beyond high school level.

Over two to four years of shipping/receiving experience including supervisory experience.

Vocational competence in the operation of mechanical and electrical/electronic equipment required.

License and Certification Requirements

Due to the physical exertion required to perform the essential duties of this job, the decision to hire is contingent on job candidate passing a pre-employment medical exam through a medical provider contracted by the library.

License

A valid Ohio Commercial Driver's license (CDL) is required and must be maintained to operate library owned vehicles and a clean driving record must be maintained at all times.

A criminal background check is required.

Tow Motor Certification must be maintained.

Disclaimers

The intent of this position description is to provide a representative summary of the major duties and responsibilities performed by incumbents of this job. Incumbents may be requested to perform job-related tasks other than those specifically presented in this description.

2.2 SHIPPING AND RECEIVING CLERK

2.2.1 Shipping and Receiving Clerk

Library Name: Clermont County Public Library
Library Location: Batavia, Ohio
Population Served: 178,749
Number of Volumes: 534,527
Number of Titles: 151,295
Number of Periodical Subscriptions: 547

Reports To

Immediate Supervisor: Co-Manager of Technical Services/Acquisitions

General Summary

Position Description: Responsible for assisting Technical Services in physical processing and distribution of materials including, but not limited to, physical processing, shuttle distribution and light clerical duties. Unpacks new shipments and materials sent in by branches for the book sale.

Essential Functions and Responsibilities

Unpacks material shipments and matches titles and quantities to the packing slips. Verifies shipment for payment or reports problems to Acquisitions Library Assistants.

Processes materials for the collection by applying appropriate labels and stamps.

Uses automated system to print spine labels and identify genre labels.

Unpacks, shelves, and sorts by subject category, books arriving from branches for book sale.

Applies plastic book jackets as needed.

Repackages audio and video materials as needed.

Sorts materials as needed including preparation of items for distribution to branches.

May perform other minor clerical tasks such as photocopying.

Uses automated system to find appropriate record for printing spine labels for reclassification projects. (proposed)

Packages and mails direct loan and other materials.

Breaks down boxes and stacks for disposal.

Knowledge, Skills, and Abilities

Manipulates stacks of books and similar materials weighing up to 50 pounds and loaded book trucks weighing up to 100 pounds.

Flexibility for reaching and bending to retrieve materials and accessing file drawers.

Establishes and maintains an effective working relationship with people within the organization.

Reaches up and down to shelve materials.

Ability to grasp materials.

Sorts accurately by alphabetical and Dewey Decimal order.

Sees, reads and understands titles and call numbers.

Follows oral and written instructions.

Education, Experience and Training:

Qualifications: Must be at least 16 years old. Preference will be given to applicants enrolled in formal education programs. Must be able to work evenings and weekends.

Disclaimers

NOTE: This job analysis describes the nature and level of assignments normally given in this position. This is not an exhaustive list of duties; additional related duties may be assigned.

XIII. Office Staff

Included in this section are secretaries, administrative and office assistants, office managers, and typists.

1.0 ASSISTANT

1.1 ASSISTANT TO DIRECTOR

1.1.1 Assistant to Director

Library Name: Ellensburg Public Library
Library Location: Ellensburg, Washington
Population Served: 15,400
Number of Volumes: 59,000
Number of Titles: 53,000
Number of Periodical Subscriptions: 188

Reports To

TYPE OF SUPERVISION RECEIVED:

Quantity and quality of employee's work is subject to reasonably close supervision by Library Director or Head of Cataloging, as appropriate.

General Summary

MISSION:

To perform library business office duties and provide clerical support to the Library Director as a confidential employee; assist in ordering and cataloging new materials

SUMMARY:

Prepare payroll and maintain related personnel records; do mail and daily cash deposits, prepare purchase orders, prepare correspondence, photocopy, file; purchase supplies, arrange equipment repair and service; assist in basic cataloging; order library materials

Essential Functions and Responsibilities

All of the following are to be performed while adhering to City of Ellensburg operational policies, safety rules, and procedures.

Office:

Record staff attendance, calculate time sheets, calculate leave

Prepare payroll monthly; distribute checks; maintain payroll records and time sheets

Sort and distribute mail; handle outgoing mail and postage machines

Prepare purchase orders for ordering and payments, file records

Count daily receipts; reconcile cash register and petty cash, prepare deposits, maintain records for auditor; implement proper cash procedures

Attend Library Board meetings to take notes and draft minutes for Director's approval

Obtain service and repair for library equipment such as copiers, VCRs, reader/printers, security system, etc.

Order needed equipment from suppliers as authorized in budget and by Director

Purchase needed supplies; contact vendors and suppliers; do errands

Maintain master list of supplies and vendors, monitor supply use and reorder as needed

Report major problems with equipment or building systems to Director/City Maintenance

Acquisitions/Cataloging duties:

Create Dynix bibliographic entries for juvenile and young adult paperbacks and other materials cataloged without MARC records

Order library materials with B & T electronic ordering system; receipt in orders

Order all library materials not available through B&T; books, audios, VHS

Order subscriptions; track annual standing orders; claim missing magazine issues;

Catalog magazine issues; help with annual magazine deletions

Perform cataloging functions on Dynix system

Add local information to WLN record online system

Batch items for further work and review by cataloging supervisor.

Miscellaneous; or special assignments:

Attend regular staff meetings

Provide backup for physical processing of cataloged materials

Staff checkout desk on rotating weekends and as substitute

Other duties may be assigned.

This is a representative sample—not to imply a complete listing of responsibilities and tasks.

Additional Job Duties

KEY RELATIONSHIPS:

The key relationships described here are representative of those an employee encounters while performing the essential functions of this job.

While performing the duties of this job, the employee will provide information to and collect information from city hall staff, vendors, suppliers, wholesalers, local businesses and the public. Contact will be made by telephone and in person.

The employee will solve problems and negotiate solutions within policy guidelines with city hall staff, vendors, suppliers, wholesalers, local businesses, and the public. Contact will be made by telephone or in person.

Knowledge, Skills, and Abilities

QUALIFICATION REQUIREMENTS:

To perform this job successfully, an individual must be able to perform each essential duty satisfactorily. The requirements listed below are representative of the knowledge, skill, and/or ability required. Reasonable accommodations may be made to enable individuals with disabilities to perform the essential functions.

LANGUAGE SKILLS:

Ability to read and interpret documents such as safety rules, operating and maintenance instructions, and procedure manuals. Ability to write routine reports and correspondence. Ability to speak effectively before groups of customers or employees of organization.

MATHEMATICAL SKILLS:

Ability to add, subtract, multiply, and divide in all units of measure, using whole numbers, common fractions, and decimals.

ADDITIONAL QUALIFICATIONS:

Knowledge of general office practice and procedures; knowledge of basic principles of library practices and procedures, knowledge of bibliographic data; ability to learn MARC cataloging and copy cataloging procedures; knowledge of personal computer software and equipment, especially word processing and spread sheets; knowledge of basic reference resources;

Skill in keyboard and computer data entry; skill in data base searching techniques; operation of listed tools and equipment; Periodically accesses sensitive information required to perform job tasks, requiring the ability to maintain confidentiality.

Ability to be courteous and tactful with the general public; Ability to communicate effectively, verbally and in writing; to implement policy and procedure; to exercise initiative and judgment in completing tasks; to organize various activities; Ability to be accurate when working with extremely detailed tasks with exact rules; ability to establish and maintain effective working relationships with employees, supervisors, and the general public.

Physical and Mental Requirements

The physical demands described here are representative of those that must be met by an employee to successfully perform the essential functions. Reasonable accommodations may be made to enable individuals with disabilities to perform the essential functions.

While performing the duties of this job, the employee is regularly required to stand; walk; sit; use hands to finger, handle, or feel objects, tools, or controls; reach with hands and arms; climb or balance; stoop, kneel, crouch, or crawl; and talk or hear. The employee is required to hear and is occasionally required to taste or smell.

The employee must regularly lift and/or move up to 25 pounds. Specific vision abilities required by this job include close vision, distance vision, color vision, peripheral vision, depth perception, and the ability to adjust focus. Tasks affected include computer work, filing, answering the telephone, processing and shelving books.

Tools and Equipment Used

Personal computer, printer, software programs, cash register, calculator, typewriter, copier; phone, fax, audio-visual equipment, microfilm reader/printer

Work Environment

The work environment characteristics described here are representative of those an employee encounters while performing the essential functions of this job. Reasonable accommodations may be made to enable individuals with disabilities to perform the essential functions.

While performing the duties of this job, the employee is regularly exposed to airborne particles. The employee occasionally is exposed to risk of electrical shock. The noise level in the work environment is usually moderate.

Supervisory Responsibilities

Non-supervisory. Acts as person in charge of library, in absence of senior staff, or when scheduled at the checkout desk, on weekends

Education, Experience and Training:

Two years of college or specialized education in appropriate skills. And one year related experience; or equivalent combination of education and experience.

License and Certification Requirements

CERTIFICATES, LICENSES, REGISTRATIONS:
First aid certification

Disclaimers

DISCLAIMERS Job profiles are not intended, nor should they be construed to be, an exhaustive list of all responsibilities, tasks, skills, efforts, working conditions or similar behaviors, attributes or requirements associated with a job. A job profile is not a comprehensive job description. It is intended for the sole purpose of acquainting a person who is unfamiliar with such position with a brief overview of the position's general direction and scope. This position profile is confidential, is intended for internal use only and may not be copied or reproduced by anyone for any purpose without written permission from the Director of Personnel or the City Manager.

NOTICE: The above job profile does not include all essential and nonessential duties of this job. All employees with disabilities are encouraged to contact the Personnel Department to review and discuss the essential and nonessential functions of the job. An employee with a disability can evaluate the job in greater detail to determine if she/he can safely perform the essential function of this job with or without reasonable accommodation.

1.2 ADMINISTRATIVE ASSISTANT

1.2.1 Administrative Assistant

Library Name: Anacortes Public Library
Library Location: Anacortes, Washington
Population Served: 14,500
Number of Volumes: N/A
Number of Titles: 55,565
Periodical Subscriptions: 126

Reports To

Library Director

General Summary

PRINCIPAL PURPOSE OF JOB: This position is responsible for providing administrative support for the library director and, as time and priorities allow, assistant directors.

LEVEL OF AUTHORITY: Performs duties with only moderate supervision following established procedures and deadlines. Has limited latitude to make decisions regarding priorities for both routine schedules and responses to non-routine and emergency situations. Responsibility for judgment, thoroughness and competence is most important due to potential disruption of Library operations, monetary loss or adverse public relations.

Essential Functions and Responsibilities

Process Library correspondence; screen and direct all incoming correspondence not specifically addressed to a staff member.

Maintain the Library accounts of receivables, expenses and purchase orders. This includes receiving requisitions for the purchase of supplies, equipment and library materials, maintaining records and files of expenditures, preparing purchase orders, obtaining approval signatures and verifying invoices.

Maintain Library supplies for office, data processing and janitorial upkeep. This includes ordering supplies and equipment and checking in deliveries of non-library materials.

Attend to minor building maintenance, acting as liaison with facilities manager, custodians, etc.

Maintain Library records, files and calendar. This includes: scheduling the use of library facilities by outside parties; posting library announcements, etc.

Prepare Director's correspondence and reports, schedule appointments, etc., as directed.

Collect and organize data for projections and preparation of Library budget, as directed.

Additional Job Duties

Attend staff, Board of Trustees and community meetings as required, often outside regular working hours.

Make deliveries and pick-ups from City Hall and drive in the course of other Library business.

Serve as secretary to the Board of Trustees and its committees, preparing and distributing meeting agendas, reports and minutes.

Knowledge, Skills, and Abilities

Must type 60 wpm with accuracy and be able to transcribe from dictation equipment, hand-written notes or verbal instructions.

Must have excellent communication skills, including an ability to proofread the work of self and others with a high degree of accuracy.

Must have broad knowledge of general office skills and equipment as evidenced by a combination of course work and responsible secretarial experience in a comparable environment.

Must be able to perform basic accounting and mathematical computations with a high degree of accuracy using 10-key calculator.

Must be familiar with standard office equipment, including personal computers and DOS-based software (including word processing, database and spreadsheet) and be able to learn and implement Library systems and procedures.

Must be bondable.

Attention to detail and accuracy.

Ability to communicate effectively, patiently and courteously with City employees, the Library Board of Trustees, patrons and other community members.

Ability to handle multiple activities or interruptions at once and to work positively and effectively within a team model.

Excellent memory and organizational ability to deal with multiple responsibilities and to meet

Physical and Mental Requirements

Ability to sit and use computer workstation, including keyboard and visual display terminal, for extended periods of time.

Ability to stand, walk and drive as needed throughout the day.

Ability to occasionally lift, carry and put away parcels weighing up to 30 pounds.

Tools and Equipment Used

Office equipment, such as; computer, modem, typewriter, adding machine, microfiche reader, paper cutter, fax, copier, telephone and postage meter.

Work Environment

Work is performed primarily in indoor office setting, in community meeting rooms and at the library.

Education, Experience and Training:

QUALIFICATIONS
Technical
Two-year degree in office technology or equivalent work experience.

Additional Qualifications

OTHER

As an absolute condition of employment, employees are required upon hire to sign a drug-free workplace agreement and an agreement not to use tobacco products of any kind while on the job.

Following an offer of employment, and prior to starting work, individuals may be required to have a pre-employment physical examination by a physician designated by the City of Anacortes. The examination will be paid for the by the City. Satisfactory clearance to perform essential job functions will be required for employment.

License and Certification Requirements

Must possess a valid Washington State driver's license.
Disclaimers
The statements contained in this job description reflect general details as necessary to describe the principal functions of this job, the level of knowledge and skill typically required and the scope of responsibility. It should not be considered an all-inclusive

listing of work requirements. Individuals may perform other duties as assigned, including work in other functional areas to cover absences or provide relief, to equalize peak work periods or otherwise to balance the work load.

1.3 OFFICE ASSISTANT

1.3.1 Office Assistant

Library Name: Manitowoc-Calumet Public Library
Library Location: Manitowoc, Wisconsin
Population Served: 58,213
Number of Volumes: 195,166
Number of Titles: N/A
Periodical Subscriptions: 395

General Summary

BROAD SCOPE OF POSITION: Working under direct supervision of Business Office Supervisor, provides clerical support for department as assigned, and performs a variety of clerical tasks.

Assists with personnel, financial, and other functions of department. Maintains confidentiality.

Uses personal vehicle for daily to semi-weekly deliveries in City and surrounding areas. May assume responsibility for departmental functions in absence of Business Office Supervisor, as delegated or assigned. May perform Assistant-level work in other departments.

Essential Functions and Responsibilities

The following list identifies principal duties and responsibilities of the job. It is not a definitive list and other similar duties may be assigned. An asterisk (*) before any of the following items indicates duties and responsibilities which are not "essential functions" of the job as defined by the Americans with Disabilities Act.

Provides clerical support for department, as assigned. Performs a variety of clerical tasks. For example: prepares administrative materials for copying and for distribution after copying (e.g., collates, separates, cuts, staples, counts, etc.); drafts simple memos; does routine word processing; maintains files; orders supplies; may shop locally for supplies on occasion; compiles statistics; replaces photocopier toner cartridges and clears jams; performs miscellaneous data and spreadsheet entry.

Performs procedures related to memorials and other donations. For example: generates donor forms; prepares receipts and acknowledgements; reconciles bills and reports; invoices donors.

Uses personal vehicle for daily to semi-weekly deliveries in City and surrounding areas. Picks up and delivers materials at City Hall, Post Office, banks, etc.

Assists with financial functions of department, as delegated or assigned. For example: prepares accounts payable; reconciles daily cash register and photocopier receipts; prepares and makes deposits; reconciles various checking accounts; may input requests for computer-generated City reports; maintains confidentiality.

May assist with personnel functions of department, as assigned. For example: prepares timecards for payroll; tracks salaries, wages, and step payments for payroll; performs new employee intake and employee termination paperwork; files confidential personnel and other administrative records; verifies accrual of sick leave and vacations; maintains confidentiality.

Assists with other functions of department, as delegated or assigned. For example: Deals with variety of people including staff, public, governmental officials, board members; refers questions to supervisor or director; answers Business Office Supervisor's and Director's phones in their absence; maintains Library's furniture and equipment inventory records; assists with refreshments; may take minutes at Library Board and other meetings occasionally; maintains confidentiality.

Deals with problem patrons, particularly those who disrupt normal use or operation of the Library, or attempt to unlawfully remove library materials from premises. Assists with maintenance of building security. For example: enforcing library policies for patron behavior; responding to alarms; completing Incident Reports and calling police or other official assistance, when necessary.

May assume responsibility for departmental functions, as assigned, in absence of Business Office Supervisor. May perform Assistant-level work in other departments.

Knowledge, Skills, and Abilities

1. Knowledge of or ability to quickly acquire knowledge of business office routines and procedures. Understanding of labor agreement and personnel manual. Skill in typing, filing, counting money, reconciling statements, compiling reports, etc. Willingness to maintain confidentiality.

2. Skill in using microcomputers and related software. Minimum skill level: accurate keyboarding at a minimum of 20 words per minute. Basic knowledge of database, spreadsheet and wordprocessing software programs. Knowledge of or ability to quickly learn Library's current software programs as these apply to tasks.

3. Ability to use other equipment associated with preparation and distribution of administrative materials, including photocopier, postage meter, staplers, paper cutter, etc.

4. Ability to communicate effectively. Must be accurate, have legible handwriting, and possess excellent arithmetical, grammatical, spelling and proofreading skills.

5. Skill in performing routine and non-routine procedures involving many steps. Ability to follow complex written and/or verbal instructions systematically and to pay close attention to detail. Ability to think and act appropriately under pressure. Ability to work with limited direct supervision.

6. Possession of valid Wisconsin driver's license and good driving record. Willingness to use personal vehicle for semi-weekly deliveries in City and surrounding areas in all weather conditions for distances up to 25 miles per trip (under 5 miles usually). May make 10 or more stops per trip. Routine trips are usually 1 stop and under 1 mile. Mileage is reimbursed as per labor agreement.

7. Ability to establish and maintain effective working relationships with Management Team members, other library staff members, sales representatives, government officials, board members, and the public. Ability to work in a team setting. Willingness to assist and support coworkers, contribute ideas, and maintain flexibility. Ability to adapt to a rapidly changing environment. Skill in interpersonal communication necessary to understand, interpret, and paraphrase questions. Capacity to be easily understood on voice telephone.

8. Ability to develop work-related goals and objectives. Willingness to develop job-related abilities, skills and knowledge. Willingness and ability to keep abreast of changing technologies and procedures and to assume responsibilities required by introduction of different services and equipment.

9. Ability to enforce the library's established policies, procedures and standards of public behavior in nondiscriminatory fashion. Ability to present clear explanations of these rules to members of public.

10. Willingness and ability to understand and support the fundamental principles of library services, such as: open access to library materials for people of all ages; the library's obligation to provide materials representing as many points of view as possible; and a patron's right to privacy in dealings with the library and with respect to records maintained by library.

Physical and Mental Requirements

Usually (up to 100% of work time) performs routines with many rapid, repeated motions.

Usually (up to 100% of work time) works with equipment and performs procedures where reasonable caution must be exercised to avoid minor cuts, bruises, or muscle strains.

Usually (up to 100% of work time) maintains work environment. For example: vacuuming computer areas, dusting, recycling paper.

Sometimes (semi-weekly, up to 25% of work time) makes deliveries by driving personal vehicle in City and surrounding areas in all weather conditions for distances at least 25 miles per trip (under 5 miles usually). May make 10 or more stops per trip. Mileage is reimbursed as per labor agreement.

Work Environment

Usually (up to 100% of work time) works in shared-office environment with occasional public contact. Sometimes (up to 25% of work time) has considerable contact with City officials and the public when running errands. Infrequently (as situation requires) deals with problem patrons.

Usually (up to 100% of work time) is in contact with personnel, financial or other administrative materials which must be kept confidential.

Usually (up to 100% of work time) works in close proximity with microcomputers, photocopiers and other similar electronic equipment.

Education, Experience, and Training:

MINIMUM QUALIFICATIONS:

General educational development at a level normally acquired through completion of high school in the United States.

3 months previous on the job, volunteer, or life experience in a business office setting.

Demonstrable possession of knowledge, skills, abilities, and capacities identified in "Job Specifications" section, above.

Capacity to work under conditions described in "Working Conditions" section, above.

Position Hours

Part-time, typically working 20 hours per two-week pay period on a flexible schedule which varies from week to week. May be scheduled to work days, evenings, Saturdays, and Sundays.

1.3.2 Office Assistant

Library Name: Ellensburg Public Library
Library Location: Ellensburg, Washington
Population Served: 15,400
Number of Volumes: 59,000
Number of Titles: 53,000
Number of Periodical Subscriptions: 188

Reports To

TYPE OF SUPERVISION RECEIVED:

Quantity and quality of employee's work is subject to a close check by the Office Manager.

General Summary

MISSION:

To assist in scheduling and serving clients using the Center; perform basic office procedures; move furnishings, equipment, and other Center and Library property; keep storage areas orderly.

SUMMARY:

Staff Center office and interview clients, schedule events, assist clients; do set up/take down of audio-visual equipment and furniture for events; assist with forms, typing purchase orders, filing. Operate some types of AV equipment; keep Center secure and in order; do housekeeping chores in kitchen/storage areas. Perform added office duties when Office Manager is on leave.

Essential Functions and Responsibilities

All of the following are to be performed while adhering to City of Ellensburg operational policies, safety rules, and procedures.

Client Service:

Interview clients in person and by telephone; refer complex requests to Office Manager

Assess rental fees according to policy

Book events; set up schedule; ensure event compatibility

Set up audio-visual equipment, tables and chairs, etc. according to client needs

Provide keys and instructions to clients

Provide on-site assistance during events when assigned by Office Manager

Office duties:

Record client bookings, equipment needs, and fees on computer; complete forms

Collect fees; prepare deposits when Office Manager is on leave if needed

Type purchase orders for Office Manager's review and Director's signature

Assist with photocopying, mailings, filing

Be responsive to needs of clients using the Center

Distribute brochures, schedules, flyers etc. to clients and community as assigned

General maintenance and Housekeeping:

Help to move books and furnishings between the Library and the Center as needed

Ensure clean appearance of Center between client events

Assist with recycling efforts

Keep kitchen, storage areas and basement clean and orderly

Miscellaneous:

Assist Office Manager with changing stage lights and set up of AV and stage

Help to set up exhibits in lobby display cases

Other duties may be assigned.

This is a representative sample—not to imply a complete listing of responsibilities and tasks.

Additional Job Duties

QUALIFICATION REQUIREMENTS:

To perform this job successfully, an individual must be able to perform each essential duty satisfactorily. The requirements listed below are representative of the knowledge, skill, and/or ability required. Reasonable accommodations may be made to enable individuals with disabilities to perform the essential functions.

KEY RELATIONSHIPS:

The key relationships described here are representative of those an employee encounters while performing the essential functions of this job.

While performing the duties of this job, the employee will provide information to and collect information from the general public. Contact will be made by telephone, or in person.

The employee will work within policy guidelines with the general public. Contact will be made by telephone, or in person.

Knowledge, Skills, and Abilities

LANGUAGE SKILLS:

Ability to read and interpret documents such as safety rules, operating and maintenance instructions, and procedure manuals. Ability to write routine reports and correspondence. Ability to speak effectively before groups of customers or employees of organization.

MATHEMATICAL SKILLS:

Ability to add, subtract, multiply, and divide in all units of measure, using whole numbers, common fractions, and decimals.

NECESSARY KNOWLEDGE, SKILLS AND ABILITIES:

Some knowledge of general office practice and procedures; some knowledge of audio-visual equipment

Skill in keyboard and computer data entry; operation of listed tools and equipment

Ability to be courteous and tactful with the general public; Ability to communicate effectively orally and in writing; ability to apply policies and procedure; ability to organize various activities; ability to establish and maintain effective working relationships with employees, supervisors, and the general public

Physical and Mental Requirements

The physical demands described here are representative of those that must be met by an employee to successfully perform the essential functions of this job. Reasonable accommodations may be made to enable individuals with disabilities to perform the essential functions.

While performing the duties of this job, the employee is regularly required to stand; walk; sit; use hands to finger, handle, or feel objects, tools, or controls; reach with hands and arms; climb or balance; stoop, kneel, crouch, or crawl; and talk or hear. The employee is occasionally required to taste or smell.

The employee must regularly lift and/or move up to 100 pounds and occasionally lift and/or move more than 100 pounds. Specific vision abilities required by this job include close vision, distance vision, color vision, peripheral vision, depth perception, and the ability to adjust focus.

Tools and Equipment Used

Personal computer, printer, calculator; copy and fax machine; phone, furniture dolly; audio-visual equipment, common hand tools; hammer, screwdriver, etc.

Work Environment

The work environment characteristics described here are representative of those an employee encounters while performing the essential functions of this job. Reasonable accommodations may be made to enable individuals with disabilities to perform the essential functions.

While performing the duties of this job, the employee occasionally works near moving mechanical parts; in high, precarious places; and in outside weather conditions and is occasionally exposed to wet and/or humid conditions and risk of electrical shock.

The noise level in the work environment is moderate when clients are using the Center.

Supervisory Responsibilities

None.

Education, Experience and Training:

High school diploma or general education degree (GED); one year related experience and/or training; or equivalent combination of education and experience.

License and Certification Requirements

SPECIAL REQUIREMENTS
First aid and CPR certification

Disclaimers

Job profiles are not intended, nor should they be construed to be, an exhaustive list of all responsibilities, tasks, skills, efforts, working conditions or similar behaviors, attributes or requirements associated with a job. A job profile is not a comprehensive job description. It is intended for the sole purpose of acquainting a person who is unfamiliar with such position with a brief overview of the position's general direction and scope. This position profile is confidential, is intended for internal use only and may not be copied or reproduced by anyone for any purpose without written permission from the Director of Personnel or the City Manager.

NOTICE: The above job profile does not include all essential and nonessential duties of this job. All employees with disabilities are encouraged to contact the Personnel Department to review and discuss the essential and nonessential functions of the job. An employee with a disability can evaluate the job in greater detail to determine if she/he can safely perform the essential function of this job with or without reasonable accommodation.

1.3.3 Office Assistant

Library Name: Groton Public Library
Library Location: Groton, Connecticut
Population Served: 40,456
Number of Volumes: 120,000
Number of Titles: N/A
Number of Periodical Subscriptions: N/A

General Summary

Position Overview

Performs general clerical work of considerable complexity and variety. Enters and retrieves information through a computer terminal. Provides information to the public requiring a knowledge of department programs and procedures. Incumbent may work autonomously in a small office/department or may work in conjunction with other clerical staff in a larger office/department. Schedules appointments and otherwise relieves officials of clerical work and minor administrative and business details by performing the following duties.

Essential Functions and Responsibilities

This position performs a variety of clerical and administrative tasks, focused on supporting the needs of the department. Enters data and word processes material including but not limited to records, reports, memoranda, minutes, lists and labels. Reads and routes incoming mail. Locates and attaches appropriate file to correspondence to be answered by supervisor. Composes and types routine correspondence. Files correspondence and other records. Provides information and referral services to public regarding Department, Unit or Town programs and procedures. Schedules appointments for supervisor. Compiles and types statistical reports. Prepares outgoing mail. Prepares requisitions for materials and supplies. Performs arithmetical computations as required.

Additional Job Duties

Performs various routine office duties such as running errands and delivering materials and supplies. Maintains routine financial and payroll records for a Department or unit. Receives and records fees. Handles circulation control. Temporarily relieves other office staff as need requires. Performs related tasks as assigned. Based upon the level of clerical staffing in a given office some or all of these additional duties may be considered essential. Schedules appointments, meetings and conferences.

Accommodations

Reasonable accommodations may be made to enable qualified individuals with disabilities to perform the essential functions of this position.

Knowledge, Skills, and Abilities

Qualifications

The skills and knowledge required would generally be acquired with a high school education and four years experience in general office work. Must posses the ability to type and operate office equipment. Demonstrated ability to read and comprehend documents necessary to the safe and effective performance of the job and the ability to compose basic correspondence. Must have sound word processing capabilities with current applications, demonstrated customer service skills. Must be well organized and able to effectively prioritize; must possess strong administrative and coordinating skills; must be accurate and attentive to detail, while meeting deadlines on a regular basis. Ability to create spread sheets and manage a data base. Incumbent will be required to apply reasoning ability to carry out detailed written and oral instructions and will be required to resolve problems with several variables in a dynamic setting.

Physical and Mental Requirements

The physical demands described here are representative of those that must be met by an employee to successfully perform the essential functions of this job.

While performing the duties of this job, the employee is regularly required to talk or hear. The employee frequently is required to stand; walk; sit; use hands to finger, handle, or feel; and reach with hands and arms. The employee is occasionally required to stoop, kneel, crouch, or crawl. The employee must occasionally lift and/or move up to 25 pounds. Specific vision abilities required by this job include close vision, distance vision, peripheral vision, and depth perception.

Work Environment

The work environment characteristics described here are representative of those an employee encounters while performing the essential functions of this job.

While performing the duties of this job, the employee is occasionally exposed to moving mechanical parts and outside weather conditions. The noise level in the work environment is usually moderate. The employee will routinely operate typical business office equipment, including computer hardware.

License and Certification Requirements

Certificates, Licenses, Registrations
N/A

2.0 OFFICE MANAGER

2.1 OFFICE MANAGER

2.1.1 Office Manager

Library Name: Ellensburg Public Library
Library Location: Ellensburg, Washington
Population Served: 15,400
Number of Volumes: 59,000
Number of Titles: 53,000
Number of Periodical Subscriptions: 188

General Summary

MISSION:

To serve clients using the Center, perform office procedures, operate and maintain audio-visual equipment, and coordinate staff and rental activities at the Hal Holmes Center.

SUMMARY:

Interview clients, coordinate and schedule bookings, do set up/take down of audio-visual equipment and furniture for events; Provide AV training and assistance for clients; Manage office procedures, including booking, billing, invoicing, record keeping, purchasing supplies and equipment; training and supervising assistant; consult with Director on policy and procedure; assist with budget and goal setting, provide reports on activities; implement marketing objectives. Provide public relations and promote use of Center. Maintain AV equipment and furnishings; keep Center secure and in order; coordinate with custodian and maintenance workers.

Essential Functions and Responsibilities

All of the following are to be performed while adhering to City of Ellensburg operational policies, safety rules, and procedures.
Client Service:
Interview clients in person and by telephone; determine needs and inform on services
Assess rental fees according to policy
Book events; set up schedule; ensure event compatibility
Set up audio-visual, tables and chairs, etc. according to client needs
Provide training and assistance for clients and staff on AV and other equipment
Provide keys and instructions to clients
Provide on-site assistance during events when needed
Post informative signs as needed; keep street sign current
Provide tourism brochures and other community information as needed
Collect and receipt rental fees
Office Management:
Prepare weekly and monthly calendar of events/schedules; inform library staff as needed
Complete contracts and invoice clients; Prepare follow-up letters
Maintain client and financial records on the computer and in paper files
Collect fees and other payments; Prepare deposits for City treasurer
Prepare purchase orders for Director's signature
Train and supervise assistant to help with clients, office procedures, maintenance, etc.
Prepare weekly, quarterly, and annual reports for Director on revenues and activities
Purchase supplies and equipment as budgeted
Update inventory of Center property annually
Prepare correspondence and do mailings
Public Relations:
Follow up with clients on service satisfaction
Develop relations with local business, Chamber of commerce, CWU, etc.
Provide referrals to clients with needs Center is unable to provide
Design and publish brochures, schedules, flyers etc. for clients and promotional mailings
Keep mailing lists up to date; send mailings to prospective users
Coordinate with local artists and others for displays and exhibits
General Maintenance and Housekeeping:
Schedule and install exhibits and displays in lobby display cases
Perform minor maintenance of audio-visual equipment, lighting and sound equipment

Ensure clean appearance of Center between clients

Encourage recycling in office and by Center clients

Keep storage areas and basement organized and clean

Miscellaneous:

Participate in budget planning and long range goals as requested by Director

Prepare advertising materials for newspaper ads as needed

Participate in interviewing for new hire or performance review as requested by director

Other duties may be assigned.

This is a representative sample—not to imply a complete listing of responsibilities and tasks.

Additional Job Duties

QUALIFICATION REQUIREMENTS:

To perform this job successfully, an individual must be able to perform each essential duty satisfactorily. The requirements listed below are representative of the knowledge, skill, and/or ability required. Reasonable accommodations may be made to enable individuals with disabilities to perform the essential functions.

KEY RELATIONSHIPS:

The key relationships described here are representative of those an employee encounters while performing the essential functions of this job.

While performing the duties of this job, the employee will provide information to and collect information from the general public, city council, state and local agencies, private enterprises, educational organizations, and clubs and civic groups. Contact will be made in writing, by telephone, in person, and through teaching or formal instruction.

The employee will negotiate solutions within policy guidelines and involving policy changes with the general public, city council, local and state agencies, private enterprises, educational organizations, and clubs and civic groups. Contact will be made in writing, by telephone, in person and through teaching or formal instruction.

Knowledge, Skills, and Abilities

A) Knowledge of general office and book keeping practice and procedures; considerable knowledge of audio-visual equipment and related electronic technology; knowledge of computer scheduling, spreadsheet, and word processing programs; knowledge of stage sound and lighting systems; some knowledge of principles of supervision, occupational safety standards, (OSHA) and requirements, and of Americans with Disabilities Act, (ADA) standards and requirements.

B) Skill in operation of listed tools and equipment; Skill in First Aid and CPR.

C) Ability to be courteous and tactful with the general public; Ability to communicate effectively orally and in writing; ability to interpret and implement policies and procedure; ability to work independently with initiative and judgment; ability to coordinate various activities; ability to establish and maintain effective working relationships with employees, supervisors, other agencies, participants, instructors, and community leaders.

LANGUAGE SKILLS:

Ability to read, analyze, and interpret general business periodicals, professional journals, technical procedures, and governmental regulations. Ability to write reports, business correspondence, and procedure manuals. Ability to effectively present information and respond to questions from groups of managers, clients, customers, and the general public.

MATHEMATICAL SKILLS:

Ability to add, subtract, multiply, and divide in all units of measure, using whole numbers, common fractions, and decimals. Ability to compute rate, ratio, and percent and to draw and interpret graphs.

Physical and Mental Requirements

The physical demands described here are representative of those that must be met by an employee to successfully perform the essential functions of this job. Reasonable accommodations may be made to enable individuals with disabilities to perform the essential functions.

While performing the duties of this job, the employee is regularly required to stand; walk; sit; use hands to finger, handle, or feel objects, tools, or controls; reach with hands and arms; climb or balance; stoop, kneel, crouch, or crawl; and talk or hear. The employee is occasionally required to taste or smell.

The employee must regularly lift and/or move up to 100 pounds and occasionally lift and/or move more than 100 pounds. Specific vision abilities required by this job include close vision, distance vision, color vision, peripheral vision, depth perception, and the ability to adjust focus.

Tools and Equipment Used

Audio-visual equipment of all kinds; Personal computer, printer, calculator; copy and fax machine; phone; common hand tools such as screwdriver, hammer, saw, drill; high ladders; platforms; light panels, dimmer boards, sound amplifiers and mixer boards.

Work Environment

The work environment characteristics described here are representative of those an employee encounters while performing the essential functions of this job. Reasonable accommodations may be made to enable individuals with disabilities to perform the essential functions.

While performing the duties of this job, the employee occasionally works near moving mechanical parts; in high, precarious places; and in outside weather conditions and is occasionally exposed to wet and/or humid conditions and risk of electrical shock.

The noise level in the work environment is usually moderate when clients are using the Center.

Supervisory Responsibilities

Directly supervises one part-time employee. Carries out supervisory responsibilities in accordance with the organization's policies and applicable laws. Responsibilities include assistance in the interview, hire and training process; plan, assign, and direct work; assist in appraising performance.

Education, Experience and Training:

Associate's degree (A. A.) or equivalent from two-year college or technical school; and one to two years related experience and/or training; or equivalent combination of education and experience.

License and Certification Requirements

CPR certification/First Aid
SPECIAL REQUIREMENTS:
Valid Washington State Driver's License or ability to obtain one.

Disclaimers

Job profiles are not intended, nor should they be construed to be, an exhaustive list of all responsibilities, tasks, skills, efforts, working conditions or similar behaviors, attributes or requirements associated with a job. A job profile is not a comprehensive job description. It is intended for the sole purpose of acquainting a person who is unfamiliar with such position with a brief overview of the position's general direction and scope. This position profile is confidential, is intended for internal use only and may not be copied or reproduced by anyone for any purpose without written permission from the Director of Personnel or the City Manager.

NOTICE: The above job profile does not include all essential and nonessential duties of this job. All employees with disabilities are encouraged to contact the Personnel Department to review and discuss the essential and nonessential functions of the job. An employee with a disability can evaluate the job in greater detail to determine if she/he can safely perform the essential function of this job with or without reasonable accommodation.

3.0 SECRETARY

3.1 SECRETARY

3.1.1 SECRETARY

Library Name: West Chicago Public Library District
Library Location: West Chicago Public Library District
Population Served: 22,337
Number of Volumes: 81,851
Number of Titles: N/A
Periodical Subscriptions: 238

Reports To

Administrative Assistant

General Summary

SECRETARY I
This is a library clerical position. The Secretary I performs a wide variety of standard secretarial duties providing secretarial support to all department managers.

Essential Functions and Responsibilities

Word processes letter, memos, and reports. Arranges meetings and effectively handles the department's calendar(s) and schedule(s) in paper and electronic formats.

Compiles the agenda, takes minutes, and types up the minutes for departmental team meetings.

Arranges special events, programs, meetings, etc. for departments. Ensures that all practical steps required to ensure a successful meeting/program are undertaken and that appropriate records are maintained accordingly. Verifies program room booking and set up.

Organizes and maintains departmental invoices, processes and checks in materials as required.

Disseminates a variety of correspondence to the appropriate department.

Photocopies and files, as required.

Maintains the database of contacts for programs and special events.

Effectively diary/schedules management to ensure the effective maintenance of a "forward/reminder" system. Brings to the attention of the department manager(s) events and meetings requiring their attention, if required.

Runs errands, as needed.

Performs other duties as required.

Knowledge, Skills, and Abilities

Skills: Secretarial and clerical skills.

Knowledge of office procedures and systems.

Knowledge of IT systems.

Accounting, work processing, spreadsheet and database software skills.

Word processing skills with the ability to word process reports, letters, memos, etc. to a minimum of 50 words per minute from handwritten drafts with a high degree of accuracy.

Organizational skills, ability to pay close attention to details.

Communication skills; ability to communicate effectively in English, both orally and in writing.

Interpersonal skills for dealing with vendors, patrons, and staff.

Telephone skills and techniques.

High standards of accuracy and confidentiality.

Must possess valid driver's license.

Ability to communicate in Spanish, both verbally and in writing, is a plus.

Physical and Mental Requirements

Ability to hear, comprehend and respond to the Library user both in person and in telephone conversations.

Visual ability to see computer screen.

Ability to manipulate computer and typewriter, keyboards, calculator.

Requires sitting, standing, stooping, bending and lifting/moving books and carts up to 40 pounds.

Ability to sit for long periods of time.

Ability to walk distances of more than 50 feet within the building.

Ability to perform repetitive hand motions for extended periods of time.

Ability to bend or stoop to reach items.

Ability to drive a car and hold a valid driver's license.

Must maintain professional manner when dealing with patrons, other staff, and vendors.

Must be a flexible team player and take actions to create a positive team climate.

Must be able to work independently and prioritize own workload.

Must be able to work well without close supervision and show attention to detail.

Must take responsibility for delivering against objectives in time and quality standards.

Must be able to follow instructions and procedures.

Must be flexible, creative, patient, and have a sense of humor.

Must have own transportation for running errands.

May be required to work evenings and weekends.

Work Environment

JOB SETTING/ENVIRONMENTAL/SOCIAL CONDITIONS:

Indoor conditions

Heavy workload at times

Education, Experience and Training:

MINIMUM QUALIFICATIONS REQUIRED: Education: High school diploma or equivalent, and some business school training and/or relevant college course work.

Experience: Two years office administration and computer experience, or secretarial experience.

3.1.2 Secretary

Library Name: Richland County Public Library
Library Location: Columbia, South Carolina
Population Served: 320,700
Number of Volumes: 1,059,806
Number of Titles: N/A
Periodical Subscriptions: 2,840

Essential Functions and Responsibilities

EXAMPLES OF WORK: (illustrative only)

Essential Functions of the Job:

Secretarial support to Personnel Office as needed; type, photocopy, and distribute letters, memos, job descriptions, vacancy notices, telephone lists, forms, salary schedules, and similar materials.

Secretarial support and assistance to Personnel Assistant and Volunteer Coordinator as needed.

Organize and maintain files for Personnel Office, and perform filing; extract and compile information as needed; utilize computerized files as well as paper files; remove and dispose of files and materials when appropriate.

Receptionist for Personnel Office; answer telephone; receive and send messages, mail, etc.

Operate office machines; instruct and assist other staff as appropriate in operation of same.

Select and order office supplies and equipment.

Handle employee evaluation process, including preparation, sending, return, monitoring, filing of forms (probationary and post-probationary employees).

Calculate and record annual and sick leave; prepare leave records bi-weekly for dissemination; communicate leave information to employees, supervisors, and Business Office as appropriate; keep abreast of correct procedures for leave calculation and recording via HR/payroll software; communicate with vendor regarding problems.

Keep up with leave requests and cards verifying leave has been taken.

Prepare, place, and remove job vacancy notices. Recipients may include RCPL website, employment agencies, placement offices, branch libraries, other libraries, schools, organizations, etc.; physically and electronically post notices to appropriate places and remove notices.

Additional Job Duties

Other Important Responsibilities

Compile personnel-related data and statistics; complete surveys as needed; process forms for Employment Security and Retirement Systems, etc., related to employee earnings; handle employment verifications.

Answer applicants' questions regarding vacancies; provide information as appropriate to supervisors; may communicate appropriate information to outside agencies and officials.

Provide information to employees, and answer questions from employees regarding personnel matters, maintaining required confidentiality.

Assist with hourly time card and volunteer time card processing.

Give pre-employment tests to applicants.

May coordinate with Divisions' staff on matters pertaining to substitutes.

May direct and oversee the work of graduate assistants, temporary employees, volunteers, etc.

Other associated duties as required or assigned.

Education, Experience and Training:

MINIMUM QUALIFICATIONS:

Bachelor's degree. Transcript of college or other post high school education must be presented upon hire.

Minimum 1 to 2 years experience in relevant personnel/secretarial/clerical work.

Equivalent combination of training/experience may be considered, in lieu of specific minimums in "1" & "2".

Specific technical training & technical skills needed to perform tasks, including word processing, computer use, etc.; 45 wpm typing required, with 35 wpm in pre-employment test.

Valid South Carolina driver's license with safe driving record.

Ability to perform job responsibilities.

3.2 BRANCH SECRETARY

3.2.1 Branch Secretary

Library Name: Cuyahoga County Public Library
Library Location: Parma, Ohio
Population Served: 607,909
Number of Volumes: 3,297,420
Number of Titles: N/A
Number of Periodical Subscriptions: 8,502

General Summary

Under general supervision, serves as principal office support to the office of the Branch/Regional Services Director. Work involves ensuring the timely provision of office support services to the office and providing secretarial services to the Branch/Regional Services Director. The worker ensures the completion of all tasks associated with office support services, following up with other offices, units, branches and others as necessary to ensure accurate and timely completion of the work. Work requires operation of desktop computer, computer terminal, typewriters, calculators and other office equipment.

Essential Functions and Responsibilities

(Note: The following functions represent the essential duties and outputs of the position.)

Complies with work scheduling and attendance requirements according to reasonable policy and practices. Staffing for branch and regional libraries and some administration (ADM) departments requires rotational scheduling, which includes evening and weekend (Saturday & Sunday) hours. Most ADM departments are weekday operations.

Consistently presents Cuyahoga County Public Library and its services in a positive manner and adheres to customer service guidelines and procedures as established by the Library.

Performs all secretarial duties, some of which are confidential.

Organizes and maintains unit files.

Compiles information from files and other sources into lists, summaries and reports.

Takes and prepares minutes of meetings.

Receives, opens, screens and routes mail; responds to routine inquiries.

Provides receptionist services for the unit; answers telephone and screens calls and visitors, refers calls and visitors to appropriate parties.

Responds to inquiries from the public; provides requested information and refers callers to appropriate offices or parties.

Prepares statistical charts and tables.

Orders and maintains supplies for the office.

Assigns work of other clerical staff.

Complies with the Customer Service guidelines.

Additional Job Duties

Other Duties:

(Duties-listed are not intended to be all inclusive nor to limit duties that might reasonably be assigned.)

Sets up meetings and cleans up after meetings are over.

Knowledge, Skills, and Abilities

(The following knowledge, abilities and skills (KASs) represent the KASs needed at time of appointment to perform Essential Job Functions.)

Knowledge of:

Standard office procedures and practices.

Office management procedures and practices.

Ability to

Perform varied office procedures independently.

Organize and provide office support services for the unit.

Skill in

Use of typewriters, word processors and other office equipment.

Qualifications

(Note: Any acceptable combination of education, training and experience that provides the above KASs may be substituted for those listed.)

Physical and Mental Requirements

Work involves sustained operation of a computer terminal and is subject to frequent interruptions.

Education, Experience and Training:

Graduation from high school or possession of a GED certificate, preferably including or supplemented by course work in office practices.

Experience:

Five years of progressively more responsible clerical experience; prefer at least two years serving as principal secretary to a unit.

License and Certification Requirements

Licenses: Ohio Driver's License and own vehicle preferred.

3.3 EXECUTIVE SECRETARY

3.3.1 Executive Secretary

Library Name: Cuyahoga County Public Library
Library Location: Parma, Ohio
Population Served: 607,909
Number of Volumes: 3,297,420
Number of Titles: N/A
Number of Periodical Subscriptions: 8,502

General Summary

Under moderate supervision, assists the Executive Director and the Board of Trustees by performing various secretarial and administrative tasks including planning and organizing meetings, preparing and typing correspondence and maintaining records, files and databases of information related to Executive Office and Board activities.

Essential Functions and Responsibilities

A. Complies with work scheduling and attendance requirements according to reasonable policy and practices. Staffing for branch and regional libraries and some Administration (ADM) departments requires rotational scheduling, which includes evening and weekend (Saturday and Sunday) hours. Most ADM departments are weekday operations.

B. Consistently presents Cuyahoga County Public Library and its services in a positive manner and adheres to customer service guidelines and procedures as established by the Library.

C. Complies with the established rules of operation, procedures, and policies when using library computers, peripheral hardware, and software. Individual passwords and any other confidential information regarding library records shall be kept confidential.

Acts as liaison between Executive Director, Division Directors, Administrators, Board members, public officials and others communicating information to and from the Director's office, clarifying Library policies and procedures and coordinating Executive Office activities.

Prepares and types various correspondence and reports from written and dictated sources.

Plans and coordinates Board of Trustees meetings including preparing agenda and report materials, handling Board member correspondence and recording, transcribing and distributing meeting minutes.

Answers phone for Executive Director, screening and directing callers, and recording messages.

Monitors office message systems including voice mail, E-mail, facsimile transmissions, etc.

Coordinates Executive Director's schedule including setting appointments, maintaining calendar of activities and events and making travel arrangements.

Organizes and maintains electronic and hard copy files of Executive Office data and information.

Receives, opens, screens and routes daily mail including responding to routine correspondence and inquiries.

Knowledge, Skills, and Abilities

Thorough knowledge of Library policies and procedures.

Knowledge of standard office procedures and practices.

Knowledge of grammar, spelling and punctuation.

Basic knowledge of Robert's Rules of Order and Ohio's Sunshine Law.

Computer literate with knowledge of, and ability to use, word processing and spreadsheet software.

Excellent communication and interpersonal skills for interacting with varying groups and individuals including staff and peers, attorneys, public officials and Board members.

Strong organizational skills with ability to coordinate multiple tasks and schedules of Executive Director and the Board.

Ability to operate basic office equipment such as word processor, typewriter, 10-key calculator, copier, fax, etc., and type 50–60 wpm.

Ability to transcribe recorded information from dictaphone tape.

Summary Minimum Education & Experience Required

Associate's degree in Office Administration or related field.

Four to six years of progressively more responsible secretarial/administrative office work.

Physical and Mental Requirements

Occasional minor discomforts form near-continuous use of a video display terminal.

Additional Qualifications

OTHER TESTING / LICENSES REQUIRED

A criminal background check is required.

Disclaimers

The intent of this position description is to provide a representative summary of the major duties and responsibilities performed by incumbents of this job. Incumbents may be requested to perform job-related tasks other than those specifically presented in this description.

4.0 TYPIST

4.1 TYPIST

4.1.1 Typist

Library Name: St. Clair County Library System
Library Location: Port Hudson, Michigan
Population Served: 160,708
Number of Volumes: 432,880
Number of Titles: 206,173
Periodical Subscriptions: 560

Reports To

SUPERVISION RECEIVED: Library Services Secretary/Library Director.

General Summary

General Duties: Works with limited supervision in the efficient operation of the Library Administrative Office and its financial services.

Essential Functions and Responsibilities

Typical Work: (An employee in this classification may be called upon to perform the following tasks which are illustrative and not exhaustive in nature.)

Responsible for accounts payable system for the Library including inputting invoices.

With Library Services Secretary alternates responsibility for inputting payroll and reconciling cash accounts. Assists in processing and distribution of checks.

Accurate data input and retrieval.

Order, pick up and distribute supplies.

Receptionist duties.

Set up meeting room for various meetings (includes monthly Library Board Meetings, systems meetings and others.)

Work at the Circulation and/or Juvenile Room Desk as is determined.

Arrange for repairs of office equipment.

Filing and typing various documents.

Knowledge, Skills, and Abilities

Desired Qualifications:

Ability to read and interpret documents.

Ability to write routine reports and correspondence.

Ability to communicate effectively with other employees, Library and County management and Vendors.

Some knowledge of basic bookkeeping.

Ability to calculate figures and amounts such as discounts, proportions and percentages. Proficiency with calculator.

Ability to apply common sense understanding to carry out instructions in written or verbal form. Ability to deal with problems and make minor decisions in accordance with established procedures.

Ability to multitask with superior skill in organization. High degree of accuracy and confidentiality is a must. Ability to operate a Personal Computer. Word processing (Microsoft Word), spreadsheet (Microsoft Excel) and e-mail experience.

Ability to type at least 45 words per minute. Ability to perform duties with awareness of all Management, Library Board and County policies and procedures. Strong customer service skills.

Physical and Mental Requirements

The physical demands described here are representative of those that must be met by an employee to successfully perform the essential functions of this position. Reasonable accommodations may be made to enable individuals with disabilities to perform the essential functions.

While performing the duties of this job, the employee is regularly required to talk, hear and operate a computer. The employee is required to sit for extensive periods of time, stand and walk. The employee is required to push carts with materials and stoop in an ergonomically correct manner. The employee must occasionally lift and/or move supplies and materials up to 50 pounds. Specific vision requirements required by the job include close vision and depth perception.

The noise level in the work environment is moderate, with varying interruptions. Position usually demands meeting deadlines with severe time constraints.

Education, Experience, and Training:

Experience Needed: High school graduate or equivalent with business training or experience desirable.

XIV. OUTREACH AND EXTENSION SERVICES

Included in this section are bookmobile personnel, outreach librarians, and programming coordinators.

1.0 BOOKMOBILE

1.1 ASSISTANT

1.1.1 Assistant

Library Name: Cass County Public Library
Library Location: Harrisonville, Missouri
Population Served: 80,000
Number of Volumes: 155,000
Number of Titles: N/A
Number of Periodical Subscriptions: 264

General Summary

Facilitate the delivery of library materials and information to various bookmobile stops.

Participate in the daily circulation operations and providing programs for all ages on the mobile unit/outreach services of the Cass County Public Library.

Prepare and drive the bookmobile or van to various locations primarily following a schedule.

Provide basic inspection and maintenance of the bookmobile to ensure proper vehicle maintenance.

Essential Functions and Responsibilities

Drive the bookmobile to specified locations on a predetermined schedule.

Performs circulation duties including checking materials in and out and maintaining borrower registration.

Makes library cards for patrons.

Collects fines and fees as appropriate.

Shelves materials according to library procedure.

Assists with programming and other outreach efforts of CCPL and especially the Bookmobile.

Perform basic inspection and maintenance of the bookmobile to ensure proper vehicle maintenance.

Drive vehicle to garage for repairs and maintenance as needed.

Knowledge, Skills, and Abilities

Ability to operate mobile library vehicles.

Ability to effectively manage vehicular emergencies.

Excellent interpersonal and customer service skills with warm, caring attributes and a sense of humor.

Must enjoy working with people of all ages and display energy and enthusiasm for this kind of work.

Computer experience helpful.

Must be physically able to operate a variety of equipment including computers and hand-held scanners.

Must be able to maneuver 40 pounds of library materials.

May include shelving materials on shelves about head level.

Requires the ability to reach and grasp materials located in all areas of the bookmobile.

Requires the ability to read, write and speak effectively in standard English.

Requires the ability to deal with people effectively when confronted with persons acting under stress.

Requires driving and working year round in a bookmobile that has heat/air conditioning.

Requires daily travel around the community and loading/unloading materials and equipment in all kinds of weather and climatic conditions.

Education, Experience, and Training

Qualifications and Requirements:

HS diploma/GED

Other Qualifications:

Must have a valid Missouri driver's license and a safe driving record.

Must be willing and able to drive the library's 33-foot bookmobile.

Position Hours

Special Requirements:

Must be able to work a flexible schedule that will include some evenings, weekends, and holidays.

1.1.2 Bookmobile Associate

Library Name: Tuscaloosa Public Library
Library Location: Tuscaloosa, Alabama
Population Served: 165,000
Number of Volumes: 161,047
Number of Titles: 98,739
Periodical Subscriptions: 234

General Summary

The Library Associate in the Bookmobile Department provides service to Bookmobile Department patrons, maintains the Bookmobile collection, and administers Bookmobile processes.

The Library Associate in the Bookmobile Department is responsible to safely drive the Bookmobile to designated locations and park it.

The Library Associate in the Bookmobile Department interacts with Bookmobile patrons to determine preferences and requests, recommends books of various genres based on patron requests, and checks materials in and out for patrons. The Bookmobile Library Associate must complete paperwork, and order and maintain mail and other supplies.

The Library Associate in the Bookmobile Department must follow all library policies and guidelines, and maintain a neat, orderly and safe work environment.

Essential Functions and Responsibilities

Major Responsibilities:

Note: (E) denotes essential function of the job

30% Develops and maintains the collection by using review sources to make recommendations about orders to the Extension Coordinator, coordinating with Circulation, Children's, and Adult Services Departments to obtain requested materials that are not resident in the Bookmobile collection, assessing the condition of returned books and discarding materials when indicated by standard library procedures. (E)

30% Solicits and registers new Bookmobile patrons, establishes and maintains patron records, and perform reader's advisory functions for patrons. (E)

20% Publicizes Bookmobile collection information to patrons by preparing bibliographies and delivering book talks. (E)

10% Maintains the bookmobile by scheduling housekeeping services for the vehicle, assuring that vehicle maintenance is timely performed, talking with mechanics to describe vehicle problems and coordinate other service for the bookmobile.

10% Completes paperwork and produce timely oral and written reports regarding Bookmobile circulation for supervisors and coworkers. (E)

Knowledge, Skills, and Abilities:

Broad knowledge of popular literature, authors and genres is necessary to perform the reader's advisory functions of this job.

Oral and written communication skills, including the ability to understand oral and written communication, to produce effective oral and written communication for such purposes as determining patron reading preferences, making recommendations to patrons, summarizing information, and producing timely oral and written reports for supervisors and coworkers.

Ability to communicate professionally, courteously and effectively with Bookmobile patrons, including children, older patrons, non-readers, new readers and non-English speakers.

Ability to maintain a neat and orderly work environment.

Ability to solve problems in ambiguous situations.

Ability to operate standard office equipment, including personal computer, bar code scanner, and postage processing equipment.

Decision Making and Planning

Guidance through access to a supervisor and well-defined procedures is available, with some latitude for independent judgment relative to choice of action.

Physical and Mental Requirements

The ability to exert moderate, though not constant physical effort such as sitting, walking or standing for at least 75% of the time, with less than 25% of the time spent climbing, balancing, stooping, kneeling, crouching, and/or crawling; repetitive motion for less than 25% of the time; some lifting of objects and materials weighing less than 50 pounds; and some pushing and/or pulling of objects and materials weighing less than 100 pounds.

The ability to perceive and discriminate visual cues or signals at least 100% of the time.

The ability to communicate verbally at least 100% of the time.

Work Environment

Exposure to environmental conditions such as heat, cold, dirt, dust, and bright/dim light for more than 50% of the time.

Education, Experience, and Training

A Bachelor's Degree, experience in customer service, basic computer and software knowledge, or an equivalent combination of education and experience is necessary to perform this job. A valid Driver's License and acceptable motor vehicle record are required.

Position Hours

The Bookmobile Library Associate must work hours as scheduled by the Extension Coordinator and/or the Director or Assistant Director, including early, evening, weekend and overtime hours from time to time.

Hours: Tuesday – Saturday, 8:00 a.m. – 5:00 p.m.

Disclaimers

This position is also required to perform all other duties as assigned.

1.2 BOOKMOBILE LIBRARIAN

1.2.1 Bookmobile Librarian

Library Name: Cass County Public Library
Library Location: Harrisonville, Missouri
Population Served: 80,000
Number of Volumes: 155,000
Number of Titles: N/A
Periodical Subscriptions: 264

General Summary

Under general supervision, performs mobile library service and outreach programs for CCPL. This work includes planning, scheduling, direct patron service, conducting programs, working with community and county agencies, driving the bookmobile and supervision of library staff and volunteers.

Essential Functions and Responsibilities

Under the general supervision of the Library Director and in consultation with the Youth Services Coordinator, coordinates and executes a mobile library program. This includes planning and development of the bookmobile program, making community contacts, conducting programs and library services at remote sites and driving the library's 33-foot bookmobile.

Performs excellent customer service and provides a safe and welcoming atmosphere for adults, teens and children aboard the bookmobile.

Provides basic reader services including reference.

Maintains the materials collection on the bookmobile.

Stocks the bookmobile with books and other materials and loads/unloads materials to and from the library.

Re-shelves materials as they are returned by patrons and keeps the collection attractive and in order.

Identifies materials needing repair or replacement.

Keeps records of collection gaps and makes purchase recommendations.

Works with the library's professional staff to weed the collection and keep materials current.

Rotates collection with materials taken from the CCPL collection.

Performs bookmobile circulation tasks using computers and computer peripheral equipment.

Maintains patron registration files.

With the help of CCPL staff, plans programs for all ages and for special population groups, including children, teens, seniors, and people with limited English skills.

Conducts programs on the bookmobile and at remote outreach sites.

Works with Library Director, adult programming staff, the Youth Services Coordinator and the

Bookmobile Assistant in the development and execution of these programs.

Under the guidance of the Library Director and the Youth Services Librarian establishes good working relationships with members of the community, community and county agencies to determine community needs, learn about other area services and resources and develop appropriate services.

Works collaboratively with other agencies or departments as appropriate.

Attends meetings and workshops associated with other community.

Acts as an advocate for literacy, reading and other life skills as appropriate.

Additional Job Duties

Works with the assistant to provide circulation and reader services and to develop and conduct outreach programs for people of all ages.

Schedules assistant as appropriate.

Works with other library staff to recruit, train, schedule and supervise community volunteers on the bookmobile and in outreach programs.

Uses computers, the library's online catalog and the Internet.

Helps patrons use computers and locate library materials.

Provides one-on-one computer help and conducts other computer training as appropriate. Works with the System Administrator to keep computers on the bookmobile in good working condition and keeps the Library Director informed of any problems.

Keeps contact with the library while at remote sites via a cell phone.

Drives the bookmobile and assists in the training of other staff drivers.

May be required to do some routine cleaning of the bookmobile interior.

Write reports and meets regularly with the Library Director and other staff.

Gives presentations for staff, the public and others as appropriate.

Follows library policy and procedure.

Attends staff meetings and training.

Participates in continuing education workshops, conferences and other training opportunities as assigned.

Keeps in contact with other public library bookmobile/outreach workers in Missouri and around the U.S. through meetings, bookmobile listservs and reading articles in library publications.

Knowledge, Skills, and Abilities

Good knowledge of both adult and children's literature; must be interested in books and must enjoy reading.

Computer experience with working knowledge of MS Office products and the Internet.

Proven experience as a supervisor, ability to train and supervise an assistant and volunteers.

Good oral and written communication skills.

Ability to work independently, make decisions and solve problems.

Maturity and ability to handle a variety of situations, including emergencies

Knowledge of computer hardware and software applications used by the staff and the ability to instruct patrons in the use of the library automation system and online databases required to take full advantage of the services offered by CCPL.

Ability to get along well and maintain effective working relationships with community groups, schools, volunteers, the public and other employees and respond in a timely, respectful, and responsive manner.

Ability to lift, move, shelve and un-shelve books and other library materials on a regular basis;

Ability to maneuver boxes of materials weighing up to 40 pounds.

Ability to pass a background check and/or criminal history check.

Ability to operate mobile library vehicles.

Valid Missouri State driver's license and driving record that meets the standards set by CCPL.

Physical and Mental Requirements

Must be able to maneuver up to 40 pounds of materials, which may include lifting and carrying books and other materials and placing books on shelves about head level.

Requires the ability to work in a variety of locations in various library branches and to reach and grasp materials located in all areas of the bookmobile.

Tools and Equipment:

Must be physically able to operate a variety of equipment including computers, hand-held scanners, calculators, photocopiers, Fax machines, audio-visual recording and playback equipment, cameras, etc.

Supervisory Responsibilities

Supervises the Bookmobile Assistant. Monitors the work of the Bookmobile Assistant and informs the Library Director about job performance, training needs, etc.

Education, Experience, and Training

Bachelor's degree preferred.

Combination of associate degree and experience may substitute.

Background in library science, education, child development and/or liberal arts helpful.

Excellent interpersonal and customer service skills with warm, caring attributes and a sense of humor.

Must enjoy working with people of all ages and display energy and enthusiasm for this kind of work.

Related experience working with children.

Additional Qualifications

Requires the ability to read, write and speak effectively in standard English.

Requires the ability to speak before groups of people with poise, voice control and confidence.

Must be able to communicate via telephone.

Requires the ability to deal with people beyond giving and receiving instructions.

Must be adaptable to performing under stress and when confronted with persons acting under stress.

Requires driving and working year round in a bookmobile that has heat/air conditioning.

Requires daily travel around the community and loading/unloading materials and equipment in all kinds of weather and climatic conditions.

Must have a valid Missouri driver's license and a safe driving record. Must be willing and able to drive the library's 33-foot bookmobile.

Position Hours

Special Requirements:

Must be able to work a flexible schedule that will include some evenings, weekends and holidays.

Disclaimers

Performs other related work as assigned.

Performs other duties as assigned.

1.3 Bookmobile Specialist

1.3.1 Bookmobile Specialist

Library Name: Burnham Memorial Library
Library Location: Colchester, Vermont
Population Served: 17,000
Number of Volumes: N/A
Number of Titles: 35,000
Number of Periodical Subscriptions: 75

General Summary

Under the administrative supervision of the Library Director, the Bookmobile Specialist performs managerial, supervisory, patron service, research, technical, planning and coordination work for the Burnham Memorial Library. The Bookmobile Specialist manages the bookmobile and library outreach program, providing mobile library service and programming throughout the community and to special populations. The Bookmobile Specialist is a permanent member of the library staff and may be assigned to work in the library.

Essential Functions and Responsibilities

Works with the Library Director and the Youth Services Librarian to plan, develop and execute a program of mobile library and outreach service for all ages.

Works with the Library Director on issues of library policy and procedure that relate to the bookmobile and outreach program. Carries out policy as established by the Library Board of Trustees and the Town of Colchester.

Schedules and oversees the daily activities of staff and volunteers assigned to the bookmobile. Creates and publishes a regular schedule of bookmobile stops.

Drives the bookmobile to regularly scheduled stops and outreach sites. May visit some sites with personal vehicle. Responsible for daily bookmobile mechanical checks and works with the Town

Garage to keep the bookmobile maintained and in good running condition. Responsible for keeping the fuel tank filled. Reports vehicle problems, accidents, etc. to Library Director and others, as required. Maintains safe driving record and assists in training other library staff to drive the bookmobile.

Circulates bookmobile materials using a remote automated system and a laptop computer. Conducts daily downloads/uploads of circulation and patron data and keeps circulation records current. Registers patrons, collects fines and fees, processes patron holds and requests and maintains a card file of bookmobile patrons. Keeps circulation and usage statistics.

Provides basic information and readers' advisory service for bookmobile patrons. Assists parents, children, teens and adults in selecting bookmobile materials and locates additional materials of interest that the library owns. Reserves library materials for bookmobile patrons and offers Interlibrary Loan service.

Works with the Library Director and the Youth Services Librarian to stock a diverse, fresh and quality collection of books and audio-visual materials on the bookmobile. Keeps track of collection gaps and makes purchase recommendations; may participate in materials selection. Rotates the collection as needed and loads/unloads materials daily. Keeps the bookmobile collection in order and re-shelves materials as they are returned.

Works with the Library Director to hire, train, supervise, schedule and evaluate a support staff person (Bookmobile Assistant) and bookmobile volunteers.

Responsible for planning, implementing and evaluating a variety of programs on the bookmobile and at outreach sites, especially story programs for pre-school children, summer craft and storytelling programs, programs for seniors and services for new immigrants and those with limited English or literacy skills, especially students of English as a Second Language (ESL). Works with other library staff and with the Bookmobile Assistant to develop and execute these programs.

Under the guidance of the Library Director and the Youth Services Librarian, establishes contacts and working relationships in the community with other organizations and agencies that focus on education, literacy, services to seniors, English as a Second Language and pre-school children. Works with the Town Parks and Recreation Department and participates with the bookmobile in town-wide functions such as Winter Carnival and the 4th of July parade. Establishes deposit collections in remote locations and encourages resource sharing, when possible. Makes presentations to library staff, the Library Board of Trustees, town officials and other community groups and acts as an advocate for literacy, reading and the acquisition of English language skills

Reads widely to become familiar with the bookmobile/library collection and works with the Library Director and the Youth Services Librarian to develop skills and techniques for marketing the bookmobile collection and encouraging reading and life-long learning. May create book lists, displays and other materials that encourage the use of bookmobile resources.

Works with the library's publicity coordinator to promote the bookmobile and outreach program. Creates flyers, posters and other publicity pieces.

Maintains the bookmobile as a safe, clean, attractive and comfortable space for children, seniors and other bookmobile patrons. Handles emergency and problem situations and completes all required paper work.

Creates a list of annual budgetary needs for the bookmobile/outreach program and is responsible for allocated funds, tracking expenditures and reviewing invoices for payment.

Creates financial, statistical, narrative, and/or other reports as required.

Attends library staff meetings and training. Participates in continuing education workshops, conferences and other training opportunities as assigned/required.

Stays informed about issues, trends and news affecting bookmobile service. Participates in the national bookmobile listserv and reads selected professional literature. Keeps in contact with public library bookmobile/outreach workers in Vermont.

Works with the Library Director to find supplementary funding and partnerships, including grants. May write and/or administer grants.

Performs other related work as required.

Knowledge, Skills, and Abilities

Mature judgment, poise, professional attitude; must be able to work independently

Administrative and organizational ability

Strong commitment to customer service and ability to work effectively and comfortably with people of all ages and abilities

Excellent driving record and valid Vermont driver's license; ability to work and drive in all kinds of weather conditions and at night

Interest in books and reading; must enjoy reading and have a good knowledge of books and authors for adults and children

Ability to handle difficult patrons and emergency situations

Excellent written and oral communication skills

Good to excellent computer skills, including basic office software and Internet searching

Good research skills

Good basic math skills; ability to keep statistical reports

Imagination and creative approach to problem solving

Physical and Mental Requirements

Physical:

Prolonged sitting and/or standing

Extensive use of computers

Lifting and carrying items weighing up to 35 pounds and moving up to 50 pounds, including up and down bookmobile steps

Stress

Bending, crouching, reaching overhead, grasping objects

Using telephones, including a cell phone

Ability to climb steps of bookmobile

Driving a 28 foot bookmobile in all kinds of weather and at night

Speaking before groups

Outside temperatures and weather conditions can be cold, wet, slippery, hot

Mental Demands:

Position requires attention to details and deadlines, which may cause stress

Ability to multi-task

Ability to handle stressful situations and difficult interpersonal encounters

Reading and writing; data and statistical analysis

Judgment/Decision-Making

Working in isolation; must work independently and with periodic quiet time with little work to do

Work Environment

Located in library, on bookmobile and at remote outreach sites (nursing homes, child care centers, etc.); can be noisy and busy with many disruptions and interruptions. Includes time outside in all kinds of weather and at night

Some bookmobile stops are at remote sites with few people around

Works with other staff and general public

Works regularly with computers and other technology

Shared office in library, accessible to staff and the public

Must be able to work a flexible schedule to include: mornings, afternoons, some evenings, weekends and occasional holidays

May be assigned temporary duty in the library

Education, Experience, and Training

Bachelor's degree required. Liberal Arts or Education background preferred. Prior work experience in a library or educational setting and experience working with children required (or a combination of education and work experience from which comparable knowledge and skills are acquired)

Experience supervising the work of other employees or volunteers

Additional Qualifications

Experience with public relations and/or marketing

Artistic ability

Special skills in storytelling, puppetry and/or booktalking

Experience driving a large vehicle and with vehicle maintenance

2.0 OUTREACH COORDINATOR

2.1 OUTREACH COORDINATOR

2.1.1 Outreach Coordinator

Library Name: Cumberland County Library System

Library Location: Carlisle, Pennsylvania

Population Served: 221,162

Number of Volumes: N/A

Number of Titles: 7,571

Periodical Subscriptions: 17

General Summary

OVERALL OBJECTIVE OF JOB:

To coordinate the STAR outreach program of library services to older and/or disabled county adult residents and to coordinate County wide library system advocacy activities.

Essential Functions and Responsibilities

Coordinates STAR home delivery service in conjunction with local member libraries.

Recruits, trains, and manages STAR volunteers.

Assesses individual STAR user needs and matches users with STAR volunteers.

Provides STAR users and volunteers with readers' advisory services; solves problems as needed.

Trains local library staff to provide STAR services and works with them to promote the

STAR program

Coordinates STAR services for retirement villages, senior organizations, and nursing homes, especially the County home in conjunction with local member libraries.

Maintains regular contacts with staff at STAR site facilities, working with facility staff, library staff and volunteers to provide rotating and deposit collections. Promoting the use of public library and community resources.

Selects new materials to support the STAR program, managing its acquisition, and distribution.

Works with local libraries on joint collection development of outreach materials.

Oversees STAR automated system and Homebound module including entering of patron and facility records, coordinating overdue notices and reports.

Provides direct service to patrons with special needs and substitutes on deliveries as needed.

Serves as the library's liaison with agencies serving the elderly, especially the County Office of Aging.

Coordinates advocacy activities as staff liaison to the Advocacy Task Force including planning for legislative breakfasts, monitoring and communicating information on library issues of concern on local, state and national level to CCLS Board, local library directors and the Advocacy Task Force.

Additional Job Duties

Attends training, meetings, seminars as required.

Participates in regional state and federal advocacy activities.

Performs other job-related duties as required.

Knowledge, Skills, and Abilities

Must be able to speak and understand the English language in an understandable manner in order to carry out essential functions of job.

Must possess good communication and interpersonal skills.

Must possess initiative and problem solving skills.

Must possess ability to function independently, have flexibility and the ability to work effectively with clients, co-workers and others.

Must possess ability to maintain confidentiality in regard to client information and records.

Position Description Non-Exempt

Must possess a willingness to travel as needed to carry out essential job duties.

Must possess the ability to make independent decisions when circumstances warrant such action.

Must possess knowledge of the principles and practices used in social service work, and the ability to apply these principles and practices within the job.

Must possess some knowledge of the medical concerns and related treatments and practices regarding the aging process.

Must possess some knowledge and ability to counsel elderly.

Must possess knowledge of community resources and the ability to interact effectively with them on clients' behalf.

Must possess a valid Pennsylvania driver's license and be willing to visit deposit collection sites and library patrons, using one's own vehicle.

Must possess ability to conduct complete assessments and to determine most appropriate level of service.

Must possess ability to deliver and evaluate appropriate services to clients and to monitor the effectiveness of such services.

Must possess knowledge of and ability to practice principles and methods of effective management and supervisory skills.

Must possess ability to read and understand legislative language, develop appropriate advocacy strategies, and work cooperatively with staff, boards and the public to influence public policy as it relates to library services.

Physical and Mental Requirements

Must possess ability to record, convey and present information, explain procedures and follow instructions.

Must be able to sit for long periods throughout the workday, with intermittent periods of standing, walking, bending, twisting, and reaching as necessary to carry out job duties.

Dexterity requirements range from simple to coordinated movements of fingers/hands; feet/legs; torso as necessary to carry out duties of job.

Medium work, with occasional lifting/carrying of objects with a maximum weight of twenty-five pounds.

Must be able to pay close attention to details and concentrate on work.

Work Environment

Works indoors with adequate work space, ventilation, lighting and temperature.

Frequent exposure to noise, disruptions and stress.

Normal indoor exposure to dust/dirt.

Periodically works beyond normal work hours or works on-call or on as-needed basis.

Travels periodically as required to perform essential functions of job.

Supervisory Responsibilities

SUPERVISION RECEIVED:

Receives minimal instruction and supervision in regard to daily work duties.

SUPERVISION GIVEN:

Supervises library volunteers.

Education, Experience, and Training

QUALIFICATIONS:

BA or BS in library science, education, or related field.

WORK EXPERIENCE:

2 years work experience with library services, including activities such as volunteer management, readers' advisory services, collection development and advocacy activities

2.2 PROGRAMMING COORDINATOR

2.2.1 Programming Coordinator

Library Name: Boston Public Library
Library Location: Boston, Massachusetts
Population Served: 574,283
Number of Volumes: 7,954,358
Number of Titles: N/A
Number of Periodical Subscriptions: 29,026

Reports To

Communications Manager

General Summary

Job Purpose:

Under the general supervision of the Communications Manager assumes responsibility for planning, coordinating and implementing all Library and non-Library sponsored events, including speakers, exhibits, receptions, and similar programs. Supervises the Library Events Planner. Assumes responsibility for the Communications Department in the absence of the Communications Manager.

Essential Functions and Responsibilities

Oversees all aspects of public programming, exhibitions, and special events including planning, implementation, and logistics. Work closely with staff, library support groups such as the Boston Public Library Foundation, the Associates of the Boston Public Library, the Citywide Friends, and branch friends groups, volunteer committees, and outside vendors as they relate to a variety of activities relating to program, exhibition, and event planning and execution.

Answers and responds (written and orally) to inquiries related to public programming, exhibitions, and special events; schedules and conducts site visits by prospective clients; organizes, coordinates and executes Library/corporate events.

Oversees internal communications necessary for execution of events such as work orders, income reports and activity reports.

Oversees generating and distributing of appropriate internal and external library calendar/s in various formats.

Manages the coordination of programming and event calendars for the Library, BPL Foundation, Associates, Citywide Friends, and other similar groups. Works with various support groups to delivery a coordinated offering of programs and exhibits for the public.

Oversees all aspects of the event, program, and exhibit planning process for all in-house events including author presentations, receptions, exhibition openings, and special events hosted by community businesses and organizations.

Oversees the updating and maintaining of program, exhibition, and event information in/on Web site, public information products, and similar communications tools.

Insures close working relationship with Public Service, Financial, and Facilities staff regarding planning for programs, events, and exhibitions to insure high quality support by the Library.

May attend programs, events, exhibition openings and other events as required by scope and nature of the event.

Supervises and develops the Tour Guide program.

Insures attention to detail and appropriateness of response to queries regarding programs, exhibitions, and events.

Perform other related duties as assigned.

Knowledge, Skills and Abilities:

Demonstrated superior oral and written communication skills; tact; excellent people skills; attention to detail

Experience organizing public programming and exhibitions

Creativity and flexibility

Dependability

Familiarity with public sector policies and procedures

Excellent interpersonal and organizational skills necessary for working with a number of constituents including library staff, trustees, volunteers, vendors, community and corporate groups, and general public

Maturity; able to work on own initiative;

Demonstrated organizational skills and the ability to manage multiple priorities.

Education, Experience, and Training

Qualifications:

Education—Requires BA degree in Communications, Journalism, or a related field.

Experience—Requires a minimum of two years experience planning and implementing successful programs, exhibitions, and events. Library experience highly desirable.

Excellent Microsoft Word/general computer skills; demonstrated flexibility with schedule (position will require some holiday, evening and week-end work), able to work independently and as a member of a team and to establish effective relationships with staff, vendors, colleagues and the public enthusiasm for the work required; energetic; good judgment; superb customer service skills; ability to motivate others; personal and professional flexibility; and excellent interpersonal skills are essential. Creative, energetic, detail oriented. Valid driver's license.

Additional Qualifications:

Requirements: Must be a Resident of the City of Boston upon first day of hire.

Position Hours

Other Requirements: This position requires night, holiday and weekend work.

2.3 REGIONAL PROGRAMMING COORDINATOR

2.3.1 Regional Programming Coordinator

Library Name: Boston Public Library
Library Location: Boston, Massachusetts
Population Served: 574,283
Number of Volumes: 7,954,358
Number of Titles: N/A
Number of Periodical Subscriptions: 29,026

Reports To

Chief of Operations

General Summary

Job Purpose:

Responsible for development and administration of a variety of core and innovative programs serving other libraries, including those belonging to the Boston Regional Library System (BRLS), other regional library systems, libraries belonging to various cooperating organizations such as the Boston Library Consortium, NELINET, OCLC, ARL, RLG, etc. Oversees the delivery of the MBLN (MetroBoston Library Network) program of service. Participates in development, implementation, and administration of Boston Public Library's program of service. Serves as member of Senior Management Team.

Essential Functions and Responsibilities

Develops and manages plans of service, budgets, program evaluation, statistical reporting for state-funded programs such as the BRLS. Works with other libraries and library organizations such as NELINET, Boston Library Consortium, ARL, RLG, and other similar organizations to develop service programs of mutual benefit.

Develops annual Regional Plan of Service.

Works collaboratively with Public Service and Finance to insure the fulfillment of services to the library and the Regional members.

Develops and manages annual BRLS line and program budgets according to Massachusetts Board of Library Commissioners (MBLC) requirements.

Works with State agency, Regional Advisory Council, other regions, other library groups, such as automated resource sharing networks, Boston Library Consortium (BLC), in joint program development and implementation.

Works with BPL Systems staff, MBLN participating libraries, MBLC, and other networks in joint program development in implementation.

Represents the Boston Public Library at board meetings and on committees for various library organizations, as assigned.

Provides leadership to the development, implementation and evaluation of new and innovative cooperative and collaborative library service programs.

Provides leadership and coordination in identifying and developing, and implementing grant programs.

Coordinates MBLN service delivery with BPL Systems' Office, including the development and management of the network Plan of Service, budget, program evaluation, statistical reporting; ensures that MBLN Long Range Plan and Collection Plan are current and meet MBLC requirements.

Responsible for convening the MBLN Policy Advisory Group and other MBLN policy and service delivery development and evaluation groups.

Participates in development, implementation, and administration of BPL's program of service.

Provides management and technical advisory service to libraries.

Recruits, evaluates, and disciplines staff as appropriate.

Administers and manages Regional Services Office, including staff, budget, and work flow.

Knowledge, Skills, and Abilities

Extensive knowledge of the principles and practices of library service. Experience working with multi-type systems and automated resource sharing networks.

Demonstrated ability to work collaboratively and proactively to develop new and creative library programs and means to deliver library services.

Demonstrated knowledge of service requirements of variety of libraries; management of staff, preferably as director of library; budget development and management; working understanding of ILS and other library technologies.

Excellent written and oral communication skills; ability to travel throughout

Massachusetts; creativity, enthusiasm, decision-making; ability to work collaboratively and proactively with various advisory groups and levels of staff in a team environment.

Initiative:

Demonstrated ability to develop and implement methods of program evaluation and analysis.

Education, Experience, and Training

Qualifications:

Education—Bachelors Degree from an accredited college or university and a Masters Degree in Library and Information Science or equivalent from an American Library Association accredited library school.

Experience—Requires 7+ years in a library work environment which includes at least 7 years of supervisory experience, and experience working in a multi-type library system and/or automated resource sharing network.

Additional Qualifications

Desired attributes—Ability to manage multiple and complex priorities. Flexibility, creativity, initiative, positive outlook, respectful, strategic thinker and implementers.

3.0 LIBRARIANS, OUTREACH

3.1 OUTREACH LIBRARIAN

3.1.1 Outreach Librarian

Library Name: LaPorte County Public Library
Library Location: LaPorte, Indiana
Population Served: 65,836
Number of Volumes: 257,000
Number of Titles: 180,000
Periodical Subscriptions: 55

General Summary

The Extension Services Program Specialist will apply skills and knowledge in providing equitable extension services, particularly in the areas of collection development and program development and implementation. In addition, the Extension Services Program Specialist will assist the Extension Services Manager with administrative duties related to the successful operation of the department. This includes supervision of assigned tasks in specific areas of responsibility requiring the exercise of sound, independent judgement.

Essential Duties and Responsibilities:

(including, but not limited to the following)

Cooperate with all staff in performing any professional or non-professional duties essential to providing quality customer service and the achievement of library objectives, goals, and mission.

Plan, promote and conduct programs for all ages for the Extension Department in cooperation with other staff.

Promote programs and services through displays, fliers, public speaking, etc.

Act as library representative to the community through local groups and by making school visits, etc.

Assume responsibility of coordinating Summer Reading Program for Extension Department; including planning, preparing, and conducting programs for all at branch locations in conjunction with branch managers.

Serve on the library's Programming committee and/or sub-committees as deemed necessary.

Be familiar with the electronic resources, including the library's automation software, the library's web site and other Internet resources. Keep pace with changes in the databases provided for use and train staff and patrons in their use. Develop path-finders for staff and patrons. Must also be capable of providing basic training for the use of the library's office software products to staff and patrons.

Keep current with library profession by reading professional publications and participating in appropriate meetings, workshops, and training sessions.

Assist Department Head in supervision of daily operations, including:

Promotion of Extension services to the community.

Development, evaluation, review, and supervision of outreach services.

Substituting on bookmobile, at branches, or in other departments as needed to maintain effective service.

Supervise the collection and tabulation of statistics for programs, and summer reading program and be able to analyze these statistics accordingly.

Collection development:

Provide reader's advisory training to staff. Plan and prepare bibliographies and booklists for the Extension Department.

Assist with selection, weeding, and rotation of materials for Extension Services collections.

Knowledge, Skills, and Abilities

Ability to exercise sound independent judgement.

Ability to communicate effectively with staff and the public.

Ability to organize and supervise personnel and/or areas of responsibility.

Knowledge of, and experience with, library materials, services, and programs.

Ability to plan and conduct library programs for all age ranges.

Strong interest in, and ability to, work well with the public.

Ability to work flexible schedule including evenings and weekends as assigned.

Experience with automated systems, and/or the ability and willingness to learn to effectively use the automated system.

Ability to solve professional level problems or to make recommendations for their solution.

Ability to sit or stand for prolonged period (1 or more hours).

Ability to travel.

Have a valid Indiana driver's license.

Physical and Mental Requirements

Language Skills

A successful Extension Services Program Specialist will have the ability to read, analyze, and interpret general business periodicals, professional journals, technical procedures, or governmental regulations and write reports, business correspondence, and procedure manuals. Further required language skills include the ability to effectively present information and respond to questions from staff members, patrons, and the general public.

Mathematical Skills

The Extension Services Program Specialist must have the ability to calculate figures and amounts such as discounts, interest, commissions, proportions, percentages, area circumference, and volume.

Reasoning Ability

The Extension Services Program Specialist must possess the ability to define problems, collect data, establish facts, and draw valid conclusions.

Physical Demands

The physical demands described here are representative of those that must be met by an employee to successfully perform the essential functions of this job. Reasonable accommodations may be made to enable individuals with disabilities to perform the essential functions.

While performing the duties of this job, the employee is regularly required to use hands to finger, handle, or feel objects, tools, or controls; reach with hands and arms; and communicate. The employee is occasionally required to stand; walk; sit; climb or balance; and stoop, kneel, crouch or crawl.

The employee must regularly lift and/or move up to 25 pounds. Specific vision abilities required by this job include close vision, distance vision, color vision, peripheral vision, depth perception, and the ability to adjust focus.

Tools and Equipment:

The employee must be familiar with, or be able to learn to function with, the following equipment in order to perform job functions:

Automated system
Computer terminals
Calculator
Photocopier
Telephone/cell phone systems
Typewriter

Work Environment

The work environment characteristics described here are representative of those an employee encounters while performing the essential duties of this job. Reasonable accommodations may be made to enable individuals with disabilities to perform the essential job functions.

While performing the duties of this job, the employee may work near moving mechanical parts and in outside weather conditions. The employee is frequently exposed to fumes or airborne particles.

While performing the duties of this job, the employee may be exposed to weather elements and fluctuating temperatures in the bookmobile.

While performing the duties of this job, the employee may work in a confined area (bookmobile).

While performing the duties of this job, the employee may work in locations where access to restrooms is not readily available.

The noise level in the work environment is usually moderate.

Supervisory Responsibilities

Supervise the department in the chain of command, assist with assigning department workload, assume responsibility for the department in the absence of the Dept. Head.

Assist in hiring, training, scheduling, assigning work, and delivering performance reviews to Extension staff in conjunction with the Head of Extension Services.

Education, Experience, and Training

Master's Degree from an accredited graduate library school, or Indiana State Certification as Librarian IV or higher, or Special training and/or experience in relevant area.

Additional Qualifications

Qualification Requirements

To satisfactorily fulfill the responsibilities of the Extension Services Program Specialist, an individual must be able to meet or exceed the requirements. Reasonable accommodations may be made to enable individuals with disabilities to perform the essential functions.

Position Hours

NOTE: This is a full time (40 hours per week) position, including evenings and weekends as assigned. This position may also include traveling to professional meetings, workshops, or other activities which may be deemed necessary for attendance.

3.1.2 Extension Services Librarian

Library Name: Tippecanoe County Public Library
Library Location: La Fayette, Indiana
Population Served: 104,310
Number of Volumes: 297,091
Number of Titles: N/A
Periodical Subscriptions: 1,947

Reports To

SUPERVISOR: Department Head

General Summary

JOB OBJECTIVE:

Plan for and provide library services and materials to those who cannot, with reasonable ease, take advantage of them at the main library.

Essential Functions and Responsibilities

Participate in developing policies and procedures for Outreach Services

Provide public service (including reference, reader's advisory, and customer account maintenance) on the bookmobile, at nursing homes, and at other off-site locations

Assume responsibility for collection management in specific areas of the circulating and reference collections

Support and contribute to overall library mission

Handle public service support routines (holds, library applications, etc)

Compile appropriate statistics

Maintain professional and technical knowledge by attending workshops, reading professional publications, and participating in individual and departmental training

Supervise projects for Outreach aides, volunteers, and work study students. May need to select, train, and evaluate volunteers.

Participate in the development and provision of programming for all age groups and ability levels. (Including making speaker contacts, developing promotional and media releases, scheduling, and making presentations)

Serve as a liaison in planning community/library programs

Act as liaison to civic and community organizations

Research and apply for grant funding for Outreach programs and services

Work cooperatively with other library departments and staff members

Maintain effective communication with library staff

Know and apply professional codes and library policies

Participate on library committees

Act as staff member in charge of library as needed

Work evenings and weekends as assigned

Deal with disturbances and problem users

Understand the necessity of, and maintain, confidentiality of library use

Conduct library tours and instructional training

Actively participate in professional organizations

Other duties as assigned and/or required

Knowledge, Skills, and Abilities

Skills: Must be dedicated to quality customer service

Must be able to plan, carry-out, and evaluate programs, develop new services

Must have good written and verbal skills, including communicating with the elderly, disabled, youth, and the foreign- born.

Proficiency in English required; ability to communicate in other language(s) preferred

Must be able to effectively juggle multiple projects and deadlines

Must have good problem-solving skills

Must be able to drive to off-site locations

Must be able to prioritize tasks and responsibilities

Must be able to work with limited supervision

Must be able to try new approaches and remain flexible

Must be able to carry out emergency procedures when necessary

Must be able to efficiently utilize word processing software and troubleshoot simple equipment problems

Must be able to learn and apply latest trends in technology and library services

Physical and Mental Requirements

Must be able to:

Lift and carry a minimum of 40 pounds

Maneuver a book cart empty or full weighing as much as 200 pounds

Adapt to several different environments

Work in a confined area (bookmobile)

Tolerate fluctuating temperatures due to patrons entering and exiting the bookmobile

Retrieve materials from shelves 6' high and stoop to retrieve items on shelving close to the floor

Lift and transport books from bookmobile to buildings

Tolerate different odors in a confined area

Tools and Equipment:

Computer

Automated library system

Calculator

Typewriter

Photocopier

General office equipment

Security System

Approved chemical cleaners and cleaning equipment

Education, Experience, and Training

QUALIFICATIONS:

Education: MLS from ALA accredited library school

Previous experience: At least 2 years of Public Library work required and an equivalent combination of knowledge and experience in working with community agencies, children, the elderly, people with disabilities, and/or foreign-born.

License and Certification Requirements

Must have a valid Indiana Drivers License

Preferred: CDL Class B with air brake endorsement (or ability to attain one)

XV. SECURITY SERVICES

Included in this section are security clerks, guards, and afternoon guards.

1.0 SECURITY GUARD

1.1 AFTERNOON SECURITY GUARD

1.1.1 Afternoon Security Guard

Library Name: Manitowoc-Calumet Public Library
Library Location: Manitowoc, Wisconsin
Population Served: 58,213
Number of Volumes: 195,166
Number of Titles: N/A
Periodical Subscriptions: 395

General Summary

BROAD SCOPE OF POSITION: Working under general supervision of Business Office Supervisor, enforces library rules for patron behavior and maintains security in building and on grounds. Performs light custodial work when guard duties permit. May be assigned to assist with building-related emergencies. May perform Guard/Custodian-level work, as assigned.

Essential Functions and Responsibilities

The following list identifies principal duties and responsibilities of the job. It is not a definitive list and other similar duties may be assigned. An asterisk (*) before any of the following items indicates duties and responsibilities which are not "essential functions" of the job as defined by the Americans with Disabilities Act.

Enforces library policies for patron behavior and maintains building security by patrolling building and grounds.

Responds to book theft detection system and other alarms.

Assists Circulation and other staff in dealing with problem patrons, particularly those who disrupt normal use or operation of the Library, or attempt to unlawfully remove library materials from premises.

Calls for police or other official assistance, when necessary.

Completes Incident Reports, when necessary, and reports informally about other security and/or public behavior problems.

Performs light custodial work, as guard duties permit, such as: changing supplies in restrooms, picking up scraps of debris, using carpet sweeper.

*Assists with emptying interior materials return bins, as necessary and as guard duties permit.

Assists with emergencies requiring additional custodial attention, as necessary and/or assigned, such as: shoveling snow accumulation, cleaning up bodily fluids, mopping after water-leaks.

Knowledge, Skills, and Abilities

Ability to perform guard duties effectively and sensitively with library patrons of various ages, personalities, and backgrounds.

Ability to recognize situations requiring attention and to handle these effectively, often defusing them before they become problems.

Ability to enforce the library's established policies, procedures and standards of public behavior in nondiscriminatory fashion. Ability to present clear explanations of these rules to members of public. Ability to work cooperatively with police or other official departments, as needed.

Capacity to patrol building and grounds efficiently and to respond to situations effectively. Must be able to complete a patrol circuit of the main floor, mezzanine, and foyer/front walk area in 10 min.

Ability to think and act appropriately under pressure.

Ability to follow multi-step written and/or verbal instructions and to perform routine procedures involving several steps.

Ability to work with limited direct supervision.

Ability to establish and maintain effective working relationships with other library staff members.

Ability to write clear and understandable Incident Reports for submission to Administration and/or for use by police department.

Capacity to lift and/or carry objects weighing 5 to 20 pounds. Capacity to push or pull return bins loaded with materials weighing more than 150 pounds

Ability to develop work-related goals and objectives. Willingness to develop job-related abilities, skills and knowledge. Willingness and ability to keep abreast of changing technologies and procedures and to assume responsibilities required by introduction of different services and equipment.

Willingness and ability to understand and support the fundamental principles of library services, such as: open access to library materials for people of all ages; the library's obligation to provide materials representing as many points of view as possible; and a patron's absolute right to privacy in dealings with the library and with respect to records maintained by library.

Work Environment

Usually (up to 100% of work time) works in environment with considerable public contact.

Usually (up to 100% of work time) patrols by making regular rounds of two public levels and grounds outside building.

Often (up to 25% of work time) works with equipment and performs procedures where carelessness may result in minor cuts, bruises, or muscle strains.

Sometimes (up to 10% of work time) lifts and/or carries objects weighing 5 to 20 pounds; pushes or pulls return bins loaded with materials weighing more than 150 pounds

Infrequently (as situation requires) assists with building emergencies which may require extensive custodial attention.

Education, Experience, and Training

MINIMUM QUALIFICATIONS:

Educational development at a level normally acquired through completion of High School in the United States.

3 months previous on the job, volunteer, or life experience enforcing public behavior or other similar rules.

Demonstrable possession of knowledge, skills, abilities, and capacities identified in "Job Specifications" section, above.

Capacity to work under conditions described in "Working Conditions" section, above.

Position Hours

Seasonal. Works a flexible schedule, averaging 16 hours per two-week pay period from September to May, generally: Monday –Thursday, 4:00 p.m.–6:00 p.m. Position terminates in May of every year and is subject to rehire the September.

1.2 SECURITY MONITOR CLERK

1.2.1 Security Monitor Clerk

Library Name: Pikes Peak Library District
Library Location: Colorado Springs, Colorado
Population Served: 448,860
Number of Volumes: 876,897
Number of Titles: N/A
Number of Periodical Subscriptions: 2,330

General Summary

BROAD SCOPE OF POSITION: Under direct supervision of the Facilities and Security Officer or Senior Security Guard, and daily supervision of the Branch Manager or Assistant Branch Manager, ensures the safety of patrons, staff and library assets by enforcing library policies, procedures, and regulations. Performs security functions, circulation duties, routine billing and clerical tasks, and assists patrons in a courteous, helpful, service-oriented manner.

Essential Functions and Responsibilities

Enforces patron and staff compliance with general safety and security rules. Monitors and secures all entry and exit ways. Responds to and investigates disturbances on library property. Assists in ending disturbances and, when necessary, escorts disruptive persons from library premises. Detains, as necessary, suspects involved with theft, vandalism or other criminal activity until police arrive. May testify in court.

Performs periodic checks of the entire facility and grounds.

Monitors fire, safety, and security systems.

Incumbent is expected to wear a PPLD-issued security guard uniform and badge.

Acts as Fire Warden for the branch and as liaison with fire and law enforcement officials.

Is responsible for in-depth knowledge of the Emergency Action Plan in order to carry out duties and responsibilities outlined therein.

Maintains all records related to security issues and prepares reports.

Provides excellent customer service by issuing library cards, by checking materials in and out of the library, and by working with patrons to resolve billing problems and answer questions about their library records.

Performs a variety of clerical duties as assigned such as searching for materials, processing transfers and holds, balancing and closing the cash register, referring patrons to appropriate staff for reference assistance sorting and shelving library materials in proper order and shelf reading as assigned.

Maintains patron confidentiality.

Understands and articulates to patrons the concept of intellectual freedom as it relates to access to materials, information, and services.

Will occasionally work the Information desk to answer general questions and assist patrons in locating materials and information. Also instructs patrons in the use of the online catalog.

Participates in projects and programs as assigned.

Keeps informed of library and departmental information and changes via electronic or written mail and by attending meetings.

May assist in circulation training of new branch employees.

Performs other duties as assigned.

Knowledge, Skills, and Abilities

Knowledge of security practices and procedures.

Knowledge of basic first aid.

Knowledge of electronic surveillance and manual alarm systems (i.e., fire and burglar systems).

Skill in remaining calm and in exercising sound judgment when making rapid decisions in emergency situations.

Ability to provide efficient, courteous public service and present a positive image of the library in attitude, appearance, and performance of duties. Demonstrates interpersonal skills necessary to establish and maintain good working relationships with patrons and staff.

Ability to explain library policy and procedures with courtesy, tact, and firmness.

Ability to stand and walk for three or more hours per day, bend and stretch without limitation, lift up to 10 pounds at a time, and push a wheeled book truck weighing up to 120 pounds.

Ability to sort and arrange four book truck rows of juvenile books in 40 minutes or Young Adult/Adult books in 20 minutes. Ability to shelve four rows of juvenile books in 70 minutes, Young Adult/Adult nonfiction in 55 minutes, and Young Adult/Adult fiction in 40 minutes with five or fewer errors.

Knowledge of general clerical practices and equipment.

Knowledge of Microsoft Office applications, MS Outlook, and standard office equipment such as copiers and fax machines.

Knowledge of general subject areas, authors, and reader interest levels.

Education, Experience, and Training

MINIMUM QUALIFICATIONS:

Requires a high school diploma or GED.

Requires 2+ years of related experience.

Prefer experience in a security field or law enforcement position requiring frequent public contact and knowledge of surveillance and alarm systems.

Prefer some experience with computers.

Additional Qualifications

Requires an excellent customer service attitude! Bilingual ability is a plus!

Requires the ability to work the schedule listed on the first page of this Vacancy Announcement.

Requires satisfactory completion of education, work history, and criminal background investigations.

1.3 SECURITY OFFICER

> ### 1.3.1 Security Officer
>
> **Library Name:** Columbus Metropolitan Library
> **Library Location:** Columbus, Ohio
> **Population Served:** 762,235
> **Number of Volumes:** 780,849
> **Number of Titles:** N/A
> **Number of Periodical Subscriptions:** 2195

General Summary

Purpose of Job:

Performs the duties intended to prevent theft of library materials; controls disruptive or offensive behavior; ensures an orderly, safe, and secure.

Essential Functions and Responsibilities

Patrols buildings and grounds at regular intervals and appropriately handles observed irregularities or problems

Uses non-violent crisis intervention techniques to diplomatically confront people using disruptive, offensive or appropriate behavior; evicts from property as necessary

Prepares and promptly submits written reports regarding accidents, thefts, vandalism, etc.

Prevents theft of Library materials and examines contents of bags, briefcases, etc. in situations where theft is indicated.

Responds to alarm calls at library facilities after regular operating hours, inspects and secures building after completing appropriate notifications

Assists physically challenged customers entering or leaving library facilities

Renders first aid in medical emergencies

Responds, investigates and reports any safety hazard or emergency

Secondary Duties and Responsibilities:

Performs other duties as assigned

Supervisory Responsibilities

No direct reports

Education, Experience, and Training

Qualifications:

High school diploma or G.E.D.

One year full-time security, public safety, corrections, youth services or social sciences experience

Additional Qualifications

Preferred Requirements:

Certification in first aid and CPR, non-violent crisis intervention techniques and self defense (If not certified at the time of employment, certification must be completed within six month probationary period).

Inter-action: Customers, law enforcement representatives and library staff

Clear conviction record (subject to periodic review after employment)

Travel Requirements: Frequent

License and Certification Requirement:

Special Requirements

Driver License and personal vehicle.

Acceptable driving record.

Completion of defensive driving course.

Position Hours

Schedule set by work location; includes rotational on-call duties

> ### 1.3.2 Security Officer
>
> **Library Name:** Richland County Public Library
> **Library Location:** Columbia, South Carolina
> **Population Served:** 320,700
> **Number of Volumes:** 1,059,806
> **Number of Titles:** N/A
> **Periodical Subscriptions:** 2,840

Essential Functions and Responsibilities

EXAMPLES OF WORK: (illustrative only)

Patrols interior and exterior grounds to protect premises, property, and equipment; grounds include all areas of library, and all exterior areas controlled by library, including parking areas; moves constantly and quickly from one area to another as appropriate.

Carefully observes all unusual behavior and activities on library property and responds appropriately.

Assists patrons and staff in emergency situations relating to security and safety.

Interprets, communicates, and enforces library policies, procedures, and rules to patrons, security workers, and other staff, as appropriate.

Communicates information related to safety, security, policies, rules, and library general information in a tactful and highly professional manner; presents a positive image of the library to the general public.

Deals effectively and appropriately with disorderly patrons whenever necessary, including effectively correcting them, removing them, preventing harm to property or persons, and calling law enforcement as appropriate.

Completes appropriate incident reports and maintains required records.

Communicates effectively to other security staff, library staff, and law enforcement officials.

Additional Job Duties

Other Important Responsibilities

Assists with administering emergency First Aid to staff and patrons.

May assist with monitoring and administering staff parking.

May assist library staff in limited aspects of their job duties, as needed.

May locate certain patrons and relay messages from outside callers, within appropriate guidelines.

May provide security to branch locations and special events, as needed.

Performs other duties as required or assigned.

Education, Experience, and Training

MINIMUM QUALIFICATIONS:

Graduation from high school.

At least two years previous experience in security and/or law enforcement.

Supervisory experience desirable.

No criminal record.

Drug free.

Ability to perform job responsibilities

1.3.3 Security Officer

Library Name: Seattle Public Library
Library Location: Seattle, Washington
Population Served: 570,800
Number of Volumes: 999,555
Number of Titles: 899,185
Periodical Subscriptions: N/A

General Summary

Overview: On a typical day, over 10,000 people enter the Central Library and branch libraries. They include parents and children, students and researchers, young and old, book lovers of all kinds, even tourists. They come as individuals and in groups. The Central Library and branch libraries are among the most highly visible and heavily visited public facilities in the city. All are welcome and all must abide by the Library's rules of conduct for their safety and comfort.

Security Officers patrol libraries and work with the public and staff to explain and, when needed, to enforce Library Rules of Conduct and policies and procedures. Their most important tools are their communication and conflict resolution skills and their ability to obtain cooperation. Security Officers must be savvy in recognizing and handling conflicts, infractions and emergencies. They must understand and appreciate the different roles of security and law enforcement personnel. And they must have good judgment in knowing when and how to apply Library policies to individual situations.

Security Officers are required to regularly patrol facilities and work with building security systems. Security Officers may work at the Central Library or branch library locations; assignments and shifts may change as needed. Security Officers who work in branches must be able to collaborate with managers and staff in order to appreciate the unique challenges, distinctive user groups and security needs of each location.

Essential Functions and Responsibilities:

Security patrol.

Patrol and monitor library facilities in order to identify, prevent and respond to violations of the Library's rules of conduct and policies and procedures. Evaluate problems related to the security of Library staff, volunteers, patrons, and property and take appropriate preventative and protective actions. Explain rules and procedures to library visitors and solicit cooperation and compliance. Investigate and handle disturbances and, as needed, obtain police and law enforcement assistance. When needed, enforce exclusion policies. Perform crowd control duties for special events.

Emergency management.

Respond to medical emergencies. Take lead roles in responding to building emergencies and evacuations.

Prevention activities.

Identify and report security and/or safety conditions and concerns. Identify and recommend procedures and methods to prevent property loss and damage. Work with Library staff to identify and resolve security problems and to keep the Security Manager informed of activities and problems.

Liaison activities.

When assigned, serve as liaison between Library staff, police agencies and personnel, contracted security personnel and the public.

Security support activities.

Obtain, record and maintain necessary documentation, records and reports. Operate security and property-related programs such as lost and found materials, staff training, building access control, and surveillance activities.

Knowledge, Skills, and Abilities

- Verbal skills: Excellent verbal communication skills are required. This includes the ability to communicate in English and to communicate with Library visitors for whom English is a second language. Knowledge of conversational Spanish, Asian languages, Eastern European languages or American Sign Language is a plus.

- Conflict resolution skills: Excellent interpersonal and conflict resolution skills.

- Ability to communicate clearly and diplomatically with Library Staff and the public while enforcing security rules, often under stressful situations.

- Ability to resolve conflicts and negotiate solutions without resorting to force or provoking unneeded conflict.

- Ability to persuade.

- Ability to elicit cooperation and compliance under difficult or stressful circumstances.

Occupation-specific skill requirements:

- Knowledge of accepted practices relating to security operations, particularly those that relate to public facilities.

- Excellent observation skills; an ability to remain alert and attentive, anticipate potential disruptive behavior and safety or security threats and take preventative action.

- Ability to prepare clear, detailed and accurately written reports.

- Ability to operate two-way radio, communications and surveillance equipment.

Physical Requirements:

- Ability to perform the physical activities inherent in security patrol duties, such as walking, running, standing, rapidly ascending and descending stairs in a hi-rise building and lifting a fully grown adult in emergency situations. Ability to engage in those physical activities for typical shift durations. Height and weight in proportion. Candidates who are offered employment may be required to successfully pass a physical examination provided by the Library as a condition of employment.

Additional Requirements:

- Possession of a currently valid driver's license. Library vehicles are available for Security use. If an officer is required to use a personal vehicle for work-related activities, mileage reimbursement is provided.

- Able to work evenings and weekends as required.

- If selected, candidates will be required to provide a driver's record abstract and to authorize a check of criminal convictions. Any offer of employment or continuation of employment is contingent on the results of these checks. A record of conviction will not automatically bar employment but the circumstances may be considered in determining if employment will be offered or continued.

- This position requires the employee to wear the supplied uniform and related security gear including, non-lethal defensive equipment and a two-way radio.

Education, Experience, and Training

- Minimum of one year of related experience performing similar duties in settings that (1) require highly visible and sensitive public contact, (2) require exercising conflict resolution and problem-solving skills and (3) require the ability to respond appropriately to critical incidents in an occupational setting. Experience in comparable security occupations is preferred, but not required.

Educational and general skills requirements:

- High School diploma or equivalent.

License and Certification Requirement:

Possession of a currently valid First Aid & CPR certification, or ability to obtain certification within sixty days of employment.

Position Hours

A typical workweek consists of 40 hours. Shifts are typically 8 hours and are staffed to provide building security during evenings and weekends.

Hours: Hours vary and may include Sunday through Saturday.

XVI. Technical Services

Included in this section are technical services administrators; catalogers; acquisitions clerks and librarians; interlibrary loan and processing clerks and assistants; book repairers; and collection development librarians, managers, and technicians.

1.0 ADMINISTRATOR

1.1 TECHNICAL SERVICES ADMINISTRATOR

1.1.1 Technical Services Administrator

Library Name: Seattle Public Library
Library Location: Seattle, Washington
Population Served: 570,800
Number of Volumes: 999,555
Number of Titles: 899,185
Number of Periodical Subscriptions: N/A

General Summary

JOB OVERVIEW:

The Director of Technical and Collection Services serves as advisor to the City Librarian and senior administrators regarding strategies for purchasing, cataloging, and processing of Library books and materials; and provides leadership and counsel regarding electronic resources and emerging issues regarding Internet use and intellectual freedom. This position also directs the work of two units, Bibliographic Services and Collection Development, through subordinate supervisors.

The incumbent will have primary responsibility for determining what methods, sources and processes would be most effective to use in adding books and materials to the Library's collection. This position shares in the responsibility for articulating the basis for selection of books and materials to the public. The Director of Technical and Collections Services reports to the City Librarian and will work closely on an on-going basis with the Director of Collection Development/Center for the Book. This position will also work with the Director of Information Technology to evaluate existing collection services processes and systems, and develop and implement new and more efficient ones.

Essential Functions and Responsibilities

Support intellectual freedom; assume responsibility for how the Library is perceived by staff and the public; and provide leadership to the Library through collaborative problem-solving.

Administer the Library's Collection Services program by ensuring timely, responsive, and well-coordinated acquisition, cataloging, inventory control, processing and preservation services for all materials currently in or being added to the Library's collections.

Ensure effective use of Collection Services Division resources by planning, organizing, controlling, evaluating and measuring impact against service objectives; monitoring the department budget and recommending appropriate annual changes; and directing the training, development, evaluation and use of staff resources, to ensure high-quality service.

Develop, recommend and implement appropriate strategies to achieve program goals; ensure effective and efficient coordination of collection services by reviewing and evaluating operations and procedures, and implementing quality improvements; and by managing related organizational projects.

Ensure the effective and efficient use of materials resources by developing a spending plan to support the collection budget prepared by the Director of Collection Development/Center for the Book.

Oversee the selection of periodicals, continuations and electronic resources for the Library and coordinate related training and communications regarding these resources.

Contribute to efficient use of resources by conducting outreach and developing cooperative efforts with other libraries or informational resources.

Knowledge, Skills, and Abilities

Knowledge of collection development standards and operations for diverse subjects and formats, and current trends in public library collection management.

Applied knowledge of principles of library management and organization including budget development, purchasing and expenditure control, and project management.

Experience supervising, including the ability to train and inspire staff, and promote enthusiastic teamwork.

Working knowledge of and ability to use relevant electronic information resources, including recent technological innovations, emerging information databases and delivery technologies, and library applications.

Excellent interpersonal and creative problem-solving skills.

Exceptional written and oral communication skills, including experience in public speaking.

Positive and enthusiastic approach to public service.

Education, Experience, and Training

An MLS from an ALA-accredited library school, or Washington State certification as a librarian, and directly related in-depth experience.

2.0 LIBRARY ASSISTANTS

2.1 CATALOGING ASSISTANT

2.1.1 Cataloging Assistant

Library Name: York County Public Library
Library Location: Yorktown, Virginia
Population Served: 57,900
Number of Volumes: 143,353
Number of Titles: 84,290
Number of Periodical Subscriptions: 450

General Summary

GENERAL STATEMENT OF JOB

Responsible for performing original and copy cataloging of library collections. Processes new materials, and assists in maintaining the library's catalog. Work is performed under regular supervision from the Library Associate-Technical Services.

Essential Functions and Responsibilities

Electronically catalogs and classifies library books and audio/visual materials.

Assists in maintaining the integrated library catalog.

Assists in processing of new materials.

Serves as a lead worker to other employees working in cataloging and processing of new materials as needed; performs routine clerical and delivery work between the cataloging, circulation, and reference departments.

Additional Job Duties

Performs other related library work as required.

Knowledge, Skills, and Abilities

General knowledge of integrated library systems and networks, online bibliographic retrieval services and cataloging services.

General knowledge of library principles and practices.

General knowledge of the Anglo-American Cataloging Rules.

General knowledge of the Dewey Decimal Classification System and Library of Congress subject headings.

General knowledge of MARC format.

Ability to communicate effectively orally and in writing.

Ability to work independently.

Ability to deal effectively and courteously with the general public and other employees.

Physical and Mental Requirements

Physical Requirements: Must be physically able to operate a variety of machinery and equipment including office equipment such as computers, calculators, copiers, facsimile machines, microfiche machines, CD ROM players, etc. Lifts boxes of up to 50 pounds.

Data Conception: Requires the ability to compare and/or judge the readily observable, functional, structural or compositional characteristics (whether similar or divergent from obvious standards) of data, people or things.

Interpersonal Communication: Requires the ability of speaking and/or signaling people to convey or exchange information. Includes receiving instructions, assignments or directions from superiors.

Language Ability: Requires the ability to read a variety of reports, publications, manuals, etc.

Requires the ability to prepare logs, reports, forms, requests, etc., using prescribed formats.

Intelligence: Ability to apply principles of logical or scientific thinking to define problems, collect data, establish facts, and draw valid conclusions.

Verbal Aptitude: Requires the ability to record and deliver information, to explain procedures, to follow oral and written instructions. Must be able to communicate effectively and efficiently.

Numerical Aptitude: Requires the ability to utilize mathematical formulas; to add and subtract; multiply and divide; utilize decimals and percentages.

Form/Spatial Aptitude: Requires the ability to inspect items for proper length, width and shape.

Motor Coordination: Requires the ability coordinate hands and eyes rapidly and accurately in using office equipment.

Manual Dexterity: Requires the ability to handle a variety of items such as office equipment.

Must have minimal levels of eye/hand/foot coordination.

Physical Communication: Requires the ability to talk and hear: (Talking: expressing or exchanging ideas by means of spoken words. Hearing: perceiving nature of sounds by ear.)

Education, Experience, and Training

Bachelor's degree including coursework in library cataloging, or any equivalent combination of education and experience which provides the required knowledge, skills, and abilities.

2.2 GENERAL LIBRARY ASSISTANT

2.2.1 General Library Assistant

Library Name: Phoenix Public Library
Library Location: Phoenix, Arizona
Population Served: 1,350,435
Number of Volumes: 2,015,587
Number of Titles: 734,921
Number of Periodical Subscriptions: 4,500

General Summary

DISTINGUISHING FEATURES OF THE CLASS:

The fundamental reason this classification exists is to perform technical library work in one or more service or support units of the library system, including bibliographic services and interlibrary loan. Assignments are varied and performed independently and in accordance with established policies and procedures, although direct supervision is received on new or difficult projects. Depending on assignment, the incumbent reports to a Librarian II*Lead, Librarian III, or other supervisor.

Essential Functions and Responsibilities

Catalogs fiction and non-fiction titles, adds copies, and modifies records in the library's computerized bibliographic and cataloging system by operating a keyboard;

Verifies book and material requests submitted by Librarians for appropriate title, ISBN, price, publisher, and edition to ensure the material can be ordered as specified;

Places orders for books and other materials to vendor using an on-line computer systems;

Searches, examines, accesses, updates and edits information found in various local, national, and international computer databases;

Communicates with library users, coworkers, other agencies, and vendors to explain policies, obtain or give information, collect fees or fines, and resolve problems or discrepancies;

Keeps records of work performed such as library materials ordered from vendors, or status of loaned or borrowed material;

Performs a variety of support tasks and other paraprofessional work, such as word processing, bookkeeping, and accounting, research, or other special projects;

Trains staff, volunteers, and library users in the use of specialized computer systems or other equipment.;

Demonstrates continuous effort to improve operations, decrease turnaround times, streamline work processes, and work cooperatively and jointly to provide quality seamless customer service.

Knowledge, Skills, and Abilities

Knowledge of:

Basic technical library materials, equipment, practices and procedures.

Library computer databases and systems.

Ability to:

Work cooperatively with other City employees and the general public.

Communicate in the English language by phone or in person in a one-to-one or group setting.

Comprehend and make inferences from written material.

Learn job-related functions such as library's computer systems and operation of specialized equipment and databases primarily through oral instruction and observation which takes place mainly in an on-the-job training setting.

Enters data or information into a computer terminal, PC, or other keyboard device.

Work safely without presenting a direct threat to self or others.

Education, Experience and Training:

Two years of technical library experience or a two-year library technician degree. Other combinations of experience and education that meet the minimum requirements may be substituted.

Additional Qualifications

Some positions will require the performance of other essential and marginal functions depending upon work location, assignment, or shift.

2.2.2. General Library Assistant

Library Name: Woodland Public Library
Library Location: Woodland, California
Population Served: 46,300
Number of Volumes: 95,372
Number of Titles: N/A
Number of Periodical Subscriptions: 237

Reports To

SUPERVISION RECEIVED AND EXERCISED

General supervision is provided by the Library Services Director. Functional supervision may also be received from higher level library staff. Functional supervision may be provided to lower level library positions.

General Summary

DEFINITION

To perform a wide variety of paraprofessional technical and clerical library work related to such activities as cataloging, classification, circulation and assisting patrons.

DISTINGUISHING CHARACTERISTICS

Library Technical Assistant I: This is the entry-level class in the paraprofessional Library Technical Assistant series. This class is distinguished from the II level by the assignment of the more routine and repetitive duties that are performed according to established procedures and under immediate supervision. Under this concept, positions assigned to the classification of

Library Technical Assistant II which become vacant may reasonably be filled at the Library Technical Assistant I level.

Library Technical Assistant II: This is the journey level class in the Library Technical Assistant series. These positions may be filled by advancement from the I level or, when filled from the outside, require prior library technical experience. Appointment to the II level requires that the employee be performing the full range of duties and meet the qualification standards. A Library Technical Assistant II is expected to perform assigned duties with only occasional instruction or assistance, and work is normally reviewed only on completion. Adequate performance at this level requires the knowledge of general department policies and procedures.

Essential Functions and Responsibilities

The following are typical illustrations of duties encompassed by the job class, not an all-inclusive or limiting list:

Serve at a circulation desk, check books in and out of library; issue library cards;, conduct and oversee inventories and processing of books and other library materials; maintain bibliographic records; and establish and maintain collection files and records.

Provide general information to the public pertaining to library services and programs.

Operate and maintain various library-related equipment and general office equipment.

Perform standard office support work such as answering telephones, ordering supplies, maintaining files and operating computer terminals.

Regular and consistent attendance.

Work cooperatively with others.

Under supervision, conduct various special programs and community outreach activities such as story hours and reading programs.

May train and assign routine tasks and provide technical instruction to part-time positions in area of responsibility.

Locate books and other materials using indices, catalog guides, and computers.

Assist patrons in completing requests for materials not available in the local collection and verify completeness of requests; receive and process inter-library loan requests; maintain inter-library loan services.

Prepare displays and exhibits.

Post, file, maintain recurring accumulative records; compile data and prepare summary activity reports including circulation statistics, user and loan survey reports and materials collection lists.

Perform related duties as assigned.

Knowledge, Skills, and Abilities

QUALIFICATIONS

Library Technical Assistant I

Knowledge of:

General types and uses of library materials, including basic reference sources and materials.

Basic arithmetic.

Basic public desk etiquette, telephone etiquette and communication skills.

Safety principles, practices and procedures.

Operation and programs of a personal computer

Skill to:

Provide information to the general public regarding library department services.

Learn library practices and procedures, and the location of materials in the libraries.

Perform a variety of library technical and clerical work with speed and accuracy.

Communicate clearly and effectively, both in oral and written form; understand and carry out both oral and written instructions.

Type at a speed necessary for adequate job performance.

Establish and maintain effective work relationships with those contacted in the performance of required duties.

Ability to:

Make use of a library automated system including indices, catalogs and other on-line research methods.

Work weekend and evening shifts as assigned.

Develop cooperative public relations with co-workers and the general public.

Meet the physical requirements necessary to safely and effectively perform the assigned duties.

Supervisory Responsibilities

SUPERVISION RECEIVED AND EXERCISED

General supervision is provided by the Library Services Director. Functional supervision may also be received from higher level library staff. Functional supervision may be provided to lower level library positions.

Education, Experience, and Training

Any combination of education and experience that would likely provide the required knowledge and abilities is qualifying. A typical way to obtain the knowledge and abilities would be:

Education

Equivalent to completion of the twelfth grade.

Experience:

One year of experience performing general clerical or related work in a public library system.

3.0 LIBRARY ASSOCIATE

3.1 SENIOR LIBRARY ASSOCIATE

3.1.1 Senior Library Associate

Library Name: Kettleson Memorial Library
Library Location: Sitka Alaska
Population Served: 8835
Number of Volumes: 57,448
Number of Titles: 54,733
Number of Periodical Subscriptions: 279

General Summary

Distinguishing Features of the Class

The principal function of an employee in this class is to provide information to the public on Library services and perform special projects in support of Library activities. This class is distinguished from the class of Library Assistant by the performance of either inter-Library loans or other related Library projects of a similar scale. The work is performed under the direct supervision of the Library Director but considerable leeway is granted for the exercise of independent judgement and initiative. Supervision is exercised over the work of employees in the class of Library Page. An employee in this class performs the duties of other employees in the City and Borough Library as required or as assigned by supervisory personnel. In the absence of the Senior Library Assistant (Acquisitions), an employee in this class may be temporarily assigned specific duties of this position. The nature of the work performed requires that an employee in this class establish and maintain effective working relationships with other Department and City employees, and the public. The principal duties of this class are performed in a public Library environment. An employee in this class may perform any one or more or any additional duties as assigned.

Essential Functions and Responsibilities

Examples of Essential Work (Illustrative Only)

Oversees circulation procedures and activities of Library Assistants, Library Pages and volunteers;

Explores all possible information sources for inquiring patrons, including all materials within the Library consortium of Sitka, other contributing Libraries in the inter-Library loan program and other related sources as necessary;

Assesses, orders and processes requests from patrons and networked institutions through inter-library loans, including the use of the Sitka, Western Network, the Internet and magazine and periodical databases;

Develops displays to promote the features of the Sitka Library;

Provides direct services to Library patrons, including answering patron questions regarding the use of Library resources and general questions relating to a wide variety of academic and related areas;

Checks books, videos, cassettes, CD's and other materials in and out of the Library, renews materials, places books on hold, notifies patrons the arrival of held books and collects overdue fines;

Maintains a knowledge of reference services within the Library, and provides reference services to patrons on a wide variety of subjects and educational levels;

Maintains a safe and secure Library environment through monitoring patrons adherence to Library procedures and guidelines and maintaining an awareness of all persons within the facility;

Registers new patrons, including advising all individuals of the requirements for obtaining a Library card and the responsibilities entailed;

Cleans books and related materials and inspects all circulating materials for damages, missing pieces or other signs of abuse;

Distributes new magazines and newspapers, coordinates the reshelving process by organizing checked-in books and reshelving books as necessary;

Prepares the Library for opening times by bringing up all computers, maintaining a clean and orderly environment and ensuring that all services are readily usable by patrons;

Prepares Library for closing time by locking doors, unlocking the bookdrop, logging off all computers and straightening the Libraries common areas;

Provides demonstrations to patrons in the use of technological aspects of the Library, including microfilm, microfiche, Library's computer systems, Infotrac magazine computer index, CD ROM computer programs and Internet systems;

Performs maintenance duties on Library materials, including replacing covers on books, replacing spine labels and pockets and cleaning and repairing videos as necessary;

Locates lost books on shelves through the use of a trace computer list;

Inventories reserve/hold shelf through the use of a computer generated report;

Distributes books to and from Sitka areas schools;

Gathers materials for special displays as necessary and requested;

Greets all Library patrons and members of the public in a courteous and professional manner;

Provides needed information and demonstrations concerning how to perform certain work tasks to new employees in the same or similar class of positions;

Keeps immediate supervisor and designated others fully and accurately informed concerning work progress, including present and potential work problems and suggestions for new or improved ways of addressing such problems;

Attends meetings, conferences, workshops and training sessions and reviews publications and audio-visual materials to become and remain current on the principles, practices and new developments in assigned work areas;

Responds to citizens' questions and comments in a courteous and timely manner;

Communicates and coordinates regularly with appropriate others to maximize the effectiveness and efficiency of interdepartmental operations and activities;

Performs other related duties as assigned.

Knowledge, Skills, and Abilities

Thorough knowledge of standard library practices and procedures;

Thorough knowledge of equipment used in library operations, including microfilm, microfiche, video and related communications equipment, CD ROM, Library computer systems and Internet services;

Ability to ascertain the needs of Library patrons and direct them to the needed resource within the Library or contact outside services to ensure all available information is obtainable to the patron;

Ability in basic math computations and alphabetic filing systems;

Ability to communicate well with others, both orally and in writing, using both technical and non-technical language;

Ability to understand and follow oral and/or written policies, procedures and instructions;

Ability to prepare and present accurate and reliable reports containing findings and recommendations;

Ability to operate or quickly learn to operate a personal computer using standard or customized software applications appropriate to assigned tasks;

Ability to use logical and creative thought processes to develop solutions according to written specifications and/or oral instructions;

Ability to perform a wide variety of duties and responsibilities with accuracy and speed under the pressure of time-sensitive deadlines;

Ability and willingness to quickly learn and put to use new skills and knowledge brought about by rapidly changing information and/or technology;

Integrity, ingenuity and inventiveness in the performance of assigned tasks.

Physical and Mental Requirements

Sufficient clarity of speech and hearing or other communication capabilities, with or without reasonable accommodation, which permits the employee to communicate effectively;

Sufficient vision or other powers of observation, with or without reasonable accommodation, which permits the employee to read books and patron requests;

Sufficient manual dexterity with or without reasonable accommodation, which permits the employee to type and record library files;

Sufficient personal mobility and physical reflexes, with or without reasonable accommodation, which permits the employee to reshelve library materials.

Education, Experience and Training

Graduation from high school or possession of a GED, preferably supplemented by an Bachelor's Degree or equivalent in a related field; and

Considerable experience using basic research techniques, library sciences or other related fields; or

Any equivalent combination of experience, education and training which provides the knowledge, skills and abilities necessary to perform the work.

Additional Qualifications

Required Special Qualifications
None

4.0 PRESERVATION—BOOK REPAIRER

4.1 BOOK REPAIRER

4.1.1 Book Repairer

Library name: San Francisco Public Library
Library Location: San Francisco, California
Population Served: 793,600
Number of Volumes: 2,327,847
Number of Titles: N/A
Number of Periodical Subscriptions: 12,533

Reports To

Under supervision of the Preservation Unit manager,
General Description:

POSITION DESCRIPTION: Under supervision of the Preservation Unit manager, the Book Repairer performs conservation treatments on books and other circulating and reference materials according to SFPL standards of appropriate treatment, quality of repair and productivity.

Essential Functions and Responsibilities

Performing book binding hinge repairs (tightening hinges, regluing cover to text, hollow tubes, new end sheet and/or super, rebacking, recasing, recording textblocks, repair of broken sewing, sewing or wire stapling pamphlets into pamphlet binders, drill and sewing for temporary use materials, side stapling temporary use paperbacks);

Performing book repair-textblock treatment (tipping in pages, hinging in pages, plates, or foldouts, hinging or tipping in pockets, photocopying replacement leaves, inserting reference plates); performing paper repair (using paste and/or paste and Japanese tissue, flattening paper, guarding folds, attaching hinges, refolding maps and charts); replacing mylar jackets soiled or torn; steaming or cleaning off spines of library materials.

Maintaining monthly production statistics and submitting them in a timely manner; answering phone inquiries.

Assisting in response to damage of library materials; monitoring use of supplies and notifying manager when low.

Maintaining tools, equipment and workspace in clean and workable condition; performing other job-related duties as assigned.

Knowledge, Skills, and Abilities

Excellent hand to eye coordination skills and the ability to perform exacting hand work with care, precision and attention to detail

Ability to work independently with minimum supervision and to meet quality standards and productivity goals

Knowledge of book structure, new and old; including methods of leaf attachment

Extensive working knowledge of techniques, tools, materials and practices in the field of Preservation Book Repair and a sensitivity to the needs and care of items

Ability to evaluate each item and to decide on the appropriate technique to use in repairing the item

Good communication (oral and written), interpersonal and organizational skills

Note:

Desirable skills are intended to describe characteristics specific to each particular position and are not intended to discourage persons from applying.

Education, Experience, and Training

MINIMUM QUALIFICATIONS: 1. Two (2) years (4,000 hours) of verifiable experience in hand binding, book repair and conservation of books and similar printed materials *; AND 2. Ability to lift and move 30 pounds.

*SUBSTITUTION: 1. College level course work in book binding or book restoration may be substituted for the required experience on a year for year basis (30 semester units/45 quarter units equal one year of experience) AND/OR 2. One (1) year of formal training through an apprenticeship or internship in bookbinding or conservation also may be substituted for one year of the required experience.

Position Description:

The normal work schedule for this position is Monday through Friday from 8:00 AM to 5:00 PM (May include evenings and weekends when necessary.)

5.0 PURCHASING

5.1 BUYER

5.1.1 Buyer

Library Name: Santa Barbara Public Library
Library Location: Santa Barbara, California
Population Served: 218,300
Number of Volumes: 193,888
Number of Titles: N/A
Number of Periodical Subscriptions: 421

General Summary

DEFINITION

Under general supervision performs a variety of complex technical duties involved in the procurement and purchasing of materials, supplies, services and equipment required in the maintenance and operation of the City.

Essential Functions and Responsibilities

Essential duties may include but are not limited to, the following:

Receive, examine and process department requisitions; answer questions and provide information to City customers, vendors, suppliers and contractors.

Contact vendors and contractors by letter, fax and telephone to obtain quotes and bids for stock and special order items; research availability, quality, and price of equipment and supplies; prepare summary and comparison documentation.

Evaluate and analyze quotes and bids; review specifications; prepare quick quotes, spreadsheets, comparisons and evaluation data from quotes and bids.

Prepare purchase orders, based on approved requisitions, requests for proposals, bids and other similar and necessary documents related to the purchasing and procurement of supplies, equipment, services and materials.

Purchase a diversified range of supplies, services and equipment for City departments; expedite the delivery of purchased materials and services; make necessary adjustments with suppliers and vendors regarding replacements, incomplete orders, damaged supplies or unsatisfactory services.

Establish schedules and methods for providing purchasing services consistent with approved policies and procedures; identify resource needs; review needs with appropriate supervisory or management staff; allocate resources accordingly.

Review, plan and prioritize daily, weekly and monthly work assignments to meet the operational goals of the division. Assist in the recommendation and implementation of division and department goals and objectives.

Investigate and develop new supply sources; stay abreast of new trends and innovations in routinely purchased supplies, material, services and equipment.

Proficiently use the computer, calculator and telephone to prepare purchase orders, memos, letters and spreadsheets showing comparison data.

Proficiently use the computer, calculator and telephone to prepare purchase orders, memos, letters and spreadsheets showing comparison data.

Maintain a variety of logs and records relating to the purchase and procurement of materials, supplies and equipment.

Maintain and use an appropriate library of catalogs, price lists and other purchasing material to support City personnel seeking current information on new products.

Maintain an inventory of general office supplies.

Make recommendations to the General Services Manager and/or immediate supervisor as necessary to maintain quality customer service to all City departments.

Perform a variety of general clerical and accounting duties as required to support procurement activities.

Maintain historical computer and hardcopy files of quotes, bids and council agenda reports to support similar purchases

Work with department representatives to develop clear, concise specifications and product needs.

Perform related duties and responsibilities as required.

Knowledge, Skills, and Abilities

QUALIFICATIONS
Knowledge of:

Public or municipal purchasing operations, services and activities.

Pertinent codes and regulations concerning municipal purchasing.

Types of materials, supplies and equipment commonly used in public municipal services.

Municipal purchasing principles and practices.

Procurement practices, specifically regarding public works, motor pool, parks, recreation and facility maintenance and repairs.

Modern office procedures, practices and methods and the use of computer equipment.

Basic mathematical principles.

Principles, procedures and practices of financial record keeping and reporting.

Ability to:

Organize and review assigned work.

Evaluate quality and price of products to judge suitability of goods and alternatives offered.

Maintain detailed and accurate operational and financial records.

Read, interpret, apply and explain City purchasing policies and procedures.

Use a computer, type at a speed necessary for successful job performance with extreme accuracy.

Work independently with assigned tasks.

Communicate clearly and concisely, both orally and in writing.

Ability to:

Establish and maintain effective working relationships with those contacted in the course of work.

Read, understand and interpret complex specifications.

Maintain physical condition appropriate to the performance of assigned duties and responsibilities this may include the following:

Walking, standing or sitting for extended periods of time

Operate assigned equipment

Maintain effective audio-visual discrimination and perception needed for:

Making safe and accurate observations

Communicating with others both orally and in writing

Reading and writing

Operating assigned equipment and vehicles

Education, Experience, and Training

Any combination of experience and training that would likely provide the required knowledge and abilities. A typical way to obtain the knowledge and abilities would be:

Experience:

Two (2) years experience in purchasing/buying or procuring goods, services and materials in a public or municipal agency.

Training:

Equivalent to the completion of the twelfth grade, supplemented by college level course work in purchasing, contract administration, accounting, or a related field.

Physical and Mental Requirements

Essential functions may require maintaining physical condition necessary for sitting or standing for prolonged periods of time.

Work Environment

Environmental Conditions:

Office/warehouse environment.

License and Certification Requirements

Possession of, or the ability to obtain an appropriate, valid driver's license.

Disclaimers

Class specifications are intended to present a descriptive list of the range of duties performed by employees in the class. Specifications are not intended to reflect all duties performed within the job.

> 5.1.2 Buyer
>
> **Library Name:** Williamsburg Regional Library System
> **Library Location:** Williamsburg, Virginia
> **Population Served:** 60,100
> **Number of Volumes:** 261,243
> **Number of Titles:** N/A
> **Number of Periodical Subscriptions:** 562

General Summary

NATURE OF WORK:

Under the supervision of the Budget Management Specialist, the Buyer II performs a variety of clerical and administrative tasks to support the activities of the Library, including responsibility for evaluating and selecting vendors for purchases of supplies and equipment, managing the formal bid process, preparing accounts payable invoices for processing, and maintaining encumbrance reports. This position also administers the Library's participation in the State's set-off debt program and assists in the preparation of payroll.

Essential Functions and Responsibilities

Responsible for evaluating, prioritizing, monitoring, negotiating, ordering, receiving, and distributing departmental requests for supplies and office equipment.

Prepares accounts payable invoices for weekly processing and assists with check disbursement and invoice filing.

Reviews and ensures accuracy of the monthly encumbrance report and provides analysis on the supply budget and other purchasing activities.

Assists in the preparation of payroll.

Responsible for coordinating and monitoring office equipment and repair and maintenance schedules for

Library copiers, fax, and other office machines to ensure their efficient operation.

Serves as in-house travel agent, coordinating plans for training workshops.

Administers Library's participation in the State's set-off debt program.

Records and deposits contributions for Friends, Williamsburg Regional Library Foundation, gifts and memorials, Adopt-A-Book and Youth Services using development software. Provides Friends administrative support for mailings and manages the membership database.

Provides an average of two hours a week of library public service.

May participate in library-wide committees or projects.

Performs other tasks as needed.

Knowledge, Skills, and Abilities

Expertise in word processing, spreadsheets and other computer software.

Ability to compile and analyze information, including statistical and financial data.

Ability to organize work, set priorities, use time effectively, works independently, and meets deadlines.

Excellent written and verbal communication skills.

Ability to maintain records in a standard, orderly, systematic fashion.

Ability to establish and maintain effective working relationships with staff members, vendors, government employees, and the general public.

Ability to analyze and to creatively solve problems related to the position.

Work Environment

Work occurs typically sitting in an office, with occasional walking, light lifting, and other limited physical activities; frequent sustained operation of office equipment is required. Traveling between the two libraries is required. Regular contact is made with employees, vendors, government agencies, and the general public.

Computer, copier, calculator, coin sorter and other office equipment as required. The job is located in two libraries.

Education, Experience, and Training

MINIMUM QUALIFICATIONS:

Undergraduate degree or combination of higher education and experience in related fields to provide necessary expertise. Extensive computer experience required, including using electronic resources (Internet) for vendor and procurement sources. Basic knowledge of government procurement processes preferred. Experience working within a library environment preferred.

Additional Qualifications

NECESSARY SPECIAL QUALIFICATIONS:

Ability to travel among various library sites.

6.0 CLERKS

6.1 ACQUISITIONS CLERK

6.1.1 Acquisitions Clerk

Library Name: Cumberland County Public Library

Library Location: Carlisle, Pennsylvania

Population Served: 221,162

Number of Volumes: N/A

Number of Titles: 7,571

Periodical Subscriptions: 17

Reports To

SUPERVISION RECEIVED:

Receives occasional instruction and some supervision from Technical Services Coordinator in regard to daily work duties.

General Summary

OVERALL OBJECTIVE OF JOB:

To provide library materials to the public in a timely manner through collecting and placing orders for library materials, receiving and processing invoices and monitoring vendor discounts and services.

Essential Functions and Responsibilities

Collects and places orders for library materials using software for acquisitions and for interfacing with vendor databases.

Electronically transmits orders and receives confirmations; monitors back orders, corrects inaccurate invoices, and purges old orders in coordination with supervisor.

Coordinates ordering schedule with all system collection development staff.

Manages standing order systems.

Monitors fund accounts to make sure that materials are ordered against the appropriate account and those adequate funds are available to make purchases.

Evaluates new vendors and discounts and reports results to supervisor.

Evaluates and recommends changes to workflow for acquisitions.

Receives shipments of new library materials, unpacks and sorts them for further processing.

Prepares invoices and member library vouchers for submission to the library system's Administrative Assistant.

Generates statistical reports and records.

Searches and loads bibliographic records from ITS and OCLC utilities.

Additional Job Duties

Attends meetings, training seminars as required.

Performs other job-related duties as needed.

Knowledge, Skills, and Abilities

Must be able to speak and understand the English language in an understandable manner in order to carry out essential functions of job.

Must possess ability to communicate effectively.

Must possess ability to function independently, have flexibility and the ability to work effectively with clients, co-workers and others.

Must possess knowledge of various computer programs, bibliographic support systems and the Internet.

Must possess the technical knowledge of operating personal computers and other office equipment with accuracy and reasonable speed.

Must have the ability to instruct others in use of a variety of computer programs and methods.

Must be able to produce required reports, printouts, data as needed by various departments and to assist others with computer needs and services.

Physical and Mental Requirements

Must possess ability to record, convey and present information, explain procedures and follow instructions.

Must be able to sit for long periods throughout the workday, with intermittent periods of standing, walking, bending, squatting, twisting, pushing, carrying, and overhead reaching to carry out essential duties of job.

Must have above average mental attention or concentration to work procedures.

Must have above average attention to detail or accuracy of bibliographic records.

Coordinated movements of fingers/hand; and simple movements of feet/legs and torso.

Medium to heavy work, with lifting/carrying of objects with weights of twenty to fifty pounds.

Must be able to pay close attention to details and concentrate on work.

Work Environment

Works indoors in adequate work space, with adequate temperatures, ventilation and lighting.

Normal office exposure to noise, stress and disruptions.

May occasionally drive to other county offices.

Supervisory Responsibilities

SUPERVISION GIVEN:

Assists with coordinating daily work of clerical staff.

Education, Experience, and Training

EDUCATION/TRAINING:

BA or BS in business, library science, or related field.

WORK EXPERIENCE:

1-2 years progressively responsible clerical experience.

6.2 GENERAL CLERK

6.2.1 General Clerk

Library Name: Anacortes Public Library
Library Location: Anacortes, Washington
Population Served: 14,500
Number of Volumes: N/A
Number of Titles: 55,565
Number of Periodical Subscriptions: 126

Reports To

Technical Services Coordinator

PRINCIPAL PURPOSE OF JOB: This position performs a variety of clerical and technical duties. Assignments typically involve preparing, introducing and maintaining materials for general circulation.

LEVEL OF AUTHORITY: Performs routine and repetitive duties independently with only general supervision and according to well-known practices and procedures. Performs relatively more complex assignments and specialized functions under close and frequent supervision. Responsibility for accuracy and courtesy is important.

Essential Functions and Responsibilities

Perform technical processing services necessary to receive, prepare and introduce materials for general circulation.

Repair damaged Library materials as required. If directed, send out to bindery for materials that cannot be repaired in-house.

Additional Job Duties

May perform portions of the work of higher or lower classified positions, as required.

Process orders for Library materials, as directed.

Knowledge, Skills, and Abilities

Other

Attention to detail and accuracy.

Ability to communicate effectively, patiently and courteously with City employees, patrons and other community members.

Ability to handle multiple activities or interruptions at once and to work positively and effectively within a team model.

Ability to work weekday, evening, weekend and morning hours.

Physical and Mental Requirements

Physical Strength, for example, to push loaded book cart weighing approximately 300 pounds on level floor and up ramp, to lift or maneuver onto cart loads up to 50 pounds and to carry cartons of books up and down stairs.

Ability to bend, stoop and lift for prolonged periods in cramped spaces.

Ability to sit and use computer workstation, including keyboard and visual display terminal, for extended periods of time.

Tools and Equipment Used

Office equipment, such as; computer, modem, typewriter, adding machine, microfiche reader, paper cutter, fax, copier, telephone and postage meter. Various tools for book repair and glue guns and lamination equipment.

Work Environment

Work is performed primarily in an indoor office setting at the library, in frequently dusty atmosphere with potential exposure to airborne pathogens.

Education, Experience, and Training

QUALIFICATIONS

Technical

Must have computer ability to adequately utilize automated library cataloging systems.

Must have a basic ability to work with numbers accurately and understand verbal and written instructions, such as would be acquired in four years of high school or equivalent.

Prior library experience preferred.

Must be bondable.

Additional Qualifications

OTHER

As an absolute condition of employment, employees are required upon hire to sign a drug-free workplace agreement and an agreement not to use tobacco products of any kind while on the job.

The statements contained in this job description reflect general details as necessary to describe the principal functions of this job, the level of knowledge and skill typically required and the scope of responsibility. It should not be considered an all-inclusive listing of work requirements. Individuals may perform other duties as assigned, including work in other functional areas to cover absences or provide relief, to equalize peak work periods or otherwise to balance the workload.

6.3 INTERLIBRARY LOAN CLERK

6.3.1 Interlibrary Loan Clerk

Library Name: Anacortes Public Library
Library Location: Anacortes, Washington
Population Served: 14,500
Number of Volumes: N/A
Number of Titles: 55,565
Number of Periodical Subscriptions: 126

Reports To

Assistant Director, Adult Collection and Staff Development

General Summary

PRINCIPAL PURPOSE OF JOB: This position performs a variety of clerical and technical duties. Assignments typically involve processing all inter-library loans and providing basic reference assistance. Depending upon schedule and workload, may perform the duties of a public services clerk.

LEVEL OF AUTHORITY: Performs routine and repetitive duties independently with only general supervision and according to well-known practices and procedures. Performs relatively more complex assignments and specialized functions under close and frequent supervision. Responsibility for accuracy and courtesy is important due to potential adverse Library patron relationships.

Essential Functions and Responsibilities

Process inter-library loans from initial patron request to delivery of borrowed material.

Keep records and statistics regarding inter-library loans, generating reports as required.

Provide basic reference assistance to patrons, seeking assistance from professional librarians as needed.

Respond to public inquiries in a courteous manner; provide information within scope of knowledge and refer to employee of higher classification as appropriate.

Enforce Library rules.

Additional Job Duties

May perform portions of the work of higher classified positions, as required.

Check out to patron and receive Library print and non-print materials.

Calculate and collect funds due from patrons.

Record receipt of returned materials and reintroduce materials into circulation system.

Process new and replacement patron cards.

Knowledge, Skills, and Abilities

Other

Attention to detail and accuracy.

Ability to communicate effectively, patiently and courteously with City employees, patrons and other community members.

Ability to handle multiple activities or interruptions at once and to work positively and effectively within a team model.

Ability to work a schedule including weekday, evening, weekend and morning hours.

Use of Tools and Equipment

Office equipment, such as; computer, modem, typewriter, adding machine, microfiche reader, paper cutter, fax, copier, telephone and postage meter. May use various tools for book repair, glue guns and lamination equipment.

Physical and Mental Requirements

Physical

Strength, for example, to push loaded book cart weighing approximately 300 pounds on level floor and up ramp, to lift or maneuver onto cart loads up to 50 pounds and to carry cartons of books up and down stairs.

Ability to bend, stoop and lift for prolonged periods in cramped spaces.

Ability to sit and use computer workstation, including keyboard and visual display terminal, for extended periods of time.

Work Environment

Work is performed primarily in an indoor office setting at the library, in frequently dusty atmosphere with potential exposure to airborne pathogens.

Education, Experience, and Training

QUALIFICATIONS

Technical

Two years of higher education required, BA or BS degree desirable.

Must have computer ability to adequately utilize automated library circulation systems and assist patrons with use of Internet.

Must have a basic ability to work with numbers accurately and understand verbal and written instructions.

Prior library experience preferred.

Must have excellent verbal and non-verbal communication skills.

Must be bondable.

Ability to keep accurate records and follow through on details.

Additional Qualifications

OTHER

As an absolute condition of employment, employees are required upon hire to sign a drug-free workplace agreement and an agreement not to use tobacco products of any kind while on the job.

The statements contained in this job description reflect general details as necessary to describe the principal functions of this job, the level of knowledge and skill typically required and the scope of responsibility. It should not be considered an all-inclusive listing of work requirements. Individuals may perform other duties as assigned, including work in other functional areas to cover absences or provide relief, to equalize peak work periods or otherwise to balance the work load.

6.4 PROCESSING CLERK

6.4.1 Processing Clerk

Library Name: Cumberland County Library System
Library Location: Carlisle, Pennsylvania
Population Served: 221,162
Number of Volumes: N/A
Number of Titles: 7,571
Periodical Subscriptions: 17

Reports To

SUPERVISION RECEIVED:

Receives occasional instruction and some supervision from Technical Services librarians in regard to daily work duties.

General Summary

OVERALL OBJECTIVE OF JOB:

To provide library materials to the public in a timely manner through processing materials for library collections.

Essential Functions and Responsibilities

Applies covers, packaging, pockets, bookplates, security strips, etcl to library materials, processing approximately 21 to 25 items per hour in a neat and thorough manner.

Stamps materials with appropriate property stamps and applies bookplates

Maintains inventory of processing supplies.

Orders and receives processing supplies.

Assists in packing and unpacking of library materials.

Assists in loading and unloading of materials in delivery area.

Sorts materials to send to member libraries.

Performs clerical functions on local database as assigned.

Additional Job Duties

OTHER DUTIES OF JOB:

Attends meetings, training seminars as required.

Performs other job related duties as needed.

Knowledge, Skills, and Abilities

Must be able to speak and understand the English language in an understandable manner in order to carry out essential functions of job.

Must possess ability to communicate effectively.

Must possess ability to function independently, have flexibility and the ability to work effectively with clients, co-workers and others.

Physical and Mental Requirements

Must be able to sit for long periods throughout the work day, with intermittent periods of standing, walking, bending, squatting, twisting, pushing, carrying, and overhead reaching to carry out essential duties of job.

Must have good mental attention or concentration to follow work procedures.

Coordinated movements of fingers/hand; and simple movements of feet/legs and torso.

Medium work, with occasional lifting/carrying of objects with weights of twenty to fifty pounds.

Must be able to pay close attention to details and concentrate on work.

Work Environment

Works indoors in adequate work space, with adequate temperatures, ventilation and lighting.

Normal office exposure to noise, stress and disruptions.

Part-time position, approximately 20 to 22.5 hours per week.

Supervisory Responsibilities

SUPERVISION GIVEN:

None.

Education, Experience, and Training

QUALIFICATIONS:

EDUCATION/TRAINING:

High school or GED.

WORK EXPERIENCE:

None

6.4.2 Processing Clerk

Library Name: Public Library of Cincinnati and Hamilton County
Library Location: Cincinnati, Ohio
Population Served: 840,443
Number of Volumes: 4,799,527
Number of Titles: 1,239,511
Number of Periodical Subscriptions: 6,782

Reports To

Processing Department Manager

General Summary

Position Summary:

This position performs clerical work associated with the processing of library materials.

Essential Functions and Responsibilities

Responsibilities (not all-inclusive) all of the duties listed below are essential job functions for which reasonable accommodations will be made. All job requirements listed indicate the minimum level knowledge, skills and/or ability deemed necessary to perform the job proficiently. This job description is not to be construed as an exhaustive statement of duties, responsibilities or requirements. Employees may be required to perform any other job-related instructions as requested by their supervisor subject to reasonable accommodations.

Essential Functions:

Performs data entry into various automated systems.

Prepares binds for commercial binders.

Processes print and non-print materials for Main Library departments and branches.

Processes returned shipments from commercial binders.

Performs complex mends of library materials and creates pamphlet binders.

Compiles statistics.

Other assigned duties.

Knowledge, Skills, and Abilities

Minimum Qualifications:

Ability to manipulate books and other media.

Knowledge of basic business mathematics.

Ability to handle multiple projects and assigns priorities.

Ability to work independently.

Ability to communicate in oral and written form.

Ability to perform detailed work.

Able to successfully operate a computer and perform data entry accurately at a speed of at least 30 wpm.

Specific Requirements:

Must be able to read, write, speak and understand the English language.

Must be able to effectively communicate with the public.

Must possess the ability to make independent decisions when circumstances warrant.

Must be able to perform basic math skills, adding, subtracting, dividing etc.

Must be able to operate office equipment including information management tools (Windows applications, database, etc.).

Must possess the ability to deal tactfully with personnel, visitors, government agencies/personnel, and the general public.

Must possess ability and willingness to work harmoniously with other personnel.

Must be willing to seek out new methods and principles and be willing to incorporate them into existing practices.

Must have patience, tact, a cheerful disposition and enthusiasm as well as the willingness to handle difficult staff and situations.

Must not pose a direct threat to the health or safety of other individuals in the workplace.

Physical and Mental Requirements

Physical and Sensory Requirements (with or without the aid of mechanical devices)

Physical and Sensory Requirements: (with or without the aid of mechanical devices)

Must be able to push and pull loaded book trucks.

Must be able to move intermittently throughout the workday.

Must be able to cope with the mental and emotional stress of the position.

Must be able to see and hear, or use prosthetics that will enable these senses to function adequately to assure that the requirements of this position can be fully met.

Must function independently and have flexibility, personal integrity, and the ability to work effectively with personnel, visitors, government agencies, and general public, etc.

Must meet the general health requirements set forth by the policies of the Public Library, which may include a physical examination.

Must be able to push, pull, move and/or lift a minimum of 60 lbs. (exclude for periodicals) to a minimum height of 2 feet and be able to push, pull, move and /or carry such weight a minimum of 5 feet.

Work Environment

Ability to manipulate books and other forms of media.

Works in assigned area, including office areas, training rooms, library, etc, as necessary.

Moves intermittently during working hours.

Works flexible hours.

Is subject to frequent interruptions.

Is subject to work beyond normal working hours, evenings, weekends and holidays when necessary.

Attends and participates in continuing educational programs designed to keep you abreast of changes in your profession.

Supervisory Responsibilities

Supervises: None

Education, Experience, and Training

High School graduate or equivalent

6.5 PROCESSING AUDIOVISUAL CLERK,

6.5.1 Processing Audiovisual Clerk

Library Name: Cuyahoga County Public Library
Library Location: Parma, Ohio
Population Served: 607,909
Number of Volumes: 3,297,420
Number of Titles: N/A
Number of Periodical Subscriptions: 8,502

General Summary

GENERAL SUMMARY

Under moderate supervision, performs specialized bibliographic and clerical tasks to research, identify, and compile information for materials purchases for branch libraries, AVB public performance collection, and individual requests; completes AVB statistics; completes processing of AVB collection materials and ordering processes for AVB and central selection media.

Essential Functions and Responsibilities

A. Complies with work scheduling and attendance requirements according to reasonable policy and practices. Staffing for branch and regional libraries and some Administration (ADM) departments requires rotational scheduling, which includes evening and weekend (Saturday and Sunday) hours. Most ADM departments are weekday operations.

B. Consistently presents Cuyahoga County Public Library and its services in a positive manner and adheres to customer service guidelines and procedures as established by the Library.

C. Complies with the established rules of operation, procedures, and policies when using library computers, peripheral hardware, and software. Individual passwords and any other confidential information regarding library records shall be kept confidential.

Researches CLIO databases, the internet and various other video print and electronic sources, including direct contact with outside vendors, for new titles, releases, re-releases, and materials availability.

Compiles information into automated acquisitions module and uses electronic word processing program to create enhanced printed selection lists for distribution to branch staff.

Orders media for public performance collection, audits order and inspects materials upon arrival for accuracy.

Orders and assigns all central selection entertainment audio visual materials for branches. Maintains updated materials lists for distribution to branches and the public as required.

Determines the physical and technical quality of public performance licensed materials using various AV equipment, and documents current condition.

Creates pre-cataloging worksheet for public performance collection materials by scanning materials using various types of equipment, completing form, and forward to Catalog Department.

Completes internal scheduling cards and specialized lists for AVB Department materials.

Assists customers with materials requests.

Compiles media materials statistics into monthly report for department Manager.

Requests materials from producers and distributors for preview and arranges materials for rental for branch programs.

Substitutes for other department staff as required.

Knowledge, Skills, and Abilities

Knowledge of general office procedures such as filing, copying and record keeping.

Knowledge of CCPL AV materials and materials sources.

Computer literate with knowledge of Windows software applications.

Ability to operate computer keyboard.

Summary Minimum Education & Experience Required

Physical and Mental Requirements

Work involves near continuous use of computer terminal.

Requires light physical effort such as stooping and bending, and occasional lifting of lightweight objects (up to 25 pounds).

Education, Experience, and Training

High school diploma or GED.

One to two years library service experience.

License and Certification Requirements

OTHER TESTING / LICENSES REQUIRED
A criminal background check is required.

Disclaimers

The intent of this position description is to provide a representative summary of the major duties and responsibilities performed by incumbents of this job. Incumbents may be requested to perform job-related tasks other than those specifically presented in this description.

7.0 ACQUISITIONS LIBRARIAN

7.1 Acquisitions Librarian

7.1.1 Acquisitions Librarian

Library Name: Williamsburg Regional Library System
Library Location: Williamsburg, Virginia
Population Served: 60,100
Number of Volumes: 261,243
Number of Titles: N/A
Number of Periodical Subscriptions: 562

General Summary

NATURE OF WORK:

Under the supervision of the Assistant Library Director, the Acquisitions Administrator is responsible for the ordering and payment of all library collection items. Duties include assisting in the selection of some library materials; tracking the materials budget; processing invoices and reconciling account balances; administering the gift, memorial, and donation program; and supervising the acquisitions assistants, the technical services clerk, and volunteers. Participates in the analysis and planning of technical services operations within the Support Services department.

Essential Functions and Responsibilities

Manages the ordering of all formats of library materials through multiple electronic vendor systems as well as by telephone, fax, and mail; maintains accurate vendor records, including fund accounts and addresses; coordinates the checking of vendor backorder reports against Dynix reports to ensure order accuracy; maintains source materials collection for special order requests.

Procures library materials based on vendor history, quality of service, and discount for best value and efficiency; negotiates purchase terms and discounts with vendors; reviews buying consortium contracts.

Supervises the receiving of library materials; oversees the resolution of missing and/or incorrect orders and shipping problems; prepares materials to be returned by writing credit slips and adjusting the computer and invoice records.

Processes invoices on the library's automated acquisitions module and creates vouchers to be forwarded, with the invoices, to the finance manager; checks monthly vendor statements to make sure all invoices and credits have been processed correctly

on the library's automated acquisitions module; maintains all automated fund accounts—budgeted and donated.

Manages the ordering, processing, routing, and payment for all serials.

Hires, trains, supervises, and evaluates acquisitions assistants and technical services clerk; trains and supervises acquisitions volunteers.

Provides pertinent budget reports to all department heads on a monthly basis, plus other reports as needed.

Coordinates interface between acquisitions system and other library automated modules with appropriate library departments.

Meets with donors and assists in selection of memorial and gift materials; develops new donor programs;

Maintains files and provides monthly reports on all memorials and gift donations; places holds on requested materials; maintains memorial fund accounts.

Acts as liaison with Friends book sale volunteers; maintains Friends grant accounts for materials.

Develops and updates policies and procedures for acquisitions, serials, and donations.

May participate in library-wide committees or projects.

Performs other tasks as assigned.

Knowledge, Skills, and Abilities

Comprehensive knowledge of books, publishers, and library vendors.

Knowledge of purchasing procedures and accounting.

Ability to maintain online financial records and generate reports.

Ability to organize work, set priorities, use time effectively, work independently, meet deadlines, and delegate tasks.

Excellent written and verbal communication skills.

Ability to establish and maintain effective working relationships with staff members, vendors, and the general public.

Work Environment

The job is located in the James City County Library. Administers work typically sitting in an office, with occasional walking, light lifting, and other limited physical activities. Frequent sustained operation of video display terminal is required. Computer, CD ROM drive/modem, fax and other office equipment as required.

Regular contact is made with employees, vendors, and the general public.

Education, Experience, and Training

MINIMUM QUALIFICATIONS:

Bachelor's degree or combination of higher education and experience in related fields to provide necessary expertise. Minimum of two years library or bookstore experience. Computer experience and business management or accounting training required. Supervisory experience preferred.

Additional Qualifications

NECESSARY SPECIAL QUALIFICATIONS:

Requires the ability to travel among various library sites.

8.0 CATALOGING LIBRARIAN,

8.1 CATALOGING LIBRARIAN–GENERAL

> ### 8.1.1 Cataloging Librarian–General
>
> **Library Name:** Cumberland County Public Library
> **Library Location:** Carlisle, Pennsylvania
> **Population Served:** 221,162
> **Number of Volumes:** N/A
> **Number of Titles:** 7,751
> **Periodical Subscriptions:** 17

Reports To

SUPERVISION RECEIVED:

Receives occasional instruction and some supervision from Technical Services Coordinator in regard to daily work duties.

General Summary

OVERALL OBJECTIVE OF JOB:

To provide library materials to the public in a timely manner through classification, cataloging, and oversight of unitís clerical staff.

Essential Functions and Responsibilities

Classifies and catalogs library materials, using OCLC cataloging module, interface software, and local automated system and equipment.

Performs original cataloging for material not found on bibliographic support systems (approximately 3 – 4 records per hour).

Performs copy cataloging for materials found on bibliographic support systems (approximately 20-22 records per hour).

Reviews processing by clerical staff as well as data entered into automated system by technical support staff, checking for quality of processing and accuracy of inputting.

Assists in local database management, including development and maintenance of local authority files and holdings deletions in both library catalog and OCLC database.

Serves on system bibliographic support committees, which meets regularly to address public access concerns.

Recommends procedural and workflow changes in department to achieve optimum materials throughput.

Assists in developing department procedure manuals.

Prepares administrative reports to meet assigned deadlines.

Assists in processing of library materials, as needed.

Assists in general re-classification projects.

Additional Job Duties

Attends meetings, training seminars as required.

Oversees the Technical Service Department in the absence of the coordinator.

Performs other job-related duties as needed.

Knowledge, Skills, and Abilities

Must possess knowledge of cataloging principles and procedures such as AACR2, USMARC, MARC21, LCSH, DDC, LCRI, and authority control issues.

Must be able to speak and understand the English language in an understandable manner in order to carry out essential functions of job.

Must possess ability to communicate effectively.

Must possess ability to function independently, have flexibility and the ability to work effectively with clients, co-workers and others.

Must possess knowledge of various computer programs, bibliographic support systems and the Internet.

Must possess the technical knowledge of operating personal computers and other office equipment with accuracy and reasonable speed.

Must have the ability to instruct others in use of a variety of computer programs and methods.

Must be able to produce required reports, printouts, data as needed by various departments and to assist others with computer needs and services.

Must possess some knowledge, principles and practices of supervision and ability to apply it to job duties.

Physical and Mental Requirements

Must possess ability to record, convey and present information, explain procedures and follow instructions.

Must be able to sit for long periods throughout the workday, with intermittent periods of standing, walking, bending, squatting, twisting, pushing, carrying, and overhead reaching to carry out essential duties of job.

Must have above average mental attention or concentration to work procedures.

Must have above average attention to detail or accuracy of bibliographic records.

Coordinated movements of fingers/hand; and simple movements of feet/legs and torso.

Medium work, with occasional lifting/carrying of objects with weights of twenty to fifty pounds.

Must be able to pay close attention to details and concentrate on work.

Work Environment

Full-time position, 37.5 hours a week. Cumberland County Library System office open
8:00 AM-4:30 PM.

Works indoors in adequate work space, with adequate temperatures, ventilation and lighting.

Normal office exposure to noise, stress and disruptions.

May occasionally drive to other county offices.

Supervisory Responsibilities

SUPERVISION GIVEN:

Assists with coordinating daily work of clerical staff.

Education, Experience and Training:

QUALIFICATIONS:

Education, Experience, and Training

Masters degree in library or information science from an ALA-accredited institution and certification as public librarian in Pennsylvania.

WORK EXPERIENCE:

1-2 years working experience in cataloging services; preferably some experience with public libraries and library automation software.

8.1.2 Cataloging Librarian—General

Library Name: Needham Free Public Library
Library Location: Needham, Massachusetts
Population Served: 28,949
Number of Volumes: 135,436
Number of Titles: N/A
Number of Periodical Subscriptions: 268

General Summary

DEFINITION

Under general supervision of the Head Cataloger, assists in cataloging, processing and ordering of library materials, utilizing computerized information and inventory systems, and provides daily guidance to staff and volunteers in book processing, mending activities, and receiving of ordered materials.

Essential Functions and Responsibilities

Assists in cataloging of Library materials. Performs data entry of received and cataloged books, AV materials and on-order books into the regional network database.

Researches information for the Head Cataloger regarding books being sent to the catalog center.

Completes forms identifying database errors and problems, for resolution by Minuteman Network staff.

Instructs staff and volunteers in book processing, preservation, repair and rebinding.

Sets up work, provides daily direction to staff, and resolves related problems in the book processing area.

Performs specialized repairs, mends and processing.

Evaluates and prepares books sent to bindery; maintains related tracking records and liaison with bindery vendors.

Develops and performs technical processing on all Library AV materials.

Compiles statistics regarding technical services activities.

Interacts with book-jobbers, establishing priorities and resolving problems with received and on-order materials.

Processes invoices for all materials received. Coordinates processing of donated materials.

Attends workshops related to processing and preservation of library materials and other technical services meetings and training sessions.

Additional Job Duties

Provides assistance to Head Cataloger, including word processing and on-line searches.

Orders supplies for Technical Services department.

Deletes lists of monthly withdrawn books that had fines attached.

Withdraws from MLN database all lost and paid, damaged and discarded materials.

Performs other related duties as assigned.

Knowledge, Skills, and Abilities

MINIMUM QUALIFICATIONS

Skills, Knowledge and Abilities

Working knowledge of library technical service functions, including basic cataloging and network automated library systems.

Knowledge of standard automated office procedures, practices, forms, and equipment.

General knowledge of standard library materials.

Ability to perform detailed work accurately and with dispatch.

Interpersonal skills to interact effectively with other library staff and volunteers.

Physical and Mental Requirements

Standing and lifting of books and related library materials.

Regularly uses computer keyboards requiring eye-hand coordination and finger dexterity.

Supervisory Responsibilities

SUPERVISION

Provides daily direction and reviews accuracy of technical processing work performed by other technical processing staff and volunteers.

Education, Experience, and Training

Duties require basic knowledge of library systems and technical skills in computerized systems equivalent to two years of college and 2-3 years experience in library operations with a focus on cataloging and technical processing.

8.1.3 Cataloging Librarian—General

Library Name: Williamsburg Regional Library System
Library Location: Williamsburg, Virginia
Population Served: 60,100
Number of Volumes: 261,243
Number of Titles: N/A
Number of Periodical Subscriptions: 562

General Summary

NATURE OF WORK:

Under the supervision of the Assistant Library Director, the Librarian I (Cataloger) provides timely cataloging for materials; assists in maintaining authority files; maintains bibliographic and holdings records for library materials in the online catalog; and participates in the analysis and planning of technical services operations within the Support Services Department.

Essential Functions and Responsibilities

Searches and claims bibliographic records on shard cataloging database (OCLC) for entry into local system.

When OCLC records are unavailable, creates bibliographic records for the local system.

Edits bibliographic records on local system; assigns Library of Congress (LC) subject headings and call numbers (Dewey Decimal or local) to materials.

Adds barcodes and call number labels to individual items, editing and verifying holdings information including call number, collection code, item type, and list price for each.

Assists in maintaining accurate authority headings in the public access catalog, using the Library of Congress online authority file.

Records cataloging and special project statistics for inclusion in monthly departmental report.

Develops and maintains procedures manuals.

May organize the department's cataloging in one or more specific areas such as authority control, system reporting and batch functions, adult nonfiction, juvenile and young adult books, serials, and audiovisual materials.

May coordinate materials processing and mending in one or more specific areas.

Assists in training technical services and other library staff and volunteers.

Attends relevant workshops, programs, and meetings.

May participate in library-wide committees or projects.

Performs other tasks as assigned.

Knowledge, Skills, and Abilities

Working knowledge of the following areas:

Cataloging principles such as AACR2, Library of Congress subject headings, the Dewey Decimal system, and local call number schemes;

Automated bibliographic and holdings records (MARC format);

Online searching in OCLC or other bibliographic databases;

Integrated library systems; and

Personal computer use and data entry.

Understanding of library and technical services operations.

Familiarity with library materials and formats.

Accurate and efficient data entry and record-keeping skills.

Ability to plan and organize daily work and special projects.

Ability to interact well with supervisor, coworkers, and the general public.

Ability to analyze and to creatively solve problems related to the position.

Ability to work with enthusiasm and initiative.

Work Environment

The job is located in the James City County Library. Administers work typically sitting in an office, with occasional movement among departments, light lifting, and other limited physical activities. Frequent sustained operation of a personal computer and other office equipment required. Regular personal and phone contact is made with employees and the general public.

Education, Experience, and Training

MINIMUM QUALIFICATIONS:

Bachelor's degree or equivalent training and experience to provide the necessary expertise.

Additional Qualifications

NECESSARY SPECIAL QUALIFICATIONS:

Requires the ability to travel among various library sites.

8.2 CATALOGING LIBRARIAN—RARE BOOKS

8.2.1 Cataloging Librarian—Rare Books

Library Name: Boston Public Library
Library Location: Boston, Massachusetts
Population Served: 574,283
Number of Volumes: 7,954,358
Number of Titles: N/A
Number of Periodical Subscriptions: 29,026

Reports To

Keeper of Rare Books

Essential Functions and Responsibilities

Under supervision, responsible for performing original cataloging and complex copy cataloging of monographs and/or serials in all subjects, in various languages from the John Adams Library.

Essential Functions and Responsibilities

Performs advanced descriptive and subject cataloging, classification, and authority work using current cataloging practices and national standards for the titles in the John Adams Library.

Remains current with existing and emerging cataloging policies, practices, standards, schema and procedures including, but not limited to, MARC 21, LC Classification, LCSH, LC Rule Interpretations, AACR2r, OCLC bibliographic standards and DCRB (Descriptive Cataloging of Rare Books).

Researches sources in several languages to insure the accuracy of bibliographical assignment

Assigns subject headings and other access points based on Library of Congress practice; assigns call numbers according to local practice.

Creates local authority records in accordance with library policies.

Reports new records to the ESTC (English Short Title Catalog) quarterly.

Coordinates and cooperates with Editor, John Adams Library Project, as needed

Meets as necessary with the Chief of Cataloging regarding the implementation of Library policies and standards.

Ability to maintain a consistent output of cataloging, classification, subject analysis and database maintenance.

Performs other related and comparable duties as assigned.

Supervisory Responsibilities

Supervises: N/A

Education, Experience, and Training

Qualifications:

Thorough knowledge of AACR2r., MARC 21 (all formats), DCRB, LC Classifications and LC Subject headings; excellent organizational, analytical and problem-solving skills; ability to maintain a high level of productivity; working knowledge of one or more foreign languages (European language or Latin preferred); prior cataloging experience essential.

Ability to work well independently and cooperatively in a group.

8.3 CATALOGING LIBRARIAN—YOUNG ADULT MATERIAL

8.3.1 Cataloging Librarian—Young Adult Material

Library Name: Williamsburg Regional Library System
Library Location: Williamsburg, Virginia
Population Served: 60,100
Number of Volumes: 261,243
Number of Titles: N/A
Number of Periodical Subscriptions: 562

General Summary

NATURE OF WORK:

Under the supervision of the Senior Library Services Director (Support), the Librarian I (Cataloger) performs timely copy cataloging; prepares original MARC work forms for juvenile and young adult books; assists in maintaining the public access catalog authority files; maintains bibliographic and holdings records for library materials in the online catalog; and participates in the analysis and planning of technical services operations within the Support Services department.

Essential Functions and Responsibilities

Searches and claims bibliographic records on shared cataloging database (OCLC) for entry onto local system.

Prepares brief original MARC records for juvenile and young adult materials.

Edits bibliographic records on local system: assigns Dewey Decimal call numbers and LC subject headings to juvenile and young adult books; assigns other call numbers using local schemes to classify fiction and picture books.

Adds barcodes and call number labels to individual items, editing and verifying holdings information including call number, collection code, item type, and list price for each.

Assists in maintaining accurate juvenile and young adult author, subject, and series authority headings in the public access catalog, using the Library of Congress online authority file.

Deletes withdrawn library holdings from OCLC.

Assists in training technical services and other library staff and volunteers.

Attends relevant workshops, programs, and meetings.

May participate in library-wide committees or projects.

Performs other tasks as assigned.

Knowledge, Skills, and Abilities

Ability to acquire working knowledge of cataloging principles such as AACR2, Dewey Decimal system, and local call number schemes.

Working knowledge of automated bibliographic and holdings records (MARC format).

Basic knowledge of personal computer use and data entry.

Accurate and efficient data entry and record-keeping skills.

Ability to plan and organize daily work and special projects.

Knowledge of online searching in OCLC or other bibliographic database.

Ability to communicate well with supervisor, co-workers, and the general public.

Understanding of library and technical services operations preferred.

Ability to analyze and to creatively solve problems related to the position.

Ability to work with enthusiasm and initiative.

Knowledge of children's and young adult literature desirable.

Work Environment

The job is located in the James City County Library. Administers work typically sitt ing in an office, with occasional movement among departments, light lifting, and other limited physical activities. Frequent sustained operation of video display terminal and other office equipment required. Regular personal and phone contact is made with employees and the general public. Computer, printer, and other office equipment as required.

Education, Experience, and Training

MINIMUM QUALIFICATIONS:

Bachelor's degree or equivalent education and experience to provide the necessary expertise.

Additional Qualifications

NECESSARY SPECIAL QUALIFICATIONS:

Requires the ability to travel among various library sites.

9.0 COLLECTION DEVELOPMENT LIBRARIAN

9.1 COLLECTION DEVELOPMENT LIBRARIAN

9.1.1 Collection Development Librarian

Library Name: Hernando County Public Library

Library Location: Brooksville, Florida

Population Served: 130,802

Number of Volumes: N/A

Number of Titles: 227,929

Number of Periodical Subscriptions: 427

General Summary

GENERAL DESCRIPTION: Analyzes community and library data to determine areas of the collection which need updating; selects materials to update the collection; performs related work as required.

Essential Functions and Responsibilities

Selects and acquires all current materials to meet the levels of development indicated by the Collection Management Policy for all library sites.

Analyzes and evaluates the existing collections to determine materials needed by each agency and identifies materials that need to be replaced, or discarded or added to the existing collection.

Consults with librarians and division heads to respond to the needs of the public.

Monitors collection management budget and its expenditures to provide sufficient funds to meet the material(s) needs of all library agencies.

Supervises and monitors the acquisition of materials for new facilities' opening day collections to ensure that all contractual provisions are being fulfilled.

In the event of an emergency or crisis situation (hurricane or flood, etc.) position is required to perform recovery duties as assigned by immediate supervisor.

Regular attendance.

Additional Job Duties

Performs other reasonably related duties as assigned by immediate supervisor or other management personnel.

Reasonable accommodation will be made for otherwise qualified individuals with a disability.

Knowledge, Skills, and Abilities

Knowledge of current public library collection management practices.

Knowledge of current trends in publishing.

Knowledge of retrospective library materials.

Knowledge of current library acquisitions procedures.

Knowledge of budgetary practices.

Knowledge of statistical methods.

Knowledge of standard bibliographic sources.

Skill in using the library automated equipment including acquisitions, databases.

Skill in using professional materials to locate items for the collection.

Skill in interpreting data from many sources in analyzing collection needs.

Skill in dealing with other library administrators in a tactful manner.

Ability to work with professional librarians and the public to analyze and provide materials for collections.

Ability to maintain materials expenditures within budgeted amounts.

Ability to utilize automated acquisitions systems.

Physical and Mental Requirements

Light lifting and carrying (under 35 lbs), walking, standing, kneeling, bending and stooping are performed frequently. Ability to operate personal computer.

Tools and Equipment Used

Personal computer, library automated circulation equipment (Sirsi), photocopier and other general office equipment.

Work Environment

Normal office/library work environment

Education, Experience, and Training

Education: Master of Library Science Degree from an ALA accredited college or university.

Experience: Two (2) years of professional related experience.

License and Certification Requirements

Licenses, Certification or Registrations: Valid Florida driver's license and a good driving record required.

9.2 COLLECTION DEVELOPMENT MANAGER

9.2.1 Collection Development Manager

Library Name: Boston Public Library
Library Location: Boston, Massachusetts
Population Served: 574,283
Number of Volumes: 7,954,358
Number of Titles: N/A
Number of Periodical Subscriptions: 29,026

Reports To

Chief Operating Officer

General Summary

Job Purpose:

Under the general direction of the Chief Operating Officer, coordinates all aspects of system-wide collection development, building collections that address the full range of public needs and interests. Supervises and oversees Collection Development. Formulates collection guidelines and oversees the selection and deselection of all formats of material for the system. Participates in managing, monitoring, and advising in the formulation of the total materials budget. Works with all parts of the organization to ensure a smooth progression for getting materials into the hands of the public. Provides system-wide leadership regarding collection issues. Member of the Senior Management Team.

Essential Functions and Responsibilities

Coordinates and manages all facets of collection development to insure comprehensive collection development responsive to public needs and interests, including selection/deselection, weeding, gifts and exchange, disposal, public input and information on selection and on order information; coordinates activities with Technical Services including acquisitions, receiving, bibliographic database development and maintenance, and distribution of library collection materials.

Works with staff in assessing public access to materials, i.e. format, location, status (i.e. circulating/non-circulating); provides leadership in developing recommended changes and improvements.

Researches new approaches and tools for selection and related activities; provides proactive leadership to organize, train, and implement new methods to improve public service delivery.

Develops relevant policies and procedures for adoption by library. Has primary responsibility for the updating and revision of the library's Collection Development Policy.

Uses management information and other professional tools to improve collection development, purchasing, weeding, and replacement programs in response to public interest and information needs. Develops mechanisms to measure effectiveness of collection development program.

Convenes and gives leadership to the Materials Acquisition Budget Committee, special projects involving acquisitions (such as Black Is bibliography, summer reading program bibliography) in conjunction with the appropriate manager/s and selector/s.

Evaluates collection use reports with managers and selectors; sets up purchase, replacement, and weeding program goals and standards

Works with Technical Services to coordinate the prioritization of ordering, receiving, cataloging and processing of materials to respond to the needs and interests of library users.

Works with Business staff and selectors to develop and oversee library financial resources for collection budgets and to maximize the return to the Library from the disposal of materials.

Selects and manages licensing and contracts for electronic database products. Represents Boston Public Library in its capacity as regional and statewide service provider in the acquisition and deployment of print and electronic collection resources. Serves as convener of the Electronic Resources Committee.

Participates actively in the development of the Web site to insure a range of content to meet user needs. Serves as a member of the Internet Committee.

Participates in the development of the library's bibliographic databases, online, and digital initiatives.

Seeks out, evaluates, and coordinates special collections with appropriate selectors and others to determine appropriateness for addition to the BPL collection. Works with Library support groups and others to promote the Library's collection needs.

Represents the Library at meetings with regional/MBLN participating libraries, outside organizations, statewide initiatives, Boston Library Consortium projects, and vendors, as appropriate.

Analyzes staff training needs regarding collection development, selection, vendor selection/ordering tools and related skills and works with library's training coordinator/committee to develop appropriate staff development/training programs.

Performs related duties as required.

Knowledge, Skills, and Abilities

Experience selecting and ordering library materials in a large public service organization with a wide range of constituent use from popular reading to scholarly research.

Demonstrated love of reading; keen intellectual curiosity and love of scholarship; appreciation for popular culture and society trends

Demonstrated ability to analyze public service needs and to develop work processes designed to respond effectively.

Ability to act as team leader and to work as part of team. Demonstrated ability to work in team environment and to be responsive to stakeholder needs.

Demonstrated ability to work collaboratively with all library units to improve library service delivery to the public.

Thorough knowledge of best practice collection development and related work processes. Skilled and knowledgeable readers advisor.

Excellent written, oral, and personal computer skills.

Thorough knowledge of, and ability to evaluate, select, and implement emerging technologies and processes designed to enhance ordering and selection process and procedures.

Initiative, creativity, and flexibility. Ability to be a change agent.

Initiative in generating new ideas; a proven ability to work well under pressure and to meet inflexible deadlines.

Education, Experience, and Training

Qualifications:

Bachelor's degree from a recognized college or university and a master's degree in library and information science from an ALA accredited library school.

10 years of related library experience, including a minimum of five (5) years senior supervisory and/or management experience in one or more aspects relevant to collection development and ordering experience.

Working knowledge of all of the elements that make up a great library collection; broad-based collection development practices, including current trends in selection, ordering, patron driven programs, and vendor services; library automated systems; practices of the national and international book trade; budget and fund accounting practices; national standards; and licensing of electronic resources. Proven ability to work with staff to analyze workflow and to implement changes to improve service delivery. Proven ability to provide leadership in a team environment, and to work with staff to effectively plan and manage the work of the department.

Additional Qualifications

Requirements: Must be a Resident of the City of Boston upon first day of hire

10.0 TECHNICAL SERVICES MANAGER/COORDINATOR

10.1 MANAGER

10.1.1 Manager

Library Name: Kettleson Memorial Library
Library Location: Sitka, Alaska
Population Served: 8,835
Number of Volumes: 57,448
Number of Titles: 54,733
Number of Periodical Subscriptions: 279

General Summary

General Statement of Duties

Administers the Technical Services function at the Library and provides administrative oversight for related Library functions; performs related work as required.

Distinguishing Features of the Class

The principal function of an employee in this class is to provide technical and administrative support in the deliverance of Library services. The work is performed under the direct supervision of the Library Director but considerable leeway is granted for the exercise of independent judgment and initiative. Direct supervision is exercised over the work of all Library personnel in the absence of the Library Director. An employee in this class performs the duties of other employees in the Library as required or as assigned by supervisory personnel. In the absence of the Library Director, an employee in this class temporarily assumes full responsibility for duties of this position. The nature of the work performed requires that an employee in this class establish and maintain effective working relationships with other Department and City employees, members of the Library Consortium, outside vendors and the public. The principal duties of this class are performed in a public Library environment. An employee in this class may perform any one or more or any additional duties as assigned.

Essential Functions and Responsibilities

Examples of Essential Work (Illustrative Only)

Monitors and maintains a central computer and equipment consortium for Libraries within the City and Borough of Sitka;

Coordinates the services of automated system equipment, software, services and maintenance with appropriate vendors;

Administers the city and school library computer network;

Provides administrative oversight for library functions;

Provides on-site system support through troubleshooting technical services, performing on-call system maintenance and repairs as needed;

Maintains a knowledge of reference services within the library and provides reference services to patrons on a wide variety of subjects and educational levels;

Maintains a safe and secure library environment through monitoring patrons adherence to library procedures and guidelines and maintaining an awareness of all persons within the facility;

Trains all Library personnel within the consortium in the use of technical services, including conducting training workshops;

Composes, produces and distributes documentation, reference manuals, training materials, memos and directives in the use of the consortium system;

Conducts research on technical services to obtain the most cost effective and valuable services for Library needs and monitors vendor's compliance with contract specifications;

Develops standard policies and procedures for technical systems security in coordination with all Library staff within the consortium;

Determines and configures software codes and settings to meet system expectations of all users;

Performs software maintenance procedures, including resizing files, index building and program updates;

Rewrites and reconfigures main system menus, help screens and display screens;

Studies system use and designs revision to minimize down time to system users;

Oversees system back-up procedures, monitors disk usage and develops emergency recovery procedures;

Performs quality control checks of the bibliographic database;

Establishes and monitors a port structure to audit proper use of software licenses;

Organizes, designs and writes original file dictionaries to generate custom database reports;

Maintains, troubleshoots, repairs, replaces and selects all hardware and peripherals within the

Library, including CPU's, file servers, monitors, barcode readers, network terminals, printers, CD-ROMS, etc;

Selects and implements all software programs within the Library, customizing packages as necessary to fit Library needs and trains Library personnel in their maximum use;

Maintains detailed reports of all technical services operations for the purpose of system analysis and the determination of future needs;

Performs professional cataloguing, technical services and bibliographic control duties, including classification and description of all acquired materials using standard Library cataloguing and classification guides and by adhering to library material standards;

Enters holdings in both the Western Library Network and Sitka library Network databases;

Maintains daily Library operations in the absence of the Library Director, including staffing and operational concerns;

Serves assigned hours at the Circulation desks and performs other duties of the Library assistants as needed;

Explores all possible information sources for inquiring patrons, including all materials within the Library consortium of Sitka, other contributing Libraries in the inter-library loan program and other related sources as necessary;

Provides needed information and demonstrations concerning how to perform certain work tasks to all employees;

Keeps immediate supervisor and designated others fully and accurately informed concerning work progress, including present and potential work problems and suggestions for new or improved ways of addressing such problems;

Attends meetings, conferences, workshops and training sessions and reviews publications and audio-visual materials to become and remain current on the principles, practices and new developments in assigned work areas;

Responds to citizens' questions and comments in a courteous and timely manner;

Trains, assigns, prioritizes, supervises, motivates and evaluates the work of assigned employees;

Communicates and coordinates regularly with appropriate others to maximize the effectiveness and efficiency of interdepartmental operations and activities;

Performs other related duties as assigned.

Knowledge, Skills, and Abilities

Comprehensive knowledge of technical services systems within a Library environment, preferably within a consortium;

Comprehensive knowledge of system software as applied to Library services;

Comprehensive knowledge of Library databases and system security;

Thorough knowledge of standard library practices and procedures;

Skill in the maintenance and repair of the various components of technical services systems;

Ability to implement hardware and software systems within a library based on the analysis of current needs;

Ability to ascertain the needs of Library patrons and direct them to the needed resource within the

Library or contact outside services to ensure all available information is obtainable to the patron;

Ability in basic math computations and alphabetic filing systems;

Ability to communicate well with others, both orally and in writing, using both technical and non-technical language;

Ability to understand and follow oral and/or written policies, procedures and instructions;

Ability to prepare and present accurate and reliable reports containing findings and recommendations;

Ability to operate or quickly learn to operate a personal computer using standard or customized software applications appropriate to assigned tasks;

Ability to use logical and creative thought processes to develop solutions according to written specifications and/or oral instructions;

Ability to perform a wide variety of duties and responsibilities with accuracy and speed under the pressure of time-sensitive deadlines;

Ability and willingness to quickly learn and put to use new skills and knowledge brought about by rapidly changing information and/or technology;

Integrity, ingenuity and inventiveness in the performance of assigned tasks.

Physical and Mental Requirements

Sufficient clarity of speech and hearing or other communication capabilities, with or without reasonable accommodation, which permits the employee to communicate effectively;

Sufficient vision or other powers of observation, with or without reasonable accommodation, which permits the employee to operate computers and related equipment;

Sufficient manual dexterity with or without reasonable accommodation, which permits the employee to maintain technical information systems;

Sufficient personal mobility and physical reflexes, with or without reasonable accommodation, which permits the employee to function in a general library environment and visit various work suites throughout the City and Borough.

Education, Experience, and Training

Graduation from an accredited college or university with a Bachelor's Degree in Computer Science, Business Communications Systems or a library related field; and

Considerable experience in both Library Sciences and/or administration and technical services systems; or

Any equivalent combination of experience, education and training which provides the knowledge, skills and abilities necessary to perform the work, with an emphasis on covering the dual functions of technical proficiency and Library administration.

Additional Qualifications

Required Special Qualifications
None

10.1.2 Technical Services Manager

Library Name: Phoenix Public Library
Library Location: Phoenix, Arizona
Population Served: 1,350,435
Number of Volumes: 2,015,587
Number of Titles: 734,921
Number of Periodical Subscriptions: 4,500

General Summary

DISTINGUISHING FEATURES OF THE CLASS:

The fundamental reason this classification exists is to assign and review the work of a group of Library Clerks and other clerical, supply, and courier employees assigned to the Processing Section of the Technical Services Division. Direct supervision is exercised over employees performing such assignments as processing library materials, ordering supplies, bookmending, sign making, and courier duties. Work is performed under the general supervision of the Library Technical Services Administrator.

Essential Functions and Responsibilities

Supervises clerical, supply, and courier employees;

Supervises and participates in the selection, training, and evaluation of employees;

Reviews and establishes work procedures;

Reviews the work products of others to ensure conformance to standards;

Plans work assignments to accomplish department objectives;

Keeps personnel and activity records and writes reports;

Supervises centralized supply ordering and warehouse operations for all libraries;

Supervises book mending operations;

Supervises edge stamping, pocketing, labeling, and jacketing of newly acquired library materials;

Supervises employees who make signs using modern sign making equipment;

Supervises the preparation of books and periodicals for commercial binding;

Demonstrates continuous effort to improve operations, decrease turnaround times, streamline work processes, and work cooperatively and jointly to provide quality seamless customer service.

Knowledge, Skills, and Abilities

Knowledge of:

Library system of circulation and collection control.

Principles and practices of supervision.

Leadership styles and skills.

Modern office procedures, practices, and equipment.

Ability to:

Perform a broad range of supervisory responsibilities over others.

Interpret and make decisions in accordance with regulations and established policies.

Work cooperatively with other City employees and the general public.

Communicate in the English language by phone or in person in a one-to-one or group setting.

Move light objects (less than 20 pounds) short distances (20 feet or less).

Produce written documents in the English language with clearly organized thoughts, using proper sentence construction, punctuation, and grammar.

Perform basic mathematical and statistical computations and analysis.

Work safely without presenting a direct threat to self or others.

Additional Requirements:

This position requires the use of personal or City vehicles on City business. The individual must be physically capable of operating the vehicles safely, possess a valid driver's license and have an acceptable driving record. Use of a personal vehicle for City business will be prohibited if the employee is not authorized to drive a City vehicle or if the employee does not have personal insurance coverage.

Some positions will require the performance of other essential functions.

Education, Experience, and Training

Three years of library clerical experience, including one year of experience performing a wide variety of responsible clerical tasks with considerable independence in a library facility. Other combinations of experience and education that meet the minimum requirements may be substituted.

> ## 10.1.3 Technical Services Manager
>
> **Library Name:** Milwaukee Public Library
> **Library Location:** Milwaukee, Wisconsin
> **Population Served:** 608,150
> **Number of Volumes:** 2,553,934
> **Number of Titles:** N/A
> **Number of Periodical Subscriptions:** 9,719

SUPPLEMENTARY INFORMATION: (Indicate any other information, which further explains the importance, difficulty, or responsibility of the position.) The vast variety of materials selected, acquired and processed contributes to a position characterized by complexity and myriad detail. Over three million volumes are in the collection with more than 50,000 titles and over 150,000 items added annually. Information technology responsibilities include overall management of seven day operation of multiple LANs in 13 city libraries and an on-line bookmobile program connected by high-speed WAN data links and supporting network traffic in TCPIIP protocols, several hundred network PC's, full Internet connectivity to all network devices, and connection to network services from the City of Milwaukee and Milwaukee County Federated Library System and other external network suppliers.

Reports To

SUPERVISION RECEIVED: (Indicate the extent to which work assignments and methods are outlined, reviewed, and approved by others.)

Is granted broad authority by the City Librarian to develop and implement new programs and to direct the operation of this bureau, subject to periodic report and evaluation.

General Summary

BASIC FUNCTION OF POSITION:

The incumbent of this position plans and implements policy for the operation and improvement of the Library's Technical Services Bureau. Responsible for administration, budgeting, and program development to support:

1) selection and acquisition of library materials;
2) automation of library operations and services;
3) cataloging and authority control;
4) bibliographic and item inventory database management;
5) binding, repair and physical preparation of materials.

The Milwaukee Public Library is committed to providing the highest quality of service to internal and external customers. In meeting this commitment, employees are expected to be knowledgeable, competent, dependable and courteous in the performance of their job responsibilities, and to work cooperatively as part of a team.

Essential Functions and Responsibilities

(Break job into component parts as you would describe it to the incumbent. Indicate the approximate percentage of time devoted to each major task or group of related tasks. List the most important duties and responsibilities first. Include responsibilities related to employee safety and affirmative action goals for management positions.)

1. Automation: Directly supervises the Library Network Manager, the Librarian III—Automation Librarian, and the Librarian III

- Computer Training Librarian and through those positions, the staff of the Automation Unit. Coordinates overall planning, budgeting, and implementation of the library's automation initiatives through the following:

a. Maintains awareness of emerging automation products and services. Plans new automation services or applications for use by library staff and patrons to improve staff effectiveness and enhance customer service.

b. With assistance from the Automation Unit staff, and in consultation with other library managers and staff:

Develops automation project and operations budget requests, including hardware, software, implementation and maintenance components.

c. With assistance from the Automation Unit staff, and in consultation with other library managers and staff: (continued)

Develops equipment specifications and orders.

Meets with hardware, software and service vendors to evaluate products and services

Plans and coordinating hardware, software. and network installation services and schedules. Works with staff from city departments and outside agencies to coordinate effective wide-area network services.

Develops network cabling specifications, plans and schedules.

a. Arranges for purchase and installation of network servers, PCs and peripherals.

b. Arranges for preventative and corrective maintenance services.

c. Provides guidance and direction for training on general network software and services, and on public services software and Internet and CD-ROM reference products.

d. Plans and provides training on software specific to Technical Services functions, including acquisitions, serials control, database maintenance and cataloging.

e. Serves as liaison to other MPL automation service providers, including ITMD, MCFLS, and project or service vendors.

f. Directs planning, implementation and support activities for MPL participation in MCFLS Innovative Interfaces library automation system.

g. Serves as Information Security Officer for Milwaukee Public Library to assure compliance with the City of Milwaukee Information Security Policies and Standards.

h. Maintains awareness of grants and other external funding programs; develops grant applications and administers funded projects to expand library automation services.

i. Serves as the MPL E Rate Coordinator

Cataloging and Authority Control: Supervises the Management Librarian—Cataloging & Metadata who develops policies and procedures related to management of the library's bibliographic and information databases. Plans and implements policies to provide cost effective access to materials in all formats. Manages original and copy cataloging, classification, and authority control functions. Ensures database integrity and consistency through application of national standards and internal procedures. Negotiates system Bibliographic Database Development and Maintenance contract with MCFLS and monitors contract performance and costs.

Database Management: Supervises the Management Librarian—Cataloging & Metadata who develops policy and directs staff in the development and maintenance of records in the library's bibliographic and item databases. Implements national standards and consistent internal policies to ensure materials are correctly represented in local databases, WISCA T, and OCLC. Provides direction and policy to ensure effective system wide coordination within MCFLS.

Acquisitions: Supervises the Management Librarian— Acquisitions who coordinates support for system-wide selection of new and duplicate materials in all formats. Recommends allocations for materials budgets and monitors expenditures of city materials budget, gift and endowment funds, grant funds, and funds received from the MPL Foundation. Directs establishment and monitoring of vendor accounts for materials suppliers. Directs systems and processes used for ordering and payment processing for firm orders, standing orders, and subscriptions in all formats. Plans and implements IT systems to provide electronic data interchange of financial transaction data and materials selection ordering data with systems operated by vendors or other city departments.

Binding and Physical Treatment: Supervises the Management Librarian—Acquisitions who oversees this department which has responsibility for preparing library materials for circulation, repairing and rebinding damaged books and binding periodicals and serials. Works with the Lead Bookbinder and the Coordinator of Humanities to develop and implement preservation program and treatment.

Related Duties: Performs other duties relative to library activity and growth by participating in system-wide committees and professional organizations and by keeping informed of current trends in library development, automation and operations. Represents the Milwaukee Public Library in committees, meetings and programs sponsored by city, regional, state or national organizations dealing with Information Technology or technical services. Knows Library's Affirmative Action responsibilities and commitments and actively assists the library in meeting its goals.

Name and title of immediate Supervisor: City Librarian

Analyst—Assistants, and one Mail Processor.

Knowledge, Skills, and Abilities

1. Strong customer service orientation.

2. Broad knowledge and demonstrated experience in implementing and managing automated networks, systems and applications including the following areas is desirable: a. Project planning and management b. Computer operating systems (Windows) c. Network operating systems (Novell NetWare and Windows NT/2000) d. LAN and WAN protocols (TCPJIP) e. Management and security of computers and networks f. Category 5 and fiber data cabling standards g. Ethernet and A TM networks h. Tl, wireless and Sonet telecommunications services i. Internet and web services j. Library automation systems k. relevant IT standards governing physical networks, data formats, network interconnectivity, and electronic commerce.

1. federal, state and private grant programs and funding sources to support library IT programs and services.

OR

Ability to identify and address technical areas where knowledge is lacking, and to identify and independently pursue opportunities to gain needed knowledge and skills.

3. Thorough knowledge of selection, acquisitions, cataloging, classification, serials control, binding and preservation standards, policies, and practices is desirable.

4. Wide knowledge of publishing trends for books, serials and other media, and of business practices of library materials vendors is desirable.

5. Ability to plan, layout, direct, coordinate and maintain large, complex, detailed operations, and to develop the potential capabilities of staff members.

6. Ability to innovate successfully in the technical services field.

7. Initiative, accuracy, good judgement, tact, orderliness, good memory, coolness under pressure.

Physical and Mental Requirements

List the physical demands which are representative of those that must be met to successfully perform the essential function of the job. Reasonable accommodations may be made to enable individuals with disabilities to perform the essential functions.

1. Usually using hand, wrist and fingers simultaneously (ex: data entry);

2. Sometimes sitting, standing, walking, reaching in front of body, and using feet/legs to control equipment.

3. On occasion stooping, kneeling, crouching, crawling, twisting, bending, squatting, reaching overhead, climbing stairs and ladders.

4. Frequently lifting items weighing up to 10 pounds and sometimes up to 25 pounds. Maximum weight lifted to hip height: 25 pounds, to shoulder height: 15 pounds.

5. Sometimes pushing/pulling without wheels or assistance items weighing up to 20 pounds. On occasion pushing/pulling with wheels or assistance items weighing up to or in excess of 100 pounds.

6. Usually talking and hearing ordinary conversation in a quiet environment and on occasion in a noisy environment. Sometimes having need to hear environmental (non-speech sounds).

7. Usual need for near vision at 20 inches or less for use of computer equipment, reading, etc. Sometimes need for far vision at 20 inches or more for moving about the building and driving.

8. Sometimes need for mobility outside headquarters library.

MENTAL REQUIREMENTS: List the mental requirements, which are, representative of those that must be met to successfully perform the essential function of the job. Reasonable accommodations may be made to enable individuals with disabilities to perform the essential functions.

1. Communication Skills: effectively communicate ideas and information both in written and oral form.

2. Reading Ability: effectively read and understand information contained in procedure manuals, reports, etc.

3. Time Management: set priorities in order to meet assignment deadlines.

4. Problem Solving: develop feasible, realistic solutions to problems, recommend actions designed to prevent problems from occurring.

5. Planning and Organizing: develop long-range plans to solve complex problems or take advantage of opportunities; establish systematic methods of accomplishing goals.

6. Analytical Ability: identify problems and opportunities; review possible alternative courses of action before selection; utilize available information resources in decision making.

7. Creative Decision-Making: effectively evaluates or makes independent decision based upon experience, knowledge or training, without supervision.

Tools and Equipment Used

List equipment, which is representative of that which would be used to successfully perform the essential function of the job. Reasonable accommodations may be made to enable individuals with disabilities to perform the essential functions.

Computer terminal or networked personal computer, and peripheral equipment; telephone, typewriter, photocopier, fax machine, calculator, LCD display unit, overhead projectors, other types of audiovisual equipment, booktruck, private motor vehicle.

Work Environment

List the conditions which are representative of those that must be met to successfully perform the essential function of the job. Reasonable accommodations may be made to enable individuals with disabilities to perform the essential functions.

1. Inside work environment.

2. Flexible work hours; some evening and weekend hours and work in excess of 40 hours/week.

3. Frequently dusty work conditions.

4. Frequent glare/improper illumination.

5. Sometimes encountering vehicular traffic.

6. Sometimes working with equipment with moveable parts and around electrical hazards.

7. On occasion working around loud noise, in confirmed spaces, and/or at heights from 10–15'.

Supervisory Responsibilities

SUPERVISION EXERCISED:

42 Total number of employees for whom responsible, either directly or indirectly,

Direct Supervision. List the number and titles of personnel directly supervised. Specify the kind and extent of supervision exercised by indicating one or more of the following: (a) assign duties; (b) outline methods; 8 direct work in process; (d) check or inspect completed work; (e) sign or approve work; (t) make hiring recommendations; (g) prepare performance appraisals; (h) take disciplinary action or effectively recommend such,

Supervises all of the library system's technical services operations by assigning duties, outlining methods, overseeing completed work in general, preparing or approving performance appraisals, taking disciplinary action as needed, issuing favorable commendations, and being available for consultation as questions arise. Directly supervises two Management Librarians, one Librarian III- Automation Librarian, one Librarian III— Computer Training Librarian, and one Network Manager. Indirectly supervises another 37 FTE staff including: one Lead Bookbinder, two Bookbinders, three Librarian III Catalogers, six Copy Cataloging Technicians II, three Library Technicians IV, three Library Technicians III, 15 Library Technicians II, one Network Analyst Sr.

Education, Experience, and Training

1. Bachelor's Degree from an accredited college or university. Master of Library Science Degree from a library school accredited by ALA or approved by the Milwaukee City Service Commission.

2. Seven years of professional library experience, with at least two years in a supervisory capacity.

3. Experience in developing grant requests and implementing grant projects involving expansion of public and staff use of computers and information technology is highly desirable.

10.1.4 Technical Services Manager/Coordinator

Library Name: Anacortes Public Library
Library Location: Anacortes, Washington
Population Served: 14,500
Number of Volumes: N/A
Number of Titles: 55,565
Number of Periodical Subscriptions: 126
Department: Library

Reports To

Assistant Director, Children's Collection and Community Programs

General Summary

PRINCIPAL PURPOSE OF JOB: This position is charged with coordinating the timely processing of the Library collection. Responsible for the day-to-day supervision of technical-services staff. Will perform processing tasks as time and workload dictate.

LEVEL OF AUTHORITY: Performs duties with only moderate supervision following established procedures and deadlines. Has limited latitude to make decisions regarding priorities for routine events and schedules. Responsibility for judgment, thoroughness and competence is most important due to potential disruption of Library operations or adverse public relations.

Essential Functions and Responsibilities

Plan, organize, schedule and direct the day-to-day work activities of the technical-services clerks (TSCs) in accordance with project or program requirements.

Assure the timely orientation of new TSCs and the progressive training of present TSCs.

Interview and hire TSCs, with the assistant director, children's collection and community programs.

Repair or direct the repair of damaged Library materials.

Evaluate the performance of TSCs.

Help prepare and process materials for general circulation.

Repair or direct the repair of damaged Library materials.

Maintain or direct the maintenance of automated catalog.

Coordinate ordering and receiving of all materials for the library collection, as directed by the assistant directors.

Maintain records and statistics related to technical services, generating reports as needed.

Serve as backup systems administrator for Dynex and Local Area Network systems.

Additional Job Duties

May perform portions of the work of higher or lower classified positions, as required.

Provide reports from the Dynix system, as required.

Must be able to drive an automobile in the course of Library business

Knowledge, Skills, and Abilities

Other

Attention to detail and accuracy.

Ability to communicate effectively, patiently and courteously with City employees, patrons and other community members.

Ability to handle multiple activities or interruptions at once and to work positively and effectively within a team model.

Excellent memory and organizational ability to deal with multiple responsibilities and to meet deadlines.

Ability to work weekday, evening, weekend and morning hours.

Physical and Mental Requirements

Strength, for example, to push loaded book cart weighing approximately 300 pounds on level floor and up ramp, to lift or maneuver onto cart loads up to 50 pounds and to carry cartons of books up and down stairs.

Ability to bend, stoop and lift for prolonged periods in cramped spaces.

Ability to sit and use computer workstation, including keyboard and visual display terminal, for extended periods of time.

Tools and Equipment Used

Office equipment, such as; computer, modem, typewriter, adding machine, microfiche reader, paper cutter, fax, copier, telephone and postage meter. Various tools for book repair and glue guns and lamination equipment.

Work Environment

Work is performed primarily in an indoor office setting at the library, in frequently dusty atmosphere with potential exposure to airborne pathogens.

Education, Experience, and Training

QUALIFICATIONS

Technical

Must have a two-year college degree or equivalent work experience.

Must have ability to plan, schedule, supervise and evaluate the work of assigned staff for proficient performance and high morale.

Must have excellent communication skills.

Must have a basic ability to work with numbers accurately and understand verbal and written instructions, such as would be acquired two years of higher education or equivalent work experience.

Prior library experience preferred.

Must have computer ability to adequately utilize automated library cataloging systems.

Must be bondable.

Must possess a valid Washington State driver's license.

Ability to understand and apply a systems approach to technical-service administration.

Additional Qualifications

OTHER

As an absolute condition of employment, employees are required upon hire to sign a drug-free workplace agreement and an agreement not to use tobacco products of any kind while on the job.

The statements contained in this job description reflect general details as necessary to describe the principal functions of this job, the level of knowledge and skill typically required and the scope of responsibility. It should not be considered an all-inclusive listing of work requirements. Individuals may perform other duties as assigned, including work in other functional areas to cover absences or provide relief, to equalize peak work periods or otherwise to balance the workload.

11.0 ACQUISITIONS TECHNICIAN

11.1 TECHNICIAN

11.1.1 Technician

Library Name: Williamsburg Regional Library System
Library Location: Williamsburg, Virginia
Population Served: 60,100
Number of Volumes: 261,243
Number of Titles: N/A
Number of Periodical Subscriptions: 562

General Summary

NATURE OF WORK:

Under the supervision of the Acquisitions Administrator, the Library Technician performs a variety of clerical and administrative tasks to support technical services activities. Duties include creating and processing library materials orders in the automated acquisitions system. Places the majority of audiovisual and youth services orders, choosing the best vendor based upon publishing and binding information. Receives some serials, claiming missing or damaged items. Processes audiovisual materials. Participates in the planning and evaluation of technical services operations within the Support Services department.

Essential Functions and Responsibilities

Searches library materials orders on the integrated system (Dynix) to avoid duplication.

Selects vendors based on publishing and binding information. Keys orders into Dynix.

Places holds on patron-requested materials.

Checks backorders and problem orders, verifying ordering and confirmation information.

Places orders via electronic order transfer, fax, phone, or mail.

Receives and claims periodicals and serials, creating and editing copy records and pub patterns on the computer.

Under the direction of the cataloging staff, updates and changes Dynix bibliographic and holdings records and re-processes affected materials.

Processes audiovisual materials.

Updates vendor information on Dynix.

May participate in library-wide committees or projects.

Performs other tasks as assigned.

Knowledge, Skills, and Abilities

Accurate and efficient typing, filing, and other clerical skills, including basic knowledge of personal computer, copier, and fax operations.

Ability to organize work, set priorities, use time effectively, and work independently.

Ability to learn searching , minor editing, and e-mail skills on the libraryís automated system.

Ability to communicate well with supervisor, staff, and the general public.

Ability to analyze and creatively solve problems related to the position.

Ability to work with enthusiasm and initiative.

An understanding of basic library operations preferred.

Work Environment

The job is located in the James City County Library. Work occurs typically sitting in an office, with occasional walking, medium lifting, and other limited physical activities. Frequent sustained use of video display terminals is required. Requires handling of library materials, including transferring materials to carts and/or shelves. Regular contact is made with employees, vendors, and the general public. Computer, typewriter, copier, fax, and other office equipment as required.

Education, Experience, and Training

MINIMUM QUALIFICATIONS:

High school diploma or equivalent. Two years college and/or public library experience or equivalent preferred.

Additional Qualifications

NECESSARY SPECIAL QUALIFICATIONS:

Requires the ability to travel among various library sites.

XVII. Training Specialists

Included in this section are training librarians, heads of training and networked resources, specialists, training coordinators, and assistants.

1.0 ASSISTANT

1.1 TRAINING ASSISTANT

1.1.1 Training Assistant

Library Name: City of Austin
Library Location: Austin, Texas
Population Served: 623,125
Number of Volumes: N/A
Number of Titles: N/A
Number of Periodical Subscriptions: N/A

General Summary

Purpose:
Under general direction, responsible for developing and delivering and departmental and/or city wide training programs.

Essential Functions and Responsibilities

Essential duties and functions, pursuant to the Americans with Disabilities Act, may include the following. Other related duties may be assigned.

Develop and deliver training modules and workshops to selected audiences.

Assist in the selection and/or develop teaching aids, such as training handbooks or materials, demonstration models, visual aides, or computer tutorials.

Conduct training sessions.

Evaluate the effectiveness of training modules, workshops, etc and assist in making changes as necessary.

Participate in identifying program needs and obtaining technical data.

Schedule training programs.

Maintain training records.

Perform other duties as assigned.

Knowledge, Skills, and Abilities

Must possess required knowledge, skills, abilities and experience and be able to explain and demonstrate, with or without reasonable accommodations, that the essential functions of the job can be performed.

Knowledge of basic training and learning principles.

Skill in oral and written communications sufficient to clearly convey and receive. information and ideas.

Skill in delivering training.

Skill in hand ling and prioritizing multiple tasks.

Supervisory Responsibilities

Responsibilities- Supervision and/or Leadership Exercised: None.

Education, Experience, and Training

Minimum Qualifications
Education and/or Equivalent Experience:
Associate's degree in related field plus one (1) year related work experience.

One (1) year of experience can substitute for the education on a one for one basis up to two (2) years.

License and Certification Requirements

Licenses or Certifications Required: None.

Disclaimers

This description is intended to indicate the kinds of tasks and levels of work difficulty required of the position given this title and shall not be construed as declaring what the specific duties and responsibilities of any particular position shall be. It is not intended to limit or in any way modify the right of management to assign, direct and control the work of employees under supervision. The listing of duties and responsibilities shall not be held to exclude other duties not mentioned that are of similar kind or level of difficulty.

2.0 COORDINATOR

2.1 TRAINING DEVELOPMENT COORDINATOR

2.1.1 Training Development Coordinator

Library Name: Cuyahoga County Public Library
Library Location: Parma, Ohio
Population Served: 607,909
Number of Volumes: 3,297,420
Number of Titles: N/A
Periodical Subscriptions: 8,502

Reports To

Human Resources Director

General Summary

Under limited supervision of the Human Resources Director with alternating periods of relative autonomy, plans, coordinates and conducts managerial, supervisory and staff training programs designed to meet the organization objectives established by the Board of Directors, Executive Director and individual divisions and departments.

Essential Functions and Responsibilities

A. Complies with work scheduling and attendance requirements according to reasonable policy and practices. Staffing for branch and regional libraries and some Administration (ADM) departments requires rotational scheduling, which includes evening and weekend (Saturday and Sunday) hours. Most ADM departments are weekday operations.

B. Consistently presents Cuyahoga County Public Library and its services in a positive manner and adheres to customer service guidelines and procedures as established by the Library.

C. Complies with the established rules of operation, procedures, and policies when using library computers, peripheral hardware, and software. Individual passwords and any other confidential information regarding library records shall be kept confidential.

Plans and organizes orientation/training center activities including scheduling training sessions, ensuring necessary training materials are available for sessions, preparing lesson plans, arranging for meeting space to meet needs of class size, etc.

Develops training programs in collaboration with division and department heads to meet both individual function and system wide training needs.

Leads and conducts various training sessions including orientation programs for new employees through oral presentation.

Monitors and evaluates effectiveness of individual training programs, maintains related records of program activities and prepares reports detailing implementation and program results.

Monitors trends in training industry and maintains file of available programs and program materials for possible use in library training program development and coordination.

Negotiates with outside training vendors to determine most cost effective programs available that meet library training and development needs.

Coordinates promotion and distribution of information regarding training programs to CCPL staff.

The intent of this position description is to provide a representative summary of the major duties and responsibilities performed by incumbents of this job. Incumbents may be requested to perform job-related tasks other than those specifically presented in this description.

Knowledge, Skills, and Abilities

Thorough knowledge of adult training methods, theories, concepts and techniques.

Knowledge of HRD policy manual regarding training and Training Center guidelines.

Excellent interpersonal and oral presentation skills for effectively presenting training programs to varying groups.

Strong organizational skills for coordinating the multiple functions and planning of the Training Center.

Ability to orally present training material to adult training/orientation classes.

Computer literate with ability to operate library word processing software programs.

Ability to develop and implement training programs from information obtained from library directors and managers, established training programs and evaluation of effectiveness of current programs.

Physical and Mental Requirements

Light physical effort required as when standing for prolonged periods of time presenting training program information, and moving and setting up equipment for presentations.

Standard work environment with no major sources of working conditions discomfort.

Supervisory Responsibilities

NA

Education, Experience, and Training

Summary Minimum Education & Experience Required

Bachelor's degree in Human Resources or related field.

Four to six years of training program development, coordination and implementation.

License and Certification Requirements

A criminal background check is required.

2.2. TRAINING COORDINATOR

2.2.1 Training Coordinator

Library Name: Cuyahoga County Public Library
Library Location: Parma, Ohio
Population Served: 607,909
Number of Volumes: 3,297,420
Number of Titles: N/A
Periodical Subscriptions: 8,502

Reports To

Human Resources Director

General Summary

Under general direction, plans, organizes, coordinates and conducts managerial, supervisory and staff training programs. Works under limited supervision of the Human Resources Director and consults with the Assistant Human Resources Director and the Continuing Education Advisory Committee in planning major projects.

Essential Functions and Responsibilities

(Note: The following functions represent the essential duties and outputs of the position.)

Complies with work scheduling and attendance requirements according to reasonable policy and practices. (Staffing for branch and regional libraries and some headquarters (HQS) departments requires rotational scheduling, which includes evening and weekend (Saturday & Sunday) hours. Most HQS departments are weekday operations.)

Assists in implementing CCPL's managerial/supervisory and staff training programs including designing the content of training programs, conducting and/or coordinating the programs' presentation, evaluating and revising programs and analyzing results of training on staff performance.

Designs and conducts periodic training needs assessment studies, analyzes results and recommends programs to meet needs.

Maintains records and monitors staff participation and attendance at CCPL training programs for EEO purposes.

Participates in budgeting processes involving planning, development and proposal of budgets involving training projects. Monitors and maintains budget expenditure rates.

Coordinates publicity and dissemination of information to CCPL staff on training programs.

Knowledge, Skills, and Abilities

(The following knowledge, abilities and skills (KASs) represent the KASs needed at time of appointment to perform Essential Job Functions.)

Knowledge of

Proven knowledge and familiarity with adult training techniques and organizational development strategies.

Skills in

Creative problem solving to recognize and analyze needs and design programs to effectively address training needs.

Excellent communications skills, oral and written.

Education, Experience, and Training

Qualifications

(Note: Any acceptable combination of education, training, and experience that provides the above KASs may be substituted for those listed.)

Possession of a bachelor's degree in Human Resource development or comparable area including study in staff development and/or adult training.

Experience:

Five years of progressively more responsible experience in staff development that included practical experience in designing and conducting training programs.

Licenses: None.

Other:

Work is subject to inflexible deadlines.

Exempt/Nonexempt: Position is exempt from FLSA.

3.0 NETWORKED RESOURCES

3.1 HEAD OF NETWORKED RESOURCES

3.1.1 Head of Networked Resources

Library Name: St. Joseph County Public Library
Library Location: South Bend, Indiana
Population Served: 172,627
Number of Volumes: 521,968
Number of Titles: 178,920
Periodical Subscriptions: 2,901

Essential Functions and Responsibilities

Working under the direct supervision of the Networking Systems Coordinator this department head will:

Essential Job Duties:

1. Supervise and provide direction for the Networked Resources Development/Training department.

2. Develop and conduct a system wide program of staff and public technology training.

3. Organize ongoing development and maintenance of libraryís web site in collaboration with Webmaster, Web advisory committee, Computer Services, and Administration.

4. Implement staff technology competencies in cooperation with Personnel Department.

5. Maintain knowledge of current and emerging technologies and their potential implications for training and web site development.

6. Maintain knowledge of principles and practice of instructional design as applied to staff and public training programs; knowledge of the principles of adult learning theory and techniques.

7. Supervise department staff members including: interviewing, training, scheduling, performance reviews, and staff meetings. Work to create customer service awareness, enthusiasm, and teamwork among staff.

8. Attend and participate in administrative committees and meetings; participate in professional activities.

9. Additional responsibilities as assigned.

Additional Qualifications

Willingness to work at or be transferred to other service areas or branches if need arises.

Knowledge, Skills, and Abilities

Positive interpersonal style;

Excellent oral and written communication skills.

Must be able to work independently, as well as in a team.

Ability to establish and maintain effective work relationships.

Must possess initiative, creativity, flexibility, organizational skills, and the ability to accept and manage change.

Education, Experience, and Training

MLS from ALA-accredited program.

Experience:

Proven experience developing and conducting technology training courses.

Experience in web site development and maintenance.

Proven management experience.

License and Certification Requirements

Valid driver's license and own personal transportation.

Position Hours

Required to work a 40 hour work week.

4.0 TRAINING AND STAFF DEVELOPMENT LIBRARIAN

4.1 STAFF DEVELOPMENT LIBRARIAN

4.1.1 Staff Development Librarian

Library Name: St. Joseph County Public Library
Library Location: South Bend, Indiana
Population Served: 172, 627
Number of Volumes: 521,968
Number of Titles: 178,920
Periodical Subscriptions: 2,901

Essential Functions and Responsibilities

Perform duties to further the development of all library staff. Under the direct supervision of the Personnel Services Administrator, the Staff Development Librarian will:

1. Coordinate and facilitate ongoing staff development opportunities with various staff members responsible for training.

2. Create and present training sessions for library staff, including but not limited to reference skills and information technology skills.

3. Develop a variety of training documents/modules and/or Web-based training for use in the library system.

4. Coordinate system-wide training efforts to insure the effective utilization of staff development opportunities.

5. Negotiate and organize outside training/development opportunities based on needs assessments.

6. Evaluate library's current training program and recommend/implement changes/improvements

7. Manage and schedule the libraryís technology training room and mobile training labs.

8. Evaluate the libraryís professional meetings program and guide staff attendance at conferences following established protocols.

9. Perform reference services at a public service location on a weekly basis.

Support the St. Joseph County Public Library mission by modeling internal and external customer services.

Perform other duties as required.

Additional Job Duties

Required to rotate to other assignments in an effort to promote professional growth and job enrichment throughout the organization.

Willingness to work at or be transferred to other service areas or branches if the need arises.

Knowledge, Skills, and Abilities

Personal Strengths and Abilities

Ability to create, compose and edit written materials, including technical writing skills.

Ability to develop or revise training materials as needed.

Familiarity with web technology.

Ability to plan and organize multi-step projects.

Ability to form and maintain excellent working relationships with library staff.

Ability to work quickly and accurately.

Ability to work independently and to adapt or devise new working methods as necessary

Ability to accept and manage change.

Ability to understand and endorse the SJCPL philosophy of public service as contained in the Mission Statement, Long Range Plan, Policy Statements and other related documents.

Education, Experience, and Training

Master's Degree in Library Science.

Three to four years experience directly related to the duties and responsibilities specified Job Description

License and Certification Requirements

Valid driver's license and own transportation.

Must be able to work independently and as part of a team; work harmoniously with staff at all levels.

Additional Requirements:

Drug Testing and Criminal History Record Check are required as a condition of employment. Any offer of employment is subject to the applicant passing a drug-screening test and

Criminal History Record Check.

Position Hours

Required to work a 40-hour week. May involve a flexible schedule.

Required to work up to six (6) Sunday afternoons per calendar year at library facilities open on Sundays.

4.1.2 Training Librarian

Library Name: St. Clair County Library System
Library Location: Port Huron, Michigan
Population Served: 160,708
Number of Volumes: 432,880
Number of Titles: 206,173
Periodical Subscriptions: 560

General Summary

General Duties: This position works with limited supervision performing Reference Department duties for the St. Clair County Library System. Responsible for developing, organizing and teaching the public and co-workers various computer programs, internet usage and e-mail methods system-wide.

Reports To

SUPERVISION RECEIVED
Reports to Adult Services Librarian.

Essential Functions and Responsibilities

Desired Qualifications: Ability to read and interpret documents. Strong interpersonal skills with the ability to relate to all diversities of employees and customers. Ability to apply common sense understanding to carry out instructions in written or verbal form. Ability to deal with problems and make minor decisions in accordance with established procedures. Ability to operate a Personal Computer and Dynix software. A wide range of word processing, spreadsheet, e-mail and internet experience. Ability to present staff and customer computer instruction in a concise and clear manner. Ability to perform duties in a professional, courteous manner with awareness of all Management, Library Board and County policies and procedures.

Additional Job Duties

Responsible for Reference Desk duties providing Library customers with requested information. Performs reader's advisory and is instrumental in the selection, organization and access of library materials. Assists Library customers in navigating public access catalog, Internet, LAN and additional technological databases.

Physical and Mental Requirements

The physical demands described here are representative of those that must be met by an employee to successfully perform the essential functions of this position. Reasonable accommodations may be made to enable individuals with disabilities to perform the essential functions.

While performing the duties of this job, the employee is regularly required to sit, talk and hear. The employee is required to stand, walk and operate a computer. The employee is required to push carts with materials and stoop in an ergonomically correct manner. The employee must occasionally life and/or move sup-plies and materials up to 35 pounds. Specific vision requirements required by this job include close vision and depth perception.

Work Environment

The noise level in the work environment is moderate with many interruptions. Position requires working with a very diverse cross-section of the public.

Supervisory Responsibilities

SUPERVISION EXERCISED
Library staff during scheduled evening and weekends when Librarian 1A is highest authority available.

Education, Experience, and Training

Experience Needed: Graduate degree in Information (Library) Science from an ALA accredited school. Knowledge of the principles and practices of professional library responsibilities.

Disclaimers

Typical Work: (An employee in this classification may be called upon to perform the following tasks which are illustrative and not exhaustive in nature.)

5.0 SPECIALIST

5.1 TRAINING SPECIALIST

5.1.1 Training Specialist

Library Name: St. Joseph County Public Library
Library Location: South Bend, Indiana
Population Served: 172,627
Number of Volumes: 521,968
Number of Titles: 178,920
Periodical Subscriptions: 2,901

Essential Functions and Responsibilities

Working in a team led by the Head of Networked Resources Development and Training Department, the person in this position will perform the following:
Essential Job
Duties:

1. Develop with and conduct staff training courses for networked reference resources (i.e. Internet, leased and in-house databases, and the OPAC), software applications, and other technology, as appropriate in conjunction with NRDT Head.

2. Assist with maintenance of web site; participate in the Web Development Team.

3. Participate in electronic resource selection committee and provide statistics to NRDT Head and committee as needed.

4. Participate in "train-the-trainer" sessions for staff public trainers; guide development of public programs; teach public programs if necessary.

5. Maintain proficiency in current instructional technologies, as well as exploring emerging ones, through formal training, conferences, trade journals, and professional activities.

6. Work at reference desks throughout the library system 2–4 hrs./wk. (usually at Main Library)

Additional Qualifications

Willingness to work at or be transferred to other service areas or branches if the need arises.

Valid driver's license and own transportation.

Must be able to work independently and as part of a team; work harmoniously with staff at all levels.

Knowledge, Skills, and Abilities

Personal Strength and Abilities:

Ability to communicate with a positive interpersonal style.

Must possess initiative, creativity, flexibility, and good organizational skills.

Must have excellent oral and written communication skills.

Ability to accept and manage change.

Education, Experience, and Training

MLS or MIS preferred.

Experience in training and producing documentation for electronic resources.

Experience in web page maintenance.

Microcomputer experience, preferably both Macintosh and Windows.

Library public service experience a plus.

Position Hours

Required to work a 40-hour week. May involve a flexible schedule.

XVIII. Volunteers—Public Service

Volunteers serving in the public areas are listed by service area.

1.0 ART PROGRAMS
1.1 ARTS PROGRAM VOLUNTEER

1.1.1 Arts Program Volunteer

Library Name: Kokomo Howard County Public Library
Library Location: Kokomo, Indiana
Population Served: 78,245
Number of Volumes: 229,030
Number of Titles: 80,000
Number of Periodical Subscriptions: 506

Task Description:

Task Assist in preparation of craft materials and assists children with crafts during the Expressions Art Programs.

When does the task have to be done? Before and during the Expressions Programs in February, May, October and December.

What day and time? Dates of Expressions Program to be announced.

Times to be coordinated with staff schedule. May include evening and Saturday hours.

How often does it need to be done? Once each month listed above.

Exchange this month's bag for the previous month's collection.

Return to the library once all stops have been made.

Take returned materials to the Homebound Desk.

Record in the volunteer log the date, time in, time out, the number of patrons you served, and the time it took to deliver.

Where does it need to be done? Branch

Approximately how much time is involved? 4 to 6 hours each session.

What skills are required? Experience working with young children.

Ability to interact well with patrons and staff.

Ability to explain directions clearly to children.

Manual dexterity required.

Personality traits needed? Friendly, patient with young children.

How many people needed? 1-2 for each program.

Who will train, supervise and evaluate the volunteer?

Comments: A criminal background check is required for this position.

Training provided:

Training on how to use laminator.

Training in using die cuts to make nametags.

Detail description of task:

Assists the staff with preparation for Expressions programs.

Cuts out and laminates nametags.

Prepares items for various crafts.

Assists in setting up room prior to program and clean up after program.

Helps with registration on the day of the program.

Assists children in making craft during the Expressions Program.

2.0 BOOK READER
2.1 SPECIAL READER

2.1.1 "Book Break" Reader

Library Name: Pikes Peak Library District
Library Location: Colorado, Springs, Colorado
Population Served: 448,860
Number of Volumes: 876,897
Number of Titles: N/A
Number of Periodical Subscriptions: 2,330

Adult readers select children's books with staff guidance and read aloud with enthusiasm to preschool children for 20 minutes.

3.0 BOOK DISCUSSIONS
3.1 BOOK DISCUSSION FACILITATOR

3.1.1 Book Discussion Facilitator

Library Name: Madison Public Library
Library Location: Madison, Wisconsin
Population Served: 207,248
Number of Volumes: 858,197
Number of Titles: 499,272
Number of Periodical Subscriptions: 2,150

Job Description: Facilitate book discussions in libraries, including helping groups decide on dates and times, reserving meeting space, suggesting reading choices and helping group members reserve books through the library's computer system

Location: Central and branches

Time Commitment: 2 hours per month at the library per book discussion; time at home for reading the book, researching the author or any other topic of interest, creating discussion questions

Qualifications: A well read person with a background in literature, the Humanities or teaching; must feel comfortable guiding and facilitating groups

4.0 BOOKSTORE

4.1 BOOKSTORE VOLUNTEER

4.1.1 Bookstore Volunteer

Library Name: San Jose Public Library
Library Location: San Jose, California
Population Served: 918,000
Number of Volumes: 424,546
Number of Titles: N/A
Number of Periodical Subscriptions: 3,186

Reports To

Book Store Manager

Time Commitment: Average of 4-8 hours per week

Book Store hours are: 1:00-4:30 Tuesday-Friday

10:00-1:30 Saturday

Purpose: Friends of the San Jose Public Library advocate the importance of Library services in our communities and through the book store and quarterly book sales raise funds to support library goals.

Qualifications: Desire and ability to work with the diverse public of San Jose

Ability to keep basic daily book sale records

Ability to interact and work with all levels of library staff, Public Safety Officials and volunteers

Able to make change accurately

Organized

Dependable

Duties include:

Is the first line contact with the public to ensure their needs are met while visiting the Friends Book Store.

Assists with the upkeep of accurate records of book store sales

Assists with the coordination of book shelf needs with volunteer book sorters

Answers phones

Assures that shelves are neat and stocked for book store customers

Training: A general library orientation will be provided and specific job training will be given on-site.

5.0 CHILDREN'S PROGRAMMING

5.1 CHILDREN'S PROGRAMMING ASSISTANT

5.1.1 Children's Programming Assistant

Library Name: Madison Public Library
Library Location: Madison, Wisconsin
Population Served: 207,248
Number of Volumes: 858,197
Number of Titles: 499,272
Number of Periodical Subscriptions: 2,150

Job Description: Assist Youth Services staff in presenting programs for children and young teens. Could include: helping librarians with craft programs for preschool story times and school-age programming, showing children's videos on a regular basis, helping with the Summer Library Program finale.

Location: Central Library, branches and off-site locations

Time Commitment: $1\frac{1}{2}$ to 2 hours per week; 10 weeks or length of program series

Qualifications: Like and respect children, work effectively with children, ability to understand and follow oral and written instructions. Training on the use of AV equipment will be provided.

5.1.2 Children's Programming Assistant

Library Name: Madison Public Library
Library Location: Madison, Wisconsin
Population Served: 207,248
Number of Volumes: 858,197
Number of Titles: 499,272
Number of Periodical Subscriptions: 2,150

Job Description: Assist professional staff to provide active, hands-on projects for a large group of school-age kids, 7-15, who come to the library with nothing to do. Set up, provide instruction, and help kids play board and card games, word games, and charades. Assist with set up, instruction, and clean up of craft projects. Can work one on one or with a group of kids.

Location:

Time Commitment: Monday afternoons, 1:30–4:30 p.m., other weekday afternoons possible

Qualifications: Like and respect children, work effectively with children, ability to understand and follow oral and written instructions.

5.1.3 Children's Programming Preparation Assistant

Library Name: Madison Public Library
Library Location: Madison, Wisconsin
Population Served: 207,248
Number of Volumes: 858,197
Number of Titles: 499,272
Number of Periodical Subscriptions: 2,150

Job Description: Assist Youth Services staff in preparing programs for children and young teens. This could include: preparing craft project material for preschool story times, using the Ellison Die machine, assembling Summer Library Program materials.

Note: Jobs may involve repetitive motion, which may be hard on elbow/wrist joints.

Location: Central Library, branches

Time Commitment: $1^{1}/_{2}$ to 2 hours per week; 10 weeks or length of program

Qualifications: Ability to work independently; ability to understand and follow oral and written instructions; ability to adapt to routine repetitive activities

6.0 COORDINATOR FOR VOLUNTEERS

6.1 VOLUNTEER COORDINATOR

6.1.1 Volunteer Coordinator

Library Name: Phoenix Public Library
Library Location: Phoenix, Arizona
Population Served: 1,350,435
Number of Volumes: 2,015,587
Number of Titles: 734,921
Number of Periodical Subscriptions: 4,500

DISTINGUISHING FEATURES OF THE CLASS:

The fundamental reason this classification exists is to plan, develop, and implement volunteer, fund raising, and/or community service programs, recruit volunteers, promote gift giving, and formulate public relations and informational programs in support of the Phoenix Public Library or the Human Services

Department. Work is performed under the general supervision of the City Librarian, Personnel Officer II, or other supervisor who reviews work plans and materials for conformance to policy.

Essential Functions and Responsibilities

Develops and implements volunteer programs in support of City services;

Recruits volunteers for support work and recommends assignments that will make the best use of individual talents;

Develops training programs for volunteers and City staff who use volunteers;

Serves on task forces and committees related to volunteerism;

Writes requests for individual, corporate or foundation donations in behalf of the City;

Receives and acknowledges gifts in conformance with policies;

Maintains public contacts in the community and public/private sectors in order to implement fund raising strategies;

Develops and implements fund raising strategies and informational programs to encourage support of City programs;

Promotes public awareness of gift giving to the City, as well as its needs for volunteers, by such means as writing press releases and making public appearances;

Coordinates the preparation and printing of publicity materials with the department's Public Information Officer or City's Public Information Department, and with graphic artists in the City's Print Shops;

Determines the most economical and efficient means to print professional quality publicity materials;

Reviews proposed legislation and City, departmental, and program policies and procedures for issues related to volunteers;

Maintains volunteer time records and applications;

Plans, organizes, and implements volunteer recognition events and activities;

Assists staff in writing grant applications for programs utilizing volunteers;

Demonstrates continuous effort to improve operations, decrease turnaround times, streamline work processes, and work cooperatively and jointly to provide quality seamless customer service.

Required Knowledge, Skills and Abilities:

Knowledge, Skills, and Abilities

Principles, techniques, tools, and media used in promoting good public relations.

Principles and practices of volunteer management.

Methods and techniques of fund raising for cultural and educational institutions or social service agencies.

Ability to:

Communicate in the English language by phone or in person in a one-to-one or group setting.

Comprehend and make inferences from written material.

Produce written documents in the English language with clearly organized thoughts using proper sentence construction, punctuation, and grammar.

Work cooperatively with other City employees and the general public.

Work safely without presenting a direct threat to self or others.

Additional Qualifications

Some positions require the use of personal or City vehicles on City business. Individuals must be physically capable of operating the vehicles safely, possess a valid driver's license and have an acceptable driving record. Use of a personal vehicle for City business will be prohibited if the employee is not authorized to drive a City vehicle or if the employee does not have personal insurance coverage.

Some positions will require the performance of other essential and marginal functions depending upon work location, assignment or shift.

Education, Experience, and Training

Two years of experience in professional fund raising, professional volunteer management, or public relations and a bachelor's degree in liberal arts, public relations, or a related field. Other combinations of experience and education that meet the minimum requirements may be substituted.

7.0 ESL AND TRANSLATION

7.1 SPANISH TRANSLATOR

7.1.1 Spanish Translator

Library Name: Madison Public Library
Library Location: Madison, Wisconsin
Population Served: 207,248
Number of Volumes: 858,197
Number of Titles: 499,272
Number of Periodical Subscriptions: 2,150

Job Description: Works with library staff to help Spanish speaking customers obtain a library card, understand how the library operates and utilize the many resources available at the library.

Location: Currently at South Madison Branch

Time Commitment: 2 hours a week; 6 months

Qualifications: Fluent in Spanish and English; good "people" skills; understanding of how the library works

7.2 "TALK ENGLISH" FACILITATORS

7.2.1 "Talk English" Facilitators

Library Name: Pikes Peak Library District
Library Location: Colorado, Springs, Colorado
Population Served: 448,860
Number of Volumes: 876,897
Number of Titles: N/A
Number of Periodical Subscriptions: 2,330

Provides a place for English language learners with intermediate or high level skill to practice conversational English in a group setting. Facilitators work together as a team to conduct a 14-week series. Groups meet weekly for two hours.

8.0 FRIENDS OF THE LIBRARY

8.1 FRIENDS OF THE LIBRARY MEMBER

8.1.1 Friends of the Library Member

Library Name: San Jose Public Library
Library Location: San Jose, California
Population Served: 918,000
Number of Volumes: 424,546
Number of Titles: N/A
Number of Periodical Subscriptions: 3,186

Board Member: Friends of the Dr. Martin Luther King, Jr. Library

Purpose: Friends of the San Jose Public Library advocate the importance of Library services in our communities and through the book store and quarterly book sales raise funds to support library goals.

Time commitment: A minimum of 2 hours required for monthly Board Meetings

Participation in quarterly used-book sales (6-8 hours) and yearly silent–auction (4-6 hours)

Qualifications: A belief in and desire to support the San Jose Public Library

Desire and ability to work with the diverse public of San Jose

Energetic

Organized

Dependable

Duties might include:

As part of a hands-on team the Friend's Board of Directors ensures the ongoing needs of the Dr. Martin Luther King Main Library Book Store and used-book sales.

Training: A general library orientation will be provided and specific job training will be given by fellow board members.

9.0 HOME SERVICE

9.1 HOME SERVICE VOLUNTEER

9.1.1 Home Service Delivery Person

Library Name: Madison Public Library
Library Location: Madison, Wisconsin
Population Served: 207,248
Number of Volumes: 858,197
Number of Titles: 499,272
Number of Periodical Subscriptions: 2,150

Job Description: Delivers books and other materials to people's homes and returns finished materials to the library; serves as the library's contact for homebound users, passing on requests and problems; promotes a positive image of the Library through all contacts with the homebound user. If interested, please call Home Service at 608-266-6314.

Location: Branches and Homebound users' residences

Time Commitment: 1 to 2 hours per week on a scheduled basis; 6 months

Qualifications: Reference check; ability to work effectively with homebound users and staff; ability to understand and follow oral and written instructions as well as possessing good oral communication skills; access to transportation as needed

9.1.2 Home Service Delivery person

Library Name: Madison Public Library
Library Location: Madison, Wisconsin
Population Served: 207,248
Number of Volumes: 858,197
Number of Titles: 499,272
Number of Periodical Subscriptions: 2,150

Job Description: Delivers books and other materials to people's homes and returns finished materials to the library; serves as the library's contact for homebound users, passing on requests and problems; promotes a positive image of the Library through all contacts with the homebound user. If interested, please call Home Service at 608-266-6314.

Location: Branches and Homebound users' residences

Time Commitment: 1 to 2 hours per week on a scheduled basis; 6 months

Qualifications: Reference check; ability to work effectively with homebound users and staff; ability to understand and follow oral and written instructions as well as possessing good oral communication skills; access to transportation as needed

9.1.3 Homebound Volunteer

Library Name: Kokomo Howard County Public Library
Library Location: Kokomo, Indiana
Population Served: 78,245
Number of Volumes: 229,030
Number of Titles: 80,000
Number of Periodical Subscriptions: 506

Task Description:
Task Pick-up and deliver library materials to Homebound Patrons

When does the task have to be done? 1 time per month

What day and time? Usually on the first Tuesday or Thursday of the month. Mornings or early afternoons are preferred.

How often does it need to be done? 12 times per year.

Where does it need to be done? Main Library, transported to individual's homes.

Approximately how much time is involved? 2-3 hours per month.

9.1.4 Home Service Helper

Library Name: Madison Public Library
Library Location: Madison, Wisconsin
Population Served: 207,248
Number of Volumes: 858,197
Number of Titles: 499,272
Number of Periodical Subscriptions: 2,150

Job Description: Under the supervision of the Home Service staff: assists in choosing appropriate library materials for homebound users, maintains records of materials for all homebound users, and assists with management of retirement loan collections. If interested, please call Home Service at 608-266-6314.

Location: Central Library

Time Commitment: 1 day a week, 2 to 3 hours a day; 6+ months

Qualifications: A wide range of reading interests, with some knowledge of genre fiction; the ability to learn to use the Library's computer system; the ability to follow oral and written instructions; the ability to work independently; detail oriented

9.1.5 Home Delivery Volunteer

Library Name: Torrance Public Library
Library Location: Torrance California
Population Served: 143,220
Number of Volumes: N/A
Number of Titles: 524,277
Periodical Subscriptions: 1,134

Home Delivery Volunteer opportunities: Importance of the Position: Significantly impact the life of Torrance residents by delivering materials to individuals who are unable to visit library facilities.

Supervisor:

Qualifications:

Be 21 years of age or older

Possess a valid California Drivers License, furnish proof of adequate automobile insurance as per City regulations, availability of personal vehicle.

Willingness to commit to an ongoing delivery schedule and pay for fuel used.

Ability to be sensitive to the needs of and communicate with elderly adults and/or individuals with disabilities.

Patience, flexibility, and dependability.

Responsibilities:

Work with Senior Librarian in Charge of Access Services to select materials for home delivery to assigned patrons based on information on file at the library. This may require using the automated catalog to locate and request particular titles.

Deliver and pick up library materials from clients' homes in a timely manner.

Complete work in a neat and accurate manner with a minimum distraction to others.

Fulfill agreed upon commitment, or give supervisor adequate notice if unable to provide service for agreed upon schedule.

Training provided:

Orientation to the Library.

Specific instructions involved in the use of the library's catalog, selection of materials, and delivering library materials to individuals' homes.

Benefits of volunteering:

Personal satisfaction in enriching the lives of individuals unable to leave their residence.

Satisfaction of providing a much needed service to the library.

Time commitment: Varies

Length of commitment: Minimum of six months

Grounds for termination: Failure to carry out assigned responsibilities or misrepresenting the Library or its policies.

10.0 HOMEWORK CENTER
10.1 HOMEWORK CENTER VOLUNTEER

10.1.1 Homework Center Volunteer

Library Name: Weld Library District
Library Location: Greeley Colorado
Population Served: 137,888
Number of Volumes: 360,019
Number of Titles: N/A
Periodical Subscriptions: 711

General Description: Help students, individually or in small groups, work on specific homework assignments, within the framework of the public library. Students drop in for help as needed.

Duties:

Help students to interpret assignments.

Actively recruit student library users to visit the Homework Center

Talking with students about an approach or method for solving problems.

Referring students who need additional assistance to the Reference Librarian.

Sharing knowledge on a subject, such as math, English, science literature, drama, music, etc.

Reviewing homework when completed.

Reporting any problems to the Project Coordinator.

Recording the assistance given to students and submitting data to the Project Coordinator.

Assist students with the use of the Internet and other computer software.

Other duties as assigned.

Qualifications and Skills Required:

A desire to work with grade primary and secondary school students.

Effective communication skills, both oral and written.

Knowledge of basic math, reading and grammar skills, higher level of skills helpful.

Ability to communicate with both adults and young people.

Reliability and flexibility is essential

Training or experience as a teacher, tutor, parent or youth volunteer helpful.

Spanish language skills helpful, but not required.

Sensitivity to ESL issues.

Requirements of the Job:

Volunteers need to commit to 2 hours 1 day per week for the length of the semester. Times very according to the schedule

Volunteers must attend a training session prior to placement. Training will consist of:

The use of library resources

Computer software

Library Policies and Procedures

Confidentiality Policies

Information on developmental issues for school age students

Training and Supervision provided by: The Volunteer Coordinator, Branch Manager and the Young Adult Associate Librarian.

Benefits to the Volunteer:

Volunteers make a real difference in the lives of the students they work with. They help create lifelong learners and library users. Volunteers will have the satisfaction of helping to encourage, motivate and support students in completing their homework and assist them in succeeding as students.

11.0 LITERACY AND LANGUAGE TUTOR

11.1 LITERACY TUTOR

11.1.1 Literacy Tutor

Library Name: Pikes Peak Library District
Library Location: Colorado, Springs, Colorado
Population Served: 448,860
Number of Volumes: 876,897
Number of Titles: N/A
Number of Periodical Subscriptions: 2,330

The LitSource Adult Literacy program can help you help someone learn to read, improve their comprehension or English language skills. Training session are at Penrose Library, 20 N. Cascade Ave.

Tutors work one-on-one with an adult learner wishing to improve his/her reading skills 2-4 hours weekly for a minimum of six months.

Training is required and a six-month commitment is expected.

Return completed LitSource Volunteer application to LitSource Office, Penrose

Click here to view a LitSource Volunteer Application. Print, fill it out, and return it to any library branch to apply.

11.1.2 Literacy Reading Tutor

Library Name: Tahlequah Public Library
Library Location: Tahlequah, Oklahoma
Population served: N/A
Number of Volumes: 32,000
Number of Titles: 30,000
Number of Periodical Subscriptions: 12

Purpose of Position

To help an adult learn to read, write and improve comprehension skills.

Qualifications

Dependable and prompt, interested in others and able to relate to them, respectful of confidentiality, flexible, friendly, patient, and optimistic. Sense of humor helpful.

Training

Completion of a certified tutor training workshop. Additional in-service training will be offered at local, state, regional and national workshops and conferences.

Place of Work

At the local public library or any other public place the tutor and student find that would be convenient.

Time Commitment

At least one year with a minimum of 6 months. Tutors and students should meet once or twice a week for one hour or an hour and a half.

Duties

Meet regularly and punctually

Prepare each lesson to meet individual needs of the student.

Provide encouragement and support to your student by: listening to what the student has to say helping develop a positive attitude toward learning being supportive rather than critical of mistakes encouraging reading beyond the tutoring sessions

Identify student's special interest areas and integrate related materials.

Inform student/tutor coordinator of problems encountered in tutoring sessions.

Inform literacy coordinator of special materials and/or training needs.

Reports Required

Keep accurate records of hours tutored.

Turn in monthly tutoring reports to local literacy efforts.

Turn in student assessment and progress reports annually.

Fringe Benefits

Heightened perception of the word around you, deepened understanding of values and lifestyles different from your own, a broadened imagination for creative problem solving, and the knowledge that you are helping another individual, your community and your state.

12.0 STORY HOUR

12.1 STORYTELLER

12.1.1 Storyteller

Library Name: San Jose Public Library
Library Location: San Jose, California
Population Served: 918,000
Number of Volumes: 424,546
Number of Titles: N/A
Number of Periodical Subscriptions: 3,186

Come help enrich children's love of literature and heighten their reading skills in a creative and exciting atmosphere.

Reports To Children's librarian

Time commitment: Approximately 1 hour per week for at least a one-year commitment

Available either

Evenings 7:00-8:00pm

Mornings 10:00-11:00am

Purpose: Through the time honored tradition of reading aloud trained volunteers will encourage the love of reading through storytime programs targeting children 2-9 years-old. The Story Teller will share a wealth of books, songs and more to help children experience their world and culture around them. Children will acquire language skills and vocabulary, develop their imaginations, achieve more success in school, realize that reading is fun and entertaining, grasp new or difficult concepts and enjoy books too difficult for them to read on their own.

Qualifications:

18 years of age or older

Excellent oral communication skills

Excellent English speaking skills, Mandarin a plus

Comfortable working with Children

Flexible use of a wide range of presentation materials (*training provided)

Available for 6 hr basic "Reading to Children" training an additional 8 hr training/mentoring on site will also be completed

Ability to work independently

Responsible

Dependable

Volunteers must be fingerprinted

Duties:

Provide a 30-minute story time each week using stories, singing and creative movement to children.

Communicate with library staff to keep current with events and library activities.

Promote library programs at the Calabazas Branch Library for children aged 2 to 9 years old.

*Free Training:

A six-hour basic training (3 two hour sessions, held on three consecutive dates) is provided which includes:

Information on why it is important to read to children

Tips on selecting books for children of all ages, interests and backgrounds

Strategies for working effectively with children and parents

Techniques for leading children to reading

Followed up with 8 hours of training/mentoring with the branch Children's Librarian which covers:

Branch resources like big books, puppets, musical instruments, and flannel stories

How to build a storytime with stories, song, movement, rhymes, and drama using props.

Practice reading skills with Children's librarian during storytimes for the Calabazas community.

Provide two solo story times to hone skills while working with children.

Ongoing training and mentoring will be available to you through the Children's librarian.

12.1.2 Story Hour Volunteer

Library Name: Kokomo Howard County Public Library
Library Location: Kokomo, Indiana
Population Served: 78,245
Number of Volumes: 229,030
Number of Titles: 80,000
Number of Periodical Subscriptions: 506

Task Description:

Task Assist with preparation of materials for story hour.

When does the task have to be done? A week before each story hour.

What day and time? Flexible. Evening and Saturday hours possible.

How often does it need to be done? Minimum of 2 hours per story time

Where does it need to be done? Approximately how much time is involved? 2-4 hours each story time. About 24 times a year.

What skills are required? Handy with simple crafts.

Sewing skills a plus.

Able to work independently.

Requires manual dexterity.

Personality traits needed? Enjoys working with hands.

How many people needed? 1-2

Comments: A criminal background check is required for this position.

Training provided:

Training on using the laminator.

Training on using die cuts.

Training on using the copier.

Detailed description of task:

Cuts out and laminates name tags.

Prepares materials for various crafts, finger plays, flannel boards and puppet shows.

May prepare materials for decorating branch in coordination with story hour, program. and summer reading themes.

May copy color and activity pages for the story hours.

Note: The Head of the Branch is responsible for furnishing all patterns and materials for the volunteers.

12.1.3 Story Hour Parent Volunteer

Library Name: Kokomo Howard County Public Library
Library Location: Kokomo, Indiana
Population Served: 78,245
Number of Volumes: 229,030
Number of Titles: 80,000
Number of Periodical Subscriptions: 506

Task Description:

Task Assists with story hour.

When does the task have to be done? At each story hour.

What day and time? During story hour parent's own child attends.

How often does it need to be done? Minimum of 2 hours per story time

Where does it need to be done?

Approximately how much time is involved? 2 hours each story time.

What skills and abilities are required? Handy with simple crafts.

Ability to explain directions clearly to children.

Requires manual dexterity.

Personality traits needed? Enjoys working with hands and children.

How many people needed? 1 parent per story hour.

Comments: A criminal background check is required for this position.

Training provided:

Provided prior to each program.

Detailed description of task:

Talks with Head of Branch prior to story hour to go over craft directions.

Assists children in making simple craft during Story Hour.

13.0 SUMMER READING

13.1 SUMMER READING PROGRAM VOLUNTEER

13.1.1 Summer Reading Celebration Volunteer

Library Name: San Jose Public Library
Library Location: San Jose, California
Population Served: 918,000
Number of Volumes: 424,546
Number of Titles: N/A
Number of Periodical Subscriptions: 3,186

Reports To

Branch/Unit volunteer liaison

Time commitment: 2 to 4 hours per week (or as arranged), June 14 through

August 9, 2003

Available primarily between 12:00 noon and 4:00 PM, or during especially busy times.

Qualifications: Must be—

15 years of age or older

Enjoy working with people of all ages and cultures

Possess good verbal communication skills

Able to commit to a pre-arranged time schedule

Duties: Sign up participants in the Summer Reading Celebration

Explain how the Summer Reading Celebration works

Award points for minutes of reading

Distribute prizes based upon points earned

Other duties as needed

Training: Training & orientation will be provided at your library.

13.1.2 Summer Reading Club Decorating Volunteer

Library Name: Kokomo Howard County Public Library

Library Location: Kokomo, Indiana

Population Served: 78,245

Number of Volumes: 229,030

Number of Titles: 80,000

Number of Periodical Subscriptions: 506

Task Description:

Task Assist with decorating the Branch for the Summer Reading Club.

When does the task have to be done? Week prior to the start of Summer Reading Club—last week of May.

What day and time? Flexible. May include evening and Saturday hours.

How often does it need to be done? Once a year.

Approximately how much time is involved? 4 hours.

What skills are required? Ability to follow oral directions.

Ability to interact well with staff.

Personality traits needed? Friendly, courteous.

Likes to decorate.

Does not need to interact with patrons.

How many people needed? 2

Comments: lifting, stooping, standing, walking, reaching overhead, and possibly climbing a ladder.

Detail description of task:

Assists in decorating Branch for Summer Reading Club.

Helps put up various decorations provided by the Branch.

Tasks can include:

Putting up background paper on bulleting boards.

Putting border around and decorations on the bulletin board.

Suspending decorations from ceiling.

Decorating interior windows behind the circulation desk.

Placing decorations on top of the stacks and on the ends of the stacks.

Putting up decorations on the wall of the conference room.

13.1.3 Summer Reading Club Program Volunteer

Library Name: Kokomo Howard County Public Library

Library Location: Kokomo, Indiana

Population Served: 78,245

Number of Volumes: 229,030

Number of Titles: 80,000

Number of Periodical Subscriptions: 506

Task Description:

Task Assist staff during Summer Reading Club programs.

When does the task have to be done? During Summer Reading Club—June-July.

What day and time? Thursday afternoons—Noon to 4 pm.

How often does it need to be done? Once a week. 5 times during Summer Reading Club.

Approximately how much time is involved? 4 hours per program

What skills are required? Ability to follow oral directions.

Ability to interact well with patrons and staff.

Personality traits needed? Friendly, courteous.

How many people needed? 1-2

Who will train, supervise and evaluate the volunteer?

Comments Lifting, stooping, standing, and walking involved. May need to provide own transportation. A criminal background check is required for this position.

Detail description of task:

Assists in setting up room for programs.

Sets up chairs and/or tables for programs.

Greets patrons and helps sign in patrons if there has been a required registration.

Assists in monitoring patron behavior (safety related). Reports problems to Head of Branch.

Assists in taking down chairs, tables, and decorations at the end of the program.

Assists in general clean up of the program area.

13.1.4 Summer Reading Club Registration Volunteer

Library Name: Kokomo Howard County Public Library
Library Location: Kokomo, Indiana
Population Served: 78,245
Number of Volumes: 229,030
Number of Titles: 80,000
Number of Periodical Subscriptions: 506

Task Description:

Task Assist with Summer Reading Club registration and prize redemption.

When does the task have to be done? During Summer Reading Program, June-July.

What day and time? Hours are flexible. May include evening and Saturday hours.

How often does it need to be done? Daily

Where does it need to be done?

Approximately how much time is involved? 2-4 hours a week.

What skills are required? Ability to interact well with patrons and staff.

Ability to communicate information in an open and friendly manner.

Ability to work well in a busy environment.

Personality traits needed? Friendly. Courteous. Service-oriented. Patient.

How many people needed? 2-4

Who will train, supervise and evaluate the volunteer? Clerical staff will supervise when Head of Branch is out of the library.

Comments:

Training provided: Orientation to the Branch.

Training on the procedures and rules for the Summer Reading Club.

A criminal background check is required for this position.

Detail description of task:

Registers patrons for the Summer Reading Club.

Registers patrons for Summer Reading Club Programs.

Answers patron questions about the Summer Reading Club.

Verifies completion of requirements for prizes.

Assists patrons in the selection of prizes.

14.0 VISITOR GREETER

14.1 GREETER

14.1.1 Greeter

Library Name: Madison Public Library
Library Location: Madison, Wisconsin
Population Served: 207,248
Number of Volumes: 858,197
Number of Titles: 499,272
Number of Periodical Subscriptions: 2,150

Job Description: A wonderful opportunity for volunteers with people skills and a love for the Library! Staff a desk at the entryway to the library. Welcome visitors, and hand out library literature such as bookmarks or event flyers. Direct visitors to requested locations or resources, or refer them to the Reference desk. Training provided.

Location: Central Library, 201 W. Mifflin St.

Time Commitment: at least 1 day per week, 2-4 hour shifts

Qualifications: Knowledge of library resources and collections; friendly, outgoing personality.

XIX. Volunteers—Support Services

Volunteers serving in the support services area are listed below.

1.0 ANNOTATOR

1.1 ANNOTATOR

1.1.1 Annotator

Library Name: Madison Public Library
Library Location: Madison, Wisconsin
Population Served: 207,248
Number of Volumes: 858,197
Number of Titles: 499,272
Number of Periodical Subscriptions: 2,150

Job Description: Writes short descriptions of books, based on information garnered from book jackets and/or reviews, for use in booklists and other library publications.

Location: Central Library

Time Commitment: 2 to 3+ hours per week; 6+ months

Qualifications: Good writing/editing skills; typing/word processing skills useful, but not essential; ability to work independently; ability to understand and follow oral and written instructions

2.0 AUDIOVISUAL VOLUNTEER

2.1 CHECK/CLEAN AV MATERIALS

2.1.1 Check/Clean AV Materials

Library Name: Kokomo Howard County Public Library
Library Location: Kokomo, Indiana
Population Served: 78,245
Number of Volumes: 229,030
Number of Titles: 80,000
Number of Periodical Subscriptions: 506

Task Description:
Check/clean Main Adult videos, CDs, and DVDs
When does the task have to be done? Ongoing

What day and time? Any time the library is open
How often does it need to be done? Ongoing
Where does it need to be done? Circulation and/or AV repair area
Approximately how much time is involved? Ongoing
What skills are required? Putting materials in machine
Personality traits needed? Likes working alone; monotony
How many people are needed? One or two people at a time
Comments
Detailed description of task:
Clean and check all Main Adult videos, CDs, and DVDs for defects by using the RTI TapeChek and RTI DiscChek machines.
Videos:
1. Start at the beginning of the collection and pull one truckload of videos at a time to be cleaned and checked.
2. Operate the RTI TapeChek macine in the Circulation workroom to clean and check videos for defects.
3. If defects are found, set aside the video with a Post-it note telling how many defects were found.
4. Give defective videos to the AV Librarian (Dawn).
5. Reshelve the videos that had no defects.
6. Continue to the end of the collection.
CDs and DVDS:
Same procedures as above, but operate the RTI DiscChek machine located in the AV Storage area.

2.1.2 Audiovisual Repair Assistant

Library Name: Madison Public Library
Library Location: Madison, Wisconsin
Population Served: 207,248
Number of Volumes: 858,197
Number of Titles: 499,272
Number of Periodical Subscriptions: 2,150

Job Description: Under the supervision of library staff, assists in the repair of broken audio and video cassettes. Cleans and inspects videocassettes, audiocassettes and compact discs. Training in the use of AV equipment will be provided.

Location: Central Library

Time Commitment: 1 day a week, 2 to 3 hours a day; 6+ months

Qualifications: Ability to work independently, ability to understand and follow oral and written instructions, must be detail oriented, must be comfortable using AV equipment

3.0 BOOK REPAIR TECHNICIAN

3.1 Book Repairer

3.1.1 Book Repairer

Library Name: Woodland Public Library
Library Location: Woodland, California
Population Served: 46,300
Number of Volumes: 95,372
Number of Titles: N/A
Number of Periodical Subscriptions: 237

Importance of Position to the Library: Assists the Library by maintaining best-loved books and materials in good repair, so they can be used by library visitors.

Qualifications:

Good small motor skills and eyesight

Good attention to detail

Willingness to work with a small group

Responsible To: Director of Volunteer Services

Responsibilities:

Attend a 3-hour training provided by the Library at no charge, on book repair and cleaning.

Work with other Spinetinglers to set monthly mending date.

Attend monthly mending date, or give supervisor sufficient notice if unable to attend.

Training Provided: Orientation to the Library as well as a three-hour training on skills and techniques for repairing, mending and cleaning library books.

Benefits of Volunteering:

Provide a much-needed service to the library and its customers by ensuring best-loved books are continually available.

Gain skills in book mending and repair.

Meet people who share similar interests.

Time Commitment: Three hours once a month

Length of Commitment: Minimum six month commitment requested

Grounds for Termination: Failure to carry out assigned responsibilities

4.0 CLERICAL WORKER

4.1 Clerical Volunteer

4.1.1 Office Assistant

Library Name: Madison Public Library
Library Location: Madison, Wisconsin
Population Served: 207,248
Number of Volumes: 858,197
Number of Titles: 499,272
Number of Periodical Subscriptions: 2,150

Job Description: Helps assemble in-house printing projects such as brochures, invitations, booklists, reports and the Library's newsletter. This may involve folding, stapling and/or collating.

Location: Central Library

Time Commitment: 2 to 4 hours at a time; could be a one time commitment. Newsletter volunteers meet quarterly.

Qualifications: Ability to understand and follow oral directions; manual dexterity required.

4.1.2 Clerical Assistant

Library Name: Madison Public Library
Library Location: Madison, Wisconsin
Population Served: 207,248
Number of Volumes: 858,197
Number of Titles: 499,272
Number of Periodical Subscriptions: 2,150

Job Description: Perfect for volunteers who enjoy the "behind the scenes" work. Assist the Development Director in prospect research, data entry, data look-ups, and fundraiser mailings.

Location: Central Library, 201 W. Mifflin St.

Time Commitment: 2-6 hours per week

Qualifications: Requires basic computer skills, and knowledge of Microsoft Word, Excel and Access is desired. Ability to work independently; ability to understand and follow oral and written instructions.

4.1.3 Clerical Worker

Library Name: Idaho State Library
Library Location: Boise, Idaho
Population Served: 1,200,000
Number of Volumes: 25,000
Number of Titles: N./A
Number of Periodical Subscriptions: N/A

Volunteer Services
Volunteers enhance the efforts of the Idaho State Library staff in all areas. We depend on our volunteers to help us meet the needs of our customers. Training will be provided for all positions.

Time Required:
2-4 hours per week during library hours, 8:00 am – 5:00 pm, Monday through Friday.

Word Processing—A variety of projects are available from transcription to production typing

5.0 NEWSPAPER SERVICES: INDEXING, NEWSPAPER CLIPPING, DATA ENTRY, AND ANNOTATION

5.1 NEWSPAPER SERVICES VOLUNTEER

5.1.1 Indexing Old Newspapers

Library Name: Kokomo Howard County Public Library
Library Location: Kokomo, Indiana
Population Served: 78,245
Number of Volumes: 229,030
Number of Titles: 80,000
Number of Periodical Subscriptions: 506

Task Description
Task Index old newspapers from microfilm
When does the task have to be done? Ongoing
What day and time? Any time the library is open
How often does it need to be done? Minimum of 2 hours per month

Where does it need to be done? Main Library
Approximately how much time is involved? Minimum of 2 hours each time
What skills are required? Indexing, writing
Personality traits needed? Likes working alone
How many people are needed? One person
Comments
Detailed description of task:
Index articles from the *Kokomo Tribune, Kokomo Perspective* and *Kokomo Herald* newspapers.

1. Every issue of the Kokomo Tribune, Kokomo Perspective and Kokomo Herald newspapers is searched for "local interest" articles. These include articles about people, events, and incidents in Howard County and the surrounding area. (The surrounding area includes those cities and counties bordering Howard County). "People" may include past and present residents, or people who have a connection to a local family or business. Events and incidents are generally fires, traffic accidents, major sporting accomplishments, etc.

2. Due to their importance to the local community, national articles about DaimlerChrysler, Delphi Delco, and General Motors are all indexed.

3. Vital statistics, editorials, columns, "in the military," and insignificant police reports are not indexed.

4. Assign subject heading(s) based upon standards provided.

5. Name of newspaper, date, page, article title, and subject headings are recorded and given to the person who keys the information into the database.

5.1.2 Indexer

Library Name: Madison Public Library
Library Location: Madison, Wisconsin
Population Served: 207,248
Number of Volumes: 858,197
Number of Titles: 499,272
Number of Periodical Subscriptions: 2,150

Job Description: Read and index articles from the Wisconsin State Journal. Note: Job involves using a microfilm and/or microfiche reader. Some people find using this equipment for long periods of time hard on the eyes.
Location: Central Library
Time Commitment: 1 day a week, 2 to 3 hours a day; 6+ months
Qualifications: Knowledge of Madison's history, past and present; experience with indexing is useful; must be detail oriented; ability to work independently; ability to understand and follow oral and written instructions

5.1.3 Newspaper Index Data Entry

Library Name: Kokomo Howard County Public Library
Library Location: Kokomo, Indiana
Population Served: 78,245
Number of Volumes: 229,030
Number of Titles: 80,000

Task Description
Task Data entry for index of old newspapers
When does the task have to be done? Ongoing/after it's indexed
What day and time? Any time the library is open
How often does it need to be done? Minimum of 2 hours per month
Where does it need to be done? Main Library
Approximately how much time is involved? Minimum of 2 hours each time
What skills are required? Typing, familiarity with ACCESS
Personality traits needed? Likes working alone
How many people are needed? One person
Comments This job is dependant on the indexer completing work first
Detailed description of task:
Enter indexed newspaper information into the database.
1. Double click on "Newspaper Index" icon located on computer desktop.
2. Enter each subject heading, article title, newspaper, date and page number exactly as written.

5.1.4 Newspaper Clipping and Indexing World War II Era

Library Name: Kokomo Howard County Public Library
Library Location: Kokomo, Indiana
Population Served: 78,245
Number of Volumes: 229,030
Number of Titles: 80,000
Number of Periodical Subscriptions: 506

Task Description
Task Cut articles from newspapers (obits, births, anniversaries, baby photos, etc.)
When does the task have to be done? Project to be completed end of 2003

What day and time? Anytime the library is open
How often does it need to be done? Minimum of 2-4 hours per week
Where does it need to be done? Genealogy and Local History Dept., Main
Library
Approximately how much time is involved? 2-4 hours each time
What skills are required? Operation of copy machine
Personality traits needed? Likes working with hands, and does not need to socialize
How many people are needed? Several volunteers are needed but each will work alone.
Who will train, supervise and evaluate the volunteer?
Equipment used Scissors, copy machine
Comments
Detailed description of task:
Volunteer will be assigned a month of newspapers to work with.
Search the newspaper for articles of a local genealogical interest.
Make sure there is not an article to be clipped on the back of the found article.
If there is, photocopy one of the articles then clip the other.
Date article.
Sort articles by type.

6.0 LABEL VOLUNTEER

6.1 LABELER

6.1.1 Labeler

Library Name: Kokomo Howard County Public Library
Library Location: Kokomo, Indiana
Population Served: 78,245
Number of Volumes: 229,030
Number of Titles: 80,000
Number of Periodical Subscriptions: 506

Task Description
Task Replace labels on books
When does the task have to be done? On-going
What day and time? Anytime the library is open
How often does it need to be done? Minimum of 2 hours per week

Where does it need to be done? Genealogy and Local History Dept., Main Library

Approximately how much time is involved? 1-2 hours each time

What skills are required? Neat hand lettering with pen

Personality traits needed? Likes working with hands, and does not need to socialize

How many people are needed? One or two volunteers are needed but each will work alone.

Equipment used Utility knife and ink pen

Comments

Detailed description of task:

Pick a section to work in (Family History, a county, etc.)

Make a sheet of new labels to match that section

Taking one book at a time, remove old label and tape (if paper cover then don't take off label and tape)

Wipe sticky spot with De-Solv-it (citrus solution)

Dry area

Put new label on

Put label protector over label

Also replace colored tape on spine if needed

7.0 MAGAZINES AND PERIODICALS

7.1 MAGAZINE AND PERIODICAL VOLUNTEER

7.1.1 Periodical Assistant

Library Name: Kokomo Howard County Public Library
Library Location: Kokomo, Indiana
Population Served: 78,245
Number of Volumes: 229,030
Number of Titles: 80,000
Number of Periodical Subscriptions: 506

Task Description:
Task Assists with pulling older newspapers and periodicals.
When does the task have to be done? Twice a month.
What day and time? Flexible. May be done in the evening or on Saturday.
How often does it need to be done? Minimum of 1 hour each time.

Where does it need to be done?

Approximately how much time is involved? 2 hours each month.

What skills are required? Able to concentrate and pay attention to details.

Personality traits needed? Dependable.

Does not need to interact with patrons.

How many people needed? 1

Who will train, supervise and evaluate the volunteer?

Clerical staff will supervise when Head of Branch is out of the library.

Comments: Requires lifting, carrying, stooping.

Training provided: Training in withdrawal of periodicals from shelf.

Detailed description of task:

Sorts through newspapers and pulls issues more than two weeks old.

Places newspapers in crates or paper bags to go to Main for recycling.

Labels crate or bag with black marker for recycling and places with courier items.

Following a rotational list of titles, the volunteer pulls magazine issues more than a year old.

Places magazines on the workroom counter for the 30-hour clerk for processing.

7.1.2 Magazine Assistant

Library Name: Madison Public Library
Library Location: Madison, Wisconsin
Population Served: 207,248
Number of Volumes: 858,197
Number of Titles: 499,272
Number of Periodical Subscriptions: 2,150

Job Description: Assist library staff in maintaining the magazine collection in an orderly manner.

Location: Branches

Time Commitment: 1 day a week, 2+ hours a day; 6+ months

Qualifications: Attention to detail; able to work independently; able to arrange materials in chronological and alphabetical order; able to push, bend, stretch and lift.

8.0 MATERIALS CLEANING ASSISTANT

8.1 MATERIALS CLEANING ASSISTANT

8.1.1 Materials Cleaning Assistant

Library Name: Madison Public Library
Library Location: Madison, Wisconsin
Population Served: 207,248
Number of Volumes: 858,197

Job Description: Assist library staff in maintaining and improving the physical condition of library materials, including cleaning, mending and covering books, videos and CD's, and covering, removing or replacing labels on any of these materials.

Location: Central Library and Branches

Time Commitment: 1 day a week, 2+ hours a day; 6+ months

Qualifications: Good manual dexterity and attention to detail; able to work independently; no allergies to commercial cleaners; ability to understand and follow oral and written instructions; ability to adapt to routine repetitive activities.

9.0 OBITUARY BOOK— MAINTENANCE

9.1 OBITUARY BOOK VOLUNTEER

9.1.1 Obituary Book Volunteer

Library Name: Kokomo Howard County Public Library
Library Location: Kokomo, Indiana
Population Served: 78,245
Number of Volumes: 229,030
Number of Titles: 80,00
Number of Periodical Subscriptions: 506

Task Description
Task Compile obituaries into book form

When does the task have to be done? On-going

What day and time? Anytime the library is open

How often does it need to be done? Minimum of 2 hours per week

Where does it need to be done? Genealogy and Local History Dept., Main Library

Approximately how much time is involved? 1-2 hours each time

What skills are required? Operation of microfilm reader/printer

Personality traits needed? Likes working with hands, and does not need to socialize

How many people are needed? Several volunteers are needed but each will work alone.

Who will train, supervise and evaluate the volunteer?

Equipment used: Microfilm reader/printer & copy machine

Comments:

Detailed description of task:

Photocopy obituaries from the microfilm

Cut obituaries apart

Divide by month

Alphabetize obituaries

Tape to sheets of paper

Make copies of these sheets using the copy machine

Label these pages with the month and year

10.0 TECHNICAL ASSISTANT

10.1 TECHNICAL ASSISTANT

10.1.1 Technical Assistant

Library Name: Idaho State Library
Library Location: Boise, Idaho
Population Served: 1,200,000
Number of Volumes: 25,000
Number of Titles: N./A
Number of Periodical Subscriptions: N/A

Volunteer Services

Volunteers enhance the efforts of the Idaho State Library staff in all areas. We depend on our volunteers to help us meet the needs of our customers. Training will be provided for all positions.

Time Required:

2-4 hours per week during library hours, 8:00 am – 5:00 pm, Monday through Friday.

Machine Repair – repair and maintenance of Talking Book equipment (tools provided)

Recording – record local interest books and magazines

Narrator – narrates book and magazine. Anyone wishing to apply for this position must pass a narration audition test.

Monitor – operates open reel recording equipment, while following the narration in a print copy of the text.

Reviewer – operates open reel playback equipment. Proof read previously recorded material.

11.0 TECHNOLOGY ASSISTANT
11.1 TECHNOLOGY ASSISTANT

11.1.1 Technology Assistant

Library Name: San Jose Public Library
Library Location: San Jose, California
Population Served: 918,000
Number of Volumes: 424,546
Number of Titles: N/A
Number of Periodical Subscriptions: 3,186

Reports To Branch/Unit Volunteer Liaison

Time commitment: 2-4 hours a week. We ask for at least a 3-6 month commitment.

Actual time commitment depending on need at specific Library Branch/Unit

Purpose: To provide direct technological support to library customers.

Qualifications: 15 years of age or older

Excellent oral communication skills

Bilingual a plus

Spanish

Chinese

Vietnamese

Organizational skills

A strong desire to work with and help people

Ability to work independently

Knowledge of basic PC and Printer maintenance (i.e. rebooting, refilling paper)

Familiarity with the following programs:

Microsoft Windows (95/98/NT)

Microsoft Word or similar word processing software

Microsoft Internet Explorer

Netscape Navigator

Duties might include: Monitor public usage of available computers

Basic computer troubleshooting and maintenance

One-on-One instruction with customers on:

Use of the OPAC and the Internet/World Wide Web

Basic "How to" use a computer

Basic "How to" word processing

Training: A general library orientation will be provided and specific job training on:

How to use the Library's on line public access catalog

Specific monitoring/sign up procedures

General maintenance of Library's Public Access Computers

Understanding the San Jose Public Library Internet Access and Use Policy

XX. Volunteers—Miscellaneous

Volunteers in various capacities are listed below.

1.0 BULLETIN BOARD

1.1 BULLETIN BOARDS AND HANDOUTS VOLUNTEER

1.1.1 Bulletin Boards and Handout Volunteer

Library Name: Kokomo Howard County Public Library
Library Location: Kokomo, Indiana
Population Served: 78,245
Number of Volumes: 229,030
Number of Titles: 80,000

Task Description:

Task Stocks the hand-out racks, arranges bulletin board by entrance and weeds outdated material from all areas.

When does the task have to be done? On-going.

What day and time? Flexible. May be evening or Saturday hours.

How often does it need to be done? Minimum of 1 hour per month.

Where does it need to be done? Branch

Approximately how much time is involved? 1-2 hours each time.

What skills are required? Able to work independently.

Personality traits needed? Does not need to interact with patrons.

How many people needed? 1

Who will train, supervise and evaluate the volunteer?

Clerical staff will supervise when Head of Branch is out of the library.

Comments: Requires reaching overhead.

Training provided: Training on appropriate materials for handout racks and bulletin board display.

Detailed description of task:

Makes certain public handouts are not covering library handouts

Removes commercial handouts from handout racks inside the library.

Checks handout racks for outdated materials.

Gives old materials to Head of Branch.

Replenishes handouts that are low.

Notifies Head of Branch if more handouts are need.

Places date on back of new public items on the bulletin board.

Removes public items after 2 months or after date of event advertised.

Makes certain that public notices are limited to the right hand side of the bulletin board.

Makes certain Library notices are recent and have not been covered by public notices.

Brings any material inappropriate for posting to the attention of the Head of the Branch.

1.1.2 Bulletin Board Organizer

Library Name: Madison Public Library
Library Location: Madison, Wisconsin
Population Served: 207,248
Number of Volumes: 858,197

Job Description: Assists library staff in maintaining community information "give away" materials and posting community information on bulletin boards.

Location: Central Library and Branches

Time Commitment: 1 day a week, 2+ hours a day; 6+ months

Qualifications: Able to work independently; good organizational skills; able to push, bend, stretch and lift.

2.0. GENERAL DUTIES

2.1 GENERAL DUTIES VOLUNTEER

2.1.1 General Duties Volunteer

Library Name: San Jose Public Library
Library Location: San Jose, California
Population Served: 918,000
Number of Volumes: 424,546
Number of Titles: N/A
Number of Periodical Subscriptions: 3,186

Reports To Branch/Unit Volunteer Liaison

Time Commitment: 2-4 hours, once a week. We ask for at least a 6-month commitment

Actual time commitment depending on need at specific Library Branch/Unit

Purpose: To support/assist staff with day to day library maintenance

Qualifications: 15 years of age or older

Responsible

Dependable

Able to file alphabetically/numerically

Able to follow directions
Able to work independently
Duties might include:
Assisting customers with the Library's Express Check Out Machine
Labeling
Media
Book Series
Children's Books
Organizing Magazines,
Children's Reading Area,
Collection Books
Cleaning books
Filing & Photocopying
Stamping Discards
Routing Slips
Assisting with programs & special projects
Watering Plants
Training: A general library orientation will be provided and specific job training will be given on-site.

3.0 HOUSEKEEPING
3.1 HOUSEKEEPING VOLUNTEER

3.1.1 Vacuum Operator

Library Name: Sheridan County Fulmer Public Library
Library Location: Sheridan, Wyoming
Population Served: 26,700
Number of Volumes: N/A
Number of Titles: 109,554
Number of Periodical Subscriptions: 225

Volunteer Impact
Volunteer will operate a vacuum cleaner in order to remove dirt, dust, etc. from the library carpets.
Duties and Responsibilities Vacuum carpets
Qualifications/Essential Attributes
Is a strong advocate of the library.
Physical Requirements
Must be physically fit to push vacuum throughout library.
Must be able to bend over repeatedly to pick up items too large to be picked up by the vacuum cleaner.
Timeframe
Minimum of one hour per week.
Benefits
Volunteer will:

Gain experience in working with the library's maintenance department.
Receive a letter of recommendation upon request.

4.0 PLANTS AND LANDSCAPING
4.1 PLANTS AND GROUNDS VOLUNTEER

4.1.1 Grounds Volunteer I

Library Name: Kokomo Howard County Public Library
Library Location: Kokomo, Indiana
Population Served: 78,245
Number of Volumes: 229,030
Number of Titles: 80,000
Number of Periodical Subscriptions: 506

Task Description:
Task Gardener
When does the task have to be done? Seasonal—April through October
What day and time? Flexible.
How often does it need to be done? Weekly.
Where does it need to be done? Branch, outside
Approximately how much time is involved? Varies. 1-2 hours a week.
What skills are required? Knowledge of plants desirable.
Able to interact well with staff.
Able to work independently.
Personality traits needed? Dependable. Cooperative. Creative. Does not need to interact with patrons.
How many people needed? 1
Comments: Physical stamina is required—bending, digging, lifting, stooping, standing, and walking.
Person may make recommendations on types of plants selected and placement of plants.
Detailed description of task:
Plants flowers and bulbs.
Weeds flower beds.
Waters plants during dry season.

4.1.2 Grounds Volunteer II

Library Name: Kokomo Howard County Public Library
Library Location: Kokomo, Indiana
Population Served: 78,245
Number of Volumes: 229,030
Number of Titles: 80,000

Task Description: Task Spreading Mulch.

When does the task have to be done? Seasonal—April or Early May

What day and time? Time coordinated with Custodian's schedule.

How often does it need to be done? Once a year.

Where does it need to be done? Branch

Approximately how much time is involved? 3-4 hours.

What skills are required? Ability to follow oral directions.

Able to work in a group to complete task.

Able to keep track of time worked by signing in and out.

Personality traits needed? Dependable. Cooperative.

How many people needed? 3-5

Comments: Physical stamina is required—lifting, stooping, standing, and walking.

Detailed description of task:

Pull weeds out of all mulched areas.

Remove trash and debris and place in trash bag.

Spread mulch over areas to be covered.

Sweep excess mulch off of sidewalks.

4.1.3 Plant Caregiver/Gardener

Library Name: Madison Public Library
Library Location: Madison, Wisconsin
Population Served: 207,248
Number of Volumes: 858,197
Number of Titles: 499,272
Number of Periodical Subscriptions: 2,150

Job Description: Helps maintain indoor plants, including watering and pruning when necessary

Location:

Time Commitment: 1-2 hours per week depending on season

Qualifications: Knowledge of house plants and their care; ability to work independently

Plant Caregiver/Gardener (Central Library)

5.0 PICKLIST AND HOLDS

5.1 PICKLIST ASSISTANT

5.1.1 Picklist Assistant

Library Name: Madison Public Library

Library Location: Madison, Wisconsin
Population Served: 207,248
Number of Volumes: 858,197

Job Description: Each day a list of materials which have been reserved that day, called a picklist, is printed from LINKcat. The picklist assistant retrieves the materials on the list from the shelves. The materials are then placed on that library's reserve shelf, or sent to other libraries, for a specific customer to check out.

Location: Branches

Time Commitment: 1 day a week, 2+ hours a day; 6+ months

Qualifications: Able to understand the arrangement of library materials in chronological or alphabetical order; able to bend, reach, stretch and lift; attention to detail; able to work independently.

5.1.2 Pick List Searcher, Processor, Retrieving Clerk

Library Name: Pikes Peak Library District
Library Location: Colorado, Springs, Colorado
Population Served: 448,860
Number of Volumes: 876,897
Number of Titles: N/A
Number of Periodical Subscriptions: 2,330

Searches shelves for items on the daily Holds list

Empties or fills bins with books (branches only)

Uses scanner to trap and print Holds slip and places item in correct bin for transfer

Must be able to maintain confidentiality, perform tasks accurately, search by alphabetical/Dewey number, stand for 2–4 hours, and commit to a schedule.

Four-hour shifts on any weekday.

6.0 BOOK AND SHELF CLEANER

6.1 BOOK AND SHELF CLEANING VOLUNTEER

6.1.1 Book and Shelf Cleaning Volunteer

Library Name: Pikes Peak Library District
Library Location: Colorado, Springs, Colorado
Population Served: 448,860
Number of Volumes: 876,897

Wipes down shelves and books to remove plaster dust due to construction

Ability to perform tasks with care, consistency and thoroughness

Three or four people could complete this in one day/ two half days.

6.1.2 Shelf Cleaner

Library Name: Madison Public Library
Library Location: Madison, Wisconsin
Population Served: 207,248
Number of Volumes: 858,197
Number of Titles: 499,272
Number of Periodical Subscriptions: 2,150

Job Description: Under direction of library staff, assist in cleaning book shelving areas to maintain a clean, healthy environment for library users.

Location: Branches

Time Commitment: 1 day a week, 2 hours a day

Qualifications: Able to push, bend, stretch and lift; able to work independently; no allergies to dust, mold, cleaning materials.

Putting decimal numbers in order and alphabetizing

Personality traits needed? Likes working alone

How many people are needed? Unlimited

Comments

Requires standing, and squatting to read on upper and lower shelves.

Detailed description of task:

Go to the assigned shelf area and make sure the items are in correct order by reading the call number on the spine or front of each item. Rearrange items as necessary

Fiction

Arrange alphabetically by the author's last name.

Small, J.

Smith, I.

Snow, B.

If two or more authors have the same last name, shelve alphabetically by the author's first name.

Stone, Irving

7.0 SHELF READER

7.1 SHELF READER

7.1.1 Shelf Reader

Library Name: Kokomo Howard County Public Library
Library Location: Kokomo, Indiana
Population Served: 78,245
Number of Volumes: 229,030
Number of Titles: 80,000
Number of Periodical Subscriptions: 506

Task Description

Task Read shelves

When does the task have to be done? Ongoing

What day and time? Any time the library is open

How often does it need to be done? Ongoing

Where does it need to be done? AYASD

Approximately how much time is involved? 1-2 hours each time

What skills are required?

Stone, James B.

Stone, James H.

If an author has more than one title, shelve the books alphabetically by the title (ignore the words A, An, The as the first word of the title).

The Passions of the Mind

Past Presidents

The President's Lady

Non-fiction

Shelve numerically by the Dewey Decimal number. The numbers after the decimal point are evaluated one number at a time.

618.034

618.135

822.008
822.03

If two or more books have identical numbers, then shelve by the author's last name.

614 Ad
614 Bl
614 De

If an author has more than one book under the same call number, shelve alphabetically by title.

158.1 Dyer, Wayne The Sky's the Limit
158.1 Dyer, Wayne Your Erroneous Zone

8.0 SHELVER

8.1 SHELVER

8.1.1 Shelver

Library Name: Pikes Peak Library District
Library Location: Colorado, Springs, Colorado
Population Served: 448,860
Number of Volumes: 876,897
Number of Titles: N/A
Number of Periodical Subscriptions: 2,330

3–5 permanent, long-term volunteers prepare book trucks alphabetically and in Dewey Decimal order and search for items on patron Holds list.

Must be able to search alphabetically/Dewey number; stand, bend, stretch, lift books, and perform repetitive tasks accurately and efficiently.

Four-hour shifts, morning or afternoon, weekdays until 6 p.m.

8.1.2 Summer Shelver

Library Name: Kokomo Howard County Public Library
Library Location: Kokomo, Indiana
Population Served: 78,245
Number of Volumes: 229,030
Number of Titles: 80,000
Number of Periodical Subscriptions: 506

Task Description:
Task Assist with shelving books and reading shelves.

When does the task have to be done? During Summer Reading Program, June-July.

What day and time? Hours are flexible but limited to the hours that the Branch is open. May include evening and Saturday hours.

How often does it need to be done? Daily

Where does it need to be done?

Approximately how much time is involved? Minimum of 2 hours a week.

What skills are required? Able to concentrate and pay attention to details.

Able to use alphabetical and numerical filing systems.

Able to follow written and oral instructions.

Able to work independently following training.

Able to keep track of time worked by signing in and out.

Able to interact well with staff.

Personality traits needed? Strong sense of order. Detail-oriented. Pleasant and courteous. Dependable.

How many people needed? 2-4

Who will train, supervise and evaluate the volunteer? Clerical staff will supervise when Head of Branch is out of the library.

Comments: Physical stamina is required—lifting, stooping, standing, walking, pushing carts, and reaching up to higher shelving, sometimes with the aid of a step stool.

Training provided: Orientation to library.

Training in Dewey Decimal System.

Training in shelving library material.

Detailed description of task:

Shelve returned books.

Make certain books are for Branch. Books for the Main Library and South Branch need to be placed in the appropriate courier crates.

Sort books into shelf location—Easy, Easy Reader, Juvenile Non-Fiction, etc.

Put books in shelf order on book truck by the Call Number.

Take cart to the shelving area.

Shelve books in the correct place by the Call Number.

Read shelves to maintain accurate book placement.

If a large number are out of order notify the supervisor.

Straighten books and keep shelves orderly.

8.1.3 Materials Shelver

Library Name: Madison Public Library
Library Location: Madison, Wisconsin
Population Served: 207,248
Number of Volumes: 858,197
Number of Titles: 499,272
Number of Periodical Subscriptions: 2,150

Job Description: Assists library staff in shelving all types of materials. May also read shelves to determine that materials are in proper order. Job may be limited to putting Qwik cases on compact discs or videos prior to shelving.

Location: Branches

Time Commitment: 1 day a week, 2+ hours a day; 6+ months.

Qualifications: Able to pass library skills and aptitude measurement test; able to accurately arrange items in alphabetical and numerical order; able to bend, stoop, reach, stretch and lift; attention to detail; able to work independently.

Job Description: This description covers a wide variety of jobs, all of which are short term and deal with a one time or once a year event such as the Book Club Café, Summer Library Program, a library anniversary, a book sale, etc. A job could last several hours, such as selling books at a sale, or 20 hours over a span of several months, such as hiring and negotiating with a caterer for the Book Club Café.

Location: Central, branches and off site

Time Commitment: 2 hours to 20 hours or more depending on the individual job

Qualifications: Vary widely depending on the specific job.

9.0 WEEDING ASSISTANT

9.1 WEEDING ASSISTANT

9.1.1 Weeding Assistant

Library Name: Madison Public Library
Library Location: Madison, Wisconsin
Population Served: 207,248
Number of Volumes: 858,197
Number of Titles: 499,272
Number of Periodical Subscriptions: 2,150

Job Description: Assists professional staff in weeding collections by removing worn, damaged materials from the shelves on the basis of condition or using other specified criteria.

Location: Branches

Time Commitment: 1 day a week, 2+ hours a day; 6+ months

Qualifications: Attention to detail; able to work independently; able to bend, stoop, stretch and lift.

THE JOB-DESCRIPTION
WRITER'S TOOL BOX

Tool 1: Basics of the Equal Employment Opportunity Commission

All jobs must comply with the laws of the Americans with Disabilities Act (ADA) as interpreted by the Equal Employment Opportunity Commission (EEOC). When constructing job descriptions, you should get a basic understanding of the key federal guidelines from the EEOC Web site (available at www.eeoc.gov). The site offers current law, practice, and advice in over 50 specific areas grouped under ten large headings:

- About Equal Employment Opportunity (EEO)
- Discrimination by Type: Facts and Guidance
- Filing a Charge of Discrimination
- Employers and EEOC
- Federal Agencies and Employees
- About the EEOC
- Laws, Regulations, and Guidance
- Statistics
- Litigation
- Training and Outreach
- Information in Print

In addition to understanding the law, you should be aware that the job description is the first place the EEOC looks when investigating a lawsuit. This is another practical and essential reason to craft job descriptions that are as precisely worded as possible.

Compliance with the Equal Employment Opportunity Commission can be quite a task to master as it requires precise job descriptions. Essential functions, duties, and responsibilities are threads that are interwoven with knowledge, skills, and abilities to make up the fabric that is the job description. You must have certain knowledge, skills, and abilities to perform the duties and responsibilities demanded by the position. Duties and responsibilities are derived from functions, which are those areas that are essential to the purpose of the job. As you work on this you will see how it is all woven together to make one complete tapestry.

Although job descriptions are not required by law, they are the first thing the EEOC looks at when ADA issues arise. EEOC pays particular attention to the essential job functions listed in the description.

Before you begin selecting your descriptions, learn the facts about the Americans with Disabilities Act:

Title I of the Americans with Disabilities Act of 1990, which took effect July 26, 1992, prohibits private employers, state and local governments, employment agencies and labor unions from discriminating against qualified individuals with disabilities in job application procedures, hiring, firing, advancement, compensation, job training, and other terms, conditions and privileges of employment. An individual with a disability is a person who:

Has a physical or mental impairment that substantially limits one or more major life activities;

Has a record of such an impairment; or

Is regarded as having such an impairment.

A qualified employee or applicant with a disability is an individual who, with or without reasonable accommodation, can perform the essential functions of the job in question. Reasonable accommodation may include, but is not limited to:

Making existing facilities used by employees readily accessible to and usable by persons with disabilities.

Job restructuring, modifying work schedules, reassignment to a vacant position; acquiring or modifying equipment or devices, adjusting modifying examinations, training materials, or policies, and providing qualified readers or interpreters.

An employer is required to make an accommodation to the known disability of a qualified applicant or employee if it would not impose an "undue hardship" on the operation of the employer's business. Undue hardship is defined as an action requiring significant difficulty or expense when considered in light of factors such as an employer's size, financial resources and the nature and structure of its operation.

An employer is not required to lower quality or production standards to make an accommodation, nor is an employer obligated to provide personal use items such as glasses or hearing aids.

(www.eeoc.gov)

The EEOC gives you some latitude in determining essential functions of the job. The Technical Assistance Manual: Title I of the ADA states: "The ADA does not limit an employer's ability to establish or change the content, nature, or functions of the job. It is the employer's province to establish what a job is and what functions are required to perform it. It is vital to have written job descriptions listing the position's essential functions before advertising or interviewing applicants for a job because it is considered evidence along with the employer's judgment in the event of a law suit.

(www.eeoc.gov)

Below is how EEOC determines essential functions, again taken from the agency's Web site:

Essential functions are the basic job duties that an employee must be able to perform, with or without reasonable accommodation. You should carefully examine each job to determine which functions or tasks are essential to performance. (This is particularly important before taking an employment action such as recruiting, advertising, hiring, promoting or firing).

Factors to consider in determining if a function is essential include:

- whether the reason the position exists is to perform that function,
- the number of other employees available to perform the function or among whom the performance of the function can be distributed, and
- the degree of expertise or skill required to perform the function.

Your judgment as to which functions are essential, and a written job description prepared before advertising or interviewing for a job will be considered by EEOC as evidence of essential functions. Other kinds of evidence that EEOC will consider include:

- the actual work experience of present or past employees in the job,
- the time spent performing a function,
- the consequences of not requiring that an employee perform a function, and
- the terms of a collective bargaining agreement.

(www.eeoc.gov)

In addition to enforcing Title I of the ADA, which prohibits discrimination against people with disabilities in the private sector and state and local governments as well as the Rehabilitation Act's prohibitions against disability discrimination in the federal government, EEOC also enforcesTitle VII of the Civil Rights Act of 1964, which prohibits employment discrimination based on race, color, religion, sex, and national origin; the Age Discrimination in Employment Act, which prohibits discrimination against individuals 40 years of age or older; the Equal Pay Act; and sections of the Civil Rights Act of 1991.

Legal compliance is vital, but you should make the requirements work for you. Let them serve as an important foundation to the entire process. The whole job description can be selected or written using essential functions as a starting point.

Tool 2: Tips for Creating Well-Written Job Descriptions

Don't make the mistake of thinking the only reason for a well-written, up-to-date description is to avoid disastrous lawsuits. The benefits begin at advertising for the job and last throughout the life of the position. Below is a partial list of the benefits of a well-written job description and, thus, reasons you cannot afford to ignore those neglected files any longer. A clear, accurate job description

- clarifies job responsibilities;
- decreases confusion over job duties;
- increases communication;
- increases objectivity;
- serves as an effective recruitment tool;
- helps you to comply with the Americans with Disabilities Act;
- decreases the likelihood of your library's being the object of a successful lawsuit;
- gives direction to training efforts;
- keeps employees from assuming responsibilities and authority without your knowledge or consent;
- assures objective job performance evaluations;
- serves as a compensation and pay-grade check;
- serves as a guide for transfers and promotions;
- serves as an important orientation tool;
- eliminates duplication in job duties;
- serves as a common document for you, the employee, and city or county officials;
- increases performance because employees know what is expected of them;
- empowers employees by involving them in the process;
- eliminates ambiguity;
- allows you to formulate effective interview questions;
- gives a job applicant an accurate picture of the job;
- increases cooperation between employees since duties are made clear;
- makes it possible to evenly distributes duties and responsibilities between employees;
- accurately places employee within the city/county's organizational structure;
- allows you to evaluate if applicants' aptitudes fit job duties; and
- helps to ensure you hire the right person for the job.

You now know the why of job descriptions. Here is the how to select those that are appropriate for you. But before you dig out those musty files and start thumbing through this book, there are other steps to be taken first.

GATHERING THE FACTS

You undoubtedly know the highlights of each job, and you may even know some details. However, the employee who has the job knows all the important details that busy eyes don't catch.

Remind the employee that this is not an appraisal or review. You are simply revamping old job descriptions so that they more accurately portray the duties and responsibilities of the position. Take notes and listen carefully for those areas that need to be probed further. Some experts recommend giving the description back to the employee to check for any last minute errors or omissions before it is finalized.

There is another advantage to this process: corralling the employee who has gathered more and more authority and power and has cleverly encroached upon other employees' duties and responsibilities. The interview process may help unearth the existence of this mini-empire, which you may have suspected for a long time but did not have the evidence for, and certainly nothing in writing like an accurate job description, which would have headed this off at the pass. You can keep other empires from being built and tear down those already firmly entrenched.

DUTIES AND RESPONSIBILITIES

What you want may already be brewing in your mind. It is now time to elaborate on essential functions in the "Duties and Responsibilities" section, clarifying for yourself, the employee, and any third party the actual tasks the position entails. This section requires a thorough treatment of what is done, how it is done, and why it is done. Pick the duties in a logical order, with the most important first. These should constitute tasks that take more than 10% of the employee's time.

Dos and Don'ts: Look for concise, direct, specific duties and responsibilities. Avoid verbose rambling sentences. Avoid confusing sentences. If your public information officer is responsible for press releases, you don't want to write "Responsible for press releases." That is too general and allows for too many interpretations. Instead, try something such as: "Creates accurate press releases about library events and news and distributes them to media outlets in a timely manner," or a similar description.

KNOWLEDGE SKILLS AND ABILITIES

All jobs, even those for employees on the lowest rung of the organizational ladder, have minimum qualifications. You might have an opening for a job as simple as taking a truck of books and putting them in correct Dewey order. Or, the job can get as complex as the Rochester Public Library and Monroe County Library System, which "seeks a resourceful library director who can manage budgets totaling $16 million and lead a team of 360 employees . . . 10 or more years experience with 5 as a director."

Ohio State University (www.osu.edu) has an excellent discussion on job descriptions. They offer easily understandable definitions:

- Knowledge is a body of information applied directly to the performance of a duty.
- Skills are a present, observable competence to perform a learned activity.
- Ability is a present competence to perform an observable behavior or a behavior that results in an observable product.

Use examples from the job to define it concisely. Certain jobs also require physical characteristics: ability to lift 50 lbs., sit for long periods of time, and manually input data into a computer for extended periods. Credentials and experience also play a role. Many positions will require a certain level of education, experience, and certifications, for example, MLS required, Archival certification required.

The dos and don'ts: Look for specifics: lifting 50 lbs., carrying 50 lbs., and moving 50 lbs. are three very different abilities. Know exactly what you want done. Be realistic so it is achievable on the job and defensible in court. Relate it to essential functions. Don't inflate specifications. Don't describe the ideal candidate. Look for preferences, such as, bilingual Spanish/English preferred or five years of progressively supervisory experience preferred.

Complete this process before advertising or interviewing, and then stick with what you decide. The EEOC frowns upon, and might possibly rule against you, if you change the rules of the game halfway through the hiring process. They do allow you to change essential functions, responsibilities, and KSA, (Knowledge Skills and Abilities) in an established position if the changes in conditions warrant it. You just can't change midstream during the hiring process. You can make a bachelor degree a requirement for future library associates and grandfather in current associates who do not have a degree. But you cannot change the requirements in the middle of the hiring process so that you can hire one person over another or disqualify a candidate.

The University of Virginia (http://staff.lib.virginia.edu/HR/policy/classify.html) compiled an excellent list of KSAs common to library positions:

- Ability to maintain good working relationships
- Ability to communicate effectively [in writing or orally]
- Ability to deal courteously and effectively with the public
- Ability to resolve [simple, complex] problems

- Ability to work within a complex system of rules and procedures
- Ability to plan and execute tasks [or projects]
- Ability to work accurately with attention to detail
- Ability to analyze and organize work procedures
- Ability to organize time and work assignments effectively
- Ability to cope with fluctuating workloads
- Ability to adapt to changes in workflow and procedures
- Ability to instruct classes and other groups
- Ability to work independently
- Ability to [hire, train, evaluate, schedule and/or supervise] staff
- Ability to work with a variety of foreign languages
- Knowledge [or skill] of [or in] [language, subject specialty, electronic information services, etc.]
- Knowledge of [basic keyboarding, word processing, computer languages and/or other computer skills]
- Ability to interpret and work with bibliographic information
- Manual dexterity [or physical stamina] sufficient to perform [task]
- Ability to maintain confidentiality

DEGREE OF SUPERVISION

The degree of supervision, states the University of California Santa Barbara Human Resource guide, (http://hr.ucsb.edu), describes the way in which work is assigned, when it is reviewed, what guidelines are followed, and which protocols are available. Other than usurping other employees' duties and responsibilities, this is where min-empires are built. Over a period of time, a long-term employee has employees reporting to him or her, sees and reviews work instead of the supervisor designated in the organizational chart, or she may even have employees reporting to him or her instead of to you. This stretches from definite limits to wide latitudes. Use whatever verbiage your organization requires.

The different degrees of supervision:

Close Supervision: assigned duties according to specific procedures and work is checked frequently.

Supervision: performs routine duties and follows established guidelines.

General Supervision: develops procedures for performance and performs complex duties within established guidelines.

Direction: develops procedures within the limits of established policy guidelines and usually only final results of work are reviewed

General Direction: Receives guidance in terms of goals and overall objectives and establishes the methods to attain them. Usually formulates policy but may not have the final authority.

PHYSICAL DEMANDS AND ENVIRONMENT

Many jobs have physical demands or operate in unusual or hostile environments, such as outdoors in the heat and cold or in a particularly noisy part of the building. If an employee is required to lift 50 lbs. or carry heavy tubs of books all day and it is related to an essential function of the job, then state it in the job description. Look for specifics and details. Librarians usually have to bend, kneel, stand, reach, walk, push, pull, and carry to do their work. Cataloging librarians sit and input records into the computer for long periods of time. Have this in the description. For some jobs reasonable accommodations can be made, and in some cases they must be made, for others it is not possible to accommodate.

OTHER DUTIES AS ASSIGNED

"Other duties as assigned" is a main stay in job descriptions. Too often we hear, "It's not my job." Job descriptions inherently cannot describe every situation. A job description that did that would be the size of a book and still leave out something. Jeniece Guy, in ALA's Toolkit *Writing Library Job Descriptions*, (www.state.sc.us/scsl/pubs/PLstandards/section2.pdf) has a wonderful catchall phrase to insert in the job description instead of the "other duties as assigned" phrase. Guy writes, "Job descriptions are meant to be general guidelines to the duties and responsibilities of the job and are not intended to list every possible task an employee may be call upon to perform." This is straightforward and notifies employees that they may be asked to work in areas they are not familiar with or do not work at on a regular basis.

STRIKING A BALANCE

Strike a balance between being overly general and dictating every small task. Look for the end results you require, but allow creativity to blossom and give your employees some freedom in finding ways to improve the workflow. Where would we be if Henry Ford did not sit on his famous couch and sketch out on a page of sheet music the idea of assembly line production? Pages may not have much latitude, but the head of children's services can be given much freer reign in how to run her department.

JOB SUMMARY

This is a snapshot of the position, and it provides a synopsis of the major purpose of the position and its role in the library. This thumbnail sketch is designed to give the reader a clear picture of the general nature, level, purpose, and objective of the job. It includes the job title and the title of the immediate supervisor. It is especially useful in job postings, recruitment ads, and salary surveys.

WRITING JOB DESCRIPTION SENTENCES

If you are using the descriptions in the book as guides and then writing your own, try to follow the guidelines below:

- Begin each sentence with an active verb.
- Use present tense verbs.
- Use clear and concise words.
- Structure sentences as verb/object/explanatory phrase.
- Avoid rambling, verbose sentences.
- Avoid words with multiple meanings or vague words, such as "handles" or "checks."
- Use explanatory phrases when necessary.
- Use non-technical terms if possible.
- Describe equipment used if necessary.
- Use generic terms, such as word processing, instead of Microsoft Word, unless you are specifying knowledge of a particular program.
- Use gender-neutral terms.
- Describe the results you expect.
- Qualify when necessary.
- Use concise, direct sentences.

CHECKLIST

Review the job description after it is written. Some experts recommend you show the employee the description before finally completing it. Ask yourself the following questions, which the Human Resources department at University of California at Berkeley (http://hrweb.berkeley.edu/supervision/.)uses:

- Is it logically organized to describe all the duties and responsibilities?
- Does it avoid using vague terms? Is it clear and current?
- Is it specific in explaining what is done and why? Are good examples used to illustrate complex and abstract issues?
- Is it concise? Does it address all major duties, rather than giving a detailed list of tasks?
- Does it include only material describing the position? Are personal references to the incumbent avoided?
- Are essential duties (as determined by the ADA) indicated with an asterisk?
- Does the description provide a valuable introduction for a new employee in the position?

RE-EVALUATING DESCRIPTIONS

Descriptions need to be re-evaluated every year. Constantly changing technology, organizational shifts, variable community needs, varying organizational needs, new programs, new responsibilities, and combining or dividing job responsibilities all require that regular attention be paid to each position. Ensuring accuracy is a top priority. Without it there are legal woes and you do not get the benefits mentioned above. Without accuracy your are back in the same position when you had those musty old files on some far away cabinet. The effect is the same. Conditions change, so should the descriptions.

Questions to Ask before Completing the Description

- To whom do the employees report?
- Do they supervise other employees?
- Whom do they specifically supervise?
- What level of experience and training do they need?
- Do they need prior library experience?
- What computer applications must they know?
- Do they need specific library knowledge, such as basic cataloging skills?
- What specific duties do they perform?
- How much contact will they have with the public?
- What skills do they need?
- Will they serve on committees?
- Is continuing education required?
- Will they be responsible for programming?
- Will they have contact with the public?
- What specific outreach responsibilities will they have?
- Do they need any type of special certification or training?
- Is a driver's license required?
- Is English language proficiency required?
- Is any other language skill necessary?
- Do they prepare reports?
- Is attention to detail an important part of the job?
- Do they have budget responsibilities?
- Do they sit or stand for long periods of time?
- Do they input data for long periods of time?
- Will they be required to work nights and/or weekends?

- Are there any special physical demands, such as lifting 50 pounds?
- Do they need reference interview skills?
- Must they know the Dewey Decimal System?
- Do they need specialized knowledge in a particular field such as art?
- Must they have the ability to read and write?
- Is a clear, understandable tone needed for the job?
- Do they answer reference questions?
- Must they be able to use specific resources?
- Do they need to be courteous and tactful?
- What type of work environment is there?
- Do they have access to sensitive information?
- Must they be able to use a telephone?
- Are there areas where reasonable accommodations can be made?
- Do they need to know how to use specific equipment?
- Do they need material conservation and preservation skills?
- Do they need experience with children?
- Does the position require an MLS?
- Does the position require specific software training?
- How much total experience is required?
- Is the description clear and concise?
- Does the description use action verbs like those found in the appendix?
- Is the description accurate?
- Are the elements achievable and realistic?
- Do the essential functions meet ADA requirements?
- How often does the job description need revision?

Tool 3: Sample Job Description Questionnaire

DALLAS COUNTY COMMUNITY COLLEGE DISTRICT

JOB DESCRIPTION QUESTIONNAIRE
PROFESSIONAL SUPPORT STAFF, INFORMATION TECHNOLOGY, FACILITIES
SERVICES, SAFETY/SECURITY EMPLOYEES

1. Employees currently holding positions on the Professional Support Staff/Information Technology/Facilities Services/Safety & Security salary schedule should use this form.
2. The employee currently holding the position to be evaluated should complete a questionnaire or the first level supervisor if the position is vacant or newly described.

Part I: To be completed by employee.

Instructions

The purpose of this form is to help you describe the duties and responsibilities of your position. Before answering any questions, please read the entire questionnaire carefully. Complete this form on your own and answer each question completely. Please forward this questionnaire to your immediate supervisor for comments upon completion.

1. Identification

Print Name: _____ SS#: _____

Current Position Title: _____

Employment Status: ____ full-time _____ Limited full-time   Email address:_____

Department: _____

Location: _____

Name of Immediate Supervisor:_____

Title of Immediate Supervisor:_____

Immediate Supervisor Telephone Number:_____

Name of Second Level Supervisor: _____

Title of Second Level Supervisor: _____

Your Office Telephone Number: _____

2. Duties and Responsibilities

Write a brief description of your position (please use only the space provided).

_____
_____
_____
_____
_____
_____
_____
_____

Please list your major duties and responsibilities beginning with the duty on which you spend most of your time (those which equate to 10% or more individually).

Major Position Duties and Responsibilities

_____
_____
_____
_____
_____
_____
_____
_____
_____
_____
_____
_____
_____

Please list other position duties and responsibilities (those requiring less than 10% individually) which are also parts of your job.

Other Position Duties and Responsibilities

_____
_____
_____
_____
_____
_____
_____
_____
_____
_____

3. Education

Check below the minimum level of education you think is necessary for performing the duties of this position satisfactorily (NOT necessarily your own level of education).

_____ (a) On-the-job training only. Basic ability to read and write and perform simple calculations.

_____ (b) Able to read, write, do arithmetic, and apply reasoning skills equal to that of the average high school graduate.

_____ (c) Knowledge/skills resulting from some business, trade, or specialized training beyond high school.

_____ (d) Knowledge/skills resulting from completion of community college or technical/vocational school; or one-half of the courses required for graduation from a college or university with a bachelor's degree.

_____ (e) Ability equal to that resulting from satisfactory completion of courses required for graduation from an accredited college or university with a bachelor's degree.

4. Experience

List the amounts and types of previous work experience you feel are necessary for a person to perform the duties of this position (DO NOT list your own years of work experience).

Example: Secretary I 1 year

Secretary II 3 years

Type of Experience Number of Years

_____

_____

_____

_____

5. Physical Effort

Physical effort includes such things as lifting, walking, or climbing needed to perform the duties of this position.

List examples of the types of materials you work with in this position and the types of work that require physical effort:

_____

_____

_____

_____

6. Supervision Exercised

List by job title the number of employees that you supervise directly. Student assistants may be included. (ONLY those employees whom you hire, evaluate, regularly sign timesheets, and assign a work schedule.)

Employee Job Title	Type Full/Part/ Limited Full-time	Number of Employees
_____	_____	_____
_____	_____	_____
_____	_____	_____
_____	_____	_____

7. Supervision Received

Supervision received can be defined as the degree to which you work independently. Describe the assistance you receive from your supervisor in successfully completing your job duties (e.g., my supervisor checks the results of job duties I perform, my supervisor works with me to complete each part of a project, etc.)

8. Human Relations Skills

Briefly describe the types of people contacts you make in your job on a daily/weekly basis (i.e., students, faculty, District staff only, outside telephone calls, etc.). Indicate levels of courtesy, understanding, ability to influence and/or motivate required.

_____

_____

_____

_____

_____

_____

_____

_____

9. Freedom to Act

Freedom to act is related to the amount and detail of instructions you are given to perform the job.

Please give specific examples of the kind of instructions you receive from your supervisor to perform a task.

_____

_____

_____

_____

_____

10. Budget Responsibilities

If you have budget responsibilities, what is the total dollar value (annual terms) of your budget?

$_____

List applicable budget numbers.

_____

11. Magnitude

To what extent does your job affect other work groups at your location or in the DCCCD?

_____
_____
_____
_____
_____
_____
_____

12. Impact

What is the level of impact your job has on the organization?

_____ (a) Substantial impact on the organization resources through decisions involving changes in policy, programs, or new services, asset/liability management, or other actions, legal or otherwise.

_____ (b) Moderate impact on organization resources through expenditures of organizational funds or other actions involving the interpretation and implementation of predetermined programs, polices, and procedures.

_____ (c) Little or no opportunity to affect organization resources in as much as position administers existing polices and procedures.

If your answer is (a), please list two specific examples which support your choice.

_____
_____
_____
_____
_____
_____

13. Innovation

Different positions require varying amounts of creativity in order to complete the assigned tasks.

Creativity/innovation includes such things as problem solving through alternative actions and solutions, and situation analysis and interpretation.

Describe three examples of typical situations that require innovativeness in your position:

1. _____

_____

2. _____

_____

3. _____

_____

14. Independence of Action

The degree of responsibility placed on your job, including how you handle both minor and major decisions, the span of results caused by those decisions, and required follow-up.

Describe two typical decisions that you make without being directed or assisted by your immediate supervisor.

_____
_____
_____
_____
_____
_____

15. Working Conditions

Describe your general working conditions, including any disagreeable elements that may affect successful completion of your job from time to time.

_____
_____
_____
_____
_____

Give any other information about your position that is important to understanding it.

_____
_____
_____
_____
_____
_____
_____

16. Job Description (Generic Job Description Included in Packet)

Do you feel that your generic job description describes accurately what you do? Yes ____ No___
If no, what does it not describe?

_____
_____
_____
_____

17. Department Breakdown (Please provide us with an organizational chart of your department.)

18. Please describe your current education level.

Degree Received: High School Diploma or G.E.D
    Associate's (indicate if A.A., A.S., etc.)   _____   Major:_____
    Bachelor's (indicate if B.A., or B.S., etc.)   _____   Major: _____
    Master's (indicate if M.A., or M.S., etc.)   _____   Major: _____
    Ph.D. Major: _____
    Technical Certification List: _____

List Other Credentials & Certifications:

I believe the information I have provided on this questionnaire is a true description of the job that I perform.

_____
Signature of Employee

_____
Date

Thank you for your assistance. Please send the completed, signed copy of the questionnaire to your supervisor for comments and signatures.

PART II: To be completed by immediate supervisor.

The immediate supervisor of the employee who completed the attached questionnaire should complete this section. Please do not change any of the information on the employee's portion of the questionnaire.

1. Note here any exceptions to the employee's responses. If you have none, please write "None."

_____

_____

_____

_____

2. Note here any additions to the employee's report. If you have none, please write "None."

_____

_____

_____

_____

Except for the items that I have indicated, I agree with the responses to the questionnaire supplied by the employee as an accurate description of the job to be performed.

_____

Signature of Immediate Supervisor

_____

Date

Please forward the completed questionnaire to your next level supervisor.

PART III: To be completed by second level supervisor.

The second level supervisor of the employee who completed the attached questionnaire should complete this section. Please do not change any information on the employee's or the immediate supervisor's portion of the questionnaire.

1. List any exceptions to the employee's or the immediate supervisor's responses. If you have none, please write "None."

_____

_____

_____

_____

2. Note here any additions to the employee's or the immediate supervisor's responses. If you have none, please write "None".

_____

_____

_____

_____

Except for the items that I have indicated, I agree with the employee and supervisor responses to the questionnaire supplied by the employee and the revisions/corrections of the attached position description as an accurate description of the job to be performed.

_____

Signature of Second Level Supervisor

_____

Date

Tool 4: Active Verbs to Use when Selecting a Job Description

Whether you are using the job descriptions in the book as a pattern and writing your own, using the following words will make your description more productive:

A

Accommodates
Accounts
Achieves
Acquires
Acts
Adapts
Addresses
Adjusts
Administers
Adopts
Advises
Advocates
Allocates
Allots
Alters
Analyzes
Answers
Applies
Appoints
Appraises
Approves
Arbitrates
Arranges
Assembles
Assesses
Assigns
Assists
Assumes
Assures
Attains
Attracts
Audits
Augments
Authorizes
Awards

B

Balances
Bargains
Batches
Bends
Budgets

C

Calculates
Calibrates
Carries
Categorizes
Certifies
Checks
Circulates
Clarifies
Classifies
Cleans
Clears
Climbs
Coaches
Codes
Collaborates
Collates
Collects
Combines
Communicates
Compares
Completes
Complies
Composes
Computes
Condenses
Conducts
Confers
Confirms
Consolidates
Constructs
Consults
Controls
Converts
Conveys
Coordinates
Correlates
Corresponds
Counsels
Creates
Customizes

D

Debates
Decides
Defends
Defines
Delegates
Deliberates
Delivers
Demonstrates
Designates
Designs
Destroys
Detects
Determines
Develops
Devises
Devotes
Diagnoses
Digs
Directs
Disburses
Disciplines
Discusses
Discovers
Dismantles
Dispatches
Dispenses
Displays
Disseminates
Distinguishes
Distributes
Documents
Drafts
Drives
Dumps
Duplicates

E

Edits
Elaborates
Elects
Eliminates
Employs
Encourages
Endorses
Enforces
Enlists
Ensures
Enters
Entertains
Escorts
Establishes
Estimates
Evaluates
Examines
Exchanges
Executes
Exercises
Exhibits
Expands
Expedites
Experiments
Explains
Explores
Extends
Extracts

F

Fabricates
Facilitates
Fastens
Feeds
Files
Forecasts
Formulates
Furnishes

G

Garners
Gathers
Gauges
Generates
Governs
Grades
Guards
Guides

H

Hauls
Highlights
Hires
Hypothesizes

I

Identifies
Illustrates
Implements
Imports
Improves
Improvises
Indexes
Incorporates
Increases
Influences
Informs
Initiates
Innovate
Inspects
Installs
Instructs
Interacts
Interfaces
Interprets
Interviews
Introduces
Inventories

Invents
Investigates
Issues
Itemizes

J

Joins
Judges
Justifies

K

Kneels

L

Lifts
Loads
Locates
Lubricates

M

Maintains
Manages
Manipulates
Manufactures
Maps
Markets
Measures
Mediates
Mends
Mixes
Modifies
Monitors
Motivates
Moves

N

Negotiates
Notifies
Nullifies

O

Observes
Obtains
Opens
Operates
Organizes
Originates
Outlines
Overhauls
Oversees

P

Packages
Participates
Performs
Permits
Persuades
Picks up
Plans
Posts
Predicts
Prescribes
Prepares
Presents
Preserves
Presides
Prevents
Processes
Procures
Produces
Programs
Promotes
Proofreads
Proposes
Provides
Publicizes
Publishes
Pulls

Purchases
Pushes

Q

Quantifies
Questions

R

Ranks
Rates
Reaches
Reaps
Rebuilds
Recognizes
Recommends
Reconciles
Records
Recruits
Redesigns
Reduces
Refers
Refines
Registers
Regulates
Reinforces
Rejects
Releases
Remits
Reorganizes
Repairs
Replaces
Reports
Represents
Rescinds
Rescues
Researches
Resolves
Retrieves
Restructures

Reviews
Revises
Rewards

S

Scans
Schedules
Scores
Screens
Seals
Searches
Secures
Selects
Sells
Sends
Serves
Services
Signs
Simplifies
Sits
Solicits
Solves
Sorts
Specifies
Stacks
Stands
Stimulates
Stores
Strategize
Streamline
Strengthen
Studies
Submits
Suggests
Summarizes
Supervises
Supplies
Supports
Surveys

Synthesizes
Systematizes

T

Tabulates
Teaches
Tends
Testifies
Tests
Totals
Traces
Trades
Trains
Transacts
Transcribes
Transfers
Translates
Transmits
Treats
Troubleshoots
Turns
Tutors
Types

U

Updates
Upgrades
Ushers

V

Validates
Verifies

W

Walks
Waxes
Weighs
Welds
Writes

BIBLIOGRAPHY

GENERAL PRINT RESOURCES

McDonough, Beverley, ed. *American Library Directory: Libraries in the United States,* 56th ed., vol.1, 2003–2004, Medford, NJ: Information Today.

PRINT RESOURCES

Guy, Jeniece, *Writing Library Job Descriptions.* Tip Kit no. 7. Chicago: American Library Association, 1985. www.state.sc.us/scsl/pubs/PLstandards/section2.pdf

Jones, Mark A. "Job Descriptions Made Easy." *Personal Journal* 5, no. 3 (May 1984): 23-25.

Klinger, Donald E. "When a Traditional Job Description Is Not Enough." *Personnel Journal* 4, no. 2 (April 1984): 32–33.

Russell, Richard S. "How to Describe a Job." *Supervisory Management* 3, no. 9 (May 1966): 134–137.

INTERNET RESOURCES

Career Search Consultants. Available at www.cscrecruiters.com. Accessed April 6, 2005.

Equal Employment Opportunity Commission. Available at: www.eeoc.gov. Accessed April 6, 2005.

Heathfield, Susan M. *Job Descriptions: Why Effective Job Descriptions Make Good Business Sense. Part Two, Five Warnings about Job Descriptions.* Available at: http://human resources.about.com. Accessed April 6, 2005.

"New Law Requires Accurate Job Descriptions." *Just Management Newsletter* (Summer 1991). Available at: www.fairmeasures.com. Accessed April 6, 2005.

Niederlander, Mary. *Writing Job Descriptions.* Available at: www.librarysupportstaff.com/whatsmyjob.html. Accessed April 6, 2005.

Ohio State University. Available at: http://ohioline.osu.edu/cd-fact/1376.html. Accessed April 6, 2005.

Online Women's Business Center. *What Are You Looking for: Writing Effective Job Descriptions.* Available at: www.onlinewbc.gov/. Accessed April 6, 2005.

Sack, Steven Mitchell. *From Hiring to Firing: The Legal Survival Guide for Employers.* 1995. Available at: http://earthlink.findlaw.com/employmentbook/ Accessed April 6, 2005.

Smith, Sarah E. "Letter Perfect: The Ins and Outs of Writing Job Descriptions." *Restaurants USA,* September 1999. Available at: www.restaurant.org/. Accessed April 6, 2005.

Technical Assistance Manual: Title I of the ADA. Equal Employment Opportunity Commission: ADA Technical Assistance Manual Addendum. Available at: www.jan.wvu.edu/links/ADAtam1.html. Accessed April 6, 2005.

University of California at Berkeley. *Supervision: A Newsletter for Managers and Supervisors.* Available at: http://hrweb.berkeley.edu/supervision/. Accessed April 6, 2005.

University of California at Los Angeles. *Guide to Writing Job Descriptions.* Available at: www.college.ucla.edu/personnel/writing/jdescip.htm. Accessed April 6, 2005.

University of California at Santa Barbara Human Resources. Available at: http://hr.ucsb.edu/. Accessed April 6, 2005.

University of Maryland, College Park. *How to Update or Write Job Descriptions.* Available at: www.personnel.umd.edu/. Accessed April 6, 2005.

University of Nebraska. *What to Write in a Job Description.* Available at: http://unebapps01.nebraska.edu/nuvalues/. Accessed April 6, 2005.

University of Texas Health Science Center at Houston. "Criteria for Job Descriptions." Available at: www.uth.tmc.edu/ut_general/admin_fin/hr/aw/jobdescriptions.html. Accessed April 6, 2005.

University of Virginia. "Guidelines for Classifying Library Employees." Available at: http://staff.lib.virginia.edu/HR/policy/classify.html. Accessed April 6, 2005.

Winning, Ethan A. "The Many Uses of the Job Description." Human Resources Zone. Available at: http://www.all-biz.com. Accessed April 6, 2005.

CONTRIBUTING LIBRARIES

Note: URLs for contributing libraries current as of April 2005.

Albany County Public Library. Laramie, Wyoming. Available at: http://acpl.lib.wy.us/.

Amherst County Public Library. Amherst, Virginia. Available at: www.acpl.us/.

Anacortes Public Library. Anacortes, Washington. Available at: http://library.cityofanacortes.org/.

City of Austin. Austin, Texas. Available at:www.ci.austin.tx.us/.

Bay County Library System. Bay City, Michigan. Available at: www.baycountylibrary.org/.

Bellevue Regional Library. Bellevue, Washington. Available at: www.kcls.org/brl/brlpage.cfm

Boston Public Library. Boston, Massachusetts. Available at: www.bpl.org.

Brentwood Library and Center for Fine Arts. Brentwood, Tennessee. Available at: http://brentwood-tn.org/library/

Burnham Memorial Library. Colchester, Vermont. Available at: www.burnham.lib.vt.us/

Cass County Public Library. Harrisonville, Missouri. Available at: www.casscolibrary.org.

Cecil County Public Library. Elkton, Maryland. Available at: www.ebranch.cecil.lib.md.us/.

Public Library of Cincinnati and Hamilton County, Cincinnati, Ohio. Available at: www.cincinnatilibrary.org/.

Clermont County Public Library. Batavia, Ohio. Available at: www.clermont.lib.oh.us/.

Columbus Metropolitan Library. Columbus, Ohio. Available at: www.columbuslibrary.org/.

Cumberland County Library System. Carlisle, Pennsylvania. Available at: www.cumberland.lib.nc.us/.

Cuyahoga County Public Library. Parma, Ohio. Available at: www.cuyahogalibrary.org/.

District Human Resources. Dallas County Community College District. Available at: www.dcccd.edu/.

Des Moines Public Library. Des Moines, Iowa. Available at: http://desmoineslibrary.com/.

Edwin A. Bemis Public Library. Littleton, Colorado. Available at: www.littletongov.org/bemis/

Ellensburg Public Library. Ellensburg, Washington. Available at: http://epl.eburg.com.

Escondido Public Library. Escondido, California. Available at: www.ci.escondido.ca.us/library/.

Fort Collins Public Library. Fort Collins, Colorado. Available at: www.fcgov.com/library/.

Genesee District Library. Flint, Michigan. Available at: www.thegdl.org/.

Glendale Public Library. Glendale, California. Available at: www.glendalepubliclibrary.org.

Goffstown Public Library. Goffstown, New Hampshire. Available at: www.goffstown.lib.nh.us/.

Gorton Public Library. Groton, Connecticut. Available at: www.seconnlib.org/.

Hartford Public Library. Hartford, Connecticut Available at: www.hplct.org/.

Helen M. Plum Memorial Library. Lombard, Illinois. Available at: www.plum.lib.il.us/.

Henderson County Public Library District. Henderson, Kentucky. Available at: www.hcpl.org/.

Hernando County Public Library. Brooksville, Florida. Available at: www.hcpl.lib.fl.us/.

Hurt-Battelle Memorial Library of West Jefferson. West Jefferson, Ohio. Available at: http://winslo.state.oh.us/publib/job.html.

Idaho State Library. Boise, Idaho. Available at: www.lili.org/.

Kettleson Memorial Library. Sitka, Alaska. Available at: www.cityofsitka.com/dept/library/library.html.

Kokomo Howard County Public Library. Kokomo, Indiana. Available at: www.kokomo.lib.in.us/.

La Porte County Public Library. La Porte, Indiana. Available at: www.lopcat.org/.

Laramie County Library System. Cheyenne, Wyoming. Available at: www.lclsonline.org/.

Leicester Public Library. Leicester, Massachusetts. Available at: www.ci.leicester.ma.us/library.htm.

Lorain Public Library. Lorain, Ohio. Available at: www.lorain.lib.oh.us/.

Madison Public Library. Madison, Wisconsin. Available at: www.madisonpubliclibrary.org/.

Manchester Public Library. Manchester, Connecticut. Available at: http://library.ci.manchester.ct.us/.

Manitowoc-Calumet Library System. Manitowoc, Wisconsin. Available at: www.manitowoc.lib.wi.us/.

Massachusetts Board of Library Commissioners. Boston, Massachusetts. Available at: www.mlin.lib.ma.us/.

Mesquite Public Library. Mesquite, Texas. Available at: www.library.mesquite.tx.us/.

Milford Public Library. Milford, Connecticut. Available at: www.milford.lib.in.us/.

Milwaukee Public Library. Milwaukee, Wisconsin. Available at: www.mpl.org/.

Mission Viejo Library. Mission Viejo, California. Available at: www.cmvl.org.

Montana State Library. Helena, Montana. Available at: http://msl.state.mt.us/.

Mount Prospect Public Library. Mount Prospect, Illinois. Available at: http://mppl.org/.

Murray Public Library. Murray, Utah. Available at: www.murray.lib.ut.us/.

Nebraska State Historical Society Library and Archives. Lincoln, Nebraska. Available at: www.nebraskahistory.org/.

Needham Free Public Library. Needham, Massachusetts. Available at: www.town.needham.ma.us/Library/index.htm.

Neill Public Library. Pullman, Washington. Available at: http://neill.lib.org/.

Newport Beach Public Library. Newport Beach, California. Available at: www.newportbeachlibrary.org/.

Norfolk Public Library. Norfolk, Virginia. Available at: www.npl.lib.va.us/.

Omaha Public Library. Omaha, Washington. Available at: www.omaha.lib.ne.us/.

Palo Alto City Library. Palo Alto, California. Available at: www.city.palo-alto.ca.us/library/.

Pasco County Library System. Hudson, Florida. Available at: http://pascolibraries.org/.

Phoenix Public Library. Phoenix, Arizona. Available at: www.phoenixpubliclibrary.org.

Pikes Peak Library District. Colorado Springs, Colorado. Available at: http://library.ppld.org/default.asp/.

Pinal County Library District Florence, Arizona. Available at: http://co.pinal.az.us/library/.

Portage County Public Library. Stevens Point, Wisconsin. Available at: www.portagelibrary.info/.

Richland County Public Library. Columbia, South Carolina. Available at: www.richland.lib.sc.us/.

Rochester Public Library. Rochester, Minnesota. Available at: www.rochesterpubliclibrary.org/.

Rowan Public Library. Salisbury, North Carolina. Available at: www.rowanpubliclibrary.org/.

St. Clair County Library System. Port Huron, Michigan. Available at: www.sccl.lib.mi.us/.

St. Joseph County Public Library. South Bend, Indiana. Available at: http://sjcpl.lib.in.us/.

Saline County Public Library. Benton, Arkansas. Available at: www.saline.lib.ar.us/.

San Francisco Public Library. San Francisco, California. Available at: www.sfpl.org/.

San Jose Public Library. San Jose, California. Available at: www.sjlibrary.org/

Santa Barbara Public Library. Santa Barbara, California. Available at: www.santabarbaraca.gov/Government/Departments/Library/

Santa Clara City Library. Santa Clara, California. Available at: www.library.ci.santa-clara.ca.us/.

Seattle Public Library. Seattle, Washington. Available at: www.spl.org.

Seminole County Public Library. Sanford, Florida. Available at: www.scpl.lib.fl.us/.

Sheridan County Public Library System. Sheridan, Wyoming. Available at: www.sheridanwyolibrary.org/.

Solano County Library. Fairfield, California. Available at: http://solanolibrary.com.

Sussex County Library System. Georgetown, Delaware. Available at: www.sussex.lib.de.us/.

Tahlequah Public Library. Tahlequah, Oklahoma. Available at: www.tahlequah.lib.ok.us/.

Tigard Public Library. Tigard, Oregon. Available at: www.ci.tigard.or.us/library/default.asp/.

Tippecanoe County Public Library. La Fayette, Indiana. Available at: www.tcpl.lib.in.us/.

Torrance Public Library. Torrance, California. Available at: www.library.torrnet.com/.

Tuscaloosa Public Library. Tuscaloosa, Alabama. Available at: http://tuscaloosa.library.org/.

Vigo County Public Library. Terre Haute, Indiana. Available at: www.vigo.lib.in.us/.

Walla Walla Public Library. Walla Walla, Washington. Available at: www.ci.walla-walla.wa.us/.

Washoe County Library System. Reno, Nevada. Available at: www.washoe.lib.nv.us/.

Weld Library District. Greeley, Colorado. Available at: www.weld.lib.co.us.

West Chicago Public Library District. West Chicago, Illinois. Available at: www.westchicago.lib.il.us/.

Westminster Public Library. Westminster, Colorado. Available at: www.westminster.lib.co.us/.

Williamsburg Regional Library. Williamsburg, Virginia. Available at: www.wrl.org.

Wisconsin Department of Public Instruction Public Library Development. Madison, Wisconsin. Available at: http://dpi.state.wi.us/dpi/dltcl/pld/.

Woodland Public Library. Woodland, California. Available at: www.ci.woodland.ca.us/library/.

York County Public Library. Yorktown, Virginia. Available at: www.yorkcounty.gov/library/.

CONTRIBUTING LIBRARIES

The following libraries are responsible for this book. This compilation would not have been possible without their willingness to share their job descriptions and hard work.

Albany County Public
Library
Linda Nofziger
Laramie, Wyoming

Amherst County Public
Library
Leona Wilkins, retired
director
Amherst, Virginia

Anacortes Public Library
Doug Everhart
Anacortes, Washington

Austin Public Library
City of Austin
Austin, Texas

Bay County Library System
Trish Burns
Bay City, Michigan

Bellevue Regional Library
Bellevue, Washington

Bemis Public Library
Littleton, Colorado

Boston Public Library
Boston, Massachusetts

Brentwood Library and
Center for Fine Arts
Charles Sherrill
Brentwood, Tennessee

Burnham Memorial Library
Martha Reid
Colchester, Vermont

Canton Public Library
Canton, Mississippi

Cass County Public Library
Jo Irwin
Harrisonville, Missouri

Cecil County Public Library
Elkton, Maryland

Public Library of Cincinnati
and Hamilton County
Cincinnati, Ohio

Clermont County Public
Library
Batavia, Ohio

Columbus Metropolitan
Library
Deb McWilliam
Columbus, Ohio

Cumberland County Library
System
Jonelle Prether Darr,
Executive Director
Carlisle, Pennsylvania

Cuyahoga County Public
Library
Debra K. Wells
Parma, Ohio

District Human Resources
Dallas County Community
College District
Dallas, Texas

Des Moines Public Library
Kay Runge

De Moines, Iowa

Ellensburg Public Library
Celeste Kline
Ellensburg, Washington

Escondido Public Library
Escondido, California

Fort Collins Public Library
Brenda Carns
Fort Collins, Colorado

Genesee District Library
Valerie A. McNiff
Flint, Michigan

Glendale Public Library
Glendale, California

Goffstown Public Library
Dianne Hathaway
Goffstown, New Hampshire

Groton Public Library
Alan G. Benkert
Groton, Connecticut

Hartford Public Library
Hartford, Connecticut

Helen M. Plum Memorial
Library
Robert A Harris
Lombard, Illinois

Henderson County Public
Library
Pam Vincent
Henderson, Kentucky

Barbara Shiflett

Hernando County Public
Library System
Brooksville, Florida

Hurt-Battelle Memorial
Library of West Jefferson
Sharon Shrum
West Jefferson, Ohio

Idaho State Library
Charles A. Bolles
Boise, Idaho

Kettleson Memorial Library
Cheryl Pearson
Sitka, Alaska

Kokomo-Howard County
Public Library
Peg Harmon
Kokomo, Indiana

La Porte County Public
Library
Judy R. Hamilton
La Porte, Indiana

Laramie County Library
Foundation
Cheyenne, Wyoming

Leicester Public Library
Leicester, Massachusetts

Lorain Public Library System
Lorain, Ohio

Madison Public Library
Barbara L. Dimick
Madison, Wisconsin

Manchester Public Library
Douglas McDonough
Manchester, Connecticut

Manitowoc-Calumet Library System
Manitowoc, Wisconsin

Massachusetts Board of Commissioners
Boston, Massachusetts

City of Mesquite Human Resources Department
Mesquite, Texas

Milford Public Library
Salvatore L. Stingo
Milford, Connecticut

Milwaukee Public Library
Kathleen Huston, City Librarian
Milwaukee, Wisconsin

Mission Viejo Library
Valerie L. Maginnis
Mission Viejo, California

Montana State Library
Helena, Montana

Mount Prospect Public Library
Mount Prospect, Illinois

Murray Library
Daniel Barr
Murray, Utah

Nebraska State Historical Society Library
Library/Archives
Lincoln, Nebraska

Needham Free Public Library
Ann MacFate
Needham, Massachusetts

Neill Public Library asked for this to be included in the Acknowledgments:
"The job descriptions for Neill Public Library were developed by BDPA, Inc. Human Resource Consultants in Boise, Idaho. The descriptions were customized for the city of Pullman and will not necessarily apply to other libraries without significant modification and analysis of job duties and responsibilities."
Neill Public Library
Pullman, Washington

Newport Beach Public Library
Newport Beach, California

Norfolk Public Library
Norman L. Maas
Norfolk, Virginia

Omaha Public Library
Rivkah Sass
Omaha, Nebraska

Palo Alto City Library
Palo Alto, California

Pasco County Library System
Hudson, Florida

Phoenix Public Library
Phoenix, Arizona

Pikes Peak Library District
Jose Aponte, Executive Director
Colorado Springs, Colorado

Pinal County Library District
Denise Keller
Florence, Arizona

Portage County Public Library
Stevens Point, Wisconsin

Richland County Public Library
Columbia, South Carolina

Rochester Public Library
Rochester, Minnesota

Rowan Public Library
Salisbury, North Carolina

St. Clair County Library System
Port Huron, Michigan

Saline County Public Library
Julie Hart
Benton, Arkansas

San Francisco Public Library
Paul Underwood, Acting City Librarian
San Francisco, California

San Jose Public Library
San Jose, California

City of Santa Barbara
Santa Barbara, California

Central Park Library
City of Santa Clara
Santa Clara, California

The Seattle Public Library
Seattle, Washington

Seminole County Government Library System
Sanford, Florida

Sheridan County Public Library System
Sheridan, Wyoming

Solano County Library
Ann Cousineau
Fairfield, California

Sussex County Department of Libraries
Pamella A. Russell
Georgetown, Delaware

Tahlequah Public Library
Georgie Drees
Tahlequah, Oklahoma

Tigard Public Library
Margaret Barnes
Tigard, Oregon

Tippecanoe County Public Library
La Fayette, Indiana

Torrance Public Library
James Buckley
Torrance, California

Tuscaloosa Public Library
Nancy C. Pack
Tuscaloosa, Alabama

Vigo County Public Library
Nancy E. Dowell
Terre Haute, Indiana

Walla Walla Public Library
Martha Van Pelt, Library Director
Walla Walla, Washington

Washoe County Library System
Nancy Cummings
Reno, Nevada

Weld Library District
Greeley, Colorado

West Chicago Public Library
Melody E. Coleman
West Chicago, Illinois

Westminster Public Library
Westminster, Colorado

Williamsburg Regional Library
Williamsburg, Virginia

Wisconsin Department of Public Instruction
"Copyright 2002 Wisconsin Department of Public Library Instruction. Duplication and distribution for not-for-profit purposes with the copyright notice."
Public Library Development
Madison, Wisconsin

Woodland Public Library
Woodland, California

York County Library
Lucinda Munger
Yorktown, Virginia

INDEX of JOB TITLES

This Index contains many cross-references because libraries do not have standard job titles.

To find a job, first look under service area, then follow the job titles and the many see also references. Look under a variety of titles and follow see also references to find those descriptions that will fill your library's particular needs. For example, if your library calls a position a "specialist," also follow the see also reference to associates, assistants, and technicians. If your library uses the term information systems manager, then follow the see also reference to systems coordinator.

ABOUT THE AUTHOR

Rebecca Brumley is a librarian in the Humanities Division at Dallas (Tex.) Public Library. Brumley enjoys writing, gardening, Texas Ranger baseball, Dallas Cowboy football, and music. She also fosters cats and kittens rescued from local animal shelters for Frisco Humane Society. Brumley has an MIS from the University of North Texas (Dallas). She is also the author of *The Public Library Manager's Forms, Policies, and Procedures Handbook, with CD-ROM* (Neal-Schuman Publishers, 2004).